A CONCEPTUAL ANALYSIS OF EUROPEAN PRIVATE INTERNATIONAL LAW

A CONCEPTUAL ANALYSIS OF EUROPEAN PRIVATE INTERNATIONAL LAW

The General Issues in the EU and its Member States

Felix M. Wilke

intersentia
Cambridge – Antwerp – Chicago

Intersentia Ltd
Sheraton House | Castle Park
Cambridge | CB3 0AX | United Kingdom
Tel.: +44 1223 370 170 | Fax: +44 1223 370 169
Email: mail@intersentia.co.uk
www.intersentia.com | www.intersentia.co.uk

Distribution for the UK and Ireland:
NBN International
Airport Business Centre, 10 Thornbury Road
Plymouth, PL6 7PP
United Kingdom
Tel.: +44 1752 202 301 | Fax: +44 1752 202 331
Email: orders@nbninternational.com

Distribution for Europe and all other countries:
Intersentia Publishing nv
Groenstraat 31
2640 Mortsel
Belgium
Tel.: +32 3 680 15 50 | Fax: +32 3 658 71 21
Email: mail@intersentia.be

Distribution for the USA and Canada:
Independent Publishers Group
Order Department
814 North Franklin Street
Chicago, IL 60610
USA
Tel.: +1 800 888 4741 (toll free) | Fax: +1 312 337 5985
Email: orders@ipgbook.com

A Conceptual Analysis of European Private International Law. The General Issues in the EU and its Member States

ISBN 978-1-78068-690-5
D/2019/7849/16
NUR 822

British Library Cataloguing in Publication Data. A catalogue record for this book is available from the British Library.

To My Family

FOREWORD

Not long ago, genuine European private international law consisted, beyond the Brussels Convention, of a few isolated choice-of-law provisions in specific EU instruments, in particular consumer directives. Since then, we have witnessed an astonishing growth in the number of instruments of European provenance, many of which directed at establishing the applicable law. EU private international law has moved from the margins to the centre. By now, it is a venerable field of its own.

While we do have European private international law, what we do not have is a comprehensive and systematically uniform approach to private international law on a European level. Different Regulations on private international law stand in sometimes unclear relation to each other. Moreover, general issues of private international law – doctrinal tools like characterisation, renvoi, and the public policy exception – are not regulated on a level that would transcend these individual instruments. Some tools, like the public policy exception, can be found in each of the Regulations. Other tools, like characterisation, exist in a form that is doctrinally different from that in domestic law, often as provisions concerning the scope of an instrument and the scope of the applicable law. And some tools, like the incidental question, find no regulation at all.

This lack of uniformity is the focus of this most welcome book. Felix M. Wilke, a young scholar from the University of Bayreuth in Germany, has focused on this topic before: he was prominently involved in a project established at a conference in 2012, and in a corresponding collection of essays published in 2013, which aimed at establishing the potential for a general part of European private international law. The project set out to produce a legislative instrument, cleverly named a "Rome 0 Regulation", that could serve as a legislative general part that would both supplement and connect the existing private international law regulations. Both book and project were in German and brought together scholars from German-speaking universities. Now, Wilke addresses this question in a comprehensive fashion in English.

And he deserves our gratitude for this. This is a thoroughly researched work that is both comparative-empirical and prescriptive in nature, a study that both surveys existing law and makes proposals on the basis of its findings. The comparison is more doctrinal than functional in nature, which seems adequate for its topic of a conceptual analysis: Wilke is interested in establishing techniques, not resolving concrete cases, so a functional approach would not have been of much use to him. He analyses not just the existing EU instruments for what they reveal regarding general issues; in addition, his study relies on a comparison of the existing domestic private international law systems, both codified and uncodified, in all EU member states. Wilke thus departs from his earlier view that only a few domestic models exist – he finds, in fact, that general issues are more thoroughly discussed and regulated in domestic legislation than in European law, and therefore finds the existing material most helpful for European concepts. He even includes the United Kingdom – despite Brexit, and despite the differences one should expect between a common law approach in England and the civil law approaches of most other member states.

The result is an impressive survey of approaches concerning these questions; and Wilke's results are surprising and interesting. One might have expected to find significant differences; after all, although private international law was once a significantly international discipline, it has, over much of the 20th century, become domestic, with the consequence of different domestic traditions. In fact, even within domestic traditions, differences exist, at least insofar as that the relevant questions have not been resolved legislatively. Although European private international law does create uniformity, it often differs from domestic law. However, Wilke proposes that there are enough commonalities to justify a common understanding. Most conflicts rules, he suggests, have a tripartite structure–subject matter, connecting factor, and applicable law. Each of these elements itself raises certain general issues that he discusses in detail; further general issues exist, too. Wilke's normative conclusion is clear: general issues are necessarily part of private international law, and the EU ought to codify them in a regulation. He does not, unfortunately, put forth a draft of what such a regulation may resemble – maybe he will do so in a later publication?

Will his argument convince the discipline? The general part of private international law, and the focus on general issues, is something of a German peculiarity (though it needs to be said that US doctrine, despite its rejection of a general part per se, is even more obsessed with general issues). Scholars and practitioners in many other European countries tend to be less interested in them, so far. The general part is viewed by many as representative of the abstract a priori character of German private international law doctrine, which Dicey juxtaposed long ago with an English pragmatic approach. Moreover, some scholars will deplore that Wilke focuses on genuine private international law and largely leaves out the role that general European Union law plays for private international law. The principle of recognition is deliberately ignored, as are the four freedoms and the country-of-origin principle. In this sense, Wilke's general issues are not as general as some may wish for.

Nevertheless, this book clearly shows its background in German thinking, and it displays that at its best. The fact that the book is written in English provides the discipline with a formidable opportunity to learn about and engage with a specific kind of position towards conceptual issues of private international law. That position will undoubtedly influence European discussions in a fruitful manner. I, for one, look forward to those further discussions, and congratulate Felix M. Wilke on his considerable achievement.

Ralf Michaels
Arthur Larson, Professor of Law, Duke University
Chair in Global Law, Queen Mary University of London
Impending Director, Max Planck Institute for
Comparative and International Private Law
January 2019

ACKNOWLEDGEMENTS

The main work for this book project – for a long time under the working title of "The General Issues of Private International Law: A European Concept" – was carried out at the Faculty of Law and Economics (*Rechts- und Wirtschaftswissenschaftliche Fakultät*) of the University of Bayreuth, Germany. It was done under the tutelage of Prof. Hannes Unberath until his untimely passing. His brilliant mind, his instructive scholarly contributions, and his great kindness have made a lasting impression on me as they have on everyone who has known him.

Prof. Stefan Leible took over my academic mentorship without hesitation. For that I would like to thank him, as well as for supporting my choice of this topic. I would also like to express my gratitude to him for giving me all the freedom I could wish for in preparing this book and for his quick review of its final version. I would further like to thank Prof. Michael Grünberger for his speedy evaluation of my work, and for defying a sudden injury that might have prevented him from showing up for the formal presentation of my work. Moreover, I would like to thank Prof. Jörg Gundel for judiciously presiding over the presentation.

The thoughtful remarks from all the people mentioned above, as well as from three anonymous peer reviewers, have afforded me the opportunity to refine some points further before the book went to the press. Legal developments up until September 2018 have been taken into account as far as possible.

I would further like to thank Prof. Oliver Lepsius. He sparked my academic career when he saw something in me after only half a year of law school and employed me as a student assistant for the entire remainder of my legal studies. His ideas and research in general, and his remarks on "general parts" in German public law (or rather the lack thereof) in particular, have strongly influenced my own understanding of law and my choice of this topic.

Many other people have supported the genesis of this book in many ways. For this I would like to thank my colleagues at the University of Bayreuth, in particular Dr. Michael F. Müller; the student assistants at the Chair for Private Law, Private International Law, and Comparative Law; the library staff at the University of Bayreuth, particularly the inter-library loan team who were able to procure almost every item I asked for, no matter how obscure; Asja Bernd for offering a non-legal and thus very welcome perspective on my writing; and the staff at Intersentia, in particular Ann-Christin Maak-Scherpe and Ahmed Hegazi, for agreeing to publish this book and for all their efforts in connection with the publication.

Finally, I would like to thank my parents, Annemarie Wilke and Gerhard M. Horstmann-Wilke, whose support I could and can always count on. My father even provided hands-on assistance with this project by proofreading an earlier version of the manuscript. The dedication of this book to my family includes them, of course, as it does the memory of my grandmother Marieluise Wilke (1914–2007). With the two world wars in her lifetime, the success story of the European Union and its legal system (which this book analyses in part) must have seemed anything but certain to her. May we keep this in mind in times of growing Euroscepticism!

Bayreuth, autumn 2018

CONTENTS

LIST OF ABBREVIATIONS

AG	Amtsgericht [German District Court]
Agency Convention	Convention on the Law Applicable to Agency (Concluded 14 March 1978)
Better Regulation Guidelines	Commission Staff Working Document, Better Regulation Guidelines, COM(2015) 215 final (available online at http://ec.europa.eu/smart-regulation/guidelines/docs/swd_br_guidelines_en.pdf, last visited 21 April 2016)
BGB	Bürgerliches Gesetzbuch [German Civil Code]
BGBl.	Bundesgesetzblatt [German Federal Law Gazette]
BGH	Bundesgerichtshof [German Federal Supreme Court]
Brussels I	Council Regulation (EC) No 44/2001 of 22 December 2000 on jurisdiction and the recognition and enforcement of judgments in civil and commercial matters, [2001] OJ L 12/1
Brussels Ibis	Regulation (EU) No 1215/2012 of the European Parliament and of the Council of 12 December 2012 on jurisdiction and the recognition and enforcement of judgments in civil and commercial matters (recast), [2012] OJ L 351/1
Brussels IIbis	Council Regulation (EC) No 2201/2003 of 27 November 2003 concerning jurisdiction and the recognition and enforcement of judgments in matrimonial matters and the matters of parental responsibility, repealing Regulation (EC) No 1347/2000, [2003] OJ L 338/1
Brussels Convention	1968 Brussels Convention on jurisdiction and the enforcement of judgments in civil and commercial matters (consolidated version: [1998] OJ C 27/1)
BT-Drucks.	Drucksache des Deutschen Bundestags [Parliamentary Materials of the German Bundestag]
BVerfGE	Entscheidungen des Bundesverfassungsgerichts [Collection of the decisions by the German Federal Constitutional Court, published by Mohr Siebeck, Tübingen]
Cass. Ass. plén.	Cour de cassation, Assemblée plénière [France]
Cass. (1re) civ.	Cour de cassation, (Première) Chambre civile [France]

Cass. req.	Cour de cassation, Chambre des requêtes [France]
CISG	United Nations Convention on Contracts for the International Sale of Goods
CISG-AC Bylaws	CISG Advisory Council Bylaws (available online at http://www.cisgac.com/default.php?ipkCat=149&sid=149, last visited 3 June 2016)
Conflict of Nationality Laws Convention	Convention on Certain Questions Relating to the Conflict of Nationality Laws of 12 April 1930
Consumer Credit Directive 1986	Council Directive 87/102/EEC of 22 December 1986 for the approximation of the laws, regulations and administrative provisions of the Member States concerning consumer credit, [1987] OJ L 42/48
Consumer Credit Directive 2008	Directive 2008/48/EC of the European Parliament and of the Council of 23 April 2008 on credit agreements for consumers and repealing Council Directive 87/102/EEC, [2008] OJ L 133/66
Consumer Sales Directive	Directive 1999/44/EC of the European Parliament and of the Council of 25 May 1999 on certain aspects of the sale of consumer goods and associated guarantees, [1999] OJ L 171/12
Consumer Rights Directive	Directive 2011/83/EU of the European Parliament and of the Council of 25 October 2011 on consumer rights, amending Council Directive 93/13/EEC and Directive 1999/44/EC of the European Parliament and of the Council and repealing Council Directive 85/577/EEC and Directive 97/7/EC of the European Parliament and of the Council, [2011] OJ L 304/64
Council Resolution on the Quality of Drafting of Community Legislation	Council Resolution of 8 June 1993 on the quality of drafting of community legislation, [1993] OJ C 166/1
DCFR	Draft Common Frame of Reference (see von Bar, Christian et al. (eds.), Principles, Definitions and Model Rules of European Private Law)
Distance Contract Directive	Directive 97/7/EC of the European Parliament and of the Council of 20 May 1997 on the protection of consumers in respect of distance contracts, [1997] OJ L 144/19

Distance Marketing of Consumer Financial Services Directive	Directive 2002/65/EC of the European Parliament and of the Council of 23 September 2002 concerning the distance marketing of consumer financial services and amending Council Directive 90/619/EEC and Directives 97/7/EC and 98/27/EC, [2002] OJ L 271/16
Doorstep Selling Directive	Council Directive 85/577/EEC of 20 December 1985 to protect the consumer in respect of contracts negotiated away from business premises, [1985] OJ L 372/31
ECJ	European Court of Justice (technically: Court of Justice of the Court of Justice of the European Union)
ECtHR	European Court of Human Rights
EGBGB	Einführungsgesetz zum Bürgerlichen Gesetzbuche [Introductory Act to the German Civil Code]
Enforcement Order Regulation	Regulation (EC) No 805/2004 of the European Parliament and of the Council of 21 April 2004 creating a European Enforcement Order for uncontested claims, [2004] OJ L 143/15
EU Charter of Fundamental Rights	Charter of Fundamental Rights of the European Union, [2012] OJ C 326/391
EU Justice Agenda for 2020	The EU Justice Agenda for 2020 – Strengthening Trust, Mobility and Growth within the Union, COM(2014) 144 final
European Convention on Nationality	European Convention on Nationality of 6 November 1997 (Council of Europe Treaty No. 166)
Framework Decision on the European Arrest Warrant	Council Framework Decision 2002/584/JHA of 13 June 2002 on the European arrest warrant and the surrender procedures between Member States, [2002] OJ L 190/1
FS	Festschrift/Festskrift [Liber Amicorum]
Geneva Refugee Convention	Convention Relating to the Status of Refugees of 28 July 1951
GG	Grundgesetz (German Constitution)
Kamerstuk	[Document of the Dutch Parliament]
Insolvency Regulation	Regulation (EU) 2015/848 of the European Parliament and of the Council of 20 May 2015 on insolvency proceedings (recast), [2015] OJ L 141/19
IPRspr.	Die deutsche Rechtsprechung auf dem Gebiete des Internationalen Privatrechts [Collection of German Jurisprudence Relating to Private International Law, published by Mohr Siebeck, Tübingen]

LA	Liber Amicorum
LG	Landgericht [German Regional Court]
Maintenance Protocol	Protocol on the law applicable to maintenance obligations of 23 November 2007 (available online at www.hcch.net, last visited 11 June 2016)
Maintenance Regulation	Council Regulation (EC) No 4/2009 of 18 December 2008 on jurisdiction, applicable law, recognition and enforcement of decisions and cooperation in matters relating to maintenance obligations, [2009] OJ L 7/1
M-Property Regulation	Council Regulation (EU) 2016/1103 of 24 June 2016 implementing enhanced cooperation in the area of jurisdiction, applicable law and the recognition and [e]nforcement of decisions in matters of matrimonial property regimes, [2016] OJ L 183/1
OGH	Oberster Gerichtshof [Austrian Supreme Court]
OJ	Official Journal of the European Union
OLG	Oberlandesgericht [German Higher Regional Court]
Order for Payment Procedure Regulation	Regulation (EC) No 1896/2006 of the European Parliament and of the Council of 12 December 2006 creating a European order for payment procedure, [2006] OJ L 399/1
Package Travel Directive	Council Directive 90/314/EEC of 13 June 1990 on package travel, package holidays and package tours, [1990] OJ L 158/59
Product Liability Directive	Council Directive 85/374/EEC of 25 July 1985 on the approximation of the laws, regulations and administrative provisions of the Member States concerning liability for defective products, [1985] OJ L 210/29
Qualification Directive (Recast)	Directive 2011/95/EU of the European Parliament and of the Council of 13 December 2011 on standards for the qualification of third-country nationals or stateless persons as beneficiaries of international protection, for a uniform status for refugees or for persons eligible for subsidiary protection, and for the content of the protection granted (recast), [2011] OJ L 337/9
Refugee Protocol	Protocol Relating to the Status of Refugees of 31 January 1967
RGBl.	Reichsgesetzblatt [German Imperial Law Gazette]
Rome I	Regulation (EC) No 593/2008 of the European Parliament and of the Council of 17 June 2008 on the law applicable to contractual obligations (Rome I), [2008] OJ L 177/6

RGZ	Entscheidungen des Reichsgerichts in Zivilsachen [Decisions of the German Imperial Court in Civil Matters]
Rome II	Regulation (EC) No 864/2007 of the European Parliament and of the Council of 11 July 2007 on the law applicable to non-contractual obligations (Rome II), [2007] OJ L 199/40
Rome III	Council Regulation (EU) No 1259/2010 of 20 December 2010 implementing enhanced cooperation in the area of the law applicable to divorce and legal separation, [2010] OJ L 343/10
Rome Convention	Convention on the law applicable to contractual obligations opened for signature in Rome on 19 June 1980, [1980] OJ L 266/1
RP-Property Regulation	Council Regulation (EU) 2016/1104 of 24 June 2016 implementing enhanced cooperation in the area of jurisdiction, applicable law and the recognition and enforcement of decisions in matters of the property consequences of registered partnerships, [2016] OJ L 183/30
Self-Employed Commercial Agents Directive	Council Directive 86/653/EEC of 18 December 1986 on the coordination of the laws of the Member States relating to self-employed commercial agents, [1986] OJ L 382/17
Small Claims Procedure Regulation	Regulation (EC) No 861/2007 of the European Parliament and of the Council of 11 July 2007 establishing a European Small Claims Procedure, [2007] OJ L 199/1
Social Security Regulation No. 1408/71	Council Regulation (EC) No 1408/71 of 14 June 1971 on the application of social security schemes to employed persons, to self-employed persons and to members of their families moving within the Community, [1997] OJ L 28/1
Stateless Persons Convention	Convention Relating to the Status of Stateless Persons of 28 September 1954
Stockholm Programme	The Stockholm Programme – An Open and Secure Europe Serving and Protecting Citizens, [2010] OJ C 115/1
Succession Regulation	Regulation (EU) No 650/2012 of the European Parliament and of the Council of 4 July 2012 on jurisdiction, applicable law, recognition and enforcement of decisions and acceptance and enforcement of authentic instruments in matters of succession and on the creation of a European Certificate of Succession, [2012] OJ L 201/107

TEC	Treaty establishing the European Community (consolidated version: [2006] OJ C 321/E37)
TEU	Treaty on European Union (consolidated version: [2012] OJ C 326/13)
TFEU	Treaty on the Functioning of the European Union (consolidated version: [2012] OJ C 326/47)
Testamentary Form Convention	Convention of 5 October 1961 on the Conflicts of Laws Relating to the Form of Testamentary Dispositions
Unfair Terms Directive	Council Directive 93/13/EEC of 5 April 1993 on unfair terms in consumer contracts, [1993] OJ L 95/29
ZPO	Zivilprozessordnung [German Code of Civil Procedure]

INTRODUCTION

It is a truth universally acknowledged that a book with a broad title such as the present one must begin with a statement as to what it is not about. Assuming that the reader is at least equally interested in learning what it *is* about, the apologetic section (2) is preceded by a section offering a positive perspective on things to come (1). Together, these first two sections delineate the scope of the book. As this is not only a book with a broad title, but also a unilingual comparative analysis in the field of private international law, there is a particular need to address quite a number of terminological issues. They are the subject of the third section.

1. THE CONCEPT OF GENERAL ISSUES

It would not seem to be a stretch to posit that most persons with a legal education will associate the notion of establishing a "general part" of one area of law with German law and German legal scholarship. "The technique of creating a General [Part] is, in its perfection, a marvel of German legal theory."[1] Nothing epitomises the "German abstract approach to law"[2] quite like the General Part of the German Civil Code, the BGB. But the idea is older and far from limited to substantive private law.[3] Codifications of criminal law separated general from specific provisions even before the 19th century. Otto Mayer, who is considered the father of "general administrative law" (*Allgemeines Verwaltungsrecht*) in Germany,[4] set forth his distinction of a "general part" and a "special part" of administrative law in 1895.[5] Even the German Constitution has occasionally been called a "general part" (of German public law or even of all German law).[6]

1 *Mansel*, in: Leible (ed.), General Principles, §8.01[A].

2 *Schmidt*, Sc. St. L. 12 (1968), 93.

3 See *infra* Chapter 6 for some historical notes and intra-disciplinary comparisons.

4 *Groß*, Die Verwaltung, Beiheft 2 (1999), 57, 61 (with further references).

5 *Mayer*, Deutsches Verwaltungsrecht I, 19–20 (with note 8), with reference to substantive private law. For the development of the general part of administrative law in Germany see *Groß*, Die Verwaltung, Beiheft 2 (1999), 57, 58–64.

6 *Hollstein*, Verfassung als "Allgemeiner Teil", 176–224, in particular 212–213, in his analysis of *Nipperdey*'s œuvre; also *Wahl*, in: Merten/Papier (eds.), Handbuch der Grundrechte I, §19 at 23 ("The 'general part' of all areas of law is written by constitutional law and its scholars."). *Lepsius*, Die Verwaltung, Beiheft 10 (2010), 179, 196, considers such a position to be beside the point.

From a German perspective, thus, it is all but unnatural that the discourse concerning European Union (EU) private international law has relatively quickly turned to its general provisions,[7] its general principles,[8] its general theory,[9] its general doctrines,[10] and/or even expressly to its (potential) general part.[11] Indeed, most contributions calling for a general part of EU private international law, or at least exploring the topic of general rules originate in Germany.[12] This is somewhat awkward from a political point of view: the idea as a whole could be in danger of being dismissed or discounted as an exclusively German brainchild of little use for the other member states.[13] Possibly even more problematic for the prospects of any such endeavour is that the vast majority of contributions to the topic thus far, German or not, merely *presuppose* the concept of general provisions of private international law.

Despite its status as one of the poster children of German law, it might surprise not just the non-German reader to learn that explanations of the establishment of a general part, even in substantive private law, are rare.[14] This state of affairs is quite similar in (EU) private international law. Only rarely does an author give details on what his or her exact idea of general issues or provisions is.[15] If the topic comes up at all, reference typically is made to the traditions of and custom within the field.[16] Tradition and custom as such, however, do not offer a particularly safe foothold with regard to *EU* private international law – perhaps the concept rests upon prerequisites that EU law does not (yet) meet or even cannot meet? To give just one example at this point, the most obvious of such potential requirements would probably be the codification issue: are general provisions inextricably linked to codes?

---

7 *Corneloup/Nourissat*, in: Fallon/Lagarde/Poillot-Peruzzetto (eds.), Quelle architecture pour un code européen de droit international privé?, 257, 265.

8 See the contributions in Leible (ed.), General Principles.

9 *Bariatti/Pataut*, in: Fallon/Lagarde/Poillot-Peruzzetto (eds.), Quelle architecture pour un code européen de droit international privé?, 337.

10 *Nehne*, Methodik und allgemeine Lehren des europäischen IPR.

11 See the contributions in Leible/Unberath (eds.), Rom 0-Verordnung; *Lagarde*, in: Fallon/Lagarde/Poillot-Peruzzetto (eds.), Quelle architecture pour un code européen de droit international privé?, 365, 368; *Heinze*, in: FS Kropholler, 105; *Sonnenberger*, ibid., 227; *Kreuzer*, in: Jud/Rechberger/Reichelt (eds.), Kollisionsrecht in der Europäischen Union, 1.

12 The foregoing footnotes provide ample illustration of this.

13 See *Lein*'s recent short review of Leible (ed.), General Principles ("the – quite Germanic – idea of an '*Allgemeiner Teil*' for the European conflict of laws"; italics in the original), <http://conflictoflaws.net/2016/general-principles-of-european-private-international-law-book> (last visited 12 October 2018).

14 *Brockmöller*, Die Entstehung der Rechtstheorie, 180.

15 For a notable exception see *Kreuzer*, in: Jud/Rechberger/Reichelt (eds.), Kollisionsrecht in der Europäischen Union, 1 – who, however, only *posits* requirements of general provisions without questioning/examining these requirements further.

16 *Trüten*, Die Entwicklung des IPR in der EU, §19 III 3 (665) ("common view"); *Bariatti/Pataut*, in: Fallon/Lagarde/Poillot-Peruzzetto (eds.), Quelle architecture pour un code européen de droit international privé?, 337, 341 ("classiquement").

It is the objective of this book to arrive at firm *conceptual* foundations for general provisions of EU private international law. It pursues this objective from a comparative point of view, taking into account the private international law of all the EU member states, as well as existing EU private international law itself. First, as a kind of prolegomenon, it provides some groundwork concerning the methodological implications of this approach, as well as its empirical foundations (Part I). It then proposes a formal and a substantive way to approach the concept of "general issues" and checks these not necessarily exclusive notions against existing private international law rules (Part II). This part aims to be exhaustive; hence the definite article in the subtitle of this book. To the extent that the two approaches prove theoretically viable, they are scrutinised as to their legal compatibility with and functional appropriateness for EU law (Part III).

2. LIMITATIONS OF THIS BOOK

The emphasis on concept in the preceding section – and, of course, in the title of this book – already indicates one of the main issues on which this book does not focus: content. This is not to suggest that the following pages are devoid of content, but rather that the content of general provisions of (EU) private international law will only be of incidental interest. The content of virtually all issues identified as in some way "general" in the course of the following analysis warrants individual monographs. Countless have already been written in relation to domestic law; many have also already been written from a European perspective; and others are currently in the works. The footnotes in the respective chapters and the bibliography provide a glimpse of all this, without even pretending to be exhaustive. Here, by contrast, there will be no annex with a draft "Rome 0" Regulation, no suggestions of how to phrase general provisions of EU private international law, no evaluation of policy reasons for and against certain solutions. Note the limitation of the foregoing limitation, contained in the word "policy": if there are *legal* reasons for or against a certain solution, which in particular means standards of EU law, they will be covered and applied. Thus, in some instances, concrete solutions do emerge – but only as a by-product of the conceptual analysis. Apart from this, where the content of certain provisions of domestic private international law appears in the following analysis, it is only intended to illustrate a point.

To the extent that EU private international law is at issue, this book is limited to the law as it stands[17] in Rome I, Rome II, and Rome III, as well as in the Succession Regulation, the M-Property Regulation, and the RP-Property[18]

---

17 The M-Property Regulation and RP-Property Regulation are already in force even though most of their provisions will become applicable only in 2019: Article 70 M-/RP-Property Regulation.

18 See *infra* 3.3. for an explanation of the nomenclature used in this book for the EU private international law regulations.

Regulation. Provisions regarding the applicable law found in other instruments of EU law, whether they be regulations or directives, only appear in isolated instances and usually in order to illustrate a point further. Moreover, there will be no long-winded abstract descriptions of the history and content of the aforementioned regulations. It seems unlikely that anybody entirely unfamiliar with them would occupy herself with this book in the first place. Questions as to the validity of the regulations[19] will not be discussed either.

In line with these regulations forming the basis of this book, it will simply be assumed that EU private international law by and large consists of omnilateral conflicts rules.[20] For one thing, this implicates a system of private international law resting not on approaches but rules. Due to the focus on *conflicts* rules,[21] the topic of recognition[22] is not covered at all, regardless of whether modern private international law as a whole requires the idea of referral to be complemented by recognition and consideration (of local and moral data).[23] Furthermore, this means a system under which the respective conflicts rules in principle can lead to any substantive law in the world, as opposed to the law of just one country (unilateral conflicts rules) or of just a group of countries (multilateral conflicts rules). To be sure, the expression "*omni*lateral" is a bit unusual.[24] It appears that "multilateral" is most often considered the exact opposite of "unilateral"; but "omnilateral" is the precise expression, even more so as there are examples of genuinely *multi*lateral conflicts rules.[25]

3. TERMINOLOGY

3.1. "PRIVATE INTERNATIONAL LAW" AND "CONFLICT OF LAWS"

"Private international law" and its direct equivalents in other languages are hardly ideal terms, this much has been widely accepted for a long time.[26]

---

19 See *Thomale*, ZEuP 2015, 517, 526–527, for noteworthy points as to Rome III being in contravention of the TFEU from a perspective of competence.

20 For the reasonableness of such an assumption in general see e.g. *Rühl*, in: Max Planck Encyclopedia of European Private Law, s. v. "Unilateralism", 1735, 1737; *Baratta*, Yearbook of Private International Law VI (2006), 155, 156; *Sonnenberger*, in: FS Kropholler, 227, 228–229.

21 See *infra* 3.1. on my use of the term "conflicts".

22 For its discussion see e.g. *Lehmann*, in: Leible (ed.), General Principles, §2; *Basedow*, The Law of Open Societies, at 496–522; *Grünberger*, in: Leible/Unberath (eds.), Rom 0-Verordnung, 81; *Sonnenberger*, in: FS Spellenberg, 371; *Fallon/Meeusen*, Yearbook of Private International Law 4 (2002), 37.

23 For the latter view in particular *M.-P. Weller*, RabelsZ 81 (2017), 747, 770–780.

24 But see *Magnus/Mankowski*, Joint Response, i (Question 3) and passim.

25 See Article 7 Insolvency Regulation: The applicable law will be that of a member state, not of any third state.

26 For a relatively early account, see *Zitelmann*, NiemeyersZ 27 (1918), 177, 180–187.

The body of legal provisions to which this title refers is neither necessarily international by its sources,[27] nor does it necessarily deal with inter-national cases, i.e. cases involving different sovereign countries.[28] Whether these provisions are to be characterised as "private" is another point for debate.[29] "Conflict of laws" is not much better, for it seems to require that there must always be an actual conflict.[30] Arguably, both terms are much too concerned with states instead of the parties whose needs and wants are at issue.[31] There are, however, one negative reason and one positive reason for sticking with them regardless.

The negative reason is that there is no evidently better alternative. "Private international law" as a term has been around for more than 180 years,[32] having been coined by the American Story.[33] It was then introduced to Germany in 1841,[34] to France in 1843,[35] and to Spain in 1846.[36] "Conflict of laws" dates back even longer, somewhat ironically originating from a European scholar.[37] Since then, many other terms have been suggested, each with their individual flaws. To name but a few: "choice of law" is difficult to distinguish from party autonomy; *Rechtsanwendungsrecht*, i.e. "law determining the applicability of law", could equally pertain to provisions of procedural, administrative or criminal law;[38] "law determining the applicability of private law" (*Privatrechtsanwendungsrecht*) would dispel these doubts to a large extent,[39] but it is simply too bulky to be of any practical use (though, admittedly, the length of "private international law" was long ago also identified as one of its flaws[40]); and "interprivate law"

27 *Cachard*, DIP, at 3.

28 See only *Neuhaus*, Grundbegriffe, §1 III 1 (5).

29 See *Symeonides*, Codifying Choice of Law, 292; for such a nature e.g. *Kropholler*, IPR, §1 V 1 (8); *Boele-Woelki*, in: LA Kurt Siehr, 61; against it e.g. *Nagy*, PIL in Hungary, at 27; for a nuanced view e.g. *Calvo Caravaca/Carrascosa González*, DIP I, 23; *Loussouarn/Bourel/de Vareilles-Sommières*, DIP, at 85–87.

30 See *Rogerson*, Collier's Conflict of Laws, 3; *Briggs*, Conflict of Laws, 1; *Calvo Caravaca/Carrascosa González*, DIP I, 23; already *Zitelmann*, NiemeyersZ 27 (1918), 177, 189.

31 *Lehmann*, Vand. J. Trans. L. 41 (2008), 381, 398–399 and passim.

32 On the history of the terminology also see *Ancel*, Éléments d'histoire du droit international privé, 20–21.

33 *Story*, §9 (according to *Neuhaus*, Grundbegriffe, §1 III (4, note 10), already in the first edition); the impact of this terminology was limited, see already *Zitelmann*, NiemeyersZ 27 (1918), 177, 178.

34 *Schaeffner*, Entwicklung des IPR; see *Neuhaus*, Grundbegriffe, §1 III (4, note 10).

35 *Foelix*, Traité du DIP; see *Cachard*, DIP, at 3; an earlier work of *Foelix's* was actually titled "Du conflit des lois [...]", see *Zitelmann*, NiemeyersZ 27 (1918), 177, 179.

36 See Calvo Caravaca/Carrascosa González, DIP I, 22.

37 See *Symeonides*, Codifying Choice of Law, 291, referring to *Huber*, De conflictu legum diversarum in diversis imperiis (1689).

38 See e.g. *Neuhaus*, Grundbegriffe, §1 III 2 (7).

39 One could doubt perhaps whether this term would only seem to encompass provisions determining the application of substantive private law, excluding foreign conflicts rules.

40 *Zitelmann*, NiemeyersZ 27 (1918), 177, 186–187.

(alternatively *droit interprivé, diritto interprivato, Zwischenprivatrecht*)[41] does not seem to have gained traction over the last century.

The positive reason is the vernacular across the EU. This being a book on EU law and the domestic law of its member states, it is reasonable to use terminology prevalent on both levels. First, the respective equivalents of "private international law" seem to be in common usage within the legal systems of many member states, in academic writings as well as in legislation: *Internationales Privatrecht, droit international privé, derecho internacional privado, diritto internazionale privato, internationaal privaatrecht*. But "conflict of laws" is not limited to the United Kingdom.[42] Nor is "conflict of laws" an exclusive term under common law. Westlake used both terms interchangeably.[43] Each of them serves as the title for one of the two leading English textbooks on the subject.[44] Two pertinent law journals in English contain "private international law" in their name,[45] and there is a "Private International Law (Miscellaneous Provisions) Act" in the United Kingdom.[46] In turn, a popular blog goes by the name "conflictoflaws.net".

Second, turning to EU law itself, "conflict of laws" is frequently used: Articles 1, 23, and 25 Rome I; Articles 1, 27, 28 and 30 Rome II; Articles 1, 14–16 and 19 Rome III; Articles 36–38 Succession Regulation; and Articles 33–55 M-/RP-Property Regulation.[47] Yet "private international law" is never far, see Article 20 Rome I, Article 24 Rome II, Article 11 Rome III, Articles 34 and 83 Succession Regulation, and Articles 9, 32, 62(3) M-Property Regulation, as well as Article 32 RP-Property Regulation.[48] Both terms also appear in the Commission's 2014 EU Justice Agenda.[49]

None of this is set in stone. It is always possible to propose new terminology for dealing with legal phenomena at the EU level. Maybe Latin is the answer,[50] although it seems rather improbable. For the time being, anyway, the terminology seems to have solidified at the EU level as well.

---

41 *Zitelmann*, NiemeyersZ 27 (1918), 177, 193–194.

42 E.g. the section "Direitos dos estrangeiros e conflitos de leis" in the Portuguese Civil Code (Article 14 et seq.). Conversely, the traditional English nomenclature was recently described by an English author as having "passed its used-by date", *Briggs*, Private International Law in the English Courts, at 1.40.

43 *Westlake*, PIL (1925), 2–3.

44 See, on the one hand, *Dicey/Morris/Collins*, Conflict of Laws, and on the other, *Cheshire/North/Fawcett*, PIL.

45 The Journal of Private International Law and the Yearbook of Private International Law.

46 More on the Private International Law (Miscellaneous Provisions) Act 1995 *infra* Chapter 2, section 1.2.1 (*United Kingdom: England*).

47 Occurrences in recitals omitted.

48 Occurrences in recitals omitted.

49 EU Justice Agenda for 2020, 4.2 and note 9.

50 *Nehne*, Methodik und allgemeine Lehren des europäischen IPR, 19 and passim; already touched upon by *Zweigert*, RabelsZ 16 (1951), 387, 396.

Thus, in the following, the terms "private international law" and "conflict of laws" will be used despite their shortcomings. Both are meant *only* to designate the area of law determining what national law governs a given case, regardless of whether these rules point to substantive law or again to rules determining the governing law. Neither "private international law" nor "conflict of laws" refers to provisions on international jurisdiction, recognition and enforcement of foreign judgments, or any other procedural matter,[51] unless stated otherwise.

I will, however, make one important distinction between the two terms in the following. National as well as European private international law legislation contains several kinds of provisions, e.g. definitions, provisions as to the scope of application (*ratione materiae, ratione temporis* etc.), and perhaps review clauses. In some sense, all of these are, simply by their being aggregated in this way, private international law rules and, by the same virtue, conflicts rules. But it will be helpful later on to separate all these rules from the smaller group of private international law/conflict of laws provisions *stricto sensu*: provisions that, if their requirements are fulfilled, determine the governing law for a subject matter.[52] In order to make this distinction immediately recognisable, but without cluttering the text with the plethoric use of "*stricto sensu*", I make use of a terminological crutch: "private international law" will be the broader term and "conflict of laws" (or simply "conflicts" instead of a compound expression) will only relate to the narrower category.[53]

3.2. FURTHER TERMS OF ART

"EU private international law" means private international law in EU instruments, predominantly in the private international law regulations mentioned above. National private international law of the member states of the EU, albeit geographically speaking also "European (Union) law", will always be designated as domestic or national law. "Member states" are the member states of the EU. "Rules" are normative statements, regardless of who made them and what form

51 Particularly English "Conflict of Laws" textbooks use the term in this much broader sense, see e.g. *Harding*, Conflict of Laws, 2; *Briggs*, Conflict of Laws, 1. But then, "private international law" and its equivalents are also often used as such an umbrella term, see *Stone*, EU PIL, 3 (for EU Law); *Audit*, in: Bermann/Picard (eds.), Introduction to French Law, 453 (France); *Boele-Woelki/van Iterson*, in: van Erp/van Vliet (eds.), Netherlands Report, 145 (Netherlands); *Calvo Caravaca/Carrascosa González*, DIP I, 44–48 (Spain); but also see *Nagy*, PIL in Hungary, at 23–27. On the place of international procedural law among other areas of law recently *Mankowski*, RabelsZ 82 (2018), 576.

52 To this extent also the ECJ, Case C-116/11, Bank Handlowy w Warszawie SA, PPHU 'ADAX'/Ryszard Adamiak v Christianapol sp. z o.o., ECLI:EU:C:2012:739 at 48: "[T]he defining characteristic of a conflict-of-laws rule is that it does not in fact answer a question of substantive law itself, but simply determines the law that governs the answer to that question."

53 Similarly *Bogdan*, Introduction to EU PIL (2016), 1.1.

they assume. "Provisions", by contrast, are *statutory* rules, in particular excluding any judge-made law.

3.3. NOMENCLATURE, CITATION, AND CITED LITERATURE

As it seems both hard to read and impractical to use the authentic names in each language, bodies of national legislation have received harmonised English names. Not all idiosyncrasies were abandoned, however. Instead of referring to all national private international law legislation simply as "codification",[54] depending on usage in the respective country, some codifications are referred to as "Act", while others are referred to as "Code". Thus the difference, e.g., between the "Austrian PIL Act" and the "Belgian PIL Code". Where private international law rules form part of a civil code, an anglicised name of that code is used, e.g. "French Civil Code". For practical reasons (only), Germany receives special treatment. As will be demonstrated in more detail later on,[55] its private international law is found in the Introductory Act to its Civil Code. A designation in accordance with the guidelines just set forth, i.e. "Introductory Act to the German Civil Code", would have been quite unwieldy. On the other hand, "German Introductory Act" would have been too imprecise. It appeared best simply to use its common abbreviation in German: "EGBGB". As "BGB" itself is an abbreviation known around the world and associated with the German Civil Code, any additional geographical reference seemed redundant.

As far as the numbering of provisions is concerned, the Dutch and Lithuanian Civil Codes deserve special mention. The numbering of the articles starts anew with each of their "books" unlike, e.g., in the BGB or the Romanian Civil Code. Hence it is necessary (and customary) to refer to them by both book and article.[56] For example, "Article 10:5 Dutch Civil Code" refers to Article 5 of Book 10 of the Dutch Civil Code, i.e. the provision on *renvoi*. Similarly, "Article 1.11(1) Lithuanian Civil Code" refers to Article 11(1) of Book 1 of the Lithuanian Civil Code, i.e. the public policy provision.

The nomenclature for the EU private international law regulations is rather straightforward for Rome I, Rome II, Rome III, and the Succession Regulation: the labels "Rome I" and "Rome II" are even found in the official titles of the respective instruments. "Rome III", albeit not a sanctioned name, has already been used widely to designate Regulation 1259/2010. "Succession Regulation" is a self-explanatory abridgment of the long title of Regulation 650/2012;

---

54 See *Symeonides*, Codifying Choice of Law, 25 with note 143.

55 *Infra* Chapter 2, section 1.3.2.1. (*Germany: Legislation*).

56 See *Struycken*, RabelsZ 78 (2014), 592, 593, for the Dutch Civil Code.

"Rome IV" would not be a suitable alternative because the Succession Regulation, unlike Rome I through III, does not exclusively deal with determining the applicable law.

Regulations 2016/1103 and 2016/1104, however, prove challenging in this regard. A name involving "Rome" would not work for the same reason just given for the Succession Regulation. "Matrimonial Property Regimes Regulation" and "Property Consequences of Registered Partnerships Regulation" would be the most telling labels, but these "short" forms would bloat the length of sentences, and thus this book in general, to an unacceptable degree. Moreover, as both regulations are extremely similar to one another, a label reflecting this similarity is preferable. While "Güterrecht" can serve as a common denominator from which to start in German, the only term common to the English designation of the corresponding field of law is "property". It is not ideal because of its many facets. Still, in order to preserve readability, "M-Property Regulation" for Regulation 2016/1103 ("M" for "matrimony") and "RP-Property Regulation" for Regulation 2016/1104 ("RP" for "registered partnerships") will be used for the purposes of this book. Where reference is made to a provision or recital which is the same in both regulations (as is often the case), the shortened designation "M-/RP-Property Regulation" will be employed.

Not strictly a matter of comparative law, but one of writing for a diverse audience, is the issue of references to cases of the European Court of Justice. For reasons of practicability, the English version of the Court Reports will be referred to. Thus, occasionally, page numbers of a translated version may differ, in particular when the respective member state only joined after the decision was published.

As far as citation of source materials in general is concerned, there has certainly been no attempt to practice "propaganda citation", i.e. citation in order to promote a certain school of thought,[57] which in this case some readers might identify as "the" German school of thought. It will become apparent later on that, perhaps contrary to common belief, there is no such school regarding general issues of private international law anyway.[58]

In the relatively rare case that non-English legal literature has been translated into English (like Zweigert and Kötz's *Introduction to Comparative Law* and Wieacker's *A History of Private Law in Europe*), this version, if available at the time of writing, will be cited for reasons of accessibility.

---

57 See *Markesinis/Fedtke*, Engaging with Foreign Law, 103–107.

58 *Infra* Chapter 2, section 1.3.2.1. (*Germany: Scholarship*).

PART I
FOUNDATIONS

Some groundwork is necessary before one can delve into conceptual, legal, and policy questions surrounding general issues of private international law in the context of the EU.

The first chapter in this part addresses questions of method. Why even approach the present topic from a comparative perspective? What kind of perspective is this? How does it deal with the various difficulties of taking into account the law of 28 states?

The next chapter then provides an overview of the legislative and scholarly material upon which Part II in particular relies. Short country reports summarise the situation of private international law in the different member states. Does domestic private international law – or at least its treatment by the cognoscenti – already reflect a distinction between "general" and "special" issues? If so, to what extent? Finally, with regard to EU private international law itself: is it possible to observe in it at least incunabula of any such systematisation?

CHAPTER 1
METHOD

Comparative law is a risky discipline. There is a danger of at least *prima facie* doubtful endeavours such as comparing New Zealand and German adoption laws, or Uzbek securities trading law with its Swiss counterpart.[59] Then there are numerous, perhaps countless,[60] pitfalls in the comparative process itself. In view of these issues, this chapter addresses three aspects. First, the reasonableness of approaching the present topic in a comparative way. Second, the extent to which this book follows the traditional notion of comparative law, the extent to which it does not, and why not. Third, the attempts that will be made in order to avoid some of the subject's pitfalls and why falling into some of them – *horribile dictu* – would not cast doubts on the book as a whole.

Radbruch's observation that "sciences which have to busy themselves with their own methodology usually are sick sciences"[61] may or may not be true.[62] If one emphasises the compulsory aspect ("have to") in the sense that those sciences do little else, it is easier to agree with Radbruch than in general, where occupation with method and methodology is a constitutive element of the scientific nature of a discipline. Even though there are excellent examples of comparative private international law,[63] i.e. the comparison of private international law rules,[64]

---

59 The pointed examples are *Derleder*'s, myops 11/2011, 12, 16.

60 *Bogdan*, Introduction to Comparative Law, 29 ("impossible to list").

61 *Radbruch*, Einführung in die Rechtswissenschaft, 283; in the translation by *Weir* (*Zweigert/Kötz*, Introduction to Comparative Law, 33), the modification "usually" ("pflegen … zu sein") is missing.

62 *Zweigert/Kötz*, Introduction to Comparative Law, 33 ("generally true", but no "diagnosis which fits modern comparative law").

63 The term "comparative private international law" is not ideal, of course. It combines the problematic "private international law" (*supra* Introduction, section 3.1.) with the equally problematic "comparative law" (for unlike "private law", "constitutional law" etc., "comparative" does not designate a particular legal subject matter).

64 See the entries in Basedow/Rühl/Ferrari/de Miguel Asensio (eds.), Encyclopedia of PIL, Volumes 1 and 2; also *Symeonides*, Codifying Choice of Law; *Kadner Graziano*, Gemeineuropäisches IPR; *Cuniberti*, Conflict of Laws; the contributions in Lipstein (ed.), The International Encyclopedia of Comparative Law, Vol. III; and, of course, *Rabel*, The Conflict of Laws. See already the voluminous entries under "Internationales Privatrecht", in: Schlegelberger (ed.), Rechtsvergleichendes Handwörterbuch (the project as a whole was not finished because of World War II, *Martinek*, in: Simon (ed.), Rechtswissenschaft in der Bonner Republik, 529, 566). See also *Rühl*, in: Zimmermann (ed.), Zukunftsperspektiven der Rechtsvergleichung,

questions of comparative law are mostly (and mostly without making mention of it) discussed in relation to comparing substantive rules. Thus, it may be of some general interest to analyse features of comparative private international law here. In order to be understood as correctly as intersubjectively possible, some remarks as to methodological preconceptions are indispensable. "Some", however, is to be taken literally; the debate on methods in comparative law has been getting out of hand,[65] it would be impossible in this context to address anything but select questions.

1. COMPARATIVE PRIVATE INTERNATIONAL LAW IN THE EUROPEAN UNION

1.1. COMPARATIVE PRIVATE INTERNATIONAL LAW

The "intimate",[66] almost "symbiotic"[67] relationship between private international law and comparative law has often been noted.[68] Usually, or at least in the first instance, the emphasis lies on the usefulness of "comparative" substantive private law when concerning oneself with private international law.[69] The quotation marks are necessary because, in these instances, "comparative law" often means little more than ascertaining the content of foreign law, without any actual comparison. Comparative law as a discipline, however, can supply this quest for information with important tools.[70]

When foreign law is deemed applicable – and with the increasing relevance of party autonomy, this becomes more and more an issue of shaping legal

---

103, 109, with further references. For a more abstract account of comparative private international law see *Kropholler*, ZVglRWiss 77 (1978), 1, 3–6.

65 See *Kischel*, Rechtsvergleichung, VII; the debate has been *en vogue* for more than thirty years, *id.*, R.I.D.C. 2016, 907.

66 *Fauvarque-Cosson*, in: LA Gaudemet-Tallon, 43.

67 *Reimann*, Bussani, Mauro/Mattei, Ugo (eds.), The Cambridge Companion to Comparative Law, 13, 16.

68 Recently *Rühl*, in: Zimmermann (ed.), Zukunftsperspektiven der Rechtsvergleichung, 103, 105 and passim; *Michaels*, in: Basedow/Rühl/Ferrari/de Miguel Asensio (eds.), Encyclopedia of PIL, s. v. "Comparative Law and Private International Law".

69 *Kischel*, Rechtsvergleichung, §1 at 43; *Siems*, Comparative Law, 4; *Bogdan*, Introduction to Comparative Law, 22–23; *Örücü*, in: ead./Nelken (eds.), Comparative Law, 43, 46; *Reimann*, in: id./Zimmermann (eds.), The Oxford Handbook of Comparative Law, 1363, 1365 and, in detail, 1380–1388; *Jayme*, Rechtsvergleichung im internationalen Privatrecht; *von Mehren*, in: Butler (ed.), International Law in Comparative Perspective, 153, 155 (and 160 for the importance of comparative efforts for American approaches to conflict of laws); *Sandrock*, Sinn und Methode, 24; but see *Rühl*, in: Zimmermann (ed.), Zukunftsperspektiven der Rechtsvergleichung, 103, 107: Comparing substantive law and comparing private international law as the two main prongs.

70 See *Kischel*, Rechtsvergleichung, §1 at 5–7.

relationships prospectively[71] – its content must be known. In this respect, the substantive rules of different legal systems constitute the "raw material of private international law".[72] Some concepts of private international law, such as characterisation[73] and public policy, *require* certain genuinely comparative efforts.[74] Private international law thus depends on comparative law.[75] In an early account, Kahn additionally advocated for the comparison of substantive private law with the goal of creating, developing and interpreting private international law, be it in international treaties or national legislation.[76]

At the same time, however, Kahn had also already touched upon the importance of comparing conflicts provisions themselves as regards the interpretation and application of such provisions, noting that several countries (even without any treaty-induced obligation) would often have identical or very similar rules.[77] It is not clear whether Kahn, by his omission, intended to exclude the *creation* of private international law rules. Indeed, a century later, the importance of comparative law for private international law legislation, even codification, has been emphasised expressly.[78]

The last line of thought is of particular relevance for the present book. One of comparative law's many[79] fields of application lies at the international or supranational level, where harmonisation or unification is at issue. When negotiating a legislative solution or developing academic model rules, the participating states/scholars will often compare existing domestic laws in order to achieve a unified result acceptable to all:[80] be it the most common solution, a solution regarded as the best, the lowest common denominator or some combination;[81] be it some middle ground between extreme positions, a more

---

71 *Flessner*, in: FS Magnus, 403, 411.

72 *Kropholler*, ZVglRWiss 77 (1978), 1, 2.

73 Recently *Rühl*, in: Zimmermann (ed.), Zukunftsperspektiven der Rechtsvergleichung, 103, 118–121.

74 See only *Flessner*, in: FS Magnus, 403, 406–407; *Reimann*, in: id./Zimmermann (eds.), The Oxford Handbook of Comparative Law, 1363, 1384–1387; *Mansel*, JZ 1991, 529, 530.

75 *Fauvarque-Cosson*, in: LA Gaudemet-Tallon, 43, 49–50.

76 *Kahn*, Zeitschrift für internationales Privat- und Strafrecht 10 (1900), 97, 98–100 and passim.

77 *Kahn*, Zeitschrift für internationales Privat- und Strafrecht 10 (1900), 97, 101; also *Rabel*, Die Fachgebiete des Kaiser-Wilhelm-Instituts, 180, 226–227, concerning the law applicable to contractual obligations.

78 *Bourdelois*, in: Puigelier (ed.), La loi, 89, 102; *Fauvarque-Cosson*, in: LA Gaudemet-Tallon, 43, 48; along similar lines already *Rabel*, Die Fachgebiete des Kaiser-Wilhelm-Instituts, 180, 225.

79 For an impressive compilation see *Reimann*, Tul. Eur. & Civ. L.F. 11 (1996), 49, 54; also e.g., *Örücü*, in: ead./Nelken (eds.), Comparative Law, 43, 53–56; *Dannemann*, in: Reimann/Zimmermann (eds.), The Oxford Handbook of Comparative Law, 383, 401–406.

80 *Reimann*, in: Bussani/Mattei (eds.), The Cambridge Companion to Comparative Law, 13, 17; *Dannemann*, in: Adams/Bomhoff (eds.), Practice and Theory in Comparative Law, 96, 97; *Zweigert/Kötz*, Introduction to Comparative Law, 24; *Zweigert*, in: Mélanges Maury, 579, 581.

81 See *Siems*, Comparative Law, 4.

general principle found behind (or indeed a more specific solution than) the different national solutions or an entirely novel solution.[82] This observation also pertains to EU private international law,[83] not least because a comparative study by the German Notary Institute forms the background for the Succession Regulation.[84]

The EU courts can be said to follow a similar approach, employing comparative law to arrive at solutions "'compatible' with the traditions of the Member States and [...] not hurting special sensitivities".[85] Somewhat paradoxically, these sensitivities may be one of the reasons why there is little explicit evidence of comparative work in EU legal instruments.[86]

Against this backdrop of the increasing harmonisation of private international law at the EU level, it seems of particular importance to have a look at the domestic private international law of the Union's member states when concerning oneself with general provisions of EU private international law. Such an approach may bring to light greater uniformity across the EU than is commonly assumed; it may point out precise differences instead of generalised assumptions. It may further help to identify gaps,[87] issues that EU law does not currently deal with or that are not even on its agenda yet.

What is more, private international law has often been dealt with internationally:[88] many scholars in this area (and in particular concerning general issues) are used to comparative efforts.[89] Private international law has been a traditional terrain for international harmonisation through conventions or nowadays by way of EU regulations. General issues of private international law may indeed be particularly suitable for a comparative analysis, as it has been said that "basic principles, problems, and solutions" in this area have long since broken free from the confines of national borders.[90] Over the course of

---

82 *Dannemann*, in: Adams/Bomhoff (eds.), Practice and Theory in Comparative Law, 96, 109–113 (from the point of view of wanting to achieve system neutrality).

83 *Rühl*, in: Zimmermann (ed.), Zukunftsperspektiven der Rechtsvergleichung, 103, 111.

84 Deutsches Notarinstitut (ed.), Les Successions Internationales dans l'UE, 1–330.

85 *Lenaerts*, ICLQ 52 (2003), 873, 879, see also 886 and 893–894 (each with further references); he goes so far as to call this "psycho-diplomacy", 906; similarly *Singer/Engel*, JDI 2007, 497, 504; also *infra* section 1.2.2. for further discussion of the relevance of comparative law for the EU courts.

86 *Smits*, in: Twigg-Flesner (ed.), The Cambridge Companion to EU Private Law, 33, 38.

87 See *Dannemann*, in: Reimann/Zimmermann (eds.), The Oxford Handbook of Comparative Law, 383, 416 (for gaps in domestic law).

88 *Trüten*, Die Entwicklung des IPR in der EU, §19 II (659). For an in-depth look at the ups and downs of the international discourse in private international law, see *Kadner Graziano*, Gemeineuropäisches IPR, 48–82.

89 *Reimann*, in: id./Zimmermann (eds.), The Oxford Handbook of Comparative Law, 1363, 1365; for a specific example, see *Erauw/Fallon*, in: Dirix/Lelen (eds.), The Belgian Reports, 227, 236–237 for the influence of comparative efforts on the drafting of the Belgian PIL Code.

90 *Reimann*, in: id./Zimmermann (eds.), The Oxford Handbook of Comparative Law, 1363, 1365; similarly *Kropholler*, ZVglRWiss 77 (1978), 1, 3. Also *Kadner Graziano*, Gemeineuropäisches

this book, it will become apparent whether this is the case, to what extent, and why this may be. At this stage, it can simply be taken as a working assumption buttressing the reasonableness[91] of a comparative approach.

1.2. COMPARATIVE LAW IN THE EUROPEAN UNION

The argument has thus far been that a comparative approach is reasonable because of the object of this analysis, private international law. At issue, however, is not private international law in general, but EU private international law. From this additional characteristic follows the second strand of the argument in favour of a comparative perspective.

1.2.1. European Legal Scholarship: Comparative Scholarship

The point of departure is the realisation: "And then Europe came along".[92] The advent of provisions of supranational European provenance has caused (even?) common law writers like Briggs to opt for a new way of presenting private international law – even though EU and domestic rules find themselves in a state of "uneasy co-existence", even though the resulting presentation appears to "look odd" to the author himself.[93] This new way openly acknowledges that EU law shapes the "infrastructure" of an area of law, and deals with it prior to domestic law.[94]

The bigger picture here is the notion that an area of law subject to manifold European influences must be dealt with in a genuinely European manner. It should be analysed, presented, and explained from a European point of view. Such a European approach should not focus "on any particular legal system or its systematics and [should] not [be] addressed to readers of any particular nation".[95] This does not amount to a top-down approach (looking at national law

IPR, 6: The "general part" (what is it?) of private international law as the main playing field of an international discourse, to the extent that, in some European universities, the "general part" of private international law is taught to all students together, whereas there are separate courses for students from abroad in the context of the "special parts".

91 One might object that the need for comparative efforts is at least less pressing where there already is a Europeanised discourse, see *infra* footnote 142 and appurtenant text. See also *infra* section 3.2. for the relationship of (near-)equivalent legal rules and unification.

92 *Briggs*, Private International Law in the English Courts, at 1.42.

93 *Briggs*, Private International Law in the English Courts, at 1.63.

94 Ibid.

95 *Zweigert/Kötz*, Introduction to Comparative Law, 29–30 (concerning substantive private law); see also *Kötz*, in: de Witte/Forder (eds.), The common law of Europe and the future of legal education, 31, 39; *idem*, FS Zweigert, 481, 498.

from the perspective of EU legal instruments), but rather a bottom-up one.[96] Accordingly, the importance of comparative efforts has often been emphasised.[97]

The arguments in support of this approach are in essence the following. The first is rooted in the present: legal harmonisation or unification in Europe, unless one day truly all-encompassing, is fragmentary. It will always leave grey areas between the scope of application of unified law and remaining national law; it will also always cause issues of interpretation from which discrepancies among national courts follow. Thus, scholarship should be comparative. It should strive for a consensus as to more general rules that can then aid in the application and interpretation of uniform law as well as national law.[98] Without a proper (general) foundation, the proliferation of fragmentary rules will lead to an unnecessarily complex mesh of domestic and supranational rules.[99] Some say that, already today, citizens and legal practitioners alike can hardly cope with the resulting difficulties.[100] It does not help that none of the venerable European codes have been drafted with a European perspective.[101]

A second argument pertains to the future: increasing European integration will at some point require a common set of rules. This set should – some would say *must* – be preceded by common European legal scholarship and legal training.[102] In this context, the US-American common law and *Ius Commune* are often mentioned. The purpose of such references seems to be two fold: they are made in order to show that a common European law and corresponding scholarship are not just lofty idea(l)s; and also in order to point to sources of inspiration.

---

96 *Zimmermann*, in: MacQueen/id. (ed.), European Contract Law, 1, 2; *Martinek*, in: Simon (ed.), Rechtswissenschaft in der Bonner Republik, 529, 562; *Mansel*, JZ 1991, 529, 533.

97 See e.g. *Twigg-Flesner*, in: id. (ed.), The Cambridge Companion to EU Private Law, 1, 2; *Zweigert/Kötz*, Introduction to Comparative Law, 28–31; *Coing*, in: Le nuove frontiere del diritto e il problema dell'unificazione, 171, 199; for a somewhat more sceptical perspective *Smits*, in: Twigg-Flesner (ed.), The Cambridge Companion to EU Private Law, 33.

98 *Kötz*, FS Zweigert, 481, 484–488; inter alia, *Kötz* exemplifies this with the Law Commission's "Report on the Proposed E. E. C. Directive on the Law Relating to Commercial Agents" (Law Com. No. 84, Cmnd. 6948, 1977) in which the Commission stated that the proposed provisions depended "upon a corpus of law which is not stated in the directive" itself (at 52); *Koopmans*, in: de Witte/Forder (eds.), The common law of Europe and the future of legal education, 43, 50; *Ulmer*, JZ 1992, 1, 7–8.

99 *Kötz*, FS Zweigert, 481, 488–489.

100 *von Bar*, JZ 2014, 473.

101 *von Bar*, JZ 2014, 473, 475.

102 *Zimmermann*, in: MacQueen/id. (ed.), European Contract Law, 1, 40–41; *idem*, JZ 1992, 8, 9; *Wurmnest*, Grundzüge eines europäischen Haftungsrechts, 4; *van Gerven*, ERPL 4 (2001), 485, 503; *Remien*, JZ 1992, 277, 282–283; *Coing*, NJW 1990, 937, 939; *Sacco*, in: Cappelletti (ed.), New Perspectives for a Common Law of Europe, 95, 101–102 and 108–109; more generally *Kötz*, RabelsZ 50 (1986), 1, 15 (the necessity of scholars accompanying legislative projects for uniform law); with an emphasis on legal education *de Groot*, in: de Witte/Forder (eds.), The common law of Europe and the future of legal education, 7, 17.

1.2.1.1. The Example of the US-American Common Law

The US-American common law is regarded as a current example that divergent legal systems can reasonably and usefully be dealt with from a broader, common perspective.[103] It is an example of "law which applies *everywhere* across the country but which, as such, is not in force *anywhere*".[104] Popular examples are Restatements by the American Law Institute and the common legal education[105] provided by the (leading, "national") law schools. Indeed, the label "restatement" itself tends to surface in European discourse.[106]

1.2.1.2. *Ius Commune*

Then and Now

With the *Ius Commune* there is a historical precedent, or even model,[107] of European "terms, principles, traditions of thinking, and rules" serving as a common foundation for differing rules and customs[108] as a "backup";[109] from a common past to a common future, to paraphrase van Gerven.[110] As the *Ius Commune* was an important aspect of shaping European legal systems,[111] it is possible even today to discuss legal concepts independently of individual, cultural settings.[112] The *Ius Commune* finds its foundation in the reception of Roman (Canon) Law from the 12th century onwards.[113] The important role that academic learning played in this process is emphasised with a view to the

---

103 *Ulmer*, JZ 1992, 1, 8; *Coing*, NJW 1990, 937, 939–940; *Kötz*, FS Zweigert, 481, 495–496.

104 *Markesinis*, ERPL 5 (1997), 519, 522 (emphases in the original).

105 See *Gray*, RabelsZ 50 (1986), 111, 132–133; *Markesinis*, ERPL 5 (1997), 519, 522; *Kötz*, RabelsZ 50 (1986), 1, 15; to this extent similar to Germany in the 19th century, *Zimmermann*, in: MacQueen/id. (ed.), European Contract Law, 1, 34–45, 40–41.

106 See *Bussani*, R.I.D.C. 2010, 7, 20; *Zimmermann*, Am. J. Comp. L. 57 (2009), 479, 481; *de Groot*, in: de Witte/Forder (eds.), The common law of Europe and the future of legal education, 7, 24.

107 *Zimmermann*, in: Reimann/id. (ed.), The Oxford Handbook of Comparative Law, 539, 547 ("point of departure"); *Coing*, in: Le nuove frontiere del diritto e il problema dell'unificazione, 171, 198 ("valuable" source of "inspiration").

108 *Kötz*, FS Zweigert, 481, 490; very similarly *Koopmans*, in: de Witte/Forder (eds.), The common law of Europe and the future of legal education. 43, 50–51; *Coing*, in: Cappelletti (ed.), New Perspectives for a Common Law of Europe, 31, 34; *David*, ibid., 113.

109 *Robbers*, Introduction, at 569.

110 *van Gerven*, ERPL 4 (2001), 485, 488–489.

111 Whether or not England formed the exception has been disputed (for this position: *Coing*, in: Cappelletti (ed.), New Perspectives for a Common Law of Europe, 31, 33 – against it: *Zimmermann*, ZEuP 1993, 4; *idem*, JZ 1992, 8, 15); the topic is of no import here.

112 See *Watson*, The Making of the Civil Law, 19–21, for what he calls "The Block Effect of Roman Law".

113 In much more detail *Zimmermann*, in: MacQueen/id. (ed.), European Contract Law, 1, 8–12; *Gebauer*, Grundfragen, 13–29; *Coing*, in: Cappelletti (ed.), New Perspectives for a Common Law of Europe, 31, 32–34; *id.*, in: Le nuove frontiere del diritto e il problema dell'unificazione, 171, 175–184; succinctly, *Robbers*, Introduction, at 567–569.

present age.[114] "[T]he European lawyer [...] preceded the European law".[115] (Incidentally: the foundations for modern private *international* law belong to the very same academic tradition.[116]) The *Ius Commune* also serves as a reminder that European law as a whole does not have to be uniform.[117]

While German scholars took the first steps down this road,[118] and to this day seem to dominate the *Ius Commune* discourse, scholars from other countries have since joined, and not only to express dissatisfaction with it.[119] Pan-European working groups have been established in which the ideas of comparative research across the EU were put to work. They have come up with principles and rules for different areas of substantive private law: the Principles of European Trust Law,[120] the Principles of European Insolvency Law,[121] the Principles of European Family Law Regarding Divorce and Maintenance Between Former Spouses,[122] the Principles of European Tort Law,[123] the Principles of European Family Law Regarding Parental Responsibilities,[124] the Principles of European Insurance Contract Law,[125] and also principles regarding Acquisition and Loss of Ownership of Goods.[126] Perhaps the most well-known are the Principles of European Contract Law[127] (and their revised version *Principes contractuels*

114 *van Gerven*, MJ 1994, 6, 40; *de Groot*, in: de Witte/Forder (eds.), The common law of Europe and the future of legal education, 7, 14–15; *Ulmer*, JZ 1992, 1, 8; *Zimmermann*, JZ 1992, 8, 9 and passim; *David*, in: Cappelletti (ed.), New Perspectives for a Common Law of Europe, 113, 133; *Coing*, in: Le nuove frontiere del diritto e il problema dell'unificazione, 171, 181–183; as to the historical development also *van Caenegem*, Judges, Legislators, and Professors, 67–111.

115 *Coing*, in: Cappelletti (ed.), New Perspectives for a Common Law of Europe, 31, 44.

116 *Gebauer*, Grundfragen, 33; *Coing*, in: Le nuove frontiere del diritto e il problema dell'unificazione, 171, 183.

117 *Gebauer*, Grundfragen, 7; see already *David*, in: Cappelletti (ed.), New Perspectives for a Common Law of Europe, 113, 144.

118 Among the earliest articles that are cited most often are *Coing*, in: Le nuove frontiere del diritto e il problema dell'unificazione; *id.*, in: Cappelletti (ed.), New Perspectives for a Common Law of Europe; one should also mention *David*, ibid.

119 See *van Gerven*, ERPL 4 (2001), 485; also the contributions from all over Europe in: de Witte/Forder (eds.), The common law of Europe and the future of legal education; in particular *Koopmans*, in: de Witte/Forder (eds.), The common law of Europe and the future of legal education, 43, 49–50, with reference to the "common legal heritage of Europe"; also the contributions in the "successor" to that volume, see *Faure/Smits/Schneider*, in: iid. (ed.), Towards a European Ius Commune in Legal Education and Research, I.

120 Hayton/Kortmann/Verhagen (eds.), Principles of European Trust Law.

121 McBryde/Flessner/Kortmann (eds.), Principles of European Insolvency Law.

122 Boele-Woelki et al. (eds.), Principles of European Family Law Regarding Divorce and Maintenance Between Former Spouses.

123 Group on European Tort Law (ed.), Principles of European Tort Law.

124 Boele-Woelki et al. (eds.), Principles of European Family Law Regarding Parental Responsibilities.

125 Basedow et al. (eds.), Principles of European Insurance Contract Law.

126 Lurger/Faber (eds.), Acquisition and Loss of Ownership of Goods.

127 Lando/Beale (eds.), Principles of European Contract Law, Parts I and II; Lando et al. (eds.), Principles of European Contract Law, Part III.

communs[128]) and the Draft Common Frame of Reference.[129] The European Law Institute and UNIDROIT are also in the process of developing European rules of civil procedure.[130] Outside of substantive private law, one can point to the ReNEUAL Model Rules 2014, a similar project concerning administrative law.[131] Additionally, textbooks on different areas of substantive private law have been published that adopt some kind of European vantage point; either by "merely" offering a description of the law of different member states together or even by proceeding from a more abstract, normative ground "above" national legal systems.[132] Again, books with a similar approach also exist for administrative law.[133]

Relevance for Private International Law in the European Union

It goes without saying that the ideas themselves, as well as the arguments in their favour, have not remained unchallenged. The projects and their results have also been criticised. At the EU level, enthusiasm for a common European substantive private law seems to have cooled recently when the Commission did not pursue the idea of a Common European Sales Law further.[134] This is not the place to even begin to sketch all these developments.[135] Nor should too much weight be placed on the references to the *Ius Commune*. The more pertinent issue here

---

128 Association Henri Capitant des Amis de la Culture Juridique Française/Société de Législation Comparée (eds.), Principes Contractuels Communs.

129 von Bar et al. (eds.), Principles, Definitions and Model Rules of European Private Law.

130 See <https://www.unidroit.org/work-in-progress/transnational-civil-procedure> (last visited 12 October 2018); *Stadler*, JZ 2017, 693.

131 See <http://www.reneual.eu> ("The ReNEUAL Model Rules 2014 are designed to reinforce general principles of EU law and identify – on the basis of comparative research – best practices in different specific policies of the EU."), last visited 12 October 2018; the parallels to the debate in the field of substantive private law are not lost on the participants, see *Schneider/Hofmann/Ziller*, JZ 2015, 265, 270.

132 For a critical overview see *Zimmermann*, in: Reimann/id. (ed.), The Oxford Handbook of Comparative Law, 539, 549–555; without any intention to provide an exhaustive picture, one can mention *Schulze/Zoll*, European Contract Law; *von Bar*, Gemeineuropäisches Sachenrecht I; *id.*, The Common European Law of Torts; *van Dam*, European Tort Law; *Kötz*, Europäisches Vertragsrecht; *id./Flessner*, European Contract Law; *Ranieri*, Europäisches Obligationenrecht; Zimmermann/Whittaker (eds.), Good Faith in European Contract Law; *Schlechtriem*, Restitution und Bereicherungsausgleich in Europa.

133 *Schwarze*, European Administrative Law (and/or its counterparts in other languages), served a pioneering function for ReNEUAL, *Schneider/Hofmann/Ziller*, JZ 2015, 265, 267; see also Auby/Dutheil de la Rochère (eds.), Traité de droit administratif européen, whose "comparative flavour" already follows from having contributors from all over Europe; to some degree also *Craig*, EU Administrative Law (see 246).

134 See the letter by six ministers of justice regarding the proposed Common European Sales Law, printed in ZEuP 2015, 433–435 with an introduction by *Basedow*, 432; also see COM(2014) 910 final, Annex 2 No. 60.

135 For copious references to several of these projects, see *Bussani*, R.I.D.C. 2010, 7, 8–11; *Zimmermann*, Am. J. Comp. L. 57 (2009), 479.

is that these ideas were mainly developed by scholars of private law, with an implied or express focus[136] on substantive private law.[137] Private international law seldom[138] features as an object of focus. Thus, the question arises: is it reasonable to approach European private international law in such a manner?

The historical *Ius Commune* only offers a partial foothold. There was no Roman law of note in the field of private international law *avant la lettre* that could have been the object of reception across Europe.[139] Nevertheless, when the statute theory/statutist approach came into existence, the latter was adopted as part of the *Ius Commune*.[140]

As far as the influence of European law is concerned, however, there are a few similarities to the *Ius Commune* discourse. Legal instruments of the European Economic Community affecting domestic substantive private law catalysed, if not sparked, the debate on a common European private law; for, consequently, "it was *practically* no longer possible to consider private law as a purely national phenomenon".[141] Yet, when, in particular, the Product Liability Directive, the Doorstep Selling Directive, the Consumer Credit Directive 1986, and the Package Travel Directive entered into force respectively, the Brussels Convention (1968) and the Rome Convention (1980) already existed. Thus, private international law (in the broad sense), that had to be treated differently to domestic law, applied across the European Economic Community. At least for the topics "affected", an isolated national approach was no longer warranted. Today, when regulations harmonise certain areas of private international law, nothing else can apply.

Even if someone were to doubt that a European perspective is necessary, or at least useful, for the areas of private international law left untouched thus far by the EU legislator, its general issues do not belong in that category.

---

136 But see, e.g., the different sections in: Faure/Smits/Schneider (eds.), Towards a European Ius Commune in Legal Education and Research; de Witte/Forder (eds.), The common law of Europe and the future of legal education. *Coing*, NJW 1990, 937, 938, had hastened to add (note 11) that his ideas about common European private law would "surely" also apply to administrative and tax law; the historical *Ius Commune* was not limited to issues of private law, anyway, *id.*, in: Le nuove frontiere del diritto e il problema dell'unificazione, 171, 178.

137 This does not necessarily include all areas of substantive private law. *Seifert*, ZEuP 2015, 241, 267–271, recently doubted the usefulness of transferring these ideas to labour law.

138 A voluminous exception is *Kadner Graziano*, Gemeineuropäisches IPR; see also *d'Oliveira*, in: de Witte/Forder (eds.), The common law of Europe and the future of legal education, 265, 267, who, however, albeit in the context of a volume on the "common law of Europe", mainly discusses the influences of European Community law on domestic private international law; similarly, *Muir-Watt*, in: Twigg-Flesner (ed.), The Cambridge Companion to EU Private Law, 44–57, mainly covers EU legal instruments instead of domestic law.

139 *Mills*, Confluence, 28–30; *Kadner Graziano*, Gemeineuropäisches IPR, 48; *Gebauer*, Grundfragen, 33; *Wolff*, PIL, at 17.

140 *Gebauer*, Grundfragen, 33.

141 *Smits*, in: Adams/Bomhoff (eds.), Practice and Theory in Comparative Law, 170, 172 (emphasis in the original); similarly *Zimmermann*, in: Reimann/id. (ed.), The Oxford Handbook of Comparative Law, 539, 543.

Whatever a reasonable understanding of "general" is – it must mean something relevant in or pertaining to more than one context. If one of these contexts is that of national law and another is that of EU law (which already provides six regulations), it seems particularly important to determine whether there is a common European understanding/content. This could then serve as a common foundation: reducing complexity for the time being and facilitating potential harmonisation in the future. This is also the reason why now is the time to tackle these general issues of private international law from a comparative perspective.[142] To this extent, the ideas behind European private law align with the present ideas of a European perspective on private international law.

1.2.2. The European Union Courts as Comparative Institutions

Such an approach to law in Europe is not only a matter for scholars and legislators, but also one for the judiciary, in particular for the Court of Justice of the European Union. By its nature, "permeated with the values of the surrounding [sic] legal systems", it is a comparative institution.[143] While there is no general provision like Article 38(1)(c) Statute of the International Court of Justice, there are several normative bases in the Treaties for the European Court of Justice (ECJ) to take account of the domestic laws of the member states:[144]

- Article 19(1) TEU (to the extent that it takes up Article 220 EC[145]);
- Article 6(3) TEU ("constitutional traditions common to the Member States");[146]
- Article 340(2) TFEU ("general principles common to the laws of the Member States").

142 *Kadner Graziano*, Gemeineuropäisches IPR, 22, saw no pressing need for the (further) Europeanisation of the private international law discourse in relation to general issues.

143 *Lenaerts*, ICLQ 52 (2003), 873, 905.

144 *Lenaerts/Gutman*, in: Andenas/Fairgrieve (eds.), Courts and Comparative Law, 141, 150–157; *id.*, ICLQ 52 (2003), 873, 876–879; *Kakouris*, in: Drobnig/van Erp (eds.), The Use of Comparative Law by Courts, 97, 99–104.

145 The Court of Justice itself based its reference to "general principles common to the legal systems of the Member States" on this provision, Joined Cases C-46/93 and C-48/93, Brasserie du Pêcheur SA v Bundesrepublik Deutschland and The Queen v Secretary of State for Transport, ex parte: Factortame Ltd and others, Reports of Cases 1996, I-1029, at 27; *Singer/Engel*, JDI 2007, 497, 501; *Kakouris*, in: Drobnig/van Erp (eds.), The Use of Comparative Law by Courts, 97, 102.

146 Adopting a principle formulated by Advocate General *Dutheillet de Lamothe* (Case 11/70, Internationale Handelsgesellschaft mbH v Einfuhr- und Vorratsstelle für Getreide und Futtermittel, Reports of Cases 1970, 1125, 1146–47) and taken up by the Court in Case 4/73, J. Nold, Kohlen- und Baustoffgroßhandlung v Commission of the European Communities, Reports of Cases 1974, 491, at 13 ("the Court is bound to draw inspiration from constitutional traditions common to the Member States"); see also the fifth paragraph of the preamble to and Article 52(4) of the EU Charter of Fundamental Rights, which shares the hierarchical status of the Treaties (Article 6(1) subparagraph 1 TEU).

The last provision is the most obvious. It constitutes an "authorisation of the court to practice evaluative comparative law".[147] To be sure, the Court has not made much use of this authorisation with regard to the liability of the Union.[148] Its first judgment concerning the liability of member states for the violation of Community law,[149] however, already prompted observers to speak of a "new *ius commune*"[150] – although the court had not even made use of any principles common to the member states.[151] Soon after, the Court did rely on the predecessor of Article 340(2) TFEU to support the establishment of criteria for the liability of member states.[152]

More generally, the Court will approach a topic from a comparative point of view when it needs to address a lacuna of EU law.[153] Moreover, when interpreting EU law, the ECJ will often opt for an autonomous understanding of legal terms.[154] "Autonomous" should not be misunderstood as "necessarily and completely removed from national law". It is not paradoxical to have an autonomous interpretation based on comparative law.[155] The expression only refers to an interpretation independent from *individual* national notions.[156] Indeed, the ECJ occasionally has recourse to national legal systems in order

147 *Gellermann*, in: Streinz (ed.), EUV/AEUV, Art. 340 AEUV at 8.

148 See *Kakouris*, in: Drobnig/van Erp (eds.), The Use of Comparative Law by Courts, 97, 100; accordingly, many (German) scholars do not pay much attention to the comparative dimension of this provision, either, *Kischel*, Rechtsvergleichung, §2 at 83.

149 Joined Cases C-6/90 and C-9/90, Andrea Francovich and Danila Bonifaci and others v Italian Republic, Reports of Cases 1991, I-5357.

150 *Caranta*, CMLRev 32 (1995), 703 (italics in the original); very similarly ("Common Law for Europe") and also with references to European legal history *van Gerven*, MJ 1994, 6.

151 It simply considered the liability for a breach of Union law "inherent in the system of the Treaty", Joined Cases C-6/90 and C-9/90, Andrea Francovich and Danila Bonifaci and others v Italian Republic, Reports of Cases 1991, I-5357, at 35.

152 Joined Cases C-46/93 and C-48/93, Brasserie du Pêcheur SA v Bundesrepublik Deutschland and The Queen v Secretary of State for Transport, ex parte: Factortame Ltd and others, Reports of Cases 1996, I-1029, at 40–43.

153 *Beck*, Legal Reasoning of the Court of Justice, 215–216; *Singer/Engel*, JDI 2007, 497, 502. See *Lenaerts*, ICLQ 52 (2003), 873, 883–894 for a typology; and *id./Gutman*, in: Andenas/Fairgrieve (eds.), Courts and Comparative Law, 141, 158–163, for a survey of more recent cases.

154 For an early example see Case 51/76, Verbond van Nederlandse Ondernemingen v Inspecteur der Invoerrechten en Accijnzen, Reports of Cases 1977, 113, at 9–11 (concerning the 1967 directive on turnover taxes); about the same time, the Court declared that Article 1 Brussels Convention had to be given an autonomous meaning, Case 29/76, LTU Lufttransportunternehmen GmbH & Co. KG v Eurocontrol, Reports of Cases 1976, 1541, at 3.

155 *Kakouris*, in: Drobnig/van Erp (eds.), The Use of Comparative Law by Courts, 97, 107; *Kerameus*, in: Hartkamp et al. (eds.), Towards a European Civil Code, 261, 270 ("Autonomous interpretation [of the Brussels Convention] pretends to be uniquely derived from the system and the purpose of the Convention but in fact draws heavily on a comparative review of national legal systems.").

156 Very clearly recently *Kohler*, IPRax 2015, 52, 53; also *Reimann*, C in: id./Zimmermann (eds.), The Oxford Handbook of Comparative Law, 1363, 1388–1389 (concerning the autonomous interpretation of conventions in general).

to arrive at an autonomous meaning.[157] In summary, Lenaerts has described the comparative approach as "a 'quasi-compelling' method of interpretation of [what was then] Community law, intrinsically linked to the continuous integration process".[158] Other insiders regularly stress the importance of comparative law for the Court.[159]

To be sure, (normative) theory and practice seem to, at least, diverge. Sometimes, "general principles of law" in the Court's jurisprudence are "of such a general nature that one does not really need comparative research to conclude that they exist".[160] Often, the Court only pays lip service to the importance of comparative endeavours; comparative efforts in the text of a decision are rare,[161] particularly since the Union has grown to encompass more than six new members.[162] Yet the lack of an express comparative analysis does not mean that such an analysis did not influence a given decision. The Advocate General,[163] the Commission or a member state can provide it.[164] Occasionally, the Court has even requested a comparative analysis from the parties.[165] Perhaps most importantly, and largely unbeknown to the public as well as the parties, the Research and Documentation Directorate also provides comparative research notes for internal use by the EU courts only.[166] Furthermore, a bench made up of judges from different countries is inherently a comparative institution.[167] Finally, the lack of any express comparative analysis may find its reason in the unwieldy style[168] of judicial opinions at the EU level.

157 *Singer/Engel*, JDI 2007, 497, 502–503; *Lenaerts*, ICLQ 52 (2003), 873, 894–897 with examples; for a more pessimistic and a more optimistic view of the success of such comparative efforts *Hess*, IPRax 2006, 348, 353, and *Kropholler*, in: 75 Jahre Max-Planck-Institut für Privatrecht, 583, 591 (at a time when there were only 15 member states), respectively.

158 *Lenaerts*, ICLQ 52 (2003), 873, 878–879; more cautiously *Beck*, Legal Reasoning of the Court of Justice, 215–217.

159 *Singer/Engel*, JDI 2007, 497, 498 and passim; *Kakouris*, in: Drobnig/van Erp (eds.), The Use of Comparative Law by Courts, 97, 102.

160 *Smits*, in: Adams/Bomhoff (eds.), Practice and Theory in Comparative Law, 170, 181.

161 *Rühl*, in: Zimmermann (ed.), Zukunftsperspektiven der Rechtsvergleichung, 103, 126–131; *Smits*, in: Twigg-Flesner (ed.), The Cambridge Companion to EU Private Law, 33, 40; *Hess*, IPRax 2006, 348, 352; *Zimmermann*, in: Reimann/id. (ed.), The Oxford Handbook of Comparative Law, 539, 576.

162 *Lenaerts*, ICLQ 52 (2003), 873, 874.

163 As to the Advocate's General role recently *Lenaerts/Gutman*, in: Andenas/Fairgrieve (eds.), Courts and Comparative Law, 141, 145–150.

164 *Lenaerts*, ICLQ 52 (2003), 873, 875; *Kakouris*, in: Drobnig/van Erp (eds.), The Use of Comparative Law by Courts, 97, 105–107.

165 E.g. Case 155/78, M. v Commission of the European Communities, Reports of Cases 1980, 1797, 1806 ("the parties provided [...] an analytical conspectus of comparative law in answer to a written question from the Court"); see Article 24 Statute of the Court of Justice of the EU.

166 Together with the Directorate Library, this Directorate makes up the Directorate General Library, Research and Documentation; as to its practice see *Singer/Engel*, JDI 2007, 497, 508–513.

167 *Wurmnest*, Grundzüge eines europäischen Haftungsrechts, 16.

168 *Nettesheim*, in: Tichý/Holländer/Bruns (eds.), The Judicial Opinion, 343, 344–345 and passim, also as to the reasons behind this style.

In any case, a questionable practice could not make a normatively predetermined and theoretically sound approach "incorrect".

In conclusion, it seems reasonable to engage with the topic of EU private international law through comparative analysis from a European vantage point. It makes sense because private international law is at issue; it makes sense because European law is at issue.[169] It makes sense from the perspectives of the European legislator, the European judge, and the European scholar.

The approach is bottom-up; otherwise, the (narrow) fixation on a national legal system would have simply been replaced with a (similarly narrow) fixation on EU law.[170] The approach, then, is in many ways similar to Kadner Graziano's.[171] The main and rather obvious difference is that he is interested in content and much less so in structure, whereas I am interested in structure and much less so in content.[172]

2. THE COMPARATIVE APPROACH IN DETAIL

2.1. THE FOUR STEPS OF A TRADITIONAL COMPARATIVE ANALYSIS

A traditional comparative analysis has four steps.[173] It begins with a functional research question, e.g. "How do different countries resolve factual problem X?",[174] and names the countries to be examined (often three).[175] The functional approach is usually traced back to Rabel;[176] Salomon is rarely mentioned,[177] although

---

169 For comparative law and EU private international law specifically, *Basedow*, JZ 2016, 269, 277–279.

170 This is how I understand *Fernández Arroyo*'s, Yearbook of PIL 11 (2009), 31, 57, criticism of "Euro-centrism"; his idea of comparative private international law on a global scale, however, seems to go even further than the present approach, ibid., 71.

171 *Kadner Graziano*, Gemeineuropäisches IPR, 26–32 (concerning his method), 45–89 (historical models).

172 *Supra* Introduction, section 2.

173 *Siems*, Comparative Law, 13–40; similarly *Dannemann*, in: Reimann/Zimmermann (eds.), The Oxford Handbook of Comparative Law, 383, 406–418. Of course, different models with fewer, more (see *Husa*, RabelsZ 67 (2003), 419, 425: five) or different steps exist. The four outlined here, however, do seem to encapsulate the most common approach.

174 *Bogdan*, Introduction to Comparative Law, 47; *Reimann*, Am. J. Comp. L. 50 (2002), 671, 679; *Zweigert/Kötz*, Introduction to Comparative Law, 34–36; *Martinek*, in: Simon (ed.), Rechtswissenschaft in der Bonner Republik, 529, 551; *Rheinstein*, Einführung, 25–28; *Zweigert*, in: Mélanges Maury, 579, 583–590.

175 *Siems*, Comparative Law, 15.

176 *Rabel*, Die Fachgebiete des Kaiser-Wilhelm-Instituts, 180, 187; one might even go back a bit farther in *Rabel*'s work to remarks made "almost in passing" (*Michaels*, in: Reimann/Zimmermann (eds.), The Oxford Handbook of Comparative Law, 339, 362): *Rabel*, Aufgabe und Notwendigkeit, 1, 3–5. In any case, *Rabel* did not really elaborate on his approach, *Gerber*, in: Riles (ed.), Rethinking the Masters of Comparative Law, 190, 198.

177 But see *Sandrock*, Sinn und Methode, 16–17.

his account[178] is at least equally elaborate.[179] The functional approach finds its standard reference text in Zweigert and Kötz's *Introduction to Comparative Law*.[180] It is employed in micro-comparative endeavours[181] in order to observe how rules actually work, as well as not to be misled by foreign terminology and formal classifications.[182] If similar to one's own, they might obscure differences; if different from one's own, they might obscure similarities. If the starting point were a legal concept or institution (usually one found in the comparatist's own legal system), one might come away empty-handed because the foreign legal system might not have this concept or institution. One could overlook that the same problem is indeed resolved under the foreign legal system, only by the means of some other legal institution.[183] "Social problems are universal",[184] legal institutions are not.

The limitation to a few countries – or to be more precise, legal systems – is based on practical constraints of time and space, in light of the goal of being able to carry out an "actual comparison".[185] The selection of the legal systems to be compared obviously depends on the research question, with preconceptions about certain legal systems acting as possible guiding factors.[186] It has also been suggested to look for phenotypical solutions and then to only compare representatives of each class of phenotypes.[187] Moreover, for reasons of "sophistication and richness of material", a focus on the major legal systems has been proposed.[188]

The second step consists of describing the different laws. The comparatist is not supposed to carry out this description from the perspective of her own

---

178 *Salomon*, Grundlegung, 33–37.

179 Some foundations for functionalism also appear in *Zitelmann*'s œuvre, see *Neuenbäumer*, Ernst Zitelmann, 233–238.

180 *Michaels*, in: Reimann/Zimmermann (eds.), The Oxford Handbook of Comparative Law, 339, 340; a bit more cautiously *Martinek*, in: Simon (ed.), Rechtswissenschaft in der Bonner Republik, 529, 552 (functionalism "for instance" "represented" by *Zweigert/Kötz).*

181 *Dannemann*, in: Reimann/Zimmermann (eds.), The Oxford Handbook of Comparative Law, 383, 388, correctly points out that the functional approach does not really lend itself to macrocomparison; similarly *Husa*, RabelsZ 67 (2003), 419, 422.

182 *Bogdan*, Introduction to Comparative Law, 47–48; *Gerber*, in: Riles (ed.), Rethinking the Masters of Comparative Law, 190, 199; *Reitz*, Am. J. Comp. L. 46 (1998), 617, 621.

183 *Siems*, Comparative Law, 14; *Zweigert*, in: Mélanges Maury, 579, 589 (the problem of "on ne trouve rien à ce sujet").

184 *Örücü*, in: ead./Nelken (eds.), Comparative Law, 43, 51; similarly, but not as succinctly *Zweigert/Kötz*, Introduction to Comparative Law, 39; but also see *Michaels*, in: Reimann/Zimmermann (eds.), The Oxford Handbook of Comparative Law, 339, 368–369, who argues to consider the formulation of a problem as a constructive rather than an empirical move.

185 *Siems*, Comparative Law, 15; *Zweigert/Kötz*, Introduction to Comparative Law, 41; already *Zweigert*, in: Mélanges Maury, 579, 584, contending that it might be possible to "consider everything" but efforts and results would be out of proportion.

186 See *Zweigert*, in: Mélanges Maury, 579, 586 (for antitrust law, it might be more fruitful to turn to U.S. law than to French law etc.); similarly *Sandrock*, Sinn und Methode, 29.

187 *Drobnig*, in: FS Rheinstein I, 221, 225.

188 *Markesinis/Fedtke*, Engaging with Foreign Law, 50.

legal system because this would likely distort the picture.[189] Whether an internal or a neutral point of view should be adopted, however, is a contested issue.[190]

In the third step, similarities and variations are identified and explained. Otherwise, according to the frequent and justified admonition,[191] comparative law would merely consist of compiling foreign law and not be deserving of its name.

The final step consists of a policy evaluation, possibly resulting in proposals *de lege ferenda*. Rabel himself distinguished this last step from comparative law, contending that evaluation is a question only *made possible* by comparative law.[192] However, if the comparatist does not provide a critical evaluation, "no one else will do it".[193] Hence, whether one considers it a question of comparative *law* as a matter of terminology or not (the question of which rule to make or adopt mostly being a matter of policy, not one of law), it should nevertheless be considered part of the comparative process.

2.2. THE STEPS UNDERTAKEN IN THIS BOOK

2.2.1. The Research Question and the Legal Systems at Issue

2.2.1.1. A Focus on Concepts (but still Functionalism)

This analysis follows the steps just outlined only in part. Already the starting point is different. It would be quite artificial to say that this analysis is about a factual situation and its different solutions. This is due, in part, to the very nature of private international law; it does not provide a substantive solution to a factual situation but only determines the law in which to find that solution. Comparative private international law *can* have the conventional factual

---

189 *Siems*, Comparative Law, 16.

190 For the internal perspective *Bogdan*, Introduction to Comparative Law, 32–34; *Grosswald Curran*, Am. J. Comp. L. 46 (1990), 43, 50–51 (notes removed); the functional approach itself seems to furnish a neutral basis to proceed from, see *Siems*, Comparative Law, 17, with reference to *Zweigert/Kötz*, Introduction to Comparative Law, 10.

191 *Kischel*, Rechtsvergleichung, §3 at 238; *Siems*, Comparative Law, 20; *Markesinis/Fedtke*, Engaging with Foreign Law, 9; *Reimann*, in: id./Zimmermann (eds.), The Oxford Handbook of Comparative Law, 1363, 1381; *Zweigert/Kötz*, Introduction to Comparative Law, 6 and 43; *Rheinstein*, Einführung, 22; similarly *Bogdan*, Introduction to Comparative Law, 16–17.

192 *Rabel*, Aufgabe und Notwendigkeit, 1, 3; for modern restrictive positions see *Valcke*, in: Adams/Bomhoff (eds.), Practice and Theory in Comparative Law, 22, 24–25, and the post-modern conception of comparative law by *Jayme*, Postmoderne Theorie, 103, 110; *von Mehren*, in: Butler (ed.), International Law in Comparative Perspective, 153–154, also stops after step three.

193 *Zweigert/Kötz*, Introduction to Comparative Law, 47; see already *Zweigert*, in: Mélanges Maury, 579, 595–596; for an evaluative final step also *Kischel*, Rechtsvergleichung, §1 at 11.

starting point where it is concerned with the question of which law different domestic conflicts provisions deem applicable to a given set of facts. Yet the comparative part of this book does not concern this. Rather, it revolves around a conceptual, legal issue: how do the EU and its member states deal with a certain class of issues of private international law, a class not made up of a common factual basis but by issues sharing a "general" quality?

Is this still functionalism? Does it not mean succumbing to the fallacy of looking through a conceptual prism? To be sure, there is no factual basis to proceed from functionally; indeed, with this objective, there cannot be. For whatever a sensible and precise understanding of "general" could be, at the very least it must mean something abstract, aggregated, broad. A factual problem cannot display any of those traits. If a focus on facts and the effects of legal rules in reality is the bedrock of functionalism,[194] the present analysis is not "functional".

However, in the first instance, the relevance of legal undertones actually moves on a sliding scale, even where factual problems are at issue.[195] Second, this book does concern the reaction of different legal systems to a common issue, with the one qualification that the issue does not directly involve social reality. Broadly speaking, the common issue here is one of structuring/conceptualising an area of law.

It is true that in order to be able to answer the question of "how", an affirmative answer to the "if" must be presupposed, just as the universality of social problems[196] must be supposed when the comparative analysis departs from a factual issue. In other words: private international law must be considered a separate area of law in all the legal systems to be examined. This, however, does not constitute misguided reliance on terminology. Rather, it is all about the *function* of private international law: a solution to the question of which law to apply to a given factual situation. It is safe to assume (and will subsequently be demonstrated) that every member state has solutions for this issue – whether in statutory form or not; whether the solution consists in the application of its own law or foreign law – and distinguishes these solutions from provisions which directly determine the outcome. Hence the danger of "on ne trouve rien à ce sujet"[197] does not exist in this respect.

The potential reverse side of the coin, i.e. overlooking (novel) solutions in the foreign legal system only because they are not found "in the same place" as

---

194 See *Siems*, Comparative Law, 26; *Michaels*, in: Reimann/Zimmermann (eds.), The Oxford Handbook of Comparative Law, 339, 342.

195 See *Kischel*, Rechtsvergleichung, §3 at 167–168.

196 At least insofar as the legal systems to be examined are concerned; see *Michaels*, in: Reimann/Zimmermann (eds.), The Oxford Handbook of Comparative Law, 339, 370, also as to the tautology contained in this statement ("not fatal once we understand functionalism as a constructive method").

197 See note 181.

in the comparatist's own law, likewise does not exist. Function determines the objects of comparison, not their place. Even if a member state did not call this area of law "private international law" or "conflicts" or any of the usual names, rules could be identified by their function. Thus, while the starting point is unusual from a traditional point of view, this book complies with several main tenets of functionalism.

An ideal functional analysis is very open-ended as it can look beyond the law even.[198] The present book cannot do so, for it only pertains to a question of law to begin with. Where matters of concept are at issue, there is no conceptual veil to be lifted. This book is not, however, entirely limited to legislation. Any domestic structure (or lack thereof[199]) of private international law rules will be taken into account. Whether a structure exists in a legislative text or has been developed by another stakeholder does not matter for the purposes of being included here. This seems to correspond to Sacco's idea of taking account of "legal formants",[200] i.e. "all the authorities a lawyer working in a given system might consult to find the law".[201] This, in any case, is one of the core concerns of functionalism.[202]

2.2.1.2. Inclusion of All Member States

The suggestion of limiting oneself to about three countries is outright ignored. The subject of this analysis is, in addition to the private international law of the EU itself, the domestic private international law rules of all its member states. For all of them (but also only for them), general issues of EU private international law are relevant. The selection, thus, was not made on a substantive basis (what legal systems will likely provide the most interesting/fruitful/inspiring solutions?) but on a politico-economic/geographical basis, against the backdrop of existing EU private international law. Choosing only legal systems which are relatively easy to research (for reasons of language, "sophistication", and availability of materials) can certainly lead to results interesting in and of themselves. There also is something to be said for the latter approach from a practical perspective, such as Markesinis and Fedtke's which focuses on the

---

198 See *Markesinis/Fedtke*, Engaging with Foreign Law, 38–39; *Michaels*, in: Reimann/Zimmermann (eds.), The Oxford Handbook of Comparative Law, 339, 364; *Dannemann*, ibid., 383, 414; *Gerber*, in: Riles (ed.), Rethinking the Masters of Comparative Law, 190, 200 ("virtually unlimited" scope); *Peters/Schwenke*, ICLQ 49 (2000), 800, 828; *Martinek*, in: Simon (ed.), Rechtswissenschaft in der Bonner Republik, 529, 551 (but also see his more sobering assessment, 552–553); already *Rabel*, Aufgabe und Notwendigkeit, 1, 5; see *Frankenberg*, Harv. Int. L. J. 26 (1985), 411, 437 for a much more critical assessment.

199 Which in this case would be a *finding* ("member state X does have private international law rules but does not structure them in any apparent way"), *not a mistake*.

200 *Sacco*, Am. J. Comp. L. 39 (1991), 1, 21–34.

201 *Reitz*, Am. J. Comp. L. 46 (1998), 617, 629.

202 See also *Kischel*, Rechtsvergleichung, 44–45.

realities for practitioners, students, and legislators.[203] Nevertheless, it would obviously not lead to an accurate portrayal of the status quo across all the EU.

A genuinely European analysis simply cannot ignore any member state *a priori*. This is not only a theoretical postulate,[204] it also has a practical side to it: if the EU legislator decided to address the issue, it might be easier to reach (political) consensus for a concept that is widely known than for a concept only known in one legal system, even if this legal system is a powerhouse of intellectual and legal tradition. Conversely, if one were to champion a concept from one of these powerhouses, one had better be aware that other positions exist. Otherwise it will be much harder to be persuasive, as one's arguments would address concerns based on other positions only by coincidence.

Finally, any accusation of "cherry-picking"[205] will be levied in vain given that the selection of legal systems to be analysed is made without looking at the content of their rules. Admittedly, several difficulties result from "blindly" including all the member states. They will be dealt with below.[206]

2.2.2. *The Descriptive Stage*

The second traditional step of descriptively juxtaposing the different laws is observed, albeit in deliberately brief fashion. The perspective taken is intended to be neutral because a truly perfect inside perspective is almost impossible to achieve.[207] At the end of each section, the findings are summarised. Certain similarities are highlighted and some differences are accounted for.

2.2.3. *Establishment of a Framework*

Instead of delving too deep into the similarities and differences, however, an attempt will subsequently be made to provide a theoretical framework for general provisions at the EU level, with examples from national law used to support these suggestions. As the framework is established on a theoretical level removed from individual solutions (although inspiration and influence cannot be denied), the rationale behind the domestic examples will usually not be explored from an internal perspective.

The approach is (in part) in line with the aforementioned notion of dealing with representative examples of certain types of solutions. It is clearly not

---

203 *Markesinis/Fedtke*, Engaging with Foreign Law, 35 and passim (49–51 for the application of their view to the question of making a selection of countries to examine).

204 I agree in this regard with what *von Bar*, JZ 2014, 473, 478, calls the "arrogance" of the notion of legal families.

205 Regardless of whether one considers such an accusation plausible; *Markesinis/Fedtke*, Engaging with Foreign Law, 49–50, clearly do not.

206 *Infra* sections 3.3. and 3.4.

207 See *Zweigert*, in: Mélanges Maury, 579, 588.

"comparative law as a method of interpretation",[208] for it does not concern the construction of any given legal rule. Yet it shares with that concept the idea that findings of comparative law can corroborate or cast doubt on results arrived at by other means.[209]

2.2.4. External Standards of Law and Policy

As this book generally does not revolve around the content of individual "general" provisions at the national level, there also is no critical evaluation in the sense of determining which national provision is the "best". As pure functionalism focuses on functional *equivalents*, it cannot be the foundation for such a decision in any case.[210] Rather, this analysis proceeds to covering the general provisions of private international law as a concept from two different perspectives, those of law and policy. Regardless of the potential content of general provisions of EU law, would the EU even allowed to make use of the framework developed in the previous step? And should it? The mere fact that there is a majority position for one way of approaching general issues of private international law in domestic law obviously cannot be the answer to the first question. Nor does it automatically tip the policy balance in its favour; although, from a political point of view, harmonisation could be easier when only a few countries need to be brought onboard.

As Zweigert has observed, a theoretician certainly could come up with the same solutions as a comparatist, but the latter's chances of doing so are much greater.[211] The present approach is of a hybrid nature: a theoretical framework is set up, both inspired and validated by examples drawn from comparative efforts.

3. POTENTIAL PITFALLS

It seems somewhat plausible to say that comparative private international law has fewer pitfalls than comparative law in general due to the "indirect character" of conflicts rules and their being more removed from the factual circumstances.[212] Yet many of comparative law's notorious problems, and some

---

208 Foundationally *Zweigert*, ZAIPR 15 (1949/50), 5–21; for a more recent and updated account in English see *Zweigert/Kötz*, Introduction to Comparative Law, 18–21.

209 *Zweigert*, ZAIPR 15 (1949/50), 5, 17–18.

210 *Michaels*, in: Reimann/Zimmermann (eds.), The Oxford Handbook of Comparative Law, 339, 374.

211 *Zweigert*, in: Mélanges Maury, 579, 581.

212 *Mádl/Vékás*, ZfRV 1982, 266, 267 ("[d]er indirekte Charakter der Kollisionsnormen, ihre größere Distanz zu den Lebensverhältnissen").

issues raised more recently also, rear their ugly heads when dealing with private international law. In the following, some of these difficulties and their impact on this book shall be expressly addressed and assessed. It will be regarded as axiomatic, however, that the member states, not least for forming part of the EU, are sufficiently similar[213] as not to warrant any discussion of comparative law's potential difficulties[214] in relation to "radically different"[215] countries.

3.1. "POST-MODERN" CHALLENGES TO TRADITIONAL COMPARATIVE LAW

Traditional comparative law has been challenged in particular since the end of the 20th century. Frankenberg had already laid much of the groundwork for the attack in 1985,[216] but the impact of his seminal article was felt only later on in light of the conference on "New Approaches to Comparative Law" at the University of Utah.[217] Relatively quickly, these challenges were aggregated and dubbed "post-modern",[218] even if not every one of them is genuinely post-modern. At roughly the same time, Jayme came forward with some remarks as to post-modern comparative law,[219] both independent from the development occurring across the Atlantic and much less critically.

The more disapproving line of criticism seems to suggest that comparative law is an almost impossible discipline. This stands in stark contrast to the experience of many comparatists that, despite the existence of issues and pitfalls that nobody denies, this branch of law often produces acceptable results.[220] It is probably for this reason that the critical post-modern approaches have occasionally been castigated as "silly",[221] and that the agenda behind them has

213 See *Zimmermann*, in: Reimann/id. (ed.), The Oxford Handbook of Comparative Law, 539, 541.

214 See *Siems*, Comparative Law, 36–37; *Bogdan*, Introduction to Comparative Law, 50–52; *Martinek*, in: Simon (ed.), Rechtswissenschaft in der Bonner Republik, 529, 563–565; *Sacco*, Am. J. Comp. L. 39 (1991), 1, 6–9.

215 "Law in Radically Different Cultures" was a class taught at Stanford University at the beginning of the 1980s, see *Gibbs*, American Behavioral Scientist 25 (1981), 37. The problems of comparative law arise in particular in relation to non-occidental law, *Kischel*, R.I.D.C. 2016, 907, 925.

216 *Frankenberg*, Harv. Int. L. J. 26 (1985), 411.

217 The contributions to the conference can be found in Utah L. R. 1997, 255–663; as to the development see *Mattei*, in: Reimann/Zimmermann (eds.), The Oxford Handbook of Comparative Law, 815, 818.

218 See *Siems*, Comparative Law, 18 ("umbrella term"); *Markesinis/Fedtke*, Engaging with Foreign Law, 53; *Reimann*, Am. J. Comp. L. 50 (2002), 671, 681–682; *Peters/Schwenke*, ICLQ 49 (2000), 800, 801 (also admitting that this label is a simplification).

219 *Jayme*, Postmoderne Theorie.

220 *Kischel*, R.I.D.C. 2016, 907, 908.

221 *Markesinis/Fedtke*, Engaging with Foreign Law, 45, 53–58.

been described as one of "liberation through disruption and disorientation".[222] Incidentally, disorientation is one of the effects that the style and language of a typical text bring about. More charitably, one can say that post-modern criticism has led to (a postulate of) "heightened reflexivity"[223] – which happens to be exactly what Frankenberg originally argued for.[224] In this spirit, the relevance of some aspects of post-modern critique[225] for the present book will be explored.

3.1.1. *Western Focus*

Traditional comparative law has been attacked for focusing on Western legal systems.[226] Even if one were to accept this as a valid criticism,[227] it would be patently unfair to challenge the choice of countries made here in this way. This book does not aim to unearth a "universal" law, but to assess the law of the member states. In light of this, it is just the other way around: to include any *other* legal system,[228] possibly some tribal law for good measure, would require justification. The only potential object to frown upon, therefore, could be the goal of this book itself. Yet the considerations made in the first half of this chapter seem to justify it sufficiently.

3.1.2. *Bias*

Post-modern critics (but not only them) have pointed out at least two biases of traditional comparative law. First, a bias for the comparatist's own law;[229] and second, a bias towards similarities (as opposed to tolerating/accepting differences).[230] To some degree, these criticisms are valid. Some distortion in the comparative process is inevitable. It is almost inconceivable that a scholar knows

---

222 *Mattei*, in: Reimann/Zimmermann (eds.), The Oxford Handbook of Comparative Law, 815, 819; how different *Jayme's* idea of post-modernist comparative law, Postmoderne Theorie, 103, 118 ("Die postmoderne Theorie der Rechtsvergleichung rüttelt nicht am Bestehenden und Bewährten.")!

223 *Peters/Schwenke*, ICLQ 49 (2000), 800, 829; similarly *de Coninck*, RabelsZ 74 (2010), 318, 335–336; *Husa*, RabelsZ 67 (2003), 419, 446.

224 *Frankenberg*, Harv. Int. L. J. 26 (1985), 411, 421 and 442–445; but see *Husa*, RabelsZ 67 (2003), 419, 436, with a different understanding of *Frankenberg*: "Why is comparative law done at all?" instead of "How should it be done?".

225 For a balanced assessment of critique of the functional method, see also *Piek*, ZEuP 2013, 60.

226 *Frankenberg*, Harv. Int. L. J. 26 (1985), 411, 414 and 422; also see *Siems*, Comparative Law, 36–37.

227 *Peters/Schwenke* do not, ICLQ 49 (2000), 800, 821.

228 This is not to suggest that looking beyond the boundaries of the EU would not be a worthwhile endeavour (for this *Rühl*, in: Zimmermann (ed.), Zukunftsperspektiven der Rechtsvergleichung, 103, 124–125 and 137).

229 See *Frankenberg*, Harv. Int. L. J. 26 (1985), 411, 425 and 432.

230 *Grosswald Curran*, Am. J. Comp. L. 46 (1990), 43, 67 and 91; similarly *Jayme*, Postmoderne Theorie, 103, 107–108 and 110.

exactly as much about a foreign legal system as she does about the one by which she was socialised.[231] The asymmetry of knowledge, minuscule as it may be, implies some bias, even if it is not pronounced. The comparatist can strive to be objective and can (and should) openly acknowledge as many of her underlying premises as possible, but "true" objectivity is impossible to achieve individually. This is where scholarly (and for comparative law in particular: international) collaboration and mutual criticism come into play.[232] Comparative efforts are doomed to imperfection[233] – but that does not make them futile. This very part of the book serves to address my substantive and methodological preconceptions transparently; critical discussion may then further purge the results of any remaining bias.

The reader might consider the occasional use of the term "general part" an indication of bias. Yet this term is only shorthand for (legislative) concepts that formally distinguish between certain "general" rules and other more specific rules; at the very least, it does not refer to a *particular* national model. Insofar as using the term at all might be construed as a bias towards any system, or all the systems employing such a distinction, the reproach is harder to refute. But it is as hard to refute as the idea that a German author is likely to have a bias towards a "general part" anyway,[234] even (and maybe particularly) where an effort has been made to avoid that term. Placed between a rock and a hard place, I made the conscious choice of sticking with the expression.

A related question is that of systematisation. Ideally, a supranational comparative analysis follows a structure independent from national preconceptions. Such a structure, however, is a (intermediary) result of the comparative efforts themselves.[235] This is a heuristic problem, yet also one of properly presenting the findings. If the results of the comparative efforts form the basis, findings may seem self-evident and arguments circular. Taking national classifications as a basis risks starting with a bias and/or ending up with results not in conformity with the structure used. Because of the aforementioned "international" characteristics of private international law, however, this concern applies with much less force. As many (of the major) private international law classifications and terms *are* in conformity, or at least commonly known, they can be presupposed without much danger of thereby tainting the results.

---

231 See *Peters/Schwenke*, ICLQ 49 (2000), 800, 833.

232 *Peters/Schwenke*, ICLQ 49 (2000), 800, 831; already *Rabel*, ZAIPR 16 (1951), 340, 359 ("If the picture presented by a scholar is coloured by his background or education, international collaboration will correct it." – as translated in *Zweigert/Kötz*, Introduction to Comparative Law, 47).

233 *Grosswald Curran*, Am. J. Comp. L. 46 (1990), 43, 48 and 91; it should be noted that *Grosswald Curran* herself does not come the result that this observation makes comparative efforts futile, either.

234 See *supra* Introduction, section 1., and *infra* Chapter 6, section 2.1.

235 *Drobnig*, in: FS Rheinstein I, 221, 228–229.

3.1.3. *"Legocentrism"*

Frankenberg in particular has criticised the focus on law, as opposed to everything that "is not formalized and not regulated under a given legal regime".[236] This appears to be a criticism of the way comparative law is actually being practised, rather than a criticism of comparative law in theory because, as pointed out above,[237] functionalism *can* go beyond the law.[238] As also already pointed out, however, for comparative private international law, this does not seem applicable. In order for things not to become hopelessly complicated, the existence of law must be presupposed – and how else but by *legal* rules would one determine the applicability of this *law*? Therefore, the analysis must be "logocentric".

3.2. FUNCTIONALISM AND UNIFICATION

Michaels argues rather persuasively that functional comparative law does not actually fare well when it comes to the unification of law.[239] First and as already mentioned, functionalism itself can provide no argument for or against a particular solution; by definition, all solutions are functionally equivalent. Second, as an anti-doctrinal method (it is designed, after all, not to rely on formalist classifications), it does not work well when making doctrinal rules. Third, when a functional comparison has revealed similarities, why unify at all? When unification is easier than previously thought, it is also less important.

These three arguments, however, apply only in part to the present context. The first one has already been dealt with.[240] Functionalism does not serve as the foundation for a policy question. As this book has an inevitable focus on *law*, its comparative approach is rather doctrinal. Therefore, the second argument is not of much concern. Finally, the third argument regarding the usefulness of unification in view of existing harmony is a policy issue that will be addressed later on. Suffice it to say at this point that harmony regarding a concept/structure is not the same as harmony regarding the individual solutions.

---

236 *Frankenberg*, Harv. Int. L. J. 26 (1985), 411, 433, 438, and 445–448.

237 *Supra* sections 2.1. and 2.2.1.1.

238 Also see *Grellette/Valcke*, Transnational Legal Theory 5 (2014), 557, 569–576, for a recent account of why a focus on "law" is less narrow than it might appear.

239 *Michaels*, in: Reimann/Zimmermann (eds.), The Oxford Handbook of Comparative Law, 339, 376–377.

240 *Supra* section 2.2.4.

3.3. THE AVAILABILITY AND RELIABILITY OF PRIMARY AND SECONDARY SOURCES

At the end of the 1960s, Rheinstein predicted that, thanks to computerisation, legal materials from all over the world and from all time periods would be available to the scholar.[241] So far, this optimistic prognosis has not come true. Even in an age like the present, where all information is seemingly available at the click of a mouse, it is not possible even for an astute cybrarian to find up-to-date legal materials, whether legislation or scholarly works, for every country subject to this analysis. Furthermore, due to the sheer amount of foreign law to be processed, there is a risk that materials which were up-to-date when research began were already out of date by the time of writing. The risk of outdated materials exists simply because of the time lag between writing and publication.

Yet, although highly desirable, currency is ultimately not as important for this conceptual analysis as it would be for a book on the content of individual rules.[242] Unless a member state has completely restructured its private international law – i.e. abolished an existing "general part" without any substitute, or created one where there had been none before – this book is not seriously compromised. The removal or addition of individual provisions from or to a "general part" would affect the results only in isolated instances. In contrast, changes made to the content of a "general" provision would not affect the findings at all, as the fact of the existence of a certain provision would remain.

Another issue is the number of available secondary, i.e. non-legislative, sources.[243] Depending on factors such as the size of the member state at issue, its tradition and culture of legal education and writing,[244] the existence of people able and willing to write about their respective private international law in a language that I at least rudimentarily understand, and the accessibility of such materials, the amount of secondary materials processed in this book unfortunately varies from member state to member state. The lower the number of sources, the greater the risk of an inadvertent misrepresentation.

---

241 *Rheinstein*, Einführung, 51.

242 See *Bogdan*, Introduction to Comparative Law, 32, who points out that relying on certain fundamental assumptions can be justifiable, even in light of possibly abrupt changes.

243 For a relatively recent practical example of the problems of assessing the developments in several European member states at the same time, see *Czepelak*, in: Campuzano Díaz et al. (eds.), Latest Developments in EU Private International Law, 49, 50 and passim.

244 See the examples in EuLF 2005, I-260–I-311, regarding, in particular, the conditions of research and teaching of *private international law* in 26 member states. For one comparative perspective on legal education around the world, see *Wilson*, The Role of Practice in Legal Education.

While this is perhaps the biggest possible systemic flaw affecting this analysis, again, its conceptual nature either makes any such misrepresentation unlikely, or at least mitigates its effects. First, questions like "is there a legislative general part of private international law in member state X?" and "what is its scope?" are unlikely subjects for a scholarly debate in which an observer from the outside might mistakenly only take account of one of many positions. One can really only envision such a situation where the validity of law is contested, maybe due to constitutional requirements or an ambiguous provision determining the date of its entering into force. Even in those extreme situations – of which there has not been any indication across the EU – the general willingness of a legislator to conceptualise private international law along certain lines would remain as a fact of relevance for present purposes. Second, where the likelihood of any such misrepresentation is greater, e.g. where scholarly concepts of a "general part" are not congruent with written law (as is arguably the case in Germany[245]), there still is the respective primary source (or, in other cases, the lack thereof) which can serve as a conceptual starting point.

Then there is the usual risk of misapprehension as to the relative importance of statutory law in other countries.[246] For conceptual purposes, however, it can be sufficient to merely note the existence of statutory private international law and its structure. Findings may be even more persuasive where these statutory provisions matter more in the daily practice of law, but their very existence already constitutes a useful baseline.

3.4. THE CHOICE OF THE ENGLISH LANGUAGE

While it may be true that genuinely European legal scholarship must be multilingual,[247] a single volume by one author should stick to one language. The main reason behind the choice of the English language is the desire to make the findings of this book as broadly accessible as possible. For this purpose, nothing other than the *de facto*[248] *lingua franca* of the EU seems appropriate. EU and private international law terminology, however, can be rather peculiar; it might be more accurate to speak of an English dialect[249] (much as "Globish" has been identified as a global English dialect[250]). The use of English also has a beneficial

245 *Infra* Chapter 2, section 1.3.2.1.
246 *Bogdan*, Introduction to Comparative Law, 33.
247 *Remien*, JZ 1992, 277, 283.
248 *Truchot*, in: Maurais/Morris (eds.), Languages in a globalising world, 99, 103–105; also *Zimmermann*, in: MacQueen/id. (ed.), European Contract Law, 1, 34 (with caveats); *idem*, Comparative Law and the Europeanization of Private Law, 539, 550.
249 See *Pozzo*, Comparative law and language, 88, 110–111.
250 The term seems to have been coined by *Jean-Paul Nerrière*, see *McCrum*, Globish, 9.

side effect. Language is likely to manifest preconceptions in a way that is hard to detect;[251] authors might not even be aware of this phenomenon themselves. My resorting to a language other than the one in which I received most of my legal training should at least have diminished this risk.

Most materials on which this book is based are written in English, French or German, while some are in Dutch, Italian, Portuguese or Spanish. The implication is twofold: on the one hand, for quite a few member states, materials in the language of their respective legal systems were used, albeit not always exclusively; on the other hand, for many states, only translations and secondary materials not in the original language were used due to linguistic limitations. If comparative scholars must be "fluent in at least one of the main languages of each of the foreign countries whose law they intend to study",[252] this becomes rather problematic.

A related question is that of the translation of legal terms in general.[253] Without translation, legal ideas rarely "spread further than [...] national boundaries".[254] But any translation runs the risk of either being unfaithful to the legal system of origin, or of being incomprehensible to the intended audience.[255] Some terms are ambiguous because they can, although seemingly identical by their letters, mean two things in two different legal systems, e.g. "jurisprudence" in English and French; not to mention that one and the same term can have different meanings even within the same legal system. Other words seem to have the same content (mainly because it is easy to translate them literally), but are different, at least around their edges: think of "property" or "contract".[256] Rather than only being a question of presentation, the issue of translation can affect the entire comparative process from the start. If it is based on a translation, at least one element of the understanding of a foreign legal system as completely as possible is lacking already.[257]

Yet again, the limited objective of this book, as well as the special case of private international law, considerably alleviate these serious issues. Even if, in

---

[251] See *Dannemann*, in: Adams/Bomhoff (eds.), Practice and Theory in Comparative Law, 96, 109 (for drafting legal rules).

[252] *Reitz*, Am. J. Comp. L. 46 (1998), 617, 632; but also see 633 ("quite legitimate for comparatists to base their comparisons on literature produced by foreign law specialists").

[253] *Kischel*, Rechtsvergleichung, §3 at 203; *Pozzo*, Comparative law and language; *Reitz*, Am. J. Comp. L. 46 (1998), 617, 620–621; *Grosswald Curran*, Am. J. Comp. L. 46 (1990), 43, 54–59; *Drobnig*, in: FS Rheinstein I, 221, 230–233.

[254] *Markesinis/Fedtke*, Engaging with Foreign Law, 44; similarly *Zimmermann*, in: Reimann/id. (ed.), The Oxford Handbook of Comparative Law, 539, 550.

[255] *Pozzo*, Comparative law and language, 88, 94.

[256] See *Sacco*, in: Cappelletti (ed.), New Perspectives for a Common Law of Europe, 95, 96 ("Le *Besitz* n'est pas la possession. Le *Vertrag* n'est pas le *contrat*, il n'est pas non plus le *contract*.") (italics in the original).

[257] See *Grosswald Curran*, Am. J. Comp. L. 46 (1990), 43, 57 and passim.

the source materials, certain terms were poorly translated,[258] this would affect a book on the content of provisions much more so than one concerned with the structural order behind them. Unless entire provisions have been literally lost in translation, even a poor translation should leave unaffected the structure in which the provision is found. Furthermore, as a consequence of the long tradition of international collaboration and thinking in private international law, many terms of art do have reliable (English) translations.[259] When non-native speakers make use of private international law terms in a foreign language, it is relatively safe to assume that they do not make mistakes on the basis of "false friends" and such.

Therefore, in most cases, only the English term in question will be used here. Where more clarity and precision is needed, however, the original word will additionally be used at least once. Where more than one term is commonly used to describe a certain phenomenon (e.g. "characterisation", "classification" or "qualification"), all will be mentioned and, where needed, expressly distinguished.

Finally, the book follows Siems' sensible advice not to underestimate the reader.[260] Where an English term is used for a phenomenon found in a legal system not operating in English, it will be assumed that the reader realises that the word does not necessarily have the exact same meaning as it would in an English environment.

---

258 It does not matter whether this is due to carelessness or whether it is near-impossible to "properly" translate a given term for the lack of a counterpart (see *Bogdan*, Introduction to Comparative Law, 36).

259 See e.g. *T. Ballarino/E. Ballarino/Pretelli*, DIP, I 6 (11).

260 *Siems*, Comparative Law, 18.

CHAPTER 2
MATERIAL

Descriptive sections in comparative studies can easily become tedious. Yet transparency dictates not making reference to the provisions of domestic and EU law only in piecemeal fashion later on, where the brunt of references is relegated to the "low rumble of the footnote".[261] I will therefore try to navigate Scylla and Charybdis by first giving a brief overview of the private international law of each member state and of the EU itself, so that later references do not point to a vacuum.

Incidentally: the decision for not having fewer references, and thus slimmer footnotes, in the first place is based on the idea that not all sources compiled for this book will be available everywhere. More references for the same point increase the probability that every reader has access to at least some of the sources relied upon for my observations.

1. DOMESTIC PRIVATE INTERNATIONAL LAW

1.1. SCOPE OF THE OVERVIEW

In accordance with the overall approach of this book, the scope does not cover the legal, constitutional, or political order of the member states as a whole. Rather, it focuses on the following issues:

- Is there a legislative act, be it part of another act or stand-alone, dealing with different aspects of conflict of laws? In short, and shunning the many possible connotations of the term, is there a "code" of private international law?
- If so, does that code contain a separate set of provisions which it itself expressly deems "general"? (This formal perspective entails that the meaning of "general" can remain open for the time being.) What issues do the provisions in such a section deal with?

---

261 *Grafton*, The Footnote, 5.

- If there is no code of private international law, are there issues which have nevertheless been identified as "general" or at least are dealt with separately from other sets of issues (and by whom/with what authority)?

Note that, in the interest of readability, I will use inverted commas as sparingly as possible outside of direct quotations (of which there will be quite a few). References to the general provisions of a member state are meant as references to what this particular member state calls "general" (or "common" etc.) provisions. Also note that the country reports had long been written when the *Encyclopaedia of PIL*, edited by Basedow, Rühl, Ferrari, and de Miguel Asensio, was published. Even without any express references to the national reports found in the third volume of said encyclopaedia, it is to be understood that information from/on all the countries analysed in the following, with the exception of Cyprus, can also be found there, with a different scope and focus of course.

1.1.1. A (Limited) Reliance on Words

One might be inclined to think that an analysis of this sort relies on words instead of issues – contrary to the core tenets of comparative law outlined above[262] – and is prone to be misinterpreted and/or misleading itself. From this perspective, it would be wise to first establish the conceptual criteria of Part II, and then have a look at the law of the member states.

A possible response to this point of contention would be that the following sections are, of course, informed by the conceptual findings presented later on in this book, and that the arrangement of chapters and sections does not necessarily reflect the order in which they were written and revised. There has been much cross-fertilisation in this undertaking (as the many cross-references in the footnotes indicate). Such a reply, however, would be somewhat disingenuous towards the reader who dutifully follows the serial order of chapters.

Rather, it is important to stress the limited nature of the following observations. Even when remarkable parallels emerge, they do so with the reservation that they really only are terminological parallels – for now. The inference of some common conceptual ground may seem plausible already, the more so because private international law terminology in general, possibly more so than any other set of legal terminology, is typically not confined to a particular set of borders.

Why not make do without this chapter then? The reason is my belief that the "material" – to which there will be many references over the following chapters – must in some way be presented first in order for the subsequent

[262] *Supra* Chapter 1, section 2.1.

analysis to be more comprehensible, even if this choice of approach has already been influenced in part by insights to be presented later on.

1.1.2. National Private International Law as an Object of Analysis

Before individual countries are discussed, some general remarks on national law – and on the law of certain member states in particular – as an object of analysis are in order.

1.1.2.1. The Continuing Relevance of National Law

To look at national law might appear to be a futile endeavour: why even bother with domestic law when the regulatory space of the member states in the area of private international law is shrinking? Regulations, directly applicable across the EU (Article 288(2) clause 2 TFEU) and enjoying primacy, crowd out national law. But domestic private international law has not become irrelevant and will not be until the EU has harmonised all areas[263] of private international law. Domestic private international law continues to apply where EU private international law does not prevail over it; this concerns all areas of private international law not yet harmonised as such, as well as those issues excluded from the substantive scope of the EU instruments (unless, of course, another EU instrument fills the respective gap[264]).

Domestic Reactions to European Union Legislation

Legislators in the member states have reacted differently to the increasingly interstitial nature of national private international law. In Germany, for example, provisions on the law applicable to non-contractual obligations were retained in order to have fallback rules for issues not covered by Rome II.[265] The entire section on the law applicable to contractual obligations, however, was simply repealed in light of Rome I.[266] This has caused some issues regarding contracts which are excluded from the scope of Rome I, notably arbitration agreements.[267] In contrast, Austria did not throw out the baby with the bath water. With §35 Austrian PIL Act, it enacted a special provision accounting for all contractual obligations not covered by Rome I.

---

263 This does *not* include a general part because many general issues need to be resolved, anyway, regardless of the existence of a legislative general part; see *infra* Chapter 3, section 8.2.

264 E.g., see the exclusion of obligations arising out of wills and succession in Article 1(2)(c) Rome I from the scope of Rome I for which the Succession Regulation now provides the applicable law.

265 See BT-Drucks. 16/9995, 6.

266 BGBl. 2009 I, 1574.

267 Article 1(2)(e) Rome I.

The Replication Prohibition

The member states cannot, however, simply reproduce the provisions of the private international law regulations in their national law within the scope of application of EU regulations, i.e. the "replication prohibition" or *Normwiederholungsverbot*. In a series of decisions in the 1970s and 80s, the ECJ has set forth restricted boundaries for the "implementation" of regulations. The ECJ first emphasised that, while it might be "useful" to draw attention to certain provisions in regulations, their application does not depend upon it.[268] Member states may not "implement" a regulation when this "[brings] into doubt both the legal nature of the applicable provisions and the date of their coming into force".[269] More generally, the contents of provisions of regulations cannot be introduced into the legal order of member states in a way which could obstruct their direct applicability or affect the Court's jurisdiction.[270] When, however, the *effet utile* of EU law depends on the interplay of provisions adopted at different levels – i.e. EU, national, and regional – it is permissible to incorporate "some elements of [...] regulations" for the sake of coherence and comprehensibility.[271] Save for this loophole, EU law values clarity as to the nature and (European) provenance of provisions higher than the (national) interest of gathering related rules in one act.[272]

Yet, as will become apparent below, several member states such as the Czech Republic, the Netherlands, and Poland have enacted codes of private international law,[273] despite impending or existing European instruments. As these codes do not contain verbatim adoptions of the regulations within their scope of application, they do not directly contravene the replication prohibition; but one might wonder if the rationale underlying the prohibition could be extended to other national legislation. Comprehensive private international law codes, in particular, could possibly run afoul of EU law requirements if, by their very existence or by their content, they dissimulated the applicability of EU regulations. A code, by its very nature, gives the impression of containing all that is required for the legal assessment of a given situation.

---

268 ECJ Case 20/72, Belgian State v NV Cobelex, Reports of Cases 1972, 1055, 1062 (at 20).

269 ECJ Case 39/72, Commission of the European Communities v Italian Republic, Reports of Cases 1973, 101, 113 (at 17).

270 ECJ Case 34/73, Fratelli Variola S.p.A. v Amministrazione italiana delle Finanze, Reports of Cases 1973, 981, 990–991 (at 10–11).

271 See ECJ Case 272/83, Commission of the European Communities v Italian Republic, Reports of Cases 1985, 1057, 1074 (at 27). Of no further interest here is the opposite scenario where an EU regulation requires the member states to make provisions which implement it. Here, it is the failure to implement the regulation which constitutes a contravention of EU law, see ECJ Case C-128/78, Commission of the European Communities v United Kingdom of Great Britain and Northern Ireland, Reports of Cases 1979, 419.

272 See *Mankowski*, in: Basedow/Kischel/Sieber (eds.), German National Reports, 133, 135.

273 Also see *Czepelak*, ERPL 2010, 705, 714, who is critical of this development.

If this semblance of comprehensiveness led people to pay less attention to EU regulations,[274] one could call this an "obstruction" of their direct applicability as prohibited by ECJ case law. The exception to the prohibition would not apply, for there would be no respective interplay: *either* EU law *or* national law would apply. As a consequence, domestic law would be in contravention of EU law and would thus be a questionable object of comparative analysis.

The risk of such a contravention actually happening or being assumed by the ECJ, however, seems rather low. The respective domestic codes acknowledge both the existence and primacy of EU private international law regulations; sometimes in a general fashion,[275] sometimes with pinpoint accuracy.[276] Furthermore, it is unlikely that domestic general provisions as such – as and to the extent that they are relevant for areas of private international law left to the member states for the time being – would be in contravention of EU law.

1.1.2.2. Denmark, Ireland, and the UK

The inclusion of Denmark, Ireland, and the UK in this survey of national laws may warrant a further short explanation. After all, the UK voted to leave the EU when the manuscript for this book had not yet even been finished.[277] Moreover, as is still the case with Denmark and Ireland, the UK did not (necessarily) participate in the adoption of measures in the "Area of Freedom, Security and Justice" (Articles 67–89 TFEU), nor was it (automatically) bound by such measures.[278] One area of law affected by this state of affairs is private international law.[279]

But a conceptualisation of general issues and rules of private international law from a European perspective must take account of the domestic law of all

274 This is the presumable policy reason behind Germany flat-out repealing the private international law provisions on contractual obligations instead of keeping them for cases beyond the scope of Rome I, see *Martiny*, RIW 2009, 737, 740.

275 §2 Czech PIL Act; Article 10:1 Dutch Civil Code.

276 §84 Czech PIL Act (with a note referring to, inter alia, Rome I and Rome II); Article 10:153 Dutch Civil Code (Rome I); Article 10:157 Dutch Civil Code (Rome II); Article 28 Polish PIL Act (Rome I), Article 33 Polish PIL Act (Rome II), Article 63 Polish PIL Act (Maintenance Regulation).

277 For an account of the impact of the eventual "Brexit" in the area of private international law see e.g. *Cachard*, DIP, at 23 ("E3"); *Cuniberti*, in: Bahurel/Bernard/Ho-Dac (eds.), Le Brexit, 197; *Sonnentag*, Die Konsequenzen des Brexits; *Rühl*, ICQL 67 (2018), 99, in particular 107–111; *ead.*, JZ 2017, 72; *Lehmann/Zetzsche*, JZ 2017, 62; *Hess*, IPRax 2016, 409; *Dickinson*, Journal of Private International Law 12 (2016), 915.

278 See Articles 1 and 2 of Protocol (No 21) on the Position of the United Kingdom and Ireland in respect of the Area of Freedom, Security and Justice, and Articles 1 and 2 of Protocol (No 22) on the Position of Denmark, respectively, both annexed to the TFEU.

279 See Recitals 44–46 Rome I, Recitals 39–40 Rome II, Recitals 46–48 Maintenance Regulation, Recitals 82–83 Succession Regulation. (Rome III is missing from this list because it implements enhanced cooperation and thus constitutes a special case independent from the positions adopted by Denmark, Ireland, and the UK.)

member states; otherwise it does not even aspire to be complete. As a matter of European politics, the likelihood of pan-European acceptance of a possible legislative endeavour increases when it is founded on common ground. Where such ground does not exist, the discourse benefits from transparency. Therefore, Denmark and Ireland will not be ignored here under the guise of Protocol Nos 21 and 22 to the TFEU. As the UK has substantially influenced the law of other member states (as will be demonstrated momentarily), it also still makes sense to include it in the following survey, even though its days as a member of the EU were already numbered at the time of writing.

1.1.2.3. The Relevance of National Law for Present Purposes

With it continuing to exist and having relevance, domestic private international law remains an object of great interest for present purposes. Domestic law has always played an important role at the EU level, be it as a source for the ECJ or as part of individual preconceptions of the members of the EU's legislative bodies. For both of these aspects the following comparative analysis can prove insightful: *de lege lata* that certain (general) categories of private international law are known everywhere – *de lege Europaea ferenda* that certain (legislative) concepts have already been employed and found to be useful, and not just in isolated instances.

In the following, therefore, national law will be an object of analysis. This is not meant to deny the importance of EU law, but only as a means of focusing more clearly on national concepts. Accordingly, where a certain legal instrument will be identified as one country's "main" source of private international law, this is meant only in relation to other legal instruments of the same country, not in relation to EU law.

1.2. MEMBER STATES WITHOUT PRIVATE INTERNATIONAL LAW "CODES"

1.2.1. Common Law Countries

United Kingdom: England

Regardless of whether one subscribes to the view that "English law flourished in noble isolation from Europe",[280] that the common law constitutes a distinct,[281] autochthonous achievement, or whether one emphasises the many influences of

[280] *Baker*, An Introduction to English Legal History, 35.

[281] *van Caenegem*, Judges, Legislators, and Professors, particularly 1–65.

continental legal developments on the common law throughout the centuries and the common foundations of European legal systems[282] – the main difference in the dichotomy of civil law and common law lies in the codification question. "If common law stands for anything, it is absence of codes [...]".[283] Nobody denies the existence of statutes and even partial, i.e. sectorial, codifications in the English common law,[284] but there are no "comprehensive and systematic exposition[s] of the norms in some important field of law".[285]

This observation holds true for the private international law of the United Kingdom. "If it is generally true of common law to say that one must look for the law in the judgments of the courts, it is doubly true in respect of the conflict of laws, for no other branch of law has been so completely a judicial creation".[286] Parliament had only served an "interstitial function"[287] in private international law before many areas became subject to EU law, usually accepting the existing "foundations and structure of the subject [...] developed at common law".[288] Although the Private International Law (Miscellaneous Provisions) Act 1995 carries a promising name for our purposes, it really is (only) very miscellaneous in nature: it covers interests on judgment debts not expressed in sterling, the validity in English law of potentially polygamous marriages, and some conflicts rules for tort cases (with the exclusion of defamation). In its Section 9, however, there is a provision covering several issues of overarching significance in tort and delict, among them characterisation and *renvoi*.

While there is no private international law code, one book has attained unusual authority – Dicey's *Conflict of Laws*, which has been deemed a "quasi-code".[289] After all, Dicey presented English private international law rules "virtually as if they were a set of sovereign commands".[290] This is also one of the reasons why "England is far closer to Continental Europe than to the US" as regards private international law.[291]

---

282 For an instructive account, see *Zimmermann*, ZEuP 1993, 4.

283 *van Caenegem*, Judges, Legislators, and Professors, 39.

284 E.g. the Sale of Goods Act 1979 whose precursor was passed in 1893.

285 *van Caenegem*, Judges, Legislators, and Professors, 42; to the same effect (but more recently) *Dannemann*, in: Adams/Bomhoff (eds.), Practice and Theory in Comparative Law, 96, 106.

286 *Graveson*, Philosophical Aspects, 14, 32; see also *Briggs*' statement (Conflict of Laws, 213) that private international law of contracts was a matter for the common law "[f]rom the beginning of time until 1991" when the Rome Convention was implemented in the UK.

287 *Graveson*, Philosophical Aspects, 14, 27.

288 *Briggs*, PIL in the English Courts, at 1.24.

289 *Graveson*, Special Character, 1, 7; see also *Rogerson*, Collier's Conflict of Laws, 3; *Fentiman*, in: Symeonides (ed.), PIL at the End of the 20th Century, 165, 169–170; see already *Rabel*, Die Fachgebiete des Kaiser-Wilhelm-Instituts, 180, 219, as to *Dicey*'s book being the most favoured one (in 1937).

290 *Mills*, Confluence, 52.

291 *Einhorn*, in: LA Siehr (2010), 3, 32.

In the textbooks, there are usually no parts expressly entitled "general". Turning to the venerable Dicey (as well as Morris and Collins) first, however, there is a first part about "preliminary matters" such as characterisation, incidental question, *renvoi*, public policy, overriding mandatory provisions, and domicile, as well as residence.[292] The same can be said about Cheshire, North, and Fawcett, only the title of the respective part is slightly different ("preliminary topics").[293] In the first edition of his textbook, Westlake did not discuss any matters but nationality and domicile separately from more specific questions like jurisdiction and the applicable law in the context of immovables, obligations etc.[294] In its seventh edition by Bentwich, almost 70 years later, *renvoi* has been added as another topic discussed separately.[295]

In one of his works, Briggs extensively discusses "common law rules of private international law: structure and methods"[296] as a subject entirely separate from specific ones like contractual obligations, non-contractual obligations etc.[297] Under this heading, he deals with topics such as foreign law in English courts, characterisation, *renvoi*, incidental questions, and connecting factors. Elsewhere, he similarly recognises "four components of the choice of law process", i.e. characterisation, *renvoi*, incidental question, and connecting factors.[298] These very issues are also discussed by Rogerson in a chapter with the heading "[c]hoice of law rules" that precedes her analysis of contractual obligations, non-contractual obligations, and property.[299] These chapters are followed by a final chapter dealing with "[a]voiding the results of the choice of law process" covering, inter alia, public policy and mandatory rules, and picking up *renvoi*.[300] Of an again slightly different scope are Harding's "technical issues relating to applicable law", which encompass characterisation, connecting factors, public policy, and *renvoi*.[301] For Hill and Ní Shúilleabháin, classification, connecting factors, *renvoi*, the incidental question, proof of foreign law, and the exclusion of foreign law (i.e. public policy) form the "mechanics of the [conflict of laws] process".[302]

292 *Dicey/Morris/Collins*, Conflict of Laws, at 1-001–6-172.
293 *Cheshire/North/Fawcett*, PIL, 41–184 (emphasis added).
294 *Westlake*, PIL (1859), 5–51.
295 *Westlake*, PIL (1925), 23–39.
296 *Briggs*, PIL in the English Courts, at 3.01–3.211.
297 *Briggs*, PIL in the English Courts, at 7.01–14.107.
298 *Briggs*, Conflict of Laws, 15 (15–20 (characterisation), 20–25 (*renvoi*), 25–27 (incidental question), 27–36 (connecting factors); see also his twelve "principles" in Private International Law in the English Courts, 3.15–3.211, which also cover these four issues. He also "undertake[s] a preliminary examination" of the issue of public policy, Conflict of Laws, 189, 208–212.
299 *Rogerson*, Collier's Conflict of Laws, 264–290.
300 *Rogerson*, Collier's Conflict of Laws, 412–434.
301 *Harding*, Conflict of Laws, 7 (characterisation; 7–8 (connecting factors), 8–9 (public policy), 9 (*renvoi*)).
302 *Hill/Ní Shúilleabháin*, Clarkson & Hill's Conflict of Laws, at 1.65–1.172.

(To refer to Wolff's book, with its extensive section on "general rules on conflict of laws",[303] would be a bit disingenuous in this context, as he was not only of German origin but also "bewildered" some of his audience with his systematic approach.[304])

So – even though it has been stressed that English private international law is much more about pragmatism than theory[305] – it seems impossible to deny a certain amount of (inevitably theoretical) structuring.[306] The adage that private international law is one of the most theoretical areas in practice seems to hold true. In particular, this concerns the dichotomy of "general" versus "special" in the sense of "relevant not just in specific instances" versus "relevant specifically at a certain point", even though the terms themselves do not appear.

United Kingdom: Scotland

While, in principle, Scots and English private international law are not the same,[307] and private international law is a devolved matter (Section 126(4)(a) Scotland Act 1998), the respective rules "are in fact very similar",[308] with both systems sharing a common Supreme Court and a common legislature. Although Scots courts initially, from the 16th century onwards, relied much on continental juristic authorities in private international law cases, this practice died down in the 19th century.[309] Dicey, Morris, and Collins, as well as Cheshire, North, and Fawcett, are still held in high regard.[310]

Beaumont and McEleavy do not expressly reserve a section for issues of overarching or recurring relevance. However, before turning to issues of contract, non-contractual obligations, marriage, divorce etc. – each in a section of its own[311] – they discuss, inter alia, the "identification of the applicable law" and "the application of statutes and limits to the application of foreign law".[312] In these two chapters, they cover characterisation, connecting factors, *renvoi*, the incidental question, and public policy. Similarly, Crawford and Carruthers do not provide for one section on issues deemed "general", "preliminary" or

303 *Wolff*, PIL, at 87–253 (i.e. pages 93–274).

304 See *Dannemann*, in: Beatson/Zimmermann (eds.), Jurists Uprooted, 441, 450.

305 *Fentiman*, in: Symeonides (ed.), PIL at the End of the 20th Century, 165, 166 and passim.

306 *Fentiman*'s statements (ibid.) are probably not meant to deny this, either, as he expressly acknowledges a "formalistic" character of English private international law (168–170).

307 *Beaumont/McEleavy*, Anton's PIL, at 1.04.

308 *Beaumont/McEleavy*, Anton's PIL, at 1.24; see also *Crawford/Carruthers*, IPL: A Scots Perspective, at 2-04, as well as *Kischel*'s sceptical assessment of the (extent of) individuality of the Scottish legal system, Rechtsvergleichung, §5 at 271–274.

309 See *Beaumont/McEleavy*, Anton's PIL, at 1.27–1.34 and at 1.38.

310 *Beaumont/McEleavy*, Anton's PIL, at 1.36.

311 *Beaumont/McEleavy*, Anton's PIL, at 10.01–27.194.

312 *Beaumont/McEleavy*, Anton's PIL, at 4.01–5.34.

the like, but they deal seriatim with the "operation of foreign law", "method", "*renvoi*", and "domicile and other personal law connecting factors"[313] before turning to jurisdiction and conflict of laws as to marriage, matrimonial causes, contracts, and so forth. These four chapters address, inter alia, public policy, characterisation, incidental questions, *renvoi* (obviously), and connecting factors.

Ireland

Ireland "inherited" the common law from the UK, including private international law.[314] They do not seem to have drifted apart much in this area. *Mutatis mutandis*, therefore, the statements made above apply to Ireland as well.

The seemingly sole Irish textbook on private international law begins with a part on "preliminary topics".[315] It includes a historical overview of the subject, as well as a short chapter on peculiarities of Irish conflict of laws. It goes on to deal with the issues of characterisation, *renvoi*, domicile and further connecting factors, and proof of foreign law,[316] before covering jurisdiction and individual areas of private international law (e.g. family law, property, and obligations).

Malta

There is no Maltese private international law act. Conflicts provisions can sometimes be found in other legislation. Apart from that, and despite the Maltese Civil Code pertaining to the Roman family,[317] private international law follows the British common law.[318]

Cyprus

Having been under British rule for almost 80 years, the Republic of Cyprus mainly follows British common law rules in the area of private international law.[319] Hence, by and large, the findings outlined above hold true for Cyprus as well. It is worth mentioning that Cypriot writers Neocleous, Koundourou,

313 *Crawford/Carruthers*, IPL: A Scots Perspective, at 3-01–6-52.
314 *Kennedy*, in: Esplugues/Iglesias/Palao (eds.), Application of Foreign Law, 231; *Hickey*, RabelsZ 42 (1978), 268; also see *Binchy*, Irish Conflicts of Law, 22–25.
315 *Binchy*, Irish Conflicts of Law, 1–120 (that is about a sixth of the length of the book as a whole).
316 *Binchy*, Irish Conflicts of Law, 27–120.
317 *Pisani*, IPRax 2007, 359.
318 *F. Sturm/G. Sturm*, in: Staudinger, Einl. zum IPR at 721; *Pisani*, IPRax 2007, 359.
319 With references to Cypriot case law *Neocleous/Koundourou/Monou*, Neocleous's Introduction, at 9-4.

and Monou discuss *renvoi*, public policy and domicile as separate issues before turning to contracts, torts, property, etc.; they do not, however, expressly label these issues as "general" or the like.[320]

1.2.2. France

A more surprising entry in this category is France. French jurists take the French tradition of codified law very seriously.[321] Others, too, recognise the French Civil Code as "intellectually the most significant and historically the most fertile" of all the codes coming into force in the late 18th and early 19th Centuries.[322] Thus, there seems to be some consternation when Cachard states that: "[N]i la France, patrie des codes et de la *Commission supérieure de la codification*, ni le Grand-Duché de Luxembourg n'ont adopté de code de droit international privé à la différence de certains États voisins de tradition civiliste".[323] It appears paradoxical that France, "the land of written law", lacks a private international law code.[324] Its private international law provisions "are scarce and scattered",[325] with the French Civil Code containing only "some laconic sentences" on private international law.[326]

From an outsider's perspective, calling Article 3 French Civil Code "incomplete"[327] is like calling a single cloud in the Parisian sky incomplete cloud cover. In any case, it certainly constitutes no semblance of a code of private international law.[328] There is no single reason for this, rather a combination of political indifference and academia contenting itself with the existence of judge-made law.[329] It has been said that the French Supreme Court has worked miracles with the little material it has at its disposal.[330] The existence of a

320 *Neocleous/Koundourou/Monou*, Neocleous's Introduction, 9-18–9-24.

321 See e.g. *Drago*, General Introduction, xxix, xxx, who points out that the Prussian General Land Law "had an altogether different content and was on an altogether different scale" than the *code civil*, and that the BGB "dates back only to 1900"; *Loussouarn/Bourel/de Vareilles-Sommières*, DIP, at 29; for a nuanced view as to "La culture juridique française", see the eponymous book by *Audren/Halpérin*.

322 *Zweigert/Kötz*, Introduction to Comparative Law, 86.

323 *Cachard*, DIP, at 30 (italics in the original); also see *Remy*, R.I.D.C. 2010, 291–292; *Loussouarn*, in: LA Droz, 191. Many consider it similarly anomalous that French administrative law has not been codified, *Drago*, General Introduction, xxix, xxxiv.

324 *Bodénès-Constantin*, La codification du DIP français, at 7.

325 *Audit*, in: Bermann/Picard (eds.), Introduction to French Law, 453.

326 *Ballarino/Bonomi*, Yearbook of Private International Law 2 (2000), 99, 107 (with note 107).

327 *Loussouarn/Bourel/de Vareilles-Sommières*, DIP, at 134.

328 Expressly *Fiorini*, ICLQ 54 (2005), 499, 502.

329 *Remy*, R.I.D.C. 2010, 291, 293; *Fiorini*, ICLQ 54 (2005), 499, 503; *Audit*, in: Symeonides (ed.), PIL at the End of the 20th Century, 191, 192; *Loussouarn*, in: LA Droz, 191, 202–203.

330 *Bourdelois*, in: Puigelier (ed.), La loi, 89, 90; apparently to the point where reference is made to Article 3 French Civil Code without it really having to do with anything, see *Remy*, R.I.D.C. 2010, 291, 315–316; also *Cachard*, DIP, at 30.

book like Ancel and Lequette's "Grands arrêts"[331] is a further indication of the importance of the Cour de cassation for private international law.

Nevertheless, there have been no fewer than three attempts to codify French private international law in the 20th century.[332] Although the most recent draft, realised by a commission of academics and practitioners,[333] dates back half a century,[334] it offers some interesting *conceptual* insights. For present purposes, most relevant is the existence of a section of eight "dispositions générales", particularly remarkable because of the scepticism towards a general part of private international law in the context of the prior draft.[335] This section covers public policy, *renvoi*, multi-nationals, non-uniform legal systems, and the establishment and application[336] of foreign law. These issues were not regarded as particularly controversial and were thus included, with the respective provisions by and large reflecting the decisions in leading cases, whereas other issues such as characterisation were deliberately excluded.[337]

French textbooks only partly follow this conceptual lead. Some authors discuss a "general theory of conflict of laws",[338] or even a "partie générale", including the history of the subject, characterisation, incidental questions, *renvoi*, and public policy;[339] whereas others cover the same issues without expressly marking them as "general", but still separately from specific areas of private international law.[340] Essentially, however, everyone ("tout le monde") is supposed to agree that there is such a thing as a "general theory" of private international law in France and that it concerns both the structure of conflicts rules and factors influencing its mechanisms.[341]

---

331 *Ancel/Lequette*, Les grands arrêts de la jurisprudence française de droit international privé.

332 *Remy*, R.I.D.C. 2010, 291, 292–293; *Fiorini*, ICLQ 54 (2005), 499, 503; *Bodénès-Constantin*, La codification du DIP français, at 6; *Bureau*, in: Beignier (ed.), La codification, 119, 124–125; *Loussouarn*, in: LA Droz, 191, 193; *Foyer*, JDI 1971, 31–32; each with further references regarding the different projects.

333 *Foyer*, JDI 1971, 31, 32.

334 The 1967 draft was published, inter alia, in Rev. crit. DIP 1970, 835–846.

335 See *Reichelt*, ZfRV 1971, 249, 250.

336 Article 2287 French Civil Code (1967 Draft) provides for the *ex officio* application of *conflicts* provisions. This could include the *ex officio* application of foreign law in case the conflicts provisions determine its applicability, see *Reichelt*, ZfRV 1971, 249, 259–260; it will be shown *infra* (Chapter 3, section 2.1.2.2., *No Room for Divergent ("Procedural") Domestic Rules under Rome I/II*), however, that the one does not necessarily follow from the other.

337 *Foyer*, JDI 1971, 31, 34–35.

338 *Loussouarn/Bourel/de Vareilles-Sommières*, DIP, at 109–416.

339 *Audit/d'Avout*, DIP, at 126–383 (the "partie générale" continues to cover procedural issues, at 384–667; *Mayer/Heuzé*, DIP, at 47–283 (the "partie générale" continues to cover [mainly] procedural issues, at 275–482).

340 See *Cachard*, DIP, at 294–369 and at 537–654 (recurring issues), on the one hand, and at 370–536 (particular conflicts rules), on the other hand.

341 *Azzi/Boskovic*, in: iidem (eds.), Quel avenir pour la théorie générale des conflits de lois?, 1, 2.

1.2.3. Luxembourg

The situation in Luxembourg is quite similar to the one in France. The *code civil luxembourgeois* with its origin in the French Civil Code[342] is almost silent on private international law issues.[343] There is no stand-alone code of private international law, either.[344] Judges relying on doctrinal writings and often referring to Belgian and French decisions have developed the law.[345]

In the doctrine, however, one finds a "théorie générale" of Luxembourg private international law comprising characterisation, *renvoi*, change of the applicable law, proof and application of foreign law, public policy, overriding mandatory provisions, and evasion of the law.[346] Of an entirely different nature is the "partie générale" of *Cuniberti*'s "code". It covers jurisdiction, procedure, and conflict of laws, but on the latter subject it only contains several treaties, little domestic law, and the Rome Convention as well as Rome I and II as a whole.[347] In relation to conflict of laws, "générale" probably must be understood along the lines of "not confined to one type of obligation", particularly against the backdrop of a later section entitled "contrats et délits spéciaux". As other non-general (an express "special part" does not exist) sections concern e.g. "droit de la famille", "droit social", "modes alternatifs de resolution des différends", and "droit des investissements",[348] it is difficult, however, to identify a homogeneous concept here.

1.2.4. The Nordic Member States

Neither Denmark nor Finland nor Sweden has a code of private international law. Nor have there ever been Nordic model laws on private international law.[349] There are, however, a handful of Nordic Conventions in this field of law,[350]

---

342 *Bernecker*, RabelsZ 27 (1962), 263, 264.

343 *Wiwinius*, DIP, 28.

344 There *is* the "Code de droit international privé luxembourgeois" with 812 pages of fine print, but it turns out to be a private compilation by (in the second edition) *Cuniberti* of Luxembourg, European, and international law relevant for Luxembourg, see *infra* footnotes 347–348. *Kinsch*, in: Cuniberti (ed.), Code de DIP, V, attributes the lack of an "entirely original" code to Luxembourg's size (or rather: its lack thereof).

345 See *Wiwinius*, DIP, 28 and 30; *Kinsch*, in: Cuniberti (ed.), Code de DIP, V; *Bernecker*, RabelsZ 27 (1962), 263, 268.

346 *Wiwinius*, DIP, 37–70.

347 Cuniberti (ed.), Code de DIP, VII–VIII.

348 Cuniberti (ed.), Code de DIP VIII–XVII.

349 *Lookofsky*, in: Symeonides (ed.), PIL at the End of the 20th Century, 147, 148.

350 See *F. Sturm/G. Sturm*, in: Staudinger, Einl. IPR at 507; *Jänterä-Jareborg*, in: LA Pintens, 733, 735–737; *Ring/Olsen-Ring*, Einführung in das skandinavische Recht, at 924; as to their development, as well as the development of Nordic/Scandinavian cooperation in general, *Philip*, Rec. des cours 96 (1959-I), 241, 246–251.

designed for inter-Nordic cases.[351] Articles 75(3) Succession Regulation and 62(3) M-Property Regulation acknowledge the existence and continuing relevance of these conventions. Scholars have occasionally taken up abstract principles of private international law, particularly from Germany, but Scandinavian courts have shown a reluctance to making use of them.[352]

Denmark's private international law was developed largely by the courts and commentators.[353] Private international law legislation is found where Denmark implements international conventions.[354] The courts practice a style of brief explanations and narrow language.[355] In determining the applicable law (at least to contracts), the courts mainly seem to have been guided by a principle similar to that of the "closest connection".[356] The issues of *renvoi*, public policy, and characterisation have come up in practice and in doctrinal works.[357]

A similar style of drafting judicial decisions has been observed in both Finland and Sweden as well.[358] As far as Finnish private international law is concerned, both legislation and judicial decisions are scarce.[359] One of the few English books on Finnish private international law does recognise some overarching features of private international law (overriding mandatory provisions, public policy, characterisation), but not necessarily as such,[360] more as part of the "procedural starting-point" as regards the application of foreign law.[361]

---

351 *Philip*, Rec. des cours 96 (1959-I), 241, 256.

352 *Sundström*, Foreign Ships and Foreign Waters, 208.

353 *Lookofsky*, Choice of Law in Denmark, I; *id.*, in: Symeonides (ed.), PIL at the End of the 20th Century, 147, 148; also see *eund.*, in: Dahl/Melchior/Tamm (eds.), Danish Law in a European Perspective, 455, 461; *Dübeck*, Einführung in das dänische Recht, 264, additionally recognises the "nature of things" as a source of private international law, but the actual meaning of this remains cryptic.

354 *Lookofsky*, Choice of Law in Denmark, I.

355 *Lookofsky*, in: Hondius, Precedent and the Law, 253, 263–265 (for the legal status of precedents in Danish law, see 254 and passim); *id.*, in: Symeonides (ed.), PIL at the End of the 20th Century, 147, 151 and passim.

356 *Lookofsky*, Choice of Law in Denmark, II B.

357 See *Lookofsky*, in: Symeonides (ed.), PIL at the End of the 20th Century, 147, 159–162.

358 *Sundström*, Foreign Ships and Foreign Waters, 215–216.

359 *Klami/Kuisma*, Finnish Law as an Option, 87; *Bergmann*, Hauptprobleme, 1. See *Liukkunen*, Recent PIL Codifications, 4–5, for a relatively recent overview as to Finnish legislation in the field.

360 For an approach to Finnish private international law which expressly makes a distinction between "general" and "special" provisions, see *Bergmann*, Hauptprobleme. For present purposes, however, his account is problematic because it is not apparent if he merely traces an existing distinction in Finnish law (or at least in Finnish doctrine) or superimposes a German perspective on Finnish law. *Liukkunen*, Recent PIL Codifications, 13, at least deems public policy a "general principle of [Finnish] private international law".

361 *Klami/Kuisma*, Finnish Law as an Option, 7–9.

While there are "numerous" private international law statutes in Sweden (particularly covering family law issues), they do not add up to a code of private international law.[362] Bogdan identifies the "general problems" of Swedish private international law as one of the main legislative gaps.[363] Similarly to Denmark and Finland, the influence of opinions of legal writers on the relatively scarce case law is emphasised.[364] But there seems to be only one up-to-date English monograph on Swedish private international law, and only a few in Swedish.[365] In the former, Bogdan does distinguish between "connection" (dealing with the elements of a conflicts provision and certain connecting factors) and "basic terms" (such as characterisation, incidental question, *renvoi*, public policy, adaptation) on the one hand, and particular choice of law rules on the other.[366] This distinction has some tradition in Swedish legal writing.[367]

1.3. MEMBER STATES WITH PRIVATE INTERNATIONAL LAW CODES

All of the other member states have some form of private international law code. One can distinguish three models. First, there are legislative acts dealing exclusively with private international law.[368] Second, (relatively) comprehensive sections on private international law can be part of a member state's civil code. Among these, one can further distinguish those parts that have a formal section for general provisions[369] and those that do not.[370] Third, there are statutory instruments that cover private international law as well as different questions of international jurisdiction and/or international civil procedure.[371]

---

362 *Bogdan*, PIL in Sweden, at 16.
363 Ibid.
364 *Bogdan*, PIL in Sweden, at 23.
365 *Bogdan*, PIL in Sweden, 123.
366 *Bogdan*, PIL in Sweden, at 24–57 and at 58–105.
367 See *Eek*, Swedish Conflict of Laws, 1–230 (dealing with overarching issues including the structure of conflicts provisions, connecting factors, *renvoi*, incidental question, public policy and so forth) vs. 231–292 (dealing with particular private law issues such as personal law, family law, property law); note, too, the stark contrast in length dedicated to each part.
368 To wit: The Austrian PIL Act, the Estonian PIL Act, the Polish PIL Act.
369 To wit: The Lithuanian Civil Code, the Dutch Civil Code, the Portuguese Civil Code, the Romanian Civil Code. As explained *infra*, section 1.3.2.1., *Germany: Legislation*, I will also consider the German EGBGB part of this category.
370 To wit: The Greek Civil Code, the Latvian Civil Code, the Spanish Civil Code.
371 To wit: The Belgian PIL Code, the Bulgarian PIL Code, the Croatian PIL Act, the Czech PIL Act, the Hungarian PIL Act, the Italian PIL Act, the Slovak PIL Act, the Slovenian PIL Act. For a global perspective see *Kadner Graziano*, Journal of Private International Law 11 (2015), 585, 588–592.

1.3.1. *Stand-Alone Codes of Private International Law Only*

Austria

The main source[372] for Austria's private international law is its 1978 Private International Law Act. The 1811 Civil Code had only contained a few scattered conflicts provisions. Codification efforts, which had already started in the 1890s and picked up steam in the 1950s, came to fruition with the 1978 Act.[373] It is divided into eight parts, the first of which covers "General Provisions". It begins with a provision setting forth the principle of the strongest connection. Despite a 1994 decision by the Austrian Supreme Court to the contrary, it is disputed whether this provision can be regarded as a general escape clause.[374] It has also been used as a means to apply domestic as well as foreign overriding mandatory provisions.[375] Additionally, there are provisions on the *ex officio* application of Austrian conflicts rules, the establishment and application of foreign law, *renvoi*, non-unified legal systems, public policy, change of the applicable law, form, and nationality.[376] There is also a provision setting forth some particulars about party autonomy. Questions of jurisdiction and of the effects of foreign decisions are not dealt with by the Act, contrary to the original draft.[377] There are no provisions on characterisation or incidental questions.[378] Despite this legislative structure, authors of Austrian textbooks are divided on whether to deal with general issues before or after the special issues.[379] In any case, they do follow the distinction between "general" and "special".

Estonia

Private international law can be traced back to 1865 in Estonia; its history is marked by vicissitudes.[380] In the 1990s, the decision was made to outsource

---

372 *Lurger/Melcher*, IPR, at 1/13; *Wendehorst*, in: Verschraegen (ed.), Austrian Law, 79.

373 In more detail see *Wendehorst*, in: Verschraegen (ed.), Austrian Law, 79, 80–82; *Siehr*, in: Reichelt (ed.), 30 Jahre österreichisches IPR-Gesetz, 9–11; *Palmer*, Am. J. Comp. L. 28 (1980), 197, 200–202.

374 See *infra* Chapter 3, section 4.1.1.

375 *Lurger/Melcher*, IPR, at 1/48; *Wendehorst*, in: Verschraegen (ed.), Austrian Law, 79, 90–92.

376 To be precise, §9 Austrian PIL Act concerns the personal law which is determined by a person's nationality; later provisions then employ the personal law (rather than nationality) as their connecting factor.

377 *Beitzke*, RabelsZ 43 (1979), 245, 246.

378 §5 Austrian PIL Act does not contain a "hidden" rule dealing with incidental questions, *Beitzke*, RabelsZ 43 (1979), 245, 250.

379 See *Verschraegen*, IPR, III, as to her decision to cover general issues only after special issues; *Lurger/Melcher*, IPR, ("§1. Allgemeine Fragen": 1–49); *Schwimann*, IPR ("Allgemeine Lehren": 19–52; "Besonderer Teil": 53–178).

380 See *Sein*, Yearbook of Private International Law 10 (2008), 459–460.

the private international law rules found in Estonia's 1994 Civil Code Act into a separate act.[381] On 1 July 2002, the Estonian PIL Act entered into force. It generally only encompasses conflicts provisions, although this characterisation of §2 and §4 Estonian PIL Act on the application and ascertainment of foreign law could be called into question.[382]

The Act begins with Part 1 on "General Provisions". It contains, inter alia, the aforementioned rules concerning foreign law, as well as provisions on *renvoi*, public policy, form, and agency. No rule on overriding mandatory provisions is to be found among the general provisions of Part 1, but §31 Estonian PIL Act concerns Estonian overriding mandatory provisions in the context of contractual obligations. Similarly, while there is no provision in Part 1 on "residence", one of the main connecting factors of the Estonian PIL Act, §10 in its Part 2 refers the issue to Estonian substantive law. Nationality is to be determined by the law of the presumable state of nationality, as per §11 Estonian PIL Act, but this provision also does not form part of the "General Provisions".

Poland

When the new act on private international law was passed in 2011, it marked the third stand-alone act on private international law in Poland in 85 years, with the first dating back to 1926 and the second to 1965.[383] While the 1965 Polish PIL Act was not comprehensive in the sense that there were quite a few conflicts rules in other legislative acts (which sometimes led to incoherence),[384] the 2011 Act expressly repeals many of them.[385] It was mainly drafted by academics.[386]

The first chapter of the 2011 Polish PIL Act covers "general provisions". There are rules on nationality, the exercise of party autonomy, *renvoi*, public policy, overriding mandatory provisions,[387] and non-unified legal systems. Like its predecessor,[388] the 2011 Polish PIL Act does not contain any provisions

---

381 *Sein*, Yearbook of Private International Law 10 (2008), 459, 460.

382 See the Estonian Supreme Court decision reported by *Sein*, Yearbook of Private International Law 10 (2008), 459, 461 with note 11. In more detail, *infra* Chapter 3, section 5.3.1.

383 The 1965 Polish PIL Act was still among the earliest national comprehensive private international law acts, see *Lasok*, Am. J. Comp. L. 15 (1967), 330; for an overview of the legal development in Poland see *Mączyński*, Yearbook of Private International Law 6 (2004), 203–205, and *Pazdan*, in: Lewaszkiewicz-Petrykowska (ed.), Rapports Polonais, 49–51; for an outline of the road to the 2011 Act, see *Ernst*, RabelsZ 76 (2012), 597, 602–605.

384 *Mączyński*, Yearbook of Private International Law 6 (2004), 203, 215–216.

385 Articles 69–79 Polish PIL Act; see *Ernst*, RabelsZ 76 (2012), 597, 605.

386 *Ernst*, RabelsZ 76 (2012), 597, 637; *Pajor*, Rev. crit. DIP 2012, 5, 6–7; *id.*, Yearbook of Private International Law 13 (2011), 381, 382.

387 A respective rule had been missing from the 1965 Act, *Pajor*, Rev. crit. DIP 2012, 5, 9–10; *id.*, Yearbook of Private International Law 13 (2011), 381, 385; *Mączyński*, Yearbook of Private International Law 6 (2004), 203, 210.

388 *Mączyński*, Yearbook of Private International Law 6 (2004), 203, 210–211.

concerning characterisation, incidental questions or evasion of the law.[389] There is also no escape clause among the general provisions; nor, for that matter, can Article 67 Polish PIL Act be regarded as a general escape clause, for it presupposes that no other conflicts provision be applicable.[390] Domicile and habitual residence are used as connecting factors, but their definition can only be found in the *travaux préparatoires*.[391] With the (arguable) exception of arbitration agreements,[392] the 2011 Polish PIL Act only deals with issues of conflict of laws; the question of the establishment of foreign law is left to the Polish Code of Civil Procedure,[393] in this respect contrary to the 2007 draft of the PIL Act.[394] There is, however, a general provision setting forth the consequences of a failure to ascertain the content of foreign law within reasonable time.

1.3.2. Private International Law as Part of a Member State's Civil Code

1.3.2.1. "General Provisions" with a Formal Section of Their Own

Germany: Legislation

The main source of German private international law is the Introductory Act to the 1896 BGB (EGBGB).[395] That it ended up there is the result of a somewhat vicissitudinous history. Originally, there had been plans to make private international law part of the BGB itself. In fact, the member of the 1874 First Commission who was in charge of drafting the future code's General Part (Gebhard) was also tasked with drafting conflicts provisions.[396] (The same approach would later be employed in Portugal en route to its 1967 Civil Code.[397]) The subject, however, is conspicuously missing from both the 1888 first draft of the BGB and the appurtenant "Motives". This remained a mystery for almost 85 years.[398] Only then it transpired that the German Foreign Office

389 *Pazdan/Gralla*, WiRO 2011, 299, 300.
390 *Ernst*, RabelsZ 76 (2012), 597, 609; *Pazdan*, IPRax 2012, 77, 81, only regards it as an "indication" ("Hinweis") as to what to do.
391 *Ernst*, RabelsZ 76 (2012), 597, 607–608.
392 *Ernst*, RabelsZ 76 (2012), 597, 605.
393 *Pazdan*, IPRax 2012, 77, 79; *id./Gralla*, WiRO 2011, 299–300.
394 *Ernst*, RabelsZ 76 (2012), 597, 612.
395 *Mankowski*, in: Basedow/Kischel/Sieber (eds.), German National Reports, 133, 134; *Kropholler*, IPR, §1 III; for German private international law outside the EGBGB see *F. Sturm/G. Sturm*, in: Staudinger, Einl. IPR at 641–653.
396 *Hartwieg*, in: id./Korkisch (eds.), Die geheimen Materialien, 23, 29.
397 See *Neuhaus/Rau*, RabelsZ 32 (1968), 500, 502.
398 See e.g. *Rabel*, Die Fachgebiete des Kaiser-Wilhelm-Instituts, 180, 214, who in 1937 only could talk of "obscure reasons".

(*Auswärtiges Amt*) had intervened with reference to Chancellor Bismarck, noting that private international law was too sensitive a subject from the perspective of international politics to be included in the code.[399] Private international law was nevertheless discussed by the 1890 Second Commission and became part of the draft BGB as a sixth book.[400] After negotiations between the Foreign Office and the Judicial Office (*Reichsjustizamt*), it was proposed to relegate private international law to the Introductory Law.[401] This was the result eventually approved by Reichstag, Bundesrat, and Kaiser en bloc with the BGB.[402]

In spite of the many subdivisions of the BGB (with, of course, an entire book devoted to the "General Part"), all of the original (mainly unilateral) private international law provisions of the EGBGB simply stood among a few other "General Provisions", dealing with, inter alia, the entering into force of the BGB on 1 January 1900, the definition of "statute" under the BGB, and Alsace-Lorraine being regarded as a German state. There was no separate section for general private international law provisions. Nor were there many which coincided with what other member states call "general provisions". Rules on *renvoi*, stateless persons, and public policy, however, were among the final private international law provisions.

A formally separate section in the EGBGB for private international law was only established in the sweeping 1986 reform.[403] Until then, private international law had largely maintained its 1896, all along "mutilated",[404] form.[405] Private international law was now given a separate chapter in the EGBGB; rules on *renvoi*, non-unified legal systems, nationality, and public policy were grouped together in the first section of that chapter. Habitual residence was and is not defined in the EGBGB, but the first chapter does contain a provision dealing with a very specific sub-topic.[406] It has sometimes been deplored that the

399 Letter from *Herbert Graf von Bismarck* (Foreign Office) to *Hermann von Schelling* (Judicial Office) (September 30, 1887), in: Hartwieg/Korkisch (eds.), Die geheimen Materalien, 159–160; as to the consequences of this intervention see *Hartwieg*, Entstehung, 23, 32–34.

400 See the drafts in Hartwieg/Korkisch (eds.), Die geheimen Materalien, 210–215 and 252–257, as well as *Hartwieg*, in: id./Korkisch (eds.), Die geheimen Materialien, 23, 38–42.

401 *Hartwieg*, in: id./Korkisch (eds.), Die geheimen Materialien, 23, 44; as a side note, this compromise also severely affected the content of the eventually adopted private international law rules, see *Korkisch*, in: Hartwieg/id. (eds.), Die geheimen Materalien, 1, 3.

402 *Hartwieg*, in: id./Korkisch (eds.), Die geheimen Materialien, 23, 55–56; for a summary of the events see *F. Sturm/G. Sturm*, in: Staudinger, Einl. IPR at 896–903; the EGBGB was published in RGBl. 1986, 604.

403 BGBl. 1986 I, 1142–1150.

404 *Gogos/Aubin*, RabelsZ 15 (1949/1950), 240, 243.

405 *F. Sturm/G. Sturm*, in: Staudinger, Einl. IPR at 904.

406 Article 5(3) EGBGB concerns the consequences of persons without or with only restricted capacity to contract changing their residence without the consent of their legal representative.

opportunity of the 1986 reform was not taken to address more general issues.[407] The title "General Provisions" was given to the first section only in 2008.[408] This was meant to clarify that the provisions of this section are always to be taken into account when applying the following provisions.[409]

Obviously, the BGB, not the EGBGB, is Germany's Civil Code. But being its Introductory Act, the EGBGB is closely connected to the BGB. Additionally, the EGBGB concerns many more issues than private international law, including questions of substantive law that arise in connection with rules of the BGB. From this perspective, the EGBGB is a supplement to the BGB. It seems justifiable, therefore, not to regard it as a stand-alone private international law code here, but rather to pigeon-hole Germany among the countries where private international law forms part of the civil code.

Germany: Scholarship

Having come to the "[r]ather sobering [realisation] that Germany's general part consists entirely of [...] a grand total of four provisions",[410] one might wonder whether German private international law scholarship provides a more comprehensive picture. The following will show that the German academic understanding of general issues of private international law is indeed much richer than the legislative material. But it will also show that the understanding of "general" is anything but uniform.[411]

In Kropholler's textbook, "general part" encompasses the history of private international law, the fundamental interests and values to be taken into account, the connection of this branch of law with public international and comparative law, the structure of conflicts provisions, the topics of characterisation, incidental questions, substitution and adaptation, *renvoi*, public policy, inter-personal and inter-local conflict of laws, and much more; in total, this "general part" makes up close to 300 pages out of 685.[412] Neuhaus, whose work Kropholler took over, had covered many of these issues as well but had not compiled them under the label of "general part".[413] Then again, his work was supposed to cover only the basic concepts of private international law ("*Grundbegriffe*"), so there was

[407] *Mankowski*, in: Basedow/Kischel/Sieber (eds.), German National Reports, 133, 150; but see *Stoll*, IPRax 1984, 1, 5, for the opposing viewpoint.

[408] BGBl. 2008 I, 2401.

[409] BT-Drucks. 16/6995, 7.

[410] *Wagner*, in: Leible (ed.), General Principles, §4.05[A].

[411] This should dispel any remaining doubts as to this book merely being a veiled attempt to impose "the" German perspective on the rest of the EU. A much shorter overview of German private international law scholarship as regards "general issues" was part of my contribution to Leible (ed.), General Principles (§1.03).

[412] *Kropholler*, IPR, §§1–40 (1–301).

[413] *Neuhaus*, Grundbegriffe.

no real need to distinguish between "general" and "special" concepts. In any case, as Neuhaus had stated himself in the preface for the second edition, he understood his book to be mainly about "questions of the general part [of private international law]".[414]

Junker deals with the terminology and the history of the discipline separately, but by and large his section on the "general part" (174 pages out of 496) covers the same issues as Kropholler's.[415] In the textbook by Kegel and Schurig, there is a separate section labelled "private international law as a whole" (242 pages out of 1147), in which they discuss the terminology, the fundamental interests, neighbouring branches of law, the history, and the sources of private international law. Under the heading "general part", they then address the remainder of the topics mentioned above, including the structure of private international law provisions.[416]

Rauscher and also von Hoffmann and Thorn distinguish "basics" from "general doctrines", but do not use the term "general part".[417] Together, the respective sections constitute a considerable portion of each book.[418] While the "basics" deal with the history of the subject, neighbouring disciplines etc., the "doctrines" concern the structure of conflicts provisions, connecting factors, characterisation, *renvoi*, non-unified legal systems, public policy etc. Firsching, the originator of the latter work, had used a different label for the latter issues ("technical basics").[419] Raape used only the term "general doctrines", covering everything from neighbouring disciplines and sources of private international law to aspects of conflicts provisions and the history of this area of law.[420]

To make matters *prima facie* more confusing, "general part" and "general doctrines" sometimes appear side by side. von Bar and Mankowski speak of "general doctrines" as the wider term, encompassing methods, history, and neighbouring branches of law; they use "general part" as the narrower term, containing "the rather technical rules [...] which are relevant in all areas of the special part [of private international law]".[421]

It seems to be this narrow understanding which Sendmeyer takes as a basis for her article on the "general doctrines" of private international law.[422] Gottschalk shows an even narrower understanding of "general doctrines" in his 2002 monograph, although it is probably not meant to be exclusive.[423]

---

414 *Neuhaus*, Grundbegriffe, VII.
415 *Junker*, IPR, 71–257.
416 *Kegel/Schurig*, IPR, §§6–16 (301–542).
417 *Rauscher*, IPR, at 159–603; *von Hoffmann/Thorn*, IPR 175–276.
418 *Rauscher*: 153 pages out of 672; *von Hoffmann/Thorn*: 276 pages out of 534 (it should be noted, however, that *von Hoffmann/Thorn's* "basics" contain a big section on procedure).
419 *Firsching*, Einführung ("Technische Grundbegriffe").
420 *Raape*, IPR, 1–168 (out of 698 pages).
421 *von Bar/Mankowski*, IPR I, §7 at 1.
422 *Sendmeyer*, Jura 2011, 588.
423 *Gottschalk*, Allgemeine Lehren, 23.

Stürner offers a similar list for the "general part" of private international law, which is probably not to be understood as exclusive either.[424] The monograph by Nehne on "general doctrines" in EU private international law is based on a broader notion of "general part" than that;[425] he seems to use both terms synonymously.[426] In essence, this is Heinze's approach as well.[427] Martinek presupposes the existence of (not just) a (German) general part of private international law, but does not tell us its extent; characterisation, the preliminary question, and evasion of the law are the only three examples he gives.[428]

Turning to German commentaries dealing with private international law, only a few sub-headings contain the word "general" in von Hein's introduction to private international law. He does deal with essentially all of the topics already mentioned in this section, however, including the history of the subject, its methods, and the structure of conflicts provisions.[429] F. Sturm and G. Sturm use the heading "Technorama" to deal with *renvoi*, characterisation, adaptation, incidental question, and public policy.[430] Lorenz's heading "Foundational mechanisms of private international law"[431] (under which he also covers the structure of conflicts rules) is quite similar to this. Looschelders designates his introductory remarks to Articles 3–6 EGBGB as the "general part of private international law". In this section, he also covers the structure of conflicts provisions, as well as the ascertainment and application of foreign law.[432] At the same time, he also demonstrates a narrower understanding of "general part" when he states that it concerns "general rules" to be taken into account when applying conflicts provisions.[433] In a more recent contribution, he seems to use "general doctrines" and "general part" interchangeably in relation to EU private international law.[434] Dörner does not seem to use any of these terms, but does address quite a few of the issues already mentioned.[435]

Even in the comparative handbook edited by Schlegelberger, one does not find a clear answer to what "general doctrines" of private international law are supposed to comprise. The eponymous entry[436] deals with a short

424 *Stürner*, in: Langenbucher (ed.), Europäisches Privat- und Wirtschaftsrecht, §8 at 19–27.
425 *Nehne*, Methodik und allgemeine Lehren des europäischen IPR, 2.
426 See *Nehne*, Methodik und allgemeine Lehren des europäischen IPR, 3.
427 *Heinze*, in: FS Kropholler, 105, 106 (with note 12).
428 *Martinek*, Seven Pillars of Wisdom, 3.1.
429 *von Hein*, in: MüKoBGB, Einl. IPR.
430 *F. Sturm/G. Sturm*, in: Staudinger, Einl zum IPR at 240–294.
431 *S. Lorenz*, in: BeckOK BGB, 40th ed. (01.11.2015), Einleitung zum Internationalen Privatrecht at 32–77.
432 *Looschelders*, IPR, Vorbem. zu Art. 3-6 EGBGB (the title is on page 27).
433 *Looschelders*, IPR, Vorbem. zu Art. 3-6 EGBGB at 2.
434 *Looschelders*, in: FS Coester-Waltjen, 531.
435 *Dörner*, in: HK-BGB, Vorbemerkung zu Artikel 3-6 EGBGB.
436 *Wahl*, in: Schlegelberger (ed.), Rechtsvergleichendes Handwörterbuch, Abschnitt II: Allgemeine Lehren.

historical overview of the discipline, main positions in the legal literature of different countries (on what exactly?), and how private international law itself is to be classified (public/private law?; national/international law?; positive/natural law?). It further addresses the questions of how to fill lacunae, the difference of conflicts provisions and provisions of substantive law, the issue of characterisation, the relation of different applicable laws among each other, and a judge's duties in relation to the application of foreign law. A footnote informs the readers that they should also have a look at the later entries concerning public policy, *renvoi*, and evasion of the law.

In summary, substantial portions of many German private international law textbooks are devoted to something called "general part" or "general doctrines". The terms also appear in all other categories of German scholarly works on private international law, albeit not in each individual contribution. Yet there is no uniform understanding of what these terms encompass, nor are the discrepancies regularly addressed.[437] While certain questions are always covered, there is no consistent picture regarding all the other issues. At the same time, even the common core is not congruent with the scope of the "general provisions" of the EGBGB.

Lithuania

The 2000 Lithuanian Civil Code, which entered into force in 2001, is divided into books, the first of which deals with "General Provisions". This book is itself divided into parts. Part One concerns "Civil Laws and their Application", dealing first with the substantive scope of Lithuanian civil law, its sources, and some methodological issues such as interpretation and analogy. A second chapter on private international law immediately follows, beginning with a section on "General Provisions". The structure of its five provisions mirrors the one found in Articles 603–607 of the Lithuanian Civil Code following the reform in 1994.[438] The articles cover the issues of *renvoi*, non-unified legal systems, public policy, Lithuanian and foreign overriding mandatory provisions, and establishment of foreign law. Jurisdiction, as well as recognition and enforcement of judgments, was originally also supposed to be subject to private international law provisions in the Civil Code, but these were instead moved to the 2002 Code of Civil Procedure.[439] The main (objective) connecting factor is domicile;[440] its definition, however, is found not only outside the "General Provisions", but also outside the private international provisions in general.[441]

---

437 But see *Heinze*, in: FS Kropholler 105, 106 note 12; *Looschelders*, Vorbem. zu Art. 3-6 EGBGB at 1; *von Bar/Mankowski*, IPR I, §7 at 1; *Kegel/Schurig*, before §6.

438 *Ravluševičius*, IPRax 2003, 272.

439 Mikelėnas, in: Yearbook of Private International Law 7 (2005), 161, 165.

440 Mikelėnas, in: Yearbook of Private International Law 7 (2005), 161, 167 and passim.

441 See Article 2.12 Lithuanian Civil Code.

The Netherlands

Since 1 January 2012, Book 10 of the Dutch Civil Code (*Burgerlijk Wetboek*) has been in force. It encompasses conflicts provisions but, in principle, does not cover questions of a procedural nature.[442] It was preceded by step-by-step legislation in the field of private international law, with Book 10 in general ultimately providing more consolidation than innovation.[443] The compilation and systematic arrangement of sixteen prior private international law acts is capped off by a new section on "general provisions" placed right at the beginning.[444] It reflects a strong academic influence.[445]

Among the seventeen articles in the first chapter, there are provisions on the application of foreign law, incidental questions, *renvoi*, public policy, overriding mandatory provisions, form, prescription, non-unified legal systems, and nationality. Furthermore, there is a general escape clause for cases in which, inter alia, a closer connection exists to a law other than the one determined by another conflicts rule. There is also a provision on the requirements for party autonomy (if it is allowed elsewhere) and a "*fait accompli* exception".[446]

Portugal

The main part of Portuguese private international law can be found in the General Part of the 1966 Portuguese Civil Code, which entered into force in 1967.[447] The chapter on "foreigners' rights and conflict of laws" is subdivided into two sections. The first section covers "general provisions", while the second, itself divided into several subsections, comprises conflicts provisions for different subject matters. The private international law provisions in the Portuguese Civil Code have been described as forming "une codification cohérente et complète",[448] but there are also quite a few conflicts provisions in separate codes and statutes.[449] The influence of academic thought on

---

442 *Struycken*, RabelsZ 78 (2014), 592, 598–599, also as to the exceptions.

443 See *Struycken*, RabelsZ 78 (2014), 592, 597–600; *ten Wolde*, Yearbook of Private International Law 13 (2011), 389, 390–392; *Boele-Woelki/van Iterson*, in: van Erp/van Vliet (eds.), Netherlands Report, 145, 146–148.

444 See *ten Wolde*, Yearbook of Private International Law 13 (2011), 389, 391 and 411.

445 *Rammeloo*, EuLF 2010, I-180, I-184.

446 See *infra* Chapter 3, section 5.9.

447 As to the development of the private international law provisions of the Portuguese Civil Code see *de Lima Pinheiro*, Yearbook of Private International Law 14 (2012/2013), 153–154; *Neuhaus/Rau*, RabelsZ 32 (1968), 500, 501–504.

448 *Moura Ramos*, in: Symeonides (ed.), PIL at the End of the 20th Century, 349, 350.

449 *de Lima Pinheiro*, Yearbook of Private International Law 14 (2012/2013), 153, 154; *Moura Vicente*, Yearbook of Private International Law 9 (2007), 257, 259.

Portuguese private international law and on the private international law provisions of the Civil Code is generally regarded as high.[450]

The collection of general provisions in no particular order,[451] sometimes expressly called "general part",[452] is regarded by some as the most remarkable feature of Portuguese private international law.[453] It encompasses rules on characterisation, *renvoi* (four formally separate provisions), non-unified legal systems, evasion of the law, public policy, and the interpretation as well as the consequence of a failure to establish foreign law. The last provision is complemented by a provision found much later in the code under which foreign law is considered law and, in general, must be applied *ex officio*.[454] There is no general escape clause. Some Portuguese scholars have argued, however, that the underlying principle of the closest connection should allow the courts to deviate from particular conflicts provisions.[455] None of the provisions recognise overriding mandatory provisions, but scholars and courts alike have discussed the issue.[456]

Romania

There used to be a separate code of private international law in Romania,[457] but the 2009 Romanian Civil Code, in force since 1 October 2011, now incorporates partially reformed conflicts provisions in Book VII.[458] Title I features an extensive section on "General Provisions", whereas Title II deals with individual subject matters. The general provisions cover almost all issues previously mentioned in the context of other member states' private international law, with the exception of incidental questions. This includes provisions on characterisation, overriding mandatory provisions (which Romanian statutory law had not dealt with before[459]), evasion of the law, the

---

450 *Moura Vicente*, Yearbook of Private International Law 9 (2007), 257, 259; *Moura Ramos*, in: Symeonides (ed.), PIL at the End of the 20th Century, 349, 351 ("Professorenrecht").

451 *Neuhaus/Rau*, RabelsZ 32 (1968), 500, 505 ("bunte Reihenfolge").

452 *Moura Ramos*, in: Symeonides (ed.), PIL at the End of the 20th Century, 349, 380; *de Lima Pinheiro*, Yearbook of Private International Law 14 (2012/2013), 153.

453 *Moura Ramos*, in: Symeonides (ed.), PIL at the End of the 20th Century, 349, 380.

454 *de Lima Pinheiro*, Yearbook of Private International Law 14 (2012/2013), 153, 170; *Moura Vicente*, Yearbook of Private International Law 9 (2007), 257, 263; Article 348 Portuguese Civil Code.

455 *de Lima Pinheiro*, Yearbook of Private International Law 14 (2012/2013), 153, 156 with further references.

456 *de Lima Pinheiro*, Yearbook of Private International Law 14 (2012/2013), 153, 160 with further references.

457 See *Aden*, RIW 2008, 700–707; *Leonhardt*, IPRax 1994, 156–159.

458 See *Avasilencei*, Rev. crit. DIP 2012, 247, 248–249; the procedural provisions also contained in the former private international law act were similarly incorporated in the Romanian Code of Civil Procedure, ibid.

459 *Avasilencei*, Rev. crit. DIP 2012, 247, 251.

establishment, interpretation and application of foreign law, and public policy, as well as the lack of a requirement of reciprocity. Furthermore, there are rules on nationality and habitual residence.

1.3.2.2. "General Provisions" without a Formal Section of Their Own

Greece

Private international law provisions form part of the 1940 Greek Civil Code which, on account of World War II, only "really" entered into force in 1946.[460] A section of Greek academia had suggested a separate code for private international law,[461] but the provisions were ultimately placed in the Greek Civil Code's First Book, its "General Part". The chapter on private international law is not subdivided any further internally. Provisions on some issues already mentioned can nevertheless be found largely in one group at the end of this chapter, i.e. after provisions determining the law applicable to questions of family, contract, tort, property, and succession law. Kozyris's outline of Greek private international law is structured accordingly, with "General Matters" being the last section of the part on Greek conflict of laws.[462] Meidanis's section on "General Questions" in a volume on Greek private international law edited by Vrellis, however, immediately follows the introduction by the editor.[463]

The cluster of provisions just mentioned encompasses rules on nationality (Greece's main connecting factor), multi-national as well as stateless persons, *renvoi*, and public policy. The drafters deliberately refrained from making, or even attempting to make, a provision on characterisation.[464] The Greek Code of Civil Procedure deals with the application of foreign law and its reviewability.[465]

Latvia

Private international law provisions can be found in the Introduction to Latvia's 1992[466] Civil Code, alongside, inter alia, a general good faith provision

---

460 *Gogos/Aubin*, RabelsZ 15 (1949/1950), 240.

461 See *Vassilakakis*, RHDI 63 (2010), 103; *Gogos/Aubin*, RabelsZ 15 (1949/1950), 240, 241.

462 *Kozyris*, in: Kerameus/id. (eds.), Introduction to Greek Law, 379, 396–397; *Gogos/Aubin*, RabelsZ 15 (1949/1950), 240, 250–255, however, mostly deal with these issues *before* turning to special ones.

463 *Meidanis*, in: Vrellis (ed.), PIL in Greece.

464 *Gogos/Aubin*, RabelsZ 15 (1949/1950), 240, 245.

465 *Kozyris*, in: Kerameus/id. (eds.), Introduction to Greek Law, 379, 397–402.

466 The 1992 Civil Code is essentially a recast of the pre-Soviet 1937 Civil Code, reinstated after Latvia regained its independence in 1991, see *Schulze*, in: Roggemann/Kuss (eds.), 187,

and a rule setting forth how provisions are to be construed. From these, conflicts rules are not formally separated; nor is there a formal substructure. Yet at the end of the Introduction, some provisions are rounded up that do not deal with any special legal relationship such as parenthood, property rights or contracts, but cover the application of foreign law: its determination (by way of referring to Latvia's Code of Civil Procedure) and the consequences when this is impossible, *renvoi*, and public policy. Furthermore, there is a provision on form.[467] One of the earlier sections provides an express definition of "place of residence", a much-used connecting factor.

Spain

Spanish private international law in statutory form has always been part of Spain's Civil Codes.[468] Its main[469] provisions are now located in the Preliminary Title to the Civil Code. The fourth chapter of said Title deals with "Normas de derecho internacional privado".[470] It only comprises rules determining the applicable law, whereas questions of jurisdiction, as well as those of the recognition and enforcement of foreign decisions, are regulated elsewhere.[471] The chapter on the applicable law has no further subdivision. Its final Article 12, however, covers several issues relevant for (potentially) all the provisions preceding it: characterisation, *renvoi*, public policy, evasion of the law, non-unified legal systems, and the *ex officio* application of Spanish conflicts provisions. Nationality is the most frequently employed connecting factor.[472] Some rules on double nationality and statelessness can be found at the end of Article 9 Spanish Civil Code, which, other than that, contains conflicts provisions concerning an individual's personal law, matrimony, adoption etc. Another provision deals with issues of form in an arguably general manner.[473] There is no escape clause for all conflicts provisions. One might be tempted to

199; *Strautins*, Yearbook of Private International Law 8 (2006), 289, mentions an upcoming Latvian private international law reform but there are still no indications of it.

467 Section 21(1) Latvian Civil Code extends to all kinds of "legal transaction[s]"; this view is confirmed by reading Section 21(2) Latvian Civil Code *a contrario*.

468 See *Esplugues Mota/Azcárraga Monzonís*, Spanish Report, 1–2; concerning the importance of case law, 8–9; see *Calvo Caravaca/Carrascosa González*, DIP I, 94, concerning the importance of legal scholarship.

469 *Calvo Caravaca/Carrascosa González*, DIP I, 92; see *Esplugues Mota/Azcárraga Monzonís*, Spanish Report, 6 for Spanish private international law provisions in other acts.

470 These rules generally apply in interregional conflict cases, too, but with modifications, see Article 16 Spanish Civil Code. I will pay no further attention to Spanish interregional conflicts here, but see *Calvo Caravaca/Carrascosa González*, DIP I, 54–65.

471 *Calvo Caravaca/Carrascosa González*, DIP I, 183 (jurisdiction) and 763 (effects of foreign decisions).

472 *Esplugues Mota/Azcárraga Monzonís*, Spanish Report, 9.

473 Article 11 Spanish Civil Code.

read Article 8 Spanish Civil Code as a general provision on national overriding mandatory provisions, but it is generally understood to cover Spanish public law only.[474]

1.3.3. Codes on Both Private International Law and Procedural Issues

Belgium

After nearly ten years of preparatory works,[475] the Belgian Code of Private International Law entered into force on 1 October 2004. Prior legislation had been piecemeal, with the case law far from clear.[476] The Belgian PIL Code thus marked a "Copernican revolution".[477] It originally had 140 articles,[478] covering jurisdiction and conflict of laws, as well as recognition and enforcement of foreign decisions (Article 2 Belgian PIL Code). The title "Code" is to be taken seriously: its authors strove for coherence in structure and terminology, as well as a level of completeness.[479] The Code commences with a chapter on "General Provisions" consisting of 31 articles, which scholars have also dubbed a "General Part".[480] Sections 4 and 6 of this chapter contain "general provisions" as to jurisdiction and the effects of foreign judgments respectively, and Section 5 concerns "general provisions" as to conflict of laws.

The section on general provisions of conflict of laws contains provisions, inter alia, on the establishment and application of foreign law, *renvoi*, overriding mandatory provisions, and public policy, as well as a general escape clause (supplemented by some specific escape clauses later on in the Code[481]). Additionally, the third section of the first chapter pertains to nationality, domicile, and habitual residence, supplying general definitions for the two latter concepts. The code provides considerable room for party autonomy, but there is no general provision dealing with it (even though a common thread can be identified).[482]

---

474 See *Calvo Caravaca/Carrascosa González*, DIP I, 413–414.

475 See *Erauw/Fallon*, in: Dirix/Lelen (eds.), The Belgian Reports, 227, 228–231; *Fiorini*, ICLQ 54 (2005), 499, 507.

476 *Erauw/Fallon*, in: Dirix/Lelen (eds.), The Belgian Reports, 227, 228 and 235; *Francq*, RabelsZ 70 (2006), 235; *Fiorini*, ICLQ 54 (2005), 499, 504; also *Reimann*, in: id./Zimmermann (eds.), The Oxford Handbook of Comparative Law, 1363, 1379 (with note 54).

477 *Pertegas*, IPRax 2006, 53.

478 The law of 10 May 2007 inserted two new articles (Article 35bis and Article 35ter) into the Belgian PIL Code.

479 *Erauw/Fallon*, in: Dirix/Lelen (eds.), The Belgian Reports, 227, 232–234 and 238; *Francq*, RabelsZ 70 (2006), 235, 240 and 242.

480 *Erauw/Fallon*, in: Dirix/Lelen (eds.), The Belgian Reports, 227, 231; *Pertegas*, IPRax 2006, 53, 54 (albeit not capitalised).

481 *Erauw/Fallon*, in: Dirix/Lelen (eds.), The Belgian Reports, 227, 241.

482 See *Pertegas*, IPRax 2006, 53, 57–58.

Bulgaria

Until the Code of Private International Law entered into force on 21 May 2005, Bulgarian private international law had been marked by gaps, piecemeal solutions, and incoherence.[483] The lack of a general part had been described as "[p]articularly sensitive".[484] *Renvoi* had not been regulated anywhere at all, whereas there had been several, but divergent, public policy clauses.[485] Now, however, the title "Code" (*kodeks*) is already supposed to indicate that this legislative instrument covers private international law as a whole, not just select areas.[486] Indeed, its 124 articles concern jurisdiction, the applicable law, and the recognition and enforcement of foreign decisions alike (see Article 1(1) Bulgarian PIL Code).

Part Three of said Code concerns the applicable law and its Chapter Four[487] (Articles 39–47 Bulgarian PIL Code) contains "General Provisions". Among these provisions are rules on characterisation, *renvoi*, public policy, overriding mandatory provisions, and the establishment and application of foreign law. Several of these rules have no predecessor in statutory Bulgarian law.[488] Furthermore, at the very beginning of the Code, there is a short section containing other "General Provisions": Article 1 Bulgarian PIL Code, setting forth the scope of the Code; Article 2 Bulgarian PIL Code, embodying the principle of closest connection; and Article 3 Bulgarian PIL Code, stating the primacy of treaty law. Although the Bulgarian PIL Code relies much on the connecting factor of habitual residence, this is not defined expressly in the Code.

Croatia

The 1982 Yugoslav PIL Act, which entered into force on 1 January 1983, is still in force (with only a few modifications) in Croatia, although there has been talk of reform for some years now.[489] At the time, Firsching praised the Act as the "most modern codification" of private international law.[490] The Act was

---

483 *Zidarova/Stančeva-Minčeva*, RabelsZ 71 (2007), 398, 401.

484 *Hessel-Jolst*, Yearbook of Private International Law 5 (2003), 143, 144.

485 *Hessel-Jolst*, Yearbook of Private International Law 5 (2003), 143, 153.

486 *Hessel-Jolst*, Yearbook of Private International Law 9 (2007), 375, 377 (with note 8).

487 It should be noted that this chapter is not the fourth chapter of the third part of the Code, as one might easily surmise; rather, the chapters of the Bulgarian PIL Code are numbered consecutively. Thus, in fact, the general provisions can be found at the very beginning of the part on the applicable law.

488 *Hessel-Jolst*, Yearbook of Private International Law 9 (2007), 375, 377; *Zidarova/Stančeva-Minčeva*, RabelsZ 71 (2007), 398, 403.

489 See *Kunda*, 477, 486 with note 79; *Hessel-Jolst*, Yearbook of Private International Law 9 (2007), 375, 377.

490 *Firsching*, IPRax 1983, 1, 5 (albeit apparently not entirely without ulterior motives in view of the reform of German private international law in the 1980s); see also *Conetti*, Riv. dir. int. priv. proc. 2000, 569, 578.

prepared over the course of 15 years.[491] The Croatian PIL Act, as it will be designated henceforth, contains rules on the applicable law and on jurisdiction, as well as on the recognition and enforcement of foreign decisions (Article 1 Croatian PIL Act). It thus groups together issues not previously found in one place in Croatian/Yugoslav law.[492]

The heading of its first chapter is sometimes translated as "basic provisions",[493] but the chapter is more often referred to as being about "general" provisions.[494] It encompasses provisions on public policy, evasion of the law, *renvoi*, formal validity, prescription, characterisation (to some degree[495]), non-unified legal systems, nationality, and the establishment and application of foreign law.

The Czech Republic

A new Czech Act on Private International Law replaced the 1963 Act in 2012 and entered into force on 1 January 2014. It forms part of the comprehensive recodification of Czech private law that took place in 2012.[496] The new Act pertains to the applicable law, jurisdiction and procedure, and recognition and enforcement of foreign judgments, as well as to the legal status of foreigners, some insolvency issues, and arbitration (§1 Czech PIL Act). This reflects the Czech legislator's desired approach to having a single piece of legislation comprising all areas of private international law.[497]

The inclusion of procedural issues in a private international law act constitutes no novelty in the Czech Republic. The 1963 Act had already covered conflict of laws, as well as procedural questions. However, a clear innovation – and one which is not only quite interesting for present purposes, but which has also already been described as a "striking structural change"[498] – is the inclusion of a part containing "general provisions", or rather: several such parts. There is Part One with "General Provisions" as such, Part Two with "General Provisions of Procedural International Law", and Part Three with "General Provisions of Private International Law". Among the 28 general provisions, there are rules

491 *Šarčević*, Am. J. Comp. L. 33 (1985), 283, 285; *Matić*, Neth. Int. L. Rev. 30 (1983), 220.

492 See *Šarčević*, Am. J. Comp. L. 33 (1985), 283, 293–294.

493 See the translation by the T. M. C. Asser Institute in Neth. Int. L. Rev. 30 (1983), 222.

494 *Šarčević*, Am. J. Comp. L. 33 (1985), 283, 285; *Cigoj*, Rev. crit. DIP 1983, 375, 376 ("generaux"); *Firsching*, IPRax 1983, 1, 2 ("[a]llgemeine Bestimmungen").

495 See *Šarčević*, Am. J. Comp. L. 33 (1985), 283, 287–288; *Cigoj*, Rev. crit. DIP 1983, 375, 376; *infra* footnote 769.

496 *Pauknerová/Pfeiffer*, Journal of Private International Law 10 (2014), 205, 209 and passim; *Dobiáš*, RIW 2012, 671; *Bohata*, WiRO 2012, 193.

497 *Pauknerová/Pfeiffer*, Journal of Private International Law 10 (2014), 205, 217; see also *Dobiáš*, Riv. dir. int. priv. proc. 2015, 109.

498 *Pauknerová/Pfeiffer*, Journal of Private International Law 10 (2014), 205, 214.

on (both Czech and foreign) overriding mandatory provisions, public policy, characterisation, incidental questions, establishment and application of foreign law, and *renvoi*. The provisions on characterisation, incidental questions, and establishment and application of foreign law are entirely novel to Czech private international law.[499] There are also a provision on evasion of the law and a general escape clause. Although the Czech PIL Act relies heavily on the concept of habitual residence,[500] it does not define the term.

Hungary: The Hungarian PIL Code 1979

Hungary has had a private international law code since 1979. The Hungarian PIL Code 1979 was adopted as a "law-decree", i.e. not by the Hungarian parliament. For all intents and purposes, however, this law-decree could be regarded as statutory law, and Hungarian writers even generally and habitually referred to it as "code".[501] In its Chapters I through VIII, the Code contained rules as to the applicable law. Later chapters addressed jurisdiction and the effects of foreign decisions. As the age of the Code already indicates, Hungarian private international law has proved remarkably stable despite Hungary's political and economic changes.[502]

The very first chapter of the Code, thus also the first chapter on the applicable law, contained "General Provisions", forming the "General Part"[503] of the Hungarian PIL Code 1979. There were rules on characterisation, *renvoi*, the establishment and application of foreign law, reciprocity (or rather: the lack of a requirement of reciprocity), public policy, evasion of the law, and the parties' right not to have foreign law applied. In the Hungarian PIL Code 1979, there were also definitions for domicile and habitual residence, as well as rules on questions of nationality. However, they were not located in the chapter with general provisions, but in Chapter II on persons. There was no escape clause among the general provisions. Rules on overriding mandatory provisions and

499 *Dobiáš*, RIW 2012, 671, 672 and 674.

500 Habitual residence appears more than 60 times in the 2012 Act as opposed to once in the 1963 Act (and in a provision which was introduced to the Act only in 2004), *Pauknerová/Pfeiffer*, Journal of Private International Law 10 (2014), 205, 221.

501 *Harsági/Kengyel/Nemessányi*, in: Esplugues/Iglesias/Palao (eds.), Application of Foreign Law, 213, 214; *Nagy*, PIL in Hungary, at 9 and passim; *Raffai/Szabó*, Acta Juridica Hungarica 51 (2010), 136, 137 and passim; *Burián*, in: Symeonides (ed.), PIL at the End of the 20th Century, 263, 264 (with note 2) and passim; *Mádl*, RHDI 44 (1991), 227; already *Mádl/Vékás*, ZfRV 1982, 266, 267.

502 See *Burián*, in: Symeonides (ed.), PIL at the End of the 20th Century, 263, 276; for a short overview of the modifications made since 1979 until 2010 see *Raffai/Szabó*, Acta Juridica Hungarica 51 (2010), 136, 137.

503 *Mádl*, RHDI 44 (1991), 227, 238.

incidental questions had to be supplied by the judiciary; a uniform practice, however, had not been observed.[504]

Hungary: The Hungarian PIL Act 2018

In 2017, Hungary passed a new Private International Law Act. It also concerns jurisdiction and other aspects of international procedure. It entered into force on 1 January 2018. It too contains "general provisions" – with 14 constituting a few more than the nine of the 1979 Code. In addition to the issues already dealt with in the old Code, there now are rules on the *ex officio* application of foreign law, non-unified legal systems, party autonomy, overriding mandatory provisions, and the *conflit mobile*. A general escape clause was introduced, as well as a subsidiary conflicts rule. Definitions for habitual residence and domicile have been included in the chapter with "general provisions". On the other hand, the rules on reciprocity and evasion of the law have disappeared.

The new Act was passed sufficiently early for it to be included in the final version of this book's manuscript; but with the act being so recent and written in Hungarian, there was almost no[505] pertinent secondary literature to take into account before the book went to press. Against this background, the references to the 1979 Code – for which many sources, at least in French, English, and German, exist – have been kept (with the designation "Hungarian PIL Code 1979"). For conceptual insights, the repeal of the Code does not matter too much. In the context of its general provisions, the new Act mainly added to the issues which the 1979 Code addresses anyway. References to the new provisions (with the designation "Hungarian PIL Act") have been included wherever necessary.

Italy

Private international law had been part of Italian Civil Codes for 130 years, first in the 1865 Code, then the 1942 Code.[506] After more than a decade of official preparatory works,[507] however, the 1995 Italian PIL Act entered into force, expressly repealing the private international law provisions in the Civil Code.[508] Although some pessimistic observers only gave it a life expectancy of ten years or fewer – not necessarily because of its quality, but because of rapid

504 *Raffai/Szabó*, Acta Juridica Hungarica 51 (2010), 136, 137.

505 At the eleventh hour, the contribution by *Csehi*, IPRax 2018, 298, was published.

506 *Giardina*, ILM 35 (1996), 760. To be precise, Italian private international law was not found in the 1942 Code itself but in its preliminary provisions ("disposizioni sulla legge in generale").

507 See *Kindler*, RabelsZ 61 (1997), 227, 229–231; *Giardina*, Rev. crit. DIP 1996, 1, 3–4.

508 Article 73 Italian PIL Act.

changes in Italian law in general at the time[509] – it still remains in force today (with modifications). While the Act has not been named a "code", it purports to be comprehensive.[510] An indication of this can perhaps even be inferred from the title the Act did receive: "Riforma del *sistema* italiano di diritto internazionale private".[511] Accordingly, the Italian PIL Act deals not only with the determination of the applicable law, but also with jurisdiction and issues of recognition and enforcement of foreign judgments.

The Italian PIL Act begins with a short section of "General Provisions" concerning the scope of the Act and the effect of international conventions. The applicable law is determined by Title III of the Act, which in turn begins with a chapter on "General Provisions". This in itself is somewhat of an innovation because prior Italian statutory private international law had only dealt with *renvoi* and public policy.[512] The chapter comprises rules on *renvoi*, establishment and application of foreign law, public policy, Italian overriding mandatory provisions, non-unified legal systems, and questions of nationality. The Act provides for more flexibility than its predecessor,[513] yet does not contain a general escape clause. The Italian legislator did not tackle the issues of characterisation and incidental questions.[514]

Slovakia

The Slovak Act on "Private International Law and Rules of International Procedure" of 1963[515] has been amended several times. Its first part deals with conflict of laws (Division 1) and the legal status of foreigners (Division 2), the latter including a rule on dual and uncertain nationality. The first part is capped off by a third Division on "common provisions", covering non-unified legal systems, *renvoi*, and public policy. A rule on the establishment of foreign law is found later in the Slovak PIL Act among procedural provisions.

---

509 See *Pesce*, RIW 1995, 977, 983.

510 *Krätschmer*, Integration von Staatsverträgen, 53–54; *Pocar/Honorati*, in: Symeonides (ed.), PIL at the End of the 20th Century, 279, 280; *Kindler*, RabelsZ 61 (1997), 227, 232; *Giardina*, ILM 35 (1996), 760, 761. The Italian PIL Act also loosely follows the structure of the Italian Civil Code: *Kindler*, RabelsZ 61 (1997), 227, 252; *Pesce*, RIW 1995, 977; with some scepticism *Ballarino/Bonomi*, Yearbook of Private International Law 2 (2000), 99, 108.

511 Emphasis added; along similar lines *Giardina*, Rev. crit. DIP 1996, 1, 6.

512 *Pocar/Honorati*, in: Symeonides (ed.), PIL at the End of the 20th Century, 279, 282; *Pocar*, IPRax 1996, 145, 150.

513 *Krätschmer*, Integration von Staatsverträgen, 55–58; *Pocar/Honorati*, in: Symeonides (ed.), PIL at the End of the 20th Century, 279, 290; *Pocar*, IPRax 1996, 145, 146–147; *Giardina*, Rev. crit. DIP 1996, 1, 10–11; *id.*, ILM 35 (1996), 760, 762; for a more sceptical view see *Ballarino/Bonomi*, Yearbook of Private International Law 2 (2000), 99, 115–116.

514 *Pocar*, IPRax 1996, 145, 150.

515 Thus, it is one of the several new acts and codes passed during the comprehensive Slovak private law reform of the 1960s, see *Fiala/Hurdík/Kirstová*, Contract Law, at 10.

Slovenia

When Slovenia gained independence in 1991, Yugoslav laws generally remained in force, provided they were not in contravention of Slovenia's legal order.[516] Accordingly, the Yugoslav PIL Act[517] continued to be applicable for questions of private international law, now as an Act of the Republic of Slovenia.[518] This changed in 1999 when the new Slovenian Private International Law and Procedural Act entered into force. Its structure closely resembles that of the Yugoslav PIL Act, but it contains quite a few content-related alterations.[519] As its name already suggests, the Act does not only cover conflict of laws but also jurisdiction, as well as recognition and enforcement of foreign decisions (and arbitral awards).

The Slovenian PIL Act begins with a first chapter consisting of 12 "Basic Provisions". It contains a general escape clause (called the "most significant innovation" of this new act[520]), as well as provisions on public policy, *renvoi*, non-unified legal systems, form, prescription, nationality, and the establishment of foreign law. Neither the characterisation provision nor the evasion of the law provision, however, were carried over from the Yugoslav PIL Act.[521] The drafters also deliberately abstained from creating rules on adaptation or incidental questions.[522]

1.4. PROVISIONAL SUMMARY

1.4.1. Private International Law Codes: A Majority Position

The EU is divided into two groups of countries as far as private international law is concerned: those with a private international law code and those without. The second group consists of countries of the common law tradition, the Nordic countries, France, and Luxembourg. The first group is the bigger one, with 19 out of the 28 member states having a private international law code. Eleven of these codes are stand-alone acts; eight form part of the respective countries' civil code.[523] The latter approach seems to more traditional in nature

---

516 *Puharič*, Yearbook of Private International Law 5 (2003), 155, 156; Geč-*Korošec*, RabelsZ 66 (2002), 710, 712.

517 See already *supra Croatia*.

518 *Rudolf*, IPRax 2003, 158.

519 *Puharič*, Yearbook of Private International Law 5 (2003), 155, 157; *Conetti*, Riv. dir. int. priv. proc. 2000, 569–570.

520 *Puharič*, Yearbook of Private International Law 5 (2003), 155, 159; see also *Conetti*, Riv. dir. int. priv. proc. 2000, 569, 570.

521 *Rudolf*, IPRax 2003, 158, 159; Geč-*Korošec*, RabelsZ 66 (2002), 710, 715–717.

522 *Rudolf*, IPRax 2003, 158, 159.

523 With Germany being in something of a grey area, but regarded here as belonging to the second group, see *supra* section 1.3.2.1. (*Germany*).

(albeit not passé, as the recent Romanian and Dutch examples show). It possibly stems from the idea that, in order to be "complete", a civil code needed to "provide the key for the territorial application of the rules it contained".[524] Incidentally, this observation also holds true on a global scale.[525]

The tally of 19 codes is slightly lower than Symeonides's, who counts 20 private international law "codifications" in (what is now) the EU.[526] Against the backdrop that his book only covers the period between 1962 and 2012,[527] this number must be adjusted by adding Greece (1940/1946).[528] The resulting discrepancy between 21 (Symeonides) and 19 (here) follows from Symeonides's approach of including "codifications" which cover "choice of law for only certain subjects".[529] He thus includes the 2001 Finnish Marriage Act, as well as the United Kingdom's Private International Law (Miscellaneous Provisions) Act in his list.[530] As such legal instruments run contrary to the criterion set up at the beginning of this chapter, i.e. that the legislative acts must comprehensively cover different areas of conflict of laws, it comes as no surprise that his number of private international law codifications in the EU is a bit higher than the number arrived at in this book. Apart from this, his approach is quite similar to the one employed here: he also does not discriminate on the basis of formal designation; on the basis of a legislative instrument standing alone or forming part of another code; or on the basis of a legal instrument covering more than just conflicts provisions.

Even in the member states without a private international law code, many scholars present the law in their textbooks along the dichotomy of "general" ("preliminary", "basic" etc.) and individual issues.

1.4.2. *Jurisdiction and Effects of Foreign Decisions*

There is no clear trend towards combining conflicts provisions and those pertaining to jurisdiction, as well as the effects of foreign decisions, in one act.[531]

524 *Fiorini*, ICLQ 54 (2005), 499, 502 with note 32; similarly *Neuhaus/Rau*, RabelsZ 32 (1968), 500, 502.

525 See *Symeonides*, Codifying Choice of Law, 21.

526 *Symeonides*, Codifying Choice of Law, 18.

527 *Symeonides*, Codifying Choice of Law, 1 and 4.

528 It does not make a numerical difference that *Symeonides* does not take account of the 2009 Romanian Civil Code, for he does take into account the 1992 Romanian PIL which was replaced by it (*supra* section 1.3.2.1. (*Romania*)).

529 *Symeonides*, Codifying Choice of Law, 25.

530 *Symeonides*, Codifying Choice of Law, 8–9; see also *Reimann*, in: id./Zimmermann (eds.), The Oxford Handbook of Comparative Law 1363, 1379.

531 See the contributions of *Dutta* and *Kadner-Graziano* to von Hein/Rühl (eds.), Kohärenz im Internationalen Privat- und Verfahrensrecht der Europäischen Union, 27 and 44, for policy questions regarding the combination or separation of the topics in legislation.

Of the ten domestic private international law codes passed in the last two decades,[532] five also contain procedural provisions (beyond questions of the establishment and application of foreign law), whereas five do not.

1.4.3. A Formally Separate Section for General Provisions (in Most Cases)

The vast majority of private international law codes reserve a special section for general provisions,[533] usually under this exact title. Only Greece, Latvia, and Spain – member states whose private international law is found in their respective civil codes[534] – do not follow this approach. In their codes, general provisions can arguably be found side by side with other conflicts provisions, without any formal separation by chapters, titles, and such.

From a functional perspective, it is not even necessary to regard any member state with a private international law code as part of this already small group of seeming outsiders. The Spanish example is particularly obvious. Its conflicts provisions consist of very long and self-contained articles;[535] other domestic codes would create separate sections for different areas of law, dividing the same content into several shorter provisions. Accordingly, Article 12 Spanish Civil Code groups in one place many of those provisions which elsewhere can be found in a separate "general" section.[536] This is functionally equivalent to a section consisting of several short general provisions. Moreover, the issues that many member states, as the analysis has shown so far, consider "general" can be found grouped together in the Greek Civil Code, as well as the Latvian Civil Code. While there is no formal separation by way of a chapter or title, the respective provisions are not scattered among specific conflicts provisions either.

It is therefore misleading at best to state that there are only a few "national models" for general provisions in private international law across the EU.[537]

---

532 Namely, the Slovenian PIL Act, the Lithuanian Civil Code, the Estonian PIL Act, the Belgian PIL Code, the Bulgarian PIL Code, the Romanian Civil Code, the Dutch Civil Code, the Polish PIL Act, the Czech PIL Act, and the Hungarian PIL Act.

533 *Audit* made a similar observation more than a decade ago in his analysis with a greater geographical scope, Rec. des cours 305 (2003), 9, 55.

534 The reverse statement is not true: there *are* member states (Germany, Portugal, the Netherlands) whose private international law is part of their civil code and which do have a formally separate section for general provisions.

535 See Article 9 Spanish Civil Code: personal law, family law; Article 10 Spanish Civil Code: property, contractual obligations, non-contractual obligations.

536 *Supra* section 1.3.2.2.

537 Unfortunately, the statement is my own: *Wilke*, in: Leible/Unberath (eds.), Rom 0-Verordnung, 23, 25, relying, as evidenced by footnote 12, on the less blanket (yet rather sceptical) statement by *Sonnenberger*, in: FS Kropholler, 227–228. My statement understandably has been misread already, see e.g. *Wandt*, Rechtswahlregelungen, 212–213. I have clarified/rectified my position since, in: Leible (ed.), General Principles, §1.02. See also *Dolinger*, in: Essays in Honor of Juenger, 23, 39, for a global sample of "general part" provisions of private international law.

Rather, as a matter of practice, however, there is not a single domestic private international law code in the EU that does not contain general provisions.

1.4.4. *Placement of General Provisions*

As a matter of structure, general provisions are usually found *before* the special conflicts provisions; textbooks usually begin with "general issues" and turn to individual conflicts rules later on. Exceptions to this observation are the codes of Greece, Latvia, Slovakia, and Spain where, similarly to the corresponding section in the 1896 EGBGB, general provisions mainly make up the final provisions. Considering that Latvia's 1992 Civil Code is essentially its 1937 Civil Code,[538] these are four of the five countries with the oldest private international law codes. Since 1979, no country has created a private international law code in which general provisions do not precede the special conflicts provisions – and Portugal had not already done so in 1966.

1.4.5. *The Newer, the Bigger*

In 1997, Conetti observed, at the time, the relative size of recent private international law codes and their relative "*systématicité*".[539] Almost twenty years later, a similar observation can be made about fleshing out general provisions in private international law codes. Of the ten codes passed in the last two decades,[540] many contain sections with more general provisions than the previous codes of other countries. Where new codes replaced prior legal instruments in the same country, or where they were drafted (and promulgated) in the absence of a predecessor, (additional) general provisions were often introduced. The Belgian PIL Code (no prior legislative instrument of private international law, now a large section with general provisions)[541] and the Czech PIL Act (no section with general provisions before, now a large one)[542] are the most striking examples in this regard. The unprecedented rules on overriding mandatory provisions in Poland (Article 8 Polish PIL Act) and Romania (Article 2.566 Romanian Civil Code) illustrate this point further.

1.4.6. *"New" Issues Tackled*

Part of the apparent trend of more extensive sections on general provisions is a slightly increased willingness to tackle issues long or often left untouched

538 *Supra* section 1.3.2.2. (*Latvia*) with footnote 467.
539 *Conetti*, in: Collisio Legum, 129, 130.
540 *Supra* footnote 532.
541 *Supra* section 1.3.3. (*Belgium*).
542 *Supra* section 1.3.3. (*The Czech Republic*).

by legislators, such as the incidental question (Article 10:4 Dutch Civil Code; §22 Czech PIL Act) and characterisation (Article 39 Bulgarian PIL Code; Article 2.558 Romanian Civil Code; §20 Czech PIL Act).

1.4.7. A Tendency of Uniformity Regarding the Scope

The country reports may have appeared to be rather repetitive. Rather than poor style, however, this turns out to be an interesting *result* – and a surprising one for those who thus far have assumed big conceptual differences among the member states. Although the extent is not yet clear at this point, there appears to be some uniformity as regards the scope of general provisions. Several issues surface in every, or almost in every, domestic private international law code, in particular *renvoi*, public policy, and non-unified legal systems. Other issues appear in more than half of the respective groups of general provisions, such as questions of ascertaining and/or applying foreign law or questions of multinational and stateless persons.

2. EUROPEAN UNION PRIVATE INTERNATIONAL LAW

2.1. LEGISLATION

2.1.1. Conceptual Observations

EU private international law, to the extent that it is analysed here,[543] consists of six regulations. The obvious finding is that there is no single legislative act dealing with different areas of conflict of laws. The regulations pertain to one (special) area of private international law each, i.e. contractual obligations (Rome I), non-contractual obligations (Rome II), divorce and legal separation (Rome III), succession (Succession Regulation), matrimonial property regimes (M-Property Regulation), and property consequences of registered partnerships (RP-Property Regulation). The first three only concern the determination of the applicable law, while the latter three also concern jurisdiction, the recognition and enforcement of decisions, and other matters. There is no separate instrument or section of these instruments that concerns all of EU private international law; nor do the Rome Regulations contain chapters designated as "general".[544]

This is not to say that EU private international law does not deal at all with issues of overarching relevance. It will be shown in detail later on that the

543 *Supra* Introduction, section 2.

544 *Infra* footnote 549 and appurtenant text for the Succession Regulation, the M-Property Regulation, and the RP-Property Regulation.

EU legislator has dealt with quite a few of the issues identified as "general" on the domestic level, just always only in the context of each regulation. Moreover, the regulations do set apart entire sections or chapters from their particular conflicts provisions:[545] all Rome Regulations have chapters with "Other Provisions"[546] and "Final Provisions".[547] Rome II has an additional chapter containing "Common Rules";[548] the Succession Regulation, the M-Property Regulation, and the RP-Property Regulation even have a chapter on "*General* and Final Provisions".[549]

Upon closer inspection of what these chapters encompass, certain parallels and divergences appear. In Rome I and Rome II, the "Other Provisions" concern habitual residence, *renvoi*, public policy, states with more than one legal system, and the relationship of the respective regulations with other (EU and international) instruments. Even the order of these provisions is almost the same in both regulations.[550] The respective "Final Provisions" contain a provision as to the date of their application/entry into force. The "Application in Time", however, is one of the "Other Provisions" in Rome I, but a "Final Provision" in Rome II.

Many of the issues found in the chapter on "Other Provisions" in Rome I and Rome II are also found clustered together in Rome III, the Succession Regulation, the M-Property Regulation, and the RP-Property Regulation, but without a formal separation from the other (conflicts) provisions.[551] In turn, many of the topics dealt with under the heading "Other Provisions" in Rome III appear in the chapter on "General and Final Provisions" of the Succession Regulation, the M-Property Regulation, and the RP-Property

545 Occasionally even called "general parts": *Czepelak*, ERPL 2010, 705, 726. Also see *Trüten*, Die Entwicklung des IPR in der EU, §19 III 3 (665) ("nucleus for a 'general part'"); *Bariatti/Pataut*, in: Fallon/Lagarde/Poillot-Peruzzetto (eds.), Quelle architecture pour un code européen de droit international privé?, 337, 338 (insertion of "des dispositions de théorie générale" into the individual regulations). In part also *Roth*, in: Remien/Kieninger (eds.), Europäische Kollisionsrechtsvereinheitlichung, 11, 48, who points to even more commonalities of Rome I and II to serve as a foundation for a potential "general part".

546 Articles 19–28 Rome I, Articles 23–28 Rome II, Articles 17–20 Rome III.

547 Article 29 Rome I, Articles 29–32 Rome II, Article 21 Rome III.

548 Articles 15–22 Rome II. *Kühn*, Die gestörte Gesamtschuld im IPR, 128, makes a distinction between these provisions and those she considers as principles belonging in a "general part" of private international law, but unfortunately does not explain why; somewhat inconsistently, she later (199) uses the positioning of Article 20 Rome II as an indication that it actually forms part of the "general part" of private international law.

549 Articles 74–84 Succession Regulation; Articles 61–70 M-/RP-Property Regulation (emphasis added).

550 The difference concerns the public policy provision: in Rome I, it is found before the rule on states with more than one legal system, in Rome II, after it.

551 These regulations contain provisions on *renvoi*, public policy, territorial conflicts of laws and inter-personal conflicts of laws, and internal conflicts of laws. See also *Looschelders*, in: FS Coester-Waltjen, 531: Articles 30–37 Succession Regulation concern "classical" issues of the "general part".

Regulation,[552] in which the counterpart of Rome III's "final provision" on its entry into force can also be found.

Moreover, the first chapter of each private international law regulation sets forth the material scope of the respective instrument. In the three Rome Regulations, this first chapter also contains a provision pertaining to the universal application of the following conflicts rules.[553] All regulations but Rome I[554] contain a provision with definitions to be used when applying the following provisions.[555] Finally, all EU private international law regulations contain review clauses in a section separate from conflicts provisions, but not always in a section of the same name.[556]

Then again, there is no provision at all for quite a few of the "general" issues that the foregoing comparative survey of domestic private international law has brought to light. For example, statutory EU private international law does not expressly deal with characterisation (as such[557]), incidental questions, or the establishment and application of foreign law.

One insight to take away from these somewhat dry observations is that, as a matter of legislative technique, the EU legislator does compartmentalise. In particular, it formally distinguishes conflicts provisions for different subject matters from all sorts of other issues by grouping the respective provisions together, often in separate chapters.

2.1.2. Resulting Problems

Even so, two caveats are in order. First, it is already an indication of some conceptual incoherence that it was rather complicated merely to *describe* the content of the different chapters. Although the regulations share chapters of the same name, they do not necessarily deal with the same issues within them. Conversely, even though all remaining regulations do cover the issues found in the chapter with "Other Provisions" in Rome I and II, a respective separate chapter is missing in each. The second proviso is of a more substantive nature. Where the EU legislator compartmentalises, it only does so in the context of

---

552 Namely transitional provisions, the relationship of each regulation with certain international conventions, and information to be provided by the member states.

553 Article 2 Rome I; Article 3 Rome II; Article 4 Rome III. In the Succession Regulation, the M-Property Regulation, and the RP-Property Regulation, the respective provision is the very first one in each Chapter III on the applicable law: Article 20 Succession Regulation/M-/RP-Property Regulation.

554 In Rome I, a single definition is part of the provision on the scope: Article 1(4).

555 Article 2 Rome II; Article 3 Rome III/Succession Regulation/M-/RP-Property Regulation.

556 Article 27 Rome I ("Other Provisions"), Article 30 Rome II ("Final Provisions"), Article 20 Rome III ("Other Provisions"), and Article 82 Succession Regulation as well as Article 68 M-/RP-Property Regulation ("General and Final Provisions").

557 But see *infra* Chapter 3, section 2.4. (*European Union: Characterisation de Lege Europaea Lata*).

each specific area of European private international law. Issues arising in more than one of these areas are thus dealt with anew each time. This causes redundancy and, where the provisions on the same issue diverge, legal uncertainty. Legal uncertainty also arises for questions that EU law does not address. At this point, one example for each category may suffice.[558]

2.1.2.1. Redundancy: The Public Policy Exception[559]

All existing private international law regulations contain a public policy exception. Foreign law specified by these regulations is to be applied unless the application is manifestly incompatible with the forum's *ordre public*. The public policy exception sometimes appears, as with Article 21 Rome I and Article 26 Rome II, in a separate chapter with "Other Provisions"; sometimes its place is simply alongside the provisions determining the applicable law, as with Article 12 Rome III (even though there *is* a chapter "Other Provisions"), Article 35 Succession Regulation, and Article 31 M-/RP-Property Regulation.

All of these public policy provisions are carbon copies of each other. To be precise: Article 21 Rome I, Article 26 Rome II, Article 35 Succession Regulation, and Article 31 M-/RP-Property Regulation are formulated in exactly the same way, whereas the wording of Article 12 Rome III contains a few marginal deviations.[560] Even these minor differences seem to be mere translation issues: in German, for example, Article 12 Rome III is perfectly in line with its counterparts in Rome I and Rome II, but Article 35 Succession Regulation is phrased slightly differently, as is Article 31 M-/RP-Property Regulation. The French and Spanish wording differs slightly from regulation to regulation (but, strangely, not in unison).[561] For all intents and purposes, the public policy exception is the same across all these regulations. Thus, there actually is *one* (general) public policy exception in European private

---

558 The question of coherence in EU private international law has been widely discussed elsewhere, see *Sánchez Lorenzo*, REDI 70 (2018), 17; *Rühl/von Hein*, RabelsZ 79 (2015), 701, 713–721; the contributions to von Hein/Rühl (eds.), Kohärenz im Internationalen Privat- und Verfahrensrecht der Europäischen Union; and *Wiedemann*, in: Vaz de Sequeira/de Almeida Ribeiro (eds.), Católica Graduate Legal Research Conference 2014 – Conference Proceedings, 175.

559 In detail *infra* Chapter 3, section 5.6.

560 "Application" instead of "[t]he application", "designated by virtue of" instead of "specified by", no "(ordre public)" after "public policy".

561 French: "la loi designee par le présent règlement" (Rome I) vs. "la loi d'un pays désignée par le présent règlement" (Rome II) vs. "la loi désignée en vertu du présent règlement" (Rome III) vs. "la loi d'un État désignée par le présent règlement" (Succession Regulation/M-/RP-Property Regulation); Spanish: "la ley de cualquier país designada por el presente Reglamento" (Rome I) vs. "la ley designada por el presente Reglamento" (Rome II) vs. "la ley designada en virtud del presente Reglamento" (Rome III) vs. "la ley de cualquier Estado designada por el presente Reglamento" (Succession Regulation) vs. "la ley de cualquier Estado determinada por el presente Reglamento" (M-/RP-Property Regulation).

international law which has been separately inserted into different regulations. From the point of view that the same rule now has been repeated six times, this approach has led to redundancy.

2.1.2.2. Legal Uncertainty Through Divergence: Overriding Mandatory Provisions[562]

The situation regarding overriding mandatory provisions stands in marked contrast to this. Rome I provides a definition of this phenomenon in its Article 9(1). Moreover, it contains both a provision concerning overriding mandatory provisions of the *lex fori*[563] and a, albeit ambiguous,[564] rule as to foreign overriding mandatory provisions.[565] Article 16 Rome II only addresses such provisions of the *lex fori* and does not define them. No rule on overriding mandatory provisions appears in Rome III.[566] While the Succession Regulation does not contain the term "overriding mandatory provisions", its Article 30 deals with "special rules [of the *situs* state] applicable irrespective of the law applicable to the succession". Hence, by its nature, it is about overriding mandatory provisions, but is strongly limited geographically as well as in terms of the provisions' content.[567] Article 30 M-/RP-Property Regulation again addresses overriding mandatory provisions of the law of the forum and also provides a definition for them.

Anyone faced with applying EU private international law thus finds herself in the unenviable position of having to decide whether these stark differences are intentional or not. Is the silence of Rome III to be understood *a contrario* that there is no room whatsoever for overriding mandatory provisions, not even for those of the *lex fori*? And when Article 16 Rome II and Article 30 M-/RP-Property Regulation do not mention overriding mandatory provisions of any other law than the forum's, does this mean all other overriding mandatory provisions are irrelevant?

2.1.2.3. Legal Uncertainty Through Silence: Incidental Questions[568]

None of the private international law regulations contains a provision regarding the incidental question, whereas domestic private international law (in some member states) provides an answer, sometimes even expressly in

562 In detail *infra* Chapter 3, section 2.9.
563 Article 9(2) Rome I.
564 See only *Sonnenberger*, in: Leible (ed.), General Principles, §7.03.
565 Article 9(3) Rome I.
566 For an in-depth discussion of Article 10 Rome III, see *infra* Chapter 3, section 2.9.5.3.
567 See *infra* Chapter 3, section 2.9.5.4.
568 In detail *infra* Chapter 3, section 2.5.

a respective provision. If an incidental question arises, can one have recourse to the domestic solutions? If so, however, seemingly harmonised EU private international law would not produce uniform outcomes irrespective of the forum as the domestic solutions are not the same.[569] A solution on the level of the EU would be preferable in light of the goal of uniformity, but what is it supposed to be in light of the presence of very little material in the regulations?

2.2. EUROPEAN UNION PRIVATE INTERNATIONAL LAW SCHOLARSHIP

Books and other contributions specifically[570] on EU private international law often contain no chapter or section on something called "general part" or "general provisions". Even the proto-compartmentalisation in the regulations themselves is not often reflected.

Stone groups public policy and overriding interests together, but does not formally treat them as an issue common to both Rome I and Rome II.[571] He does not make any further generalisations. Van Calster adopts a similar approach in this regard, dealing with public policy and mandatory law in one sweep, but individually for Rome I and Rome II.[572] In his prelusive chapter, however, he does isolate characterisation, *renvoi*, and incidental question from individual conflicts rules.[573]

Bogdan, in his 2016 introduction to EU private international law, does not reserve any overarching section for general questions. He does, however, expressly mention *renvoi* and public policy as "some of the general problems" of private international law with which Rome I deals.[574] His list of examples of "general problems" grows longer in the context of Rome II, also including rules on overriding mandatory provisions and on non-unified legal systems.[575] This essentially reflects Bogdan's approach of outlining EU private international law in 2006 before the Rome Regulations were in force.[576] The casebook on EU private

569 Also see more generally *de Lima Pinheiro*, Yearbook of Private International Law 14 (2012/2013), 153, 155.

570 The qualification is important. Nowadays, no reputable textbook on *domestic* private international law can forgo elaborating on *EU* private international law. Accordingly, there already are quite a few textbooks that distinguish certain "general" or "preliminary" issues from individual questions of private international law, including EU private international law. At this point, however, exclusive accounts of EU private international law are at issue.

571 *Stone*, EU PIL, 334–342 (Rome I), 388 (Rome II); there only is a footnote noting the accord of Article 26 Rome II with Article 21 Rome I.

572 *van Calster*, European PIL, 3.2.8 (Rome I), 4.10 (Rome II).

573 *van Calster*, European PIL, 1.4.

574 *Bogdan*, Introduction to EU PIL (2016), 7.1.

575 *Bogdan*, Introduction to EU PIL (2016), 8.1.

576 See *Bogdan*, Introduction to EU PIL (2006), 119 and 148.

international law by Bogdan and Maunsbach is structured only chronologically, i.e. it does not follow any (other) overarching system.

Conversely, Weller reserves an entire section[577] for "general doctrines" of EU private international law. In it, he covers peculiarities of conflicts provisions, questions of the determination of foreign law (he classifies characterisation, incidental questions, adaptation, substitution, transposition, *renvoi*, overriding mandatory provisions, public policy, the treatment of foreign law, and non-unified legal systems as topics of this kind), connecting factors, and the recognition of public documents and records.

Wilderspin deals with "Common Principles" before turning to Rome I and Rome II.[578] In particular, he addresses the recurring issues of characterisation, habitual residence, *renvoi*, and inter-local conflict of laws under this heading. He reserves, however, a separate chapter each for (of all issues) "mandatory rules" and public policy.[579]

Trüten clearly considers the structure of conflicts rules, characterisation, adaptation, incidental question, *renvoi*, non-unified legal systems, and public policy to be issues of the "general part" of EU private international law, but he does not explain why (beyond stating that this is the "common" view), nor does he say whether this list is meant to be exhaustive.[580] Hausmann regards different connecting factors, characterisation, and *renvoi* as general questions of EU private international law, without stating which other topics belong in this category.[581]

Article-by-article commentaries of the regulations in the German tradition[582] are an unlikely place to find sections that group together general observations (except perhaps in a lengthier introduction). Their very structure is preordained by the structure of their respective legal instrument; their primary purpose is to shed light on the *particular* provisions at hand. Two examples in English support this hypothesis. The contributors to the commentary edited by Calliess on the three Rome Regulations usually stick

577 In fact, his *entire* contribution deals with "general doctrines", in which he first covers the EU's competence for private international law and the historical development on the EU level: *Weller*, in: id. (ed.), Europäisches Kollisionsrecht, A I–V (at 1–47). Terminologically somewhat confusingly, he proceeds to cover EU private international law from the perspective of the "general doctrines" of the field as *part* of the "general doctrines": A VI (at 48–149). As this contribution is an updated version of *Weller*, in: Teichmann/Gebauer (eds.), Europäisches Privat- und Unternehmensrecht, §8 A, the latter will not be cited here further.

578 *Plender/Wilderspin*, European PIL of Obligations, vii.

579 *Plender/Wilderspin*, European PIL of Obligations, xii ("Chapter 12 – mandatory rules and ordre public") and xiv ("Chapter 27 – mandatory rules and ordre public").

580 *Trüten*, Die Entwicklung des IPR in der EU, §19 III 3 (665).

581 *Hausmann*, Riv. dir. int. priv. proc. 2015, 499.

582 See *Calliess*, in: id. (ed.), Rome Regulations, xi.

to the respective provision, often only noting in passing that there are certain parallels between the regulations.[583] Similarly, the contributors to the Rome I commentary edited by Ferrari make almost no reference to an arguably general nature of some of the issues Rome I covers. Schmidt-Kessel provides for an exception, noting the absence of a "general part" of EU private international law and its effect on terminological issues in the context of overriding mandatory provisions.[584]

2.3. PROVISIONAL SUMMARY

Unlike many domestic legal systems, EU private international law does not have a separate set of "general" provisions relevant for the entire field. Scholars who deal with EU private international law as a whole do not distinguish (yet), at least not on a broad scale, between individual conflicts provisions and general issues in all of private international law, although this approach is also common in the member states. On the lower level of each private international law regulation, however, both the EU legislator and scholars do show a tendency to separate individual subject matters from other provisions, in part uniformly across the regulations. In doing so, however, the legislator has created redundancy as well as incoherence.

---

583 *Renner*, in: Calliess (ed.), Rome Regulations, Art. 21 Rome I at 2, and *Roth*, in: Calliess (ed.), Rome Regulations, Art. 12 Rome III at 2, provide for limited exceptions, the former calling public policy a "general concept", the latter pointing out that the standards developed for public policy under Rome I and II (as well as in German domestic law, which is questionable when stated in this blanket manner) apply to public policy in Rome III.

584 *Schmidt-Kessel*, in: Ferrari (ed.), Rome I Regulation, Article 9 at 9.

PART II
APPROACHES

The survey of the material in the preceding part has shown several parallels among the member states, as well as between the domestic and EU levels – not only as to the idea of dealing with certain issues of private international law separately from individual conflicts rules, but also as to the scope of these issues. In domestic law, they are even often designated as "general". Only rarely, however, does a legislator or scholar give an explanation for proceeding in this way. When there is one, it is usually along the lines of the respective issues/rules being "technical" and/or of relevance for the remainder of private international law.

Ordinarily, one can content oneself with such a short explanation. The distinction between "general" and "special" is a traditional device to structure all sorts of accounts, not just the law. In many aspects, it can (thus) be grasped intuitively and requires no further analysis. For present purposes, however, a closer look is necessary.

What is actually meant by "general"? What does "technical" mean, and what kind of "relevance" is at issue? To what extent do the resulting descriptions explain the scope of "general" provisions in the (written) law and of sections on "general" issues in scholarly works? If the answer to the last question is a (relatively) high percentage, the implication for the future of European (Union) private international law is twofold. First, there would be a model that could feasibly be used for all of EU private international law because it would make sense for all member states. Second, the model could direct the attention of domestic legislators, as well as that of the EU, to issues not yet on their respective agendas.

Accordingly, this part focuses on approaches to the term "general". Borrowing from ideas first advanced in the context of the theory of legislation,[585]

585 The distinction between a "general part" in a "systematic" sense (here called "formal") and one in a "fundamental" sense (here called "substantive") seems to have been proposed by *Rödig*, in: id./Baden/Kindermann, Vorstudien, 17 (where he even proposes more categories). *Rödig* died before he had a chance to flesh out his theories further. *Kindermann*, in: GS Rödig, 99, 103 and 106, provides a more elaborate picture of the two manifestations. The conceptualisation does not seem to have become mainstream, not even in other works on the theory of legislation, but it was relatively recently picked up by *Schärdel*, Bücherkodifikation, 168–171.

it addresses whether and to what extent it makes sense to look at "general" issues of private international law from a formal perspective (Chapter 3) and whether and to what extent it makes sense to look at them from a substantive perspective (Chapter 4). While these are not the only ways to understand "general",[586] they seem to be the most promising.

[586] For example, one could understand "general" to mean "regular" or "without considering all the details". "General rules of private international law" would thus be private international law rules that concern garden-variety legal relations, excluding more complex ones; in this sense apparently *Wortley*, Rec. des cours 71 (1947), 3–109. Yet none of the examples of "general" provisions or issues mentioned in the preceding part would meet such a definition, with the possible exception of the structure of *Cuniberti*'s code (*supra* Chapter 2, section 1.2.3.). Therefore, it seems futile to cover this approach in any more detail.

CHAPTER 3
THE FORMAL APPROACH

"General" can be understood in a formal way. The generality of an issue or a rule in this formal[587] sense means that it is relevant in more than one legal context. Relevance in more than one *factual* context would hardly suffice.[588] What exactly constitutes a "legal context" depends upon each legal system and is also a question of perspective/level of abstraction. Thus, for example, a substantive rule on the formation of contracts is formally general because this issue arises with regard to more than one type of contract, be it a sales contract, a construction contract or a service contract. Yet it would still only be a rule about contracts and of no importance in tort law.

The same can be said for EU private international law. At EU level, for example, each of the Rome Regulations and the Succession Regulation can be seen as constituting one legal context. Formally general issues or rules would thus be issues or rules relevant for more than one EU private international law regulation. This is the level with which this chapter deals for the most part. But one can also move one level lower: there are issues or rules that are formally general *within* each EU private international law regulation because they are relevant for more than one of their conflict's provisions, e.g. not only for consumer contracts but also for employment contracts, not only for torts but also for unjust enrichment. Symeonides has called this problem of shifting frames of reference the "blurred line" between special and general rules.[589] As long as the frame of reference is made explicit, however, one is able to say whether an issue exists in (or a rule applies to) only one context or more.

This chapter, then, is about issues arising for more than one rule – or, if there is already a solution for the issue in question intended to operate in more than one context, about rules that are the same for more than one conflicts rule. For reasons of efficiency and effectivity, be it in legislation or in legal

587 This approach has also been called "systematic", see *Schärdel*, Bücherkodifikation, 169; *Kindermann*, in: GS Rödig, 99, 103.

588 A law limiting basic rights that can apply only to one set of facts would even be unconstitutional in Germany: Article 19(1) clause 1 GG; BVerfGE 13, 225, 229 [1961]; for details see e.g. *Dreier*, in: id. (ed.), Grundgesetz, Art. 19 I at 9–18.

589 Codifying Choice of Law, 191 (in the context of escape clauses).

education, such *common*[590] issues or rules are often considered separately from the individual contexts. This mathematical idea of "factoring out" will reappear later.[591]

1. DEVELOPING THE FORMAL APPROACH

1.1. "FORMALLY GENERAL" vs. "FORMALLY GENERAL IN THE STRICT SENSE"

It will be useful to distinguish between two types of issues/rules: on the one hand, those that (can) arise in every context, i.e. for conflicts rules in every area of private international law; and on the other hand, those that cannot arise in every context, but (can) arise in more than one.[592] The former will be designated as "formally general in the strict sense", the latter as only "formally general".

1.2. THE TRIPARTITE STRUCTURE OF CONFLICTS RULES

When looking for formally general issues (in the strict sense) of private international law, it seems reasonable to start with features common to all conflicts rules. Issues arising in connection with any of these features are likely candidates to be formally general.[593] This brings us to the structure of conflicts rules as a fundamental characteristic common to all conflicts rules.

Conflicts rules[594] are analysed largely in the same way in the member states; the terminology differs in part, but the content is essentially identical.[595]

---

590 See *Corneloup/Nourissat*, in: Fallon/Lagarde/Poillot-Peruzzetto (eds.), Quelle architecture pour un code européen de droit international privé?, 257, 265, who prefer the term "common provisions" to "general provisions" as the former one is supposed to express most clearly that "common" and "special" provisions interlock.

591 *Infra* section 8.3.

592 But see *Kreuzer*, in: Jud/Rechberger/Reichelt (eds.), Kollisionsrecht in der Europäischen Union, 1, 3, according to whom only rules of the former kind belong in a "general part" of EU private international law.

593 Broader still (and arguably too broad) *Zidarova/Stančeva-Minčeva*, RabelsZ 71 (2007), 398, 407 (general provisions of private international law important for all relationships under private – and not: private international – law).

594 To reiterate: only conflicts rules of a generally omnilateral approach are at issue here, *supra* Introduction, section 2.

595 *Basedow*, in: id./Rühl/Ferrari/de Miguel Asensio (eds.), Encyclopedia of PIL, s. v. "Choice of Law", III; *Nehne*, Methodik und allgemeine Lehren des europäischen IPR, 19–22 (comparing Austria, England, France, Germany, and Spain); for Austria, also see e.g. *Verschraegen*, IPR, at 1131; for Spain, also see e.g. *Garcimartín Alférez*, DIP, at 20.6. Furthermore, see *Rigaux/Fallon*, DIP, at 3.37–3.46 (Belgium); *Nagy*, PIL in Hungary, at 46; *Vonken*, Algemeen deel IPR, at 302 (The Netherlands); *Bogdan*, PIL in Sweden, at 27; already *Philip*, Rec. des Cours 96

A conflicts rule has three elements: namely the subject matter, the connecting factor, and the governing law.[596] This more or less corresponds to the three-step analysis that Falconbridge suggested in 1937 to courts faced with a case involving a foreign element.[597]

It seems that the first two elements are virtually ubiquitous in academic writing, whereas the last one is not always mentioned.[598] Maybe this is because the actual "sanction" only follows from the substantive law determined by a conflicts rule,[599] and/or because the determination of the governing law appears to be a self-evident part of any conflicts rule. Yet looking at conflicts rules from the dichotomous perspective of "requirements" and "legal consequence" common to all legal rules,[600] the determination of the applicable law, by way of the connecting factor, marks the legal consequence. As such, it should be analysed as a separate third element.

This does not qualify as a particularly innovative insight. The three elements of a conflicts rule have long been recognised. In light of this, however, it comes as somewhat of a surprise that the tripartite structure of conflicts rules is not consistently used to conceptualise and structure private international law, in particular general issues of private international law. This is not to say that many authors habitually disregard this structure or do not explain sufficiently how an issue is connected to one of the three elements. Many volumes on private international law do appear to be structured *partially* along these lines. Only rarely, however, does the structure of the analysis expressly and consistently follow this framework. Notable exceptions are the recent works of Nehne, Leible, and Müller.[601] Earlier examples that partially (but expressly) adhere

(1959-I), 241, 253 ("Rules of private international law are generally formulated in accordance with a certain traditional scheme") and, from a global perspective, *Rabel*, The Conflict of Laws, 47–72.

596 *Leible/Müller*, Yearbook of Private International Law 14 (2012/2013), 137, 142; *van Calster*, European PIL, 1.3.2.1–1.3.2.3; this appears to be what *Sagi*, The Foundation of Choice of Law, 2–3, calls the "methodology of connecting factors".

597 *Falconbridge*, Law Q. Rev. 53 (1937), 235–236: "Characterization, Selection and Application".

598 See *Rogerson*, Collier's Conflict of Laws, 9 ("Choice of law rules usually have the form of an issue plus a connecting factor.") and 265; *Dicey/Morris/Collins*, Conflict of Laws, at 1-079. Differently *Rabel*, The Conflict of Laws, 47–48 (dichotomy of "operative facts" and "legal consequence", although he recognises the connecting factor as "an essential element" that can form part of either component).

599 See *Nagy*, PIL in Hungary, at 46.

600 In French: "hypothèse" (or "présupposé de fait", *Franceskakis*, Riv. dir. int. priv. proc. 1967, 691) and "dispositif", see *Rigaux/Fallon*, DIP, at 4.7; in Spanish: "supuesto de hecho" and "consecuencia jurídica", see *Calvo Caravaca/Carrascosa González*, DIP I, 424.

601 *Nehne*, Methodik und allgemeine Lehren des europäischen IPR, 170–228, 229–306, 307–318; Leible (ed.), General principles; *Leible/Müller*, Yearbook of Private International Law 14 (2012/2013), 137, 142–144, 145–147, 147–150; *Müller*, in: von Hein/Rühl (eds.), Kohärenz im Internationalen Privat- und Verfahrensrecht der Europäischen Union, 243–278, in which he applies this framework to the jurisdictional rules of the Brussels I regime.

to the tripartite structure are Kahn-Freund's *General Problems of Private International Law*[602] and Lewald's *Règles générales des conflits de lois.*[603]

1.3. OVERVIEW

In the following, I will attempt to stick as closely to the tripartite structure as possible. If one wants to establish formally general issues, one had better proceed as formally as possible. Accordingly, issues arising in connection with the subject matter of conflicts rules will be addressed first (2.), then those in the context of the connecting factor (4.), and finally those pertaining to the governing law (5.). As a kind of maverick, evasion of the law will be dealt with *between* the section on the subject matter and the one on the connecting factor (3.), for reasons expounded there.[604] After the governing law, some issues will be analysed that, for one reason or another, are not connected to one particular element of conflicts rules (6. and 7.).

Generally, a further three-step analysis will be employed. First, the issue to be examined will be identified and described. Second, there will be an explanation of its formally general relevance and, especially if it is not obvious, of why it should be allocated to that particular element in the tripartite framework. Third, comparative examples will underpin the theoretical findings: do the private international law codes and/or academics of the member states likewise consider the respective issue as one to be dealt with separately from individual conflicts rules? Is there any indication that the EU legislator has recognised its recurring relevance, either within one regulation or even beyond the limits of any particular regulation? To the extent that the influence of EU law on domestic law or the content of EU private international law is at issue, the *solution* for the respective issue will also be examined.[605]

One final caveat: the tripartite structure of conflicts rules is a model. The reality is messier. A private international law analysis will not always start by delineating different subject matters in complete nescience of what the

602 *Kahn-Freund*, General Problems, 223–241 ("The classification of the issue"), 242–275 ("The choice of the connecting factor"), 276–317 ("The application of the chosen law") – but note that this means that 222 pages of "general problems" are outside of the tripartite structure.

603 *Lewald*, Règles générales, deals with the structure of a conflicts rule first in three chapters (5–65) and then (66–1119) again deals with special questions of the subject matter, the connection, and the determination of foreign law in three separate chapters. He does add, however, a fourth chapter on public policy and an entire (albeit short) third *part* on the application of foreign law. From the perspective adopted here, the latter two issues in particular are not beyond the tripartite framework, see *infra* sections 5.3. and 5.6.

604 *Infra* section 3.2.

605 To do so for all domestic solutions – and then to determine the "best" solution – would be desirable but is impossible for linguistic limitations. See already *supra* Chapter 1, sections 3.3. and 3.4.

governing law could be, but perhaps with the substantive rule that might be applicable in the end. Even if one has "arrived at" the governing law, sometimes it will be necessary to "go back" to the subject matter and correct a potential mistake at the characterisation stage.[606] As the structure and some of the findings of the following remarks are tied inextricably to this model, they cannot claim to represent reality exactly either. It is important to keep this in mind, particularly at points in this analysis where an issue is allocated to an element of a conflicts rule with which it has not (often) been associated thus far. It is submitted, however, that the model developed in the following explains – or at least illuminates – rather a lot.

2. THE SUBJECT MATTER

The first element of a conflicts rule is the subject matter. It concerns the juridical category or the legal concept which this rule is meant to cover.[607] If a conflicts rule determines the law applicable to contracts for the sale of goods, as does Article 4(1)(a) Rome I, its subject matter is contracts for the sale of goods. If a conflicts rule determines the law applicable to non-contractual liability arising out of damage caused by a product, as does Article 5(1) Rome II, its subject matter is non-contractual liability arising out of damage caused by a product.

Sundry questions arise as regards the subject matter: is a given subject matter relevant even when no party has raised it during court proceedings (2.1.)? In which situations, at which point in time, and to which persons does it apply (2.2.)? How does it relate to the same subject matter found in a legal instrument of a different hierarchical status (2.3.)? What is the meaning/scope of a given subject matter (2.4.)? How do subject matters of the same legal instrument interact, particularly if one issue implicates or could implicate at least two of them at once (2.5.–2.7.)? How do specific and general subject matters relate to one another (2.8.)? How do special subject matters, perhaps even those of another legislator, affect regular subject matters (2.9.)? Is it possible that no subject matter covers a given case – and, if so, what happens then (2.10.)?

2.1. THE MANDATORY APPLICATION OF CONFLICTS RULES

The very first question one can ask about the subject matter of any conflicts rule is if it is to be relevant regardless of whether any party has raised it. As this concerns all subject matters, the issue is formally general in the strict sense.

606 See *Schurig*, in: FS Kegel, 549, 567; *id.*, Kollisionsnorm und Sachrecht, 176–184, for the idea that application of (conflict of laws) rules always requires a "tentative" approach, one in which one jumps back and forth between several levels that can be separated analytically.

607 *Rogerson*, Collier's Conflict of Laws, 265; *Dicey/Morris/Collins*, Conflict of Laws, at 1-079.

2.1.1. *Member States*

Only four member states with a private international law code have among their general provisions an express rule on the *ex officio* application of private international law (or foreign law).[608] In other member states, a general rule of private international law setting forth the *ex officio* ascertainment of the law[609] *determined* by a conflicts provision can be interpreted to require the *ex officio* application of the conflicts provision itself.[610] Elsewhere, a rule of procedural law provides the answer,[611] or the *ex officio* application of conflicts rules simply follows from them being rules of law.[612] Several member states, however, do not attribute mandatory character to their national conflicts rules in general.[613]

2.1.2. *European Union*

None of the EU regulations on private international law thus far contain any provision on the application of their conflicts rules. Hence there are two ways to think about the issue: one might interpret EU private international law as leaving the question as an essentially procedural matter to national law (2.1.2.1.). Even in this scenario, however, it would be a misconception to assume that EU law does not set any boundaries for the application of its conflicts provisions. Yet it is also possible, and arguably more persuasive, to consider the matter as not excluded from the ambit of EU private international law (2.1.2.2.).

2.1.2.1. European Union Limitations on National Rules of Procedure

Assuming for the moment that the question of the (non-)mandatory nature of EU conflicts provisions is left to the member states, they would not enjoy unfettered discretion in their response. As always when procedural issues are

608 §2 Austrian PIL Act (its wording could be clearer; but see e.g. *Verschraegen*, IPR, at 1088); Article 10:2 Dutch Civil Code; Article 12(6) Spanish Civil Code; §7(1) Hungarian PIL Act seems to provide for the *ex officio* application of foreign law.

609 For national rules on the ascertainment of foreign law see *infra* section 5.3.2.

610 See e.g. for Italy *Queirolo et al.*, in: Esplugues/Iglesias/Palao (eds.), Application of Foreign Law, 237, 241.

611 E.g. in Portugal, see *Moura Vicente/Brito*, in: Esplugues/Iglesias/Palao (eds.), Application of Foreign Law, 301, 302.

612 E.g. in Germany: BGH NJW 1993, 2305, 2306, in accordance with the legislative materials. See also *Mankowski*, in: Basedow/Kischel/Sieber (eds.), German National Reports, 133, 148: the German constitution mandates that courts are bound by all laws – and the provisions of the EGBGB are law.

613 See *Esplugues*, in: id./Iglesias/Palao (eds.), Application of Foreign Law, 3, 19, with further references. For Hungary see *infra* footnote 635.

left to the member states,[614] they need to make sure that the respective rules "are not less favourable than those governing similar domestic actions (principle of equivalence) and [...] that they do not render virtually impossible or excessively difficult the exercise of rights conferred by [EU] law (principle of effectiveness)".[615] As long as domestic private international law is also regarded as non-mandatory in the state at issue, considering EU private international law to be non-mandatory would not discriminate against EU rules. In other words, the principle of equivalence would not be infringed. This analysis finds support in *van Schijndel* where the ECJ was concerned with the converse case: where national courts must raise points of law on their own motion regarding certain rules of domestic law, they are under the same duty regarding similar rules of EU law.[616]

The situation is more complex with regard to the principle of effectiveness. In *van Schijndel*, the ECJ further held that national courts with the discretion to apply rules of law are obligated to apply directly applicable binding rules of EU law.[617] Even if the Court did not expressly say so at the time (it did so later, however[618]), this is an emanation of the principle of effectiveness.[619] Other cases are in line with the application of the principle in *van Schijndel*.[620] It would seem to follow for EU private international law that domestic courts must apply its rules if they either have a duty or the discretion to apply domestic private international law – to the extent that the respective provisions of EU law can be considered "binding" under *van Schijndel*.[621] The only courts

614 Unless one were to read Article 1(3) Rome I/II as an exemption from the general requirements of EU law. Such an interpretation, however, is not plausible in the end. See *Trautmann*, Europäisches Kollisionsrecht und ausländisches Recht im nationalen Zivilverfahren, 286–289.

615 ECJ Joined Cases C-222/05 to C-225/05, J. van der Weerd and Others v Minister van Landbouw, Natuur en Voedselkwaliteit, Reports of Cases 2007, I-4233, at 28.

616 ECJ Joined Cases C-430/93 and C-431/93, Jeroen van Schijndel and Johannes Nicolaas Cornelis van Veen v Stichting Pensioenfonds voor Fysiotherapeuten, Reports of Cases 1995, I-4705, at 13.

617 ECJ Joined Cases C-430/93 and C-431/93, Jeroen van Schijndel and Johannes Nicolaas Cornelis van Veen v Stichting Pensioenfonds voor Fysiotherapeuten, Reports of Cases 1995, I-4705, at 14.

618 ECJ Joined Cases C-222/05 to C-225/05, J. van der Weerd and Others v Minister van Landbouw, Natuur en Voedselkwaliteit, Reports of Cases 2007, I-4233, at 28, referring to *van Schijndel* when stating the principles of equivalence and effectiveness.

619 *Trautmann*, Europäisches Kollisionsrecht und ausländisches Recht im nationalen Zivilverfahren, 296.

620 *Trautmann*, Europäisches Kollisionsrecht und ausländisches Recht im nationalen Zivilverfahren, 296–297, with reference to ECJ Case C-72/95, Aannemersbedrijf P.K. Kraaijeveld BV e.a. v Gedeputeerde Staten van Zuid-Holland, Reports of Cases 1996, I-5403, and Case C-2/06, Willy Kempter KG v Hauptzollamt Hamburg-Jonas, Reports of Cases 2008, I-411.

621 At the very least, such "binding" rules would be the ones which cannot be derogated from by party autonomy (a set of rules that partly overlaps with the one concerning groups of

unaffected by this approach – and thus seemingly not compelled to apply EU private international law – would be those neither required nor authorised to apply domestic rules of private international law *ex officio*.[622]

Yet, there are further gateways for EU law into national proceedings. The ECJ has held in particular that the Unfair Terms Directive "entails the national court being able to determine of its own motion whether a term of a contract before it is unfair".[623] It seems reasonable to extrapolate this kind of reasoning from consumers and apply it to more classes of people especially protected by EU law. Employees quickly come to mind, other groups are less obvious.[624] Under this approach, it would at least seem that the application of Articles 6 and 8 Rome I is mandatory, regardless of a country's stance regarding its own private international law provisions. Finally, it is conceivable that the Court's case law on important public interests of the EU, requiring national courts to apply rules of their own motion,[625] could be extended to some rules of private international law.[626]

In conclusion, no uniform solution exists under the premise that the matter is left to the member states. A yet to be exhaustively determined set of EU private international law rules is to be applied mandatorily by every court in the EU. All "binding" rules must be applied as long as the court in question at least has discretion to apply domestic private international law.[627] As most member states consider domestic private international law as mandatory,[628] the *practical* outcome is that most have to apply EU private international law mandatorily.

---

especially protected people), see e.g. *Herb*, Europäisches Gemeinschaftsrecht und nationaler Zivilprozess, 21–23 – but it seems preferable to consider all EU private international law "binding" at least in this sense, essentially for the reasons set forth in the next section. See also *Trautmann*, Europäisches Kollisionsrecht und ausländisches Recht im nationalen Zivilverfahren, 298–303.

622 Similarly, but only with regard to courts which do not apply foreign law *ex officio*, *McParland*, The Rome I Regulation, at 8.73.

623 ECJ Joined Cases C-240/98 to C-244/98, Océano Grupo Editorial SA v Roció Murciano Quintero et al., Reports of Cases 2000, I-4941, at 29. The restriction to the point in time of a "preliminary assessment as to whether a claim should be allowed to proceed before the national courts" later disappeared, see e.g. ECJ Case C-473/00, Cofidis SA v Jean-Louis Fredout, Reports of Cases 2002, I-10875, at 32.

624 *Trautmann*, Europäisches Kollisionsrecht und ausländisches Recht im nationalen Zivilverfahren, 303–312.

625 See ECJ Case C-168/05, Elisa María Mostaza Claro v Centro Móvil Milenium SL, Reports of Cases 2006, I-10421, at 38 (consumer protection under the Unfair Terms Directive, again).

626 See *Trautmann*, Europäisches Kollisionsrecht und ausländisches Recht im nationalen Zivilverfahren, 312–319, who, however, by and large answers the question in the negative.

627 For this outcome also *Herb*, Europäisches Gemeinschaftsrecht und nationaler Zivilprozess, 279–289 (without a specific private international law context).

628 *Supra* section 2.1.1., and *Esplugues*, in: id./Iglesias/Palao (eds.), Application of Foreign Law, 3, 18–19, with further references.

2.1.2.2. The Mandatory Nature of European Union Private International Law

The result just arrived at indubitably can be established *lege artis*. But is this solution, fraught with complexities and uncertainties, truly viable? In the following, an alternative solution[629] will be expounded according to which EU private international law is mandatory for all member states.

Rules Found in European Union Regulations

First, there is the nature of EU private international law. As far as it is at issue here, it is enshrined in regulations. A regulation is "binding in its entirety and directly applicable in all Member States" (Article 288(2) TFEU). But, strange as it may seem at first, this alone is not conclusive for the mandatory nature of EU private international law; neither "binding" nor "directly applicable" necessarily mean "applicable *ex officio*".[630] The former criterion can be read to mean only that all parts of a regulation are relevant (as opposed to a directive which, at least notionally, is only binding "as to the result to be achieved", Article 288(3) TFEU), and that a regulation does not allow for any contradictory domestic rule. The latter criterion can be understood as meaning that there is no need for any implementation. Furthermore, the case law outlined above[631] clearly also only applies the principles of equivalence and effectiveness to "binding" EU law. The ECJ could simply have held that "binding" law must be applied, end of story. On the other hand, the case law is not exactly on point, either: none of the cases mentioned above concern an EU regulation of private (international) law.

The Goal of Supranational Harmonisation

What would be the point of supranational private (international) law harmonisation if the harmonised rules did not have to be applied in practice? Several authors, including some partial to the idea of facultative conflicts rules, have relied on this idea to attribute mandatory character to conflicts rules in international conventions, in part with the reservation that this only applies

---

629 In light of existing differences in domestic law, I do not share *Esplugues*' optimistic assertion (in: id./Iglesias/Palao (eds.), Application of Foreign Law, 3, 19) that there already is a general rule across Europe that EU private international law is mandatory.

630 But see *Kreuzer*, in: Jud/Rechberger/Reichelt (eds.), Kollisionsrecht in der Europäischen Union, 1, 6; *Oppermann/Classen/Nettesheim*, Europarecht, §9 at 78 (even for regulations in general).

631 *Supra* section 2.1.2.1.

to those rules under which the parties cannot make a choice of law.[632] Does anybody suggest that the evolution from the Rome Convention to Rome I was supposed to be a step backwards in this regard? Rather, the rules found in the EU private international law regulations are mandatory *a fortiori* in light of the goal of legal certainty through harmonisation.[633] The regulations themselves amply stress this aim.[634] In any case, against the backdrop of facultative private international law being a minority position in the member states,[635] would one not expect the Convention or the regulations to provide for a facultative nature expressly if it was the desired solution?

True, such a broad line of reasoning, relying in essence on the idea of *effet utile*,[636] is not without problems. Where the enforcement of EU law in national courts is concerned, *effet utile* boils down to the principle of effectiveness.[637] As demonstrated above, however, the decisions by the ECJ so far do not suggest that this principle requires the *ex officio* application of EU private international law. But there is a loophole. If the application of EU private international law is no issue left to domestic procedure in the first place, the relative leeway granted by the principle of effectiveness does not even exist.

A Nuanced and Internalised System of Party Autonomy

One reason why the issue has indeed not been left to domestic law lies in the nuanced system of party autonomy set up by the EU private international

632 *F. Sturm/G. Sturm*, in: Staudinger, Einl. zum IPR at 228; *Hausmann*, EuLF 2008, I-1, I-7; already *Fentiman*, Foreign Law in English Courts, 93–94. The position is widely but not universally accepted, see *Jänterä-Jareborg*, Rec. des cours 304 (2003), 181, 253–255.

633 See also *Remien*, in: FS Roth, 431, 433 (who concedes a possible limitation to those rules not allowing a choice of law by the parties or which intend a certain protection); *von Hein*, in: MüKoBGB, Einl. IPR at 292; *Sonnenberger*, in: FS Kropholler, 227, 245; probably also *Illmer*, C. J. Q. 28 (2009), 237, 258–259 (who only is concerned with the application of foreign law). Also *Hausmann*, EuLF 2008, I-1, I-13 (but apparently – only – from the point of view of policy).

634 Recital 6 Rome I/Rome II, Recital 9 Rome III; Recital 37 Succession Regulation.

635 See already *supra* footnote 613 and accompanying text; also e.g. *ten Wolde*, Yearbook of Private International Law 13 (2011), 389, 394; *Moura Vicente*, Yearbook of Private International Law 9 (2007), 257, 262–263; *Giardina*, Rev. crit. DIP 1996, 1, 14. Pursuant to §9 Hungarian PIL Code 1979, the parties could mutually agree during judicial proceedings to have Hungarian law apply to their case even where party autonomy is permitted; *Harsági/Kengyel/Nemessányi*, in: Esplugues/Iglesias/Palao (eds.), Application of Foreign Law, 213, 220; *Nagy*, PIL in Hungary, at 85–87.

636 Expressly along these lines *von Hein*, in: MüKoBGB, Einl. IPR at 292; *id.*, RabelsZ 73 (2009), 461, 507; *Bariatti/Pataut*, in: Fallon/Lagarde/Poillot-Peruzzetto (eds.), Quelle architecture pour un code européen de droit international privé?, 337, 345; *Illmer*, C. J. Q. 28 (2009), 237, 259.

637 *Trautmann*, Europäisches Kollisionsrecht und ausländisches Recht im nationalen Zivilverfahren, 320.

law regulations. As will become apparent later on,[638] party autonomy is one of their main features. But it is not boundless. Party autonomy is restricted in some areas to begin with, and in others for certain categories of cases. To make the application of EU private international law dependent upon a party pleading it, or to allow the parties to choose the *lex fori* in every case, would subvert these limitations.[639]

Flessner, however, as one of the main proponents of facultative private international law, has argued forcefully that (also) in EU private international law the parties can have an interest in the application of the *lex fori*, one that prevails over the purportedly weak interests of the legislator.[640] As a consequence, the parties should (almost) never be denied the choice of the *lex fori*.[641] Yet this cannot work at all for the Succession Regulation.[642] If its conflicts provisions were not mandatory, how could a person ever know for certain (Recital 37 Succession Regulation) which law applies to her succession? The proceedings in which the parties would perhaps choose the *lex fori* take place after her death. Hence, for one entire regulation already, the parties cannot be allowed to choose the *lex fori*.

More generally, the parties' interest in being able to make a choice of law has been internalised in EU private international law.[643] It may have been internalised imperfectly, implausibly or inconsistently because of the different restrictions and prohibitions – but as long as it has not been internalised illegally, there is no *legal* reason for a model that allows a choice of the *lex fori* externally, i.e. outside of the scope and restrictions of the regulations.

The need for a normative reason for such a model perhaps explains a further strand of Flessner's reasoning, his reliance on Articles 67 and 81 TFEU.[644] But even if Article 67(4) TFEU was adversely affected by restricting the possibility of choosing the *lex fori*, and even if Article 81(2)(f) TFEU had an effect on the competence under its (c) that is at issue here, it is far from clear that other interests would not be capable of forming a sufficient counterweight. Contravention of the TFEU is too harsh a verdict. It follows that the nuanced system of party autonomy must not be bypassed.

---

638 *Infra* section 4.3.4.

639 *von Hein*, in: MüKoBGB, Einl. IPR at 292; *Kropholler*, IPR, §7 II 2 (45–46).

640 *Flessner*, in: FS Magnus, 403, 412; *id.*, in: LA Pintens, 593, 598–600.

641 *Flessner*, in: LA Pintens, 593, 605–606 (individual analysis for each provision not allowing a choice of law); for this position also *Maultzsch*, Journal of Private International Law 12 (2016), 466, 482–483.

642 Admittedly, *Flessner* does not take the Succession Regulation (or, at the time, the proposal for it) into account.

643 One might also reason *a contrario* from Article 15 Maintenance Regulation with Article 7(1) Maintenance Protocol, as the EU legislator here, by way of the Protocol, expressly does allow the parties to a particular proceeding to choose the *lex fori*.

644 *Flessner*, in: FS Magnus, 403, 412; *id.*, in: LA Pintens, 593, 601–603.

No Room for Divergent ("Procedural") Domestic Rules under Rome I/II

One might still maintain that the *ex officio* application of EU private international law is a particular feature of all regulations except for Rome I and II,[645] for (only[646]) the latter two instruments make a reservation for domestic law in the sphere of "evidence and procedure". This approach would dovetail with the comparative finding[647] that several member states distinguish in a similar manner between areas of law with regard to the mandatory nature of their conflicts rules. Arguably, it would also be the only way to disregard the wording of the conflicts provisions themselves, as even those found in Rome I and II seem rather to suggest that they are to be applied ("shall apply", "shall be governed", "shall be determined", "the law applicable shall be"[648]).

In order to decide about the validity of this nuanced hypothesis, closer scrutiny of the reservation for "evidence and procedure" is required. Now found in Article 1(3) Rome I and II, it first appeared in European private international law as Article 1(2)(h) Rome Convention. According to Giuliano and Lagarde, this exclusion requires no individual comment.[649] The same authors do expound, however, that "questions of evidence are in principle subject to the law of the forum" and that Article 1(2)(h) Rome Convention affirms – "[i]n order that there should be no doubt" – that questions of evidence "not decided by the Convention" are left to the contracting states.[650] It appears that others interpret this as meaning that the definition of "evidence and procedure" is left to the contracting states, and now, under Rome I and II, to the member states.[651] Yet this would be rather strange. Not only are terms in conventions and legal acts of the EU generally to be given an autonomous meaning,[652] there is also no room for any national definition of "evidence and

---

645 For Rome I and II the approach just outlined (*supra* section 2.1.2.1.) would still be relevant so that no member state would be *entirely* free in its decision whether or not to apply them.

646 To be sure, Recital 17 Rome III seems to presuppose the existence of divergent procedures at the national level. But, at the same time, it seems to presuppose that the parties designate the applicable law *under* Rome III; then, however, the "procedures" cannot include the question of the nature of the rules of Rome III. They must be applicable to begin with.

647 In some member states, the nature of conflicts rules depends on the issue at stake, in particular, whether the rights at issue are available for a settlement by the parties or not. *Esplugues*, in: id./Iglesias/Palao (eds.), Application of Foreign Law, 3, 20–21.

648 Just see Articles 1(1), 3(1), 4(1), 5(1) clause 1 Rome I.

649 *Giuliano/Lagarde*, Report on the Convention on the law applicable to contractual obligations, 13.

650 *Giuliano/Lagarde*, Report on the Convention on the law applicable to contractual obligations, 36.

651 *Dicey/Morris/Collins*, Conflict of Laws, at 9-011; *Fentiman*, Foreign Law in English Courts, 92.

652 See also *infra* section 2.4. (European Union: The European Dimension of Characterisation). For this question in particular *Halfmeier*, in: Calliess (ed.), Rome Regulations, Art. 1 Rome II at 64; *Illmer*, C. J. Q. 28 (2009), 237, 243; *Dickinson*, The Rome II Regulation, at 14.57. For Article 1(3) Rome I see *Weller*, in: Calliess (ed.), Rome Regulations, Art. 1 Rome I at 44.

procedure", in particular because its terminological counterpart, "substance" (to be governed by the *lex causae*), is quite clearly defined by Rome I and II themselves: Article 12 Rome I, Article 15 Rome II, which are both not exhaustive ("in particular"). If one of only two complementary pieces is to be understood autonomously, the other must simply be understood autonomously too. It follows that it is not the *definition* of "evidence and procedure" that is left to the member states, but all *matters* of "evidence and procedure" *as defined* independently. The matters themselves are "not decided" by Rome I and II; thus, such an understanding is perfectly in line with the statements made by Giuliano and Lagarde.

This raises the pivotal question: understood independently from domestic preconceptions, does "evidence and procedure" include the issue of whether the conflicts rules of Rome I and II are to be applied *ex officio*?[653] At the outset, the question causes some unease. This is because the nature of a conflicts rule is certainly no issue of the *lex causae* determined by the conflicts rule; it is thus hard to state that it is a substantive issue. But nor is it a typical case of the *lex fori* either when the conflicts provision is one of EU law.

Even if one allocates EU conflicts rules to the *lex fori*, is their nature necessarily an issue of procedure? Or *tertium datur* – particularly as conflicts rules themselves are neither substantive nor procedural rules?[654] Extrapolating from Article 12 Rome I and Article 15 Rome II, it could be said that an issue is one of "procedure" if it is not directed at (not: does not affect in any way) the decision on the merits, i.e. is "neutral" in this regard.[655] Examples of procedural issues then are the "formalities of bringing a claim, summons, service, types of proceedings, a stay of proceedings, consolidation of claims, admissibility of counterclaims, functions of judge and jury, costs and appeals".[656] While the result could be seen as intuitively persuasive, the approach is at least borderline circular when it relies on the concept of "merits" to define "procedure". Similarly narrowly, it has been suggested that "procedure" should include (only) those rules that are an "integral and indispensable element of the forum's legal framework for the judicial determination of disputes".[657] It would seem that the quality of a legal rule, even of a conflicts rule, of being mandatory (or not) is very much directed at the outcome of a given case. Moreover, a country's legal *framework*

653 Answering the question in the affirmative: *Calliess*, in: id. (ed.), Rome Regulations, Art. 3 at 47; *Kieninger*, in: Leible (ed.), General Principles, §17.03[A]; *Dickinson*, The Rome II Regulation, at 14.71–14.75.

654 *Michaels*, in: FS Kropholler, 151, 156; *Kropholler*, IPR, §13 I (103–104).

655 *Illmer*, C. J. Q. 28 (2009), 237, 246.

656 *Illmer*, C. J. Q. 28 (2009), 237, 247 (footnotes removed); in favour of this interpretation *Halfmeier*, in: Calliess (ed.), Rome Regulations, Art. 1 Rome II at 65.

657 *Dickinson*, The Rome II Regulation, at 14.61 (who, however, assumes that pleading and proof of foreign law are left to national law, at 14.71–14.75).

for the resolution of disputes by definition cannot affect the question of whether the rules made by another lawmaker are mandatory or not. Nor is the nature of a conflicts provision an issue concerning the administrative efficiency of the courts.[658] Hence, the issue is not one of procedure – and is thus not allocated to be decided by domestic law.

To be sure, there is something to be said for interpreting Article 1(3) Rome II in particular against the backdrop of Article 30(1)(i) Rome II. The treatment of foreign law has arguably not yet been harmonised on the EU level.[659] But this concerns a step in the conflicts analysis in which a conflicts rule has already been applied and has led to the choice of foreign law. The example of Article 12(6) Spanish Civil Code in particular informs us[660] that the questions of the mandatory nature of conflicts rules and of the ascertainment, as well as application, of foreign law can be distinguished. Therefore, the position of the regulations as to the treatment of the governing law can offer no conclusive counterpoints at this point.

2.1.2.3. Conclusion

Everybody seems to agree that at least certain *parts* of EU private international law must be applied *ex officio*. However, as the exception for matters of procedure in Rome I and II cannot be read as addressing the matter, as the supranational harmonisation of conflicts rules is at issue, and as the regulations themselves provide for different levels of party autonomy, the preferable view is to regard *all* EU private international law as mandatory.[661] This also keeps it from providing a merely "decorative" scheme of governance[662] for private transactions occurring across borders. It is a different kettle of fish whether foreign law determined by the conflicts rule must also be ascertained *ex officio*. This is a question of the governing law and, accordingly, will be discussed later on.[663]

2.2. THE SCOPE OF APPLICATION

A natural, even seemingly self-evident, issue of recurring relevance is the scope of application of conflicts rules. Before any rule can apply, the criteria for its

658 For this criterion (in connection with Section 14(3)(b) Private International Law (Miscellaneous Provisions) Act 1995 [UK]) see *Rogerson*, Cambridge L. J. 2006, 515, 517.
659 The topic will be discussed in context *infra* section 5.3.3.1.
660 See *infra* footnote 1567.
661 For this view also *Weller*, in: id. (ed.), Europäisches Kollisionsrecht, at 112.
662 For this criticism of contemporary private international law see *Muir-Watt*, Transnational Legal Theory 2 (2011), 347, 375.
663 *Infra* section 5.3.

scope of application must be met. The issue is thus of a formally general nature in the strict sense. Moreover, the scope of application can be reformulated as a question of the subject matter. A conflicts rule on contracts for the sale of goods is not merely about contracts for the sale of goods, but about contracts for the sale of goods in a particular (e.g. cross-border, substantive) context, in a particular time frame, and so forth. Hence, one can consider all these subtopics issues of the subject matter.

2.2.1. *Requirement of an International Element?*

To even mention the requirement of an international element as an issue of relevance, for more than one (indeed: all) conflicts rules may seem hackneyed at first. Is this not as obvious for a field called private *international* law (or conflict of *laws*, plural) as insisting that all rules of private international *law* are *legal* rules? Yet the statement actually raises serious doubts, at both the domestic and the EU level.[664]

The criterion of an international element is used to distinguish conflicts cases from "purely domestic cases". It is said that internal substantive law applies to the latter group of cases as a matter of course, whereas private international law is needed to decide which law applies if a case contains at least one international element.[665] Even where such an element is present, however, internal substantive law might apply: it could very well turn out that the existing international element is not relevant from the point of view of particular conflicts rules.[666] A case might have the international elements A, B, and C, but the pertinent conflicts rule might only lead to foreign law if element D is foreign. Hence, the *lex fori* would apply despite the existence of three international elements. From the perspective of the resulting "application of internal law", it does not matter whether a case is "purely domestic" or has international elements, as long as they are not relevant for the pertinent conflicts rule. Only by looking at the rules of private international law can one know whether an international element is relevant or not. In other words: whether or not a case is "purely domestic" can only be answered by taking note of the pertinent conflicts rules. If there *is* a relevant international element,

664 Advocate General Szpunar recently analysed the issue as well: Opinion, Case C-54/16, Vinyls Italia SpA v Mediterranea di Navigazione SpA, ECLI:EU:C:2017:164, at 92–115.

665 E.g. *Dicey/Morris/Collins*, Conflict of Laws, at 1-002 ("English court will naturally apply English internal [...] law" if there is no international element); *Sagi*, The Foundation of Choice of Law, xv (requirement of "foreign element(s)" for private international law); *Cuniberti*, Conflict of Laws, 3 ("domestic legal relationships are obviously governed by the law of the single state to which they are connected"); *Hohloch*, in: Erman BGB, Art. 3 EGBGB at 4 (no need to justify the application of provisions of the *lex fori* by way of conflicts rules; it simply follows from the legislator's competence to regulate purely domestic cases); *Stürner*, in: Langenbucher (ed.), Europäisches Privat- und Wirtschaftsrecht, §8 at 1.

666 Very clearly *Lopes Pegna*, in: Baratta (ed.), DIP, s. v. "criteri di collegamento", 91, 92.

any prior, and thus additional, inquiry as to whether the case has an international element serves no purpose. All this calls into question the usefulness of distinguishing "purely domestic" and international cases in the abstract.

Moreover, thus far nobody has been able to demonstrate with precision the line of demarcation between a "purely domestic" and an international case. Authors who (seem to) attribute independent meaning to the international element as a general requirement quickly *exemplify* such elements with a list of potential connecting factors.[667] Similarly, when the "international situation" required by Article 2 Belgian PIL Code is described as encompassing all situations that can raise a question of determining the applicable law,[668] the tautology is palpable. In a globalised world, some connection to another state can almost always be found,[669] even if it is simply that the pen used to sign a contract was manufactured abroad. To rely on the experience of a judge informing her that there *could* be a relevant connection to another state,[670] or to require that one "would seriously think about the law of state A or B" in a given case,[671] may have some practical merit, but it does not amount to a legal standard. A list of *all* potentially relevant connecting factors would be such a standard, but one of questionable usefulness and/or feasibility.

In light of this, it appears preferable *not* to consider private international law a special field of law for cases with international elements.[672] Rather, the application of *any* substantive rule of law, internal or foreign, is preceded by – and in this way depends on – a conflicts rule.[673] If there is no *relevant* foreign element, the rule will simply lead to domestic law, but a conflicts decision has been made nevertheless. This means that the requirement of an international element is actually *no* commonality of conflicts rules.

Member States

This theoretical insight, however, is clearly at odds with empirical findings. More than half of the member states with a private international law code have among their general provisions a rule on the applicability of

667 See *Neumayr*, in: ABGB-Kurzkommentar, §1 IPRG at 2; *Hohloch*, in: Erman BGB, Art. 3 EGBGB at 3; *Mosconi/Campiglio*, DIPP, III 5 (157).

668 *Fallon*, in: Het Wetboek Internationaal Privaatrecht becommentarieerd, Art. 2 IV ("Est visée toute situation qui peut soulever une question [...] de désignation du droit national applicable [...]").

669 *Lehmann*, Vand. J. Trans. L. 41 (2008), 381, 422.

670 *Koch*, in: FS Magnus, 475, 477 and passim.

671 *Lehmann*, Vand. J. Trans. L. 41 (2008), 381, 422–423.

672 *von Hein*, in: MüKoBGB, Art. 3 EGBGB at 12; *Hausmann*, in: Staudinger, Art. 3 EGBGB at 7; *Neuhaus*, Grundbegriffe, §11 IV (104–105); at least for Rome I also Opinion by AG Szpunar, Case C-54/16, Vinyls Italia SpA v Mediterranea di Navigazione SpA, ECLI:EU:C:2017:164, at 106.

673 *Köhler*, Eingriffsnormen, 6; *Schurig*, Kollisionsnorm und Sachrecht, 51–57.

conflicts provisions.[674] They require an "international" or "cross-border element" (Croatia, Czech Republic, Romania, Slovakia, Slovenia), an "international situation" (Belgium), or a connection of the case to another state (Bulgaria, Estonia, Germany,[675] Poland). Hungary even combined two of these options: §1 Hungarian PIL Code 1979 required both an international element and the potential applicability of the law of several states; §1 Hungarian PIL Act now only requires a foreign element. Although not exactly concerning the applicability of conflicts provisions,[676] §1(1) Austrian PIL Act can also be counted among these provisions because of its requirement of a case with a connection to a foreign state ("Sachverhalt mit Auslandsberührung").[677] In any case, several Austrian scholars, without recourse to §1(1) Austrian PIL Act, postulate the requirement of a connection to a foreign state.[678] A "case with a foreign element" is also seen as constitutive of a conflicts case under common law.[679] In French law, private international law is commonly said to concern "international relations of private parties",[680] and/or situations connected to more than one country.[681] Even in a member state such as Italy, whose respective provision on the object of its private international law act seems more lenient in this regard,[682] scholars affirm the requirement of an international connection.[683]

European Union

All three Rome Regulations likewise expressly set forth the requirement of a conflict of laws in many languages ("conflit de lois", "conflitto di leggi", "conflicto de leyes"), each in its Article 1(1) clause 1.[684] This way of phrasing

674 Article 2 Belgian PIL Code, Article 1(2) Bulgarian PIL Code, Article 1(1) Croatian PIL Act, §1(a) Czech PIL Act, §1 Estonian PIL Act, Article 3 EGBGB, §1 Hungarian PIL Code 1979/§1 Hungarian PIL Act, Article 1 Polish PIL Act, Article 2.557(2) Romanian Civil Code, Article 1 Slovak PIL Act, Article 1(1) Slovenian PIL Act.

675 In line with the theoretical statements above, however, prevailing opinion in Germany has it that no abstract analysis of international elements is necessary, in spite of Article 3 EGBGB: *von Hein*, in: MüKoBGB, Art. 3 EGBGB at 12; *Hausmann*, in: Staudinger, Art. 3 EGBGB at 7 (both with further references).

676 Judging by its consequence, §1(1) Austrian PIL Code only seems to be about the "closest connection".

677 In this sense apparently *Neumayr*, in: ABGB-Kurzkommentar, §1 IPRG at 2.

678 *Lurger/Melcher*, IPR, at 1/3; *Verschraegen*, IPR, at 1066.

679 *Dicey/Morris/Collins*, Conflict of Laws, at 1-001–1-002; *Rogerson*, Collier's Conflict of Laws, 1; *Crawford/Carruthers*, IPL: A Scots Perspective, at 1-01.

680 See e.g. *Loussouarn/Bourel/de Vareilles-Sommières*, DIP, at 1; *Cachard*, DIP, at 3; *Mayer/Heuzé*, DIP, at 2.

681 *Loussouarn/Bourel/de Vareilles-Sommières*, DIP, at 5; also see *Mayer/Heuzé*, DIP, at 5 (requirement of an "élément d'extranéité").

682 Article 1 Italian PIL Act, as translated in ILM 35 (1996), 765: "This law shall [...] lay down the criteria to identify the applicable law [...]".

683 *Mosconi/Campiglio*, DIPP, III 5 (154).

684 For the history of Article 1(1) clause 1 Rome I in particular see *McParland*, The Rome I Regulation, at 6.02–6.06.

is even more obviously tautological than the one found in different domestic laws. Stripped down to the essentials, each Article 1(1) clause 1 only says, "The following conflict of laws provisions apply in situations involving a conflict of laws". Doubts regarding any independent meaning of these terms are again in order.[685] The international element seems to be a yeti on the EU level as well: everybody has heard of it, nobody has seen it.[686]

The respective German versions offer no way out either. To be sure, as they require a connection to the law of different states, they are not as plainly tautological as their siblings. But they are as questionable as the provisions of domestic law outlined above – even more so because the connection to the *law* of another state is the *result* of the application of a conflicts provision. It cannot be a general *requirement* at the same time.[687]

One might now object that an international element must be a general requirement (at least) for EU private international law because, under Article 81 TFEU, the EU only has the competence to adopt measures "in civil matters having cross-border implications". One therefore might say that the (abstract) determination of an international element is necessary: without it, none of the regulations can apply[688] and domestic law is not preempted.

The observation as such is correct, of course. But one can still question if it affects the dimension discussed here. The present question is whether an international element is a criterion relevant for *conflicts* rules specifically. By contrast, the perspective of the TFEU implicates the question of whether a rule made by the EU is *binding on* domestic authorities. An affirmative answer can only be given if the rule does not contravene the TFEU. For provisions whose sole basis could be Article 81 TFEU, this means that they must indeed concern matters with cross-border implications. But this condition does not follow from a provision being a conflicts rule, but from its being an *EU law* rule.

---

685 To the same effect *von Hein*, in: MüKoBGB, Art. 3 EGBGB at 12; *Spickhoff*, in: BeckOK BGB, 39th ed. (01.02.2013), Art. 1 VO (EG) 593/2008 at 24; *Halfmeier*, in: Calliess (ed.), Rome Regulations, Art. 1 Rome II at 19. *Plender/Wilderspin*, European PIL of Obligations, at 4-008, occupy some sort of middle ground when they contend that there is no objective test of identifying a situation of an international character (as formulated by the Draft Rome Convention), but by determining "whether the judge [is] confronted with a relevant choice of law". These remarks concern the Rome Convention, but the author expressly extends them to Rome I, at 4-010. Finally, see the recent assessment by *Hau*, in: GS Unberath, 139.

686 This is a transplant of *Lippert*'s metaphor, ZEuS 2014, 273, 274. Neither there nor in his monograph on the same subject, Der grenzüberschreitende Sachverhalt im Unionsrecht, does he deal with the requirement of a cross-border case in *private international* law (although he mentions Article 81 TFEU in passing, 12). The monograph covers "only" the context of the fundamental freedoms of the TFEU (25–94), EU competition law (94–149) and Article 18 TFEU (149–195); the article concerns the first two topics.

687 Similarly *von Hein*, in: MüKoBGB, Art. 3 EGBGB at 9 with note 32 (regarding an earlier version of Article 3 EGBGB).

688 To this effect apparently also recently *Magnus*, ZEuP 2018, 507, 509–512.

The three most recent private international law regulations reinforce this view. The Succession Regulation did not mention any requirement for a conflict of laws anymore. Nor does any provision of the M-Property Regulation or the RP-Property Regulation.[689] Moreover, when the two latter regulations do mention "cross-border implications" in Recital 14, they do so with express reference to Article 81 TFEU, i.e. not as a question of private international law but as one of competence.

This distinction dovetails with the ECJ case law concerning the Brussels I regime. Neither the Brussels Convention nor Brussels I(bis) contains the written requirement of an international element akin to Articles 1(1) Rome I–III. The *Jenard Report* nevertheless stressed that the rules of jurisdiction of the Brussels Convention only applied in cases involving an international element.[690] In accordance with this statement, the Court of Justice has required an international element for the application of the Brussels I regime.[691] Crucially, it later expressly distinguished this element from "the conditions under which the rules of jurisdiction […] must apply".[692] It thus uncoupled the criterion for the application of Brussels I[693] from the connecting factors establishing jurisdiction in given cases. Indeed, even though a party's nationality is not relevant for any head of jurisdiction under Brussels I(bis), the Court seems[694] to have held that the foreign nationality of one of the parties sufficed in order for Brussels I to apply.[695]

Perhaps because the Court's line of argument started with the Brussels Convention, it did not expressly rely on the idea of EU competence. However, it did refer to applicable Brussels provisions *replacing* domestic rules of jurisdiction.[696] Thus, the idea of EU law prevailing over national law is present in

689 See, however, *Martiny*, ZfPW 2017, 1, 6, with a different explanation: no conflict of laws needed (yet) at the relevant point in time because party autonomy is to be allowed even in purely domestic situations with a view to the future and because, due to the limited nature of party autonomy in these regulations, a sufficient connection to the chosen law will exist.

690 *Jenard*, Report on the Convention on jurisdiction and the enforcement of judgments in civil and commercial matters, 8.

691 ECJ Case C-281/02, Andrew Owusu v N. B. Jackson, trading as "Villa Holidays Bal-Inn Villas" and Others, Reports of Cases 2005, I-1383, at 25.

692 ECJ Case C-327/10, Hypoteční banka a.s. v Udo Mike Lindner, Reports of Cases 2011, I-11543, at 31.

693 There is no indication that the decision would come out differently for Brussels Ibis, *Lith*, in: Dickinson/Lein (eds.), Brussels I Recast, at 3.03.

694 But perhaps the statement is less sweeping than it might appear (*Requejo/Cuniberti*, Rev. crit. DIP 2012, 421, 430): the case at hand concerned a defendant whose domicile was unknown – it *could* have been abroad (*Hau*, in: GS Unberath, 139, 152); or perhaps the known foreign nationality of the defendant was enough reason to speculate that his domicile might also be foreign.

695 This seems to be how *Grimm*, GPR 2012, 87–88, understands ECJ Case C-327/10, Hypoteční banka a.s. v Udo Mike Lindner, Reports of Cases 2011, I-11543, at 35.

696 ECJ Case C-327/10, Hypoteční banka a.s. v Udo Mike Lindner, Reports of Cases 2011, I-11543, at 33.

the decision. This is a further indication that the Court considered the question of the international element to be one of the application of the Brussels regime *in relation to* domestic rules, and not so much as one of an *inherent feature* of rules of international jurisdiction. In any case, it is submitted that the former way of looking at the issue is preferable.

In conclusion, while the existence of an international element *is* a requirement of relevance for all EU conflicts rules, it is one linked to their EU provenance, not to their private international law nature. It originates in the TFEU; as such, it is actually already set forth (also hierarchically) separately from individual conflicts rules. There is no legal[697] reason for EU private international law itself to reiterate the requirement.

2.2.2. *Scope of Application* Ratione Materiae

Member States

Domestic private international law typically contains no general rule setting forth requirements *ratione materiae* (other than the international element and its functional counterparts). It is not difficult to see why. Assuming that no legal system in the EU tolerates that there is no law whatsoever applicable to a given case, domestic law must provide for rules on the applicable law for all potential situations – even if the decision of domestic law merely consists in not making any existing international element relevant, and thus in applying the *lex fori*. Where private international law concerns all fields of private law, a rule on the scope *ratione materiae* is unnecessary. In systems whose private international law is statutory only in part,[698] or not found in only one legal instrument, however, one might envision a declaratory provision on the scope *ratione materiae* of the written parts or of the respective instrument. Article 1 Croatian PIL Act, in fact the "Act concerning the resolution of conflict of laws with the provisions of other countries *in certain matters*",[699] may serve as an example of the latter.

European Union

For EU private international law, however, things are different. If and to the extent that it is not applicable, domestic rules apply. Hence, as long as it is not all-encompassing, EU private international law needs to delineate its scope

[697] For a potential *policy* reason to have such a rule, *infra* Chapter 6, section 2.4.1.

[698] See e.g. Germany, where there are no statutory conflicts provisions regarding companies.

[699] Translation in Neth. Int. L. Rev. 30 (1983), 222 (emphasis added); as to possible misunderstandings caused by the wording of Article 1 (the German translation in IPRax 1983, 6, is much clearer) see *Matić*, Neth. Int. L. Rev. 30 (1983), 220, 221.

of application in relation to national private international law. Accordingly, there is a first chapter entitled "scope" in all of the regulations. Each Article 1 of the six regulations specifies that their respective body of rules shall apply to contractual obligations and non-contractual obligations in civil and commercial matters, to divorce and legal separation, to the estate of deceased persons, to matrimonial property regimes, and to the property consequences of registered partnerships. Their conflicts provisions do not apply, in particular, to "revenue, customs or administrative matters".[700] The regulations further expressly exclude certain matters from their scope.[701] These are formally general rules in the strict sense in relation to the respective regulation.

2.2.3. *Scope of Application* Ratione Temporis/*Change in the Applicable Conflicts Rules*

Every legal rule begins to be applicable at some point in time. A rule on the application *ratione temporis*, however, is missing from all sections with general provisions in domestic private international codes. Rather, such rules are usually found at the very end of the legislative instrument[702] or in a provision that is not formally part of the instrument.[703] This seems to be a matter of legislative custom. Domestic legislators typically seem to recognise that such provisions do not belong among specific conflicts rules, as evidenced by them often being located in a separate section.[704] To some extent, this also reflects the idea, first put forth by none other than von Savigny,[705] of intertemporal law as a discipline of conflict of laws, whether in relation to substantive law or private international law.[706]

The principle is clear, in any case, that the law of the forum[707] decides questions about the application of its conflicts rules in time, i.e. decides how

---

700 Article 1(1) clause 2 Rome I/Rome II/Succession Regulation/M-/RP-Property Regulation.

701 Articles 1(2) and (3) Rome I and Rome II; 1(2) Rome III/Succession Regulation/M-/RP-Property Regulation.

702 E.g. Article 140 Belgian PIL Code, §125 Czech PIL Act, Article 74 Italian PIL Act, Article 81 Polish PIL Act, Article 70 Slovak PIL Act, Article 119 Slovenian PIL Act.

703 E.g. Article V of the Dutch Law of May 19, 2011, i.e. the law that contains Book 10 of the Civil Code in its Article I. Book 10 of the Dutch Civil Code also contains particular temporal provisions at the end of several of its chapters.

704 Article 140 Belgian PIL Code is the only provision in the section on "Entry into Force", §125 Czech PIL Act is in the section of "Transitional and Final Provisions", Article 74 Italian PIL Act is the final "transitional provision", Article 81 Polish PIL Act, Article 70 Slovak PIL, and Article 119 Slovenian PIL Act are among the respective instrument's "Final Provisions". See also Articles 220 and 236 EGBGB, located among intertemporal provisions. As to German intertemporal private international law in general, see *Heß*, Intertemporales Privatrecht, 237–249.

705 *von Savigny*, System VIII, VI.

706 See in particular *Heß*, Intertemporales Privatrecht, 23–27, 325–382, and passim; *Schröder*, Die Verweisung auf Mehrrechtsstaaten, 59–81.

707 *Grodecki*, Intertemporal Conflict of Laws, at 2; *Calvo Caravaca/Carrascosa González*, DIP I, 529; *Mayer/Heuzé*, DIP, at 252–257; *Audit/d'Avout*, DIP, at 311–312.

to resolve this *conflit transitoire*. Private international law scholars generally discuss it separately from specific conflicts rules, although not necessarily together with other issues called "general" and the like.[708]

The observation for EU private international law is very similar: Rome I, Rome II, and Rome III each have a final chapter with "Final Provisions", the Succession Regulation, the M-Property Regulation, and the RP-Property Regulation have one with "General and Final Provisions". Each of these chapters contains provisions on when the respective regulation enters into force and/or from when it shall apply,[709] sometimes supplemented by transitional provisions.[710]

2.2.4. *Scope of Application* Ratione Personae

Both domestic and EU private international law apply regardless of any requirements as to the person involved or affected. This statement is so obvious that usually neither private international law legislators nor scholars in the field make any mention of it. The legislator of the BGB, for example, expressly declined to make any legislative statement to this effect.[711] Historically speaking, however, the idea of letting foreigners participate in domestic legal dealings found its way into private international law codes specifically.[712] It still resounds among the general provisions of a few current domestic private international law codes.[713] Moreover, the French tradition commonly considers the *conditions des étrangers* a sub-topic of *droit international privé*.[714] They are discussed as such in private international law textbooks, independently

708 *Dicey/Morris/Collins*, Conflict of Laws, at 3-003–3-007 (special chapter on the "time factor", but as part of the "preliminary matters"). *Rogerson*, Collier's Conflict of Laws, 288–290 (special section on the "time factor" in the chapter on conflicts rules in general). *Calvo Caravaca/Carrascosa González*, DIP I, 528–530 (as one of the general issues of applying a conflicts rule). *Bogdan*, PIL in Sweden, at 53 (as part of the chapter on "connection", i.e. mainly connecting factors, together with the change of the *lex fori*). *Mayer/Heuzé*, DIP, at 252–257 (in the "partie générale", yet not in the part on the application of foreign law, but together with other intertemporal issues as "facteurs de complication"). *Cachard*, DIP, at 602–604 (as part of a section on the influence of "time" on private international law). *von Bar/Mankowski*, IPR I, §4 at 171 (in the context of German private international law as part of the German legal system, together with other questions of intertemporal law).

709 Article 29 Rome I, Article 32 Rome II, Article 21 Rome III, Article 84 Succession Regulation, Article 70 M-/RP-Property Regulation.

710 Article 31 Rome II, Article 83 Succession Regulation, Article 69 M-/RP-Property Regulation; see also Article 28 Rome I that is found in the chapter with "Other Provisions".

711 See Mugdan I, 370; *Schmoeckel*, in: HKK-BGB, vor §1 at 7.

712 *Gogos/Aubin*, RabelsZ 15 (1949/1950), 240, 248–250.

713 §§26–27 Czech PIL Act; Article 14 Portuguese Civil Code. Also see Article 4 Greek Civil Code (at the beginning of the provisions on private international law) and Article 32 Slovak PIL Act (not among the "common" provisions, but right in between them and individual conflicts provisions (Articles 3–31 Slovak PIL Act), i.e. at least separate from the latter ones.

714 *Chetail*, JDI 2014, 447, 451.

from conflicts rules.[715] To this day, the *Revue critique de droit international privé* has a separate section labelled "condition des étrangers".

Admittedly, these provisions and principles have a range of implications, which may encompass immigration law (including asylum, residence, and deportation), political rights,[716] and all positions of substantive private law. To consider them from the perspective of "scope" means to disregard big parts of their range. Yet if one continues to follow the formal[717] approach pursued presently, there are two ways of conceptualising these rules. The first is an internal approach limited to private *international* law. If one asks how these rules are relevant for more than one *conflicts* rule, their function and indeed their raison d'être do boil down to a question of scope *ratione personae*: private international law also applies to foreigners. The second approach is broader. It would consider the relevance of such rules for *substantive* private law. Relevant for more than one rule of substantive private law, they would stand *next to* conflicts rules – the latter would determine the *spatial* applicability of substantive private law, and the former its *personal* applicability. Either approach, however, renders it possible to explain from a formal perspective the existence of such rules on foreigners among the general provisions of an instrument on private international law (or in a separate chapter in a private international law textbook).

2.3. THE HIERARCHY OF INSTRUMENTS OF PRIVATE INTERNATIONAL LAW

Particularly since private international law has been a traditional object of international harmonisation efforts, even domestic codes for "all" areas of private international law do not necessarily provide the complete picture. In a given case, perhaps also only in relation to one particular other country, a special conflicts rule from an international convention might take precedence over purely domestic legislation. Nowadays, of course, rules of domestic codes might additionally take second billing to EU private international law. The issue is thus one of the relationship of private international law rules of instruments of different provenance or nature, typically characterised by a different hierarchical status. It arises in every field of private international law as defined by the respective subject matters. It is a formally general issue in the strict sense.

715 *Loussouarn/Bourel/de Vareilles-Sommières*, DIP, at 1121–1206 (also for the historical development of the topic and its connection with private international law); *Audit/d'Avout*, DIP, 93–115; *Mayer/Heuzé*, DIP, at 992–1082. Also see Article 11 French Civil Code.

716 For both see e.g. *Loussouarn/Bourel/de Vareilles-Sommières*, DIP, at 1133–1175.

717 For a conceptualisation as a general provision of a *substantive* nature *infra* Chapter 4, section 4.4.1.

Member States

The interaction of domestic rules with rules established by a convention or by the EU is a fundamental question not confined to private international law. The answer depends on each country's concept of the effect of international conventions on domestic law (implementation necessary or direct effect?), although the EU itself (in the form of the ECJ) may have some say regarding the effect of its law. It is therefore no theoretical necessity to address this issue specifically in private international law legislation, although the replication prohibition may require some respective efforts in a given instance.[718] In any case, since 1979 no private international law code has been passed that does not in some way acknowledge other sources of private international law.[719] In fact, most member states deal with the issue formally separately from individual conflicts rules, and often among the "general provisions".[720]

European Union

There is a certain need for EU private international law to establish or clarify its status, especially in relation to international conventions. It is one thing to claim precedence over domestic law, but another to potentially make member states contravene existing duties under their conventions with third states. On the other hand, where a convention has been concluded exclusively among member states, there is little reason for the EU to have "[r]espect for international commitments".[721] To this extent, the goal of uniform private international law among the member states can be said to prevail.[722] All EU private international law regulations address both issues, and all do so in a chapter separate from individual conflicts rules: the chapter on

---

718 *Supra* Chapter 2, section 1.1.2.1.

719 The existence of other sources of private international law is mentioned by §2(1) Estonian PIL Act and Article 67 Polish PIL Act. The Polish PIL Act additionally refers to EU regulations individually, see e.g. Article 28 Polish PIL Act (reference to Rome I), Article 33 (reference to Rome II). The Belgian PIL Code operates in a similar way, see e.g. Article 98(4) Belgian PIL Code (reference to Rome II). Together with the following footnote, all fifteen private international law codes passed since 1979 (plus Slovakia) are accounted for.

720 Among the "general provisions" concerning the applicable law only: Article 3 Croatian PIL Act, Article 3 EGBGB, §2 Hungarian PIL Code 1979/§2 Hungarian PIL Act, Articles 1.10(1), 1.13 Lithuanian Civil Code, Article 10:1 Dutch Civil Code, Article 2.557(3) Romanian Civil Code, Article 4 Slovenian PIL Act. See also Article 25 Latvian Civil Code (very last provision of the introduction to the civil code, right after *renvoi* and public policy). Among the "general" (or "introductory") provisions of the entire code: Article 3 Bulgarian PIL Code, §2 Czech PIL Act, Article 2 Italian PIL Act, Article 2 Slovak PIL Act. The pertinent §53 Austrian PIL Act is one of the "final provisions" of that act.

721 Recital 41 clause 1 Rome I, Recital 36 clause 1 Rome II, Article 73 clause 1 Succession Regulation.

722 Recital 73 clause 3 Succession Regulation.

"Other Provisions" in the Rome Regulations,[723] and the chapter on "General and Final Provisions" in the Succession Regulation, the M-Property Regulation, and the RP-Property Regulation.[724] The regulations honour international commitments involving third states, but override commitments exclusively among member states.[725] This is also what Lagarde has proposed as a general provision for all of EU private international law.[726]

Only Rome II contains any indication as to *future* international conventions concluded by the member states. Pursuant to Recital 37 Rome II, "sectoral matters" can still be subject to international conventions with third states. Regulation 662/2009 lays down the respective "procedures and conditions". It is obvious that the EU legislator assumes that this is the only way in which member states can still conclude international agreements. It is not necessary to argue *a contrario* in respect of the other regulations, as the supremacy of EU law,[727] and the AETR decision by the ECJ,[728] already prohibit member states from assuming divergent obligations through international conventions.

2.4. CHARACTERISATION

The term "characterisation" was apparently coined by Falconbridge.[729] The phenomenon is also called "qualification"[730] or "classification". It relates to a "conundrum"[731] often regarded as one of the most complex, difficult, and contentious issues in private international law,[732] and as an "enigma in a complicated and mysterious field of law".[733] Indeed, while *renvoi* is regularly the target of disparaging epithets,[734] everybody at least agrees as to what *renvoi* is about. With characterisation there is already "very great debate

723 Article 25 Rome I, Article 28 Rome II, Article 19 Rome III.

724 Article 75 Succession Regulation, Article 62 M-/RP-Property Regulation.

725 For the special case of Rome I in relation to the Rome Convention, see Article 24 Rome I, likewise among the "Other Provisions" of Rome I.

726 *Lagarde*, RabelsZ 75 (2011), 673 (Article 112).

727 *Halfmeier*, in: Calliess (ed.), Rome Regulations, Art. 28 Rome II at 21.

728 ECJ Case C-22/70, Commission of the European Communities v Council of the European Communities (European Agreement on Road Transport), Reports of Cases 1971, 263, at 22.

729 *Falconbridge*, Law Q. Rev. 53 (1937), 235, 239, with further references to his earlier works. For the history of the issue of characterisation in the English-speaking world see *Weber*, Theorie der Qualifikation, 90–92 and 164–181.

730 This is how one of its intellectual fathers called it in French: *Bartin*, JDI 1897, 225, 227.

731 *Juenger*, in: LA Siehr (2000), 288, 295.

732 *Rogerson*, Collier's Conflict of Laws, 268; *Dicey/Morris/Collins*, Conflict of Laws, at 2-008; *von Bar/Mankowski*, IPR I, §7 at 138 (note 3); *Nehne*'s flow charts provide ample illustration of this point, Methodik und allgemeine Lehren des europäischen IPR, 173–177.

733 *Siehr*, Yearbook of Private International Law VII (2005), 17, 39.

734 See *infra* section 5.5.

and confusion as to what it is that is characterised".[735] Facts?[736] A legal issue?[737] A rule of law?[738] A combination of factual and legal elements?[739] Is characterisation a question of interpretation of a conflicts rule,[740] of applying it to the facts at hand,[741] of both?[742] All of this despite the insight that characterisation "was not invented" by private international law,[743] but is rather, and has always been, part of everyday legal reasoning in domestic substantive (private) law, i.e. determining if a case is one of tort, contract, family law etc.[744] And all of this despite the issue being anything but new:[745] it truly appeared on the map through the seemingly independent[746] studies by Kahn and Bartin at the end of the 19th century.[747]

At least from a functional perspective, and at an abstract level, however, a common thread has been identified in the EU:[748] characterisation is a method to allocate an issue (regardless of whether it is factual or legal) to a conflicts rule. In essence, characterisation is about determining the pertinent conflicts rule.[749] A rather clear example of this is Article 12(1) Spanish Civil Code: "La calificación

---

735 *Rogerson*, Collier's Conflict of Laws, 269; also *Vonken*, Algemeen deel IPR, at 308, and *Weber*, Theorie der Qualifikation, 215, declaring in unison everything in this context to be contentious ("alles omstreden", "alles umstritten").

736 See e.g. *Esplugues Mota/Azcárraga Monzonís*, Spanish Report, 24; *Mádl*, RHDI 44 (1991), 227, 238; *Rabel*, The Conflict of Laws I, 55; *id.*, ZAIPR 5 (1931), 241, 245.

737 *Metzger*, in: Max Planck Encyclopedia of European Private Law, s. v. "Characterization", 167.

738 *Dicey/Morris/Collins*, Conflict of Laws, at 2-009.

739 *Leible/Müller*, Yearbook of Private International Law 14 (2012/2013), 137, 142.

740 See e.g. *Reimann*, in: id./Zimmermann (eds.), The Oxford Handbook of Comparative Law, 1363, 1385; *Nowicka*, in: Dajczak/Szwarc/Wiliński (eds.), Handbook of Polish Law, 17.2.1.1.; *Rabel*, The Conflict of Laws, 50.

741 See *von Hoffmann/Ortiz-Arce*, RabelsZ 39 (1975), 647, 653.

742 See *Heiss/Kaufmann-Mohi*, in: Leible (ed.), General Principles, §5.02[A][1]; *Heinze*, in: FS Kropholler, 105, 107–108 with further references; *Dicey/Morris/Collins*, Conflict of Laws, at 2-006–7, make a (further) distinction between characterisation in and outside the context of EU regulations.

743 *Dolinger*, in: Essays in Honor of Juenger, 23, 28.

744 *Rogerson*, Collier's Conflict of Laws, 267–268; *von Bar/Mankowski*, IPR I, §7 at 141; *Binchy*, Irish Conflicts of Law, 27.

745 It is often said that *Dumoulin* was the first to touch upon the question, see *Loussouarn/Bourel/de Vareilles-Sommières*, at 123.

746 *Bartin* professes that no one before him seems to have discussed the issue, JDI 1897, 225; *Kahn*'s analysis does not appear in his article (at the time, it seems not to have been noticed in France at all: *Weber*, Theorie der Qualifikation, 34).

747 To wit: *Kahn*, Gesetzeskollisionen, 92–123; *Bartin*, JDI 1897, 225, 466, 720. See *Loussouarn/Bourel/de Vareilles-Sommières*, at 259; *Lipstein*, Characterization, at 11; in great detail *Weber*, Theorie der Qualifikation, 14–51 and passim.

748 *Nehne*, Methodik und allgemeine Lehren des europäischen IPR, 170–171.

749 *McParland*, The Rome I Regulation, at 3.07; *Leible/Müller*, Yearbook of Private International Law 14 (2012/2013), 137, 142; *Cachard*, DIP, at 558; *Calvo Caravaca/Carrascosa* González, DIP I, 465; *Garnett*, Substance and Procedure in PIL, at 3.02; *Wendehorst*, in: Verschraegen (ed.), Austrian Law, 79, 98; *Bogdan*, Rec. des cours 348 (2010), 9, 134–135; *Nowicka*, in: Dajczak/Szwarc/Wiliński (eds.), Handbook of Polish Law, 17.2.1.1.; *Pazdan*, in: Lewaszkiewicz-Petrykowska (ed.), Rapports Polonais, 49, 61–62; *von Bar/Mankowski*, IPR I, §7 at 138;

para determinar la norma de conflicto aplicable se hará siempre con arreglo a la ley Española".[750]

It should become apparent that this is a formally general issue in the strict sense.[751] It has even been described as constituting "one of the most general institutions of private international law".[752] The correct identification/selection of a conflicts rule is simply relevant in every conflicts case; indeed, in many ways,[753] it marks the starting point.[754] As the relevance of a conflicts rule for a given case depends on the scope of its subject matter, the allocation of characterisation to the subject matter requires no further explanation.

The Peculiarity of Characterisation in Private International Law

The determination of the pertinent legal rule forms a necessary part of all areas of law. As such, it is rarely subject to discussion, although the relevance of a particular rule of statutory or case law *for a given case* certainly will be. Generally, it would seem that finding the pertinent rule is a function of one's knowledge of the law in the respective field. The law itself will usually give no specific instructions on how to do so. Nor is it a novel phenomenon that one and the same word can have different meanings even *within* one legal system, depending on the respective field of law.[755]

On the face of it, then, it should come as a surprise that so much has been made of this issue in private international law specifically. Yet here it has a qualitative dimension lacking in areas of substantive law. A conflicts rule typically relies on broad terminology, on "broad categories of typical legal institutions".[756] As such, it refers to entire sets of substantive rules. The category

presumably also *Harding*, Conflict of Laws, 7; *Baratta*, Yearbook of Private International Law VI (2006), 155. While broader notions of "characterisation" existed in the 20th century, they seem to have all but vanished – and rightfully so, see *Philip*, Rec. des cours 96 (1959-I), 241, 266.

750 Emphasis added.

751 See *Baratta*, in: id. (ed.), DIP, s. v. "Qualificazioni", 315 ("un'esigenza imprescindibile dell'attivazione della normativa di d.i.p."). *Juenger* regarding characterisation as one of the "self-inflicted difficulties of the multilateral approach" (in: LA Siehr (2000), 288, 296 with note 28) implicitly confirms this view, as he refers to multilateralism in general, not to any individual rules.

752 *Mádl*, RHDI 44 (1991), 227, 238.

753 One could argue, however, that for conflicts provisions in EU regulations or treaties the scope of application is an issue that must be dealt with prior.

754 *Beaumont/McEleavy*, Anton's PIL, at 1.18 and 4.01; *Baratta*, Yearbook of Private International Law VI (2006), 155, 156.

755 A telling example is the recognition of a tenant's right to possession of the rented item as "property" under the German constitution, Article 14 GG (BVerfGE 89, 1). To consider that right as property under private law, however, would be a colossal mistake.

756 *Lipstein*, Characterization, at 4.

and the class of substantive rules it refers to depend on the conflicts interests implicated, whereas the terminology used is only a linguistic tool.[757] This is because, more often than not, a legislator will use terms and concepts borrowed from its substantive law in order to designate a conflicts category, while at the same time intending – as long as it wants to draft a multi- or omnilateral rule – the category to be capable of encompassing foreign substantive law.[758] It follows that one can theoretically approach the determination of the pertinent rule in private international law from at least three perspectives: the perspective of the (substantive) *lex fori*, the perspective of the (foreign) *lex causae*, or a perspective removed from these two. It is the peculiarity of private international law[759] that there even is room to consider from which perspective to approach the question.

Member States

Characterisation as an issue surfaces virtually everywhere across the EU, typically discussed separately from individual conflicts rules. Examples can be found in works on common law,[760] in continental legal literature from the Nordic member states,[761] in Greece,[762] and everything in between.[763]

---

757 *Köhler*, Eingriffsnormen, 84–86; *Kegel/Schurig*, IPR, §6 II 2 (315–316); *von Bar/Mankowski*, IPR I, §7 at 139–140; for a similar French perspective see *Audit/d'Avout*, DIP, at 261.

758 *Kegel/Schurig*, IPR, §7 III 1, 2 a (336–339); see already *Rabel*, ZAIPR 5 (1931), 241, 247 and passim.

759 See also *Weber*, Theorie der Qualifikation, 223–224. For an entirely different qualitative take see *Gaudemet-Tallon*, in: Essays in Honor of Juenger, 317, 330: the connection between the identity of a state and its legal system exists in all areas of law, but it is particularly strong in private international law, for here decisions on the very essence of its institutions are necessary.

760 *Briggs*, Private International Law in the English Courts, at 3.48–3.63 (as part of the "structure and methods" of private international law); *id.*, Conflict of Laws, 15–20 (as a "technique" of "common law choice of law"); *Hill/Ní Shúilleabháin*, Clarkson & Hill's Conflict of Laws, at 1.66–1.101 (as part of the "meachnis" of private international law); *Harding*, Conflict of Laws, 7 ("technical issue"); *Rogerson*, Collier's Conflict of Laws, 267–277; *Dicey/Morris/Collins*, Conflict of Laws, at 2-001–2-047 (as a "preliminary matter"), *Cheshire/North/Fawcett*, PIL, 41–50 (as a "preliminary topic"). *Beaumont/McEleavy*, Anton's PIL, at 4.06–4.26 (in the chapter on the "identification of the applicable law"). Characterisation has also been recognised by the English legislator in a formally general way for tort and delict, see Section 9(2) Private International Law (Miscellaneous Provisions) Act 1995.

761 Denmark: *Lookofsky*, in: Symeonides (ed.), PIL at the End of the 20th Century, 147, 160–162 (implicitly acknowledging the issue to be of relevance for more than one conflicts rule). For Finland see *Bergmann*, Hauptprobleme, 16–20. Sweden: *Bogdan*, PIL in Sweden, at 58–65 (as one of the "basic terms"); *Eek*, Swedish Conflict of Laws, 112–119 (as part of the "structure and construction of choice of law rules").

762 *Meidanis*, in: Vrellis (ed.), PIL in Greece, at 59–60; implicitly *Vassilakakis*, RHDI 63 (2010), 103, 108; *Vrellis*, in: Symeonides (ed.), PIL at the End of the 20th Century, 243, 255–256.

763 Austria: *Lurger/Melcher*, IPR, at 1/100–1/109 (as one of the "general questions"); *Verschraegen*, IPR, at 1170–1177 (in the "general part"). France: *Loussouarn/Bourel/de Vareilles-Sommières*,

Provisions on characterisation, however, are relatively rare. Fewer than half of the member states with a private international law code have enacted a rule *on characterisation as such*[764] among their general provisions.[765] Notably, out of the seven codes that do, six deal with characterisation at the beginning of the general provisions, in line with the idea stated above that characterisation concerns one of the very first steps of any private international law analysis. In the Bulgarian PIL Code, the Czech PIL Act, and the Spanish Civil Code, the respective provision is the very first general provision on private international law;[766] whereas the respective provision in the Hungarian PIL Act, the Portuguese Civil Code, and the Romanian Civil Code follows the first provision(s) that either concern(s) the scope and purpose of the subsequent provisions,[767] or the equal treatment of foreigners.[768]

There is no clear temporal trend: three out of the six oldest codes of private international law in the EU (Portugal 1966, Spain 1974, Croatia/Yugoslavia 1982[769]) contain such a provision, as do three out of the five most recent

DIP, at 259–277 (as part of the "théorie générale des conflits de lois); *Audit/d'Avout*, DIP, at 258–273 (in the "partie générale", more specifically as part of the interpretation of conflicts rules); *Cachard*, DIP, at 558–573 (as part of the "sélection de la règle de conflit"); *Mayer/Heuzé*, DIP, at 154–174 (as part of the "choix de la règle de conflit"). Germany: *Kropholler*, IPR, §13 (in the chapter on the "general part", specifically in the section on the subject matter of conflicts rules); Kegel/Schurig, IPR, §7 (under the heading "general part"); *von Bar/Mankowski*, IPR I, §7 II (with §7 as such concerning the "general part"). Italy: *T. Ballarino/E. Ballarino/Pretelli*, DIP, IV 3 (96–99) (as part of the "messa in opera" of (any) conflicts rule). Luxembourg: *Wiwinius*, DIP, at 73–109 (in the "partie générale"). Portugal: *de Lima Pinheiro*, DIP I, 571–597 (as part of the "parte geral"). The Netherlands: *Vonken*, Algemeen deel IPR, at 302–324.

764 There are few more general provisions concerning different *aspects* of characterisation: Pursuant to Article 10:13 Dutch Civil Code and Article 6(2) Polish PIL Act, presumptions or provisions of the *lex causae* as to the burden of proof apply. Pursuant to Article 6(1) Polish PIL Act, provisions of public law of the *lex causae* apply as well. As to the scope of a foreign *lex causae* also see Article 1.10(2) Lithuanian Civil Code.

765 To wit: Article 39 Bulgarian PIL Code, Article 9 Croatian PIL Act, §3 Hungarian PIL Code 1979/§4 Hungarian PIL Act, Article 15 Portuguese Civil Code, Article 2.558 Romanian Civil Code, Article 12(1) Spanish Civil Code.

766 Article 39 Bulgarian PIL Code, §20 Czech PIL Act, Article 12(1) Spanish Civil Code.

767 §4 Hungarian PIL Act (similarly already §3 Hungarian PIL Code 1979), Article 2.558 Romanian Civil Code.

768 Article 15 Portuguese Civil Code. That the respective provision in Croatia is only the ninth general provision, found after public policy and *renvoi*, as well as immediately before non-unified legal systems, may be another reason to doubt that it belongs in the present context, see the following footnote.

769 Article 9 Croatian PIL Act, albeit often considered without any qualification to be a provision on characterisation (*Lipstein*, Characterization, at 20; *Šarčević*, Am. J. Comp. L. 33 (1985), 283, 285; *Cigoj*, Rev. crit. DIP 1983, 375, 376; also see the German translation in IPRax 1983, 6), is a doubtful candidate. Its draft concerned the issue more clearly than its final form (see *Firsching*, IPRax 1983, 1, 2), as it now (only) concerns *how* foreign law is

ones (Bulgaria 2005, Romania 2009,[770] Czech Republic 2012). The relative elaborateness of the three characterisation provisions passed since the turn of the century stands out, however. They have three (Bulgaria), four (Czech Republic), or even five (Romania) paragraphs with specific provisions for rights *in rem* supplementing the abovementioned two provisions.[771] Of course, this conceptual observation does not imply that the shorter provisions passed much earlier are *per se* any less complex, or that they have not been the subject of much discussion.[772]

The Belgian PIL Code serves as a still recent example of a different approach to the issue of characterisation. It contains no pertinent general provision, but offers guidance for particular questions. It itself expressly defines several concepts not found in Belgian substantive law.[773] Furthermore, the Code regularly sets forth the scope of its conflicts rules,[774] providing "non-exhaustive enumeration[s] of the legal issues covered by the specific rule".[775] In light of this two-pronged approach, a general theoretical framework for characterisation was deemed unnecessary.[776]

European Union: The European Dimension of Characterisation

For EU private international law, things are both easier and more complicated at the same time. They are relatively easy because the solution must be an autonomous approach to characterisation; otherwise, i.e. if one made recourse to the respective domestic *lex fori* or *lex causae*, uniform interpretation of EU private international law could not be achieved. It appears that everyone agrees with this elementary statement.[777] Preference for autonomous interpretation

---

to be applied. Such a provision also could be considered a question belonging in the context of the ascertainment and application of foreign law.

770 The Romanian stand-alone private international law code of 1992 contained a respective provision, too: *Aden*, RIW 2008, 700, 701.

771 Article 64(2) Bulgarian PIL Code (see *Zidarova/Stančeva-Minčeva*, RabelsZ 71 (2007), 398, 407); §69(1) Czech PIL Act (see *Dobiáš*, Riv. dir. int. priv. proc. 2015, 109, 116). In the Romanian Civil Code, this issue has been dealt with by the general characterisation provision itself, Article 2.558(3) Romanian Civil Code.

772 Article 15 Portuguese Civil Code in particular seems to have sparked (or anything but stopped) a vigorous academic debate, see in particular Ferrer-Correia, ZfRV 1970, 114 (with note 1), already soon after the provision went into force. But §3 Hungarian PIL Code 1979 has figured prominently in scholarly discussions as well, with – surprise, surprise – mixed evaluations; see e.g. *Raffai/Szabó*, Acta Juridica Hungarica 51 (2010), 136, 143–144; *Burián*, in: Symeonides (ed.), PIL at the End of the 20th Century, 263, 275–276; *Mádl*, RHDI 44 (1991), 227, 238; *Conetti*, in: Collisio Legum, 129, 132.

773 Such as the trust, see Article 122 Belgian PIL Code.

774 See e.g. Articles 48(2), 53, 56, 63, 76, 80 Belgian PIL Code.

775 *Pertegas*, IPRax 2006, 53, 55.

776 *Erauw/Fallon*, in: Dirix/Lelen (eds.), The Belgian Reports, 227, 266.

777 See e.g. *McParland*, The Rome I Regulation, at 3.08; *Rühl*, in: Zimmermann (ed.), Zukunftsperspektiven der Rechtsvergleichung, 103, 120; *Leible/Müller*, Yearbook of

when concerned with terms of EU law (that does not itself refer to national law[778]) is also a core precept of the ECJ's case law.[779]

To practise what one preaches becomes difficult rather quickly, however. There is little to no EU (substantive private) law that could at least serve as an indication of how to understand EU private international law. Autonomous interpretation thus (partially) lacks a foundation.[780] International (private international law) conventions, which face the same issue, often provide definitions and expressly determine their own scope.[781] A comparative approach would be ideal where no other guidance can be found.[782]

European Union: Characterisation *de Lege Europaea Lata*

No Rome Regulation employs any of the terms "characterisation", "classification", or "qualification". The Succession Regulation does mention "qualification", but only in relation to *personal* qualifications, later also called "personal conditions".[783] Similarly, while "classification" appears in the M-Property Regulation and the RP-Property Regulation, it does not use the term in the

Private International Law 14 (2012/2013), 137, 143; *de Lima Pinheiro*, Yearbook of Private International Law 14 (2012/2013), 153, 165; *Vonken*, Algemeen deel IPR, at 324; *Calvo Caravaca/Carrascosa González*, DIP I, 472–475; *Metzger*, in: Max Planck Encyclopedia of European Private Law, s. v. "Characterization", 167, 169; *Mankowski*, in: Basedow/Kischel/Sieber (eds.), German National Reports, 133, 148; *Baratta*, Yearbook of Private International Law VI (2006), 155, 164; *Kreuzer*, in: Jud/Rechberger/Reichelt (eds.), Kollisionsrecht in der Europäischen Union, 1, 53; *Kropholler*, in: 75 Jahre Max-Planck-Institut für Privatrecht, 583, 590; *von Bar/Mankowski*, IPR I, §7 at 171.

778 As Article 63(3) Brussel Ibis still does, unfortunately.

779 *Basedow*, JZ 2016, 269, 277. In the context of cross-border cases of private law, this goes back at least to ECJ Case 29–76, LTU Lufttransportunternehmen GmbH & Co. KG v Eurocontrol, Reports of Cases 1976, 1541, at 3–5, concerning the interpretation of the Brussels Convention. See also ECJ Case C-443/03, Götz Leffler v Berlin Chemie AG, Reports of Cases 2005, I-9637, at 44–45, for a line of reasoning based both on uniformity and on the treaties.

780 See *Baratta*, in: id. (ed.), DIP, s. v. "Qualificazioni", 320; *Hess*, IPRax 2006, 348, 352. Hinted at by *Leible/Müller*, Yearbook of Private International Law 14 (2012/2013), 137, 143.

781 *von Bar/Mankowski*, IPR I, §7 at 171. This presumably is what *Juenger* means when he states that a private international law convention could "indeed avoid some of the embarrassments of the 'General Part', such as characterization", in: LA Siehr (2000), 288, 303.

782 *Metzger*, in: Max Planck Encyclopedia of European Private Law, s. v. "Characterization", 167, 169; generally for a comparative approach to characterisation famously *Rabel*, e.g. The Conflict of Laws I, 54–66; ZAIPR 5 (1931), 241, 255 and passim. It has already been shown that characterisation is one of the points of contact between comparative law and private international law, *supra* Chapter 1, section 1.1.

783 Article 27(3) Succession Regulation. Also see e.g. Recital 53 clause 1 Succession Regulation, referring to rules "limiting the permitted forms of dispositions of property upon death by reference to personal qualifications" such as age, somewhat ironically *characterising* pertinent legal rules as being matters of form.

meaning at issue here.[784] No regulation provides for a general provision on its interpretation, or on the determination of its pertinent conflicts rule, either, unlike Article 18 Rome Convention.

Yet the regulations do not leave their end users high and dry in the characterisation context. First, one can regard their chapter headings that mention "uniform" rules determining the applicable law[785] as a formally general prompt for an autonomous approach. Second, Recital 11 Rome II expressly points to the need for an interpretation independent from domestic concepts.[786] Third, several recitals in the regulations also refer to the uniform or harmonised nature of their respective conflicts rules,[787] which one can likewise interpret to implicate an overall autonomous approach. Fourth, some provisions are clearly aimed by way of their content at a uniform interpretation of the concepts used. For Article 26 Succession Regulation, a further recital expressly emphasises this background.[788] Even without such a recital, "characterisation by way of example"[789] is a common feature of EU private international law: Articles 12 Rome I, 15 Rome II, Article 23(2) Succession Regulation, and Article 27 M-/RP-Property Regulation provide non-exhaustive ("in particular"/"inter alia") lists of issues to be decided by the respective *lex causae*. Accordingly, these provisions have been dubbed "(specific) characterisation rules".[790] Moreover, Article 18(1) Rome I and Article 22(1) Rome II supplement[791] these provisions as regards the burden of proof and presumptions. As these provisions refer to the law applicable under the entire regulation in question, they are formally general provisions.[792] The position of Articles 15 and 22 Rome II among the

---

784 Article 27(a) M-/RP-Property Regulation, making the classification of property into different categories during and after marriage/the registered partnership subject to the *lex causae*.

785 Chapter II Rome I, Chapter II Rome III.

786 "Autonomous concept" of non-contractual obligations.

787 Recitals 13 and 16 Rome II, Recitals 12 and 21 Rome III, Recital 37 clause 2 Succession Regulation, Recital 43 clause 2 M-Property Regulation, Recital 42 clause 2 RP-Property Regulation.

788 Recital 48 clause 2 Succession Regulation: "To ensure the uniform application of that rule, this Regulation should list which elements should be considered as elements pertaining to substantive validity."

789 *Calvo Caravaca/Carrascosa González*, DIP I, 471 ("calificación ejemplificativa").

790 For Rome I and II see *Metzger*, in: Max Planck Encyclopedia of European Private Law, s. v. "Characterization", 167, 169; also *Mankowski*, in: Basedow/Kischel/Sieber (eds.), German National Reports, 133, 148; *Sonnenberger*, in: FS Kropholler, 227, 239. For the Succession Regulation see *Dutta*, in: MüKoBGB, Art. 23 EuErbVO at 1.

791 See e.g. *Junker*, in: MüKoBGB, Art. 22 Rom II-VO at 1.

792 Article 12(1) Rome I: "The law applicable to a contract by virtue of this Regulation"; Article 15 Rome II: "The law applicable to non-contractual obligations under this Regulation". Article 23(2) Succession Regulation merely refers to "that" law; pursuant to Article 23(1) Succession Regulation, this turns out to be the "law determined pursuant to Article 21 or Article 22", i.e. the main conflicts provisions of the Succession Regulation.

"Common Rules"[793] further underlines this insight. Finally, Article 3(1)(a) through (d) Succession Regulation, located in the separate chapter on "Scope and Definitions", expressly defines several of its subject matters.

2.5. THE INCIDENTAL QUESTION

The legal rules governing a given issue may themselves depend[794] on a legal concept (as opposed to purely factual requirements[795]). A tort rule may require that "property" has been damaged in some way, a succession rule may require that somebody was "married" to somebody else. In such a situation, the answer to the issue at hand (i.e. the main or principal question) depends on the answer to the other issue (i.e. the incidental question). Outside of private international law, this phenomenon should not raise any eyebrows, although it may have implications in procedural law.[796] Within private international law, however, one is faced with the question of which conflicts rules to apply to the incidental question: those of the legal system of the *lex fori* or those of the legal system of the *lex causae*.[797] This issue can arise in any context; it is formally general.[798]

2.5.1. Terminology: The Preferability of "Incidental" Question

Gotlieb observed in the 1970s "differing descriptions and terminological confusion" as regards the issue just outlined.[799] Much of this confusion seems

793 Oddly, the French title of Articles 12 Rome I ("Domaine de la loi du contrat") and 15 Rome II ("Portée de la loi applicable") is not the same, unlike in English, German, Italian, and Spanish.

794 If the legal *consequences* of the rule refer to a legal concept, some German authors have suggested that another peculiar (general) issue of private international law arises, the "Nachfrage" (recently *Reuter*, ZfPW 2017, 475; previously *Kegel/Schurig*, IPR, §9 II 3; *von Bar/Mankowski*, IPR I, §7 at 182 in note 763). The term seems impossible to be translated properly, being the result of wordplay with the German term for the incidental question ("Vorfrage"). "Postliminary question" would be the best approximation if one accepted that the incidental question rather should be called "preliminary question" (but see the following paragraphs in the main text on terminology). I am still not convinced that the concept of "Nachfrage" is necessary. See also *von Hein*, in: MüKoBGB, Einl. IPR at 168.

795 This is a broad-brush statement, for one very well can doubt that a "purely factual requirement" exists anywhere in the law. Even if it is at the outermost edge, at some point every term has a normative dimension. On the other hand, the notion of "legal concept" or "prejudicial relationship" has its ambiguities, too, *Mäsch*, in: Leible (ed.), General Principles, §6.04[A].

796 See *von Bar/Mankowski*, IPR I, §7 at 184.

797 It is at least almost universally acknowledged that the *automatic*, immediate application of either the *lex fori* or the *lex causae* is not correct, see only *Weller*, in: id. (ed.), Europäisches Kollisionsrecht, at 71; *Bernitt*, Die Anknüpfung von Vorfragen, 35–36.

798 See *Dicey/Morris/Collins*, Conflict of Laws, at 2-049 (incidental question "a fundamental problem that can arise in any conflicts system"); *Schuz*, A Modern Approach, 4; implicitly *Juenger*, in: LA Siehr, 288, 296 (with note 28).

799 *Gotlieb*, ICLQ 26 (1977), 734, 741.

to have abated in national law. Nowadays, only two terms are commonly used to designate the problem: "incidental question" and "preliminary question" ("Vorfrage", "question préalable", "cuestión previa", "questione preliminare", "voorvraag"). The latter term has the advantage of pedigree; it originates with Melchior and Wengler who are generally regarded as pioneers in this field,[800] although occasionally other scholars have been credited with the "discovery" of the issue.[801] Yet when Wolff – presumably Marguerite, not Martin[802] – coined the former term,[803] common law writers immediately considered it superior to that of "preliminary question" in particular.[804] This common law preference persists until today,[805] while the respective terms for "preliminary question" continue to dominate on the continent.[806]

"Incidental question" is indeed the *mot juste*. While "preliminary" correctly implies that an incidental issue must be resolved before there can be an answer to the *main issue*, it is prone to causing the misunderstanding that it must be resolved before the *determination of the law* applicable to the main question. From the perspective of determining that law, however, the incidental question is clearly "postliminary".[807] It is submitted that the terminology at EU level is not set in stone (yet),[808] and that it is therefore not improper to insist on a term that is unusual for continental Europe.

2.5.2. A Formally General Question of the Subject Matter

In light of the foregoing insight, the appropriateness of discussing the topic in the context of the subject matter is not beyond doubt at first. As the existence of an incidental issue depends on the governing law, the latter could appear to be the preferable context. Express examples of either of these two potential views can be found in academic literature, although usually no explanation is given.[809]

---

800 *Melchior*, Grundlagen, 245–265; *Wengler*, ZAIPR 8 (1934), 148–251.

801 *Gotlieb*, ICLQ 26 (1977), 734, 735, with a detailed analysis in note 5.

802 See *Dannemann*, in: Beatson/Zimmermann (eds.), Jurists Uprooted, 441, 451.

803 *Wolff*, PIL, at 196.

804 See *Dannemann*, in: Beatson/Zimmermann (eds.), Jurists Uprooted, 441, 451 with further references.

805 See e.g. *Dicey/Morris/Collins*, Conflict of Laws, at 2-048 (note 89).

806 See the references *infra* in footnote 827.

807 *Wolff*, PIL, at 196 (note 1); also see *Kropholler*, IPR, §32 I (221); *Neuhaus*, Grundbegriffe, §46 I (344): "subsequent question" in relation to the conflicts issue.

808 See *infra* section 2.5.5.1.; expressly for sticking with continental terminology for EU private international law as well, however, *Bernitt*, Die Anknüpfung von Vorfragen, 20.

809 In the context of the governing law: e.g. *Kropholler*, IPR, §32; *Schwimann*, IPR, 42–44; *Kahn-Freund*, General Problems. In the context of the subject matter: e.g. *Garcimartín Alférez*, DIP, at 21.6; *Calvo Caravaca/Carrascosa González*, DIP I, 481; *Mansel*, in: FS Kropholler,

To discuss the issue in the present context seems preferable because it also concerns the content and the relationship of internal conflicts rules. How so? If one takes the position that the conflicts rules of the legal system of the *lex fori* determine the law applicable to the incidental question, this should be obvious. This approach boils down to the realisation that the main issue also implicates the subject matter of another internal conflicts rule. The same is true, albeit not as obvious, for the other approach – to apply to the incidental question the conflicts rules of the legal system of the *lex causae*. The application of a foreign (conflicts) rule necessarily presupposes an *internal* conflicts decision.[810] Thus, two things occur at once if one applies a foreign conflicts rule to an incidental question: the internal conflicts rule whose subject matter, in principle, covers the issue is disregarded when that issue only arises incidentally; instead, a new (internal) conflicts rule is created that leads to the foreign conflicts rule.[811] The topic thus revolves around the interplay of several internal conflicts rules, i.e. the interplay (and respective scope) of several subject matters. The resulting allocation to the subject matter does not negate the relevance of the governing law for the existence of an incidental issue; this is simply an instance where one reaches the boundaries of the model[812] developed here.

2.5.3. *Similar Phenomena*[813]

Preliminary Question (in the Strict Sense)

Quite a few scholars (not only) in the German-speaking world of private international law distinguish the incidental question from the "primary incidental question" ("Erstfrage").[814] Pursuant to the terminological considerations above, one would also be justified in calling *this* question "preliminary": it concerns a legal concept presupposed by an internal *conflicts* rule.[815] One might say that such a question must be resolved (even) "before" the law applicable to the main question is determined. As there is no *lex causae* "yet", the solution

---

353, 360 (who does explain his position); presumably (*a contrario*) also *Mosconi/Campiglio*, DIPP, III 19 (200).

810 Also *infra* section 2.9.3.4. in the context of overriding mandatory provisions.

811 *Mäsch*, in: Leible (ed.), General Principles, §6.02; *Schurig*, in: FS Kegel, 549, 563–564.

812 *Supra* section 1.2.

813 As to the relationship of the incidental question with the issue of substitution, *infra* section 5.7.

814 For the translation see *Wendehorst*, in: Verschraegen (ed.), Austrian Law, 79, 100; for the distinction in Dutch law see *Vonken*, Algemeen deel IPR, at 456.

815 The term "Erstfrage" was coined by *Jochem*, FamRZ 1964, 392, 393, in order to distinguish it from questions only arising as part of a substantive provision of the governing law.

for the preliminary question in this sense can only be the application of the conflicts rules of the legal system of the *lex fori*.[816] (A special treatment of the preliminary question of nationality is nevertheless widely accepted.[817]) Others maintain that the term is merely an *ignis fatuus*.[818] A general provision on how to deal with preliminary questions in this sense does not exist in the EU; occasionally, however, there are rules on how to approach particular preliminary questions like nationality.[819]

Collateral Question

More commonly accepted is the distinction between the incidental question and the "collateral question" ("Teilfrage", literally: "partial question"), although some only seem to use the second term when there is a special conflicts rule for the collateral question.[820] A collateral question is one that cannot arise independently from another (main) question.[821] While, in the examples given above, "property" and "marriage" are incidental questions because they could be main questions as well, questions such as capacity or form can only arise in connection with another issue. While the collateral question is more similar to the incidental question than is often acknowledged, there appears to be broad consensus that it does not raise the same problem. (Of course, many of those who would resolve incidental questions by resorting to the conflicts rules of the *lex fori* would say that the incidental question does not actually raise any problem either.) If there is a special internal conflicts rule for the collateral question, it applies; if not, the *lex causae* does.[822]

2.5.4. Member States

There may not be a European discussion of the incidental question (yet), in the sense of scholars from different member states examining the incidental question from a European point of view.[823] Despite its German origins, however,

---

816 *Lurger/Melcher*, IPR, at 1/91; *Wendehorst*, in: Verschraegen (ed.), Austrian Law, 79, 100 (note 106); *Kropholler*, IPR, §32 III (223–224); *von Bar/Mankowski*, IPR I, §7 at 186.

817 See *infra* section 4.4.1.1.

818 *F. Sturm/G. Sturm*, in: Staudinger, Einl. zum IPR at 290; *Verschraegen*, IPR, at 1211; *Bernitt*, Die Anknüpfung von Vorfragen, 17.

819 See *infra* section 4.4.2.2.

820 *von Bar/Mankowski*, IPR I, §7 at 185.

821 *von Hein*, in: MüKoBGB, Einl. IPR at 103; *Bernitt*, Die Anknüpfung von Vorfragen, 11.

822 See *infra* section 2.6. (The Collateral Question *de Lege Lata*).

823 *Mäsch*, in: Leible (ed.), General Principles, §6.01; looking at the authors cited *infra* (footnotes 836–856), it is hard to escape this conclusion.

it does appear in doctrinal writings on domestic private international law all over the EU, typically as a question of relevance independent from any particular conflicts rule.[824] Its origins are often mentioned,[825] but far from consistently. This suggests that the issue has been recognised in other countries to be relevant on its own,[826] instead of by being an idea only pursued elsewhere.

General legislative solutions for the incidental question are rare. It did appear on the agenda during, or in light of, the process of (re-)codification of private international law in some member states,[827] but it usually did not crystallise into a general provision. Of the four domestic private international law codes that entered into force in the EU in the 2010s, however, two now expressly deal with the incidental question in a provision among the general ones.

---

824 Austria: *Verschraegen*, IPR, at 1210–1214; *Lurger/Melcher*, IPR, at 1/89–1/99. Belgium: *Rigaux/Fallon*, DIP, at 6.29–6.37. France: *Ancel*, Éléments d'histoire du droit international privé, 554; *Audit/d'Avout*, DIP, at 316–317; *Cachard*, DIP, at 594–599; *Loussouarn/Bourel/de Vareilles-Sommières*, DIP, at 281–282; *Mayer/Heuzé*, DIP, at 272. Notably, *Azzi/Boskovic* apparently considered the topic to be of sufficient relevance to include it in their volume on the general theory of private international law even though they made the conscious choice to exclude certain other topics, see in: iidem (eds.), Quel avenir pour la théorie générale des conflits de lois?, 1, 3. Germany: *Kropholler*, IPR, §32 (221–230); *Kegel/Schurig*, IPR, §9 (371–386); *von Bar/Mankowski*, IPR I, §7 III (at 182–213). Greece: *Meidanis*, in: Vrellis (ed.), PIL in Greece, at 61–64 ("an important issue in Greek private international law"). Hungary: *Raffai/Szabó*, Acta Juridica Hungarica 51 (2010), 136, 154. Italy: *T. Ballarino/E. Ballarino/Pretelli*, DIP, IV 4 (99–101); *Mosconi/Campiglio*, DIPP, III 19 (200–203). The Netherlands (before Article 10:4 Dutch Civil Code came into existence): *Strikwerda*, Inleiding, 2 F; *van Hoogstraten*, NILR 9 (1962), 209–225. Poland: *Mączyński*, Yearbook of Private International Law 6 (2004), 203, 210 ("such [incidental] questions are dealt with thoroughly in doctrinal studies"); see also the references listed by *Ernst*, RabelsZ 76 (2012), 598, 612. Portugal: *de Lima Pinheiro*, DIP I, 608–619. Spain: *Calvo Caravaca/Carrascosa González*, DIP I, 481–486; *Garcimartín Alférez*, DIP, at 21.6. Sweden: *Bogdan*, PIL in Sweden, at 66–70. For Scandinavian law in general: *Schmidt*, Sc. St. L. 12 (1968), 93–113. Common Law: *Cheshire/North/Fawcett*, PIL, 51–54; *Beaumont/McEleavy*, Anton's PIL, at 4.71–4.79; *Dicey/Morris/Collins*, Conflict of Laws, at 2-048–2-067; *Briggs*, PIL in the English Courts, at 3.80–3.83 (= *id.*, Conflict of Laws, 25–27); *Hill/Ní Shúilleabháin*, Clarkson & Hill's Conflict of Laws, at 1.131–1.137; *Rogerson*, Collier's Conflict of Laws, 277–280.

825 See e.g. *Calvo Caravaca/Carrascosa González*, DIP I, 481; *Ancel*, Éléments d'histoire du droit international privé, 554; *Loussouarn/Bourel/de Vareilles-Sommières*, DIP, at 281; *Sana-Chaillé de Néré*, in: Azzi/Boskovic (eds.), Quel avenir pour la théorie générale des conflits de lois?, 123; *Vonken*, Algemeen deel IPR, at 453; *Beaumont/McEleavy*, Anton's PIL, at 4.71 (note 110); *Rigaux/Fallon*, DIP, at 6.29.

826 Even though it is forty years old, the comparative list of writers and cases dealing with the incidental question assembled by *Gotlieb* does not fail to impress, ICLQ 26 (1977), 734, in particular 753–754 and 761–779.

827 See *Ernst*, RabelsZ 76 (2012), 598, 612; *Zidarova/Stančeva-Minčeva*, RabelsZ 71 (2007), 398, 412; *Pocar*, IPRax 1997, 145, 150; *Stoll*, IPRax 1984, 1, 5, and BT-Drucks. 10/504, 32.

Article 10:4 Dutch Civil Code broke ground.[828] Soon after, the arguably less jumbled §22 Czech PIL Act followed suit. (While the exact *content* of general provisions is beyond the scope of this book, it may be of interest that both provisions opt for the solution *independent* from the conflicts rules of the *lex causae*.[829])

2.5.5. *European Union*

2.5.5.1. Terminological Confusion

While the "incidental question" only appears in a procedural context in the EU private international law regulations,[830] several of their recitals contain the term "preliminary question". Recital 10(3) Rome III refers to "preliminary questions such as legal capacity and the validity of the marriage". Recital 41 Succession Regulation refers to "the determination of the nationality or the multiple nationalities of a person [...] as a preliminary question". The M-Property Regulation and the RP-Property Regulation each contain a counterpart of the former recital.[831] The EU legislator thus seems to have a rather wide understanding of "preliminary" questions, encompassing preliminary (marriage, nationality), as well as collateral questions (capacity),[832] while not exactly addressing incidental questions as of yet.

But serious doubts arise as to whether one is to accord any weight to this terminology. Recital 50 M-Property Regulation and Recital 49 RP-Property Regulation identify the question of "how to consider a person having multiple nationalities" as a "preliminary question". Under no traditional definition of "preliminary" or "incidental" does this issue constitute such a question. Furthermore, the terminology of Rome III is itself much less obvious in other languages. One does come across "Vorfragen", "questions préalables", and "questioni preliminari", but also "cuestiones prejudiciales" (instead of "previas") and "prealabele zaken" (instead of "voorvraagen"). The ground becomes even shakier in the Succession Regulation: "question préliminaire"

---

828 The Dutch legislator was aware that it was about to make a virtually unprecedented rule, but stated that legal certainty was a good reason to do so: Kamerstukken II 2009/2010, 32317, No. 3, 12. See also *Struycken*, RabelsZ 78 (2014), 592, 608 ("bold general provision [...] which has no parallel in other codifications" – at the time that article was published, however, there did exist a "parallel" in §22 Czech PIL Act).

829 See *Struycken*, RabelsZ 78 (2014), 592, 608; *Rammeloo*, EuLF 2010, I-180, I-185; *Dobiáš*, Riv. dir. int. priv. proc. 2015, 109, 117; *Bohata*, WiRO 2012, 193, 196.

830 Articles 39(3), 59(4) Succession Regulation, Articles 36(3), 58(4) M-/RP-Property Regulation: recognition and acceptance.

831 Recital 21 M-Property Regulation, Recital 21 RP-Property Regulation.

832 Recital 21 M-/RP-Property Regulation confirms this when it refers to "*other* preliminary questions" (emphasis added) than that in the preceding recital, i.e. capacity.

(instead of "préalable"), "cuestión preliminar" (instead of "previa"), "preliminaire vraag" (instead of "voorvraag"); the German and Italian versions lack a noun as *terminus technicus* altogether, certain matters simply "have to be dealt with in advance" ("vorab geklärt werden", "risolvere in via preliminare"). As the examples show, terminology in the two regulations is not even uniform within the same language. In sum, there is no consistent vernacular yet at the EU level.

2.5.5.2. A Uniform Solution Through Interpretation?

Even in absence of uniform terminology, is there perhaps a uniform solution? To begin with, no express provision on the incidental question exists in EU private international law. In the Succession and Wills Green Paper, the Commission had seemed inclined to draft such a rule,[833] as it had asked "what" conflicts provision should be adopted for "preliminary" questions instead of *whether* such a rule should be adopted. In the end, the provisions of the Succession Regulation are as silent as the ones in Rome I through III.

Turning to interpretation, it is important to keep in mind the two dimensions of the incidental question at the EU level.[834] First, does EU law itself provide an answer or does it leave the entire issue to domestic law? Second, if EU law provides an answer, what is it? The difficulty in distinguishing these two levels lies in the insight that the reply to either question can lead to the private international law of the forum. Either EU law leaves *the entire topic* to the forum's private international law (which now can decide whether to directly determine the applicable law to the incidental question or do so by way of foreign private international law), or it only leaves *the determination of the applicable law* to the forum's private international law (i.e. without allowing it to rely on foreign private international law).

The Four Most Recent Regulations in Particular

As already shown, there are at least some textual indications, albeit inconsistently formulated, in the four most recent regulations. Recital 10(3) Rome III sets forth that "preliminary questions such as legal capacity and the validity of the marriage [...] should be determined by the conflict-of-laws rules applicable in the participating Member State concerned". Recital 21 M-/RP-Property Regulation states that (all?) "other preliminary questions [...] continue to be covered by the national law of the Member States, including

---

[833] COM(2005) 65 final, 8 (question 13 – contrast, e.g., with questions 11 and 12 on the same page; its understanding of preliminary questions also clearly was not limited to nationality, see *infra* at footnote 841); see *Bernitt*, Die Anknüpfung von Vorfragen, 5; *Heinze*, in: FS Kropholler, 105, 113.

[834] *Heinze*, in: FS Kropholler, 105, 112.

their rules of private international law". Both could be statements regarding the first dimension of the problem. They would then have to be read as: "Each member state itself decides ("by", i.e. pursuant to, its conflicts rules) how to deal with incidental questions".[835] But they could also be statements regarding the second dimension: "EU private international law mandates that the conflicts rules of the forum – and not of the legal system of the *lex causae* – apply in order to determine the law applicable to incidental questions".

The reference solely to rules of member states is inconclusive. While it clearly does not *mandate* a solution pursuant to *lex causae* conflicts rules (as the applicable law could be that of a third state[836]), it could still leave the question of whether or not to rely on the *lex causae* to the member states, i.e. to their "conflict-of-laws rules". If one reads the reference to "conflict-of-laws rules" to mean *statutory* rules, however, it is more reasonable to consider it a rule under which the conflicts rules of the forum determine the applicable law to incidental questions,[837] as there are almost no statutory rules on how to deal with incidental questions in general in the member states.

Recital 41 Succession Regulation exclusively deals with the "preliminary question" of nationality. For this reason alone, it is far from an ideal basis for a general answer for incidental questions in the context of successions. As the Green Paper had already exemplified "preliminary questions" as "validity of a marriage or partnership, establishment of paternity, etc.",[838] it is hard to see why the Succession Regulation should not contain similar examples (also similar to Recital 10(3) Rome III and Recital 21 M-/RP-Property Regulation) if a statement of a broader scope had been intended. Finally, the wording of these recitals essentially suffers from the same ambiguity as Recitals 10(3) Rome III and 21 M-/RP-Property Regulation: it is not obvious whether they provide no answer of their own, or whether they provide the answer that only the law of a certain state applies.

European Union Private International Law in General[839]

As not even the regulations that expressly mention "preliminary questions" yield a clear indication of how to approach incidental questions within

---

835 To this effect e.g. *Gruber*, IPRax 2012, 381, 389; apparently also (because of her reference to *Gruber*) *Lein*, in: Calliess (ed.), Rome Regulations, Art. 8 Rome III at 20.

836 Article 4 Rome III, Article 20 M-/RP-Property Regulation.

837 *von Hein*, in: MüKoBGB, Einl. IPR at 155.

838 COM(2005) 65 final, 8.

839 Also see *Álvarez González*, REDI 69 (2017), 19; *Weller*, in: id. (ed.), Europäisches Kollisionsrecht, at 75–87; *Sana-Chaillé de Néré*, in: Azzi/Boskovic (eds.), Quel avenir pour la théorie générale des conflits de lois?, 123, 133–138.

their context,[840] a general solution for each regulation, or even for EU private international law as a whole, can only be found through purposive interpretation, if at all. Yet this means that close to a century's worth of highly specialised discussion is (back) on the table.[841] In the course of this broad analysis, it remains for some base lines to be established.

First, in light of the goal of uniform conflicts provisions,[842] it is hard to imagine that the entire topic of incidental questions has been left to the member states. Member state A could apply its own conflicts rules to determine the law applicable to an incidental question, while member state B could apply the *lex causae* conflicts rules, even though both apply EU private international law as regards the main question. Despite harmonised conflicts rules for the main question, a given case might come out differently depending on the forum. In order to avoid such a situation, EU private international law must be understood in order to give an answer as to whose conflicts rules are decisive.[843]

Second, as far as an EU conflicts rule exists for a particular incidental question, the default solution will lie in its application. Where the *lex causae* is the law of a (participating) member state, this would be the outcome anyway:[844] even if one relied on the *lex causae* conflicts rules, these would be the EU rules again. Where the *lex causae* is that of a third state, predictability and legal certainty also suggest the application of EU law, as opposed to third state private international law.[845] Moreover, the far-reaching exclusion of *renvoi* in EU private international law[846] can be regarded as a statement against the reliance on third state private international law.[847]

Third, where there is no EU conflicts rule for a particular incidental question yet, it might seem that application of the conflicts rules of the *lex causae* is the most appropriate solution. All member states would apply the same conflicts rules for the main question (i.e. EU rules), and all of them would apply the same conflicts rules for the incidental question (i.e. *lex causae* rules).[848]

840 To this effect also *Sinay-Cytermann*, in: Azzi/Boskovic (eds.), Quel avenir pour la théorie générale des conflits de lois?, 83, 87.

841 See *Solomon*, in: FS Spellenberg, 355, 369, who contends that nothing in EU private international law (as it stood in 2010) implies a different treatment of incidental questions than in domestic law.

842 See already *supra* sections 2.1.2.2. (The Goal of Supranational Harmonisation) and 2.4. (European Union: The European Dimension of Characterisation).

843 *Heinze*, in: FS Kropholler, 105, 113; *Sonnenberger*, in: FS Kropholler, 227, 241.

844 This is why ECJ Case C-191/15, Verein für Konsumenteninformation v Amazon EU Sàrl, ECLI:EU:C:2016:612, is inconclusive for the present issue; see *Wilke*, GPR 2017, 21, 23.

845 *Heinze*, in: FS Kropholler, 105, 114.

846 See also *infra* section 5.5.4. (General Exclusion of *Renvoi*).

847 *Gössl*, Journal of Private International Law 8 (2012), 63, 75; *Bernitt*, Die Anknüpfung von Vorfragen, 131–133.

848 See *Kropholler*, §32 VI (229–230). Ultimately, however, he also considers the conflicts rules of the *lex fori* to be the default approach.

To apply *lex fori* conflicts rules could lead to non-uniform outcomes. Even so, the interests of predictability, as well as legal certainty, and the prospect of the *lex fori* approach one day prevailing in most instances in any case (because of the ongoing harmonisation of EU private international law), can be regarded as sufficient counterweights.[849] Additionally, the harmonisation of private international law, be it in conventions or in EU law instruments, is limited to its respective scope. To the extent of the limitation – in the present context: to the extent of incidental questions of a non-harmonised area – international decisional harmony is no objective of the given instrument.[850] Remember that one would need to *develop* a separate conflicts rule leading to foreign private international law if one wanted to apply the *lex causae* conflicts rules to the incidental question.[851] Because of the limited scope, there is simply no room for such an additional rule.

In conclusion, it is justifiable to consider the determination of the law to be applicable to incidental questions by conflicts rules of the *lex fori* as the default solution of EU private international law.[852] Without further analysis, however, it cannot be excluded that certain questions or contexts require an exception.[853]

2.6. THE COLLATERAL QUESTION

As already described,[854] the collateral and the incidental questions have in common that they arise in connection with another question, the main question. Yet unlike the incidental question, the collateral question *only* arises in connection with another issue. If there is no separate internal conflicts provision whose subject matter covers the collateral question, the issue is whether the governing law for the collateral question is to be determined via the conflicts rule for the main question; if there is a separate provision, does it

849 *Gössl*, Journal of Private International Law 8 (2012), 63, 69–71; with the same result *Heinze*, in: FS Kropholler, 105, 114–115; *Dörner*, in: HK-BGB, Vorbemerkung zu Artikel 3–6 EGBGB at 25.

850 *Gössl*, Journal of Private International Law 8 (2012), 63, 73; *Solomon*, in: FS Spellenberg, 355, 368; *Heinze*, in: FS Kropholler, 105, 114; *von Bar/Mankowski*, IPR I, §7 at 208.

851 *Supra* section 2.5.2.

852 This also seems to be in line with at least a majority position in domestic law, *Mäsch*, in: Leible (ed.), General Principles, §6.01; also see the comparative overview by *F. Sturm/G. Sturm*, in: Staudinger, Einl. zum IPR at 292, and *supra* section 2.5.4.

853 The Succession Regulation has become the focus of much debate in this regard. See *von Hein*, in: MüKoBGB, Einl. IPR at 188 (for the default rule); *Dutta*, in: MüKoBGB, vor Art. 20 EuErbVO at 50–53 (for the conflicts rules of the *lex causae*) – both with many further references.

854 *Supra* section 2.5.3. (Collateral Question).

(have to) apply? As the scope and relation of subject matters is again concerned, the topic is most appropriately discussed in this context. It is not limited to any particular area of private international law and is thus formally general in the strict sense.

The Collateral Question *de Lege Lata*

There appears to be consensus that the *lex causae* is applicable to collateral questions unless a special conflicts rule of the *lex fori* says otherwise.[855] If there is such a rule, a (not often mentioned[856]) structural similarity to the incidental question exists: the relationship of two internal conflicts rules is now at issue. Nevertheless, and unlike for the incidental question, it would not make any sense at all to consider whether or not to apply the internal conflicts rule. A conflicts rule for an issue that can be a main question would remain relevant even if one were to rely on foreign conflicts rules where that issue arises incidentally. The rule would be relevant when the issue arises as the main question. To disregard the conflicts rule for a collateral question that can never be the main question, however, would implicate an extreme reduction of its relevance: it could only apply when the *lex fori* is also the *lex causae*. Such an interpretation of conflicts rules for collateral questions is generally unreasonable.[857] On the contrary, *lex fori* conflicts rules for collateral questions are always to be applied.[858]

A general provision to this effect does not exist in domestic or EU private international law. Both the EU and its member states, however, have enacted conflicts rules for certain collateral questions, in particular for form, capacity, and prescription. As these issues in particular can arise in more than one area of private law, they can also be regarded as formally general.[859] In domestic law, some of these provisions can indeed be found among the general ones.[860]

855 Also see *Weller*, in: id. (ed.), Europäisches Kollisionsrecht, at 66.

856 But see *Bernitt*, Die Anknüpfung von Vorfragen, 11.

857 *Bernitt*, Die Anknüpfung von Vorfragen, 12.

858 *F. Sturm/G. Sturm*, in: Staudinger, Einl. zum IPR at 291; *Verschraegen*, IPR, at 1215; *Kropholler*, IPR, §32 II (222).

859 *Infra* section 6.

860 Form: §8 Austrian PIL Act; Article 7 Croatian PIL Act; §8 Estonian PIL Act; Article 10:12 Dutch Civil Code; Article 7 Slovenian PIL Act. See also the special case of Article 4(4) Polish PIL Act on the interplay of formal requirements and party autonomy. Section 21 Latvian Civil Code constitutes a borderline case as it is located right in the middle (remember: no formal separation between general and special provisions in the introduction to the Latvian Civil Code) of provisions one could call special and others one could call general, such as on the ascertainment of foreign law, *renvoi* etc. Capacity: Article 11 Dutch Civil Code. Many other codes deal with questions of capacity immediately *after* the general provisions in a part concerning personal issues, e.g. §10 Hungarian PIL Code 1979, Article 1.15–16 Lithuanian Civil Code, Article 11 Polish PIL Act, Article 25 Portuguese Civil Code, Article 2.572 Romanian Civil Code. Prescription: Article 8 Croatian PIL Act; Article 10:14 Dutch Civil Code; Article 8 Slovenian PIL Act.

In the "Common Rules" of Rome II, there are Article 15(h) (*lex causae* governs issues of prescription) and Article 21 (formal validity of certain unilateral acts). Similar provisions exist in the other regulations, but these are not located in a separate section.[861] There is a conceptual overlap with the topic of characterisation:[862] if the conflicts rules of the forum determine that the *lex causae* governs certain (collateral) questions, it can be considered to be both a rule on the particular collateral question and an express characterisation decision.

2.7. ADDENDUM: *DÉPEÇAGE*

In a broad sense, the phenomenon of *dépeçage* refers to the application of the law of different legal systems to parts/aspects/questions/issues of the same cause of action.[863] This can happen for several reasons. There may be several subject matters (with differing connecting factors) within the same general field. European scholars seem hesitant to call such a (legislative) fragmentation of conflicts rules a genuine *dépeçage*, however.[864] As typically one rule will be more specific than the others *from the same field* of private international law and will thus prevail, it is indeed not immediately obvious that a differentiation of subject matters will lead to the application of several laws to one and the same cause of action.[865] Yet when the cause of action implies an incidental question and one considers the *lex fori* approach correct, different conflicts rules of the forum, even from different areas of private international law, apply at the same time. If it now leads to more than one applicable law, this scenario meets the broad definition of *dépeçage*. The application of more than one law to one cause of action can also occur – and this is where the present and the prior issue connect – when there are special conflicts provisions for certain, typically traditional collateral questions:[866] form, capacity, prescription.

---

861 E.g. Articles 11 and 12(1)(d) Rome I, Article 7 Rome III, Articles 12(2)(c), 27 Succession Regulation, 25 M-/RP-Property Regulation.

862 See already *supra* section 2.4. (European Union: Characterisation *de Lege Europaea Lata*).

863 *Symeonides*, Codifying Choice of Law, 221; *Siehr*, Yearbook of Private International Law VII (2005), 17, 37. For a detailed analysis of many, if not all, phenomena that one might consider under the heading of *dépeçage*, see *Aubart*, Die Behandlung der *dépeçage*, 5–27.

864 *Erauw/Fallon*, in: Dirix/Lelen (eds.), The Belgian Reports, 227, 250 ("substitute for *dépeçage*"); *Mankowski*, in: Basedow/Kischel/Sieber (eds.), German National Reports, 133, 138; *Boele-Woelki/van Iterson*, in: van Erp/van Vliet (eds.), Netherlands Report, 145, 160; differently *Remy*, R.I.D.C. 2010, 291, 302 (legislative *dépeçage* as "*dépeçage* naturel").

865 Under Rome I, e.g., a cause of action *either* is one of a consumer contract *or* one of an insurance contract *or* one of an employment contract etc., but never one of all of the foregoing.

866 For such an understanding of *dépeçage* e.g. *Aubart*, Die Behandlung der *dépeçage*, 12; *Siehr*, Yearbook of Private International Law VII (2005), 17, 37–38; *Burián*, in: Symeonides (ed.),

(If these provisions only determine/clarify that the *lex causae* applies, no *dépeçage* occurs, of course.) Furthermore, there may be a rule of private international law that allows the application of a different law for a *part* of the subject matter, or that allows the parties themselves to make a partial choice of law. This final category is the most narrow definition of *dépeçage*: more than one applicable law for one "general" subject matter.[867]

Dépeçage de Lege Lata

There is no general rule on *dépeçage* as such in domestic or EU private international law. But its non-existence does not come as a big surprise. The relationship of several conflicts rules is an issue of specificity, of overriding mandatory provisions, of the incidental question, or of collateral questions.[868] If a judge is allowed to treat a part of a cause of action differently from the rest, this would (likely) be a case of a partial "escape clause" such as Article 4(1) clause 2 Rome Convention. If the parties are allowed to choose the law for parts of the respective subject matter, this will be due to a rule allowing for party autonomy; some do allow a partial choice (see Article 3(1) clause 3 Rome I[869]), but others do not (see Article 22(1) clause 1 Succession Regulation). Maybe the law applicable to a given subject matter consists in part in the law chosen by the parties and in part in mandatory provisions of another law that the parties could not deselect.[870]

In all of these situations, *dépeçage* is only the *result* of the application of – written or unwritten, general or specific – conflicts rules. To this extent, there is no room for a general rule on *dépeçage*.[871] All it could say is that the application of more than one law to one cause of action is possible where so provided by law: a matter of course. The need for a rule that itself mandates or allows for

PIL at the End of the 20th Century, 263, 276; apparently also *Liukkunen*, Recent PIL Codifications, 9.

867 To this effect *Mankowski*, in: Basedow/Kischel/Sieber (eds.), German National Reports, 133, 138.

868 See *infra* sections 2.8. and 2.9. as to the former two, *supra* sections 2.5. and 2.6. as to the latter two.

869 The wording only refers to (one) "part" (with the consequence that the rest would be governed by the law applicable in absence of a choice), but everybody seems to assume that the provision also allows the parties to choose the law for more than one part, see only *Martiny*, in: MüKoBGB, Art. 3 Rom I-VO at 72. In such a case, one might say that the parties make use of Article 3(1) clause 3 Rome I more than once.

870 See Article 3(3) Rome I.

871 For a similar position see *Dolinger*, in: Essays in Honor of Juenger, 23, 37 ("I would not include *dépeçage* among the basic principles of conflicts law, because [...] it simply tells us that different rules can be implemented concomitantly and harmoniously regarding one single legal relationship", italics in the original).

the application of more than one law to one cause of action in general, but that does not fit into any of the aforementioned categories, is not apparent.

2.8. SPECIFIC CONFLICTS RULES

Just like all other kinds of legal rules, conflicts rules can be organised in accordance with their degree of specificity. A more specific rule has all the requirements of a more general rule, but with at least one more in addition. For example, a rule concerning contracts for the sale of goods by auction is more specific than a rule only concerning contracts for the sale of goods. Accordingly, Article 4(1)(g) Rome I is more specific than Article 4(1)(a) Rome I.[872]

When the requirements of a more specific rule are met, *ex hypothesi* the requirements of the more general rule are also met. Typically, however, both rules cannot apply at once. It is up to each legal system to decide which rule prevails, although one can suspect that the more specific rule will usually prevail. As the subject matter is the element of a conflicts rule in which its requirements are set forth, the issue of the relationship of more specific conflicts rules with more general ones is appropriately discussed here.

Member States

The sections of general provisions in domestic private international law codes do not contain any rules on the relationship of *lex fori* conflicts rules with diverging degrees of specificity. The existence of such a rule, e.g. setting forth the principle of *lex specialis derogat legi generali* in a private international law code would be rather surprising. It is unlikely that any country would provide for a different solution in its private international law than it does in its other areas of law. If at all, then, one would look for such a rule in codes of substantive law, but even here one generally searches in vain. At issue is a question of often non-codified legal method.

Conflicts rules of *foreign* legal systems that are seemingly more specific than a conflicts rule of the *lex fori* typically cause no problem. Usually, courts only apply their own conflicts rules; foreign conflicts rules are not applied nor even taken account of. The case of *renvoi* is no exception. To be sure, foreign conflicts rules can be applied in its context – but only those of the governing law, i.e. *after* the conflicts rule of the *lex fori* has determined the governing law. Hence, the foreign conflicts rule does not apply because it is more specific than the one found in the private international law of the *lex fori*, but because the

---

872 *Gebauer*, in: Calliess (ed.), Rome Regulations, Art. 4 at 30.

latter allows the former to be applicable. It would be inadequate to frame their relationship in terms of "general vs. specific".[873]

European Union

A general statement on the relationship of more specific EU conflicts rules with more general ones is also missing from EU private international law. Occasionally, however, individual provisions themselves identify other provisions that would, if applicable, prevail over them. Examples can be found in Article 4(1) Rome I ("without prejudice to Articles 5 to 8")[874] and Article 5(1) Rome II ("[w]ithout prejudice to Article 4(2)"). One can also consider Article 4 Rome II as the general provision and Articles 5 through 9 Rome II as the specific ones in the tort context.[875]

2.9. SPECIAL CONFLICTS RULES: OVERRIDING MANDATORY PROVISIONS

The phenomenon of overriding mandatory provisions has been the "favourite pastime of academic discussion ever since the 1980s".[876] They go by many names such as (literal translations into other languages omitted): "lois d'application immédiate, norme di applicazione necessaria, Exklusiv- [or] Eingriffsnormen, mandatory [sic] rules, rechtstreeks toepasselijke regels";[877] "règle[s] internationalement impérative[s]", "loi[s] de police";[878] "peremptory rules";[879] "interventionist norms";[880] "derogatory, hyper-mandatory rules".[881] As "Gesetze von streng positiver, zwingender Natur" they already appear in von Savigny's work.[882] While some call into question that all these terms

---

873 *Among* the *foreign* conflicts rules, once they are to be applied because of the admission of *renvoi*, the question of one rule perhaps being more specific than another can arise again. Yet this obviously is no instance of a foreign rule being more specific than a domestic rule, either.

874 Expressly *Martiny*, in: MüKoBGB, Art. 4 Rom I-VO at 3 ("leges speciales"); *Briggs*, Conflict of Laws, 243 ("special legislative provision is made" for certain contracts).

875 *de Lima Pinheiro*, Riv. dir. int. priv. proc. 2008, 5, 15.

876 *Mankowski*, in: Basedow/Kischel/Sieber (eds.), German National Reports, 133, 146 (note with many further references omitted); similarly *Roth*, in: FS Dauses, 315–316; *Remien*, in: FS von Hoffmann, 334; see also *Symeonides*, Codifying Choice of Law, 303–304 (note 61); *Vassilakakis*, RHDI 63 (2010), 103, 106 (for Greece specifically).

877 *Siehr*, in: FS Drobnig, 443, 447–448.

878 *Remy*, R.I.D.C. 2010, 291, 305.

879 *Wendehorst*, in: Verschraegen (ed.), Austrian Law, 79, 90 (as a translation of the German "Eingriffsnormen").

880 *Schurig*, RabelsZ 54 (1990), 217, 249 (as a translation of the German "Eingriffsnormen").

881 *Muir-Watt*, Transnational Legal Theory 2 (2011), 347, 415.

882 *von Savigny*, System VIII, 33.

really mean one and the same thing,[883] others maintain that they do.[884] It seems, however, that the *issue* that private international law faces is always the same.[885] Since this book concerns issues, it is preferable to ignore any distinctions based on the particular features of different rules[886] raising the same issue.[887]

The issue of overriding mandatory provisions concerns rules that are intended to apply regardless of the otherwise applicable law. On the face of it, this appears to be a question of substantive law, "apply regardless of the otherwise applicable law" seemingly clearly referring to the governing law. Yet such an assumption would seriously obstruct one's understanding. It is important to keep in mind at this point that rules of substantive law by definition contain no statement as to their applicability. "They are simply neutral; the answer is not in them. Generally, therefore, what is needed [...] is not an interpretation of the [substantive] statute *but a rule of private international law* to accompany and delimit the rule of private law".[888]

As the application of any rule of substantive law requires a prior determination at the conflicts level,[889] the application of a substantive rule *intended* to apply regardless of the otherwise applicable law presupposes a conflicts decision as well.[890] This realisation at least goes back to von Savigny.[891]

---

883 See e.g. *Remy*, R.I.D.C. 2010, 291, 305; *Mankowski*, in: LA Schurig, 159, 163–165; *Esplugues Mota/Azcárraga Monzonís*, Spanish Report, 17–19.

884 *Kühne*, in: LA Schurig, 129, 140 (e.g. "selbstgerechte" or "autolimitierte Sachnormen" as only a predecessor of the idea of overriding mandatory provisions); *Bonomi*, in: Baratta (ed.), DIP, s. v. "Norme di applicazione necessaria", 233 (*lois de police* and *lois d'application immédiate* as the predecessors of overriding mandatory provisions); *van Calster*, European PIL, 3.2.8.3; *Rühl*, in: Max Planck Encyclopedia of European Private Law, s. v. "Unilateralism", 1735, 1737; *Bonomi*, Yearbook of Private International Law I (1999), 215, 218–219.

885 Also see *Michaels*, in: LA Schurig, 191, 192, as to one of *Schurig's* contributions to the topic: demonstrating that there is one underlying concept.

886 See e.g. *Köhler*, Eingriffsnormen, 11, who considers auto-limited rules and/or *lois d'application immédiate* as overriding mandatory rules in a formal sense and distinguishes them from overriding mandatory rules in a substantive sense. *Both*, however, are overriding mandatory provisions.

887 Yet to the extent that the term "lois d'application immédiate" is meant to refer to *substantively* self-limiting rules, i.e. substantive rules that require and indeed presuppose that a conflicts rule determines their application but then themselves contain some spatial limitation (*Kahn-Freund*, General Problems, 93–97; also see *Dicey/Morris/Collins*, Conflict of Laws, at 1-049–1-052, clearly distinguishing this type of rule from "lois d'application immédiate", at 1-054), the respective rules indeed can be excluded from the present discussion. They are a mere matter of substantive law. But see *Garcimartín Alférez*, DIP, at 20.15, who considers "normas materiales autolimitadas" unilateral (conflict of laws) rules.

888 *Rabel*, The Conflict of Laws I, 103 (emphasis added).

889 *Supra* section 2.2.1.

890 *Mansel*, in: FS Roth, 375, 376; *Köhler*, Eingriffsnormen, 11; *Kropholler*, IPR, §13 V (109); *von Bar/Mankowski*, IPR I, §4 at 12.

891 *von Savigny*, System VIII, 34–35.

This is why the term "règle d'application immédiate" is rather problematic. It suggests that a substantive rule applies "immediately", i.e. without a decision at the conflicts level.[892] But, of course, the decision *that* a particular rule applies, and not the rule of another legal system, *is* a conflicts decision, albeit perhaps one not always made consciously. Franceskakis, the originator of the term "règle d'application immédiate",[893] occasionally seems to say so himself,[894] even though elsewhere he seems to claim just the opposite.[895] The Commission also might have had substantive rules in mind that somehow apply by themselves.[896] But the EU legislator appears to have become aware of at least some connection to conflicts rules since then, otherwise it would not have needed to specify in Recital 54 clause 4 Succession Regulation that certain *conflicts* rules cannot be considered overriding mandatory provisions.[897]

It follows that the issue of overriding mandatory provisions must first and foremost be framed in terms of private international law, not in the categories of substantive law. So what happens at the conflicts level when a rule is intended to apply regardless of the otherwise applicable law? This can only mean that the substantive rule in question is accompanied by a (perhaps unwritten) conflicts rule (a) mandating that the former be applied and (b) that is intended to take precedence over any other conflicts rule. "Overriding" serves as shorthand for "associated with a particular conflicts decision intended to always prevail". Typically, then, this conflicts rule will be both limited and unilateral:[898] it will only determine when one particular substantive rule is applicable, and this substantive rule will be one from the same legal system as the conflicts rule. But it does not have to be either.

---

892 See e.g. *Symeonides*, Codifying Choice of Law, 299 (overriding mandatory provisions apply "regardless of whether a choice-of-law rule authorizes their application") and 301 (an overriding mandatory provision applies "without considering whether such a rule is made applicable by a choice-of-law rule"); *Cachard*, DIP, at 326 and passim; *Audit/d'Avout*, DIP, at 176 (application "indépendamment de sa désignation par une règle de conflit").

893 *Francescakis*, La théorie du renvoi, 11.

894 *Franceskakis*, Rev. crit. DIP 1966, 1, 9; *id.*, La théorie du renvoi, 19.

895 *Franceskakis*, Riv. dir. int. priv. proc. 1967, 691, 695; *id.*, Rev. crit. DIP 1966, 1, 3 (as a description of how French courts proceeded). As to these seemingly contradictory statements *Köhler*, Eingriffsnormen, 7–8, with further references; *Schurig*, Kollisionsnorm und Sachrecht, 319 (note 211).

896 Rome I Green Paper, COM(2002) 654 final, 45 ("Unlike the mechanism of the international public-policy [sic] exception, the court does not look to its conflict rules to ascertain the applicable law and evaluate whether its content may be incompatible with the system of values of the forum but automatically applies its own rules.").

897 As to Article 30 Succession Regulation concerning overriding mandatory provisions, see *infra* section 2.9.5.4.

898 See e.g. *Mansel*, in: FS Roth, 375, 376; *Köhler*, Eingriffsnormen, 11. Also see *Rogerson*, Collier's Conflict of Laws, 433, who makes the reverse statement: unilateral conflicts rules of the *lex fori* are internationally mandatory provisions.

Theoretically, the conflicts rule could determine the application of an entire group of substantive rules instead of just one substantive rule; it could also be a rule determining the application of more than one law.[899]

2.9.1. "Special", Not Necessarily "Specific"

At issue is thus a conflicts rule (typically determining the application of one substantive rule) that potentially interferes with a conflicts rule determining the application of another law (the "otherwise applicable" law). This is rather obvious for those cases where the substantive rule at issue is accompanied by an express conflicts provision. If, at the same time, the facts of a given case fulfil the requirements of a general conflicts rule,[900] the scenario boils down to the relatively simple relationship between a specific and a more general rule. Accordingly, the principle of *lex specialis derogat legi generali* has been applied to this situation.[901] No problem at all arises if a regular conflicts rule already refers to the overriding mandatory provision (some assume this to be the general solution regarding all overriding mandatory provisions of the *lex causae*[902]).

There can be a bit of a complication, however. Overriding mandatory provisions are typically based on public interests of a country, "such as its political, social or economic organisation" (Article 9(1) Rome I). They implicate conflicts interests based on these public interests. By contrast, run-of-the-mill private international law rules are based on conflicts interests derived from[903] private interests. It follows that overriding mandatory provisions can implicate conflicts rules with entirely different interests to regular conflicts rules.[904] At least from a formal perspective, then, it would not be appropriate to call the former conflicts rules "specific" in the sense of "narrower". In light of

899 *Neuhaus*, Grundbegriffe, §11 V (106); *id.*, RabelsZ 33 (1969), 194, 195.

900 Or in the long version from the perspective of substantive law: "If the facts of a given case fulfil the requirements of rules of substantive law that in turn fulfil the requirements of a general conflicts rule …".

901 *Köhler*, Eingriffsnormen, 11; *Bonomi*, Yearbook of Private International Law I (1999), 215, 234; *Siehr*, RabelsZ 46 (1982), 357, 375 (381 in English, 382 in Spanish); arguably also *Neuhaus*, Grundbegriffe, §11 V (106).

902 But see *infra* section 2.9.3.2. for doubts as to this approach.

903 The step of derivation is important: substantive interests underlie substantive rules, conflicts interests underlie conflicts rules. To *directly* infer a conflicts rule from substantive interests is impossible; see only *Köhler*, Eingriffsnormen, 18–19.

904 This is (supposed to be) a very short account particularly of *Schurig*'s approach to overriding mandatory provisions, see Kollisionsnorm und Sachrecht, 322–230; *id.*, RabelsZ 54 (1990), 217, 226–233 (also see the English abstract, 248–250); *Kegel/id.*, IPR, §2 IV 2 (153). It recently was taken up in by *Köhler*, Eingriffsnormen, 87, 92–97. Also see *Roth*, in: FS Dauses, 315, 16; *id.*, CMLRev 39 (2002), 369, 378.

this realisation, I will designate the conflicts rules for overriding mandatory provisions as "special", implying that they can also be "isolated" rules.

2.9.2. *A Formally General Issue of the Subject Matter*

The position of the issue of overriding mandatory provisions within the tripartite structure of conflicts rules follows from the foregoing insights. Overriding mandatory provisions implicate special conflicts rules. To say that a conflicts rule is special is a relational statement; it makes no sense without an object of comparison. This object can only be the subject matter. As the subject matter of a conflicts rule depends on the interests at issue,[905] it constitutes the element in which the relation to another rule with different interests becomes relevant. Accordingly, the issue is discussed most appropriately in the present context.

This understanding is in line with statements according to which overriding mandatory provisions "exclude certain areas of law from the scope of operation of 'ordinary' choice-of-law rules",[906] "override, pre-empt, or displace the ordinary *choice-of-law* rules",[907] "circumvent the 'normal' *choice of law* rules",[908] or interfere with the scope of a general conflicts rule.[909] Furthermore, the idea of special conflicts rules conforms to the realisation that overriding mandatory provisions often *flank* the *lex causae*,[910] rather than completely excluding the normally applicable conflicts rule and with it the *lex causae*: the "regular" subject matter continues to be relevant for everything not covered by the special subject matter. In this sense, special conflicts provisions for overriding mandatory provisions form a (potential or actual) restriction of the subject matter[911] of other conflicts rules. This is why they are a formally general

---

905 *Supra* section 2.4.

906 *Sagi*, The Foundation of Choice of Law, 205.

907 *Symeonides*, Codifying Choice of Law, 307 (emphasis added). Admittedly, the entire statement reads, "[overriding mandatory provisions] override, pre-empt, or displace the ordinary choice-of-law rules *and* the substantive law that would apply under those rules" (emphasis added). But the second part, pertaining to the governing law, is merely a necessary consequence of the first part of the statement: if (the subject matter of) a conflicts rule is displaced, it cannot determine the applicable law anymore.

908 *Muir-Watt*, Transnational Legal Theory 2 (2011), 347, 415 (note 331) (emphasis added).

909 *Roth*, in: FS Dauses, 315, 316; *Köhler*, Eingriffsnormen, 11; in this sense probably also *Cordero Álvarez*, CDT 2017, 174, 176.

910 *Bonomi*, in: Baratta (ed.), DIP, s. v. "Norme di applicazione necessaria", 233, 235; see also *eund.*, Yearbook of Private International Law I (1999), 215, 226–228; *Biagoni*, NLCC 2009, 768, 798; *Briggs*, Conflict of Laws, 248 ("operation [of a conflicts rule] is to this extent overridden"); *Chong*, Journal of Private International Law 2 (2006), 27, 32 ("superimposed onto the [otherwise still] applicable law").

911 *Leible/Müller*, Yearbook of Private International Law XIV (2012/2013), 137, 144; also see that *Sonnenberger*'s contribution to Leible (ed.), General Principles, §7, was placed in the context of the subject matter.

issue. It is even formally general in the strict sense,[912] as there is no telling in which area of law an overriding mandatory provision might surface.[913]

Yet this understanding of overriding mandatory provisions does not seem to be particularly prevalent. Rather, they are often discussed in connection with/in close proximity to public policy, or in other ways (at least implicitly) as a question of the governing law.[914] This conceptualisation, however, ultimately proves less persuasive.

2.9.2.1. Overriding Mandatory Provisions as an Escape Device?

To begin with, quite a few scholars frame overriding mandatory provisions as an escape device.[915] There is no denying that overriding mandatory provisions can have this effect and that they can be used as such. If a (general) conflicts rule determines the application of foreign law, but an overriding mandatory provision of the *lex fori* exists, the latter will probably prevail. As a result, not foreign law but the *lex fori* applies to the case. Likewise, the application of a foreign overriding mandatory provision means (partially) escaping the otherwise applicable law, even if that is the *lex fori* – although such an escape is probably not particularly interesting for a judge.

To adopt the vantage point of the consequence or outcome of the application of conflicts rules, however, is a relatively weak conceptual device

---

912 It is, of course, not the existence of overriding mandatory provisions which is inherent in every conflicts rule. Rather, every conflicts rule has a subject matter that might be affected by another, special conflicts rule. Some reaction of the private international law system at issue to these substantive rules is necessary, and be it disregard, i.e. abstaining from making a special conflicts rule. Likewise, the substantive provision itself that is supposed to have an overriding effect would not be found in a collection of general rules of private international law. Such provisions are usually not even part of the respective general codification of substantive private law (if any), *Mankowski*, in: Basedow/Kischel/Sieber (eds.), German National Reports, 133, 142.

913 *Mansel*, in: FS Roth, 375, 377 and 381 (overriding mandatory provisions as an institute of the "general part" of private international law); *Mankowski*, in: Basedow/Kischel/Sieber (eds.), German National Reports, 133, 140 ("the (mistaken) belief that [overriding mandatory provisions] only exist in contract and possibly in tort"); *Kühne*, in: FS Heldrich, 815, 830 (but critical of this phenomenon); *Junker*, IPRax 2000, 65, 73 (who nevertheless argued against transferring the German implementation of Article 7(2) Rome Convention from contractual obligations to the general part of the EGBGB).

914 *Ernst*, RabelsZ 76 (2012), 597, 610; *Verschraegen*, IPR, at 1310–1336 ("Ordre Public und Eingriffsnormen"); *Plender/Wilderspin*, European PIL of Obligations, xii ("chapter 12 – mandatory rules and ordre public") and xiv ("chapter 27 – mandatory rules and ordre public"); also see *infra* footnote 931.

915 See e.g. *Schmidt-Kessel*, in: Ferrari (ed.), Rome I Regulation, Article 9 at 32; *Briggs*, Private International Law in the English Courts, at 7.244–7.251 (as one instance of the "displacement of the applicable law"); *id.*, Conflict of Laws, 248 (an instance of "general displacement"); *Cheshire/North/Fawcett*, PIL, 143–144 (in the chapter on "exclusion of foreign law") and 743–752 (as a "limitation on the dominance of the applicable law"); *Boele-Woelki/van Iterson*, in: van Erp/van Vliet (eds.), Netherlands Report, 145, 155.

for present purposes. As the application of some law is the legal consequence of all conflicts rules, it can be affected by modification to any of its requirements. Hence, many if not all of the issues discussed here as formally general can be reformulated to pertain in some way to the (non-)application of (foreign) law. For example, characterisation can be carried out in a way so that a conflicts rule leading to one's own law is applicable instead of one leading to foreign law.[916] Illicit manipulations of the connecting factor can be sanctioned by applying the *lex fori* instead of the foreign law applicable after the manipulation.[917] Even party autonomy has been regarded as a way of excluding the application of the otherwise, i.e. objectively, applicable law.[918] To cluster these topics is reasonable for an analysis of how courts, for whatever reason, avoid the application of foreign law ("homeward trend"); it is reasonable if one is looking for all kinds of "escapes".[919] Indeed, the entire "general part" of private international law has been said to have the purpose of blocking the application of foreign law.[920] Yet such an approach obfuscates an analysis like the present one, which is concerned with a relatively precise delineation of general issues of private international law. Instead, it is necessary to find an intrinsic reason for the allocation to a particular element of a conflicts rule.

2.9.2.2. Overriding Mandatory Provisions as an Issue of Public Policy?

To be sure, some relation between the topic of overriding mandatory provisions and the public policy exception cannot be gainsaid. Both are based on considerations of public interest,[921] as several recitals of the private international law regulations also express.[922] Furthermore, not too long ago, public policy was not only used as a shield against foreign provisions, but in many countries also as a sword: applying forum provisions to govern an issue regardless of the otherwise applicable law.[923]

---

916 Accordingly, characterisation has also been considered an escape device, see *Michaels*, in: FS Kropholler, 151, 152–153, for the American "conflicts revolution".

917 *Infra* section 3.4.

918 *Carruthers/Crawford*, Edin. L. R. 9 (2005), 65, 82.

919 See e.g. *Muir-Watt*, Transnational Legal Theory 2 (2011), 347, 380 (note 163).

920 *Dolinger*, in: Essays in Honor of Juenger, 23, 25.

921 *McParland*, The Rome I Regulation, at 15.01; *Bonomi*, in: Baratta (ed.), DIP, s. v. "Norme di applicazione necessaria", 233, 235.

922 Recitals 37 Rome I, 32 Rome II, and 53 (in conjunction with 54) M-/RP-Property Regulation.

923 See *Kegel/Schurig*, §2 IV 2; *Spickhoff*, Der ordre public im IPR, 128–129; *Remy*, R.I.D.C. 2010, 291, 310, and *Francescakis*, La théorie du renvoi, 13, for examples from France; *de Lima Pinheiro*, Yearbook of Private International Law 14 (2012/2013), 153, 161 for examples from Portugal; *Pajor*, in: Symeonides (ed.), PIL at the End of the 20th Century, 337–338, for the example of a 1969 decision by the Polish Supreme Court; in a singular English instance, public policy was even employed to apply *foreign* law which would otherwise have been inapplicable, *Dicey/Morris/Collins*, Conflict of Laws, at 5-007. *Zitelmann*, IPR I,

The latter "positive" or "offensive" effect of public policy,[924] however, is by now largely[925] defunct.[926] Instead, it is ascribed to the context of overriding mandatory provisions.[927] From the point of view of terminological clarity, it would be best if one got rid of the term "positive public policy" altogether. It is likely to mislead as ("negative"[928]) public policy and overriding mandatory provisions *operate* entirely differently.[929]

As will be demonstrated in more detail later on,[930] public policy concerns the question of whether it is possible to ultimately deny the application of foreign law. Its determination is accepted at first, but it turns out that it leads to an outcome offensive to the *lex fori*. In contrast, overriding mandatory provisions (are supposed to) apply regardless of what other law applies. Since they (are meant to) "override" everything else, it is simply irrelevant to determine what they override. The content of the law determined by the "general" conflicts rule does not matter. Hence, it is not correct to say that overriding mandatory provisions constitute a means to remediate an unwelcome *outcome* produced by the application of foreign law.[931] "[T]he public policy exception operates *a posteriori* […] Mandatory rules that claim

325–326, seems to have led the way in this regard: *Spickhoff*, Der ordre public im IPR, 41 (with note 28).

924 *Renner*, in: Calliess (ed.), Rome Regulations, Art. 9 Rome I at 6; *Symeonides*, in: id. (ed.), PIL at the End of the 20th Century, 3, 17 (note 48).

925 But see *Thoma*, in: Basedow/Rühl/Ferrari/de Miguel Asensio (eds.), Encyclopedia of PIL, s. v. "Public Policy (*Ordre Public*)", IV *Lüttringhaus*, IPRax 2014, 146, 149 and 150; *id.*, Grenzüberschreitender Diskriminierungsschutz, 191 (while admitting, note 4, that "at least terminologically" overriding mandatory provisions and public policy have developed to be separate subjects) and passim; *Lurger/Melcher*, IPR, at 1/48; *van Calster*, European PIL, 3.2.8.3. Also see *Basedow*, The Law of Open Societies, at 715–722 (distinguishing overriding mandatory provisions and positive public policy, but ultimately noting that the distinction "is fading away").

926 From the perspective of public policy *Wurmnest*, in: Leible (ed.), General Principles, §14.03[A] ("this concept [positive public policy] has become practically meaningless for the modern public policy reservation").

927 See, e.g., *Symeonides*, Codifying Choice of Law, 311–12; *Burián*, in: Symeonides (ed.), PIL at the End of the 20th Century, 263, 269–270; already *Schurig*, Kollisionsnorm und Sachrecht, 249.

928 The adjective could be dropped, of course, once there is no need for the contradistinction anymore.

929 Expressly making the following distinction between public policy and overriding mandatory provisions *Bogdan*, Introduction to EU PIL (2016), 7.5; similarly *Cachard*, DIP, at 331; also see *von Hein*, in: Calliess (ed.), Rome Regulations, Art. 16 Rome II at 7 (positive function of public policy "superfluous").

930 *Infra* 5.6.

931 But see *Hauser*, 42, who states that the purpose of *both* is to remediate the *outcome* ("das Ergebnis") of the application of foreign law; *Lurger/Melcher*, IPR, at 1/49 ("thrusting aside the governing law"); *Rogerson*, Collier's Conflict of Laws, 434 (mandatory rules as a means of "[a]voiding the *results* of the choice of law process", emphasis added); *Rammeloo*, EuLF 2010, I-180, I-185 (correction to the "outcome of the process of finding the applicable law"); *Bonomi*, Yearbook of Private International Law I (1999), 215, 226 ("correcting the results"); possibly also *Pesce*, RIW 1995, 977, 980.

applicability *a priori*, displacing the operation of the choice-of-law-system, fall under the concept of overriding mandatory rules [...]".[932] The Commission, regardless of its erroneous idea of *lois d'application immédiate*, also had this contradistinction in mind when drafting the first Rome Regulations.[933]

2.9.2.3. Substantive Solutions as a Counterargument?

One might object that, in certain legal systems, overriding mandatory provisions of a foreign legislator only have any effect if the substantive *lex causae* makes room for them.[934] Consequently, there might be reason to allocate the issue to the governing law. Yet this is merely one of the ways a legal system can react to (foreign) overriding mandatory provisions. One should not confuse one of several *solutions* with the *issue*. If the solution of a legal system consisted in flat-out refusing to give any effect to foreign overriding mandatory provisions, one would not say that the *issue* does not exist, would one?

2.9.2.4. Conclusion

It would not be sound to locate overriding mandatory provisions in the third element, i.e. the governing law.[935] Neither their potential use as an escape device nor their shared (substantive and historical) foundation with the issue of public policy warrant such an approach. Public policy is a *corrective mechanism* after a conflicts rule has been applied; whereas, where an overriding mandatory provision is at issue, a special conflicts rule is intended to (partially) *replace* the normally applicable conflicts rule.[936] The element of the governing law does not even reach the point of becoming an object of consideration if an overriding mandatory provision prevails in the way it is supposed to operate. As no statement whatsoever is made about the content of foreign law, one might say that the application of overriding mandatory provisions constitutes a relatively

---

932 *de Lima Pinheiro*, Yearbook of Private International Law 14 (2012/2013), 153, 170 (italics in the original); very clearly also *Cachard*, at 304; *Bonomi*, in: Baratta (ed.), DIP, s. v. "Norme di applicazione necessaria", 233, 235–236 and 239; *Chong*, Journal of Private International Law 2 (2006), 27, 30; similarly *Mankowski*, in: Basedow/Kischel/Sieber (eds.), German National Reports, 133, 144; *Pocar*, IPRax 1996, 145, 153; to this effect also already *Francescakis*, La théorie du renvoi, 13.

933 Rome I Green Paper, COM(2002) 654 final, 45 (see already *supra* footnote 896); Rome II Proposal, COM(2003) 427 final, 28.

934 See *Schacherreiter*, ZEuP 2015, 497, 500–502, with references from Austria, Germany, and France.

935 Similarly already *Eek*, Swedish Conflict of Laws, 197: "This solution [what he calls "absolute" domestic rules] is therefore more properly dealt with in another context [i.e. *not* the public policy context]."

936 Pellucidly *Junker*, IPRax 2000, 65, 66; also see *Mansel*, in: FS Roth, 375, 377 (partial replacement of the general conflicts provision); *Neuhaus*, Grundbegriffe, §11 V (106).

uncontroversial judicial move;[937] but then, the interference with applicable "normal" conflicts rules is far greater than if there was merely some correction to the substantive outcome.

2.9.3. *Preliminary Inferences from the Nature of the Problem*

As the issue of overriding mandatory provisions boils down to the reaction of a system of private international law to special conflicts rules, either of the same system or of a foreign system, some preliminary inferences are possible. Against this backdrop, private international law of the member states and of the EU will be examined.

2.9.3.1. Overriding Mandatory Provisions by the Private International Law Legislator

If the legislator of the overriding mandatory provision is the same as that of the private international law rules, their relationship does not cause problems. Presumably, the special conflicts rule will prevail over the regular one.[938] This can simply be a question of the principle of *lex specialis derogat legi generali*,[939] but the outcome is the same if one does not suppose a relationship of formal specificity. After all, the point of a *special* rule is to apply instead of a regular rule. The application of overriding mandatory provisions originating from the same legislator as the regular conflicts rules is a matter of course.[940] As long as private international law is firmly in the hands of domestic legislators, overriding mandatory provisions of the *lex fori* will apply.

2.9.3.2. Overriding Mandatory Provisions by Another Legislator

The default solution is also very simple when an overriding mandatory provision by another legislator is at issue. The conflicts decisions by the other legislator are not binding on whoever is in the process of applying internal private international law. Hence, the foreign overriding mandatory provision will not be applied either – unless an *internal* conflicts rule determines its application.[941]

---

937 *Mills*, Confluence, 191.

938 *Francq*, RabelsZ 70 (2006), 235, 256 (for Article 20 Belgian PIL Code).

939 *Supra* section 2.8.

940 *Köhler*, Eingriffsnormen, 16; *Schurig*, RabelsZ 54 (1990), 217, 233; *Drobnig*, RabelsZ 52 (1988), 1, 4 (with the only – and rather obvious – proviso that the overriding mandatory provision at issue really covers the case at hand); also see *von Bar/Mankowski*, IPR I, §4 at 100 (no *practical* difference to the issue of specific vs. general conflicts rules); *Dicey/Morris/Collins*, Conflict of Laws, at 1-054.

941 *Köhler*, Eingriffsnormen, 192.

This is *not* already the case if the overriding mandatory provision in question is found in the legal system of the *lex causae*. The idea is certainly rather popular[942] and tempting because of its simplicity: "If internal private international law determines the law of state X to apply to a given subject matter, it means *all* law of state X". But this approach, unfortunately also presupposed without any discussion by Advocate General Szpunar in the context of Rome I recently,[943] is too broad. One would overlook that it depends on the underlying interests which foreign rules exactly are determined to apply. If the purported overriding mandatory provision implicates different conflicts interests than those underlying the conflicts rule, the overriding mandatory provision is not part of the *lex causae*.[944] *Only if* the underlying interests align does the conflicts rule (also) lead to the overriding mandatory provision;[945] it does *not necessarily* do so. To be clear: it is an entirely tenable position that e.g. Rome I refers to all rules found in the legal system of the *lex causae*. But this would be an interpretation of Rome I specifically, not one based on a general idea.

It should thus become apparent why the issue of overriding mandatory provisions is of tremendous importance in the context of EU private international law. The legislator for conflict of laws is now largely the EU. From its perspective, *all* domestic overriding mandatory provisions are foreign, for they originate with another legislator. Hence, in the absence of any particular rule, overriding mandatory provisions of a member state do not apply – even if they are part of the *lex fori*.[946]

Yet this is merely the default solution. A private international law legislator is at liberty to provide for some sort of opening for foreign overriding mandatory provisions. Why, when, and how[947] it should do so is a policy question. Suffice it to say at this point that a legislator can plausibly claim that justice requires foreign overriding mandatory provisions to have some effect

942 *Roth*, IPRax 2018, 177, 181–183 (with a detailed analysis of the arguments advanced against this approach in the context of Rome I); *Mansel*, in: FS Roth, 375, 378; *Symeonides*, Codifying Choice of Law, 309 (with note 90); *Audit/d'Avout*, DIP, at 181; *Bonomi*, in: Baratta (ed.), DIP, s. v. "Norme di applicazione necessaria", 233, 240–241.

943 Opinion by AG Szpunar, Case C-135/15, Hellenic Republic v Grigorios Nikiforidis, ECLI:EU:C:2016:281 at 76.

944 *Freitag*, in: Reithmann/Martiny (eds.), Internationales Vertragsrecht, at 5.24; *Köhler*, Eingriffsnormen, 282–283; *Kegel/Schurig*, IPR, §2 IV 2 (155); *Schurig*, RabelsZ 54 (1990), 217, 244; *von Bar/Mankowski*, IPR I, §4 at 120; also *Remien*, in: FS von Hoffmann, 334, 341.

945 See e.g. *Roth*, in: FS Spellenberg, 309, 324–236; *Lando/Nielsen*, CMLRev 45 (2008), 1687, 1719.

946 See *von Bar/Mankowski*, IPR I, §4 at 100, already for the Rome Convention.

947 See *Schacherreiter*, ZEuP 2015, 497, 500–507, for a recent comparative overview of how domestic law deals with foreign overriding mandatory provisions; see also the account by *Chong*, Journal of Private International Law 2 (2006), 27, 40–47.

in certain instances, e.g. if otherwise a court "might find itself called upon to order a defendant to pay damages for not committing a crime".[948]

2.9.3.3. Overriding Mandatory Provisions and Party Autonomy

No "Limitation" on Party Autonomy

Allocating the issue of overriding mandatory provisions to the subject matter makes it easy to explain that they also "prevail over" the law chosen by the parties.[949] Party autonomy is best considered a question of the connecting factor.[950] Overriding mandatory provisions operating at the stage of the subject matter cut off the conflicts analysis *before* any connecting factor can even be considered. From this perspective,[951] it is misleading to consider overriding mandatory provisions as a *limitation* on (existing) party autonomy.[952] To the extent that an overriding mandatory provision applies, there is no room for party autonomy in the first place. In any case, as overriding mandatory provisions are not just relevant where the applicable law has been chosen, they should not be merely considered against the backdrop of party autonomy.[953]

Simple Mandatory Provisions and Overriding Mandatory Provisions

It is likewise relatively easy now to explain the operative difference[954] between simple[955] mandatory provisions and overriding mandatory provisions – a difference clearly envisioned by Recital 37 clause 2 Rome I. Simple mandatory

---

948 *Briggs*, Private International Law in the English Courts, at 7.250, assuming an overriding mandatory provision of a third state to penalise the behaviour about which the parties validly made a contract under the *lex causae*.

949 See e.g. *Reimann*, in: Verschraegen (ed.), Rechtswahl, 1, 5 (who bases the statement on the purported independence of overriding mandatory provisions from conflicts rules); *Symeonides*, Codifying Choice of Law, 307. Similarly to the approach proposed here, but still with a reference on the governing law, *Michaels*, in: LA Schurig, 191, 194–195.

950 *Infra* section 4.3.2.

951 Similarly to the statements above regarding overriding mandatory provisions as an escape device, it *is* reasonable to consider overriding mandatory provision a limitation on party autonomy if one is concerned with all the different ways party autonomy *ultimately* does not come to fruition.

952 Similarly *Michaels*, in: LA Schurig, 191, 195; but see *Cordero Álvarez*, CDT 2017, 174, 179–182.

953 *Mankowski*, EWiR 2014, 11, 12; *Bonomi*, Yearbook of Private International Law I (1999), 215, 226. But see *Renner*, in: Calliess (ed.), Rome Regulations, Art. 9 Rome I at 1 (Article 9 Rome I as an attempt to balance party autonomy with regulatory interests); also ECJ Case C-184/12, United Antwerp Maritime Agencies (Unamar) NV v Navigation Maritime Bulgare, ECLI:EU:C:2013:663, at 49 (although the Court's focus on party autonomy simply may have been due to the case at hand).

954 On the difference e.g. *Hartley*, in: LA Kohler, 171; *Bonomi*, in: Baratta (ed.), DIP, s. v. "Norme di applicazione necessaria", 233, 236.

955 Or "relatively mandatory": *Lehmann*, Vand. J. Trans. L. 41 (2008), 381, 419–421.

provisions are legal standards "which cannot be derogated from by agreement" (Article 3(3) Rome I). *Within* one legal system, the parties cannot escape them, but if the respective law is not applicable, they are typically ineffective. To wit, mandatory provisions set a limit to private autonomy, but not to party autonomy. They are relevant *once* the *lex causae* has been determined. Overriding mandatory provisions, however, (are supposed to) operate even *before* the *lex causae* has been determined, independently from its determination.

When simple mandatory provisions are supposed to apply in spite of a choice by the parties, however, a structural parallel to overriding mandatory provisions emerges.[956] A separate conflicts decision regarding the application of the respective provisions is as necessary here as it is there.[957] A provision like Article 3(3) Rome I rather deceptively states that a choice "shall not *prejudice* the application"[958] of mandatory provisions. Yet as these provisions are not applicable *per se*, it is actually Article 3(3) Rome I itself that serves as the necessary conflicts rule making them applicable.[959]

2.9.3.4. A "Victory for Unilateralism"?

It has often been observed that the phenomenon of overriding mandatory provisions is "attributable to unilateralist thinking",[960] that it constitutes a "contemporary use" of unilateralism,[961] or even that it is "a small but clear victory of unilateralism over multilateralism".[962] To the extent that such an expression reflects that the typical conflicts rule pertaining to an overriding mandatory provision is unilateral, the statement is correct but rather innocuous. Moreover, as a written special conflicts rule for the purported overriding mandatory provision will often be missing,[963] there is really no other way of

956 See *Michaels*, in: LA Schurig, 191, 199–200 and passim.

957 There is a potential difference in that the conflicts decision that makes a provision "overriding" typically only concerns that very provision, whereas a provision like Article 3(3) Rome I concerns an entire set of provisions (i.e. *all* mandatory provisions of a particular country). The structure remains the same, however, see *Michaels*, in: LA Schurig, 191, 200.

958 Emphasis added.

959 *Michaels*, in: LA Schurig, 191, 197.

960 *Symeonides*, in: id. (ed.), PIL at the End of the 20th Century, 3, 16.

961 *Muir-Watt*, Transnational Legal Theory 2 (2011), 347, 415.

962 *Symeonides*, Codifying Choice of Law, 310; similarly *Pajor*, in: Symeonides (ed.), PIL at the End of the 20th Century, 340 ("proof of the resurgence [of the unilateral method]"); *Juenger*, in: LA Siehr (2000), 288, 302 ("renaissance", but "hardly [...] a return to statutism").

963 The dichotomy "written – unwritten" may be a reason why the issue truly emerged in the uncodified private international law of France (see *supra* footnotes 893–895). Where an overriding mandatory provision of the *lex fori* can be said to apply, a judge does not have to develop a (multilateral) conflicts rule, *Siehr*, Yearbook of Private International Law VII (2005), 17, 56; *id.*, in: FS Drobnig, 443, 448.

approaching the issue than to start the conflicts analysis with the substantive rule in question,[964] as opposed to the facts of the case (as would be the omni-/multilateralist ideal).[965]

If the reference to unilateralism is meant to express, however, that the application even of a foreign overriding mandatory provision only depends on *that* provision's "intent to be applied", i.e. only on the *foreign* conflicts decision, it would be rather questionable. This would amount to a (partial) system change.[966] Yet it remains for each private international law legislator to decide whether to allow a foreign overriding mandatory provision to apply or not. If it conditions the application of such a provision on the existence of a foreign conflicts rule for it, then fine[967] – but, in such a scenario, it is still the *internal* private international law legislator making the decision to attribute relevance to the *foreign* conflicts decision. It would appear that the system is still intact.[968]

It *is* correct, however, that a growing number of overriding mandatory provisions at one point undermines the consistency of a system of conflict of laws.[969] The ECJ itself has demonstrated its awareness of this problem.[970] To be sure, overriding mandatory provisions can have the advantage of replacing the shotgun with the sniper rifle,[971] of operating with "pinpoint accuracy and express[ing] the precise and special policy considerations in the respective field".[972] But there is no point in having general rules if the system set up by them frays out because of exceptions in abundance. At least from a "traditional" point of view, the enforcement of the substantive rules of the *lex fori* cannot be the objective of conflict of laws, even if one considers one's own solutions extremely progressive or superior to others.[973]

---

964 *Ballarino/Bonomi*, Yearbook of Private International Law 2 (2000), 99, 111.

965 *Köhler*, Eingriffsnormen, 99. To start with the rule ultimately is equivalent to starting with the facts, *Köhler*, Eingriffsnormen, 61; *Schurig*, Kollisionsnorm und Sachrecht, 89. *von Savigny* himself seems to have considered both approaches to be sides of the same coin, System VIII, 1-3 and 10-11.

966 To this effect e.g. *Symeonides*, Codifying Choice of Law, 301.

967 And quite reasonable too – why have a foreign rule apply that was not intended to apply in a given case?

968 See *Köhler*, Eingriffsnormen, 87; *Schurig*, RabelsZ 54 (1990), 217, 237; *id.*, Kollisionsnorm und Sachrecht, 325–327.

969 *Kühne*, in: FS Wegen, 451, 461; *id.*, in: FS Heldrich, 815, 830; *Mankowski*, EWiR 2014, 11–12.

970 ECJ Case C-135/15, Hellenic Republic v Grigorios Nikiforidis, ECLI:EU:C:2016:774 at 45 ("to restrict disturbance to the system of conflict of laws caused by the application of overriding mandatory provisions other than those of the State of the forum").

971 *Kühne*, in: LA Schurig, 129, 140.

972 *Mankowski*, in: Basedow/Kischel/Sieber (eds.), German National Reports, 133, 144. Arguably, the application of more than one law to a case (*lex causae* plus overriding mandatory provisions of another law) also more accurately reflects the multi-national nature of a cross-border case; *Drobnig*, RabelsZ 52 (1988), 1, 7.

973 *Kühne*, in: FS Heldrich, 815, 830.

2.9.3.5. Establishing Overriding Mandatory Provisions

In summary, overriding mandatory provisions do not actually raise a terribly difficult conceptual issue at the level of private international law. To the extent that general/regular conflicts rules do not refer to the overriding mandatory provisions already, the question is one of special conflicts rules (perhaps even those of another legislator), and whether and how they can have an effect in light of an applicable general/regular conflicts rule. Much more problematic is the identification and establishment of these special conflicts rules.[974] They will often not be written and thus have to be determined through interpretation.[975] The danger of inappropriately conflating substantive interests (underlying the substantive rule) and conflicts interests (necessary to determining the pertinent conflicts rule) is great. Special rules of substantive law with underlying private interests deemed particularly important by the respective legislator, such as consumer protection provisions, seem to form a constant bone of contention in this context.[976] Additionally, the relevance of overriding mandatory provisions of another legislator will likely be subject to further conditions set forth by the internal legislator (otherwise it would "helplessly" be subject to foreign whimsicalities[977]), again necessitating interpretation. These questions, however, are largely beyond the scope of the present book.

2.9.4. Member States

At least because of Article 7 Rome Convention,[978] the topic of (not yet officially denominated "overriding") mandatory provisions was known to many member states in the field of contractual obligations.[979] Yet today, more than half of the domestic private international law codes deal with them among their general provisions.[980] Closer inspection of the class of codes that do so shows that all of them have been passed since 1995. Conversely, of the eleven private international law codes passed since then, only Slovenia and Estonia do not have such a provision.

---

974 See only *Bonomi*, in: Baratta (ed.), DIP, s. v. "Norme di applicazione necessaria", 233, 236.

975 See in particular *Köhler*, Eingriffsnormen, 88–101.

976 See only the recent examples by *Kinsch*, in: LA Kohler, 215, and *Sinay-Cytermann*, in: Azzi/Boskovic (eds.), Quel avenir pour la théorie générale des conflits de lois?, 83, 85.

977 *Schurig*, Kollisionsnorm und Sachrecht, 326.

978 The Rome Convention was among the first legislative texts to deal with the phenomenon, *Bonomi*, in: Baratta (ed.), DIP, s. v. "Norme di applicazione necessaria", 233, 234.

979 See e.g. *Lookofsky*, Choice of Law in Denmark, VII B, who discusses the topic of (overriding) mandatory provisions in Denmark *only* as a question of the Rome Convention.

980 To wit: Article 20 Belgian PIL Code, Article 46 Bulgarian PIL Code, §§3 and 25 Czech PIL Act, §13 Hungarian PIL Act, Article 17 Italian PIL Act, Article 1.11(2) Lithuanian Civil Code, Article 10:7 Dutch Civil Code, Article 8 Polish PIL Act, Article 2.566 Romanian Civil Code.

All domestic general provisions on overriding mandatory rules deal both with such of the *lex fori* as well as of some foreign law, with the exception of Article 17 Italian PIL Act (only *lex fori* overriding mandatory provisions[981]). The parallels to the Rome Convention and/or Rome I are unmistakable in many cases.[982] Article 10:7 Dutch Civil Code, for example, clearly imitates Article 9 Rome I,[983] but is not limited to contractual obligations, of course.[984] The Polish legislator made a conscious decision against carrying over Article 9 Rome I and instead opted for Article 7 Rome Convention as the model for Article 8 Polish PIL Act.[985]

Occasionally, there still is certain proximity between provisions on overriding mandatory provisions and public policy provisions. Article 1.11 Lithuanian Civil Code is a particularly strong example, combining public policy, overriding mandatory provisions, and an escape clause in one statutory article. Article 20 Belgian PIL Code speaks of "règles impératives *ou d'ordre public*".[986] Mostly, however, both topics are dealt with in separate provisions *and*[987] without overlapping terminology.

The Austrian PIL Act does not contain a rule specifically concerning overriding mandatory provisions, but one of its general provisions (§1) has been used to apply domestic as well as foreign overriding mandatory provisions.[988] With Article 3(1) French Civil Code, the issue of overriding mandatory provisions as *lois de police* has one of the few legislative bases in French private international law, although the modern use of the term is probably not in line with what its drafters had in mind.[989] French scholars typically discuss the issue separately from individual conflicts provisions – but with a clear focus on the (purportedly) different *method* that overriding mandatory provisions implicate, i.e. not necessarily in the context of other issues identified as general, such as characterisation or *renvoi*.[990]

---

981 See *Pocar/Honorati*, in: Symeonides (ed.), PIL at the End of the 20th Century, 279, 291; but *lex causae* overriding mandatory provisions are to be applied, anyway, *Kindler*, RabelsZ 61 (1997), 227, 258; *Pocar*, IPRax 1996, 145, 153.

982 Also see *Erauw/Fallon*, in: Dirix/Lelen (eds.), The Belgian Reports, 227, 258, for Article 20 Belgian PIL Code.

983 *ten Wolde*, Yearbook of Private International Law 13 (2011), 389, 398.

984 *Boele-Woelki/van Iterson*, in: van Erp/van Vliet (eds.), Netherlands Report, 145, 155.

985 *Pazdan*, IPRax 2012, 77, 79.

986 Emphasis added. Critical of this terminology *Francq*, RabelsZ 70 (2006), 235, 257.

987 Belgium does have a separate public policy exception, Article 21 Belgian PIL Code.

988 *Lurger/Melcher*, IPR, at 1/48; *Wendehorst*, in: Verschraegen (ed.), Austrian Law, 79, 90–92.

989 *Audit/d'Avout*, DIP, at 177; *Mayer/Heuzé*, DIP, at 124 (note 31).

990 *Audit/d'Avout*, DIP, at 177–183 (as part of the unilateral method that itself forms part of the "partie générale"); *Loussouarn/Bourel/de Vareilles-Sommières*, DIP, 168–183 (as part of the "diversification of the conflicts method" that itself forms part of the "théorie générale des conflits de lois"); *Mayer/Heuzé*, DIP, at 124–135 (as part of the "plurality of methods" in private international law).

Germany does not have a general provision on overriding mandatory provisions.[991] Where overriding mandatory provisions surface in German academic writings, however, they usually do so in sections separate from individual conflicts rules, but not necessarily among the issues designated as "general".[992] Many common law writers make only very brief mention of the issue in sections on overarching topics, if at all.[993]

2.9.5. *European Union*

It has already been shown that even overriding mandatory provisions of the forum could not be applied anymore where the respective area of private international law is subject to EU provisions.[994] It is up to the EU whether and to what extent it allows domestic overriding mandatory provisions to prevail over its general conflicts rules. It constitutes the "referee" at a higher level, deciding which national law applies.[995] Some scholars have already expressly acknowledged this issue to be a general one for all EU private international law.[996]

2.9.5.1. Rome I

In the tradition of the Rome Convention, Rome I expressly deals with overriding mandatory provisions, both of the law of the forum as well as of the law of certain other states. The provision in question, Article 9 Rome I, is located among the "Uniform Rules" and not among the "Other Provisions",

---

991 Some, however, consider Article 3a(2) EGBGB ("Where referrals in the third and fourth sections make the property of a person subject to the law of a country, they shall not relate to items which are not located in that country and are governed by special provisions under the law of the country where they are located.") as referring to foreign overriding mandatory provisions, see e.g. *Winkler von Mohrenfels*, in: FS Martiny, 595, 597; *Kegel/Schurig*, IPR, §12 II 2 b) aa) aaa) (427).

992 *Kropholler*, IPR, §3 II (18–24); *Kegel/Schurig*, IPR, §2 IV 2 (150–158); *von Bar/Mankowski*, IPR I, §4 at 80–129.

993 *Briggs*, Private International Law in the English Courts, at 3.22–3.23 ("mandatory rules" of the English *lex fori* as part of the "structure and methods" of the common law rules of private international law); *Cheshire/North/Fawcett*, PIL, 143–144 (short overview among the "preliminary topics" in the chapter on the "exclusion of foreign law"); *Rogerson*, Collier's Conflict of Laws, 323–326 and 365–366 (only in the context of Rome I and Rome II); but see *Dicey/Morris/Collins*, Conflict of Laws, at 1-053–1-062 (even in the very first chapter of the book). Section 14(4) of the Private International Law (Miscellaneous Provisions) Act 1995 presupposes the existence of overriding mandatory provisions: *Dickinson*, The Rome II Regulation, at 15.15.

994 *Supra* section 2.9.3.2.

995 See *Basedow*, in: LA Borrás, 175, 181; already *id.*, RabelsZ 73 (2009), 455, 458–459, although not in the context of overriding mandatory provisions.

996 *Sonnenberger*, in: FS Kropholler, 227, 241–243; *Kreuzer*, in: Jud/Rechberger/Reichelt (eds.), Kollisionsrecht in der Europäischen Union, 1, 39–43.

i.e. *not* in the section of Rome I that, in principle, rather clearly pertains to all of its conflicts rules. As both Article 9(1) and (2) Rome I expressly mention the entire regulation, however, there is no reason to doubt that it is intended to be a formally general rule in the strict sense within Rome I.[997] Many consider the definition found in Article 9(1) Rome I also relevant for Rome II, which would make it a formally general rule in the strict sense for two regulations already. This position proves persuasive particularly because Article 9 Rome I and Article 16 Rome II share the same title, and because Recital 7 of each regulation mandates a consistent interpretation of both instruments.[998]

In addition, there is Article 11(5) Rome I. Because of the phrase "requirements [...] imposed irrespective of the country where the contract is concluded and irrespective of the law governing the contract", it is plausible to regard the provision as a special rule on certain overriding mandatory provisions.[999] Its scope is narrow, however, as it only pertains to "contract[s] the subject matter of which is a right *in rem* in [...] or a tenancy of immovable property", i.e. contracts subject to Article 4(1)(c) Rome I.[1000] It thus makes sense that Article 11(5) Rome I is not found among the "Other Provisions" if one subscribes to the idea that that chapter is essentially a place for formally general provisions.

2.9.5.2. Rome II

Rome II deals with overriding mandatory provisions in its Article 16; its wording does not use the exact term, but its title does. The provision is placed among the "Common Rules" of Rome II. As if to remove any remaining doubts, Article 16 Rome II expressly refers to "[n]othing in this Regulation", underlining that the provision is relevant for the entire regulation, i.e. formally general in the strict sense. Overtly, the provision only covers overriding mandatory provisions of the forum. Does this exclude foreign overriding mandatory provisions or is this merely a gap to be filled? As the proposal for Rome II did deal with them,[1001] and Rome II itself does not, there is

---

997 Also see e.g. *Renner*, in: Calliess (ed.), Rome Regulations, Art. 9 Rome I at 2 ("applies to all types of contractual claims envisaged by the Rome I Regulation").

998 *von Hein*, in: Calliess (ed.), Rome Regulations, Art. 16 Rome II at 12; also *Junker*, RIW 2010, 257, 268. For relevance in all EU private international law *Magnus*, in: Staudinger, Art. 9 Rom I-VO at 48.

999 *Freitag*, in: Reithmann/Martiny (eds.), Internationales Vertragsrecht, at 5.25; *Renner*, in: Calliess (ed.), Rome Regulations, Art. 9 Rome I at 7; *Schmidt-Kessel*, in: Ferrari (ed.), Rome I Regulation, Article 9 at 22; *Magnus*, in: Staudinger, Art. 9 Rom I-VO at 29; in detail *Loacker*, in: Calliess (ed.), Rome Regulations, Art. 11 Rome I at 81–82.

1000 *Loacker*, in: Calliess (ed.), Rome Regulations, Art. 11 Rome I at 80 (italics in the original).

1001 Article 12(1) in COM(2003) 427 final.

something to be said for the former alternative.[1002] This would not necessarily exclude overriding mandatory provisions found in the legal system of the *lex causae*, for at least here (and at least for torts) the "*lex causae* theory" makes sense: conflicts rules for tort in Rome II can be said to take account of public interests, i.e. conduct regulation.[1003] Then again, one can also question whether the deletion of the respective provision really means a conscious decision in favour of blocking foreign overriding mandatory provisions. Maybe the question has simply been left to the member states for the time being.[1004]

2.9.5.3. Rome III

Rome III makes for a tricky case. On the face of it, it is silent as regards overriding mandatory provisions. None of its provisions or recitals even mention the term. Rome III having been passed after Rome I and Rome II, one could have expected it to contain the same terminology if the EU legislator had intended to create a rule on overriding mandatory provisions.

Article 10 Rome III, however, determines the *lex fori* to be applicable if the chosen law or the law applicable in the absence of a choice "makes no provision for divorce or does not grant one of the spouses equal access to divorce or legal separation on grounds of their sex". This is a – from the perspective of the court seised: unilateral – conflicts rule meant to take precedence over other conflicts rules of Rome III. Thus, it has characteristics at least reminiscent of the present context. Accordingly, it is necessary to analyse Article 10 Rome III more closely here.

Article 10 Rome III as a Traditional Public Policy Provision?

With the ECJ having not yet given a ruling on this provision,[1005] prevailing German opinion (which recently seems to waver, however) considers Article 10

1002 See e.g. *Liukkunen*, Recent PIL Codifications, 14; *Plender/Wilderspin*, European PIL of Obligations, at 27-007–27-008; *de Lima Pinheiro*, Riv. dir. int. priv. proc. 2008, 5, 32; *Wagner*, IPRax 2008, 1, 15.

1003 *Remien*, in: FS von Hoffmann, 334, 342; *Wagner*, IPRax 2008, 1, 15.

1004 See *von Hein*, in: Calliess (ed.), Rome Regulations, Art. 16 Rome II at 20; *Remien*, in: FS von Hoffmann, 334, 345; *Junker*, RIW 2010, 257, 268; *Leible/Lehmann*, RIW 2007, 721, 726; *Heiss/Loacker*, JBl 2007, 613, 644.

1005 The Higher Regional Court of Munich had raised the question twice, but the ECJ first had declared that it manifestly lacked jurisdiction, then that Rome III did not apply to the private divorce in question, making it unnecessary to answer the question as to Article 10 Rome III: ECJ Case C-281/15, Sahyouni v Mamisch, ECLI:EU:C:2016:343 and ECJ Case C-372/16, Sahyouni v Mamisch, ECLI:EU:C:2017:988. Advocate General Saugmandsgaard Øe, however, had stated that he does not consider Article 10 Rome III a traditional public policy provision: Opinion, Case C-372/16, Sahyouni v Mamisch, ECLI:EU:C:2017:686 at 70–89.

Rome III a special but traditional public policy provision.[1006] As public policy clauses traditionally only concern the result of the application of foreign law, not its content as such,[1007] this characterisation entails a restrictive interpretation: Article 10 Rome III only would apply if, in particular, unequal access to divorce led to an adverse result for one of the partners.[1008] This view would also dovetail with the traditional conflicts perspective that all legal systems are equal.[1009]

Ultimately, however, this approach proves unconvincing. To be sure, the idea that an abstract evaluation of foreign law is an automatic, more direct, and quicker way to reject foreign law, and that it is less politically charged than a concrete analysis of the outcome of its application,[1010] would not be persuasive if they were meant as *legal* counterarguments. Both merely concern *policy*,[1011] and the second one is weak even as such. What is the politically more dangerous move: to reject a foreign legal system as improper from the start, or only where it leads to highly problematic results?[1012]

But the sole reason to enact Article 10 Rome III in addition to and completely separately[1013] from the public policy clause in Article 12 Rome III must be that the outcome of the individual case is *not* to be decisive for the former provision.[1014] While Article 12 Rome III refers to the "application" of a provision of (foreign) law, which can only mean the application of a provision "in a given case",[1015] Article 10 Rome III refers to foreign law as such.[1016] Recitals 24 and 25 Rome III also clearly make a distinction between Article 10 Rome III and public policy,[1017] Recital 24 clause 2 even does so expressly.

1006 *Coester-Waltjen*, IPRax 2018, 238, 241–242; *Basedow*, JZ 2016, 269, 279; *Wurmnest*, in: Leible (ed.), General Principles, §14.03[C][1]; *Hau*, FamRZ 2013, 249, 254; *Helms*, FamRZ 2011, 1765, 1771–1772; *Henrich*, in: LA Pintens, 701, 707; *Schurig*, in: FS von Hoffmann, 405, 410; apparently also *Kohler/Pintens*, FamRZ 2011, 1433, 1434. Ambiguously *Finger*, FuR 2011, 313, 314 (with note 8), who states that recourse to Germany's public policy clause is unnecessary where Article 10 Rome III applies – the inapplicability Article 6 EGBGB in divorce matters, however, already follows from the existence of Rome III.

1007 *Infra* 5.3.6. (Public Policy is Results-Oriented).

1008 *Helms*, FamRZ 2011, 1765, 1772; *Henrich*, in: LA Pintens, 701, 707; *Schurig*, in: FS von Hoffmann, 405, 410.

1009 *Gössl*, EuLF 2017, 68, 72, who herself, however, ultimately does not follow this view.

1010 *Calvo Caravaca/Carrascosa González*, CDT 2009, 36, 67.

1011 To the same effect *Winkler von Mohrenfels*, in: MüKoBGB, Art. 10 Rom III-VO at 5.

1012 See already *supra* section 2.9.2.

1013 The *renvoi* provision of Article 11 Rome III separates both provisions, maybe indicating the lack of an inherent connection between them.

1014 *Antomo*, NJW 2018, 435, 437; *M.-P. Weller/Hauber/Schulz*, IPRax 2016, 123, 129–130; *Winkler von Mohrenfels*, in: FS Martiny, 595, 599; for a similar systematic perspective see *Gössl*, EuLF 2017, 68, 72.

1015 Recital 25 Rome III.

1016 Also see *Lein*, in: Calliess (ed.), Rome Regulations, Art. 10 Rome III at 6.

1017 Although there is some ambiguity (only) in the German version of Recital 24, see *Lein*, in: Calliess (ed.), Rome Regulations, Art. 10 Rome III at 11.

To be sure, a rule like Article 13(2) EGBGB[1018] also exists separately from the general public policy provision of Article 6 EGBGB, and nobody considers it anything but a special public policy provision of the traditional ilk.[1019] But Article 13(2) EGBGB has several cumulative requirements; it expressly depends upon the circumstances of the concrete case. This distinguishes it sufficiently from Article 10 Rome III. In light of all this, it is unreasonable to consider Article 10 Rome III to merely be a faultily drafted regular public policy provision that one could perfect through restrictive interpretation. Rather, the unusual[1020] and highly questionable[1021] policy decision to have an abstract evaluation of foreign law must be accepted.

Article 10 Rome III as an Overriding Mandatory Provision?

What, then, is Article 10 Rome III? Some consider Article 10 Rome III to be a special type of rule on overriding mandatory provision, even as an overriding mandatory provision itself.[1022] The main consideration behind this approach seems to be the effect of Article 10 Rome III: replacing the "regular" *lex causae* with another law.[1023] Yet, as already explained,[1024] the way that a provision operates is of greater importance to characterising its nature than its (ultimate) effect. What makes the operation of Article 10 Rome III unusual is its conditioning upon the content of the otherwise applicable law. While it is hardly exceptional for a rule on overriding mandatory provisions to be conditioned upon the content of the legal system of the purported overriding mandatory provision,[1025] the application of the *lex fori* pursuant to Article 10 Rome III depends on the content of the *lex causae*. As demonstrated above, an overriding mandatory provision is supposed to (partially) cut off the application of another conflicts rule, instead of presupposing its application.[1026]

1018 The provision determines the application of German law if a requirement for the conclusion of marriage is not fulfilled under the law applicable to it pursuant to Article 13(1) EGBGB, provided that three further conditions are met.

1019 See only *Coester*, in: MüKoBGB, Art. 13 EGBGB at 24.

1020 But this does not make it *illegal*, of course; *Winkler von Mohrenfels*, in: FS Martiny, 595, 599.

1021 Emphatically *Schurig*, in: FS von Hoffmann, 405, 410 ("Unding", which one might translate roughly as "preposterous"); also *Gruber*, IPRax 2012, 381, 391.

1022 *Winkler von Mohrenfels*, in: FS Martiny, 595, 597 and 602 (but he now seems to have dissociated himself from this position: *id.*, in: MüKoBGB, Art. 10 Rom III-VO at 6); *Verschraegen*, IPR, at 138. To be precise, both have called it an overriding mandatory provision of a conflicts nature ("Eingriffsnorm kollisionsrechtlicher Natur"), probably due to its peculiarities, see *infra* footnote 1027 and accompanying text. Also see *M.-P. Weller/Hauber/Schulz*, IPRax 2016, 123, 130.

1023 *Winkler von Mohrenfels*, in: FS Martiny, 595, 597.

1024 *Supra* section 2.9.2.

1025 In particular: is the provision to be applied regardless of the otherwise applicable law? Is "the respect for [it] regarded as crucial by a country for safeguarding its public interests, such as its political, social or economic organisation" (Article 9(1) Rome I)?

1026 Similarly *Leandro*, NLCC 2011, 1503, 1508.

It is also remarkable that Article 10 Rome III does not seem to be conditioned upon the content of the *lex fori*. As the *lex fori* will be the law of a member state, it is probably unnecessary to specify that the *lex fori* must give equal access to divorce to both partners in order to be applicable. Still, its application does not depend on whether – "on its own" – it would apply regardless of the otherwise governing law.[1027] Article 10 Rome III makes this decision entirely independently. Finally, Article 10 Rome III determines that the *lex fori* replaces the *lex causae* in its entirety, not just in part, whereas overriding mandatory provisions typically only concern a part.

In conclusion, Article 10 Rome III operates thus: first, the *lex causae* must be determined; and second, it must undergo an abstract assessment as to its content. If it fails this analysis, Article 10 Rome III determines the application of the *lex fori* instead of the *lex causae*, regardless of whether the latter would internally be considered as "overriding". All in all, this is sufficiently different from the usual operation of overriding mandatory provisions not to consider Article 10 Rome III as belonging in this context.

Article 10 Rome III as an Anomalous Public Policy Provision?

Because of the focus on the governing law just demonstrated, one might be tempted to consider Article 10 Rome III as a public policy provision after all, just as an anomalous one.[1028] But there are further differences between this provision and the usual public policy reservation. Not the *lex fori* but EU law (in fact, Article 10 Rome III itself) provides the yardstick against which the incompatibility of foreign law is to be decided. While there is no European public policy (yet) in general,[1029] Article 10 Rome III sets forth a (isolated) substantive standard. Furthermore, the immediate recourse to the *lex fori* instead of a more nuanced approach – for example, if the law chosen by the parties does not meet the requirements of Article 10 Rome III, Article 8 Rome III might still provide for a more adequate law than the *lex fori* – is not the necessary consequence of a public policy violation.

Article 10 Rome III as a "Replacement Clause"

In the end, Article 10 Rome III does not fit well into any existing category of private international law.[1030] Hence, one can understand why some have

---

[1027] Presumably, this is why Article 10 Rome III itself has been called an overriding mandatory provision instead of being considered a gateway for domestic law.

[1028] For this result apparently *Leandro*, NLCC 2011, 1503, 1509.

[1029] *Winkler von Mohrenfels*, in: FS Martiny, 595, 601, who seems to consider this a further reason against the characterisation of Article 10 Rome III as a public policy clause.

[1030] To the same effect ("Article 10 Rome III does not fit in the traditional conflict of laws system.") *Gössl*, EuLF 2017, 68, 73.

dubbed Article 10 Rome III a "rejection clause" ("cláusula de rechazo"),[1031] without assigning it to an existing, traditional type of rule. The only downside of the expression is its focus on the negative effect of the rule, whereas its positive side – making the *lex fori* the governing law – takes a back seat. If one were to coin a new term, it should rather be something along the lines of "replacement clause", containing both the negative and the positive effect. In any case, Article 10 Rome III does not belong in the context of overriding mandatory provisions.

2.9.5.4. The Succession Regulation

The Succession Regulation does not use the term "overriding mandatory provisions" either. Its Article 30, however, concerns certain rules of the state where immovable property is located that "are applicable irrespective of the law applicable to the succession". The phrase "applicable irrespective of the law applicable" is telling. Almost everybody agrees, hence, that Article 30 Succession Regulation concerns certain overriding mandatory provisions.[1032] Contrary to Article 9 Rome I and Article 16 Rome II, the wording does not refer to the entire regulation, which would have been an express indication of the formally general nature of the rule. But its location close to Articles 31 through 38 Succession Regulation, all of which will turn out to be formally general over the course of this analysis,[1033] serves as an indication of such a character. Recital 54 clause 2 Succession Regulation states that it is intended to "ensure the application of" the respective domestic provisions. This only works if Article 30 Succession Regulation takes precedence over any other conflicts provision of the Succession Regulation (to the extent necessary[1034]). Hence, it is a formally general rule.

1031 *Calvo Caravaca/Carrascosa González*, CDT 2009, 36, 67; now also *Winkler von Mohrenfels*, in: MüKoBGB, Art. 10 Rom III-VO at 6.

1032 *Lagarde*, in: Bergquist et al., EU-ErbVO, Art. 30 at 4; *id.*, in: Bonomi/Schmid (eds.), Successions internationales, 11, 17–18; *Dutta*, in: MüKoBGB, Art. 30 EuErbVO at 1; *Wilke*, RIW 2012, 601, 607; *MPI*, RabelsZ 74 (2010), 522, 644; more cautiously, however, *Martiny*, IPRax 2012, 119, 129 ("resembles the application of overriding mandatory provisions"); but see *Kramer et al.*, A European Framework for private international law, 81, stating that the Succession Regulation does not address overriding mandatory provisions at all.

1033 Article 31 Succession Regulation: *infra* section 5.8. (European Union); Articles 32 and 33 Succession Regulation: *infra* section 5.10.; Article 34 Succession Regulation: *infra* section 5.5.3.; Article 35 Succession Regulation: *infra* section 5.6.2.; Articles 36–38 Succession Regulation: *infra* section 5.2.

1034 "[T]hose special rules shall apply to the succession *in so far as*, under the law of that State, they are applicable irrespective of the law applicable to the succession." (Article 30 Succession Regulation, emphasis added.)

2.9.5.5. The M-Property Regulation and the RP-Property Regulation

After two regulations that either do not deal with overriding mandatory provisions at all (Rome III) or solely to a limited degree (Succession Regulation), the M-Property Regulation and the RP-Property Regulation essentially pick up where Rome I left off. Article 30(1) M-/RP-Property Regulation is a copy of Article 9(2) Rome I; the definition for overriding mandatory provisions found in Article 30(2) M-/RP-Property Regulation has clearly been transferred from Article 9(1) Rome I. A counterpart of Article 9(3) Rome I is missing, however. Hence, the treatment of foreign overriding mandatory provisions will likely prove as contentious as it does under Rome II.

2.9.5.6. Who Makes the Conflicts Decision?

If a rule of substantive law is to *apply* regardless of the otherwise governing law, its application must be determined by another rule, *per definitionem* by a conflicts rule. The question thus arises whether this conflicts rule is to be found at the EU level or (only) in domestic law. For present purposes, it is particularly interesting to see whether the answer to this question is formally general for EU private international law.

Article 30 Succession Regulation

The Succession Regulation provides the clearest answer.[1035] Article 30 Succession Regulation itself determines the respective domestic provisions to apply. To be sure, it sets forth that the respective rules of domestic law must be "applicable irrespective of the law applicable to the succession". But this is merely a *requirement* of its own legal consequence that "those special rules shall apply". In other words, Article 30 Succession Regulation is a conflicts provision conditioned upon domestic conflicts rules. This is why the exclusion of *renvoi* by Article 34(2) Succession Regulation is useless to the extent that it refers to Article 30 Succession Regulation. Article 30 Succession Regulation only determines the applicable law under the condition that the respective state would apply its own rules. The applicable law thus *cannot* refer to foreign law, so it is utterly redundant to exclude *renvoi*.[1036]

[1035] If one were to consider Article 10 Rome III relevant in this context, it provides a clear answer, too. As already demonstrated (*supra* section 2.9.5.3. (Article 10 Rome III as an Overriding Mandatory Provision?)), it itself determines the application of the *lex fori*, even regardless of the *lex fori*'s own conflicts decisions.

[1036] *Wilke*, RIW 2012, 601, 608; *Solomon*, in: LA Schurig, 237, 262.

There seems to be no opening for other overriding mandatory provisions, i.e. no possibility to develop another EU conflicts rule (or to rely on a domestic conflicts rule) to determine the applicability of any substantive rule deemed applicable, neither by Article 30 Succession Regulation nor by any of the regulation's ordinary conflicts provisions.[1037] When Recital 54 clause 3 Succession Regulation calls for "a strict interpretation" of Article 30 Succession Regulation, this is an indication not only that other foreign overriding mandatory provisions must be excluded, but also that overriding mandatory provisions of the *lex fori* cannot apply unless determined by the Succession Regulation. In particular, *lex fori* overriding mandatory provisions cannot apply because they "themselves" – i.e. domestic *conflicts* rules – determine their application.[1038] As the Succession Regulation in Article 30 itself determines the application of domestic overriding mandatory provisions, it is more persuasive to assume that it does not leave any gateway for domestic overriding mandatory provisions.

Rome I, Rome II, the M-Property Regulation, and the RP-Property Regulation

A similarly clear conflicts decision at the EU level is missing from the other regulations dealing with overriding mandatory provisions. On the contrary, when Article 9(2) Rome I, Article 16 Rome II, and Article 30 M-/RP-Property Regulation state in unison that "[n]othing in this Regulation shall restrict the application" of overriding mandatory provisions of the law of the forum, it is quite obvious that they *presuppose* a respective conflicts rule.[1039] They do not (even) mandate the application of an overriding mandatory provision of the *lex fori*.[1040] This corresponds to the notion of Articles 9 Rome I and 16 Rome II as "gateways",[1041] or "blocking rules",[1042] that provide for an opening for overriding mandatory provisions.[1043] But do these Articles presuppose a domestic or (also) an EU conflicts rule?

1037 Overriding mandatory provisions of the legal system of the *lex causae* thus could be applicable, *Dutta*, in: MüKoBGB, Art. 30 EuErbVO at 11.

1038 But see *Dutta*, in: MüKoBGB, Art. 30 EuErbVO at 11, who agrees with the first part of the statement, but allows for some kind of "influence" of overriding mandatory provisions of the *lex fori*. Admittedly, if a public policy violation (Article 35 Succession Regulation) leads to the application of the *lex fori*, *this* could include overriding mandatory provisions.

1039 See e.g. *Köhler*, Eingriffsnormen, 8; *von Bar/Mankowski*, IPR I, §4 at 86 (for Article 34 EGBGB). The account of *Renner*, in: Calliess (ed.), Rome Regulations, Art. 9 Rome I appears to be self-contradictory. First, he considers Article 9(2) Rome I a unilateral conflicts rule (at 22), but then states that it does not itself determine the applicable law (at 23).

1040 *Schmidt-Kessel*, in: Ferrari (ed.), Rome I Regulation, Article 9 at 39.

1041 *Sonnenberger*, in: Leible (ed.), General Principles, §7.01; *Freitag*, in: Reithmann/Martiny (eds.), Internationales Vertragsrecht, at 5.56; *Roth*, in: FS Dauses, 315, 319; *Kroll-Ludwigs*, Die Rolle der Parteiautonomie, 72 (note 475).

1042 *von Bar/Mankowski*, IPR I, §4 at 86.

1043 *Schmidt-Kessel*, in: Ferrari (ed.), Rome I Regulation, Article 9 at 3; *Biagoni*, NLCC 2009, 768, 797.

Little is to be gained from looking at the recitals. Recitals 37 Rome I and 32 Rome II are rather unclear in their English[1044] version. They only refer to the possibility of the courts "applying exceptions based on public policy and overriding mandatory provisions". Yet a court will typically not apply an exception *based* on overriding mandatory provisions, but the provisions themselves[1045] – after all, Articles 9 Rome I and 16 Rome II mention the "application of" overriding mandatory provisions.

Many authors who deal with the nature of Articles 9 Rome I and 16 Rome II appear to understand them in the way that only domestic law provides the necessary conflicts rule.[1046] But their statements are not entirely without ambiguity. There often is a way to read them as merely referring to domestic law being required to determine the application of its own substantive rules in order for them to qualify as overriding mandatory provisions. This does not necessarily mean that the domestic conflicts rule is the *only* one relevant from the perspective of EU law. Put differently, it is not clear whether these authors refer to one (necessary) condition and make no mention of another (sufficient) condition, or whether they mean to imply that there is one condition only.

By contrast, thus far only Köhler seems to have stated expressly and plausibly, albeit controversially,[1047] that the necessary conflicts rule is one to be found/determined at the EU level.[1048] Of his many noteworthy points I will only mention a few. If EU law gave *carte blanche* to domestic legislators as regards the creation of unilateral conflicts rules, overriding mandatory provisions (at least of the *lex fori*) meeting the standards of Article 9(1) Rome I could also apply in cases where Article 6 Rome II has determined the governing law. As Article 6 Rome II itself takes account of certain public interests, this cannot be the correct outcome. At least in certain instances,

---

1044 In Italian and Spanish, one comes across the same problem, whereas the French and German versions are phrased more clearly.

1045 *von Hein*, in: Calliess (ed.), Rome Regulations, Art. 16 Rome II at 7.

1046 E.g. *Freitag*, in: Reithmann/Martiny (eds.), Internationales Vertragsrecht, at 5.59; *Magnus*, in: Staudinger, Art. 9 Rom I-VO at 53; *Lüttringhaus*, Grenzüberschreitender Diskriminierungsschutz, 194. In any case, this is how *Köhler*, Eingriffsnormen, 106, understands these authors. See also *Schmidt-Kessel*, in: Ferrari (ed.), Rome I Regulation, Article 9 at 7; *Lüttringhaus*, IPRax 2014, 146, 148; *Kroll-Ludwigs*, Die Rolle der Parteiautonomie, 72 (with note 475); *Briggs*, Conflict of Laws, 248 ("operation [of Article 9(1) Rome I] entirely determined by the court in which the trial takes place") and 249 (a British court may not even be bound by the restrictions of Article 9(1) Rome I); *Rühl*, in: Max Planck Encyclopedia of European Private Law, s. v. "Unilateralism", 1735, 1737–1738; *Remien*, in: FS von Hoffmann, 334, 335; *Lando/Nielsen*, CMLRev 45 (2008), 1687, 1719. Expressly against an EU conflicts decision now *Roth*, in: FS Dauses, 315, 329. *Martiny*, in: MüKoBGB, Art. 9 Rom I at 108, now considers that Article 9(2) Rome I should be regarded as having conflicts implications itself.

1047 See *Roth*, in: FS Dauses, 315, 328–329, for several objections; *Schurig*, in: Mansel (ed.), IPR im 20. Jahrhundert, 5, 20, however, endorses *Köhler*'s approach.

1048 *Köhler*, Eingriffsnormen, 165, 264, and passim.

then, EU private international law seems to decide itself *whether or not* a domestic overriding mandatory provision applies, even if that rule stays within the framework of Article 9(1) Rome I.[1049] It is no cogent counterargument that Article 9(1) Rome I itself refers to the perspective of the country whose purported overriding mandatory provision is at issue ("regarded by a country").[1050] This could be a mere reference to domestic law serving an indicative function.[1051] In the words used here: it could merely be a reference to a necessary condition without mentioning the sufficient condition. A consistent and coherent solution for the entire EU can only be found if the conflicts rule is determined at the EU level in light of EU private international law policies.[1052]

To illustrate Köhler's approach with one of his examples:[1053] if a domestic rule of cartel law leads to the voidness of a contract, no written conflicts rule in Rome I refers to it[1054] because of the different underlying interests. If the domestic rule is to apply regardless, a(nother) *EU* conflicts rule is required. In this particular case, instead of developing a completely new rule at EU level, Article 6(3) Rome II can be applied by analogy: if the domestic rule is one of the country whose market is affected, it can apply. On the other hand, to the extent that an EU conflicts rule already takes certain interests into account and determines the application of the law of country A, there is no room for (another) special conflicts rule for a purported overriding mandatory provision of the law of country B, even if B is the forum state. This is particularly relevant for Articles 6 and 8 Rome I, i.e. consumers and employees.[1055]

Conclusion

Following the approach just outlined for Rome I and Rome II, and in light of Article 30 Succession Regulation, the necessary conflicts rule for a domestic overriding mandatory provision is to be found or developed at the level of the EU.

2.9.5.7. Application of Overriding Mandatory Provisions of the European Union

If EU law contains overriding mandatory provisions, there can be little doubt that the respective conflicts rules prevail over the conflicts rules of the six private

1049 *Köhler*, Eingriffsnormen, 112.
1050 For this view, however, *Plender/Wilderspin*, European PIL of Obligations, at 12-014.
1051 *Köhler*, Eingriffsnormen, 117.
1052 *Köhler*, Eingriffsnormen, 124.
1053 *Köhler*, Eingriffsnormen, 128–129.
1054 Not even if this rule is part of the legal system of the *lex causae*, *supra* section 2.9.3.2.
1055 *Köhler*, Eingriffsnormen, 141–143. With the same outcome, but from a different perspective *Roth*, in: FS Dauses, 315, 319.

international law regulations. This is merely the easy case of overriding mandatory provisions by the same legislator that created the regular conflicts rules. Recourse to the EU provisions on overriding mandatory provisions is unnecessary where binding EU law provides a special conflicts rule.[1056]

As usual, the real problem arises where an express special conflicts rule is missing; an additional factor of complication is introduced where a rule of a directive is supposed to have an overriding mandatory nature. Two opposing forces are at issue:[1057] from the vantage point of conflict of laws, exceptions to the regular system should be avoided; from the vantage point of EU law, the notion of its *effet utile* might seem to mandate as many exceptions as possible. In the controversial *Ingmar* decision, the ECJ identified the protection of "the operation of undistorted competition in the internal market" – rather than, or at least in addition to,[1058] the balancing of private interests – as the purpose of Articles 17 through 19 Self-Employed Commercial Agents Directive.[1059] It held that these provisions[1060] must be "applied where the situation is closely connected with the Community [...] irrespective of the law by which the parties intended the contract to be governed".[1061] From the perspective adopted here, this implicates a special EU conflicts rule because the provisions of Rome I are not based on the public interests as identified by the Court.[1062]

In the more recent *Unamar* case, the ECJ unequivocally refers to Article 7 Rome Convention when concerned with the application of national law

---

1056 For Rome I *Magnus*, in: Staudinger, Art. 9 Rom I-VO at 35; *Roth*, in: FS Spellenberg, 309, 320; presumably also *Renner*, in: Calliess (ed.), Rome Regulations, Art. 9 Rome I at 26. But see *Freitag*, in: Reithmann/Martiny (eds.), Internationales Vertragsrecht, at 5.39; *Remien*, in: FS von Hoffmann, 334, 338; both essentially rely on the idea that binding EU law forms part of the legal system of the forum and thus must be applied in accordance with Article 9(2) Rome I.

1057 *Kühne*, in: FS Wegen, 451, 454–455.

1058 Some have understood the Court to hold the protection of the commercial agent to be a further purpose of the rules, e.g. *Freitag*, in: Reithmann/Martiny (eds.), Internationales Vertragsrecht, at 5.45; *Jayme*, IPRax 2001, 190, 191.

1059 ECJ Case C-381/98, Ingmar GB Ltd v Eaton Leonard Technologies Inc., Reports of Cases 2000, I-9305, at 24.

1060 The Court rather clearly refers to the application of the provisions *of the directive* rather than of the domestic provisions transposing the directive. Only the latter option can be correct, however (for this see e.g. *Magnus*, in: Staudinger, Art. 9 Rom I-VO at 42; *Roth*, CMLRev 39 (2002), 369, 374). It would be highly doubtful to apply domestic law as it should be (according to the directive) instead of how it actually is (as implemented in national law, albeit perhaps influenced by interpretation in conformity with the directive). Private international law does not serve the purpose of compensating inherent disadvantages of certain types of legal acts of the EU; *Köhler*, Eingriffsnormen, 152–153. In *Unamar*, the Court now refers to "national law transposing Articles 17 and 18 of the directive", too; ECJ Case C-184/12, United Antwerp Maritime Agencies (Unamar) NV v Navigation Maritime Bulgare, ECLI:EU:C:2013:663, at 41.

1061 ECJ Case C-381/98, Ingmar GB Ltd v Eaton Leonard Technologies Inc., Reports of Cases 2000, I-9305, at 25.

1062 *Köhler*, Eingriffsnormen, 160–161.

transposing a directive[1063] – even though *Unamar* concerns a domestic *substantive extension* of the scope of the Self-Employed Commercial Agents Directive. The Court also points to Article 9 Rome I, although this provision was not yet applicable.[1064] This suggests that the Court will not change its approach if faced with the same issue in the Rome I context.[1065] It must be regarded as settled, then, that it is a question belonging in the context of overriding mandatory provisions whether domestic provisions implementing an EU directive are to be applied regardless of the otherwise governing law.[1066] It follows that purported overriding mandatory provisions based on a directive must conform to the requirements of Article 9 Rome I in the context of contractual obligations. As the Court insists on the intent of national legislatures,[1067] however, it seems that they enjoy a wide margin of appreciation when attributing a rule with an overriding nature.[1068] While it is not clear at which level the Court would locate the necessary conflicts rule, a domestic "claim for application" would seem to go a long way towards actual application. On the other hand, the ECJ has at least paid lip service to a "strict interpretation" of Article 9(1) Rome I and has made sibylline reference to the "uniform application of the Rome Convention".[1069] There could still be a chance of the ECJ reining in the application of domestic overriding mandatory provisions, at least in cases of a directive providing for full harmonisation or of an only *gradual* extension of a directive.[1070]

2.9.5.8. No Obligation to Apply Overriding Mandatory Provisions of Other Member States

Finally, the question arises whether one member state is required to (at least) apply overriding mandatory provisions of another member state.

1063 ECJ Case C-184/12, United Antwerp Maritime Agencies (Unamar) NV v Navigation Maritime Bulgare, ECLI:EU:C:2013:663, at 41; for a case note in English with copious references to other case notes in different languages see *Rühl*, CMLRev. 53 (2016), 209.

1064 ECJ Case C-184/12, United Antwerp Maritime Agencies (Unamar) NV v Navigation Maritime Bulgare, ECLI:EU:C:2013:663, at 48.

1065 *Kühne*, in: FS Wegen, 451, 456; *Schilling*, ZEuP 2014, 842, 847.

1066 *Lüttringhaus*, IPRax 2014, 146, 148. In the wake of *Ingmar*, this had been doubted, see e.g. *Freitag*, in: Reithmann/Martiny (eds.), Internationales Vertragsrecht, at 5.47.

1067 ECJ Case C-184/12, United Antwerp Maritime Agencies (Unamar) NV v Navigation Maritime Bulgare, ECLI:EU:C:2013:663, at 50 and 52.

1068 *Kühne*, in: FS Wegen, 451, 460; *Schmidt-Kessel*, in: Ferrari (ed.), Rome I Regulation, Article 9 at 18; *Renner*, in: Calliess (ed.), Rome Regulations, Art. 9 Rome I at 20; *Lüttringhaus*, IPRax 2014, 146, 148; *Mankowski*, EWiR 2014, 11, 12; *Schilling*, ZEuP 2014, 842, 847 and 859; more cautiously *Mansel*, in: FS Roth, 375, 376 (note 10); for a high threshold for domestic legislators *Roth*, in: FS Spellenberg, 309, 327, but now seemingly more leniently *id.*, in: FS Dauses, 315, 319.

1069 ECJ Case C-184/12, United Antwerp Maritime Agencies (Unamar) NV v Navigation Maritime Bulgare, ECLI:EU:C:2013:663, at 49 and 51.

1070 *Lüttringhaus*, IPRax 2014, 146, 150.

If a positive answer is to be found in the Treaties, only the principle of sincere cooperation laid down in Article 4(3) TEU suggests itself.[1071] Yet this provision contains a clear reference to EU law, i.e. serves as a safeguard for existing EU law, rather than as a basis to developing new duties without a connection to such law.[1072] Thus, one might refer to the internal market, indubitably a Treaty goal (Article 26 TFEU), and its requirement of harmony of decisions.[1073] As long as there are different national systems, however, harmony of decisions is to be achieved by harmonisation and duties of recognition through secondary EU law.[1074] Article 26 TFEU itself expressly requires *the Union* to take action "with the aim of establishing or ensuring the functioning of the internal market".[1075] Again, it seems difficult to come up with a stand-alone rule of primary EU law *for the member states*.

By now, the ECJ has answered part of the question. It has held that Article 4(3) TEU does not allow a member state to *apply* overriding provisions of another member state beyond Article 9(3) Rome I, arguing that Article 4(3) TEU does not authorise the circumvention of duties imposed by EU law.[1076]

If one adopts the view that the conflicts rule leading to the application of the overriding mandatory provision is to be found or developed in EU private international law, however, a basis in the Treaties is not even necessary. The conflicts rule would be binding on all member states simply by being a rule of EU private international law.[1077] From a conceptual point of view, then, the issue would be easy – the problem would "only" be the correct interpretation or development of the EU private international law rules.

1071 See e.g. *Bonomi*, Yearbook of Private International Law I (1999), 215, 240–241; to this effect recently also the Austrian Supreme Court in a dictum, JBl 2013, 363, 364. *Roth*, in: FS Dauses, 315, 334, and in: Remien/Kieninger (eds.), Europäische Kollisionsrechtsvereinheitlichung, 11, 44, considers Article 9(3) Rome I to contravene Article 4(3) TEU to the extent that it does not allow member states to take account of all overriding mandatory provisions of other member states – the ECJ now implicitly has taken the opposing view, Case C-135/15, Hellenic Republic v Grigorios Nikiforidis, ECLI:EU:C:2016:774 at 54; against this again *Roth*, IPRax 2018, 177, 185–186.

1072 *Roth*, in: FS Dauses, 315, 331; *Köhler*, Eingriffsnormen, 296; *von Bar/Mankowski*, IPR I, §4 at 117.

1073 *Roth*, in: FS Dauses, 315, 322 (with further references); *Bonomi*, in: Baratta (ed.), DIP, s. v. "Norme di applicazione necessaria", 233, 241; *id.*, Yearbook of Private International Law I (1999), 215, 240.

1074 *von Bar/Mankowski*, IPR I, §4 at 117; for a nuanced approach *Remien*, in: FS von Hoffmann, 334, 340.

1075 *Köhler*, Eingriffsnormen, 304 (with further references).

1076 ECJ Case C-135/15, Hellenic Republic v Grigorios Nikiforidis, ECLI:EU:C:2016:774 at 54. It is possible to take overriding mandatory provisions into account as *matters of fact*, ibid. at 51–53 and 55.

1077 *Köhler*, Eingriffsnormen, 309–311. One might still wonder whether Article 9 Rome I does not suggest a very restrictive approach in this regard; from a different perspective *Freitag*, in: Reithmann/Martiny (eds.), Internationales Vertragsrecht, at 5.41.

2.10. SUBSIDIARY CONFLICTS RULES

Particularly if private international law has been subject to codification efforts, one would expect to find a conflicts provision for every case. What, however, if – after characterisation – it turns out that none of the different subject matters applies? The governing law still has to be determined. This distinguishes the lack of an applicable conflicts rule from the lack of a substantive provision. In substantive law, it is entirely conceivable that a "gap" implies that something is not supposed to exist. A conflicts provision, however, must exist. At most, one might interpret a gap in private international law as an implicit determination of the *lex fori* as the governing law; yet where a system is based on the closest connection, such a flat-out rule would seem out of place.

Thus, the issue is the determination of the applicable law in absence of a pertinent subject matter: what is the subsidiary conflicts rule? Described in this way, it is obvious that the topic concerns the subject matter of conflicts rules. To be sure, conflicts rules also occasionally do not work because their *connecting factor* does not exist in real life.[1078] But these instances will be dealt with below in the context of the respective connecting factor. As it is typically impossible to tell "in advance" where a subject matter is missing, the issue is formally general.

The topic should not be confused with the idea of "escape clauses". These conflicts rules apply *even though* another conflicts rule *is* applicable. Theirs is an issue of disregarding the typified connecting factor of another conflicts rule in favour of a connecting factor deemed more appropriate in the given case. As such, it will be discussed later.[1079]

2.10.1. Member States

It will become apparent that many member states expressly address certain issues of *connecting factors* failing to work, and that they often do so in a formally general manner. By contrast, only few domestic private international law codes deal with the case in which no subject matter applies. In fact, only five member states have such a provision among their general ones.[1080]

1078 This may sound implausible at first if one thinks of a connecting factor like one person's habitual residence or the location of property. It might be problematic to ascertain such a connecting factor, but there is little doubt that it *exists*. If, however, the conflicts rule requires a common habitual residence of two people, such a thing really might not exist. Moreover, the connecting factor could be nationality and the person concerned might have more than one or none at all.

1079 *Infra* section 4.1.

1080 Article 2(2) Bulgarian PIL Code; Article 2 Croatian PIL Act; §24(2) Czech PIL Act; §11 Hungarian PIL Act; Article 3 Slovenian PIL Act.

While §1 Austrian PIL Act does not presuppose any gaps, and thus constitutes no express subsidiary conflicts rule, it is said to operate as one if there is indeed a gap.[1081]

There is also Article 67 Polish PIL Act. It is one of two provisions in the chapter on "other" legal relationships: legal relationships falling within the scope of the Polish PIL Act but not covered by (the subject matter of) another conflicts rule. This position underscores that a question of the subject matter is at issue. One could also imagine the place of this provision to be among the general provisions of the Polish PIL Act.[1082]

2.10.2. European Union

The starting point is already different for EU private international law. It does not (yet) cover all areas of private international law, nor is an EU conflicts rule legally necessary for all areas not yet covered. Gaps exist because of the limited scope of application of each regulation; domestic private international law applies where there is no EU private international law ("external gap").[1083] Thus, one might only wonder if a situation can occur in which the scope of application (as also defined by the expressly excluded matters) of a private international law regulation is met, but no pertinent subject matter exists for a given case ("internal gap"). For such a situation, a subsidiary conflicts rule would be necessary.

All Regulations Except for Rome II

In Rome I, an internal gap seems impossible. Even if there is no other conflicts rule for a "contractual obligation" (Article 1(1) clause 1 Rome I), Article 4(4) Rome I will determine the applicable law. It is a subsidiary conflicts rule,[1084] relevant for all of Rome I – not so much by its position but by its function.[1085] There is no contractual obligation in the sense of Rome I for which it does not determine the governing law.[1086]

Pursuant to Article 1(1) Rome III, its scope of application covers "divorce and legal separation". Its conflicts rules in Article 5 and Article 8 Rome III

1081 *Lurger/Melcher*, IPR, at 1/68; *Neumayr*, in: ABGB-Kurzkommentar, §1 IPRG at 4.

1082 *Ernst*, RabelsZ 76 (2012), 597, 610.

1083 Accordingly, it is up to each domestic legal system whether it uses EU conflicts rules *as conflicts rules of its own* in areas to which those rules would not apply from an EU perspective, as long as this does not mean that another applicable EU private international law rule is disregarded.

1084 *Gebauer*, in: Calliess (ed.), Rome Regulations, Art. 4 Rome I at 75.

1085 Article 4(4) Rome I itself requires that neither Article 4(1) nor Article 4(2) applies, and the former of those two paragraphs refers to Articles 5 to 8. Article 4(4) Rome I thus only applies if no subject matter of Rome I is relevant for a given case.

1086 *Martiny*, in: MüKoBGB, Art. 4 Rom I-VO at 310.

likewise have the subject matter of "divorce and legal separation". Scope of application and subject matter are congruent; an internal gap cannot exist. The result in the succession context is exactly the same: Article 1(1) clause 1 Succession Regulation determines its application to "succession to the estates of deceased persons"; its conflicts provisions always rely on the notion of "succession" too. A subsidiary conflicts provision is unnecessary for both regulations. The same applies for the M-Property Regulation and the RP-Property Regulation: their conflicts provisions require a "matrimonial property regime"/"property consequences of registered partnerships". This coincides with their respective scope of application set forth in Article 1(1) clause 1 M-/RP-Property Regulation.

Rome II

Rome II raises more doubts than the other five regulations. It seems to apply to "non-contractual obligations" (Article 1(1) clause 1 Rome II) in general, i.e. *all* obligations in civil and commercial matters *with the exception of* contractual ones. Yet its conflicts provisions only cover individually named obligations: torts/delict (Articles 4–9), unjust enrichment (Article 10), *negotiorum gestio* (Article 11), and *culpa in contrahendo* (Article 12). Perhaps a non-contractual obligation exists that none of these categories covers?[1087]

German and Austrian courts were recently occupied with the statutory liability for somebody else's debts after taking over the latter's commercial business.[1088] The supreme courts of both countries, as well as scholars, agree that this liability cannot be characterised as contractual.[1089] If Rome I and Rome II are supposed to be complementary instruments – as their wording,[1090] the Commission's intentions,[1091] and the purpose of uniform private international law for obligations do suggest[1092] – the characterisation as non-contractual would follow, i.e. the application of Rome II.

So far, however, everybody agrees that no conflicts rule of Rome II applies as regards the statutory liability for debts incurred by a business prior to takeover.[1093] If at all, it is said, Article 4 Rome II could apply, but it is usually

1087 For an overview of problematic scenarios in this regard see *Freitag*, IPRax 2016, 418, 421–425. He comes to the conclusion that a gap between Rome I and Rome II exists.

1088 BGH IPRax 2015, 257; OGH IPRax 2015, 541. The cases do not concern the Rome regulations yet, so they merely serve as an illustration.

1089 *Kramme*, IPRax 2015, 225, 227–228; *Freitag*, in: FS Spellenberg, 169, 175.

1090 See the binary distinction in each Article 1(1) clause 1: "contractual" vs. "*non*-contractual".

1091 COM(2003) 427 final, 8.

1092 *Lehmann*, IPRax 2015, 495, 496–497, as to all of these aspects in more detail.

1093 *Lehmann*, IPRax 2015, 495, 498; *Kramme*, IPRax 2015, 225, 227–228; *Weller*, in: Calliess (ed.), Rome Regulations, Art. 1 Rome I at 2 (with note 6); *Freitag*, in: FS Spellenberg, 169, 175.

discarded quickly. First, because "tort" is supposed to imply unlawful behaviour.[1094] Second, because "tort" is understood in line with the ECJ's decisions regarding what is now Article 7(2) Brussels Ibis[1095] to mean "liability for damages not related to a contract". Liability as it is at issue here (typically) does not concern any wrongful conduct or damages in the ordinary sense.[1096]

The result would thus be that there can be a third category next to contractual and non-contractual obligations (*tertium datur*),[1097] one not covered by either Rome I or Rome II.[1098] One would take recourse to domestic private international law to determine the governing law; or one would maintain that Rome I and II are exhaustive and apply domestic liability rules such as the present ones as overriding mandatory provisions.[1099] *De lege ferenda*, one would need to think about a special conflicts rule for particular cases of non-contractual liability not covered by any of the subject matters of Rome II – or about introducing a subsidiary conflicts rule.

The problem with this position from the German-speaking world is that the ECJ's decisions in other languages do not mention "damages". Here, the definition merely covers "liability of a defendant"/"la responsabilité d'un défendeur" not related to a contract. Statutory liability for somebody else's debts triggered by the takeover of a business could meet this description more easily. One might object that at least the connecting factor requires "damage" to have occurred, and that at least at this stage wrongful conduct is implied. But Article 2(1) Rome II sets forth that "damage" is meant to describe the consequences of tort/delict, unjust enrichment, *negotiorum gestio*, and *culpa in contrahendo*. Hence, it does not imply wrongful conduct *per se*; its content merely depends on the respective non-contractual category. If "tort/delict" can be understood to include the liability at issue here, the requirement of "damage" does not pose an obstacle of its own. The more persuasive objection would be to doubt that the ECJ's decisions on the

1094 *Freitag*, in: FS Spellenberg, 169, 175; presumably also *Lehmann*, IPRax 2015, 495, 498.

1095 See only ECJ Case C-189/87, Athanasios Kalfelis v Bankhaus Schröder, Münchmeyer, Hengst and Co. and others, Reports of Cases 1988, 5565, at 18; Case C-261/90, Mario Reichert, Hans-Heinz Reichert and Ingeborg Kockler v Dresdner Bank AG, Reports of Cases 1992, I-2149, at 16.

1096 *Kramme*, IPRax 2015, 225, 228; *Weller*, in: Calliess (ed.), Rome Regulations, Art. 1 Rome I at 2 (with note 6).

1097 *Freitag*, in: FS Spellenberg, 169, 175; *Kramme*, IPRax 2015, 225, 228; *Dickinson*, The Rome II Regulation, at 3.262; at least considering the possibility of a third category of obligations *Dicey/Morris/Collins*, Conflict of Laws, at 34-016.

1098 This pill might be easier to swallow in light of those exceptions to Rome II that otherwise certainly would fulfil the respective scope of application, such as Article 1(2)(f), (g) Rome II. In other words, there are non-contractual obligations that remain subject to domestic private international law for the time being, anyway.

1099 *Lehmann*, IPRax 2015, 495, 498–499, who admits that this is far from ideal; also see *Freitag*'s critique, IPRax 2016, 418, 420–421.

interpretation of "tort, delict *or quasi-delict*" in the Brussels context are conclusive for the interpretation of (only) "tort/delict" in the Rome II context. The former concept is residual,[1100] the latter does not have to be. If one is still willing to characterise liability such as the present one as tort/delict for the purposes of Rome II, the result is admittedly painful to the ears of everyone who has thus far associated these terms with the occurrence of some wrong. Yet it does have the double policy advantage of congruence between the scope of application and the subject matters of Rome II,[1101] and of leaving no room between Rome I and II. A subsidiary conflicts rule in Rome II would not be necessary if one assumes that any non-contractual obligation (unless excluded by Article 1(2) Rome II) will be covered by one of its conflicts rules.

Conclusion

While Rome I closes any internal gaps with a subsidiary conflicts rule, such gaps cannot even occur in Rome III, the Succession Regulation, the M-Property Regulation, and the RP-Property Regulation. For Rome II, however, the possibility of an internal gap cannot be disregarded easily. Its scope of application could be broader than its subject matters. In light of the lack of a subsidiary conflicts rule in Rome II, one might employ the notion of overriding mandatory provisions (or even have a new EU conflicts rule developed judicially) if one still wants to achieve a solution at least in part shaped by EU private international law. Yet two other ways of dealing with the problem seem more persuasive. The first is to contend that the scope of "non-contractual obligations" is exhaustive and that any non-contractual obligation must be considered as one of the subject matters of Rome II. The second solution works just the other way around: one assumes that the subject matters of Rome II shape its scope of application, and that therefore "non-contractual obligations" is not exhaustive. Either way, a subsidiary conflicts rule is not necessary.

3. THE SPECIAL CASE OF EVASION OF THE LAW

3.1. TERMINOLOGY

In the following, "evasion of the law" and "*fraude à la loi*" will be considered synonymous. This might seem to be at variance with EU vernacular. Recital 26

1100 *Plender/Wilderspin*, European PIL of Obligations, at 2-023.

1101 See *Unberath/Cziupka*, in: Rauscher (ed.), EuZPR/EuIPR, Art. 1 Rom II-VO at 28, who determine the scope of application of Rome II by the subject matters of its Chapters II and III.

Succession Regulation states, "Nothing in this Regulation should prevent a court from applying mechanisms designed to tackle the evasion of the law, such as *fraude à la loi* in the context of private international law".[1102] If *fraude à la loi* were only an example of evasion of the law ("such as"), they could not be synonyms. It is, however, also possible to read this recital in the sense that evasion of the law is a general legal issue that often goes by the French name of *fraude à la loi* in the context of private international law. The term originates in French private international law anyway.[1103] This understanding would also be in line with the French wording of Recital 26, that clearly supposes *fraude à la loi* to be the general term.[1104]

3.2. AN ISSUE CONCERNING THE SUBJECT MATTER *OR* THE CONNECTING FACTOR

Evasion of the law is not only germane to private international law. The topic is rather one of law in general,[1105] of general legal theory, of the *Allgemeine Rechtslehre*.[1106] Yet within the same legal system, there is typically *relatively* little room for evasion and/or the need for very complex manoeuvres, whereas there is the opportunity in private international law to leave that legal system behind altogether.[1107] This is perhaps why the issue enjoys a certain renown in private international law particularly.

A typical definition of *fraude à la loi* in private international law would be that "a party by artifice or subterfuge creates a connecting factor in order to attract or prevent the application of the rules of a particular system".[1108] This focus on the (manipulation of the) connecting factor[1109] is probably statistically warranted – the two standard historical examples of the

1102 Italics in the original.

1103 *Schurig*, in: FS Ferid, 375, 387.

1104 "Aucune disposition du présent règlement ne devrait empêcher une juridiction d'appliquer les mécanismes destinés à lutter contre la fraude à la loi, *par exemple dans le cadre* du droit international privé." (Emphasis added.)

1105 See *Audit*, La fraude à la loi, at 1; *Loussouarn/Bourel/de Vareilles-Sommières*, at 411.

1106 *Kegel/Schurig*, IPR, §14 I (477).

1107 See *Kegel/Schurig*, IPR, §14 I (477).

1108 *Kahn-Freund*, General Problems, 284.

1109 E.g. *von Hein*, in: MüKoBGB, Einl. IPR at 282; *Bariatti/Pataut*, in: Fallon/Lagarde/Poillot-Peruzzetto (eds.), Quelle architecture pour un code européen de droit international privé?, 337, 347; *Sonnenberger*, in: FS Kropholler, 227, 244; *Vonken*, Algemeen deel IPR, at 383 (but also see the more nuanced view at 384); *Rigaux/Fallon*, DIP, at 5.73; *Traest*, in: Het Wetboek Internationaal Privaatrecht becommentarieerd, Art. 18 I; *Calvo Caravaca/Carrascosa González*, DIP I, 492; *Garcimartín Alférez*, DIP, at 21.10; *Bodénès-Constantin*, La codification du DIP français, at 430; *Wolff*, PIL, at 134.

Princess de Bauffrement[1110] and *Helene Böhlau*[1111] from more than a century ago also concern the connecting factor – but not theoretically. There is no reason why evasion of the law should not be attempted, and deemed illicit, in regard to the subject matter. It is conceivable that somebody, instead of having the same conflicts rule apply to her case but lead to a different law through a change in the connecting factor, tries to have a different conflicts rule apply. French writers in particular have pointed out this possibility,[1112] not least because of a pertinent French case in the 1980s:[1113] prior to his death, the deceased had attempted to "ameublir l'immeuble",[1114] to have the rule on succession in movable property apply to his immovable property, by setting up a company, transferring his shares to a trust, and selling his apartment to that company. It seems he would have succeeded but for the French courts that found this to be *fraude à la loi*, although they arguably did not even notice the conceptual difference of this manoeuvre to an alteration of the connecting factor.[1115] Finally, most[1116] domestic *fraude à la loi* provisions do not mandate a limitation to the connecting factor either. They only require an evasion of provisions[1117] or some manipulation of facts[1118] in general without specifying the manner in which this can or must be carried out. Accordingly, the definition should be broadened to include a change in the subject matter.

As the issue can thus pertain either to the subject matter or to the connecting factor of a conflicts rule, it will be discussed at this point, right between issues of the subject matter and the connecting factor, as a "special case". *A priori*, any subject matter and any connecting factor could be the object of evasive manoeuvres. Hence the issue is of theoretical relevance for every conflicts provision, and thus formally general in the strict sense.

1110 Cass. Civ. S. 1878.1.193 = *Ancel/Lequette*, Les grands arrêts, No. 6; *Audit*, La fraude à la loi, at 3 and 199; *Cachard*, DIP, at 651; *Loussouarn/Bourel/de Vareilles-Sommières*, at 411; for an English version, see *Cuniberti*, Conflict of Laws, 85–86.

1111 OLG München, ZIR 20 (1910), 529; *Kegel/Schurig*, IPR, §14 I (475–476); the case ultimately was decided in favour of the party who had committed the evasive manoeuvre, and *fraude à la loi* did not appear in the reasons.

1112 *Loussouarn/Bourel/de Vareilles-Sommières*, at 413 (as the third option of committing a *fraude à la loi*, they refer to (fraudulent) forum shopping; this procedural topic is of no further interest here); *Cachard*, DIP, at 651; but also *Stuij*, NIPR 2015, 217, 219; *von Bar/Mankowski*, IPR I, §7 at 130 and 135 (in passing); *Meidanis*, in: Vrellis (ed.), PIL in Greece, at 85.

1113 Cass. civ. Rev. crit. DIP 1986, 66.

1114 *Lequette*, Rev. crit. DIP 1986, 71, 75.

1115 *Niboyet-Hoegy*, JDI 1987, 87, 92; *Lequette*, Rev. crit. DIP 1986, 71, 74.

1116 §8(1) Hungarian PIL Code 1979 formed a potential exception as it required a manipulation of a "foreign element".

1117 Article 5 Croatian PIL Act, Article 12(4) Spanish Civil Code. Article 2.564(1) Romanian Civil Code simply requires "fraud".

1118 Article 18 Belgian PIL Code, §5 Czech PIL Act, Article 21 Portuguese Civil Code.

3.3. FURTHER QUESTIONS OF THE CORRECT DEFINITION

The problems do not stop with the object of manipulation. The entire concept seems to slip through one's fingers like sand:[1119] looking at a case of a potential evasion of the law *ex post*, the result is either the application of the "evaded" rule (i.e. disregarding the evasive manoeuvre) or, nevertheless, the non-application of the "evaded" rule (i.e. "condoning" the evasive manoeuvre). Thus, in the first alternative, there was no evasion at all, just an unsuccessful attempt; whereas, in the second alternative, the stigma of "evasion" cannot stand. In either case, then, there was actually no evasion. "Evasion of the law" hence should be considered a legal issue to be tackled, instead of the description of a result.[1120]

To be clear: neither the subject matter or the connecting factor as *legal* requirements are at the disposal of private parties. Only a legislator or judge (by interpretation or development of the law) can make changes to them. Whenever a manipulation or change effected by private parties is mentioned above and in the following, this is just an abbreviated version of saying that the *facts* to be subsumed under the subject matter or the connecting factor have been altered. This is also how I understand the authors who phrase their definitions similarly.

Finally, it is also important to note that the factual element must actually exist. If a party merely pretends that it does, even if she produces well-forged documents, only an issue of correctly ascertaining the facts arises;[1121] no legal question is implicated.[1122] The strange use of the term *renvoi* aside, a 2011 decision[1123] can be seen as evidence that the ECJ thinks along the same lines in this regard.[1124]

1119 *Kegel/Schurig*, IPR, §14 I (478); already *Schurig*, in: FS Ferid, 375, 384.

1120 *Benecke*, Gesetzesumgehung, 246; *Kegel/Schurig*, IPR, §14 I (478); *ex ante*, the issue exists: *Schurig*, in: FS Ferid, 375, 384. See also Bullen v. Wisconsin, 240 U.S. 625, 630 (per Justice Holmes): "We do not speak of evasion, because, when the law draws a line, a case is on one side of it or the other, and if on the safe side is none the worse legally that a party has availed himself to the full of what the law permits."

1121 See *Bogdan*, PIL in Sweden, at 99; *id.*, Rec. des cours 348 (2010), 9, 199–200.

1122 *Klöpfer*, Missbrauch im Europäischen Zivilverfahrensrecht, 15; *Benecke*, Gesetzesumgehung, 239; *Schurig*, in: FS Ferid, 375, 386; but see *Dobiáš*, Riv. dir. int. priv. proc. 2015, 109, 113, as to §5 Czech PIL Act ("applies to false facts which have been feigned"); *Vonken*, Algemeen deel IPR, at 388 (simulation as a type of *fraude à la loi*).

1123 ECJ Case C-384/10, Jan Voogsgeerd v Navimer SA, Reports of Cases 2011, I-13725, at 49: "It is only if matters relating to the engagement procedure support the conclusion that the undertaking which concluded the contract in actual fact acted in the name of and on behalf of another undertaking that the referring court might consider that the linking factor in Article 6(2)(b) of the Rome Convention makes a *renvoi* to the law of the country in which the latter undertaking's place of business is situated." (Italics in the original).

1124 *von Hein*, in: MüKoBGB, Einl. IPR at 285.

3.4. EVASION OF THE LAW AND PUBLIC POLICY

To deal with *fraude à la loi* in the present context may require further explanation in the eyes of some. After all, the topic often appears in academic writings right alongside public policy in the context of the non-application of foreign law.[1125] The justification, sometimes expressly stated, is supposed to lie in this being the common result of both.[1126] And there is more. With Article 2.564(1) Romanian Civil Code, there exists a domestic private international law provision combining public policy (1st alternative) and *fraude à la loi* (2nd alternative). Article 12(4) Spanish Civil Code, although containing an evasion of the law rule separate from the public policy provision, goes back to the Spanish court practice of using evasion of the law as an auxiliary argument in the public policy context.[1127] The drafters of the Slovenian PIL Act deemed a *fraude à la loi* provision unnecessary and therefore did not keep Article 5 Yugoslav PIL Act because public policy (or escape clauses) could be used to resolve the issue.[1128] Recent French cases first relied on public policy,[1129] then on *fraude à la loi*,[1130] when dealing with the effects in France, or rather the lack thereof,[1131] of surrogacy in foreign countries. In light of all this, it would be futile to gainsay some connection between public policy and *fraude à la loi*.

Conceptually speaking, however, public policy (and hence the governing law) is not the best place to discuss evasion of the law. First, all member states with a *fraude à la loi* provision additionally have a separate public policy provision, which is at least an indication that two different topics are at issue here. Article 16(1) No. 2 Spanish Civil Code underlines this. It prevents the public policy exception from applying in interregional conflict of laws, but not the *fraude à la loi* provision.[1132] The Succession Regulation also indicates that evasion of the law and public policy are two different issues, as it covers them completely separately: *fraude à la loi* in Recital 26, public policy in Recital 58 and Article 35. Second, the non-application of foreign law *can* be

1125 *Loussouarn/Bourel/de Vareilles-Sommières*, at 372; *Cachard*, DIP, at 650.

1126 *Loussouarn/Bourel/de Vareilles-Sommières*, at 372; similarly *Kahn-Freund*, General Problems, 285.

1127 *von Hoffmann/Ortiz-Arce*, RabelsZ 39 (1975), 647, 654.

1128 *Rudolf*, IPRax 2003, 158, 159 with note 11 (with reference to the parliamentary materials); *Geč-Korošec*, RabelsZ 66 (2002), 710, 715.

1129 Cass. 1re civ., April 6, 2011, No. 09-66.486; see *Mirkovic*, Sem. Jur. G. 2013, 1731, for an overview and further references.

1130 Cass. 1re civ., September 13, 2013, No. 12.30.138.

1131 In light of the ECtHR decisions *Mennesson v. France* (application No. 65192/11), NLMR 2014, 221, and *Labassee v. France* (application No. 65941/11), the French stance had to change, and it has, see Cass. ass. plén., JDI 2016, 103–104, and *Guillaumé*, JDI 2016, 104, 106–107.

1132 See also *von Hoffmann/Ortiz-Arce*, RabelsZ 39 (1975), 647, 654.

the common result of both *fraude à la loi* and public policy, but does not have to be. As will be demonstrated later,[1133] neither does *fraude à la loi* necessarily pertain to foreign law nor does public policy necessarily result in the non-application of foreign law. Third, there is broad consensus across the EU that public policy targets the application of foreign substantive law because of its *content*.[1134] However, evasion of the law – albeit from a party's perspective motivated by the content of different laws – concerns the *way* the requirements of a conflicts rule are fulfilled.[1135] Finally, even if one were to accept that the non-application of foreign law is the only possible result of *fraude à la loi*, it has already been pointed out that the point of view of the outcome is a relatively weak conceptual device for present purposes.[1136] Hence, *fraude à la loi* will be treated entirely separately[1137] from public policy here.

3.5. "EVASION" AND "ABUSE"

There seems to be consensus that evasion of the law and abuse of the law are related concepts.[1138] But related how? That both concepts are ultimately impossible to define[1139] can hardly be enough. In his monumental monograph on *fraude à la loi*, Audit merely states that no fundamental distinction between abuse of law and evasion of the law is possible.[1140] For Bogdan, "abuse of private international law" and *fraude à la loi* seem to be synonyms.[1141] The difference according to Gaudemet-Tallon is that *fraude à la loi* presupposes a manipulation, whereas *abus de droit* does not, as the

1133 *Infra* sections 3.6. and 5.6.3. (The Consequences of a Violation of Public Policy).

1134 *Infra* section 5.6.3. (Public Policy is Results-Oriented).

1135 *Vonken*, Algemeen deel IPR, at 394; *Bogdan*, Rec. des cours 348 (2010), 9, 201; *Benecke*, Gesetzesumgehung, 242; *Spickhoff*, Der ordre public im IPR, 82; *Schurig*, in: FS Ferid, 375, 386; but see *Neuhaus*, Grundbegriffe, §25 II 2 (199), who expressly considers it possible to apply the public policy exception in this regard, too.

1136 *Supra* section 2.9.2.1.

1137 To the same effect *von Hein*, in: MüKoBGB, Einl. IPR at 282; *Voltz*, in: Staudinger BGB, Art. 6 EGBGB at 70; *Bogdan*, PIL in Sweden, at 98–105; *Schurig*, in: FS Ferid, 375, 386.

1138 *Tichý*, in: FS Martiny, 851, 853; *Bariatti*, in: LA Borrás, 161, 162; see also *Klöpfer*, Missbrauch im Europäischen Zivilverfahrensrecht, 25–92; *Schurig*, in: FS Ferid, 375, 390.

1139 *von Bar/Mankowski*, IPR I, §7 at 131. In particular, the same problem arises for abuse of law that causes difficulties in the context of evasion of the law (*supra* section 3.3.): if the sanction of an "abuse" is that the "abuser" cannot exercise a right in the way she wants to, she apparently does not *have* such a right in the first place, so there is no abuse; if not, there was no abuse, either. Similarly *Gordley*, in: de la Feria/Vogenauer (eds.), Prohibition of Abuse of Law, 33, 45.

1140 *Audit*, La fraude à la loi, at 539 with note 1. According to him, the only possible difference could be that *fraude à la loi* is a mediate exercise of a prerogative, abuse of law an immediate one.

1141 *Bogdan*, Rec. des cours 348 (2010), 9, 196.

latter (only) requires the exercise of a right in a way not corresponding to its purpose, causing disproportionate wrong to another.[1142] In private international law, then, there could not be any "abuse", for it does not itself confer any substantive rights.[1143]

Under Tichý's conception, however, abuse of law, defined as a contravention of *boni mores* (*gute Sitten*) aiming at a disproportionate result, can be based on evasion of the law or illegal behaviour.[1144] He further expressly considers the artificial creation of a connection in order to trigger a different jurisdictional rule as a case of *abuse* of procedural law.[1145] Yet this comes extremely close to a manipulation of the connecting factor in private international law that most would consider an obvious candidate for *fraude à la loi*.

No member state has a provision on abuse of law among its general private international law provisions.[1146] The topic seems to be, if at all, rarely discussed in the field of conflict of laws (unlike in the field of jurisdictional rules[1147]), possibly because *fraude à la loi* suffices to cover/explain all cases,[1148] or possibly because there is sufficiently widespread consensus that the lack of substantive rights in private international law means that there cannot be any "abuse". EU private international[1149] law does not contain anything on abuse of the law either. It therefore appears justifiable not to pursue the topic here any further.

3.6. PREVENTION OF EVASION OF THE LAW

In order to prevent illicit manipulation of facts, one can make conflicts rules with connecting factors that are not easy to manipulate.[1150] The standard

---

1142 *Gaudemet-Tallon*, in: Mélanges Audit, 383, 385.

1143 *Benecke*, Gesetzesumgehung, 240–241.

1144 *Tichý*, in: FS Martiny, 851, 853. One would like to know what example he has in mind when considering illegal behaviour a possible basis for abuse of law. If the act is illegal, there seems to be no law to be abused in the first place.

1145 *Tichý*, in: FS Martiny, 851, 857.

1146 A Greek court once used the substantive Greek provision on abuse of the law in a private international law case: *Vassilakakis*, RHDI 63 (2010), 103, 111.

1147 See, e.g., *Leible*, in: Rauscher (ed.), EuZPR/EuIPR I, Art. 29 Brüssel Ia at 36; *Tichý*, in: FS Martiny, 851; *Metzger*, in: de la Feria/Vogenauer (eds.), Prohibition of Abuse of Law, 235, 243–246; *Briggs*, ibid., 261; *Cuniberti*, ibid., 279.

1148 For *Audit*, Fraude à la loi, at 199, e.g., the case of the Princess de Bauffrement could and should be properly analysed as one of abuse of law – yet it is the paradigmatic *fraude à la loi* case.

1149 For the prohibition of abuse of the law in EU law in general, see the contributions in de la Feria/Vogenauer (eds.), Prohibition of Abuse of Law.

1150 See only *Neuhaus*, Grundbegriffe, §25 III (200).

example is the choice between nationality and habitual residence.[1151] The respective debate flared up again in the context of the drafting of the Succession Regulation, where the shift from nationality (for many member states the connecting factor for succession matters and typically not really easy to change) to habitual residence (supposedly easy to change) caused concern over manipulations.[1152] Yet habitual residence has become *the* connecting factor in EU private international law.[1153] Connecting factors for which a point in time is fixated, or to which other conditions are attached, can also be regarded as instances of prevention of evasion of the law.[1154]

Some provisions in the EU private international law regulations can be characterised as a more precise way of safeguarding the application of a certain law, i.e. prevention of attempts to evade it,[1155] namely Articles 3(3), (4) Rome I and 14(2) Rome II.[1156] Broadening the scope of this book for a moment, there are also a few provisions in directives with a relevance for private international law and that likewise can be regarded as preventive mechanisms: Article 6(2) Unfair Terms Directive, Article 7(2) Consumer Sales Directive, Article 12(2) Distance Marketing of Consumer Financial Services Directive, and Article 22(4) Consumer Credit Directive 2008.[1157]

3.7. MEMBER STATES

3.7.1. *Pertinent Provisions in the Member States*

Using the parameters of the law to be evaded and the law sought to be applied, there are three possible constellations of evasion of the law. The *lex fori* can be evaded in favour of some foreign law, foreign law can be evaded in favour of the *lex fori*, or one foreign law can be evaded in favour of another foreign law. Several member states have rules pertaining to these situations

1151 *Schurig*, in: FS Ferid, 375, 387.

1152 See only *Lechner's* report on the proposal for a regulation of the European Parliament and of the Council on jurisdiction, applicable law, recognition and enforcement of decisions and authentic instruments in matters of succession and the creation of a European Certificate of Succession (06.03.2012), 57–58 (PE441.200v03-00); *MPI*, RabelsZ 74 (2010), 522, 605–606.

1153 *Infra* section 4.5.2.

1154 *Parra-Aranguren*, in: Essays in Memory of Nygh, 263, 297.

1155 The Rome I proposal made express reference to "fraudulent evasion of the law" in this context, COM(2005) 650 final, 5; but see *Stuij*, NIPR 2015, 217, 222, who doubts that this term was meant technically.

1156 See *Bariatti*, in: LA Borrás, 161, 166; *von Hein*, in: MüKoBGB, Einl. IPR at 283; *Kluth*, Die Grenzen des kollisionsrechtlichen Verbraucherschutzes, 314.

1157 See *von Hein*, in: MüKoBGB, Einl. IPR at 283, who refers to Article 46b EGBGB, the German provision implementing all these provisions.

(Raape had doubted that such things could exist[1158]) among their general provisions of private international law.

The general *fraude à la loi* provisions of some member states only pertain to the evasion of the *lex fori*,[1159] a limitation that scholars of the respective legal systems have occasionally criticised or tried to overcome by analogy.[1160] While the 1967 Draft is entirely silent, the first French private international law codification project of the late 1940s was not, but also only sanctioned *fraude à loi française*.[1161] The Greek cases on evasion of the law reported by Vassilakakis only contain instances where Greek law was found to have been evaded.[1162] Only the Romanian provision expressly states that the consequence of the evasion of Romanian law is the application of Romanian law[1163] – but really, what else could it be other than applying the *lex fori* that has been fraudulently evaded?

If there is an evasion of foreign law, its aim might have been to have the lex fori apply. §8(1) Hungarian PIL Code 1979 rather clearly condoned such an act.[1164] In the Hungarian PIL Act, there is now no longer any rule on evasion of the law among the general provisions.

Provisions in other member states are drafted more broadly. Article 18 Belgian PIL Code, for example, is supposed to cover all evasions without any distinction.[1165] Other broad *fraude à la loi* provisions can be found in the Czech Republic[1166] and Portugal.[1167] It seems that the draft Bulgarian PIL Code contained a similarly broad provision.[1168] The sanction of those

1158 *Raape*, IPR, §18 I 6 (131).

1159 Article 5 Croatian PIL Act; Article 2.564(1) clause 1 Romanian Civil Code; Article 12(4) Spanish Civil Code (see *Carrascosa González*, El reglamento Sucesorio Europeo, 275, for examples from the Spanish Supreme Court). See the next section as to §8 Hungarian PIL Code 1979.

1160 *Avasilencei*, Rev. crit. DIP 2012, 247, 261–262 (as regards Romania, with further references); *Calvo Caravaca/Carrascosa González*, DIP I, 499 (as regards Spain, with further references).

1161 See *Makarov*, in: FS Wolff, 247, 251–252.

1162 *Vassilakakis*, RHDI 63 (2010), 103, 111–112.

1163 Article 2.564(1) clause 2 Romanian Civil Code.

1164 *Nagy*, PIL in Hungary, at 83; *Burián*, in: Symeonides (ed.), PIL at the End of the 20th Century, 263, 266. §8 Hungarian PIL Code 1979 also seemed to cover the situation of the evasion of foreign law in favour of another foreign law, but *Nagy* read it more narrowly so as to only cover the evasion of Hungarian law, *Nagy*, PIL in Hungary, at 82; but see *Burián*, in: Symeonides (ed.), PIL at the End of the 20th Century, 263, 266 ("intention of having [the parties'] case governed by a foreign law *other than the one* normally applicable" (emphasis added)).

1165 *Rigaux/Fallon*, DIP, at 5.73 (final paragraph).

1166 §5 Czech PIL Act; see *Pauknerová/Pfeiffer*, Journal of Private International Law 10 (2014), 205, 220.

1167 Article 21 Portuguese Civil Code; see *de Lima Pinheiro*, Yearbook of Private International Law 14 (2012/2013), 153, 166: prevention of "normally applicable law from being displaced, regardless of whether or not it is forum law or foreign law".

1168 *Zidarova/Stančeva-Minčeva*, RabelsZ 71 (2007), 398, 412 (with note 17).

provisions consists in disregarding or deeming irrelevant the facts constituting the evasive manoeuvre.[1169]

The traditional French position on the evasion of foreign law is indifference.[1170] The French judiciary could possibly sanction an evasion of foreign law, however, to the extent that it is perpetrated in favour of another foreign law.[1171] The Luxembourg judiciary sanctions both the evasion of foreign law and the evasion of Luxembourg law.[1172] Bogdan reports no Swedish case but submits that the courts have authority to deal with every evasion of the law.[1173]

3.7.2. *Further Positions on Evasion of the Law*[1174]

The English (non-)Position

In 1962, Graveson wrote that "English law sometimes causes a feeling of surprise, pity or despair among our continental friends by its failure to include any doctrine of evasion of the law".[1175] More than a decade later, Kahn-Freund could detect no developed doctrine in the English courts concerning evasion of the law either.[1176] Today, nothing seems to have changed. One searches in vain for the terms "evasion of the law" and "*fraude à la loi*", even only in the index of Dicey's, Morris' and Collins' *Conflict of Laws*.[1177] Nor is there a respective entry in the index of other textbooks.[1178] Cases that might have been of concern in other member states *sub specie* "evasion of the law" were either condoned or handled by application of the public policy exception.[1179]

1169 Article 18 Belgian PIL Code; §5 Czech PIL Act; Article 21 Portuguese Civil Code; by its wording, this was also the effect of §8(2) Hungarian PIL Code 1979.

1170 *Cachard*, DIP, at 654; *Rigaux/Fallon*, DIP, at 5.73 (final paragraph); but *Audit/d'Avout*, DIP, at 305 ("proposition erronée").

1171 *Cachard*, DIP, at 654; *Audit/d'Avout*, DIP, at 305–309. This raises the question whether it can only do so if the "evaded" law itself provides for a *fraude à la loi* exception, *Audit/d'Avout*, DIP, at 309, with further references.

1172 *Wiwinius*, DIP, at 226–228.

1173 *Bogdan*, PIL in Sweden, at 103.

1174 For an international perspective see *Parra-Aranguren*, in: Essays in Memory of Nygh, 263 and passim (American hemisphere), 294 (rest of the world).

1175 *Graveson*, Philosophical Aspects, 37; in more detail already *id.*, J. Comp. Leg. Int. L. 21 (1937), 27–30.

1176 *Kahn-Freund*, General Problems, 285.

1177 The entry for "fraud" only covers issues of procedure.

1178 Examined were *Briggs*, Private International Law in the English Courts (there is an entry for "fraud", but none of the references concern the manipulation of a connecting factor); *Rogerson*, Collier's Conflict of Laws; and *Briggs*, The Conflict of Laws.

1179 *Kahn-Freund*, General Problems, 285; *Graveson*, Philosophical Aspects, 37–38.

Germany

Germany does not have a private (international) law provision covering evasion of the law – and in the opinion of most, it does not need to have one anyway. Some say that there is not even any principle that connecting factors created with the intention of evading a law are to be ignored. When a legislator makes a conflicts provision with a certain connecting factor that can be manipulated, it knowingly creates leeway; without any special precautions against manipulation, an *a contrario* argument is warranted.[1180] (Incidentally, a similar position seems to be the reason why the Bulgarian PIL Code does not have such a provision either.[1181]) For others, the issue of an evasion of the law is merely a question of interpretation:[1182] does the "evaded" rule "still" apply? Evasion of the law thus becomes an issue of applying a legal rule to an unusual set of facts[1183] – and, conversely, of not applying a legal rule despite it being applicable based on its wording. In accordance with this view, provisions in German substantive consumer law that do expressly prohibit evasive tactics are often said to produce results that could have been reached through interpretation anyway.[1184] When private international law textbooks nevertheless deal with the issue, however, it appears among other topics designated as general.[1185]

There are no reported German private international law cases relying on *fraude à la loi*.[1186] A 2008 lower court decision concerning an adoption abroad does mention it in passing, but actually seems to rely on public policy.[1187] In the appellate decisions of the same case,[1188] *fraude à la loi* does not appear.

1180 *von Bar/Mankowski*, IPR I, §7 at 131 and 133. Similarly *M.-P. Weller/Benz/Thomale*, ZEuP 2017, 250, 272. For a rather lenient perspective from Austria, see *Schwimann*, IPR, 37–38. A 1997 German monograph on evasion of the law, however, paints a grim, apocalyptical even (*Schurig*, RabelsZ 65 (2001), 746, 755), picture of what is going to happen if evasive manoeuvres are not sanctioned: *Heeder*, Fraus legis, 322. Not only in light of zero reported German cases relying on *fraude à la loi* (see *infra* footnote 1186 and the accompanying text), the persuasive force of *Heeder*'s argument is rather low.

1181 *Zidarova/Stančeva-Minčeva*, RabelsZ 71 (2007), 398, 412 (with note 17).

1182 *Basedow*, The Law of Open Societies, at 523; *von Hein*, in: MüKoBGB, Einl. IPR at 284; *Kegel/Schurig*, IPR, §14 IV (483); *Schurig*, in: FS Ferid, 375, 384. *Klöpfer*, Missbrauch im Europäischen Zivilverfahrensrecht, 64–79, strictly distinguishes between interpretation and analogy as methods to deal with evasion of the law.

1183 *Neuhaus*, Grundbegriffe, §25 II 3 (199).

1184 See *Basedow*, in: MüKoBGB, §306a at 3; *S. Lorenz*, in: MüKoBGB, §475 at 39; but see *Maume*, in: BeckOK BGB, 45th ed. (01.11.2017), §312k at 8, who points out that the room for interpretation shrinks where EU directives require full harmonisation.

1185 *Kropholler*, IPR, §23; *Kegel/Schurig*, IPR, §14; *von Bar/Mankowski*, IPR I, §7 at 128–135.

1186 *von Bar/Mankowski*, IPR I, §7 at 131; *von Hein*, in: MüKoBGB, Einl. IPR at 282–285, does not refer to any, either.

1187 AG Köln, decision of 01.09.2008, Az. 60 XVI 187/07, at 11–14 (unpublished).

1188 LG Köln, decision of 07.01.2009, Az. 1 T 381/08; OLG Köln, decision of 29.05.2009, Az. 16 Wx 8/09 = IPRspr. 2009, Nos. 97a and 97b (230–235).

The Netherlands

Evasion of the law appeared on the agenda in the Netherlands in the context of the plans for private international law harmonisation among the Benelux countries.[1189] It did not resurface in the context of Dutch private international law codification,[1190] nor is there a pertinent provision in Book 10 of the Dutch Civil Code. Cases are rare, while the doctrine is not uniform.[1191] The question, however, does seem to be uniformly regarded as a "general" one, as one deserving discussion separate from individual conflicts rules.[1192]

3.8. EUROPEAN UNION

The Succession Regulation

In the EU private international law regulations, there is no provision dealing with evasion of the law. There is, however, the aforementioned Recital 26 Succession Regulation. To be sure, one could doubt that it even pertains to fraudulent behaviour as regards the applicable law. Systematically speaking, this recital is far removed from recitals dealing with the applicable law (Recital 37 onwards). Rather, it is in close proximity to the ones on jurisdiction. Ultimately, however, it is more convincing to consider Recital 26 Succession Regulation as extending to (at least also) issues of the applicable law. The use of the *terminus technicus* "*fraude à la loi*" with its history in French *conflicts* cases is a first indication for this. Second, the wording "private international law" has been used in other regulations only in the context of the applicable law.[1193] Third, one can emphasise the proximity of Recital 26 to Recitals 24 and 25 dealing with habitual residence. Habitual residence being a connecting factor important for both jurisdiction and the applicable law under the Succession Regulation, one can infer that Recital 26 is also intended to cover both aspects. Thus, Recital 26 concerns all conflicts provisions of the Succession Regulation. In its context, it is a formally general rule in the strict sense.

1189 See *Stuij*, NIPR 2015, 217, 220, with further references.

1190 *Stuij*, NIPR 2015, 217, 220.

1191 *Stuij*, NIPR 2015, 217, 221. He himself contends, similar to *von Bar/Mankowski*'s position regarding German law (*supra* footnote 1180), that a correction by way of *fraude à la loi* is of diminishing importance where there are other special mechanisms to fine-tune the determination of foreign law, 224.

1192 See *Vonken*, Algemeen deel IPR, at 383–394; also the references provided by *Stuij*, NIPR 2015, 217 (with note 4).

1193 Article 20 Rome I, Article 24 Rome II, Article 11 Rome III, Articles 9 and 32 M-Property Regulation, Article 32 RP-Property Regulation.

Whether it creates an opening for domestic notions of *fraude à la loi* or presupposes a European concept,[1194] Recital 26 Succession Regulation at the very least acknowledges the existence of the issue. The reason for the creation of this recital in the European Parliament's Committee on Legal Affairs[1195] is up to speculation. Without any apparent connection to this recital, and thus rather paradoxically, Lechner's report even states in the context of public policy that "Individuals intent on evading the law at all costs will find ways and means of doing so under the legislation in force".[1196]

The Court of Justice

The ECJ has a certain tradition of leaving room for national authorities to combat fraudulent actions in cross-border cases.[1197] The Court requires a combination of objective and subjective elements for a finding of fraud/abuse.[1198] Yet it was usually quick to point out that certain aspects could *not* be considered indicia of fraud. In *Centros* – which some deem a blatant case of evasion of the law[1199] – and *Inspire Art*, two famous cases regarding freedom of establishment, the Court did allow domestic authorities to prevent abuse and fraud on a case by case basis. It also held, however, that establishing a company in one member state, and then only or principally conducting its business in another member state, does not suffice to constitute either.[1200] Furthermore, the Court underlined in *Hadadi* that there cannot be any "abuse" if all a party does is rely on a connecting factor as provided for by law.[1201]

1194 For an opening *Carrascosa González*, El reglamento Sucesorio Europeo, 272; *Dutta*, in: MüKoBGB, vor Art. 20 EuErbVO at 64 (but limitations by the principles of equivalence and effectiveness).

1195 *Lechner's* report on the proposal for a regulation of the European Parliament and of the Councilon jurisdiction, applicable law, recognition and enforcement of decisions and authentic instruments in matters of succession and the creation of a European Certificate of Succession (06.03.2012), 11 (PE441.200v03-00).

1196 *Lechner's* report on the proposal for a regulation of the European Parliament and of the Councilon jurisdiction, applicable law, recognition and enforcement of decisions and authentic instruments in matters of succession and the creation of a European Certificate of Succession (06.03.2012), 58 (PE441.200v03-00).

1197 To this effect also *Stuij*, NIPR 2015, 217, 222–223. See *Klöpfer*, Missbrauch im Europäischen Zivilverfahrensrecht, 113–121 and passim, for respective ECJ cases and their analysis.

1198 See only the recent example of ECJ Case C-54/16, Vinyls Italia SpA v Mediterranea di Navigazione SpA, ECLI:EU:C:2017:433, at 52.

1199 *Lequette*, in: LA Gaudement-Tallon, 503, 537; *Schurig*, RabelsZ 65 (2001), 746, 754; also but see e.g. *Benecke*, Gesetzesumgehung, 311, with further references.

1200 ECJ Case C-212/97, Centros Ltd v Erhvervs- og Selskabsstyrelsen, Reports of Cases 1999, I-1459, at 25–29; Case C-167/01, Kamer van Koophandel en Fabrieken voor Amsterdam v Inspire Art Ltd., Reports of Cases 2003, I-10155, at 105 and 139.

1201 ECJ Case C-168/08, Laszlo Hadadi (Hadady) v Csilla Marta Mesko, épouse Hadadi (Hadady), Reports of Cases 2009, I-6871, at 57.

In *CDC*, the ECJ recently allowed national courts not to apply Article 6(1) Brussels I (= Article 8(1) Brussels Ibis) if there is "firm evidence to support the conclusion that the applicant artificially fulfilled, or prolonged the fulfilment of that provision's applicability".[1202] If one replaces "Article 6(1) Brussels I" in the last sentence with any provision of the Rome Regulations, the outcome sounds a lot like *fraude à la loi*. The Court does not explain where this exception comes from and, in particular, does not (expressly) base its reasoning on the terms "so closely connected" found in Article 6(1) Brussels I,[1203] i.e. on the specific wording of the provision at issue. Hence, it does not seem impossible that the Court will one day transfer this statement to EU conflicts rules. On the other hand, "in light of a legal environment favouring mobility" such as the EU, it is also very much conceivable that the relevance of *fraude à la loi* will decline steadily[1204] – even in those member states that consider a special provision for it necessary.

4. THE CONNECTING FACTOR

The second element of every conflicts rule is the connecting factor.[1205] It designates which of all the circumstances of a given case is/are the one(s) relevant to determine the applicable law. The choice of a specific connecting factor such as nationality, habitual residence of a person, or the location of goods, reflects a policy decision with regard to the specific subject matter. While every conflicts rule must have a connecting factor, there is no need for all to have the same one. Indeed, if they had, the results would range from the implausible (why should the nationality of one of the parties be decisive for the law governing a sales contract?)[1206] to the nonsensical (succession as a whole to be governed by the law of the franchisee's habitual residence?). Party autonomy might appear to be an exception, for it is theoretically conceivable that a system of private international law allows the parties to choose the

---

1202 ECJ Case C-352/13, Cartel Damage Claims (CDC) Hydrogen Peroxide SA v Akzo Nobel NV and Others, ECLI:EU:C:2015:335, at 29. That a national court really is allowed not to apply a Brussels I provision can be seen at 31 ("[i]n order to be able to exclude the applicability") and at 33 (Article 6(1) Brussels I can apply "unless" such a circumvention is found).

1203 As has been suggested, e.g., by *Leible*, in: Rauscher (ed.), EuZPR/EuIPR I, Art. 8 Brüssel Ia at 17.

1204 *Basedow*, The Law of Open Societies, at 529; *Siehr*, Yearbook of Private International Law VII (2005), 17, 58.

1205 *Falconbridge* seems to have coined the English term, L. Q. R. 53 (1937), 235, 236. The EU legislator has also been using it, see e.g. Recital 14 clause 2 Rome II and Article (!) 36(2)(c) Succession Regulation.

1206 See *Giuliano/Lagarde*, Report on the Convention on the law applicable to contractual obligations, 20 ("element [...] unrelated to the essence of the obligation").

applicable law for all subject matters. However, as long as one does not force the parties to make such a choice – and this would rather defeat the idea of party autonomy – there must always be a fallback rule that is applicable in the absence of choice. In other words, there must be objective connecting factors.

In a system of private international law that thus very conceivably uses more than one connecting factor, issues regarding a specific factor are not formally general in the strict sense. But the question of whether one can deviate from one connecting factor to another that seems more appropriate in the given case potentially concerns all connecting factors: it is a formally general issue in the strict sense (4.1.). Moreover, at an intermediate level, a question arises at least for an entire class of connecting factors: the *conflit mobile* (4.2.). Finally, as long as a factor is used more than once, formally general issues can arise (4.3.–4.5.),[1207] the most obvious being the meaning of the specific term. (That this, as a matter of principle, is to be decided according to the *lex fori*[1208] – more precisely, taking into account a possible *renvoi*, according to the law whose conflicts provision is applied – is in fact the answer to a formally general issue in the strict sense again.)

As far as general issues of individual connecting factors will be concerned, the focus will lie on party autonomy and personal connecting factors, as opposed to connecting factors concerning an object (e.g. the location of chattel) or behaviour (e.g. the place where a contract is concluded). Comparative findings – or rather the lack thereof in regard to any general rules for the latter group of connecting factors – inform this choice. A possible explanation for this is that many, if not all, of these latter factors are hardly equivocal.

4.1. THE EXISTENCE OF A MORE APPROPRIATE CONNECTING FACTOR

The legislator's choice of a particular connecting factor is a policy decision. When a legislator determines one connecting factor to be decisive for one subject matter, this policy decision necessarily concerns a typified case.

1207 See *Verwilghen*, in: Het Wetboek Internationaal Privaatrecht becommentarieerd, Art. 3 I: as the Belgian PIL Code relies on certain connecting factors in several of its articles, "le Code prend soin de commencer par donner [...] quelques explications sur le sens de ces mots ou expressions et sur la manière de résoudre les principaux problems que suscite leur détermination".

1208 *Kahn-Freund*, General Problems, 242–243; *Wolff*, PIL, at 131. Also see *infra* section 7. From the conceptual viewpoint adopted here, it is obvious that the interpretation of the connecting factor, being a distinct question from the interpretation of the subject matter, is not to be confused with the issue of characterisation. Also see *Mann*, JZ 1956, 466, 470 (with note 55); *Wolff*, PIL, at 131.

For example, a legislator may want the law with which a contract is most closely connected to govern that contract, and decide that this is *typically* the law of the country where the party required to effect the characteristic performance has her habitual residence. (This is, of course, the situation of Article 4 Rome I.) Yet what if in a given case the habitual residence of the party effecting the characteristic performance is the only aspect of the case pointing to the law of that country, whereas the case is more closely connected with another law? Do the applicable private international law rules allow for the disregard of the connecting factor in favour of one that, in the given case, *actually* leads to the law more closely connected with the contract?[1209] More generally, do the applicable private international law rules provide an opening to disregard the typified connecting factor in favour of one deemed more appropriate? This is the issue referred to here as the "existence of a more appropriate connecting factor".

The more usual name for this issue would be "escape clauses". As already mentioned, however, to analyse private international law from the point of view of whether it allows an escape from the otherwise applicable (usually foreign) law is inappropriate for present purposes.[1210] The proximity of "escape clause" to "escape device" is thus one reason to shun the term. Another reason is that the term "escape clause" connotes the idea of a closer connection because its most famous examples, such as Article 15 Swiss PIL Act, rely on it. While this notion does make up the main category of cases (in the EU, anyway[1211]),[1212] it unnecessarily narrows the perspective. Therefore, the issue is initially described in broader terms here. Later on, it will become virtually impossible to ignore the terminology used by both scholars and legislators.

As it is not the way or outcome of the application of some law that causes concern,[1213] but the fact that this law should be applicable in the first place, it would not be entirely reasonable to consider the issue one of the governing law. It rather pertains to the connecting factor: can one connecting factor

---

1209 In line with this reasoning, *Francq* calls Article 19 Belgian PIL Code "the ultimate expression" of the principle of closest connection, RabelsZ 70 (2006), 235, 266.

1210 *Supra* section 2.9.2.1.

1211 See *Symeonides*, Codifying Choice of Law, 198–201, for examples from all over the world of "escapes based on other factors" than the closer connection, with only three examples from the EU. Two of these EU examples will be dealt with in the present context. It is submitted, however, that Article 10:19 Dutch Civil Code can be analysed from a different perspective, *infra* section 5.9.

1212 *Pauknerová*, Yearbook of PIL 18 (2016/2017), 61, 62, seems to consider only rules based on a closer connection to be "escape clauses". Along these lines also *Hirse*, Die Ausweichklausel im IPR, 5, 11, and passim (for the purposes of his 446-page analysis); *Geisler*, Die engste Verbindung, 86–88.

1213 To the same effect *Remien*, in: Leible (ed.), General Principles, §11.03[B][1]; see also *Lagarde*, Public Policy, at 1, for a similar distinction between the "technique of determining the applicable law" (a question of escape clauses) and the "substance of the laws conflict" (a question of public policy).

be replaced by another? This question arises for any conflicts rule, for every conflicts rule has a connecting factor. Accordingly, it is formally general in the strict sense.[1214]

Member States

The private international law codes of several member states contain a provision among their general ones allowing for a deviation from the respective conflicts provisions that in principle would apply, not for reasons of the content of the law determined by them, but because the purpose of the connecting factor would otherwise be missed.[1215] This is particularly obvious for Article 10:8 Dutch Civil Code. It is only possible to deviate from another Dutch conflicts rule for reasons of a closer connection if that other rule is based on the idea of a presumed close connection and this close connection does not actually exist. Conversely, substantive considerations relating to the outcome of the case do not matter when applying Article 10:8 Dutch Civil Code.[1216] Similarly, Article 19(2) clause 2 Belgian PIL Code *excludes* the application of the law of a state to which the case has a closer connection if the conflicts rule from which one would deviate determines the governing law for reasons of that law's content, i.e. not because of its (presumed) close connection.[1217]

There are a couple of general provisions in other member states that *could* serve as rules providing a more appropriate connecting factor, but do not unambiguously say so. §24(1) Czech PIL Act makes it possible not to apply the law designated by another Czech conflicts provision if this would seem "unreasonable and contrary to the fair and reasonable arrangement of the legal relationship in question".[1218] Czech commentators have expressly placed this provision in the context of traditional "escape clauses".[1219] §24(2) Czech PIL Act, with its reference to the closest connection, on the other hand, seems

1214 See *Pauknerová*, Yearbook of PIL 18 (2016/2017), 61, 66, for a similar assessment, distinguishing "general escape clauses" which apply to *all* conflicts rules of a given legal instrument from "specific escape clauses" which only apply to a particular issue or rule.

1215 Article 19 Belgian PIL Code; §11 Hungarian PIL Act; Article 1.11(3) Lithuanian Civil Code (only if the law governing the case in principle is foreign, however); Article 10:8 Dutch Civil Code; Article 2.565 Romanian Civil Code; Article 2 Slovenian PIL Act.

1216 *ten Wolde*, Yearbook of Private International Law 13 (2011), 389, 400; *Boele-Woelki/van Iterson*, in: van Erp/van Vliet (eds.), Netherlands Report, 145, 157.

1217 See *Pertegas*, IPRax 2006, 53, 55, and *Fiorini*, ICLQ 54 (2005), 499, 513–514, as to how the restrictive wording of this provision in general reflects worries and critiques lodged against the introduction of such a general rule.

1218 *Dobiáš*, Riv. dir. int. priv. proc. 2015, 109, 118.

1219 *Pauknerová*, Yearbook of PIL 18 (2016/2017), 61, 67; *Dobiáš*, Riv. dir. int. priv. proc. 2015, 109, 118; *Pauknerová/Pfeiffer*, Journal of Private International Law 10 (2014), 205, 219–220. §24(1) Czech PIL Act also can be analysed in a different context, however, see *infra* section 5.9.

to be a subsidiary conflicts rule rather than an escape clause[1220] because it requires that the application of another conflicts rule is impossible.

§1 Austrian PIL Act sets forth the principle of the closest connection as the foundation for Austrian private international law. Its nature (also) as a subsidiary conflicts rule seems to be accepted,[1221] but it is disputed whether it can override other connecting factors.[1222] A very similar provision enshrining the principle of the closest connection is Article 2(1) Bulgarian PIL Code. It comes as no surprise, therefore, that it has been suggested to use this provision if the state designated by a Bulgarian conflicts rule does not have the closest connection to a case.[1223] Such a general provision, however, would render unnecessary other conflicts rules of the Bulgarian PIL Code containing special deviations in favour of the closest connection.

Other member states might have considered a general provision along these lines, but did not enact one.[1224] The notion as such seems to be known in all member states.[1225] It is not always discussed as an overarching issue.[1226]

European Union

No EU private international law regulation contains a provision that allows for a deviation from all of its conflicts rules in favour of a more appropriate connecting factor. Yet with the exception of Rome III, there are quite a few (often expressly designated as such[1227]) escape clauses for particular conflicts rules – to such an extent, in fact, that one wonders if a general escape clause for each regulation naming the provisions to which it *does not* apply might not have been more efficient. While the Succession Regulation only provides one escape clause,[1228] Rome I has four,[1229] and Rome II has five (applying to six of its Articles).[1230] While Article 26(3) subparagraph 1 M-Property Regulation

---

1220 *Supra* section 2.10.1. But see *Pauknerová/Pfeiffer*, Journal of Private International Law 10 (2014), 205, 220, who at first expressly call it an escape clause, too.

1221 *Supra* section 2.10.1.

1222 For this view *Verschraegen*, IPR, at 1391; similarly *Siehr*, in: Reichelt (ed.), 30 Jahre österreichisches IPR-Gesetz, 9, 13; against it OGH 3 Ob 549/94, SZ 67/147; *Lurger/Melcher*, IPR, at 1/67; in general see *Wendehorst*, in: Verschraegen (ed.), Austrian Law, 79, 84–85.

1223 *Symeonides*, Codifying Choice of Law, 194–195.

1224 See e.g. *Pazdan*, IPRax 2012, 77 (for Poland); *Burián*, in: Symeonides (ed.), PIL at the End of the 20th Century, 263, 270 (for the Hungarian PIL Code 1979); BT-Drucks. 10/504, 29 (for Germany).

1225 See also Section 12 Private International Law (Miscellaneous Provisions) Act 1995, and *Fentiman*, in: Symeonides (ed.), PIL at the End of the 20th Century, 165, 184–186.

1226 But see e.g. *Mayer/Heuzé*, DIP, at 512; *Loussouarn/Bourel/de Vareilles-Sommières*, DIP, at 193; *von Bar/Mankowski*, IPR I, §7 at 93.

1227 See Recital 20 Rome I, Recitals 14 and 18 Rome II.

1228 Article 21(2) Succession Regulation.

1229 Articles 4(3), 5(3), 7(2) subparagraph 2 clause 2, 8(4) Rome I.

1230 Articles 4(3) (which also applies to Article 6(2), see the latter's reference to Article 4), 5(2), 10(4), 11(4), 12(2)(c) Rome II.

and Article 26(2) subparagraph 1 RP-Property Regulation are not typical escape clauses,[1231] they do allow[1232] "by way of exception" the application of another law than that determined by the regular conflicts provision. The application of one of the parties is required, the spouses/partners must have had their last common habitual residence in the other state for a "significantly" long period of time, and both must have relied[1233] on the law of that state with regard to their property relations.

At any rate, in light of this nuanced approach to escape clauses,[1234] it would be highly questionable to deviate from any EU conflicts rule without its own escape clause;[1235] no unwritten general escape clause exists. The debate *de lege ferenda* has begun already.[1236]

4.2. CHANGE OF THE CONNECTING FACTOR (CHANGE OF THE APPLICABLE LAW, *CONFLIT MOBILE*)

Connecting factors can change. If this change is of a legal nature, i.e. if a legislator or court changes the (interpretation of the) connecting factor for a certain subject matter, this is a question for the application in time of the conflicts provision.[1237] If the connecting factor stays the same as a question of law, but the corresponding situation changes, this leads to the issue of a change in the applicable law. The expression is not unambiguous, either, as "change *of* the applicable law" could also mean a change *in* the *lex causae*.[1238] It is supposed to mean, however, that a connecting factor that

1231 Particularly because they do not necessarily rely on a closer connection, see *Goldstein*, Rev. crit. DIP 2018, 3, 10, in the context of Article 10:9 Dutch Civil Code (infra section 5.9.).

1232 The word "may" suggests that a judicial authority has discretion whether to make this decision. Recital 51 M-Property Regulation and Recital 50 RP-Property Regulation ("should [...] be able to arrive at the conclusion") likewise insinuate discretion. Still, if the conditions of the respective provisions are fulfilled, it is hard to see on which grounds a judicial authority should be allowed to refuse the application of the other law.

1233 At this point, there is an overlap with the idea of "erroneous assumptions concerning the applicable law", see *infra* section 5.9.

1234 Also *Remien*, in: Leible (ed.), General Principles, §11.03[C][1].

1235 In such a general way also *Siehr*, Yearbook of Private International Law VII (2005), 17, 28.

1236 For a general escape clause *Pauknerová*, Yearbook of PIL 18 (2016/2017), 61, 82; *Lagarde*, RabelsZ 75 (2011), 673, 675 (Article 137); *Siehr*, Yearbook of Private International Law VII (2005), 17, 29; *Kreuzer*, in: Jud/Rechberger/Reichelt (eds.), Kollisionsrecht in der EU, 1, 38–39; against it *Remien*, in: Leible (ed.), General Principles, §11.03[D]. For policy considerations as to escape clauses in general see *Symeonides*, Codifying Choice of Law, 201–204; *Hirse*, Die Ausweichklausel im IPR, 101–138 (domestic law), 436–446 (EU law).

1237 *Supra* section 2.2.3. This is what *Bogdan*, PIL in Sweden, at 53, discusses as "[c]hanges in the connecting factor". As to the similar ambiguity of the term "Statutenwechsel" in Austrian and German law, *Neumayr*, in: ABGB-Kurzkommentar, §7 IPRG at 1; *Neuhaus*, Grundbegriffe, §39 I (293).

1238 For this issue see *infra* section 5.4.

led to the law of state A now leads to the law of state B because of a change in the real world. For example: a rule with habitual residence as the connecting factor used to determine the law of state A as the applicable law because the person in question was habitually resident in state A; now, however, the person is habitually resident in state B. Without the conflicts rule having undergone any change – and irrespective of whether the substantive laws of states A and B have changed – a different law, that of state B, potentially applies. If a person brings about a change in the applicable law in order to evade the application of a certain law, the issue of *fraude à la loi* arises.[1239]

Whether or not the law of a state other than the "original" one really applies depends on the connecting factor in question. For some, the issue cannot arise at all because they necessarily refer to an event fixed in or to a place that is constant over time. The place where a tort has been committed or where a marriage has been celebrated cannot change over time. Nor, save for extraordinary circumstances, does the location of immovable property change. Other connecting factors, such as the aforementioned habitual residence or nationality, can change over time – unless they are supplemented by a criterion fixating a point in time. An express example of such a supplemental rule is Article 19(3) Rome I, referring to the time of the conclusion of the contract. Its predecessor in Article 4(2) Rome Convention was drafted specifically in order "[t]o counter the possibility of changes in the connecting factor".[1240]

A supplemental rule is, in fact, necessary for any variable connecting factor. A conflict of law rule must designate the applicable law. As far as it would lead to two or more different laws because it does not specify the relevant point in time, the rule is incomplete.[1241] It is to be completed by either making one point in the past decisive or recognising the (most recent) change as relevant. The legislator must provide an express solution for this *conflit mobile*,[1242] or one must be found by interpretation. As the lines between an express provision and interpretation are blurry, it seems preferable to use "change of the connecting factor"/*conflit mobile* as a term for the entire issue, as opposed to only those instances with a lack of an express provision.[1243]

1239 *Supra* section 3.

1240 *Giuliano/Lagarde*, Report on the Convention on the law applicable to contractual obligations, 21.

1241 *Kahn-Freund*, General Problems, 252; *Mayer/Heuzé*, DIP, at 261; *Grodecki*, Intertemporal Conflict of Laws, at 55.

1242 The term was apparently coined by *Bartin*, Principes I, 193 (see also 28–33). The Spanish equivalent is "conflicto móvil", see *Garcimartín Alférez*, DIP, at 21.9. The German term "Statutenwechsel" for the *conflit mobile* originates with *Zitelmann*, IPR I, 151. He expressly doubted that the term would be misunderstood (but see already *supra* footnote 1237 and accompanying text).

1243 Ambiguously *Mayer/Heuzé*, DIP, at 261, who describe the phenomenon as one of a "lacune dans l'énoncé de [la règle du conflit]".

From the focus on the elements of conflicts rules adopted here, it is moot to discuss whether a *conflit mobile* is actually very similar to a change in the *lex causae* or in the conflicts rules of the *lex fori* (because the result can be said to be functionally equivalent),[1244] or entirely different (because "[t]he factor of space overshadows that of time").[1245]

It was just demonstrated that not every connecting factor entails a *conflit mobile*. Hence, the issue is not formally general in the strict sense. While it is a formally general issue whether to fixate a *per se* variable connecting factor or recognise its change over time, it does not seem susceptible to a general rule. The *conflit mobile* "cannot be solved dogmatically by reference to an all-embracing general principle or formula".[1246] A general determination of the relevant point in time, albeit theoretically possible,[1247] is at least as implausible as the same connecting factor for all conflicts rules would be.

Yet a qualification should be added: subsets of the *conflit mobile* could be open to a general solution. In particular, when a system of private international law deems the change of a variable connecting factor relevant for the determination of the applicable law, the question arises whether this affects legal relationships or situations that occurred or began in the past. As long as this happens more than once, there is another formally general issue, just at a lower level. (The potential *consequence* of "transposition" will be discussed later on.[1248]) It therefore becomes of interest whether any system of private international law within the EU deals with the issue as a general one.

4.2.1. Member States

Only the private international law codes of Austria, Bulgaria, and now Hungary have a rule regarding the change of the connecting factor among their general provisions.[1249] It would be hard to argue that the problem simply has not been recognised elsewhere, as special provisions on the effects of a change of the connecting factor exist here and there. An example found in several codes is the rule *semel capax semper capax*.[1250] Several specific private international

1244 E.g. *Kegel/Schurig*, IPR, §1 VII 2 b (45); *von Bar/Mankowski*, IPR I, §4 at 172.

1245 *Grodecki*, Intertemporal Conflict of Laws, at 58; see also *Schröder*, Die Verweisung auf Mehrrechtsstaaten, 81–82.

1246 *Grodecki*, Intertemporal Conflict of Laws, at 56–58.

1247 See *von Bar/Mankowski*, IPR I, §4 at 172.

1248 *Infra* section 5.8.

1249 §7 Austrian PIL Act; Article 42 Bulgarian PIL Code; §14 Hungarian PIL Act. Because of the (problematic) connection of the *conflit mobile* and the idea of recognition of acquired rights (see e.g. *Audit/d'Avout*, DIP, at 294; *Grodecki*, Intertemporal Conflict of Laws, at 56), one might place Article 2.567 Romanian Civil Code in this context, too.

1250 Article 34(1) subparagraph 3 Belgian PIL Code; Article 7(2) EGBGB; §12(2) Estonian PIL Act; Article 1.16(5) Lithuanian Civil Code. A comparable provision appeared in the draft for the Greek private international law; its eventual omission is not to be read *a contrario*,

law provisions on real rights have to be seen against the backdrop of the *conflit mobile* too.[1251] There are also the respective Articles 12(2) of the Geneva Refugee Convention and of the Stateless Persons Convention that are binding on most member states.[1252] Scholars often discuss the *conflit mobile* separately from specific conflicts rules, in particular often in connection with general statements on connecting factors.[1253]

4.2.2. European Union

4.2.2.1. Rome I

As already mentioned in passing, Article 19(3) Rome I contains a rule fixating a point in time so as to avoid any change of the connecting factor. Due to the location of this rule at the end of the article, one might wonder whether it only applies to the cases covered by Article 19(1) and (2) Rome I, i.e. companies and business people. If so, it would not be formally general in the strict sense for all instances of habitual residence under Rome I. The systematic argument, however, is ambiguous, as one could argue as well that the rule is clearly separate from both preceding paragraphs. It is equally possible, hence, to read Article 19 Rome I as a whole to cover distinct dimensions of "habitual residence": a personal dimension in paragraphs 1 and 2, and a temporal dimension in paragraph 3. This would also be a sensible explanation of its broad title. The history of the rule as part of Article 4(2) clause 1 Rome Convention supports this view further because that provision was evidently not limited

however (*Gogos/Aubin*, RabelsZ 15 (1949/1950), 240, 257). Also see Article 29 Portuguese Civil Code, Article 2.575 Romanian Civil Code, and Article 9(1) Spanish Civil Code on coming of age.

1251 See Article 43(2), (3) EGBGB; Article 10:130 Dutch Civil Code. The latter provision even appears under the heading "conflit mobile" in the Explanatory Memorandum, Kamerstukken II 2009/2010, 32317, No. 3, 72. In other member states, the existence of real rights has been coupled with a specific point in time to begin with, e.g. Article 1.48(1) Lithuanian Civil Code, Article 2.617 Romanian Civil Code, Article 6 Slovak PIL Act; there is no statutory provision in the Slovenian PIL Act, but a solution akin to the aforementioned provisions has been suggested in scholarly literature, see *Rudolf*, IPRax 2003, 158, 160.

1252 See *infra* sections 4.4.1.3. and 4.4.1.4. for some more details.

1253 See *von Hein*, in: MüKoBGB, Einl. IPR at 78–82; *Garcimartín Alférez*, DIP, at 21.9; *Audit/d'Avout*, DIP, at 293–296; *Kahn-Freund*, General Problems, 252–257. Somewhat differently *Mayer/Heuzé*, DIP, at 259–263, who discuss the *conflit mobile* as one of the temporal aspects (along with changes of the private international law of the *lex fori* as well as changes in the *lex causae*) forming part of the "facteurs de complication" (like *renvoi* and *fraude à la loi*); *Cachard*, DIP, at 606–610 (as part of the interpretation of conflicts rules). *Bogdan*, PIL in Sweden, at 53–54 discusses "[c]hanges in the connecting factors" (by which he means the change of the private international law of the *lex fori*) and "[c]hanges in the *lex causae*" as part of the general principles, but not the *conflit mobile*.

to the personal dimension. In conclusion then, Article 19(3) Rome I is a formally general provision as far as Rome I is concerned, relevant for the determination of habitual residence whenever this connecting factor is at issue.[1254] A later change of habitual residence has no effect. Still, the parties can always subject their contract to a law other than was previously applicable, but such a change of the applicable law by way of party autonomy is limited in some regards (see Article 3(2) Rome I).

4.2.2.2. Rome II

No General Provision

A similar provision is missing from Rome II. Several of Rome II's connecting factors designate a particular point in time by referring to an event anyway.[1255] Moreover, a reference to the relevant point in time often accompanies the reference to a person's habitual residence in specific conflicts provisions.[1256]

The Problem of Article 5(1) Subparagraph 2

With regard to the foreseeability clause of Article 5(1) subparagraph 2 Rome II, however, the regulation does not provide an express answer as to the point in time relevant for the habitual residence of the person claimed to be liable. A solution must be found by interpretation. This, in turn, depends on how Article 5(1) subparagraphs 1 and 2 Rome II interact. The wording seems to indicate that subparagraph 2 applies whenever the foreseeability defence is raised against *any* of the applicable options in subparagraph 1. For example, if subparagraph 1(a) is applicable, but the person claimed to be liable could not reasonably have foreseen the marketing of the product there, subparagraph 2 would apply immediately.[1257] This outcome is questionable, as other potentially applicable options of subparagraph 1 would be ignored outright, even though the provision seems to indicate a pro-claimant favour.[1258] It is therefore preferable to read the lack of foreseeability into "failing that" of each option of subparagraph 1. If the foreseeability defence is raised for (a), (b) applies; if it is then raised for (b), (c) applies; only if it is then also

---

1254 To the same effect *McParland*, The Rome I Regulation, at 5.68 ("any person"); implicitly *Gebauer*, in: Calliess (ed.), Rome Regulations, Art. 4 Rome I at 14; he also applies it to Article 4(4) Rome I, Art. 4 Rome I at 77.

1255 See Articles 4(1), 5(1) subparagraph 1(b) and (c), 7 Rome II.

1256 E.g. Articles 4(2), 5(1) subparagraph 1(a), 10(2), 11(2), 12(2)(b) Rome II.

1257 To this effect *Junker*, in: MüKoBGB, Art. 5 Rom II-VO at 43–45.

1258 See *Schmid/Pinkel*, in: Calliess (ed.), Rome Regulations, Art. 5 Rome II at 40.

raised for (c) does the conflicts rule in subparagraph 2 apply.[1259] (Of course, any of the options could also simply "fail" because their objective requirements are not met.)

As a consequence, the determination of the relevant point in time for the defendant's habitual residence becomes tricky. Were subparagraph 2 to apply separately and immediately for each option of subparagraph 1, it would be very reasonable indeed to make the relevant point in time dependent upon the point in time found in the respective *littera* of subparagraph 1.[1260] Under the view set forth here, however, this works solely in those cases where only one of the options is applicable and the foreseeability defence is raised against it. In the four other theoretically possible situations in which subparagraph 2 applies,[1261] at least two of the options of subparagraph 1 are applicable, but each is eliminated by the foreseeability defence. The simplest solution would be to rely on the time when the damage occurred in these four situations; for, *per definitionem*, at least (a) or (c) are applicable in each. A more complicated approach would entail determining whether (b) applies as the "highest-ranking" option in the cascade and, if so,[1262] view the time of acquisition as decisive.

Equally difficult is the determination of the relevant point in time for Article 5(1) subparagraph 2 Rome II, as applied analogously. The need for an application by analogy stems from the rather obvious regulatory gap in Article 5(1) Rome II: all options in Article 5(1) subparagraph 1 have an objective marketing requirement, whereas the exception of subparagraph 2 requires subjective reasonable foreseeability. Hence, the case where the objective marketing requirement is not fulfilled under any option falls through the cracks.[1263] To simply rely on Article 4(1) Rome II cannot be the correct solution.[1264] The law of the country where the damage occurred would apply even though the product was not marketed there. This would

---

1259 To the same effect *Schmid/Pinkel*, in: Calliess (ed.), Rome Regulations, Art. 5 Rome II at 40; *Plender/Wilderspin*, European PIL of Obligations, at 19-107–19-108; probably also *Wagner*, IPRax 2008, 1, 6.

1260 *Junker*, in: MüKoBGB, Art. 5 Rom II-VO at 45.

1261 Situation 1: (a), (b), and (c) all apply, but the defence is raised against every one of them. Situation 2: (a) applies, the defence is raised, (b) applies, the defence is raised, (c) does not apply. Situation 3: (a) applies, the defence is raised, (b) does not apply, (c) applies, the defence is raised. Situation 4: (a) does not apply, (b) applies, the defence is raised, (c) applies, the defence is raised. The potential fifth situation in which neither (a) nor (b) nor (c) applies will be dealt with immediately below.

1262 This would only be "situation 4" (preceding footnote).

1263 See *Schmid/Pinkel*, in: Calliess (ed.), Rome Regulations, Art. 5 Rome II at 51; *Junker*, RIW 2010, 257, 266; *Wagner*, IPRax 2008, 1, 7; *Leible/Lehmann*, RIW 2007, 721, 728.

1264 But see *Hartley*, ICLQ 57 (2008), 899, 904–905 ("correct solution", "but strange consequences").

be an absurd outcome as Article 5(1) subparagraph 1(c) Rome II refers to the law of the country where the damage occurred *only if* the product was marketed there. Why then have Article 5(1) subparagraph 1(c) Rome II at all? Rather, *a maiore ad minus*, Article 5(1) subparagraph 2 Rome II must be applied analogously.[1265]

In this situation, Article 5(1) subparagraph 2 Rome II does not serve as an exception to any of the options in subparagraph 1. Unlike above, it is thus not at all possible to link it to any of the points in time relevant there. A solution must be found independently from subparagraph 1. The starting point should be the rule itself. It would read: "The law applicable to a non-contractual obligation arising out of damage caused by a product shall be the law of the country in which the person claimed to be liable is habitually resident if the product has not been marketed in any country indicated by subparagraph 1".[1266] In the absence of any other indication, the relevant point in time can only be the moment when the damage occurred, in this respect in line with e.g. Article 4(2) and Article 5(1) subparagraph 1(a) Rome II.

Conclusion

This little but rather complex detour into some specifics of Rome II has underlined that there are no formally general solutions in Rome II. The relevant point in time is always fixated but differently from rule to rule. Later changes of a connecting factor are irrelevant.

4.2.2.3. The Other Four Regulations

Rome III always specifically indicates the point in time relevant for habitual residence or nationality.[1267] The same is true for the M-Property Regulation and the RP-Property Regulation.[1268] Likewise, the Succession

1265 *Wagner*, IPRax 2008, 1, 7; *de Lima Pinheiro*, Riv. dir. int. priv. proc. 2008, 5, 23; *Leible/ Lehmann*, RIW 2007, 721, 728; also *Schmid/Pinkel*, in: Calliess (ed.), Rome Regulations, Art. 5 Rome II at 561; *Junker*, RIW 2010, 257, 266; *Plender/Wilderspin*, European PIL of Obligations, at 19-105–19-106; *Huber/Illmer*, Yearbook of Private International Law 9 (2007), 31, 43–44.

1266 In this regard, also see *Junker*'s revision of the entire provision, RIW 2010, 257, 266.

1267 Article 5(1)(a)–(c) ("at the time the agreement is concluded"), Article 6(2) ("at the time the court is seized"), Article 7(2)–(4) ("at the time the agreement is concluded"), Article 8(a)–(c) ("at the time the court is seized") Rome III.

1268 Article 22(1)(a)–(b) M-/RP-Property Regulation ("at the time the agreement is concluded"); Article 26(1)(a) ("first common habitual residence after the conclusion of the marriage"), (b)–(c) ("at the time of the conclusion of the marriage") M-Property Regulation. Additionally, Articles 22(1)(c) and 26(1) RP-Property Regulation refer to the creation of the registered partnership so that a change of the connecting factor is impossible. Also see Recital 46 M-Property Regulation and Recital 45 RP-Property Regulation.

Regulation sets forth the relevant point in time regarding habitual residence,[1269] nationality,[1270] and domicile.[1271] As far as this is the time of death, the law potentially applicable to the succession can change during the life of the decedent; for dispositions of property upon death, however, legal certainty is largely achieved by further fixating a relevant point in time.[1272] Article 26(2) Succession Regulation safeguards the capacity to modify or revoke a disposition from changes of the applicable law. To the extent that other provisions refer back to Articles 21 and 22 Succession Regulation in particular, their determination of the relevant point in time is of recurring relevance, along with the rest of the content of these provisions. A change of the connecting factor is only to be taken into account if specific provisions allow it.[1273] The respective provisions concern the options for party autonomy or express a *favor testamenti*; they are rather innocuous cases of a factual change of a connecting factor, if at all.[1274]

4.2.2.4. Summary

In summary, the EU private international law regulations generally provide a relevant point in time for their respective connecting factors. In most cases, therefore, a later change cannot even occur. The few instances where a change in the connecting factor can be of relevance under the Succession Regulation are also exhaustively dealt with.

4.3. PARTY AUTONOMY

4.3.1. The Rise of Party Autonomy

Even at the very beginning of the third millennium, it could still be considered an "unusual measure" to have the parties determine the applicable law for

[1269] Article 21(1) Succession Regulation ("at the time of death"); Article 27(1) subparagraph 1(d) Succession Regulation ("either at the time when the disposition was made or the agreement concluded, or at the time of death").

[1270] Article 22(1) subparagraph 1 Succession Regulation ("nationality at the time of making the choice or at the time of death"); Article 27(1) subparagraph 1(b) Succession Regulation ("either at the time when the disposition was made or the agreement concluded, or at the time of death").

[1271] Article 27(1) subparagraph 1(c) Succession Regulation ("either at the time when the disposition was made or the agreement concluded, or at the time of death").

[1272] Articles 24–25 Succession Regulation; see also Recital 48 Succession Regulation.

[1273] See the quotations providing for alternative points in time in footnotes 1272–1274.

[1274] The odd second alternative of Article 22(1) subparagraph 1 Succession Regulation seems to presuppose a (future) change of nationality; its main function, however, seems to be to facilitate the determination of a valid choice of law *ex post*, see *Wilke*, RIW 2012, 601, 605–606. Article 27(1) Succession Regulation does not even presuppose a change of the connecting factor, but *can* apply when there has been one.

contractual obligations.[1275] One should hasten to add that "unusual" was not to be confused with "innovative" – courts across Europe had (arguably) recognised party autonomy for contractual obligations much earlier,[1276] to say nothing of private international law scholars,[1277] but to be understood quite literally. As its main relevance across Europe and the world was the field of contracts, party autonomy was *not a usual* solution in private international law. About a decade later, however, the "unloved ugly duckling"[1278] has triumphed;[1279] the freedom to choose the applicable law in nearly every area of private international law has become an international trend,[1280] a "true revolution".[1281]

The justification for party autonomy, however, continues to be debated despite its ubiquity in modern times.[1282] For some, party autonomy is famously a mere "stopgap".[1283] Again, however, a clarification is in order. This (albeit common[1284]) translation of "Verlegenheitslösung" arguably pejoratively connotes a makeshift solution. Yet "Verlegenheit" has to do with embarrassment. The German expression can also be read to only refer to the "embarrassment" of a legislator that cannot find a reasonable balance of the parties' interests pointing to several potentially applicable laws. As a consequence, the legislator leaves it up to the parties themselves to break the deadlock.[1285] This expedient is not of a temporary character as the term

1275 *Kegel/Schurig*, IPR, §18 I 1 c (652).

1276 England: Robinson v. Bland, 97 E.R. 717 (1760); France: Cass. Civ. 5.12.1910 = *Ancel/Lequette*, Les grands arrêts, No. 11; Germany: RGZ 9, 225 [1882]; 14, 235; concerning the latter decisions see *von Bar/Mankowski*, IPR I, §7 at 69. On the historical foundations of party autonomy also *Mills*, Party Autonomy, 44–66.

1277 Party autonomy has been traced back to ancient times by some, see *Symeonides*, Codifying Choice of Law, 112; *F. Sturm/G. Sturm*, in: Staudinger, Einl. zum IPR at 135. More often, party autonomy is traced back to Dumoulin, see e.g. *Ancel/Lequette*, Les grands arrêts, No. 11 at 3; *Mayer/Heuzé*, DIP, at 64; also *Yntema*, Am. J. Comp. L. 2 (1953), 297, 304–305 ("anticipation" of modern doctrines); ultimately, however, this is far from indubitable, see *Kroll-Ludwigs*, Die Rolle der Parteiautonomie, 156–158; on Dumoulin and party autonomy also *Mills*, Party Autonomy, 46–48.

1278 *Mansel*, in: Leible (ed.), General Principles, §8.04[G].

1279 *Rösler*, RabelsZ 78 (2014), 155, 160 ("Siegeszug der Rechtswahlfreiheit").

1280 *Bonomi*, Explanatory Report on the Maintenance Protocol, at 109; for a global perspective also see *Symeonides*, Codifying Choice of Law, 114–115.

1281 *Lehmann*, Vand. J. Trans. L. 41 (2008), 381, 385.

1282 For relatively recent comprehensive accounts see *Mills*, Party Autonomy, 66–90; *Basedow*, The Law of Open Societies, at 183–446; *Mandery*, Party Autonomy in Contractual and Non-Contractual Obligations, 85–98; *Kroll-Ludwigs*, Die Rolle der Parteiautonomie, 148–302; also the summary by *M.-P. Weller/Benz/Thomale*, ZEuP 2017, 250, 264–267.

1283 *Kegel/Schurig*, IPR, §18 I 1 c (653); also *Raape*, IPR, §40 II 2 (458) ("Verlegenheit" of the *lex fori*).

1284 *Mansel*, in: Leible (ed.), General Principles, §8.04[G]; *von Hein*, in: Calliess (ed.), Rome Regulations, Art. 14 Rome II at 1; *Lehmann*, Vand. J. Trans. L. 41 (2008), 381, 394.

1285 Similarly *Kühne*, in: LA Schurig, 129, 136; *id.*, in: FS Heldrich, 815, 818 (note 20), assuming that *Kegel/Schurig* had the pejorative version in mind. Against the pejorative connotation

"stopgap" might suggest. Rather, the "Gordian knot" is cut,[1286] i.e. resolved permanently.

In recent times, many have abandoned this genuine conflicts perspective on party autonomy for a substantive one.[1287] Partly overlapping but with different emphases, the value of free will in liberal(-democratic) legal systems,[1288] fundamental/constitutional rights,[1289] private international law serving the parties' interests – as opposed to resolving conflicts between states,[1290] legal certainty as a core tenet of private law,[1291] a decreasing number of restrictions on private autonomy in substantive private law,[1292] implications of Enlightenment for human freedom and self-commitment,[1293] and/or the increased mobility of European citizens[1294] are supposed to provide ample justification for party autonomy.[1295] Many EU private international law regulations[1296] expressly rely on the idea of legal certainty in the party autonomy context (Recitals 31 Rome II, 15 Rome III, 38 Succession Regulation[1297]), although the idea of party autonomy as a "cornerstone" (Recital 11 Rome I) also has a more fundamental connotation. Party autonomy may also occasionally have been a compromise solution at the EU level.[1298] (In any case, to expect a *legislator* to expound a *theory* of party autonomy would be fatuous.[1299])

Schurig, in: Mansel (ed.), IPR im 20. Jahrhundert, 5, 22 (with note 92). Also see *Roth*, CMLRev 39 (2002), 369, 380 ("beyond the parties' choice there is no truly convincing objective connecting factor").

1286 *Lehmann*, Vand. J. Trans. L. 41 (2008), 381, 385.

1287 For this distinction see in particular *Kühne*, ZVglRWiss 114 (2015), 355, 364–366.

1288 *Leible*, in: FS Jayme I, 485, 488.

1289 *Hellgardt*, RabelsZ 82 (2018), 654, 670–676 (party autonomy as a fundamental right under EU law); *Lüttringhaus*, IPRax 2014, 146, 149 (party autonomy concerning contractual obligations covered by Article 16 EU Charter of Fundamental Rights); *Kroll-Ludwigs*, Die Rolle der Parteiautonomie, 148–302; *Añoveros Terradas*, in: LA Borrás, 119, 129; *F. Sturm/ G. Sturm*, in: Staudinger, Einl. zum IPR at 135–136; *Moura Vicente*, Yearbook of Private International Law 9 (2007), 257, 261; to this effect also *Hohloch*, FS Thue, 257, 263; see also ECJ Case C-184/12, United Antwerp Maritime Agencies (Unamar) NV v Navigation Maritime Bulgare, ECLI:EU:C:2013:663, at 49 (relation of party autonomy and freedom of contract). For at least some connection of party autonomy to fundamental rights also *Audit/d'Avout*, DIP, at 211.

1290 *Lehmann*, Vand. J. Trans. L. 41 (2008), 381, 413–425 and passim.

1291 *Flessner*, in: FS Magnus, 403, 410 (with further references).

1292 See *Mansel*, in: Leible (ed.), General Principles, §8.04[G].

1293 *Basedow*, The Law of Open Societies, at 183–261, in particular at 234–255; *id.*, RabelsZ 75 (2011), 38, 50–52, 54–56.

1294 *Schmitz*, Die Rechtswahlfreiheit im europäischen Kollisionsrecht, 92–106.

1295 Rather sceptical towards all of these approaches *Kühne*, LA Schurig, 129, 136.

1296 Also *Mansel*, in: Leible (ed.), General Principles, §8.04[G] ("full range of inner reasons for the legitimacy of party autonomy").

1297 Recital 45 M-Property Regulation and Recital 44 RP-Property Regulation speak of facilitating the spouses'/partners' management of their property.

1298 *Hausmann*, Riv. dir. int. priv. proc. 2015, 499, 503.

1299 See *Mansel*, in: Leible (ed.), General Principles, §8.04[G].

Even if one agrees with the gist of these approaches, however, it seems hard to escape the sobering reality of party autonomy,[1300] in which choices are made in boilerplate provisions without much consideration as a result of "compound inertia".[1301]

4.3.2. *Party Autonomy as a Formally General Issue*

For present purposes, two aspects deserve particular attention. First, against the backdrop of the tripartite structure of conflicts rules, the appropriate place for party autonomy is the context of the connecting factor.[1302] To be sure, party autonomy seems to raise certain questions, particularly in regard of the governing law,[1303] but these can arguably be rephrased as possible limitations on party autonomy.[1304] More fundamentally, the conflicts function of party autonomy is that of a connecting factor. Instead of determining the applicable law through an objective factor such as the location of a person or thing, a person's nationality etc., the parties themselves make that determination. Their decision provides the link between the subject matter and the governing law. They themselves declare that their subject matter is to be governed by a certain law; with a salient feature of party autonomy being that mandatory provisions of one law can be "deselected"[1305] – just as an "ordinary" conflicts rule, if it determines foreign law to be applicable, leads to the inapplicability of mandatory provisions of the *lex fori*. From this point

1300 *Mankowski*, Interessenpolitik, 18–22 ("myth and reality").

1301 *Johns*, Law & Contemp. Probs. 71 (2008), 243, 255.

1302 See *Junker*, IPR, §6 at 44–51; *Weller*, in: id. (ed.), Europäisches Kollisionsrecht, at 120; *Kohler*, Rec. des cours 359 (2012), 285, 304. Expressly *Kegel/Schurig*, IPR, §13 IV (474); the discussion of particular issues of party autonomy, however, is relegated likewise expressly to later parts of the textbook. *Kropholler*, IPR, §40 (292–301), together with the connecting factors "nationality" (§38) and "habitual residence" (§39); the topic "connecting factors" as such, however, is discussed much earlier (§20). Already *Neuhaus*, Grundbegriffe, §33 (251–263), with §§26–34 covering different connecting factors. See also *Basedow*, The Law of Open Societies, at 439 ("instead of objective connecting factors"); *Sonnenberger*, in: FS Kropholler, 227, 234 ("nothing else but an instrument of connection") and *Hohloch*, FS Thue, 257, 262 (party autonomy as the "third cornerstone" together with nationality and habitual residence); *Leible/Müller*, Yearbook of Private International Law XIV (2012/2013), 137, 145 (implicitly); *von Bar/Mankowski*, IPR I, §7 at 67–87 (implicitly); furthermore the position of *Mansel*'s contribution, §8, in Leible (ed.), General Principles. It seems much less plausible to say that a rule like Article 3 Rome I concerns "contracts which contain a [...] choice of law" as if such contracts were a *subject matter* of their own; but see *Carruthers/Crawford*, Edin. L. R. 9 (2005), 65, 79, who appear to make exactly this statement.

1303 *Renvoi* where the parties have chosen the applicable law? Which law can they choose when the legal system at issue is not unified?

1304 *Infra* sections 4.3.5. and 4.3.6.

1305 See only *Lehmann*, Vand. J. Trans. L. 41 (2008), 381, 388.

of view, party autonomy is all but "beyond the traditional unilateral or multilateral approaches".[1306]

To further underline this position, one can point out that *overriding* mandatory provisions and public policy exceptions affect the determination and application of the governing law in cases of party autonomy in the same way as they do for other conflicts rules.[1307] From the formal perspective adopted here, it is obvious that this must be the case: overriding mandatory provisions and public policy concern elements of conflicts rules other than (and independent from) the connecting factor.[1308]

Second, party autonomy is of formally general relevance. As already stated in the introduction to this section, party autonomy *could* be used as a general connecting factor for all subject matters. In such a case, the admission of party autonomy would be a formally general rule in the strict sense. While no domestic system of private international law in the EU seems to have gone that far, all EU private international law regulations permit party autonomy, albeit in some instances with rather big limitations. Even so, the issues raised by party autonomy are formally general as long as party autonomy is allowed more than once within a system of private international law. And in terms of issues there are quite a few.[1309] Can the parties choose any law or is their choice limited (e.g. to laws to which the parties already have some connection such as nationality)? What about non-state "law"? Do they have to submit the entire subject matter to one law or can they make a partial choice? When can they choose the applicable law? How can they make this choice? How is the validity of an agreement concerning the applicable law to be determined?

This list of issues already serves as an indicator of some of the peculiarities of party autonomy. The word "determined" in the last question is particularly telling: to the extent that the formal or material validity of an agreement is to be determined according to one law or another (see Articles 3(5), 10, 11 Rome I), a genuine conflicts provision resolves the issue. In other words, the connecting factor itself depends on other conflicts rules (with their subject matter "formal/material validity"). This is unusual, for almost all issues discussed in the context of a formal understanding of "general" do not require a determination of the applicable law themselves, and are rather

1306 For this view *Juenger*, in: LA Siehr (2000), 288, 306; against this position also see *Basedow*, The Law of Open Societies, at 439; *Michaels*, in: LA Schurig, 191, 196.

1307 See e.g. *Reimann*, in: Verschraegen (ed.), Rechtswahl, 1, 5 and 28; *Rühl*, in: FS Kropholler, 187, 205–207 (calling them "technische Grenzen"/"technical limitations" on party autonomy).

1308 See already *supra* section 2.9.2.

1309 See *Mansel*, in: Leible (ed.), General Principles, §8.05; *Coester-Waltjen/Coester*, in: LA Schurig, 33, 35–45; *Symeonides*, Codifying Choice of Law, 115–160; *Rühl*, in: FS Kropholler, 187, 189–205.

part of the overall process of determining the applicable law. Then again, none of the other connecting factors, nor other elements of a conflicts rule generally, are a legal act themselves[1310] like party autonomy.

Another peculiarity in the context of party autonomy is that issues are occasionally resolved by substantive provisions. For example, to the extent that a rule allows party autonomy to be exercised expressively or impliedly, it amends[1311] (or rather: supersedes[1312]) the applicable substantive law.

4.3.3. *Member States*

Only four member states have a provision on party autonomy among their general private international law provisions: Austria, Hungary, the Netherlands, and Poland. Notably, the latter three are among the most recent private international law codes.

§11 Austrian PIL Act and Article 10:10 Dutch Civil Code are of a rather limited scope. The former includes a rule of interpretation,[1313] excludes any implied choice of law once court proceedings have started, and shields third parties from negative effects of *ex post* choices; the latter requires a choice to be made, expressly or otherwise,[1314] sufficiently clearly. §9 Hungarian PIL Act is quite similar to these provisions, except that it also pertains to forum selection clauses.

Article 4 Polish PIL Act is much more fleshed out. It stops short of making party autonomy relevant for all of Polish private international law, but simply states that it is allowed where the Act allows it.[1315] (From the formal perspective, one can see why this provision has already been considered redundant.[1316]) Apart from that, however, there are rules on the "how" of a choice (expressly or clearly demonstrated), on the protection of third parties from choices made *ex post*, on the determination of the existence and validity of a choice, and on modification and revocation of a choice, as well as a special form provision relating to the respective subject matter.[1317] Parallels to Article 3 Rome I are obvious.[1318]

1310 See *Ömür*'s book on the basis of "Rechtswahl als Rechtsgeschäft".

1311 *Mansel*, in: Leible (ed.), General Principles, §8.05[F].

1312 *Calliess*, in: id. (ed.), Rome Regulations, Art. 3 Rome I at 27.

1313 *Infra* section 4.3.5.

1314 An implied choice is not off the table, *ten Wolde*, Yearbook of Private International Law 13 (2011), 389, 408; any determination of the applicable law by reference to the hypothetical intentions of the parties is excluded, however, *Struycken*, RabelsZ 78 (2014), 592, 608.

1315 Article 4(1) Polish PIL Act; the Act does allow it in several places, but partly only with limitations, *Ernst*, RabelsZ 76 (2012), 597, 608–609.

1316 See *Ernst*, RabelsZ 76 (2012), 597, 608; but also see *infra* Chapter 4, section 4.3.

1317 Article 4(2)–(6) Polish PIL Act.

1318 *Ernst*, RabelsZ 76 (2012), 597, 608.

The lack of general provisions on party autonomy in other codes does not allow the inference that parties can necessarily choose the applicable law only in very few, isolated instances under these codes – if at all. On the contrary, several member states have extended party autonomy to new fields of private international law when drafting their new codes. Examples include the Belgian PIL Code,[1319] the Czech PIL Act,[1320] the Bulgarian PIL Code,[1321] and the Italian PIL Act.[1322] Conversely, in some instances of national private international law, it is the lack of party autonomy that has puzzled scholars.[1323]

The overarching relevance of party autonomy is not (yet) apparent everywhere in scholarly literature. Even those who reserve a special section for "general" or "preliminary" matters as such do not necessarily cover party autonomy in it.[1324]

4.3.4. *European Union*[1325]

The chapters on "other" provisions in Rome I and Rome II contain no rules on party autonomy, nor are there any among the provisions forming the functional equivalent to these chapters in Rome III, the Succession Regulation, the M-Property Regulation, and the RP-Property Regulation.[1326] This occasions no surprise. Each of the Rome Regulations has its own conflicts rule allowing party autonomy for (in principle[1327]) *all* of the subject

---

1319 See *Erauw/Fallon*, in: Dirix/Lelen (eds.), The Belgian Reports, 227, 273–274; *Francq*, RabelsZ 70 (2006), 235, 253; *Fiorini*, ICLQ 54 (2005), 499, 518.

1320 *Pauknerová/Pfeiffer*, Journal of Private International Law 10 (2014), 205, 220.

1321 *Hessel-Jolst*, Yearbook of Private International Law 9 (2007), 375, 378 (party autonomy in new fields of private international law a "striking feature" of the Bulgarian PIL Code).

1322 *Pocar/Honorati*, in: Symeonides (ed.), PIL at the End of the 20th Century, 279, 293; *Kindler*, RabelsZ 61 (1997), 227, 263–265 and 269–274; *Giardina*, Rev. crit. DIP 1996, 1, 12 ("une innovation importante").

1323 *Carruthers/Crawford*, Edin. L. R. 9 (2005), 65, 83; *Fentiman*, in: Symeonides (ed.), PIL at the End of the 20th Century, 165, 182.

1324 See e.g. *Mayer/Heuzé*, DIP, at 730–759, well within the "partie spéciale"; *Dicey/Morris/Collins*, Conflict of Laws, at 1-079–1-087, discuss various aspects of connecting factors as part of their "preliminary matters", but make no mention of party autonomy here or elsewhere in that part; *Cheshire/North/Fawcett*, PIL, do not refer to party autonomy as part of their "preliminary topics", either. But see *Kropholler*, IPR, §40 (292–301); the chapter marks the final one before the "special part" (§§41–55).

1325 Also see *Schmitz*, Die Rechtswahlfreiheit im europäischen Kollisionsrecht, 108–301, and *Maultzsch*, Journal of Private International Law 12 (2016), 466, 470–474, for an overarching analysis of party autonomy in the Rome Regulations and the Succession Regulation.

1326 Articles 11–16 Rome III, Articles 34–38 Succession Regulation; Articles 31–35 M-/RP-Property Regulation.

1327 Special conflicts provisions in the respective regulation occasionally prohibit or (further) limit party autonomy.

matters that the respective regulation covers. Likewise, the M-Property Regulation and the RP-Property Regulation have one provision each on party autonomy in respect of their entire subject matter.[1328] No further abstraction is possible *within* one and the same instrument.[1329]

The case of Article 14 Rome II is particularly instructive. It was actually the first of the "Common Rules" for all non-contractual obligations in the first Rome II Proposal.[1330] In the amended proposal, the provision was moved up to the beginning of the proposed regulation as the very first conflicts rule,[1331] like Article 3 Rome Convention.[1332] Ultimately, the provision on party autonomy for non-contractual obligations ended up in a chapter on its own:[1333] Chapter IV, entitled "Freedom of Choice". By its wording and its being positioned separately, it is obvious that Article 14 Rome II covers all non-contractual obligations under Rome II (unless another Rome II rule denies the parties a choice of law, such as Articles 6(4) and 8(3) Rome II[1334]). Accordingly, it has even been called a small general part.[1335]

In this context, the Succession Regulation is the odd one out. It contains three separate conflicts rules admitting party autonomy.[1336] Since these provisions correlate with most[1337] of the subject matters of the private international law part of the Succession Regulation, it might have been possible to draft a single pertinent provision for this regulation too. It seems that Recital 38 Succession Regulation identifies party autonomy as (formally) generally relevant for succession matters anyway.

In light of this – and in light of a by and large coherent approach of EU private international law to party autonomy[1338] – it is not surprising that many authors have identified the topic as one of general relevance at

1328 Article 22 M-/RP-Property Regulation.

1329 Similarly *Mansel*, in: Leible (ed.), General Principles, §8.03[A], according to whom a general provision only would be appropriate in case of the creation of a complete code. In this scenario, further abstraction would be possible.

1330 Article 10 COM(2003) 427 final (36).

1331 Article 4 COM(2006) 83 final (13).

1332 And, of course, like Article 3 Rome I just 11 months later.

1333 The removal from the very start of Rome II is reasonable because party autonomy is less relevant for non-contractual obligations from a practical (and substantive) perspective; but where the parties have made a valid choice under Rome II, it will prevail, *Leible/Lehmann*, RIW 2007, 721, 726; also e.g. *de Lima Pinheiro*, Riv. dir. int. priv. proc. 2008, 5, 12.

1334 In regard to some contentious issues in this regard see *von Hein*, in: Calliess (ed.), Rome Regulations, Art. 14 at 4–7.

1335 *Mansel*, in: Leible (ed.), General Principles, §8.03[A] ("small General Section").

1336 Articles 22, 24(2), 25(3) Succession Regulation.

1337 For example, the "formal validity of dispositions of property upon death made in writing" (Article 27 Succession Regulation) is a subject matter of its own.

1338 *Rühl*, in: FS Kropholler, 187, 188 and passim.

the EU level.[1339] Views are divided, however, as to whether party autonomy makes a suitable candidate for a potential general part,[1340] or not.[1341]

4.3.5. *Party Autonomy and* Renvoi*: An Issue of Limitation*

As will be shown,[1342] the general stance on *renvoi* varies greatly from member state to member state, as well as from the Rome, M-Property, and RP-Property Regulations to the Succession Regulation. The area where *renvoi* is most frequently prohibited, regardless of this stance, however, is where the parties have chosen the applicable law,[1343] or where they could do so.[1344] One can doubt, however, whether it is correct to even regard this as an issue of *renvoi*,[1345] i.e. one of the governing law, rather than one of a limitation on party autonomy. In the dichotomy of limitations on the choice and limitations on the effects of a choice, it would be a limitation of the former kind.[1346] The parties are told that they can choose the law of state A but not all of its law, i.e. not its private international law. A good example of this perspective is Article 4(2) EGBGB. Although found in the context of *renvoi*, its wording makes it clear that it sets a (formally general) limit[1347] to what parties can choose as the applicable law: "Where the parties can choose the law of a certain country, that choice may only relate to the substantive provisions".

1339 But see *Heinze* and *Sonnenberger*, in: FS Kropholler, 105–127 and 227–246, respectively, who both do not mention party autonomy as a stand-alone issue although they discuss the "general part".

1340 *Wandt*, Rechtswahlregelungen, 214–216; *Rösler*, RabelsZ 78 (2014), 155, 191 (his doubts concern the feasibility of the project "general part"/"Rome 0 Regulation" as such, not party autonomy as an element of it); *Nehne*, Methodik und allgemeine Lehren des europäischen IPR, 269–270; *Jayme*, in: Leible/Unberath (eds.), Rom 0-Verordnung, 33, 40; still rather favourably *Mansel*, in: Leible (ed.), General Principles, §8.07.

1341 *Schmitz*, Die Rechtswahlfreiheit im europäischen Kollisionsrecht, 302–303 (against a rule merely confirming the existence of party autonomy: "little use"); *Kreuzer*, in: Jud/Rechberger/Reichelt (eds.), Kollisionsrecht in der EU, 1, 4; *Siehr*, Yearbook of Private International Law VII (2005), 17, 34; sceptically *Wagner*, in: Leible (ed.), General Principles, §4.05[C][2][d]; for a separate extensive provision in each regulation (in spite of her own proposal for a general provision) *Ömür*, Rechtswahl als Rechtsgeschäft, 230–232.

1342 *Infra* section 5.5.4.

1343 Article 13(2)(a) Italian PIL Act, Article 1.14(4) Lithuanian Civil Code, Article 5(2)(1) Polish PIL Act, Article 19(2) Portuguese Civil Code, Article 2.559(3) Romanian Civil Code; Article 34(2) Succession Regulation.

1344 Article 6(3) Slovenian PIL Act, see *Rudolf*, IPRax 2003, 158, 159.

1345 But see *Mansel*, in: Leible (ed.), General Principles, §8.03[A]; implicitly for the view put forth here *Schmitz*, Die Rechtswahlfreiheit im europäischen Kollisionsrecht, 247–257.

1346 For this view apparently also *Reimann*, in: Verschraegen (ed.), Rechtswahl, 1, 12.

1347 This also the prevailing view among German scholars, see *von Hein*, MünchKommBGB, Art. 4 EGBGB at 23. To this effect also *Corneloup*, IPRax 2017, 147. Incidentally, this seemed to be the Hungarian position, too, in absence of a specific rule in the Hungarian PIL Code 1979 *Nagy*, PIL in Hungary, at 61.

To be sure, parties will *mostly* want to choose substantive law.[1348] Choosing private international law might even be "a symptom of madness".[1349] Yet where *renvoi* is flat-out prohibited, parties *cannot* even extend their choice to private international law. To allow them to do so is not necessarily a "contradiction"[1350] of party autonomy. In particular, where party autonomy is limited to begin with, e.g. to the law of the state whose nationality a person possesses (Article 22(1) clause 1 Succession Regulation), the exclusion of *renvoi* does not appear preordained. A legislator providing for the application of the law of a person's habitual residence, including its conflicts rules, could also have made the law of that person's nationality, including its conflicts rules apply. It does not follow that allowing the party to select the respective alternative must exclude *renvoi*.[1351]

These are not merely theoretical observations. There are also examples among the general provisions of domestic private international law codes taking a more lenient view.[1352] §21(2) clause 2 Czech PIL Act, in the *renvoi* context, does allow *renvoi* in cases of party autonomy under the condition that the parties so agreed. §11(1) Austrian PIL Act, in the context of party autonomy, states that a choice of law by the parties refers to substantive law when there are doubts regarding the correct interpretation of their choice. Therefore, Austrian private international law in principle allows the parties to choose conflicts rules.[1353]

4.3.6. *Party Autonomy and Non-Unified Legal Systems: Another Issue of Limitation*

Likewise, the question of whether parties can choose the law of a territorial unit or personal sub-system of a state can be analysed as an issue of limitations to party autonomy, rather than as one of the governing law.[1354] Where the parties are only allowed to choose the law "of a country", one would

---

1348 *Reimann*, in: Verschraegen (ed.), Rechtswahl, 1, 12; *Kindler*, RabelsZ 61 (1997), 237, 253 (regarding Article 13(2)(a) Italian PIL Act).

1349 See *Briggs*, PIL in the English Courts, at 7.98.

1350 But see *Puharič*, Yearbook of Private International Law 5 (2003), 155, 159; a similarly rigid stance is taken by *Loussouarn/Bourel/de Vareilles-Sommières*, DIP, at 317, although they admit an exception for the private international law of companies, at 319.

1351 *Solomon*, in: LA Schurig, 237, 259–260; for a similar perspective see *Briggs*, PIL in the English Courts, at 7.98. It is also a contested issue whether Rome I and II allow the parties to choose conflicts rules, see only *Rödl*, in: Calliess (ed.), Rome Regulations, Art. 20 Rome I at 6–7 and Art. 24 Rome II at 8.

1352 Also see *Rugullis*, ZVglRWiss 106 (2007), 217 with a detailed analysis of the position of many German scholars that, under the rules of the EGBGB (now not in force anymore), the parties could choose private international law for contractual obligations in spite of Article 4(2) EGBGB.

1353 Also *Verschraegen*, IPR, at 1406.

1354 For other aspects of non-unified legal systems see *infra* section 5.2.

probably need to note a *prima facie* limitation of their autonomy and then look for a supplemental rule providing for a solution. Arguably, provisions pursuant to which the parties can simply choose "law" contain no such limitation. Article 3(1) clause 1 Rome I and Article 14(1) Rome II could be interpreted in this way.[1355,1356]

4.4. NATIONALITY

When a conflicts rule uses nationality as its connecting factor, four questions arise: how is nationality to be determined? What happens if it is determined that a person has more than one nationality? What if a person has no nationality? Is nationality really to be used as the connecting factor if the person concerned is a refugee from the country of her nationality? As all of these issues can occur regardless of the particular conflicts rule, they are formally general issues. As they can occur only where a conflicts rule relies on nationality, however, they are not formally general issues in the strict sense. They would only constitute such issues in a system based exclusively on nationality and no such system exists within the EU. Conversely, with Latvia, there is only one member state that does not rely at all on nationality as a connecting factor in its private international law code. There, the aforementioned issues do not arise.

4.4.1. Member States

4.4.1.1. The Determination of Nationality

The connecting factor of nationality is a legal issue relevant at the level of a conflicts rule. It is therefore a preliminary question[1357] (if one accepts this

---

1355 That Articles 3 Rome I and 14(1) Rome II rather clearly do not allow the parties to choose non-state "law" such as PECL or the Unidroit Principles (see only *Calliess*, in: id. (ed.), Rome Regulations, Article 3 Rome I at 33; *von Hein*, in: Calliess (ed.), Rome Regulations, Article 14 Rome II at 32; also Recital 13 Rome I) is no argument against this view. Nor is it entirely persuasive to argue that the existence of Articles 22 Rome I and 25 Rome II shows that only the law of a *country* can be chosen under Articles 3 Rome I, 14(1) Rome II. As there would be plenty of other instances in which these articles would still apply, they do not necessarily refer to party autonomy. To say so is a *petitio principii*, for their applicability is exactly the issue here. Admittedly, however, Article 3(3) Rome I and Article 14(2) Rome II are indications that the respective first paragraphs presuppose the law of a *country* to be the object of party autonomy.

1356 To this effect arguably (implicitly) also *Fumagalli*, in: Baratta (ed.), DIP, s. v. "Rinvio ad ordinamenti plurilegislativi", 431, 438, who states that Article 22 Rome I is relevant where the parties *do not* choose the law of the respective unit. But see *Gebauer*, in: Calliess (ed.), Rome Regulations, Article 22 Rome I at 6 and Article 25 at 6; *Calliess*, in: id. (ed.), Rome Regulations, Article 3 Rome I at 34, according to whom Articles 22 Rome I and 25 Rome II are necessary for parties wanting to choose the law of the unit of a state.

1357 *Mankowski*, IPRax 2017, 130, 132; *id.*, in: Leible (ed.), General Principles, §10.01[D]; *Nordmeier*, GPR 2013, 148, 149.

category next to the incidental question[1358]). This is even expressly set forth in Recital 41 clause 1 Succession Regulation; although, as demonstrated above,[1359] one should probably not put too much weight on this terminology. Several member states have enacted a special rule dealing with this preliminary question among their general conflicts provisions.[1360] Estonia also has a provision on this issue in its Private International Law Act, just not formally among its general provisions.[1361]

To Greece goes the credit of being among the first countries to enact such a rule, even if the content of Article 29 Greek Civil Code reflected existing widespread international consensus when it was created.[1362] Indeed, its solution – nationality to be determined according to the rules of the state whose nationality is at issue – is also the one adopted in the provisions of other member states. It seems to be the solution even of those member states that lack a (pertinent provision in their) private international law code.[1363]

As the determination of nationality is dealt with essentially everywhere in this way, one might wonder whether not only the issue but also its solution are formally general across all private international law systems. But the answer is "no". It is not *theoretically* necessary that the law of the state at issue determines a person's nationality.[1364] Any system of private international law could define nationality *for its purposes* differently from the state whose nationality is at issue. In some exceptional cases, e.g. mass denaturalisations contrary to international law,[1365] justice might even warrant such an approach.

In general, however, legal certainty is a good *policy* reason to have the rule. If one is inclined to agree with those who contend that public international law mandates it,[1366] there would obviously also be a *legal* reason for it. Nevertheless, some scepticism is in order. To be sure, a few member states are

---

1358 See *supra* section 2.5.3. (Preliminary Question (in the Strict Sense)) as to the distinction.

1359 See *supra* section 2.5.5.1.

1360 Article 3(1) Belgian PIL Code, Article 29 Greek Civil Code, Article 2(3) Polish PIL Act (in part), Article 2.569 Romanian Civil Code.

1361 §11(1) Estonian PIL Act.

1362 *Gogos/Aubin*, RabelsZ 15 (1949/1950), 240, 251.

1363 Austria: *Verschraegen*, IPR, at 1393; Germany: *Kegel/Schurig*, IPR, §13 II 4 (452) (also for "foreign countries" in general); France: *Mayer/Heuzé*, DIP, at 892–895; Spain: *Calvo Caravaca/Carrascosa González*, DIP I, 439 (with further references); also in general: *Kahn-Freund*, General Problems, 243.

1364 *Neuhaus*, Grundbegriffe, §27 II (210 with note 573); *Kegel/Schurig*, IPR, §9 II 2a (382); but see *Mankowski*, IPRax 2017, 130, 132; *Verwilghen*, in: Het Wetboek Internationaal Privaatrecht becommentarieerd, Art. 3 I and II; ambiguously *Kahn-Freund*, General Problems, 243.

1365 *Nordmeier*, GPR 2013, 148, 149 with reference to Kropholler, IPR, [§38 II 2] 272; but see *Mankowski*, in: Leible (ed.), General Principles, §10.03 ("The purposes of PIL are too limited for such an enterprise […]").

1366 *Basedow*, IPRax 2011, 109, 116 (with note 38); *Mayer/Heuzé*, DIP, at 892–895; somewhat ambiguously *Weis*, Nationality and Statelessness in International Law, 198, who states that such a customary rule exists, but who also allows for the possibility that states apply any other law.

bound[1367] in this regard by the specific rule of Article 2 Conflict of Nationality Laws Convention. Furthermore, there *is* a general rule of public international law, as evidenced by Article 3(1) European Convention on Nationality,[1368] that every state determines under its own law who its nationals are, that only the state at issue can confer or revoke its nationality.[1369] Yet it does not[1370] follow that every state, for the purposes of private international law, must look to the state whose nationality is at issue. This would be tantamount to saying that a state can only choose nationality as a connecting factor in the way it is understood by the foreign state, or that it would otherwise be barred from using a concept called "nationality" at all – absurd propositions! Article 3 European Convention on Nationality itself recognises in paragraph 2 possible limitations on the "acceptance" of foreign law on nationality.

4.4.1.2. Multiple Nationalities

Domestic Legislation As Such

With relaxing attitudes toward (at least) dual nationality, and an increasing number of respective cases, the issue of multiple nationalities is not merely theoretical.[1371] When a conflicts rule uses nationality (or, like in the Austrian PIL Act or Hungarian PIL Code 1979, the personal law[1372] determined primarily via a person's nationality[1373]) as its connecting factor,

---

1367 But only as regards other contracting states, Article 18(1) Conflict of Nationality Laws Convention.

1368 Also see Article 1(1) Stateless Persons Convention.

1369 *von Hein*, in: MüKoBGB, Art. 5 EGBGB at 14; *Loussouarn/Bourel/de Vareilles-Sommières*, at 976; *Verwilghen*, Rec. des cours 277 (1999), 9, 122–129; ECJ Case C-200/02 Kunqian Catherine Zhu and Man Lavette Chen v Secretary of State for the Home Department, Reports of Cases 2004, I-9925, at 37, with references to further cases. More recently, the Court dropped the reference to international law, but still referred to this very line of cases: ECJ Case C-135/08, Janko Rottman v Freistaat Bayern, Reports of Cases 2010, I-1449, at 39.

1370 But see *de Lima Pinheiro*, DIP I, 510.

1371 *Fuchs*, in: FS Martiny, 303, 304–306; *Vonk*, Dual Nationality in the EU, 48–58 (practical relevance), 58–64 (attitudes), and passim; see *Verwilghen*, Rec. des cours 277 (1999), 9, 183–196 (typology), 315–350 (modern attitudes).

1372 "Personal law" or "personal status" (*Personalstatut*) is a rather problematic term apt to cause misunderstandings. Depending on the context, it can mean the law applicable to status and capacity or the law applicable to all "personal" issues (perhaps also including capacity, but also including issues of family and succession law – see *Rabel*, The Conflict of Laws, 110), or it can designate a (set of) connecting factor(s). See *von Bar/Mankowski*, IPR I, §1 at 23; similarly *Müller*, Jura 2015, 1319, 1322; *von Hein*, in: MüKoBGB, Art. 5 EGBGB at 2–5; *Mansel*, Personalstatut, Staatsangehörigkeit und Effektivität, at 36.

1373 See, e.g., §§12–15 Austrian PIL Act (with the general provisions of §§9, 10 Austrian PIL Act determining the personal law for natural and juridical persons) and *Neumayr*, in: ABGB-Kurzkommentar, §9 IPRG at 1; §§10–11, 16 Hungarian PIL Code 1979. The Bulgarian PIL Code and the Romanian Civil Code provide for a similar solution that uses the *lex patriae*, generally determined pursuant to Article 48(1) Bulgarian PIL Code/Article 2.568

a supplemental rule is required for cases of a person having two or more nationalities. It must set forth what "nationality" is supposed to mean in such a case.[1374]

Not only is there a pertinent provision of general relevance in most domestic private international law codes, in most instances it is also found among that code's general provisions.[1375] In the Slovak PIL Act, the respective provision is formally separate from special conflicts rules, but also separate from the "common" provisions: it is located right *between* those two sections, together with other rules on foreigners.[1376] The only member states without such a general rule in their private international law code are Latvia, where the issue does not arise, as well as Lithuania, the Netherlands, and Portugal.

The Netherlands are a particularly interesting case. A general provision on the issue of multiple nationalities had been proposed, but the Dutch legislator deliberately refrained from enacting it.[1377] Instead, Book 10 of the Dutch Civil Code now contains individual provisions dealing with the issue in each context in which it appears.[1378] As these individual provisions are not uniform – while, for example, Article 10:19(2) clause 1 Dutch Civil Code refers to the state of the person's habitual residence, Article 10:95(1) clause 2 refers to the more favourable law – one can understand the Dutch legislator's stance against one and the same overarching rule. Nevertheless, there would have been no legal reason against such a provision, for any individual provision deviating from it would have prevailed as *lex specialis*.

The existing general rules usually follow a two-step approach. If one of the concerned person's nationalities is that of the *lex fori*, it prevails without any further analysis[1379] (not so in Estonia and Romania[1380]). If the person

Romanian Civil Code by a person's nationality (see the general provision of Article 2.571 Romanian Civil Code for the nationality of a juridical person), as a connecting factor.

1374 *Kahn-Freund*, General Problems, 243.

1375 Among the general provisions: §9(1) clause 2, 3 Austrian PIL Act; Article 3(2) Belgian PIL Code; Article 11 Croatian PIL Act; §28(1), (2) Czech PIL Act; Article 5(1) EGBGB; Article 31 Greek Civil Code; Article 19(2) Italian PIL Act; Article 2(1), (2) Polish PIL Act; Article 2.568 Romanian Civil Code; Article 10 Slovenian PIL Act. Elsewhere in the code: Article 48(2), (3) Bulgarian PIL Code; §11(2) Estonian PIL Act; Article 33(1), (2) Slovak PIL Act; Article 9(9) Spanish Civil Code; also §11(2), (3) Hungarian PIL Code 1979.

1376 Article 33(1), (2) Slovak PIL Act. The "common" provisions are Articles 34–36 Slovak PIL Act, the special conflicts provisions are Articles 3–31 Slovak PIL Act.

1377 See Kamerstukken II 2009/2010, 32317, No. 3, 6.

1378 See Articles 10:11, 10:19-10:21, 10:37, 10:92(2), 10:95(1), 10:97(2), 10:105(2) Dutch Civil Code.

1379 §9(1) clause 2 Austrian PIL Act; Article 3(2) No. 1 Belgian PIL Code; Article 48(2) Bulgarian PIL Code; Article 11(1) Croatian PIL Act; §28(1) Czech PIL Act; Article 5(1) clause 2 EGBGB; Article 31(1) Greek Civil Code; §11(2) Hungarian PIL Code 1979; Article 19(2) clause 2 Italian PIL Act; Article 2(1) Polish PIL Act; Article 33(1) Slovak PIL Act; Article 10(1) Slovenian PIL Act; Article 9(9) paragraph 2 clause 1 (with reservations) Spanish Civil Code. Also Article 2285(1) French Civil Code (1967 Draft). See also for Sweden *Bogdan*, PIL in Sweden, at 35.

1380 Always the law of the state to which the person, as a citizen of that state, is most closely connected: §11(2) Estonian PIL Act; Article 2.568 Romanian Civil Code (indicated, inter alia,

concerned is a citizen of two or more other states, a decision between these nationalities is made, often in favour of the "effective" nationality: applicable is the law of the state to which the person is more closely connected.[1381] Slovakian private international law instead refers to the law of the nationality acquired last,[1382] Spanish private international law to the state of habitual residence[1383] (regardless of whether the person even has the nationality of that state[1384]).

Limitations by European Union Law: Party Autonomy

In the *Hadadi* case, the ECJ held that jurisdiction under Article 3(1)(b) Brussels IIbis cannot be made dependent upon the most effective nationality in cases of dual nationalities, stating that the spouses may choose among the courts of both the member states whose nationalities both of them have.[1385] This being a decision on jurisdiction and one largely based upon an interpretation of Brussels IIbis,[1386] domestic conflicts provisions do not seem directly affected. In passing, however, the Court did rely on the idea that requiring an effective nationality "would restrict individuals' choice of the court having jurisdiction, particularly in cases where the right to freedom of movement for persons had been exercised".[1387] If this is a hint that the Court considers restrictions to parties' options contrary to Article 21 TFEU, domestic provisions limiting choice of law for multi-nationals to the law of the effective nationality could become inapplicable as well.[1388]

---

by habitual residence). On the other hand, Hungary even favoured a Hungarian domicile and habitual residence in Hungary when these subsidiary factors applied: §11(3), (4) Hungarian PIL Code 1979.

1381 §9(1) clause 3 Austrian PIL Act; Article 3(2) No. 2 Belgian PIL Code; Article 48(3) Bulgarian PIL Code; Article 11(3) Croatian PIL Act (only if no domicile in one of the states at issue); §28(2) Czech PIL Act (closest connection prevails over default rule of "nationality acquired last"); Article 5(1) clause 1 EGBGB (habitual residence as an indicator of the closest connection); Article 31(2) Greek Civil Code; Article 19(2) clause 1 Italian PIL Act; Article 2(2) Polish PIL Act; Article 10(3) Slovenian PIL Act (only if no domicile in one of the states at issue). Also Article 2285(2) French Civil Code (1967 Draft): effective nationality.

1382 Article 33(2) Slovak PIL Act.

1383 Article 9(9) paragraph 2 clause 2 Spanish Civil Code.

1384 *Garcimartín Alférez*, DIP, at 22.6.

1385 ECJ Case C-168/08, Laszlo Hadadi (Hadady) v Csilla Marta Mesko, épouse Hadadi (Hadady), Reports of Cases 2009, I-6871, at 58.

1386 ECJ Case C-168/08, Laszlo Hadadi (Hadady) v Csilla Marta Mesko, épouse Hadadi (Hadady), Reports of Cases 2009, I-6871, at 44–52, 54–57.

1387 ECJ Case C-168/08, Laszlo Hadadi (Hadady) v Csilla Marta Mesko, épouse Hadadi (Hadady), Reports of Cases 2009, I-6871, at 53.

1388 *von Hein*, in: MüKoBGB, Art. 5 EGBGB at 77; *Hohloch*, in: Erman BGB, Art. 5 Rom III-VO at 7; possibly also *Bariatti*, Yearbook of Private International Law 13 (2011), 1, 14; but see the sceptical stance adopted by *Coester-Waltjen/Coester*, in: LA Schurig, 33, 39.

Rules giving preference to the nationality of the *lex fori*, whether it is the effective nationality or not, also eliminate an option (if they even apply to party autonomy[1389]) and are thus likewise suspect.[1390]

Limitations by European Union Law: Applicable Law in the Absence of Choice

National provisions that, in the absence of a choice by the party involved, give preference to the law of the state to which the multi-national is most closely connected are not in danger of running afoul of EU law. In the absence of a choice by the parties, it is for the legislator and/or judge to determine the consequences of multiple nationalities. In the end, one law must apply. (A "law mix", albeit not unheard of in private international law,[1391] is hardly feasible – and even if it were, in the case of conflicting results one law still would have to prevail.) Unless one contends that this law must necessarily be the law of a state whose nationality the person concerned does *not* have – which sounds rather absurd – it must be possible to give precedence to one nationality. The criterion of the closest connection is sound.[1392] In particular, as every person with more than one nationality is treated the same regardless of which nationalities she has, there is no discrimination.

Much more problematic, however, and not just from the point of view of policy,[1393] are those provisions automatically giving preference to the nationality of the *lex fori*. A person with the effective nationality of member state A and the *lex fori* nationality is treated differently from a person who also has the effective nationality of member state A plus the nationality of a third member state B. Even though both persons have the effective nationality of member state A, its law is only applicable to the latter; the *lex fori* applies to the former. As the former is treated differently only because of the nationality she has, this constitutes discrimination on the grounds of nationality, as prohibited by Article 18 TFEU. At the very least, where EU private international law regulations apply (that leave room for national law to deal with multi-nationals[1394]), this discrimination also occurs "within the scope

1389 In German private international law, for example, several provisions expressly exclude Article 5(1) EGBGB, the rule that makes one of the nationalities decisive: see Articles 10(2) No. 1, 10(3) No. 1, and 14(2) EGBGB.

1390 Primary EU law also is one of the reasons for *von Hein*, in: MüKoBGB, Art. 5 EGBGB at 67, to suggest that Article 5(1) EGBGB should never apply in situations of party autonomy, even where the EGBGB does not say so (see the preceding footnote).

1391 See Article 6(2) Rome I.

1392 *Basedow*, IPRax 2011, 109, 116; but see *Michaels*, in: FS Kropholler, 151, 167.

1393 See only the German example of Article 5(1) clause 2 EGBGB that already ran afoul of prevailing scholarly opinion as well as of jurisprudence when it was created, see *Mansel*, Personalstatut, Staatsangehörigkeit und Effektivität, at 112–128 and at 231–238.

1394 See Recital 22 Rome III and *infra* section 4.4.2.2.

of application of the Treaties". As the exercise of the right to free movement pursuant to Article 21 TFEU also makes a case fall "within the scope of application of the Treaties", many more instances of discrimination are covered by Article 18 TFEU too.[1395] At one point, the Court of Justice even considered it sufficient for the application of Article 18 TFEU that a national of one member state lawfully resided in another member state.[1396] In a later case, its wording was more cautious.[1397]

Admittedly, the situation just outlined is different from the prototypical Article 18 TFEU case in which a state discriminates against *foreigners*; here, a state discriminates against its own nationals. It does so – and this is what makes the case seem almost paradoxical – by treating them *as its own nationals*. Yet even if one does not subscribe to the idea that Article 18 TFEU applies to nationals in relation to their very own state (as long as it is not a purely internal case),[1398] it is important to keep in mind that a multi-national *per definitionem* also is a national of another state. At least if that state is another member state, it seems hard to gainsay that Article 18 TFEU applies.

There is no justification for this discrimination. To be sure, as the Court of Justice has by now clarified, even direct discrimination can be justified "if it is based on objective considerations independent of the nationality of the persons concerned and is proportionate to the objective being legitimately pursued".[1399] Yet at one stage or another, every objective fails the proportionality test.

If member states somehow tried to justify the preference for their own nationality with wanting to "protect" their own nationals,[1400] they would be doomed from the beginning. Protecting one's own nationals is not even a legitimate objective as far as the TFEU is concerned.[1401] If it were, it would not

1395 *Fuchs*, in: FS Martiny, 303, 311.

1396 ECJ Case C-148/02, Carlos Garcia Avello v Belgian State, Reports of Cases 2003, I-11613, at 27.

1397 ECJ Case C-434/09, Shirley McCarthy v Secretary of State for the Home Department, Reports of Cases 2011, I-3375, at 56: "It follows that Article 21 TFEU is not applicable to a Union citizen who has never exercised his right of free movement, who has always resided in a Member State of which he is a national and who is also a national of another Member State, provided that the situation of that citizen does not include the application of measures by a Member State that would have the effect of depriving him of the genuine enjoyment of the substance of the rights conferred by virtue of his status as a Union citizen or of impeding the exercise of his right of free movement and residence within the territory of the Member States."

1398 See only *Epiney*, in: Calliess/Ruffert (eds.), EUV/AEUV, Art. 18 AEUV at 29; *Troge*, Europarecht und das Staatsangehörigkeitsprinzip im IPR, 43–44.

1399 See only ECJ Case C-123/08, Dominic Wolzenburg, Reports of Cases 2009, I-9621, at 54–74; *Epiney*, in: Calliess/Ruffert (eds.), EUV/AEUV, Art. 18 AEUV at 37. The quotation is from ECJ Case C-524/06, Heinz Huber v Bundesrepublik Deutschland, Reports of Cases 2008, I-9705, at 75.

1400 See *Kruger/Verhellen*, Journal of Private International Law 7 (2011), 601, 607.

1401 *Troge*, Europarecht und das Staatsangehörigkeitsprinzip im IPR, 202.

be proportionate. As the public policy exception guarantees a certain minimum level of protection anyway, it is hard to imagine that balancing will always come out in favour of a different treatment.[1402]

The main objective pursued by member states when preferring their own nationality to a foreign one seems to be the efficiency and correctness of judicial and administrative proceedings. If officials can apply the *lex fori*, proceedings will presumably come along more speedily and the result will be more likely to be correct than if they had to establish and apply foreign law. Typically, they will also be able to resolve the preliminary question of nationality itself more quickly: as soon as a person's *lex fori* nationality has been determined, there is no need to consider any other nationality or to determine an effective one.[1403] Because of the overtones of justice ("correct" results), it is not possible to dismiss these objectives immediately as purely economic ones; as such, they would be illegitimate.[1404] Still, the danger of conflicting decisions (many other member states would not give preference to the same nationality, unless it was the effective one[1405]) and possible problems of recognition are particularly grave in personal matters where nationality is most often used as a connecting factor. Relatively minor efficiency benefits cannot outweigh them in a balancing test.[1406] The famous *Garcia Avello* case is also an indication of this result. The ECJ in part relied upon the "serious inconvenience" of having divergent surnames in different countries in order to hold that a member state contravenes Articles 12 and 17 TEC (= Articles 18 and 20 TFEU) if it refuses to change a dual-national's surname to that under the other member state's law.[1407] The Court did not even discuss possible efficiency benefits.[1408]

In conclusion, rules that give preference to the *lex fori* only for the reason that it is the *lex fori* constitute prohibited discrimination under Article 18 TFEU in relation to people with multiple nationalities of member states.[1409]

1402 *Troge*, Europarecht und das Staatsangehörigkeitsprinzip im IPR, 203, considers a different treatment not even necessary to pursue a member state's objective of protecting its nationals.

1403 *Troge*, Europarecht und das Staatsangehörigkeitsprinzip im IPR, 200–201.

1404 As to the illegitimacy of economic aims as a justification for discrimination, see *Epiney*, in: Calliess/Ruffert (eds.), EUV/AEUV, Art. 18 AEUV at 38; ECJ Case C-388/01, Commission of the European Communities v Italian Republic, Reports of Cases 2003, I-721, at 19–22.

1405 In which case there would be no discrimination in the first place, as all multi-nationals would be treated alike.

1406 *Troge*, Europarecht und das Staatsangehörigkeitsprinzip im IPR, 202 (but apparently only in regard to the more efficient determination of nationality).

1407 ECJ Case C-148/02, Carlos Garcia Avello v Belgian State, Reports of Cases 2003, I-11613, at 36; the actual holding, at 45, is subject to a few reservations not reproduced here.

1408 To the same effect *von Hein*, in: MüKoBGB, Art. 5 EGBGB at 86.

1409 *Fuchs*, in: FS Martiny, 303, 312–313; *Rösler*, RabelsZ 78 (2014), 155, 184; *Gruber*, IPRax 2012, 381, 386; *Basedow*, IPRax 2011, 109, 116; *Looschelders/Smarowos*, VersR 2010, 1, 5; *Troge*, Europarecht und das Staatsangehörigkeitsprinzip im IPR, 203; *Michaels*, in FS Kropholler, 151, 167;

To this extent, the numerous, respective, domestic private international law rules found among the general provisions cannot be applied.

4.4.1.3. Statelessness

With 3.3 million reported cases of stateless persons, and a dark figure at least[1410] three times bigger,[1411] statelessness is no niche issue in practice. In private international law, if a person is stateless, or if her nationality cannot be determined, the connecting factor "nationality"[1412] does not work. This, however, is a legal problem only if there is no fallback provision, i.e. if there is only one pertinent conflicts rule and it only uses nationality as its connecting factor. In this case, the applicable law simply cannot be determined without a supplemental rule setting forth how the connecting factor "nationality" should work when a person does not have one. In all other cases, the lack of such a rule may indicate the acceptance that the connecting factor (and therefore the particular conflicts rule) does not work and that, as a consequence, another conflicts rule should apply. As it is possible to determine the applicable law, a supplemental rule is not legally necessary. It is an entirely different matter that policy considerations, in particular: non-discrimination, or obligations under public international law, can militate for such an additional rule.

All this should not distract from the realisation that the issue of stateless persons is formally general. Interpreting the lack of any special provision on statelessness in the way just outlined is akin to interpreting it as a rule of its own: "In the case of a stateless person, the otherwise applicable conflicts rules apply instead of the ones requiring nationality". The lack of any express provision on stateless persons does not indicate the lack of an issue; it is the unwritten *solution* to that issue.

Like in the context of multi-nationals, almost all member states have provided a pertinent provision in their private international law code.

Benicke/Zimmermann, IPRax 1995, 141, 147. See also *von Hein*, in: MüKoBGB, Art. 5 EGBGB at 86 (contravention of Article 18 TFEU "suggests itself"); *Meeusen*, Eur. J. Migr. L. 9 (2007), 287, 295; *von Bar/Mankowski*, IPR I, §3 at 41. From the perspective of Rome III *Hausmann*, Riv. dir. int. priv. proc. 2015, 499, 509; *Hau*, FamRZ 2013, 249, 253; *Helms*, FamRZ 2011, 1765, 1771. But see *Hohloch*, in: Erman BGB, Art. 8 Rom III-VO at 4; *Stürner*, Jura 2012, 708, 710 (without discussion or explanation); *Bariatti*, Yearbook of Private International Law 13 (2011), 1, 15–16 (with some noteworthy systematic considerations, but without even mentioning Article 18 TFEU).

1410 See *Conklin*, Statelessness, 7.

1411 The numbers are from 2012, even though the report is from 2014/2015: *UNCHR*, Global Appeal 2014–2015, 55 (available online at <www.unhcr.org/528a0a1316> last visited 12 October 2018).

1412 Or, again, the connecting factor of the "personal law" determined by a person's nationality, see *supra* section 4.4.1.2. (Domestic Legislation As Such).

The majority of these states have placed it among their general provisions.[1413] Only Latvia (which does not need one) and Lithuania[1414] have not made a general provision. Most[1415] member states are bound by Article 12(1) Stateless Persons Convention anyway. Therefore, even in the absence of any statutory rule at all, a general solution exists nearly everywhere in the EU, substituting domicile or residence for nationality.[1416]

4.4.1.4. Refugees

The practical relevance of the topic of refugees in the EU needs no elaboration in the 2010s. Under private international law, refugees do not raise a "technical" issue, unlike people with more than one nationality or none at all. All conflicts rules that use nationality as a connecting factor could apply to refugees who (still) have a nationality; if a refugee has multiple nationalities,[1417] or is stateless, the respective supplementary rules could fulfil their function. Rather, the question is: *should* rules relying on nationality even apply? It would be rather strange, perhaps ethically wrong, to apply the law of their home country to people who "have fled from that very country, have been living abroad for a long time[,] and have severed genuine personal links with [it]".[1418] One of the main policy arguments for nationality as a

1413 Among the general provisions: §9(3) Austrian PIL Act; Article 3(3), (4) Belgian PIL Code; Article 12 Croatian PIL Act; §28(3) Czech PIL Act; Article 5(2) EGBGB; Article 30 Greek Civil Code; Article 19(1) Italian PIL Act; Article 10:16 Dutch Civil Code; Article 3(1) Polish PIL Act; Article 11 Slovenian PIL Act. Elsewhere in the code: Article 48(4) Bulgarian PIL Code; §11(3) Estonian PIL Act; §11(4) Hungarian PIL Code 1979; Article 32 Portuguese Civil Code; Article 33(3) Slovak PIL Act (see *supra* at footnote 1379 as to its peculiar positioning); Article 9(10) Spanish Civil Code.

1414 Lithuanian private international law does mention stateless people here and there: Articles 1.15, 1.16, 1.18 and 1.25 Lithuanian Civil Code. Some of these provisions determine the law for stateless people in specific situations; others cover stateless people only in connection with "foreign citizens". As these provisions merely require the determination that a given person does *not* have Lithuanian citizenship, it is irrelevant whether they have any other or none.

1415 Cyprus, Estonia, Malta, and Poland are not parties to the Stateless Persons Convention; Sweden ratified it in 1965 but declared, among others, a reservation in relation to its Article 12(1).

1416 Article 12(1) Stateless Persons Convention provides: "The personal status of a stateless person shall be governed by the law of the country of his domicile or, if he has no domicile, by the law of the country of his residence." As to its meaning – obnubilated by the term "personal status"/"statut personnel", see footnote 1375 – *von Hein*, in: MüKoBGB, Art. 5 EGBGB, Anh. I, StaatenlosenÜbk at 5; *von Bar/Mankowski*, IPR I, §1 at 24–25 (regarding the identical Article 12(1) Geneva Refugee Convention).

1417 To even be a refugee under the Geneva Refugee Convention, a person with more than one nationality must meet the requirements of its Article 1A No. 2(1) in relation to *each* state, see Article 1A No. 2(2) Geneva Refugee Convention; Article 1(2) Refugee Protocol has removed the limitation to events prior to 1951 in the latter provision.

1418 *Mankowski*, in: Leible (ed.), General Principles, §10.04; also see *Nagy*, PIL in Hungary, at 97; *Lurger/Melcher*, IPR, at 1/30; *Hathaway*, The Rights of Refugees, 210; for a more nuanced picture see *Bogdan*, in: Essays Melander, 311, 319–320.

connecting factor – that, generally speaking, there exists some kind of strong bond between a person and the law of her nationality, at least as far as personal matters are concerned[1419] – simply falls flat under these circumstances.

Several member states have enacted a provision relating to refugees in their private international law codes; again, often among their general provisions.[1420] A quasi-general solution exists regardless of the existence of a provision in national codes: as almost[1421] all member states are bound by it, Article 12(1) Geneva Refugee Convention applies. Under this rule, domicile (which many actually read as "habitual residence"[1422]) or residence replaces nationality[1423] as the connecting factor.[1424]

Some even contend that Article 12(1) Geneva Refugee Convention is a fully-fledged conflicts provision. As such, it would not only replace connecting factors in domestic rules, but supersede the rules themselves as far as they relate to issues covered by the subject matter (to be autonomously interpreted) "personal status".[1425] As this can lead to discriminatory results, some further suggest a more flexible application of the rule.[1426] To be sure, this understanding has the advantage of not leaving it up to the contracting

---

1419 See only *Kegel/Schurig*, IPR, §13 II (447–448); *Loussouarn/Bourel/de Vareilles-Sommières*, DIP, at 222; *Vonk*, Dual Nationality in the EU, 117, with further references, in particular to *Jayme* and *Mancini*; *Mansel*, Staatsangehörigkeitsprinzip, 119, 134–135.

1420 Among the general provisions: §9(3) Austrian PIL Act; Article 3(3) Belgian PIL Code; §28(4) Czech PIL Act; Article 19(1) Italian PIL Act; Article 10:17 Dutch Civil Code; Article 3(2) Polish PIL Act; Article 2.568(4) Romanian Civil Code. (§28(4) Czech PIL Act simply refers to the pertinent international conventions.) Elsewhere in the code: Article 48(5) Bulgarian PIL Code, §11(3) Estonian PIL Act; §13 Hungarian PIL Code 1979.

1421 Sweden entered a reservation; its legislation does contain a similar rule, however, at least for marriage and guardianship; see *Bogdan*, in: Essays Melander, 311, 312. Spain entered a reservation, too. The *solution* of Article 12(1) Geneva Refugee Convention nevertheless has been suggested in Spanish literature, see *Calvo Caravaca/Carrascosa González*, DIP II, 60.

1422 *von Hein*, in: MüKoBGB, Art. 5 EGBGB, Anh. II, Flüchtlinge, Vertriebene, Verschleppte, Asylberechtigte, at 62; *Gottschalk*, Allgemeine Lehren, 72–73; *Lass*, Der Flüchtling im deutschen IPR, 119–124; more cautiously *Hathaway*, The Rights of Refugees, 216 ("the distinction […] may not long survive").

1423 In line with the purpose of the provision (that the law of the country from which a person has fled should not apply to her affairs), a respective *domicile* of origin also should be replaced: *von Hein*, in: MüKoBGB, Art. 5 EGBGB, Anh. II, Flüchtlinge, Vertriebene, Verschleppte, Asylberechtigte, at 61.

1424 Article 12(1) Geneva Refugee Convention provides: "The personal status of a refugee shall be governed by the law of the country of his domicile or, if he has no domicile, by the law of the country of his residence." Article 12(1) Stateless Persons Convention clearly was modelled after this provision; the remarks made *supra* in footnote 1419 apply here as well. See also *von Hein*, in: MüKoBGB, Art. 5 EGBGB at 6, and Art. 5 EGBGB, Anh. II, Flüchtlinge, Vertriebene, Verschleppte, Asylberechtigte, at 61.

1425 *Chetail*, JDI 2014, 447, 467–468; *Metzger*, in: Zimmermann (ed.), The 1951 Convention, Art. 12 at 24; *Gottschalk*, Allgemeine Lehren, 75; *Lass*, Der Flüchtling im deutschen IPR, 102–107 and 117–118 (only little room for divergent national concepts of "personal status").

1426 *Chetail*, JDI 2014, 447, 468–469; *Metzger*, in: Zimmermann (ed.), The 1951 Convention, Art. 12 at 24.

states as to which areas of law Article 12(1) Geneva Refugee Convention affects, thus ensuring uniform protection of refugees. Yet it is rather clear from the drafting history that the issue was deliberately left to the contracting states in anticipation of disagreement.[1427]

4.4.1.5. The Common Law Tradition and the French Tradition

The aforementioned issues of nationality are usually not discussed along with general issues of private international law in common law or French textbooks (as far as they even have a separate section for such issues). The reasons for this are rather different, however.

The common law has been rather hostile towards nationality as a connecting factor to begin with. "Nationality is, in general, both artificial, insufficiently personal and unsatisfactory despite its general use by civilian [sic] law countries".[1428] In accordance with the preponderance of domicile as the connecting factor under common law,[1429] there is thus not much need to deal with nationality as far as domestic law is concerned. Where the issues of multiple nationalities or statelessness do appear in the books, their potential occurrence usually only functions as an argument against the use of nationality.[1430] Still, any mention of nationality is often found at a place formally separate from specific conflicts rules.[1431]

In French legal literature, issues relating to the connecting factor "nationality" are often discussed in a section of their own, i.e. a section on nationality as a concept.[1432] These sections are usually not subordinate to

---

1427 *Hathaway*, The Rights of Refugees, 217–221. *Metzger*, in: Zimmermann (ed.), The 1951 Convention, Art. 12 at 24, seems to give too much weight to the position of (only) a group of the drafters.

1428 *Rogerson*, Collier's Conflict of Laws, 29; see also *Dicey/Morris/Collins*, Conflict of Laws, at 6-167–6-171; *Cheshire/North/Fawcett*, PIL, 171.

1429 *Briggs*, PIL in the English Courts, at 3.121; *Cheshire/North/Fawcett*, PIL, 170; see also *Dicey/Morris/Collins*, Conflict of Laws, at 6-167–6-168.

1430 *Rogerson*, Collier's Conflict of Laws, 29; *Dicey/Morris/Collins*, Conflict of Laws, at 6-170; *Cheshire/North/Fawcett*, PIL, 1171; critical of this way of reasoning *Briggs*, PIL in the English Courts, at 3.121 ("susceptible to English over-statement") and 3.124. But see *Westlake*, PIL (1859), 21–22, who had raised the issue of multiple nationalities under private international law without offering any apparent solution. In latest edition of his book, *Westlake*, PIL (1925), 378–379, both multiple nationalities and statelessness are discussed with reference to case law.

1431 *Rogerson*, Collier's Conflict of Laws, 29: Separate Chapter 3 on domicile and habitual residence. *Dicey/Morris/Collins*, Conflict of Laws, at 6-170: Chapter 6 on domicile and residence, in the part on "preliminary matters". *Cheshire/North/Fawcett*, PIL, 181: Chapter 9 on domicile, nationality, and residence, in the part on "preliminary topics". *Briggs*, PIL in the English Courts, at 3.121: Section 6 on personal connecting factors, part of "Common Law Rules of Private International Law: Structure and Methods", such as characterisation, *renvoi*, incidental question etc.

1432 *Loussouarn/Bourel/de Vareilles-Sommières*, at 977; *Audit/d'Avout*, DIP, at 64–103; *Mayer/Heuzé*, DIP, at 891–991.

sections on conflicts rules. The reason lies in the idea of nationality being a fourth branch of everything named "droit international privé".[1433] This understanding is functionally equivalent to that of considering nationality a general issue of conflicts rules only insofar as it recognises that nationality is of overarching importance. As far as it places questions of nationality *next to* conflicts rules under the umbrella term of *droit international privé*, instead of as part of or subordinate to general conflicts issues, however, there is a conceptual divide. It did not stop the drafters of the French Civil Code (1967 Draft), however, from inserting a provision on multi-nationals into the general provisions.[1434]

4.4.2. *European Union*

4.4.2.1. No General Rule in Rome I or Rome II

Neither Rome I nor Rome II use nationality as a connecting factor. In one sole instance, however, nationality does appear as *part* of the connecting factor: Article 7(3) subparagraph 1(c) Rome I allows the parties to a life assurance contract to choose the law of the member state of which the policy holder is a national. As a solitary provision cannot raise a formally general issue, Rome I could hardly be expected to provide a formally general answer. Yet all[1435] the questions outlined above still arise in connection to this one provision without there being an express specific answer.

Commentators have suggested that (at least) the question of dual nationalities should not be subject to individual domestic laws, that under Article 7(3) subparagraph 1(c) Rome I a multi-national policy holder is able to choose the law of all the member states whose national she has.[1436] This is indeed the most persuasive position. First, as Article 7(3) subparagraph 2 Rome I does contain a reference to domestic private international law,[1437] one can argue *a contrario* that subparagraph 1 is not supposed to leave any room for domestic law. Second, as any further systematic interpretation fails in light of the incoherent approach to multi-nationals under the other regulations (as will become apparent momentarily), the policy reason of ensuring uniform interpretation of Article 7(3) subparagraph 1(c) Rome I tips the balance in favour of this view.

1433 Expressly *Loussouarn/Bourel/de Vareilles-Sommières*, at 23; similarly *Audit/d'Avout*, DIP, at 63; *Gaudemet-Tallon*, in: Essays in Honor of Juenger, 317, 321.

1434 Article 2285 French Civil Code (1967 Draft).

1435 For the case of statelessness, however, the issue is not as pressing, see *supra* section 4.4.1.3.

1436 *Gruber*, in: Calliess (ed.), Rome Regulations, Art. 7 Rome I at 39; *Looschelders/Smarowos*, VersR 2010, 1, 5; *Armbrüster*, in: Staudinger, Art. 7 Rom I-VO at 13.

1437 Also see *infra* section 5.5.4. (General Exclusion of *Renvoi*).

4.4.2.2. No General Rule in Rome III

Rome III uses nationality as a connecting factor (as the second lowest rung in the *Kegel* ladder: Article 8(c)) and as one of the spouses' options for choosing the applicable law (Article 5(1)(c)). Both provisions raise the issues outlined above, and as the number of provisions is greater than one, the issues are formally general in the Rome III context. Again, however, the regulation is largely silent – with the exception of one statement in Recital 22 concerning multi-nationals: "Where this Regulation refers to nationality as a connecting factor for the application of the law of a State, the question of how to deal with cases of multiple nationality should be left to national law, in full observance of the general principles of the European Union". Does it relate to both Article 5 and Article 8 Rome III, i.e. set forth a formally general solution?

On the face of it, Recital 22 is rather clearly a general statement. Both its wording ("Where *this Regulation* refers to nationality as a connecting factor (…)")[1438] and its being a recital, instead of a specific clause annexed to either Article 5 or 8 Rome III, militate for this view. Its location alone does not constitute a particularly strong counterargument. To be sure, the recital is located *after* Recitals 15–20 on party autonomy[1439] and, what actually seems to be more relevant for this view,[1440] also *after* Recital 21 on the applicable law in the absence of choice. One could therefore assume that it only relates to the latter topic.[1441] If the recital were placed *before* Recital 15, however, would it only relate to party autonomy? Would it only relate to both topics if it were located *between* both? In domestic private international law, general provisions are found sometimes at the very beginning before specific conflicts provisions, sometimes at the very end after specific conflicts provision.[1442] Does anybody think that their relative location in any way influences their effect?

The more promising approach is to underline "as a connecting factor" in the wording of Recital 22 Rome III. Only Article 8 Rome III uses nationality as a "pure" connecting factor, whereas it is linked to party autonomy in Article 5 Rome III. Furthermore, only Recital 21 on the applicable law in the absence of choice even mentions connecting factors; none of the prior recitals on party autonomy do. Seen against this backdrop, the relative location becomes a rather persuasive argument. There seems to be an intrinsic

1438 Emphasis added; see *Lein*, in: Calliess (ed.), Rome Regulations, Art. 8 Rome III at 44; *Gruber*, IPRax 2012, 381, 385.
1439 BT-Drucks. 17/11049, 8.
1440 See *Gruber*, IPRax 2012, 381, 385 (note 65).
1441 BT-Drucks. 17/11049, 8; *von Hein*, in: MüKoBGB, Art. 5 EGBGB at 79.
1442 See *supra* Chapter 2, section 1.4.4.

connection between Recital 21 and Recital 22. It provides justification to read "Where this Regulation refers" narrowly, i.e. as "Where this Regulation in its Article 8(c) refers".

In conclusion, Recital 22 is no general statement on the treatment of multi-nationals under Rome III. It is a rule for cases of multiple nationalities specifically in the context of Article 8(c) Rome III. Here, there is room for national law, "in full observance of the general principles of the European Union". After the analysis above,[1443] it is rather obvious that this somewhat cryptic admonition (at least) refers to Article 18 TFEU and its limits for national law. Conversely, the option for party autonomy in Article 5(1)(c) Rome III is to be interpreted independently from any national rules on multiple nationalities. In line with the course set by *Hadadi*, the law of every nationality a person has can be chosen.[1444]

4.4.2.3. No General Rule in the M-Property Regulation and the RP-Property Regulation

The results just arrived at apply *mutatis mutandis* to the M-Property Regulation and the RP-Property Regulation. Both state in their recitals that the issue of multiple nationalities (as a supposed "preliminary question"[1445]) is left to national law, "in full observance of the general principles of the Union".[1446] The M-Property Regulation uses nationality as a connecting factor (Article 26(1)(b) M-Property Regulation) and as an option for a choice of law by the spouses (Article 22(1)(b) M-Property Regulation). Accordingly, the situation is essentially the same as under Rome III.

The RP-Property Regulation, however, only employs nationality as an option in the party autonomy context (Article 22(1)(b) RP-Property Regulation). This calls into question the idea of relying on the wording "as a connecting factor" as put forth in the preceding section, as Recital 49 RP-Property Regulation uses the very same phrase even though nationality is no "pure" connecting factor in any of its conflicts provisions. The outcome stands

---

1443 *Supra* section 4.4.1.2. (Limitations by European Union Law: Party Autonomy).

1444 *Kroll-Ludwigs*, in: Calliess (ed.), Rome Regulations, Art. 5 Rome III at 33; *Winkler von Mohrenfels*, in: MüKoBGB, Art. 5 Rom III-VO at 7; *Hausmann*, Riv. dir. int. priv. proc. 2015, 499, 507–508; *Rösler*, RabelsZ 78 (2014), 155, 183; *Hohloch*, in: Erman BGB, Art. 5 Rom III-VO at 7; *Fuchs*, in: FS Martiny, 303, 318; *Helms*, FamRZ 2011, 1765, 1770–1771; *Kruger/Verhellen*, Journal of Private International Law 7 (2011), 601, 619; also *Boele-Woelki*, Yearbook of Private International Law 12 (2010), 1, 18–19 (but under the premise that Recital 22 in principle also applies to Article 5(1)(c) Rome III). But see *Coester-Waltjen/Coester*, in: LA Schurig, 33, 39, who support this solution for policy reasons, but also assume that Recital 22 applies here and express scepticism whether the "general principles" include *Hadadi*.

1445 See already *supra* section 2.5.5.1. regarding this terminological confusion.

1446 Recital 50 M-Property Regulation, Recital 49 RP-Property Regulation.

nevertheless. For one thing, the EU legislator may simply have been a bit too eager when copying and pasting material from the M-Property Regulation (or back and forth between the two regulations). For another, both regulations also use the term "connecting factor" in a jurisdictional context,[1447] and Article 6(d) RP-Property Regulation does depend on nationality in a jurisdictional context. In other words, while nationality is not used as a genuine connecting factor in the private international law part of the RP-Property Regulation, it is used as one in a different part. Hence, one can read Recital 49 RP-Property Regulation in a way in which it does not have to apply to Article 22(1)(b) – and the findings concerning Rome III and the M-Property Regulation can still be transferred to the RP-Property Regulation.

4.4.2.4. General Rules in the Succession Regulation?

Chapter III of the Succession Regulation on the applicable law mostly does not use nationality as a "pure" connecting factor either. It does use it, however, as the only option for a choice of law by the person whose succession is at issue,[1448] or as the option for a choice of law in an agreement as to succession.[1449] In Article 22(1) subparagraph 2 Succession Regulation, one comes across an express provision on multi-nationals: "A person possessing multiple nationalities may choose the law of any of the States whose nationality he possesses at the time of making the choice or at the time of death". By its wording and its position, this provision only covers the choice of law under Article 22(1) subparagraph 1, but both Article 24(2) and Article 25(3) Succession Regulation refer to "the conditions set out" in Article 22. Thus, Article 22(1) subparagraph 2 turns out to be a formally general rule for these questions of party autonomy for a multi-national.

Nationality appears as a connecting factor in Article 27(1) subparagraph 1(b) Succession Regulation regarding the formal validity of dispositions of property upon death made in writing. As such a disposition is valid if it complies with the law "of *a* State whose nationality the testator […] possessed",[1450] the provision itself resolves the issue of multi-nationals without recourse to Article 22 Succession Regulation: any state suffices of which the testator was a national.[1451] This textual argument is supported by comparing Article 27(1) subparagraph 1(b) Succession Regulation with subparagraph 1(a), as the

1447 Recital 35 clause 2 M-Property Regulation, Recital 35 clause 3 RP-Property Regulation.
1448 Article 22(1) subparagraph 1 Succession Regulation; see also Article 24(2) Succession Regulation.
1449 Article 25(3) Succession Regulation.
1450 Emphasis added.
1451 Also relying on the wording *Lagarde*, in: Bergquist et al., EU-ErbVO, Art. 27 at 5.

latter begins with "of *the* State".[1452] The same distinction between "the" and "a" appears in French, German, Italian, and Portuguese, making the narrower wording in Dutch and Spanish seem to be an editing or translation error. Article 1 Testamentary Form Convention, on which Article 27 Succession Regulation is modelled, further supports this view, as it reflects this distinction.[1453]

Unlike Rome III then, the Succession Regulation itself makes the decision on how to deal with multiple nationalities and does not leave the question to national law. It does not, however, contain a provision on *how* nationality should be determined in the first place. In this respect, the Succession Regulation is in line with the Rome Regulations. Yet it is not entirely silent either. Recital 41 clause 2 sets forth that "[t]he issue of considering a person as a national of a State [...] is subject to national law". For some this means that the determination of nationality is up to the state concerned.[1454] This understanding of Recital 41 is too generous. In particular, as Recital 41 also states that the "national law" applies only "in full observance of the general principles of the European Union", it can only refer to law of member states. If it actually said that the law of the state whose nationality is at issue determines whether a person possesses it, this limitation would be inappropriate, as Article 22(1) Succession Regulation also allows choosing the law of a third state. Therefore, Recital 41 clause 2 should rather be read merely as a clarification that the Succession Regulation does not contain any rule on the question of which nationality a person has.[1455]

4.4.2.5. Conclusion

In EU private international law, nationality as a connecting factor has become less important, but not irrelevant.[1456] As far as the formally general issues of nationality are concerned, only the Succession Regulation takes up the question of the determination of nationality, but provides no answer at the EU level. With regard to multiple nationalities, the finding is somewhat strange: Recital 22 Rome III looks like a general rule, but is not; Article 22(1) subparagraph 2 Succession Regulation does not look like a general rule, but is.

1452 Emphasis added.

1453 See also *Mann*, ICLQ 35 (1986), 423, 424–425, who additionally relies on the *travaux préparatoires*.

1454 *Mankowski*, in: General Principles, §10.01[D]; *Lagarde*, in: Bergquist et al., EU-ErbVO, Art. 22 at 8; *Cach/Weber*, ZfRV 2013, 263, 268. *Nordmeier*, GPR 2013, 148, 149, reads Recital 41 clause 2 to refer to the European Convention on Nationality.

1455 To the same effect *Dutta*, in: MüKoBGB, Art. 22 EuErbVO at 4.

1456 *Mankowski*, in: Leible (ed.), General Principles, §10.01; *Kruger/Verhellen*, Journal of Private International Law 7 (2011), 601, 604–606 ("not [even] declining").

No EU private international law regulation contains any provision on stateless persons or refugees.[1457] As pointed out above, one could regard this silence as a statement. For example, one might say that the *options* for choosing the applicable law in Article 7(3) subparagraph 1(c) Rome I or Article 5(1)(c) Rome III are simply not available to stateless persons. If they do not make use of any other options,[1458] or if there are no other options,[1459] the conflicts rules determining the governing law in the absence of choice would apply.[1460] *Mutatis mutandis*, one can say the same about the Succession Regulation.[1461] The opposite standpoint identifies a gap at the EU level that it wants to fill by relying on the Stateless Persons Convention or on policy.[1462]

In the case of refugees, it is particularly convincing to rely on the solution of Article 12 Geneva Refugee Convention at the EU level, as EU law expressly acknowledges the importance of the Convention in Recital 3 Qualification Directive (Recast). The absence of any provision in the private international law regulations can thus be filled by systematic interpretation.[1463]

4.5. (HABITUAL) RESIDENCE AND DOMICILE

The private international law of every member state relies at some point on the place where a person can be located; by simply being there, by residing there, by residing there habitually, or by being domiciled there. Obviously, much of this is a mere question of semantics. What state A calls "residence", State B could call "domicile". For present purposes, thus, the question is merely whether the issue of the meaning of connecting factors relating to a person's location is formally acknowledged as general.

4.5.1. *Member States*

Only a few member states provide for an express rule in their private international law codes setting forth the meaning of one or more of their

1457 *Mankowski*, in: General Principles, §10.05[A].

1458 As in the case of Article 5(1) Rome III.

1459 As in the case of Article 7(3) subparagraph 1(c) Rome I.

1460 Here: Article 7(3) subparagraph 3 Rome I; Article 8 Rome III.

1461 *Geimer*, in: Hager (ed.), Die neue europäische Erbrechtsverordnung, 9, 18; *Leitzen*, ZEV 2013, 128; ambiguously *Nordmeier*, GPR 2013, 148, 149: when he says that the Succession Regulation does not deal with the question of whether stateless people can make a choice of law, does he mean that there could be an unwritten rule or that they cannot?

1462 For Rome III see *Winkler von Mohrenfels*, in: MüKoBGB, Art. 5 Rom III-VO at 9, and Art. 8 Rom III-VO at 9, as well as *Gruber*, IPRax 2012, 381, 386 (public international law and domestic law); for the Succession Regulation see *Dutta*, in: MüKoBGB, Art. 22 EuErbVO at 5 (policy: as a matter of autonomous interpretation and development of the law, stateless people *should* be allowed to choose the law of their habitual residence).

1463 In more detail see *Mankowski*, in: Leible (ed.), General Principles, §10.07.

connecting factors relating to a person's location. Only three of them do so among their general provisions. First, Belgium uses both "domicile" (*le domicile/woonplaats)* and "habitual residence" (*la résidence habituelle/gewone verblijfplaats*) as connecting factors. Both are defined in Article 4(1) and (2) Belgian PIL Code, respectively, among the Code's general provisions. Second, Romania relies on habitual residence as a connecting factor (*resedinta obisnuita*); its definition can be found among the general provisions in Article 2.570(1) and (2) Romanian Civil Code. Third, Hungary provides for definitions of both habitual residence and domicile in §3 Hungarian PIL Act among its general provisions.

Bulgaria defines its connecting factor of habitual residence not among the general provisions, but in connection with the rules on nationality in Article 48(7) Bulgarian PIL Code. By the express reference of this provision to the entire Code, however, it is rather obvious that it is intended not only as a specific rule for the status of natural persons (as one could surmise from its position). Indeed, later provisions in the Code that are not concerned with "status" issues rely on habitual residence.[1464]

The Latvian example constitutes a borderline case. Latvian private international law frequently uses (Latvian) residence as a connecting factor. Residence is defined in Section 7 Latvian Civil Code, thus not in the small cluster of general conflict of law rules toward the end of the introduction to its civil code. Its position, however, could either be described to be at the very beginning of the set of conflicts provisions, or at the very end of the set of general substantive provisions.[1465]

In other codes, there is no express definition of the locational connecting factor(s) among the private international law rules, even where the factor(s) is (are) used many times. This lack of a provision is readily comprehensible in some instances because the term is defined elsewhere in the law of the respective country. An obvious instance is the Lithuanian Civil Code: the first specific conflicts provision[1466] of Article 1.15(2) expressly refers to Article 2.12 of the Code in which "domicile" is defined. Likewise, the conflicts provision of §10 Estonian PIL Act, according to which Estonian law determines the residence of a natural person, is a reference to §§14

1464 See, e.g., Article 62(2) No. 1, No. 2 (agency), Article 67(2) (rights *in rem* concerning objects of personal use) Belgian PIL Code. The approach of the Hungarian PIL Code 1979 was very similar: §12 Hungarian PIL Code 1979 defined domicile and habitual residence. The provision was not located among the general provisions, but in connection with the "personal law" (see *supra* footnote 1372). Yet the terms also appeared in contexts that hardly related to "status", such as §25 Hungarian PIL Code 1979 (contractual obligations).

1465 Section 8 Latvian Civil Code concerns the applicable law to capacity, while Section 6 sets forth that general provisions (of substantive law) regarding obligations apply to other areas of law as well.

1466 Article 1.14 is the final provision in the section "general provisions".

and 15 Estonian General Part of the Civil Code Act that defines residence.[1467] Elsewhere, the legislator deliberately refrained from providing a definition.[1468]

English textbooks conventionally deal with the common law notion of domicile in chapters or sections separate from specific conflicts rules, often together with other personal connecting factors.[1469] A look at French textbooks reveals a somewhat inconsistent conceptual picture, although locational personal connecting factors are generally discussed separately from specific conflict of laws.[1470]

4.5.2. *European Union*

It is a truism that only a person who has been living under a rock for the last decade could have missed: habitual residence is *the* connecting factor in EU private international law. The "point of no return" seems to have been reached in the battle between nationality and habitual residence.[1471] Against the backdrop of Hague Conventions (but also of the Rome Convention) eschewing domicile and using habitual residence as a less contentious connecting factor,[1472] its use in Rome I[1473] and Rome II[1474] is perhaps not particularly significant; nationality was no viable connecting factor for (most of) the Rome I and II issues anyway.[1475] Now that habitual residence features prominently

1467 *Sein*, Yearbook of Private International Law 10 (2008), 459, 462.

1468 E.g. Germany, see BT-Drucks. 10/504, 41–42. The German legislator, however, did voice its principal approval for the German Federal Supreme Court's definition in NJW 1975, 1068, that, in turn, had relied on scholarly opinion and other courts.

1469 *Rogerson*, Collier's Conflict of Laws, Chapter 3 (11–39); *Dicey/Morris/Collins*, Conflict of Laws, Chapter 6, in the part on "preliminary matters"; *Cheshire/North/Fawcett*, PIL, Chapter 9, as a "preliminary topic"; *Briggs*, PIL in the English Courts, Section 6, part of "Common Law Rules of Private International Law: Structure and Methods", such as characterisation, *renvoi*, incidental question etc.

1470 *Cachard*, DIP, at 5 ("E1"), discusses habitual residence along with domicile and nationality as the "principaux facteurs de rattachement" on the third page of text, i.e. in the context of his introduction to the object of private international law. *Audit/d'Avout*, DIP, at 195–210, discuss personal connecting factors as part of the questions relating to the *statut personnel* in the "general part" of their book. *Loussouarn/Bourel/de Vareilles-Sommières*, at 232, also discuss domicile and (habitual) residence in the context of the connecting factors regarding the *statut personnel*, with this section forming part of the "general theory". *Mayer/Heuzé*, DIP, at 176–179, briefly deal with domicile as part of their discussion of the interpretation of connecting factors (while they cover nationality entirely elsewhere); said section is found among the issues of "la méthode du conflit de lois" in the "general part" of their book.

1471 *Dutta*, IPRax 2017, 139, 144.

1472 *Mann*, JZ 1956, 466, 468–469.

1473 Articles 4(1)(a), (b), (d), (e), and (f), 5(1), (2), 6(1), 7(2) subparagraph 2, 11(2), (3), and (4) clause 2 Rome I.

1474 Articles 4(2), 5(1)(a) and (1) subparagraph 2, 10(2), 11(2), 12(2)(b) Rome II.

1475 See already *supra* footnote 1206 with the appurtenant text.

in Rome III,[1476] the Succession Regulation,[1477] the M-Property Regulation, and the RP-Property Regulation[1478] as well, however, its relevance for EU private international law is unmistakable.[1479]

Despite the preponderance of habitual residence as a connecting factor – and despite its supposed advantage for the EU of having control over its definition, as opposed to the connecting factor of nationality[1480] – there is still no statutory definition to be found in EU private international law: none for all regulations, obviously, but also none for each regulation.[1481] The Hague Conference has not provided a definition[1482] either that could have been taken up.

4.5.2.1. Rome I and Rome II

Article 19 Rome I and Article 23 Rome II bear a very promising broad title ("Habitual residence"), but only cover select aspects of the issue: the determination of the habitual residence of "companies and other bodies",[1483] and of natural persons "acting in the course of [their] business activity".[1484] Both articles also contain a special rule on secondary establishments, with the one in Rome I applying to both companies and natural persons, the one in Rome II only to the former.[1485] Finally, Article 19(3) Rome I sets forth the relevant point in time for the determination of habitual residence.[1486] In any case, although Article 19 Rome I and Article 23 Rome II are limited as to their personal dimension, by their relative position in the regulations they are clearly intended to be relevant for the entire regulation. Both spearhead the respective chapters on "Other Provisions".

1476 Articles 5(1)(a) and (b), 6(2), 7(2), (3), and (4), 8(a) and (b) Rome III.

1477 In regard to the applicable law: Articles 21(1), 27(1)(d), 28(b) Succession Regulation.

1478 In regard to the applicable law: Articles 22(1)(a), 23(2)–(4), 24(2), 25(2), 26(1)(a), (3), 28(2) M-Property Regulation; Articles 22(1)(a), 23(2)–(4), 24(2), 25(2), 26(2), 28(2) RP-Property Regulation.

1479 See e.g. *Dutta*, IPRax 2017, 139, 140–142 (for the "triumph" of habitual residence), and *Mankowski*, IPRax 2017, 130, 136–139 (for the other side of the coin: the demise of nationality as a connecting factor).

1480 *Dutta*, IPRax 2017, 139, 143. According to the approach put forth here, however, there is room for a private international law legislator with regard to nationality: *supra* section 4.4.1.1.

1481 Very – and excessively – critical of this *Holliday*, in: Bergé/Francq/Gardeñes Santiago (eds.), Boundaries of European Private International Law, 297, 302.

1482 *Baetge*, in: Max Planck Encyclopedia of European Private Law, s. v. "Habitual Residence", 813.

1483 Article 19(1) subparagraph 1 Rome I; Article 23(1) subparagraph 1 Rome II.

1484 Article 19(1) subparagraph 2 Rome I; Article 23(2) Rome II.

1485 Article 19(2) Rome I, Article 23(1) subparagraph 2 Rome II; see *Baetge*, in: Calliess (ed.), Rome Regulations, Art. 19 Rome I at 23.

1486 See already *supra* sections 4.2. and 4.2.2.1.

4.5.2.2. The Succession Regulation

There is no provision defining habitual residence in the Succession Regulation, but there are two pertinent recitals. Both the wording of Recital 23 clause 1 ("*this Regulation* should provide that the general connecting factor for the purposes of determining both jurisdiction and the applicable law should be the habitual residence of the deceased at the time of death")[1487] and the position of Recitals 23 and 24 (before recitals regarding more specific issues of jurisdiction and the applicable law) support the idea that they relate to "habitual residence" wherever this term appears in the Regulation. They are to be understood as formally general for the purposes of the Succession Regulation.

While the recitals stop short of explaining what "habitual residence" *is*, they offer some guidance as to *how* to determine it, i.e. which factors to take into account when making the "overall assessment of the circumstances of the life of the deceased".[1488] Pursuant to Recital 23 clause 2 Succession Regulation, the authority concerned is to examine "the duration and regularity of the deceased's presence", as well as the "conditions and reasons" for it. When the deceased has lived abroad, she may still have her habitual residence in her state of origin if[1489] she has her centre of interest of her family and social life there (Recital 24 clause 2). It would not be very reasonable to argue *a contrario* that the "centre of interest" and the "social life" can only be taken into account in such a special case.[1490] For a peripatetic, her nationality,[1491] and the location of all her main assets, can be relevant (Recital 24 clause 4).

4.5.2.3. Rome III, the M-Property Regulation, and the RP-Property Regulation

Rome III, the M-Property Regulation, and the RP-Property Regulation are entirely silent as to the determination of habitual residence. For the two latter regulations, this finding is rather perplexing as they follow the Succession Regulation in so many other regards. Surely, one is not to assume that the indicators mentioned in the Succession Regulation are useless for the purposes of the M-Property Regulation and the RP-Property Regulation just because they have not been reiterated?

1487 Emphasis added.

1488 Recital 23 clause 2 Succession Regulation.

1489 The recital does not formulate a condition here, but it is submitted that the following factors do constitute requirements.

1490 *Wilke*, RIW 2012, 601, 603.

1491 To this extent in line with the statement of the ECJ in Case C-523/07, A, Reports of Cases 2009, I-2805, at 44.

4.5.2.4. A Definition of Habitual Residence for All Regulations?

Advocate General Warner has stated that the term "habitual" in English law "is more often applied to drunkards than to residence".[1492] The meaning of the statement was apparently entirely lost on the German translator. A German reader would learn the rather amazing fact that English law more often concerns the habitual residence of drunkards than that of other people.[1493] This is perhaps why, at least in Germany, Warner's following statement has gained much more fame: "It seems to me that habitual residence is, rather like an elephant, easier to recognize than to define".[1494] He thus refrained from providing a (full) definition, implying that it is very hard indeed to define an elephant. As even small children could give a workable definition of an elephant, the statement sounds implausible at first. Yet it turns out to be ingenious particularly for that reason. In comparison to a mastodon or mammoth, the definition (even) of an elephant becomes harder.[1495]

Because of the many instances of habitual residence as a connecting factor in recent legislation, however, the courts, ultimately the European Court of Justice,[1496] will increasingly face the term and will not be able to refuse to determine its content. Will they dare to provide a formally general answer for all EU private international law (and perhaps beyond), or will they limit themselves to the regulation – or even only the particular provision – at hand?

The 2009 case *A* might appear as an indication of the latter option. The European Court of Justice was concerned with the interpretation of "habitual residence" in Article 8(1) Brussels IIbis. It stated that

> The case-law of the Court relating to the concept of habitual residence in other areas of European Union law [...] cannot be directly transposed in the context of the assessment of the habitual residence of children for the purposes of Article 8(1) of the Regulation.[1497]

Upon closer inspection of the cases referred to, however, the "other areas of European Union law" turn out to be unrelated to questions of habitual

---

1492 *AG Warner*, Opinion in Case 42-75, Jean-Louis Delvaux v Commission of the European Communities, Reports of Cases 1976, 167, 179.

1493 *AG Warner*, Opinion in Case 42-75, Jean-Louis Delvaux v Commission of the European Communities, Reports of Cases 1976, 167, 178 (German version). The French translator did understand *Warner* correctly, even clarifying for the French reader, "signifiant dès lors 'invétéré'".

1494 *AG Warner*, Opinion in Case 42-75, Jean-Louis Delvaux v Commission of the European Communities, Reports of Cases 1976, 167, 179.

1495 Then again, this is probably only correct for a *textual* definition. A rather precise definition on the level of DNA should be possible.

1496 For a more detailed analysis of the case law of the ECJ regarding habitual residence see *Rentsch*, Der gewöhnliche Aufenthalt, 228–273.

1497 ECJ Case C-523/07, A, Reports of Cases 2009, I-2805, at 36.

residence in private international or jurisdictional law. *Magdalena Fernández* was the case of an official of the Commission proceeding against the Commission for refusing to grant him expatriation allowance.[1498] *Adanez-Vega* concerned the Social Security Regulation No. 1408/71,[1499] *Kozłowski* pertained to the Framework Decision on the European Arrest Warrant.[1500] Even closer inspection reveals that the two latter cases concern the interpretation of "residence" or "resident" only. The reluctance of the ECJ to "directly transpose" the definitions found in those judgments to "*habitual* residence" is thus quite understandable. It is no reason to suppose that a general definition for the purposes of private international law (and/or international civil procedure) could not be found.

In *A*, the Court interpreted "habitual residence" "in the light of the context of the provisions and the objective of the [particular] Regulation", specifically relying on its Recital 12 that emphasises the best interests of the child.[1501] This particularistic approach, resumed in *Mercredi*,[1502] could be another reason to assume that the Court will not develop an overall definition for (at least) the applicable law. Yet this argument would not be completely persuasive, either. First, *A* and *Mercredi* are about jurisdiction, not the applicable law. Second, Rome I and Rome II were relatively new when *A* and *Mercredi* were decided; Rome III had not been passed or, as far as *Mercredi* is concerned, only passed two days prior to the judgment; the other three regulations obviously did not yet exist. It is therefore hard to imagine that the judges had any of these regulations in mind, the more so as they were concerned with the fate of several children.[1503] As such, the approach taken in the judgments is no conclusive indicator of future development (if such a thing exists at all).

It is therefore submitted that the dice have not yet been cast at EU level as to a potential general definition of habitual residence for (at least) the purposes of private international law. To be sure, it may not be possible to transfer a definition from jurisdictional rules to rules on the applicable law. While one could allow for more than one habitual residence for jurisdictional purposes, such a result would be awkward for conflicts issues

1498 ECJ Case C-452/93 P, Pedro Magdalena Fernández v Commission of the European Communities, Reports of Cases 1994, I-4295 (definition of habitual residence at 22).

1499 ECJ Case C-372/02, Roberto Adanez-Vega v Bundesanstalt für Arbeit, Reports of Cases 2004, I-10761 (definition of residence at 37).

1500 ECJ Case C-66/08, Proceedings concerning the execution of a European arrest warrant issued against Szymon Kozłowski, Reports of Cases 2008, I-6041 (definition of resident at 54).

1501 ECJ Case C-523/07, A, Reports of Cases 2009, I-2805, at 35.

1502 ECJ Case 497/10 PPU, Barbara Mercredi v Richard Chaffe, Reports of Cases 2010, I-4309, at 46.

1503 Also see *Rogerson*, ICLQ 49 (2000), 86, 87–88 and 102–103, for the particular policy concerns in different areas of jurisdiction.

where *one* legal system must be identified eventually,[1504] as Recital 39 clause 2 Rome I underlines. Yet there is no reason to exclude *a priori* the option of a common definition for all conflicts rules.[1505] It would seem that such a position reflects the stance of some member states too: Belgium and Bulgaria rather obviously follow European influences with their general definitions of habitual residence.[1506] At the very least, there is no reason to exclude the option of a core definition, with potential variations depending on the context in marginal cases.[1507] This understanding would also be in line with the precept of Recital 23 clause 3 Succession Regulation, urging the authority concerned to identify "a close and stable connection with the State concerned taking into account *the specific aims of this Regulation*".[1508]

5. THE GOVERNING LAW

The third and final element of a conflicts rule is its legal consequence, the determination of the governing law. The meaning of "law", however, can become problematic from several perspectives: territorially speaking, does it truly mean every law in the world (as long as the connecting factor leads to it) (5.1.)? Moreover, what does "law of a state" mean where the "state" does not have any pertinent law (because only its subsystems do) (5.2.)? Temporally speaking, when there has been a change in the applicable law, does "law" refer to rules currently in force or older rules (5.3.)? Systematically speaking, does it refer to substantive rules or to conflicts rules (5.4.)? Substantively speaking, does it also include foreign law incompatible with the *lex fori*, or is there at least some limit (5.5.)?

Furthermore, a conflicts rule may mandate that *foreign* law is to be applied. But how and by whom is its content to be ascertained and applied (5.6.)? What if the cross-border situation at issue casts doubts as to the fulfilment of requirements of the applicable substantive law (5.7.)? What if a position established under one law must now be evaluated under a different law (5.8.)? What if the parties themselves relied on the application of another law (5.9.)?

1504 *Rogerson*, ICLQ 49 (2000), 86, 104.

1505 To this effect also *Rentsch*, Der gewöhnliche Aufenthalt, 191–228 (for the Rome Regulations); *ead.*, ZEuP 2015, 288, 311 (with examples from the practice of the Austrian Supreme Court pertaining to a common understanding of "habitual residence" in the *jurisdictional* rules in different EU regulations). Also *Briggs*, PIL in the English Courts, at 2.101, who doubts that the Court of Justice "would approve the existence of divergent meanings of […] habitual residence". But see *Hausmann*, Riv. dir. int. priv. proc. 2015, 499, 505–506.

1506 *Baetge*, in: FS Kropholler, 77, 78 (with further references).

1507 See *Baetge*, in: Max Planck Encyclopedia of European Private Law, s. v. "Habitual Residence", 814; *id.*, in: FS Kropholler, 77, 82 and 88. For functional variations already *Kahn-Freund*, General Problems, 258–260. But see *Dutta*, IPRax 2017, 139, 145.

1508 Emphasis added.

Finally, what if the application of more than one law to a case leads to an absurd result that neither law would have produced on its own (5.10.)?

5.1. THE AMBIT OF POTENTIALLY APPLICABLE LAWS/RECIPROCITY

Every conflicts rule makes one law govern its subject matter. This does not contradict the existence of conflicts provisions with alternative connecting factors. Such provisions simply encapsulate more than one separate conflicts rules (e.g. the second, the third etc.) depending on the prior rule(s) not applying for some reason. In the end, however, the provision deems only one law applicable. The insight does not deny the possibility of *dépeçage* either. Here, for one reason or another,[1509] more than one law must be applied to a given case. The application of each law, however, once again depends on a *separate* conflicts decision. Even if there was a rule that determined the application of one law to parts of its subject matter, and the application of another law to other parts, it could be split up analytically into two separate rules each with their own subject matters.

Furthermore, this does not make all conflicts rules unilateral. A unilateral conflicts rule can only deem the law of one particular legal system applicable: this law, typically the *lex fori*, will govern a given case. By contrast, a multi- or omnilateral conflicts rule *can* lead to multiple or all laws in the world. In a given case, however, only one of them is determined to be applicable, for the connecting factor will typically lead to one and only one legal system. In the rare case that a connecting factor leads to more than one legal system (e.g. the connecting factor "nationality" in case of a multi-national[1510]), a further rule will resolve the question in favour of one legal system.

Thus, for every non-unilateral conflicts rule, the question arises of whether every law in the world is potentially applicable, or whether there is some limitation to only certain laws. Is all law "law" or is only some law "law"? To wit: is the conflicts rule multi- or omnilateral? Therefore, in non-unilateralist systems of private international law, the question of the scope of potentially applicable laws is a formally general issue in the strict sense.

Member States

Domestic private international law codes in the EU do not contain any general rule expressly setting forth what laws are eligible. Presumably, no (general) limitation is intended.

1509 *Supra* section 2.7.

1510 *Supra* section 4.4.1.2.

A less overt way of curtailing the set of potentially applicable laws would be to require reciprocity. In the context of conflict of laws, this would mean that a certain foreign law would only be applied if the conflicts rules of that foreign law led to the *lex fori* in a respective case. No such rule exists, or has existed, in domestic private international law.[1511] On the contrary, a few general provisions of private international law expressly state that no reciprocity is required. The European examples are Bulgaria and Romania.[1512] In private international law systems based on applying the law that has the closest connection to the case at hand, reciprocity is out of place.[1513] From the perspective of private parties, reciprocity in private international law is inappropriate anyway, as a private actor "is taken hostage" for the behaviour of "her" state.[1514] But reciprocity occasionally does surface in cross-border contexts: some member states still condition recognition and enforcement of foreign judgments upon reciprocity,[1515] some the exemption of foreigners from court fees.[1516]

European Union

The matter stands somewhat differently for conflicts provisions in a convention or an EU regulation. For it is less obvious here that "law" necessarily means "every law". In particular, it is conceivable that such an instrument would only extend to the laws of the contracting/member states, leaving domestic private international law to decide the remaining cases. Indeed, this is how, at the beginning of the 20th century, the first generation of Hague Conventions in the field of private international law operated.[1517] Against this backdrop, many conventions and the EU regulations clarify that the law determined by the respective instrument applies, whether or not it is the law of a (contracting

1511 *Basedow*, in: FS Coester-Waltjen, 335, 337; but see *Dutta*, in: Basedow/Rühl/Ferrari/de Miguel Asensio (eds.), Encyclopedia of PIL, s. v. "Reciprocity", II, with an example from Kazakhstan.

1512 Article 47 Bulgarian PIL Code, Article 2.561 Romanian Civil Code. Until 2018, also §6 Hungarian PIL Code 1979 (with a presumption in paragraph 2 that, should a special rule require reciprocity nevertheless, reciprocity would be presumed until proved otherwise).

1513 *Dutta*, in: Basedow/Rühl/Ferrari/de Miguel Asensio (eds.), Encyclopedia of PIL, s. v. "Reciprocity", II; *Zidarova/Stančeva-Minčeva*, RabelsZ 71 (2007), 398, 412 (for Bulgaria); *Nagy*, PIL in Hungary, at 69.

1514 *Basedow*, in: FS Coester-Waltjen, 335, 336.

1515 E.g. Article 92 Croatian PIL Act, Article 15(1)(f) Czech PIL Act, Article 101 Slovenian PIL Act; outside the scope of the codes at issue here, see also §328(1) No. 5 ZPO. Notably, Bulgaria has abolished this requirement, see Article 117 Bulgarian PIL Code and *Zidarova/Stančeva-Minčeva*, RabelsZ 71 (2007), 398, 412.

1516 §10 Czech PIL Act; Article 50 Slovak PIL Act; Article 93 Slovenian PIL Act.

1517 *Basedow*, in: FS Coester-Waltjen, 335, 338; e.g. Article 18(1) Conflict of Nationality Laws Convention.

or participating) member state.[1518] This omnilateralism is called, by evidence of the respective headings, "universal application"/"caractère universel".[1519] By contrast, Article 7(1) Insolvency Regulation determines only the application of law of the member states. This is multilateralism in the literal sense.

The respective provisions setting forth omnilateralism in the EU regulations are found in their very first chapter on the scope of each Rome Regulation,[1520] and spearhead the chapter on applicable law in the Succession Regulation, the M-Property Regulation, and the RP-Property Regulation.[1521] In other words, the EU legislator has dealt with this issue in provisions somewhat removed from conflicts provisions.

5.2. NON-UNIFIED LEGAL SYSTEMS

The legal consequence of a conflicts rule often consists in the application of the law *of the country/state* identified by the connecting factor. This is obvious at the EU level where most conflicts provisions refer to the "law of the country where ..." (Rome I, Rome II) or the "law of the State where ..." (Rome III, Succession Regulation, M-Property Regulation, and RP-Property Regulation); yet express examples also abound in domestic private international law legislation.[1522] These rules do not work, however, when there is no such thing as law *of* the country/state, i.e. when there is no pertinent law on the level of the country itself. This is the case where different (or at least: distinct) law applies in the country's territorial units and/or[1523] to distinct categories of persons.

1518 *Audit/Bermann*, in: Nuyts/Watté (eds.), International Civil Litigation in Europe and Relations with Third States, 55, 60. See Article 2 Rome I, Article 3 Rome II, Article 4 Rome III, Article 20 Succession Regulation; Article 2 Maintenance Protocol; Article 4 Agency Convention. For the background of Article 2 Rome Convention, see *Giuliano/Lagarde*, Report on the Convention on the law applicable to contractual obligations, 8 ("The Group took the view that its main purpose was to frame general rules such as those existing in legislative provisions currently in force in Italy and in the Benelux Treaty and the French draft law.").

1519 The question of the EU's competence to make such a provision will be dealt with *infra* Chapter 5, section 1.2.

1520 Article 2 Rome I, Article 3 Rome II, Article 4 Rome III.

1521 Article 20 Succession Regulation; Article 20 M-/RP-Property Regulation.

1522 Just to give a few motley examples: §35(2) Austrian PIL Act; Article 47(1) Belgian PIL Code; Article 64(1) Bulgarian PIL Code; Article 14(1) Croatian PIL Act; §87(1) clause 1 Czech PIL Act; §14(1) Estonian PIL Act; Article 10(1) EGBGB; Article 27 Greek Civil Code; Article 25(1) Italian PIL Act; Article 11(2) Latvian Civil Code; Article 1.15(2) Lithuanian Civil Code; Article 10:92(1) Dutch Civil Code; Article 17(1) Polish PIL Act; Article 33(1) Portuguese Civil Code; Article 2.642(1) Romanian Civil Code; Article 23(1) Slovak PIL Act; Article 14 Slovenian PIL Act; Article 10(11) Spanish Civil Code.

1523 See *Schröder*, Die Verweisung auf Mehrrechtsstaaten, 2; also *Geuenich*, Verweisung auf einen territorialen Mehrrechtsstaat, 2–4, for the different dimensions of the issue.

In other words, the issue is the effect (if any) of interlocal and interpersonal conflict of laws within a country on private international law.[1524] Canada, India, Mexico, Spain, the UK, and the USA are well-known examples of the former; examples for the latter are primarily found in the Middle East and Africa.[1525] The reasons for these phenomena are manifold.[1526]

Omnilateral[1527] private international law rules referring to a country or state all face the potential challenge just outlined. Arguably less problematic are references to the law of a *place* (like, e.g., in many Spanish conflicts provisions[1528]) because they can be read to refer directly to a particular territorial unit.[1529] Yet, to the extent that the pertinent law is not linked to the territory, this does not work either. Conflicts provisions allowing for a choice by the parties *can* also constitute easier cases, as long as they do not require the parties to choose the law "of a country", but simply "law".[1530] The issue of a reference to non-unified legal systems[1531] is thus not (necessarily) formally general in the strict sense; but, as long as more than one conflicts provision of a given system refers to the law *of* a country/state, it is at least formally general.

Member States

With the exception of now[1532] only Greece and Latvia, all private international law codes in the member states deal with the reference to a non-unified legal system – and do so with a provision among their "general" ones. While some countries employ what seem to be catch-all provisions for references to

1524 As to the terminology, see *Vitta*, Interlocal Conflict of Laws, at 1. *Kahn-Freund*, General Problems, 148–149, distinguishes among interstate/interprovincial, interlocal and interpersonal conflict of laws.

1525 *Eichel*, in: Leible (ed.), General Principles, §13.01; *Vitta*, Interlocal Conflict of Laws, at 4–19; *Lipstein/Szászy*, Interpersonal Conflict of Laws, at 1.

1526 *Schröder*, Die Verweisung auf Mehrrechtsstaaten, 2–3; *Borrás*, Rec. des cours 249 (1999), 145, 161–186; *Vitta*, Interlocal Conflict of Laws, at 4–19.

1527 Or multilateral, but not limited to countries with unified legal systems.

1528 Article 10(1), (2), (3), (5), (6), (9), (10) Spanish Civil Code.

1529 See *Calvo Caravaca/Carrascosa González*, DIP I, 523; *Garcimartín Alférez*, DIP, at 21.14 (in the section with "ejemplos"); in general *Christandl*, Journal of Private International Law 9 (2013), 219, 223; *Rigaux/Fallon*, DIP, at 6.7. It is not self-evident, but very likely, that a reference to the habitual residence or domicile of a person is also intended to refer to the specific territory as opposed to the country as a whole. More generally *Leible*, in: Reichelt (ed.), Europäisches Gemeinschaftsrecht und IPR, 31, 52–53. Also Article 4(3) EGBGB and *von Hein*, in: MüKoBGB, Art. 4 EGBGB at 184–185 for a German perspective.

1530 *Supra* section 4.3.6.

1531 See *Eichel*, in: Leible (ed.), General Principles, §13.01 regarding this preferable terminology.

1532 Hungary introduced a pertinent provision with the Hungarian PIL Act whereas the Hungarian PIL Code 1979 had been silent on this issue.

countries with legal sub-systems (whether personal or territorial),[1533] others expressly distinguish the two types of sub-systems,[1534] although some of them proceed to treat both types in the same way.[1535]

Despite the apparent agreement that the issue of non-unified legal systems is one to be dealt with in a general provision, assessments as to the most appropriate context vary. Many member states have made a stand-alone rule, but the relative position of such a provision is different from code to code. Moreover, Austria and Germany have annexed a provision on non-unified legal systems to their *renvoi* provisions.[1536] Lithuanian private international law follows a similar solution. The rules on non-unified legal systems are found in paragraphs of the provision on the application of foreign law, together with the Lithuanian *renvoi* rule.[1537] The Czech PIL Act covers the topic in a paragraph of the provision that otherwise concerns the determination and application of foreign law (but not *renvoi*).[1538] Functionally similar is the Estonian solution. The stand-alone rule on non-unified legal systems is situated between the provision on the application of foreign law and the one on the ascertainment of foreign law.[1539] The common denominator of these latter solutions is that they define the appropriate place for the issue as a question of the governing law, in line with the conceptualisation followed here.

French scholars generally discuss the implications of non-unified legal systems for private international law separately from specific conflicts rules; the exact location among such general issues differs greatly, however.[1540]

1533 §5(3) Austrian PIL Act; Article 10 Croatian PIL Act; §3 Estonian PIL Act; Article 4(3) EGBGB; Article 9 Polish PIL Act; Article 2.560 Romanian Civil Code; Article 34 Slovak PIL Act; Article 9 Slovenian PIL Act; Article 12(5) Spanish Civil Code. For the proposition that the Austrian, German, and Spanish provisions are intended to cover all cases of non-unified systems see *Neumayr*, in: ABGB-Kurzkommentar, §5 IPRG at 3; *von Hein*, in: MüKoBGB, Art. 4 EGBGB at 242; *Calvo Caravaca/Carrascosa González*, DIP I, at 525, respectively. See also Article 2286 French Civil Code (1967 Draft).

1534 Article 17 Belgian PIL Code; Article 41(1),(2) vs. (3) Bulgarian PIL Code; §23(4) Czech PIL Act; §6(1) vs. (2) Hungarian PIL Act; Article 18 Italian PIL Act; Article 1.10(4) vs. (5) Lithuanian Civil Code; Article 15 Dutch Civil Code (that further distinguishes between the connecting factors at issue); Article 20(1),(2) vs. (3) Portuguese Civil Code.

1535 See, for example, Article 18 Italian PIL Act, and *Fumagalli*, in: Baratta (ed.), DIP, s. v. "Rinvio ad ordinamenti plurilegislativi", 431, 435.

1536 §5(3) Austrian PIL Act; Article 4(3) EGBGB. Similarly e.g. the stand-alone rules of Article 17 Belgian PIL Code and Article 41 Bulgarian PIL Code that immediately follow the respective provision on *renvoi*. As to the relationship of this topic with *renvoi* also see *Eichel*, in: Leible (ed.), General Principles, §13.02[A][3]; *Fumagalli*, in: Baratta (ed.), DIP, s. v. "Rinvio ad ordinamenti plurilegislativi", 431, 435–436.

1537 Article 1.10(4)–(6) Lithuanian Civil Code.

1538 §23(4) Czech PIL Act.

1539 §3 Estonian PIL Act, between §2 (application of foreign law) and §4 (ascertainment of foreign law).

1540 *Audit/d'Avout*, DIP, at 355–364, discuss the issue as one of the determination of the applicable foreign rule of law (together with changes in the *lex causae*). *Loussouarn/Bourel/de Vareilles-Sommières*, DIP, at 159–161, discuss it as an issue of the nature of conflicts

Their English counterparts do not seem to reserve a separate space for the discussion of non-unified systems. If at all, the topic surfaces in the context of a discussion of the pertinent provisions of Rome I and Rome II, and more or less in passing.[1541] If one were to hazard a guess as to the reason for this (from the perspective of many other member states) negligent treatment of non-unified legal systems, the preponderance of domicile as a connecting factor in the common law[1542] could be a decisive factor. As it is interpreted to refer to a particular place, the issue simply appears to be less pressing.[1543]

European Union

Articles 22(1) Rome I and 25(1) Rome II are nearly identical provisions on states whose territorial units have their own legal rules in respect of (non-) contractual obligations. For the purposes of these two regulations, the foreign territorial unit is to be regarded as a country of its own. Both provisions are located among the "Other Provisions" of Rome I and II, separately from their specific conflicts rules. They indubitably apply in respect of all[1544] specific conflicts rules in Rome I and II. Despite the broad titles of each of these provisions ("States with more than one legal system"), neither Rome I nor Rome II cover legal sub-systems for different categories of persons. In the field of (non-)contractual obligations, this issue is extremely rare in any case.[1545]

rules, in connection with interpersonal and interlocal conflict of laws. *Mayer/Heuzé*, DIP, at 92–95 *and* at 247–250, first discuss interpersonal and interlocal conflict of laws as a kind of introductory issue (the necessity of more than legal system being at issue) and come back to these conflicts as "facteurs de complication" in the context of taking account of foreign conflicts rules (i.e. alongside *renvoi*).

1541 *Briggs*, PIL in the English Courts, at 7.27 (as part of an outline of Rome I), at 8.27 ("ancillary issues" of Rome II), 8.68–8.69 (Article 25(1) Rome II); *Cheshire/North/Fawcett*, PIL, 788 (Article 25 Rome II); see also the brief reference to "sub-division[s] of the political state", 8; *Rogerson* mentions Article 22 Rome I once, Collier's Conflict of Laws, 300–301, and, as evidenced by the table of statutes, liv, does not refer to Article 25 Rome II at all. *Dicey/Morris/Collins*, Conflict of Laws, at 1-065–1-071, discuss the meaning of "(foreign) country/state" as a general ("preliminary") matter, but this is only one segment of the larger topic of non-unified legal systems. Later on, at 32-030, Article 22(1) Rome I is discussed, but without any reference to the larger topic.

1542 See already *supra* sections 4.4.1.5. and 4.5.1.

1543 See *Vitta*, Interlocal Conflict of Laws, at 28; already *supra* text at footnote 1532.

1544 They do not work, however, when the parties have chosen the applicable law and made reference to the state comprising the units instead of a particular unit. Whether they are even needed in the reverse situation where the parties have chosen the law of the unit instead of the law of the state, is debatable, *supra* section 4.3.6.

1545 *Eichel*, in: Leible (ed.), General Principles, §13.03[B]; *von Bar/Mankowski*, IPR I, §4 at 167; see *Fumagalli*, in: Baratta (ed.), DIP, s. v. "Rinvio ad ordinamenti plurilegislativi", 431, 438, for an example how to deal with the issue if it does arise.

By contrast, Rome III, the Succession Regulation, the M-Property Regulation, and the RP-Property Regulation have separate provisions for the two types of legal sub-systems.[1546] While the provisions on non-unified legal systems in respect of different categories of persons are nearly identical, the provisions on territorial sub-systems diverge.[1547] All of these provisions are located in close proximity to the provisions on *renvoi* and public policy, thus somewhat removed from the specific conflicts rules of Rome III and the Succession Regulation. Again, there can be no doubt that they are to cover all specific conflicts rules of the respective regulation. This is underlined by the provisions on territorial sub-units accommodating themselves to different connecting factors and, of course, by the wording "law specified by this *Regulation*",[1548] "*any* reference",[1549] and "pursuant to *any* other provisions referring to other elements as connecting factors".[1550] It appears possible to arrive at a uniform provision for all EU private international law.[1551]

Furthermore, all of the regulations contain a provision clarifying that the aforementioned rules need not be applied by the member states in respect of their purely internal conflict of laws.[1552] If at all,[1553] the "referee" at the next hierarchical level (i.e. the central, federal legislator) is to make a decision regarding the applicable law,[1554] not the one two levels removed (i.e. the EU).[1555] For the EU, this already follows from Article 81(1) TFEU: "[C]ross-border implications" presuppose a *national* border.

1546 Articles 14 Rome III, 36 Succession Regulation, and 33 M-/RP-Property Regulation ("Territorial conflict of laws"); Articles 15 Rome III, 37 Succession Regulation, and 34 M-/RP-Property Regulation ("Inter-personal conflict of laws").

1547 Article 14 Rome III (with the exception of (c)) determines the relevant territorial unit primarily itself, whereas the primary solution of Article 36 Succession Regulation/Article 33 M-/RP-Property Regulation is to leave this determination to the state concerned (paragraph 1) and only to provide for a solution itself in the absence of pertinent internal conflicts rules (paragraph 2).

1548 Article 36(1) Succession Regulation; Article 33(1) M-/RP-Property Regulation (emphasis added).

1549 Article 14(a)–(c) Rome III; Article 36(2)(a)–(c) Succession Regulation; Article 33(2)(a)–(c) M-/RP-Property Regulation (emphasis added).

1550 Article 36(2)(c) Succession Regulation; Article 33(2)(c) M-/RP-Property Regulation (emphasis added).

1551 In particular *Geuenich*, Verweisung auf einen territorialen Mehrrechtsstaat, 462.

1552 Article 22(2) Rome I, Article 25(2) Rome II, Article 16 Rome III, Article 38 Succession Regulation, Article 35 M-/RP-Property Regulation.

1553 See *Basedow*, in: LA Borrás, 175, 181.

1554 See Article 16(1) Spanish Civil Code.

1555 Whether the ECJ has jurisdiction where a member state does use the Rome provisions for internal conflicts, is a different matter; see *Dicey/Morris/Collins*, Conflict of Laws, at 32-031. Arguably, the question is to be answered in the affirmative, following ECJ Case C-280/06, Autorità Garante della Concorrenza e del Mercato v Ente tabacchi italiani – ETI SpA and Others and Philip Morris, Reports of Cases 2007, I-10893, at 21–26.

5.3. THE ASCERTAINMENT AND APPLICATION OF FOREIGN LAW

The legal consequence of a conflicts rule makes some law applicable to the case at hand. If this law is the *lex fori*, its application raises only few further issues genuinely connected to private international law.[1556] If foreign law is supposed to govern a case, however, the ground quickly becomes shaky. Typically, the first question addressed[1557] concerns the nature of foreign law from the perspective of the *lex fori*: is it law[1558] or is it fact[1559] – or is it part of some third category?[1560] At first glance, the answer to this question alone seems to allow many inferences, in particular as to who must introduce it into the proceedings, whether it can/must be proved, and whether a resulting decision can be challenged on legal grounds.[1561] Yet an (express) answer to this fundamental question is not necessarily to be expected from any country's legislation, for it turns out that legal reality is much more convoluted. The classification of foreign law "does not usually elicit a straightforward extrapolation in relation to some questions very much linked to the procedural treatment of foreign law".[1562] Those who treat foreign law as a fact cannot completely gainsay its normative quality (it forms the *standard* by which the case at hand is to be decided, after all);[1563] those who treat it as law still often treat it differently from domestic law. A general statement on the

1556 See in particular the discussion of substitution, *infra* section 5.7.

1557 *Esplugues*, in: id./Iglesias/Palao (eds.), Application of Foreign Law, 3, 8; *Pauknerová*, RHDI 64 (2011), 5, 6 and 13 (with the same observation); *Hausmann*, EuLF 2008, I-1; *Hood*, Journal of Private International Law 2 (2006), 181, 182–183 (as the first "theoretical" issue); *Fentiman*, Foreign Law in English Courts, 3 (as the first principle); *Zajtay*, The Application of Foreign Law, at 2–10.

1558 This is the position of most member states; common law countries, Luxembourg, and Spain form the exceptions: see *Esplugues*, in: id./Iglesias/Palao (eds.), Application of Foreign Law, 3, 10–16. Arguably, this also is the position of EU private international law itself, *Köhler*, Eingriffsnormen, 6 (with note 4).

1559 Rather famously, this is the position under common law: *Dicey/Morris/Collins*, Conflict of Laws, at 9-002; *Cheshire/North/Fawcett*, PIL, 105. Equally famously, however, the statement is to be attenuated: "[T]he question of foreign law, although a question of fact, is a question of fact of a peculiar kind […]", Parkasho v Singh [1968] P. 233, 250. See *Fentiman*, Foreign Law in English Courts, 4, for necessary qualifications, culminating in the delightful realisation, 66, that "it is not so much that foreign laws are facts (although technically they are), but that they are laws which cannot, for practical reasons, be treated exactly like domestic laws".

1560 See *Esplugues*, in: id./Iglesias/Palao (eds.), Application of Foreign Law, 3, 8.

1561 See *Hausmann*, EuLF 2008, I-1–I-2.

1562 *Esplugues*, in: id./Iglesias/Palao (eds.), Application of Foreign Law, 3, 18 (and passim for examples); also see *Lalani*, MJ 2013, 75, 77–78 and passim; *Hausmann*, EuLF 2008, I-1, I-3; *Jänterä-Jareborg*, Rec. des cours 304 (2003), 181, 264–271; *Zajtay*, The Application of Foreign Law, at 9.

1563 *Fentiman*, in: Andenas/Fairgrieve (eds.), Courts and Comparative Law, 79, 94.

nature of foreign law thus would not be automatically helpful.[1564] To be sure, the requirement of usefulness has not been known to keep legislators from making provisions. But there is indeed no express example of a provision on the nature of foreign law in the member states.[1565]

It is more likely to find answers to more concrete questions:[1566] must foreign law be applied even though the parties did not request it? (It is not even certain that a judicial duty to apply conflicts rules implies a duty to apply foreign law *ex officio*.[1567]) Who is charged with ascertaining foreign law, and how – and with what means – does this process work?[1568] What if this process fails/is not completed within a given time frame? And if it has worked, how is foreign law applied? Moreover, is there recourse to a court of higher instance on the grounds that foreign law has not been applied correctly?

5.3.1. The Questions as Formally General Issues of Private International Law

All these issues associated with the topic of ascertaining and applying foreign law have obvious strong undertones of procedural law. It is not self-evident to consider them (general) questions of conflict of laws specifically. First, however, there is an inextricable link to conflict of laws: the questions arise only where foreign law is deemed to govern a legal issue. If the law determined by a conflicts rule is ultimately not applied, why even make an omni-/multilateral rule in the first place? The application of foreign law "is the very object, the terminus of the choice of law process".[1569] To treat harmonised private international law provisions differently in national legal proceedings also puts the harmonisation effort itself at risk. Second, to the extent that rules provide for another law, usually the *lex fori*,[1570] to be applicable in cases

---

1564 See *Mádl*, RHDI 44 (1991), 227, 240 (deliberately no "quibble" over this question in the Hungarian PIL Code 1979).

1565 In this regard, the general report by *Esplugues*, in: id./Iglesias/Palao (eds.), Application of Foreign Law, 3, 10–12, is misleading. To be sure, there are many provisions requiring a judge to apply foreign law *ex officio*, but this does not amount to "an explicit and plain manner" of ascribing a certain *nature* to foreign law.

1566 See the contributions to Société de legislation comparée (ed.), L'application du droit étranger, for recent answers to these questions (from France).

1567 Article 12(6) Spanish Civil Code only pertains to the *ex officio* application of Spanish conflicts provisions. While a foreign observer probably would assume that the *ex officio* application of foreign law is a necessary consequence – see *von Hoffmann/Ortiz-Arce*, RabelsZ 39 (1975), 647, 656 – this is not the case: *Calvo Caravaca/Carrascosa González*, DIP I, 536; *Esplugues*, in: id./Iglesias/Palao (eds.), Application of Foreign Law, 3, 16. Contrast Article 10:2 Dutch Civil Code that expressly covers both conflicts rules and foreign law.

1568 See *M. Stürner/Krauß*, Ausländisches Recht in deutschen Zivilverfahren, on how German courts *actually* deal with foreign law; also *M. Stürner*, ZVglRWiss 117 (2018), 1.

1569 *Fentiman*, in: Andenas/Fairgrieve (eds.), Courts and Comparative Law, 79, 81.

1570 This is the prevailing solution across the EU, see the overview by *Esplugues*, in: id./Iglesias/Palao (eds.), Application of Foreign Law, 3, 67–72. Now also see §23(5) Czech PIL Act – an

where foreign law cannot be established (within a certain period of time), a genuine conflicts issue arises: the determination of the applicable law. To find pertinent rules among the member states' *conflicts* provisions thus occasions little surprise. Third, parts of the question of pleading foreign law, seemingly of a procedural nature as a whole, can and should be framed as a conflicts issue too: as far as not pleading foreign law implicates the application of the *lex fori*, the question of the applicable law is at issue.[1571] For these reasons, and in line with a certain tradition within the discipline,[1572] the topic of ascertaining and applying foreign law will be discussed here. It is formally general, for it occurs whenever foreign law is deemed to apply, entirely regardless of the legal context.

Ascertainment and application of foreign law is furthermore an issue of considerable practical significance for EU private international law. To be sure, the statement that harmonisation of private international law in the EU "will directly lead to an increasing number of cases involving the application of foreign law"[1573] requires the qualification that many instruments rather promote synchronisation of forum and *ius*, see e.g. Articles 4 and 21(1) Succession Regulation.[1574] Yet it suffices that EU private international law does entail courts having to apply foreign law, and not just in isolated instances.[1575] (And they cannot simply ask their foreign counterparts, not even in another member state (yet?[1576]).)

innovation of the new PIL Act, *Dobiáš*, Riv. dir. int. priv. proc. 2015, 109, 117 – and Article 10(2) Polish PIL Act. See *infra* footnote 1626 for a list of general provisions in the member states regarding this sub-issue.

1571 *Fentiman*, Foreign Law in English Courts, 71.

1572 The topic also was included in the volume on private international law in the International Encyclopedia of Comparative Law: *Zajtay*, The Application of Foreign Law. It was also included in Leible (ed.), General Principles (*Kieninger*, §17). For EU private international law see e.g. *Lagarde*, RabelsZ 75 (2011), 673, 675 (Article 133); *Bariatti/Pataut*, in: Fallon/Lagarde/Poillot-Peruzzetto (eds.), Quelle architecture pour un code européen de droit international privé?, 337, 343–347 (including the question of the mandatory nature of conflicts rules); *Sonnenberger*, in: FS Kropholler, 227, 245–246; *Kreuzer*, in: Jud/Rechberger/Reichelt (eds.), Kollisionsrecht in der Europäischen Union, 1, 6–13.

1573 *Esplugues*, in: id./Iglesias/Palao (eds.), Application of Foreign Law, 3, 5.

1574 There are further examples of parallels e.g. between Rome I and II on the one side and Brussels I on the other; indeed, German judges at the local court level have reported that Rome III already has led to fewer cases involving foreign law, see *M. Stürner/Krauß*, Ausländisches Recht in deutschen Zivilverfahren, at 149.

1575 Also see *Lalani*, MJ 2013, 75–76; *Trautmann*, Europäisches Kollisionsrecht und ausländisches Recht im nationalen Zivilverfahren, 404–405; *Pauknerová*, RHDI 64 (2011), 5, 20.

1576 *Remien*, ZVglRWiss 115 (2016), 570, 582, with further references, who is a big proponent of the idea of a transnational preliminary reference procedure among the member states; also see the recent ambivalent assessment by *M. Stürner*, ZVglRWiss 117 (2018), 1, 17–20; *id./Krauß*, Ausländisches Recht in deutschen Zivilverfahren, at 515–518.

5.3.2. *Member States*

5.3.2.1. General Rules

A vast majority of member states with private international law codes have a provision among their "general" ones that covers (at least aspects of) the ascertainment of foreign law, including the question of whether this must occur *ex officio*.[1577] In some cases, the motivation behind these rules seems to have been to thwart unwanted developments in the courts.[1578] Only few member states with a private international law code have left the issue to another part of the code,[1579] or to another statutory instrument altogether.[1580] This has not stopped a few authors from these legal systems from dealing with the topic among general issues of private international law.[1581] Some common law authors likewise consider the issue of foreign law to be one most appropriately discussed among general issues of private international law.[1582] Similarly, in the Nordic member states, pertinent provisions are also found in statutes on procedure,[1583] but the topic appears among "general principles" of (at least) Swedish private international law in scholarly writings.[1584] Many French (and Luxembourg) authors share this latter view.[1585]

1577 §§3–4 Austrian PIL Act; Article 15(1) clause 1, (2) Belgian PIL Code; Article 43 Bulgarian PIL Code; Article 13 Croatian PIL Act; §23(1) clause 1, (2), (3), (5) Czech PIL Act; §4 Estonian PIL Act; §5 Hungarian PIL Code 1979/§§7(2), 8 Hungarian PIL Act; Article 14 Italian PIL Act; Article 1.12(1)–(3) Lithuanian Civil Code; Article 10:2 Dutch Civil Code; Article 10(2) Polish PIL Act; Article 23(2) Portuguese Civil Code; Article 2.562 Romanian Civil Code; Article 12 Slovenian PIL Act. Section 22 Latvian Civil Code for the most part simply refers to the Latvian rules of civil procedure.

1578 In particular, see the Italian example: *Ballarino/Bonomi*, Yearbook of Private International Law 2 (2000), 99, 110; *Kindler*, RabelsZ 61 (1997), 227, 255; *Pocar*, IPRax 1996, 145, 151; *Giardina*, Rev. crit. DIP 1996, 1, 14; *Pesce*, RIW 1995, 977, 980 with note 38.

1579 Namely the section on procedure: Article 53 Slovak PIL Act.

1580 §293 ZPO; Article 337 Greek Code of Civil Procedure; Article 281(2) Spanish Act of Civil Procedure. For details, see the respective reports in: Esplugues/Iglesias/Palao (eds.), Application of Foreign Law.

1581 *Leible/Müller*, Yearbook of Private International Law 14 (2012/2013), 137, 149–150; *Kegel/Schurig*, IPR, §15 I–III (495–508). See also the inclusion of this topic in: Leible (ed.), General Principles, as well as already in: Leible/Unberath (eds.), Rom 0-Verordnung.

1582 *Briggs*, PIL in the English Courts, at 3.18–3.47 (even as the very first issue of "structure and methods" of private international law under common law); *Cheshire/North/Fawcett*, PIL, Chapter 7, as a "preliminary topic". Contrast *Rogerson*, Collier's Conflict of Laws, 46–51 (as part of "[s]elected aspects of procedure"); *Dicey/Morris/Collins*, Conflict of Laws, Chapter 9 (in a separate part on procedure).

1583 See *Ervo et al.*, in: Esplugues/Iglesias/Palao (eds.), Application of Foreign Law, 327, 330.

1584 *Bogdan*, PIL in Sweden, at 5–11.

1585 For France: *Audit/d'Avout*, DIP, at 319–337 (as part of the "partie générale", more specifically part of the issues of the application of foreign law); *Cachard*, DIP, at 614–628 (as part of the application of the law determined by the conflicts rule); *Loussouarn/Bourel/de Vareilles-Sommières*, at 349–363 (as part of the "théorie générale", more specifically part of the

Incidentally, the French Civil Code (1967 Draft) also contained two articles on this topic among its "dispositions générales".[1586]

With the exception of Ireland, all member states are parties to the 1968 European Convention on Information on Foreign Law and, with the additional exception of Slovakia, to the 1978 Protocol to said convention. These conventions, however, only play a puny role in practice.[1587]

Much fewer member states with a private international law code also have a statutory provision setting forth how to interpret and apply foreign law, even though the solutions are rather similar across the EU (i.e. application in accordance with the application in the legal system of origin[1588]). If such a provision exists, however, it is found among the general provisions of the private international law code and not anywhere else.[1589] Only Bulgaria has a statutory rule on the reviewability of the application of foreign law among its general provisions of private international law.[1590] In many other member states, more or less unequivocally phrased provisions found in legal instruments on civil procedure deal with this issue in one way or another.[1591] French (and Luxembourg) authors commonly discuss both these aspects as a general issue of private international law.[1592] However, even the common

---

application of foreign law); *Mayer/Heuzé*, DIP, at 184–195 (part of the "partie générale" that concerns conflict of laws, more specifically part of the application of foreign law). For Luxembourg: *Wiwinius*, DIP, at 148–167 (as part of the "théorie générale", more specifically part of the application of foreign law).

1586 Articles 2288 and 2289 French Civil Code (1967 Draft).

1587 *Esplugues*, in: id./Iglesias/Palao (eds.), Application of Foreign Law, 3, 56. The German judges at the level of the local courts interviewed for the study by *M. Stürner/Krauß* had not made use of the Convention or had not even heard of it, Ausländisches Recht in deutschen Zivilverfahren, at 207–208. *Remien*, ZVglRWiss 115 (2016), 570, 577, *id.*, in: Schmidt-Kessel (ed.), German National Reports, 223, 240–241, and *Basedow*, in: id./Pißler (eds.), PIL in Mainland China, Taiwan and Europe, 85, 92, take a somewhat more charitable position ("useful in simple cases"); *Jänterä-Jareborg*, Rec. des cours 304 (2003), 181, 317–318, views the Convention even more favourably.

1588 See *Esplugues*, in: id./Iglesias/Palao (eds.), Application of Foreign Law, 3, 64–67.

1589 §3 Austrian PIL Act; Article 15(1) clause 2 Belgian PIL Code; Article 44(1) Bulgarian PIL Code; §23(1) clause 2 Czech PIL Act; §2(2) Estonian PIL Act; Article 15(1) Italian PIL Act; Article 23(1) Portuguese Civil Code; Article 2.563 Romanian Civil Code. Article 1.12(1) Lithuanian Civil Code mentions the "interpretation [...] of foreign law" but does not expressly provide for a standard. For the remaining countries with a private international law code, see *Esplugues*, in: id./Iglesias/Palao (eds.), Application of Foreign Law, 3, 63–67, as well as the respective national reports.

1590 Article 44(2) Bulgarian PIL Code.

1591 See the overview by *Esplugues*, in: id./Iglesias/Palao (eds.), Application of Foreign Law, 3, 75–78. For an express exclusion see Article 79(1)(b) Dutch Act on Judicial Organisation ("Wet op de rechterlijke organisatie"). The wording of the pertinent German provision, §545 ZPO, seems less strict than before 2009, but see *infra* footnote 1596 and the appurtenant text.

1592 For France: *Audit/d'Avout*, DIP, at 338–343; *Cachard*, DIP, at 614–624; *Loussouarn/Bourel/de Vareilles-Sommières*, at 364–371; *Mayer/Heuzé*, DIP, at 196–199. For Luxembourg: *Wiwinius*, DIP, at 168–171. As to the relative position of these sections in the respective books see already footnote 1588.

law writers who deal with the ascertainment of foreign law as an issue of private international law barely mention, or only touch upon, these additional issues in the same context.[1593]

5.3.2.2. Review of the Application of Foreign Law and European Union Law

This section only concerns how EU law affects *domestic* (private international) law in the context of the application of foreign law. This means that the principles of equivalence and effectiveness are irrelevant here, for they only concern the treatment of *EU* law in national courts. Rather, the standards relevant here mainly follow from the prohibition of discrimination and the freedoms of the TFEU.[1594] The most relevant issue in this regard seems to be the review of the application of another member state's law by a superior judicial body.

If the application of the law of another member state cannot be reviewed, but the application of the *lex fori* can, there is a problem from the perspective of primary EU law. To be sure, discrimination of foreign *law* as such does not run afoul of Article 18 TFEU; this prohibition does not require just any discrimination, but discrimination on the grounds of nationality, and there is no universal nexus between the application of foreign law and nationality.[1595] Along similar lines, the German Federal Supreme Court denied any discrimination under Article 18 TFEU when it held in 2014 that German law (still) does not allow a review of the application of foreign law: the application of foreign law follows from conflicts provisions that apply to nationals, as well as to foreigners.[1596] Yet it is rather questionable whether one can stop at this point already. There are cases in which the application of foreign law does follow from a person's nationality, namely where the nationality (or, for companies, place of incorporation) of a person is the connecting factor. Thus, that person ultimately cannot appeal the application of foreign law *because of* her nationality.[1597]

Such discrimination cannot be justified.[1598] To protect one's supreme court from the possible embarrassment of getting foreign law wrong does not

---

1593 See *Briggs*, PIL in the English Courts, at 3.39–3.46; *Cheshire/North/Fawcett*, PIL, 108–113.

1594 See the detailed analysis by *Hübner*, Ausländisches Recht vor deutschen Gerichten, 158–174.

1595 But see *Flessner*, ZEuP 2006, 737, 740, who infers a general prohibition of discrimination of intra-EU cross-border cases from the very nature of the EU treaties; apparently also *Kieninger*, in: Leible (ed.), General Principles, §17.04[C][7].

1596 BGH IPRax 2014, 431, 433; to this effect already *Sturm*, JZ 2011, 74, 78; *Weckesser-Georgi*, Die letztinstanzliche Überprüfung, 277. For more on the decision see *Remien*, in: Schmidt-Kessel (ed.), German National Reports, 223, 250–253 (in English); *Hau*, IPRax 2014, 397; *Riehm*, JZ 2014, 73.

1597 *Gotsche*, Der BGH im Wettbewerb der Zivilrechtsordnungen, 163–165; *Flessner*, ZEuP 2006, 737, 739.

1598 But see *Remien*, ZVglRWiss 115 (2016), 570, 584.

even appear to be a legitimate objective.[1599] The role of a supreme court of ensuring the uniform application of the law in the lower courts, however, would be a legitimate objective. Yet, on its own, it is unrelated to the review of foreign law; this would simply be an *additional* task.[1600] A supplemental argument is necessary to end up with a more promising ground of justification: one could say that more duties would put the functioning of the entire appeals system in danger. The operability of this part of a judicial system certainly is a legitimate objective. Moreover, to exclude an entire class of cases from review furthers this goal: fewer cases mean less risk of judicial overload. Such an exclusion is not, however, necessary to achieve the aim. There are other ways in which the caseload of a supreme court can be managed, e.g. by tightening the requirements for all appeals.[1601] At the very least, this would tip the scales of the balancing process to the detriment of the objective pursued by the member state.[1602] Similar considerations apply in regard to the freedoms guaranteed by the TFEU.[1603]

In conclusion, rules that prohibit the review of the application of another member state's law are in contravention of the TFEU. They are not void, but they cannot be applied in these situations.

5.3.3. *European Union*

There is no express provision in EU private international law containing a general normative statement on the ascertainment and application of law foreign from the perspective of the forum. Nor does it contain a provision regulating any of this issue's sub-topics. Therefore, the question is whether a statement can be won through interpretation, or whether EU law at least sets some boundaries for those cases in which national courts apply its provisions of private international law.

5.3.3.1. Ascertainment and Application of Foreign Law: Left to the Member States

In line with the aim of harmonisation in order to bring about legal certainty, the policy decision is obvious: foreign law should be ascertained and applied

1599 *Gotsche*, Der BGH im Wettbewerb der Zivilrechtsordnungen, 178.

1600 *Flessner*, ZEuP 2006, 737, 739. But see *Remien*, in: FS Roth, 431, 441, who relies on the very different role of a supreme court with regard to foreign law in order to flat-out deny any discrimination to begin with.

1601 For Germany see *Gotsche*, Der BGH im Wettbewerb der Zivilrechtsordnungen, 178.

1602 *Hübner*, Ausländisches Recht vor deutschen Gerichten, 173–174.

1603 In detail *Gotsche*, Der BGH im Wettbewerb der Zivilrechtsordnungen, 179–191; already *Flessner*, ZEuP 2006, 737, 739–740; *Schwartze*, in: FS Fenge, 127, 141–144; but see *Weckesser-Georgi*, Die letztinstanzliche Überprüfung, 290–298.

in a uniform manner across the EU. If EU private international law is mandatory,[1604] it is only reasonable[1605] to require the courts to apply foreign law and to ascertain it for that purpose.[1606] Is this perhaps how the law stands already?

Once again, the interpretation of the exclusion of "evidence and procedure" from the scope of Rome I and II by Article 1(3) of each regulation is at issue. Unlike above,[1607] however, there is now is an additional argument on the table: Article 30(1)(i) Rome II. Pursuant to this provision, the Commission report (supposed to be submitted in 2011) was to include "a study on the effects of the way in which foreign law is treated in the different jurisdictions and on the extent to which courts in the Member States apply foreign law in practice pursuant to this Regulation". Reading this *a contrario*, it seems that Rome II itself presupposes that member states treat – and for the time being will continue to treat – foreign law differently.[1608]

To be sure, Article 30(1)(i) Rome II still makes sense if one does not interpret it this way. It could simply mean that the Commission is supposed to ascertain whether the member states treat foreign law in accordance with EU law requirements – and whether these requirements suffice to reach the goals pursued by the regulations, or whether there should be more.[1609] Even the Commission statement annexed to Rome II[1610] – "being aware of the different practices followed in the Member States as regards the treatment of foreign law" etc. – would still make sense. It would mean that the Commission was aware of existing differences *prior* to Rome II, and therefore saw a particular need to make sure Rome II works in this regard.

On the whole, however, Article 30(1)(i) Rome II and the Commission statement point in the opposite direction. This view finds further support in legislative history.[1611] Giuliano and Lagarde had expressly extended

---

1604 If one does not follow the approach outlined *supra* (section 2.1.2.2.), it would be reasonable to have the court apply foreign law and ascertain it for that purpose *to the extent* that EU private international law is mandatory.

1605 But, again, no logical or theoretical necessity, *supra* section 2.1.2.2. (No Room for Divergent ("Procedural") Domestic Rules Under Rome I/II) and footnote 1570.

1606 *Kieninger*, in: Leible (ed.), General Principles, §17.04[C][4]; see also Principle IV in Esplugues/Iglesias/Palao (eds.), Application of Foreign Law, 95; *Jänterä-Jareborg*, Rec. des cours 304 (2003), 181, 368; but see *Geeroms*, Foreign Law in Civil Litigation, at C.01–C.03, who doubts that any ideal harmonising solution exists because judicial cultures are just too different.

1607 *Supra* section 2.1.2.2. (No Room for Divergent ("Procedural") Domestic Rules Under Rome I/II).

1608 To this effect *Dickinson*, The Rome II Regulation, at 14.73.

1609 *Hübner*, Ausländisches Recht vor deutschen Gerichten, 178; *Trautmann*, Europäisches Kollisionsrecht und ausländisches Recht im nationalen Zivilverfahren, 286.

1610 [2007] OJ L 199, 49.

1611 In more detail see *Dickinson*, The Rome II Regulation, at 14.67–14.69; *Wagner*, in: FS Kropholler, 715, 728.

"evidence" not covered by the Rome Convention to the question of foreign law.[1612] After the first reading regarding Rome II, the European Parliament had suggested two articles concerning the present issue.[1613] Pursuant to Article 13 in particular, courts would have had to establish the content of foreign law of their own motion. Later, the Parliament relegated the question to the recitals, but the relevant content had not changed.[1614] As nothing of this ended up in Rome II, while both Article 30(1)(i) and the Commission statement do appear in it, it is difficult to escape the conclusion that the treatment of foreign law is still up to the member states under Rome II. As the issue does not surface in any of the other regulations,[1615] it cannot be argued that the situation has changed since Rome II. In particular, the absence of the issue of treatment of foreign law from the "report provisions" of the other regulations[1616] does not necessarily indicate that the issue has ceased to be relevant by now (because a common European solution has somehow emerged in the meantime); the Rome II report could simply be regarded as sufficient for revealing all problems, so that there is no need to re-examine the same question from the perspective of any other regulation. For the time being, the issue of ascertaining and applying foreign law is left to the member states in principle – with the following qualifications.

5.3.3.2. First Caveat: Equivalence and the Ascertainment of Foreign Law

It is rather obvious, however, that a distinction between foreign law determined by domestic private international law and foreign law determined by EU private international law would be incompatible with EU law, to the extent that the former is ascertained *ex officio* and the latter is not. This would constitute a less favourable treatment of EU law and violate the principle of equivalence.[1617]

1612 *Giuliano/Lagarde*, Report on the Convention on the law applicable to contractual obligations, 36.

1613 Articles 12 and 13 in P6_TA(2005)0284.

1614 See in particular the proposed Recital 30a clause 2 in Council Document ST 5516/07 (24 January 2007), 9–10.

1615 Rome III and the Succession Regulation do contain some references to the European Judicial Network, "existing networks" in general, and "other means" to ascertain foreign law in their recitals (Recital 14 clause 2 Rome III; Recital 16 clause 4 Succession Regulation). This is too vague to allow any inference as to the question whether and how a court or the parties are to approach these issues.

1616 Article 27(1) Rome I, Article 20(1) Rome III, Article 82 Succession Regulation, Article 68 M-/RP-Property Regulation. Of course, reports pursuant to these provisions *could* also cover this issue – it is not warranted to read them *a contrario*.

1617 See, *a contrario*, *Hübner*, Ausländisches Recht vor deutschen Gerichten, 157; to the same effect *Herb*, Europäisches Gemeinschaftsrecht und nationaler Zivilprozess, 271 (but without a specific private international law context).

5.3.3.3. Second Caveat: Effectiveness and the Ascertainment of Foreign Law

The ECJ held in *Laboratoires Boiron* that the principle of effectiveness requires a court to make use of all procedures available under its national law if it considers it likely that its rules concerning the burden of proof "make it impossible or excessively difficult for [certain] evidence to be produced".[1618] Although the case was one in the state aid context, it seems possible to transfer its fundamentals to EU private international law.[1619] Accordingly, a court of a member state cannot simply ignore that a party required to prove foreign law faces difficulties to do so, and proceed as if there has been a failure to produce the evidence. Rather, it has to rely on further means under its domestic law to procure evidence. This is particularly reasonable in cases where EU law serves the protection of certain classes of people.[1620]

The question remains what would happen if domestic law does not provide for any other means to establish foreign law than proof by the parties. The issue is unlikely to surface in practice, however, as even the English rules of civil procedure – being the European legal system most closely associated with the idea of having the parties prove foreign law – provide for further means.[1621]

5.3.3.4. Third Caveat: Impossibility of the Ascertainment of Foreign Law

In light of the mandatory nature of EU private international law and judicial duties to resort to all available means under domestic law,[1622] a court should not quickly arrive at the conclusion that it is impossible to ascertain the law determined by EU private international law.[1623] Yet if it does, a supplemental conflicts rule is required.[1624] In the interest of uniform application of EU private international law, it would be preferable to resolve the issue at this level instead of resorting to national law.[1625] In particular, if national law immediately makes the *lex fori* apply in such a situation, as is the case in

---

1618 ECJ Case C-526/04, Laboratoires Boiron SA v Union de recouvrement des cotisations de sécurité sociale et d'allocations familiales (Urssaf) de Lyon, assuming the rights and obligations of the Agence centrale des organismes de sécurité sociale (ACOSS), Reports of Cases 2006, I-7529, at 55 and 57.

1619 *Trautmann*, Europäisches Kollisionsrecht und ausländisches Recht im nationalen Zivilverfahren, 377–378.

1620 *Hübner*, Ausländisches Recht vor deutschen Gerichten, 148, who infers a duty to ascertain foreign law *ex officio* in these situations; along similar lines *Remien*, in: FS Roth, 431, 439.

1621 *Trautmann*, Europäisches Kollisionsrecht und ausländisches Recht im nationalen Zivilverfahren, 383; see in particular *Dickinson*, The Rome II Regulation, at 14.76.

1622 *Supra* sections 2.1.2. and 5.3.3.3.

1623 Similarly *Stürner*, in: Langenbucher (ed.), Europäisches Privat- und Wirtschaftsrecht, §8 at 17 (contrary to principle of effectiveness if *lex fori* were to apply too quickly/easily).

1624 Already *supra* 5.3.1.

1625 *Kreuzer*, in: Jud/Rechberger/Reichelt (eds.), Kollisionsrecht in der Europäischen Union, 1, 13.

many member states,[1626] the outcome would depend on the court seised, contrary to what harmonised conflicts rules are intended to achieve. It does not seem entirely far-fetched – albeit not terribly common either – that a party will seise a court before which it expects the ascertainment of the applicable law to fail in order to have the respective *lex fori* apply.

It is doubtful, however, whether this gap in the private international law regulations can be filled at the EU level *de lege lata*. To be sure, one could resort to the law designated by a subsidiary connecting factor by way of analogy.[1627] EU private international law itself occasionally recognises that one of its conflicts rules can fail to work because its requirements are not met, and provides for another conflicts rule.[1628] It is only a small step to declare the situation in which a conflicts rule fails to work because the governing law cannot be ascertained sufficiently similar. In particular, such a solution still would follow the policy decisions by the EU legislator instead of introducing a foreign object in the form of a domestic conflicts rule.[1629] Moreover, such a solution would take precedence over any domestic rule simply by being an EU solution.[1630] Yet the key word in the preceding lines is "occasionally". In many cases, there is no subsidiary conflicts rule.[1631] Then, the base for any analogy is missing.

At the most, thus, one could say rather narrowly that the question is left to the member states from the outset, but that the principle of effectiveness requires that they, where possible *within their legal system*,[1632] apply subsidiary EU conflicts rules.[1633] Or one could say that the need for uniform

---

1626 Rules among the general provisions of private international law: §4(2) Austrian PIL Act, Article 15(2) clause 2 Belgian PIL Code; §23(5) Czech PIL Act; §4(4) Estonian PIL Act; §5(3) Hungarian PIL Code 1979/§7(3) Hungarian PIL Act; Article 1.12(3) Lithuanian Civil Code; Article 10(2) Polish PIL Act; Article 2.562(3) Romanian Civil Code; Article 12(4) Slovenian PIL Act. Similarly, Section 22 Latvian Civil Code: Presumption that foreign law is the same as the *lex fori*. Article 14(2) Italian PIL Act envisions a more nuanced approach: *Lex fori* only as the last resort if potential other connecting factors fail, too. However, as such a rule requires that the conflicts provision at issue actually has alternative or subsidiary connecting factors, its scope is rather limited; *Pocar/Honorati*, in: Symeonides (ed.), PIL at the End of the 20th Century, 279, 294. Article 23(2) Portuguese Civil Code enshrines a similar rule.

1627 *Trautmann*, Europäisches Kollisionsrecht und ausländisches Recht im nationalen Zivilverfahren, 388–392.

1628 Article 5(1) clause 2 Rome I ("If those requirements are not met ..."); Article 10(2) Rome II ("Where the law applicable cannot be determined on the basis of paragraph 1"); Article 8 Rome III ("or, failing that").

1629 *Trautmann*, Europäisches Kollisionsrecht und ausländisches Recht im nationalen Zivilverfahren, 391.

1630 But see *Trautmann*, Europäisches Kollisionsrecht und ausländisches Recht im nationalen Zivilverfahren, 392, who seems to suggest otherwise.

1631 Or a related rule also would lead to the law that cannot be ascertained. It would be pointless, e.g., to resort to Article 4(2) Rome I if the law determined by Article 4(1)(a) Rome I cannot be ascertained. Article 4(2) Rome I would lead to the same law.

1632 See in particular Italy and Portugal, *supra* footnote 1626.

1633 To this effect *Trautmann*, Europäisches Kollisionsrecht und ausländisches Recht im nationalen Zivilverfahren, 392–393.

application of EU private international law mandates that courts proceed by analogy where possible *within EU law* – and only resort to their domestic rules where impossible. The latter approach is consistent with the solution adopted here in regard to the mandatory nature of EU private international law,[1634] and is therefore suggested as the one to be preferred.

If the law to be ascertained is one of another member state, one could furthermore flat-out prohibit a court to consider it impossible to ascertain, as soon as the European Judicial Network is sufficiently reliable.[1635]

5.4. CHANGE OF THE *LEX CAUSAE*

The meaning of "law" is further called into question when the applicable law[1636] has undergone a change.[1637] Does the *lex prior* (e.g. the rules in force when the conflicts rule was made) still, or does the *lex praesens*[1638] already, apply? In the latter case, what if the new rules are supposed to apply retrospectively? As all law can change,[1639] these issues can arise in connection with any conflicts rule;[1640] they are formally general in the strict sense. Scholars generally discuss them separately from specific conflict of law issues, although not always together with other issues called "general" and the like.[1641]

5.4.1. *A Lack of Formally General* Statutory *Solutions*

There is no provision focused entirely on this point in the private international law of the members, nor do the EU private international law regulations deal

1634 *Supra* section 2.1.2.2.

1635 *Hübner*, Ausländisches Recht vor deutschen Gerichten, 181. Less strictly *Michaels*, in: FS Kropholler, 151, 166–167, who nevertheless holds the courts of member states to higher standards as regards the ascertainment and correct application of the law of other member states.

1636 Substantive or (in case of a *renvoi*) foreign private international law.

1637 *Grodecki*, Intertemporal Conflict of Laws, at 22.

1638 Regarding the terminology see *Heß*, Intertemporales Privatrecht, 10 (with note 65).

1639 For a short typology with further references see *Heß*, Intertemporales Privatrecht, 2–3.

1640 Expressly *Dicey/Morris/Collins*, Conflict of Laws, at 3-014 ("it must be emphasised that the problem is always basically the same").

1641 *Calvo Caravaca/Carrascosa González*, DIP I, 586, and *Kahn-Freund*, General Problems, 295–300 (as one of the general issues concerning the application of foreign law). *Bogdan*, PIL in Sweden, at 54 (as part of the chapter on "connection", i.e. mainly connecting factors, together with the change of the *lex fori*). *Rogerson*, Collier's Conflict of Laws, 288–290 (special chapter on the "time factor"). *Dicey/Morris/Collins*, Conflict of Laws, at 3-013–3-032 (special chapter on the "time factor", but as part of the "preliminary matters"). *Cheshire/North/Fawcett*, PIL, 5–6 (special section on "space and time" as part of the introduction). *Mayer/Heuzé*, DIP, at 256–258 (in the "partie générale", yet not in the part on the application of foreign law, but together with other intertemporal issues as "facteurs de complication). *Cachard*, DIP, at 605 (as part of a section on the influence of time on private international law). *von Bar/Mankowski*, IPR I, §4 at 171 and 190–192 (in the context of German private international law as part of the German legal system, together with other questions of intertemporal law).

with this type of *conflit transitoire*. If one ascribes a temporal meaning to rules that require the judge to apply foreign law as it is or would be applied by the respective foreign judge, however, some pertinent provisions among domestic general private international law provisions do exist.[1642]

5.4.2. *The Formally Generally* Accepted *Solution*

It seems to be the general solution to the issue, anyway, that the *lex causae* itself decides about its application in time.[1643] This is particularly reasonable under the premise that – but actually only to the extent that – private international law refers to foreign law not because of its content, but because of another factor such as a close connection.[1644] The assumption that conflicts rules are generally supposed to refer to law in force, to "living" law, further underpins the reasonableness of this idea.[1645] It follows that retrospective foreign law will also be applied.[1646] If this leads to absolutely unbearable consequences from the point of view of the *lex fori*, the normal public policy exception should suffice;[1647] a separate solution is unnecessary. In principle, public policy is also the appropriate analytical viewpoint for the converse idea of applying old foreign law, even though its intertemporal provisions determine the application of the new rules ("petrification").[1648]

5.5. *RENVOI*

The meaning of "law" in a conflicts rule faces another challenge from the binary perspective of "substantive law vs. private international law".[1649]

1642 See *supra* section 5.3.2.1.

1643 Already *Bartin*, Principes I, 299; also *Grodecki*, Intertemporal Conflict of Laws, at 22 and 26; *Dicey/Morris/Collins*, Conflict of Laws, at 3-013 and 3-028; *Kahn-Freund*, General Problems, 295; *Mayer/Heuzé*, DIP, at 256; *Calvo Caravaca/Carrascosa González*, DIP I, 586; *von Bar/Mankowski*, IPR I, §4 at 171 and 190. There can also be an intertemporal *renvoi*, see *Schröder*, Die Verweisung auf Mehrrechtsstaaten, 76–79; *Heß*, Intertemporales Privatrecht, 351–353.

1644 Without the caveat *Grodecki*, Intertemporal Conflict of Laws, at 22 (with note 79).

1645 *Neuhaus*, Grundbegriffe, §39 III 1 (295–296).

1646 Ibid.

1647 *Dicey/Morris/Collins*, Conflict of Laws, at 3-028–3-031; *Grodecki*, Intertemporal Conflict of Laws, at 24 (with the somewhat problematic addition that the "content" of the *lex causae* can be offensive by itself); *Kahn-Freund*, General Problems, 295. See also *Mayer/Heuzé*, DIP, at 256, who seem to assume that retrospectivity itself can be "choquante"; similarly *Calvo Caravaca/Carrascosa González*, DIP I, 586. Ambiguously in this regard *von Bar/Mankowski*, IPR I, §4 at 190.

1648 *von Bar/Mankowski*, IPR I, §4 at 192.

1649 Expressly for a discussion of the issue as one of the meaning of "law" also e.g. *Briggs*, Private International Law in the English Courts, at 3.64; in a way also *Cachard*, DIP, at 580, who mentions *renvoi* as an issue of the *interpretation* of a conflicts provision.

Does it mean the substantive law of the state referred to or ("also"[1650]) that state's private international law? This, of course, is the issue of *renvoi*, deemed by Rabel to be "the most famous dispute in conflicts law".[1651] The term *renvoi*, albeit taken literally only one of the possible answers,[1652] has since a long time become a shibboleth for the entire question.

Renvoi has been the *cause célèbre* of private international law ever since the *Forgo* decision by the French Cour de cassation in the 19th century.[1653] The earlier English case dealing with the issue *avant la lettre*, *Collier v Rivaz*,[1654] did not attract as much attention. The topic enjoys a particularly bad reputation. It "is viewed in some quarters with a distaste which sometimes borders on mania".[1655] Mäsch suggested getting rid of *renvoi* in the long term, and limiting it as much as possible for the time being.[1656] Henrich began to sing its epicedium[1657] in the tradition of Foyer, who had proposed a "requiem" for *renvoi* thirty years earlier.[1658] Corneloup recently explored its waning relevance.[1659] Yet nobody can ignore or abolish the *issue*. As every conflicts provision determines that some law is applicable to its subject matter, the meaning of "law" must be established for each rule.[1660] Hence, *renvoi* is a formally general issue in the strict sense.

5.5.1. Structural and Terminological Observations

It is common to say that a certain conflicts rule "also" (i.e. in addition to referring to substantive law) refers to conflicts rules if *renvoi* is allowed. Phrases with this content can also be found in legislative texts, see e.g. §5(1) Austrian PIL Act, Article 4(1) EGBGB, and Article 2.559(1) Romanian Civil Code. Yet these statements are utter nonsense as a rule can only refer to *either* conflicts rules *or* substantive law.[1661]

1650 See *infra* section 5.5.1. for the problem of this common expression.

1651 *Rabel*, The Conflict of Laws, 75.

1652 "Renvoyer" as opposed to "envoyer" means "to return" or "to send back".

1653 Cass. civ. S. 1878. 1. 429 and Cass. req. S. 1882. 1. 393 = *Ancel/Lequette*, Les grands arrêts, Nos. 7–8.

1654 (1841) 2 Curt. 855, cited in *Rogerson*, Collier's Conflict of Laws, 280, and *Dicey/Morris/Collins*, Conflict of Laws, at 4-011.

1655 *Briggs*, The Conflict of Laws, 24.

1656 *Mäsch*, RabelsZ 61 (1997), 285 and passim.

1657 *Henrich*, in: FS von Hoffmann, 159, 167.

1658 *Foyer*, Trav. com. fr. DIP 1980/81, 105.

1659 *Corneloup*, IPRax 2017, 147.

1660 From different perspective, *renvoi* concerns the question which of different connecting factors in domestic and foreign private international law ultimately prevails; see already *Rabel*, Die Fachgebiete des Kaiser-Wilhelm-Instituts, 180, 231. One then might allocate *renvoi* to the element of the connecting factor. *Lipstein*, in: LA Siehr, 405, 406, could be understood in this way, although he also states two paragraphs later that the question arises after a conflicts rule has led to some other law.

1661 *Kegel/Schurig*, IPR, §10 II (391); also see *Neumayr*, in: ABGB-Kurzkommentar, §5 IPRG at 1.

If "law" is understood to refer to substantive law, no further question arises in this context. If, however, a conflicts rule is construed to refer to private international law, there is the need to distinguish. If the rule refers to the *lex fori* in the given case, it means the substantive *lex fori* for all intents and purposes.[1662] If it refers to foreign law, one of three scenarios ensues:[1663]

(1) The foreign law "accepts" the reference, i.e. considers its own law applicable.
(2) The foreign law refers back to the referring law. This is *renvoi* in the strict sense,[1664] a remission: *renvoi au premier degré* or *renvoi rémission*, *Rückverweisung*, *rinvio indietro*, *reenvío de primer grado* or *reenvío de retorno*. This might be a reference to the substantive *lex fori*, but it also might be a reference to the forum's private international law. (In order to prevent a never-ending circle of references in the latter case, it is obvious that an additional rule is required.)
(3) The foreign law refers to the law of a third country. This is *renvoi* in the wider sense,[1665] a *trans*mission: *renvoi au deuxième degré*, *Weiterverweisung*, *rinvio altrove* or *rinvio oltre*, *reenvío de segundo grado* or *reenvío ulterior*. This can be a reference to the substantive law of a third state or to that state's private international law (which then might be called *renvoi au troisième degré* and so forth).

English authors in particular seem to prefer another framework for analysing *renvoi*. If a conflicts rule is construed to refer to foreign private international law, they distinguish two situations,[1666] using multiples for their designation instead of ordinal numbers like in French and Spanish terminology:

(1) Single or partial *renvoi*: the court decides the case according to its own substantive law (remission) or according to the substantive law of the third country (transmission).
(2) Double or total *renvoi* (foreign court theory): the court decides the case as a court in the country referred to would decide the case – which seems to boil down to being able to take into account that foreign conflicts rules themselves might refer to conflicts rules instead of substantive law.

1662 *Kegel/Schurig*, IPR, §10 II (391).

1663 As to the terminology in different languages in the following, see only *Cachard*, DIP, at 581; *Kegel/Schurig*, IPR, §10 II (392); *Malatesta*, in: Baratta (ed.), DIP, s. v. "Rinvio", 422/*Pocar*, IPRax 1996, 145, 150; *Calvo Caravaca/Carrascosa González*, DIP I, 502, respectively.

1664 *Wolff*, PIL, at 178.

1665 Ibid.

1666 *Rogerson*, Collier's Conflict of Laws, 282; *Dicey/Morris/Collins*, Conflict of Laws, at 4-009–4-4010; *Briggs*, Private International Law in the English Courts, at 3.66; *id.*, The Conflict of Laws, 21; *Hill/Ní Shúilleabháin*, Clarkson & Hill's Conflict of Laws, at 1.113–1.116.

5.5.2. *Member States*

Every member state that has a private international law code also has one or more provisions concerning *renvoi* among its general provisions.[1667] In light of the history of the issue touched upon above, it is no surprise that *renvoi* is a known phenomenon under both French and common law.[1668] The same is true for Denmark, Finland, and Sweden.[1669] The authors in the countries just named deal with *renvoi* separately from individual conflicts rules.

5.5.3. *European Union*

As far as EU private international law is concerned, every regulation contains a *renvoi* provision. In Rome I and Rome II, the respective rule is found in the separate chapter of "Other Provisions".[1670] While Rome III does have such a chapter, its *renvoi* provision is not formally separated from other conflicts provisions,[1671] nor are Article 34 Succession Regulation and Article 32 M-/RP-Property Regulation. All of the latter provisions, however, are located among other provisions identified in the course of this analysis as formally general. It is of little wonder then that authors covering more than isolated parts of EU private international law likewise tend to discuss *renvoi* separately from specific conflicts rules, or even expressly as a general issue.[1672]

1667 To wit: §5(1) and (2) Austrian PIL Act, Article 16 Belgian PIL Code, Article 40 Bulgarian PIL Code, Article 6 Croatian PIL Act, §21 Czech PIL Act, §6 Estonian PIL Act, Article 4(1) and (2) EGBGB, Article 32 Greek Civil Code, §4 Hungarian PIL Code 1979/§5 Hungarian PIL Act, Article 13 Italian PIL Act, Section 23 Latvian Civil Code, Articles 1.10(3) and 1.14 Lithuanian Civil Code, Article 10:5 Dutch Civil Code, Articles 16–19 Portuguese Civil Code, Article 2.559 Romanian Civil Code, Article 35 Slovak PIL Act, Article 6 Slovenian PIL Act, Article 12(2) Spanish Civil Code. The 1967 Draft for the French Civil Code also contained a *renvoi* provision: Article 2284 French Civil Code (1967 Draft).

1668 France: *Audit/d'Avout*, DIP, at 274–292; *Loussouarn/Bourel/de Vareilles-Sommières*, DIP, at 285–321; *Cachard*, DIP, at 580–593; *Mayer/Heuzé*, DIP, at 223–240. For Luxembourg see *Wiwinius*, DIP, 44–47. For the common law see already *supra* footnote 1666, and *Beaumont/McEleavy*, Anton's PIL, at 4.40–4.68.

1669 See *Lookofsky*, Choice of Law in Denmark, VIII; *eund.*, in: Symeonides (ed.), PIL at the End of the 20th Century, 147, 159 (Denmark); *Ring/Olsen-Ring*, Einführung in das skandinavische Recht (1999), at 949 (Finland and Sweden); *Bogdan*, PIL in Sweden, at 71–74 (Sweden).

1670 Article 20 Rome I; Article 24 Rome II.

1671 Article 11 Rome III.

1672 *van Calster*, European PIL, 1.4; *Heinze*, in: FS Kropholler, 105, 115–119; *Sonnenberger*, in: FS Kropholler, 227, 238; *Siehr*, Yearbook of Private International Law VII (2005), 17, 41–44; *Kreuzer*, in: Jud/Rechberger/Reichelt (eds.), Kollisionsrecht in der Europäischen Union, 1, 20–29; *Plender/Wilderspin*, European PIL of Obligations, at 3-029–3-031.

5.5.4. *Excursus: Four Models of How to Deal with* Renvoi

Whether, and if so, when to admit which form of *renvoi* is a question of policy and, as far as existing rules are concerned, a question of content. As such, it is beyond the scope of this book. It seems relatively "safe",[1673] however, to make a short comparative excursus to the content of *renvoi* provisions across the EU; for *renvoi* is a topic so well-known and so widely discussed that the risk of misunderstandings based on language appears at least smaller than in the context of other issues.

General Admission of *Renvoi*

§5(1) Austrian PIL Act, Article 40 Bulgarian PIL Code, Article 6 Croatian PIL Act, Articles 3a(1) and 4(1) clause 1 EGBGB, and Article 6(1) Slovenian PIL Act generally admit *renvoi* in both its form as remission and transmission. For most of these cases, this follows directly from the wording of the provision. In Germany, the admission of *renvoi* as the principle is more a matter of interpretation: while Article 4(1) EGBGB has German conflicts rules refer to foreign private international law subject to an "incompatibility" condition, Article 3a(1) EGBGB stipulates that when German private international law refers to substantive provisions, it excludes conflicts provisions. *A contrario*, one can deduce that references to foreign law in general are to *include* conflicts provisions as a matter of principle.[1674] Whether *renvoi* empirically constitutes the general rule, or whether it actually forms the exception,[1675] is an entirely different question.

Furthermore, some national provisions set forth the consequences of remission and transmission. Remission usually means application of internal substantive provisions.[1676] Transmission "stops" where the foreign law "accepts" it,[1677] or when one law is referred to again for the first time.[1678]

Despite this general admission of *renvoi*, there are sometimes general exceptions to,[1679] or deviations from, this general rule in special conflicts provisions.[1680] In Germany, an exception is already inherent in the general

---

1673 See *supra* Chapter 1, section 3. for the potential pitfalls of the present comparative efforts.

1674 *Hausmann*, in: Staudinger, Art. 3a EGBGB at 1; also see *eund.*, in: Staudinger, Art. 4 EGBGB at 47 with further references.

1675 See *Mankowski*, in: Basedow/Kischel/Sieber (eds.), German National Reports, 133, 147.

1676 §5(2) Austrian PIL Act, Article 40(3) Bulgarian PIL Code, Article 6(2) Croatian PIL Act, Article 4(1) clause 2 EGBGB, Article 6(2) Slovenian PIL Act.

1677 §5(2) Austrian PIL Act, Article 40(3) Bulgarian PIL Code.

1678 §5(2) Austrian PIL Act.

1679 E.g. Article 40(2) Bulgarian PIL Code, Article 4(2) EGBGB, Article 6(3) Slovenian PIL Act.

1680 E.g. §§11(1), 8, 16(2) Austrian PIL Act (see *Neumayr*, in: ABGB-Kurzkommentar, §5 IPRG at 1), Article 83(3) Bulgarian PIL Code.

principle because Article 4(1) clause 1 EGBGB allows *renvoi* where it is not incompatible with the purpose of the conflicts rule at stake.[1681] Note the double negative and contrast this with Article 35 Slovak PIL Act (*renvoi* admitted when it "corresponds with the reasonable and just regulation of the relation concerned").

General Exclusion of *Renvoi*

Other member states generally exclude any form of *renvoi*. A very clear example is Article 32 Greek Civil Code. It is so clear, in fact, that both Vassilakakis and Vrellis devote no more than three sentences to the subject in their reports on Greek private international law.[1682] A less obvious case is Article 1.11(1) and (2) Lithuanian Civil Code. It only allows remission and transmission where the Civil Code provides for it.[1683] Similarly, Article 16 Belgian PIL Code prohibits *renvoi*, but special provisions later in the code expressly allow it,[1684] often under an additional (substantive) condition. Accordingly, commentators have called this *renvoi* of a substantive kind.[1685] Dutch private international law follows the same conceptual approach.[1686] Finally, the exclusion of *renvoi* also represents the stance of Danish[1687] and Swedish[1688] private international law.

While Article 24 Rome II, Article 11 Rome III, and Article 32 M-/RP-Property Regulation flat-out prohibit any *renvoi*, Article 20 Rome I expressly allows for the possibility of one of its provisions referring to foreign private international law. While Rome I does not actually contain such a provision, domestic law allowing *renvoi* could be relevant *by way of* Article 7 subparagraph 2 Rome I.[1689]

Only Remission Allowed

In some instances, domestic private international law only allows remission. The wording for this seemingly easy consequence, however, is often rather

1681 The main examples are alternative connecting factors and escape clauses, but the devil is in the details, see *von Hein*, MüKoBGB, Art. 4 EGBGB at 19.

1682 *Vassilakakis*, RHDI 63 (2010), 103, 108; *Vrellis*, in: Symeonides (ed.), PIL at the End of the 20th Century, 243, 254 (noting two exceptions in special legislation).

1683 See *Mikelėnas*, Yearbook of Private International Law 7 (2005), 161, 167.

1684 Articles 34(1) clause 2, 78(2) clause 2, and Article 110 clause 2 Belgian PIL Code.

1685 *Traest*, in: Het Wetboek Internationaal Privaatrecht becommentarieerd, Art. 78 III B; *Tubeuf*, in: Het Wetboek Internationaal Privaatrecht becommentarieerd, Art. 110 II C.

1686 Article 10:5 Dutch Civil Code, but Articles 10:19(1) clause 2, 65, 71(2) Dutch Civil Code; arguably also some "recognition provisions" allow *renvoi*, see *Boele-Woelki/van Iterson*, in: van Erp/van Vliet (eds.), Netherlands Report, 145, 175.

1687 *Lookofsky*, Choice of Law in Denmark, VIII; *id.*, in: Symeonides (ed.), PIL at the End of the 20th Century, 147, 159.

1688 *Bogdan*, PIL in Sweden, at 73.

1689 *Martiny*, in: MüKoBGB, Art. 20 Rom I-VO at 4.

convoluted. Arguably, the worst example – "caótica redacción" and "uno de los preceptos peor redactados del Derecheo español"[1690] – is Article 12(2) Spanish Civil Code.[1691] A similar case is §6 Estonian PIL Act; paragraph 1 clause 1 seems to admit *renvoi* in general, but paragraph 2 states that the law of a third state should not be taken into account. §4 Hungarian PIL Code 1979[1692] constituted the opposite way of bringing about this result: its first clause excluded *renvoi*, but the second clause admitted it if it led to Hungarian law.[1693] Both Section 23 Latvian Civil Code and §5(1) Polish PIL Act only deal with remission; the prohibition of transmission is a matter of interpretation.[1694] Again, general[1695] or specific exceptions[1696] may apply. As the consequence of *trans*mission in Romanian private international law seems to be the application of Romanian law,[1697] it seems justifiable to count Article 2.559(1) Romanian Civil Code among the provisions only allowing remission.

Remission Allowed, Transmission not Automatically Allowed

Finally, some member states unconditionally allow remission but make transmission dependent upon further conditions. A rather complex example of such an "intermediary position"[1698] is the Portuguese Civil Code, which contains four articles on *renvoi*. The general rule is an exclusion of *renvoi*.[1699] Yet remission is allowed and transmission accepted if the third state accepts it as well.[1700], Both latter provisions, however, are subject to exceptions in the further paragraphs of each provision and a general exclusion.[1701]

1690 *Calvo Caravaca/Carrascosa González*, DIP I, 512–513; see also *Esplugues Mota/Azcárraga Monzonís*, Spanish Report, 22.

1691 "La remisión al derecho extranjero se entenderá hecha a su ley material, sin tener en cuenta el reenvío que sus normas de conflicto puedan hacer a otra ley que no sea la española."

1692 After many changes throughout the history of Hungarian private international law; see *Burián*, in: Symeonides (ed.), PIL at the End of the 20th Century, 263, 273.

1693 A "Solomonic solution" (*Mádl*, RHDI 44 (1991), 227, 240)? The provision being of a general nature, later special provisions could deviate from it, and, in fact, this happened at least in one instance (Article 21/A Hungarian PIL Code 1979), see *Nagy*, PIL in Hungary, at 61; *Raffai/Szabó*, Acta Juridica Hungarica 51 (2010), 136, 144. The new *renvoi* provision in §5 Hungarian PIL Act is more complex.

1694 See (for the Polish provision) *Pazdan/Gralla*, WiRO 2011, 299, 300.

1695 Article 5(2) Polish PIL Act.

1696 Article 17(2) Polish PIL Act; in Spain, there are special *renvoi* provisions in other pieces of legislation, *Esplugues Mota/Azcárraga Monzonís*, Spanish Report, 22.

1697 Article 2.559(2) Romanian Civil Code: "Daca legea straina retrimite la dreptul roman sau la dreptul altui stat, se aplica legea romana, daca nu se prevede in mod expres altfel." This should not be confused with §21(1) clause 2 Czech PIL Act pursuant to which Czech law applies when transmission "fails".

1698 *Moura Ramos*, in: Symeonides (ed.), PIL at the End of the 20th Century, 349, 366.

1699 Article 16 Portuguese Civil Code.

1700 Article 18(1) Portuguese Civil Code, Article 17(1) Portuguese Civil Code, respectively.

1701 Article 19 Portuguese Civil Code.

This complexity could be the reason why de Lima Pinheiro considers only Articles 17(1) and 18(1) Portuguese Civil Code as suitable model rules for a European general part of private international law.[1702] §21 Czech PIL Act can be regarded as a condensed version of the Portuguese model: its first paragraph accepts remission and transmission where the third state accepts it too;[1703] the second paragraph contains general exceptions.

Italian private international law, which used to reject *renvoi*,[1704] now generally allows remission. It also allows transmission if the third state accepts it.[1705] Observers have hailed this as the most significant innovation of the Italian PIL Act.[1706] Article 13(2) Italian PIL Act generally excludes *renvoi* for some areas, whereas Article 13(3) Italian PIL Act makes transmission dependent upon further substantive conditions in certain cases.

The Succession Regulation follows a similar concept. For third states, Article 34(1) Succession Regulation allows a broad version of remission (not only to the member state applying the Succession Regulation in the given case, but also to any other member state), and transmission insofar as the third state accepts it. Article 34(2) Succession Regulation contains general exceptions (of which one is useless[1707]).

The Exclusion of *Renvoi* in Cases of Party Autonomy

The widespread "exclusion" of renvoi in cases of party autonomy has already turned out to be a topic more appropriately discussed in the context of party autonomy.[1708]

5.6. PUBLIC POLICY

Through the eyes of an omnilateral conflicts rule, every foreign law is potentially applicable. There are no *a priori* reservations. The rule is "blind".[1709] It leads to Raape's famous "leap into the dark".[1710] But what if the foreign

1702 *de Lima Pinheiro*, Yearbook of Private International Law 14 (2012/2013), 153, 169; to the same effect already *Neuhaus/Rau*, RabelsZ 32 (1968), 500, 506.
1703 *Dobiáš*, Riv. dir. int. priv. proc. 2015, 109, 117.
1704 *Ballarino/Bonomi*, Yearbook of Private International Law 2 (2000), 99, 108.
1705 Article 13(1)(a) and (b) Italian PIL Act, respectively.
1706 *Pocar*, IPRax 1997, 145, 150; *Giardina*, Rev. crit. DIP 1996, 1, 15.
1707 *Supra* section 2.9.5.6. (Article 30 Succession Regulation).
1708 *Supra* section 4.3.5.
1709 *Esplugues Mota/Azcárraga Monzonís*, Spanish Report, 16; very similar already *Cavers*, Harv. L. Rev. 47 (1933), 173, 180 ("blindfold test").
1710 *Raape*, IPR, §13 I (90).

law, or at least its application, contravenes the law of the forum? For private international law that in principle leads to foreign law, it would be inconsistent if any kind of divergence from the *lex fori* constituted a problem. Then why refer to foreign law at all? However, should a judge also be forced to make a decision under foreign law that conflicts with core tenets of the *lex fori*? This, of course, is the issue of public policy (*ordre public*,[1711] *ordine pubblico*, *orden público*, *ordem pública*) – the "lifeline"[1712] when leaping into the dark. The question of perhaps not applying foreign law despite having been referred to it arises in the context of every conflicts rule: public policy is a formally general issue in the strict sense.

5.6.1. Member States

Every member state that has a private international law code also has a provision on public policy among its general provisions.[1713] (In fact, it seems that every private international law code *in the world* has such a provision.[1714]) The topic is also known in Cypriot,[1715] English,[1716] Danish,[1717] Finnish,[1718] French,[1719] Luxembourg,[1720] Scots,[1721] and Swedish[1722] private international law – and is typically discussed separately from individual conflicts rules.

1711 The term long has left French boundaries, see e.g. the official title of Article 6 EGBGB: "Öffentliche Ordnung (ordre public)".

1712 *Wurmnest*, in: Leible (ed.), General Principles, §14.01.

1713 To wit: §6 Austrian PIL Act, Article 21 Belgian PIL Code, Article 45 Bulgarian PIL Code, Article 4 Croatian PIL Act, §4 Czech PIL Act, §7 Estonian PIL Act, Article 6 EGBGB, Article 33 Greek Civil Code, §7 Hungarian PIL Code 1979/§12 Hungarian PIL Act, Article 16 Italian PIL Act, Section 24 Latvian Civil Code, Article 1.11(1) Lithuanian Civil Code, Article 10:6 Dutch Civil Code, Article 7 Polish PIL Act, Article 22 Portuguese Civil Code, Article 2.564 Romanian Civil Code, Article 36 Slovak PIL Act, Article 5 Slovenian PIL Act, and Article 12(3) Spanish Civil Code.

1714 See *Symeonides*, Codifying Choice of Law, 156–157; also the comparative overview by *Lagarde*, Public Policy, at 3.

1715 *Neocleous/Koundourou/Monou*, Neocleous's Introduction, at 9-19.

1716 *Briggs*, Private International Law in the English Courts, at 3.202–3.211; *Dicey/Morris/Collins*, Conflict of Laws, at 5R-001–5-018; *Harding*, Conflict of Laws, 9; *Rogerson*, Collier's Conflict of Laws, 424–433; *Hill/Ní Shúilleabháin*, Clarkson & Hill's Conflict of Laws, at 1.155–1.172.

1717 *Lookofsky*, Choice of Law in Denmark VII A; *id.*, in: Symeonides (ed.), PIL at the End of the 20th Century, 147, 160.

1718 *Klami/Kuisma*, Finnish Law as an Option, 9; *Bergmann*, Hauptprobleme, 29.

1719 *Audit/d'Avout*, DIP, at 367–377; *Cachard*, DIP, at 630–649; *Loussouarn/Bourel/de Vareilles-Sommières*, DIP, at 374–410; *Mayer/Heuzé*, DIP, at 204–220. The 1967 Draft for the French Civil Code also had a public policy provision, Article 2283 French Civil Code (1967 Draft).

1720 *Wiwinius*, DIP, 60–65.

1721 *Beaumont/McEleavy*, Anton's PIL, at 5.22–5.24.

1722 There are even a few statutes with public policy exceptions, *Bogdan*, PIL in Sweden, at 82; *Eek*, Swedish Conflict of Laws, 197–205.

5.6.2. *European Union*

Every EU private international law regulation has a public policy clause. It is located in the chapter on "Other Provisions" in Rome I and II.[1723] In Rome III and the Succession Regulation, the respective clauses are found between the provision on *renvoi* and non-unified legal systems,[1724] i.e. provisions that have already been identified as dealing with formally general issues – and not only that, but with formally general issues of the governing law. In the M-Property Regulation and the RP-Property Regulation, the public policy provisions are positioned between the ones on overriding mandatory provisions and on *renvoi*,[1725] likewise provisions on formally general issues. The EU legislator has clearly separated the provisions on public policy from individual conflicts provisions. Authors covering more than isolated parts of EU private international law likewise tend to discuss public policy independently from specific conflicts rules, or even expressly as a general issue.[1726]

5.6.3. *Excursus: The Content of Public Policy Exceptions*

Due to the tradition and prominence of the issue, some remarks as to the *content* of public policy at the domestic and EU levels may be ventured here.[1727]

Public Policy is Result-Oriented

Almost all of the domestic public policy provisions require that the "result" or the "consequences" of the application – or at the very least the application itself – of foreign law is contrary to public policy, i.e. not foreign law in general, or even only the particular foreign rule to be applied.[1728] Take Article 12(3)

1723 Article 21 Rome I, Article 26 Rome II.

1724 Articles 12 and 13 Rome III, Article 35 Succession Regulation.

1725 Article 31 M-/RP-Property Regulation.

1726 *Wurmnest*, in: Leible (ed.), General Principles, §14; *Heinze*, in: FS Kropholler, 105, 121–126; *Sonnenberger*, in: FS Kropholler, 227, 244; *Siehr*, Yearbook of Private International Law VII (2005), 17, 53–57; *Kreuzer*, in: Jud/Rechberger/Reichelt (eds.), Kollisionsrecht in der Europäischen Union, 1, 43–47; but see *van Calster*, European PIL, 3.2.8.4 and 4.10, and *Plender/Wilderspin*, European PIL of Obligations, at 12-055–12-061 and at 27-018–27-039, who only discuss the issue in the context of *each* Rome Regulation – even though they approach e.g. *renvoi* from a more abstract perspective, see already *supra* footnote 1672.

1727 See *supra* section 5.5.4. regarding the relative lack of "risk" of such an endeavour. See also *Symeonides*, Codifying Choice of Law, 156–157, for a global comparative survey.

1728 §6 clause 1 Austrian PIL Act; Article 21 clause 1 Belgian PIL Code; Article 45(1) Bulgarian PIL Code; Article 4 Croatian PIL Act; §4 clause 1 Czech PIL Act; §7 clause 1 Estonian PIL Act; Article 6 clause 1 EGBGB; Article 33 Greek Civil Code; Article 16(1) Italian PIL Act; Article 1.11(1) clause 1 Lithuanian Civil Code; Article 7 Polish PIL Act; Article 22(1) Portuguese Civil Code; Article 2.564(2) Romanian Civil Code; Article 36 Slovak PIL Act; Article 5 Slovenian PIL Act; Article 12(3) Spanish Civil Code. Article 10:6 Dutch Civil Code likewise refers to the application of foreign law, but there have been voices who consider

Spanish Civil Code as an example: "En ningún caso tendrá aplicación la ley extranjera cuando resulte contraria al orden público". The important word here is "resulte"; the rule does not say "sea".[1729] Another clear example is Article 16(1) Italian PIL Act: "La legge straniera non è applicata se i suoi effetti sono contrari all'ordine pubblico". The operative word here is "effetti". The concrete character of the provision has accordingly been emphasised.[1730] Similar positions can be observed for English and Swedish law.[1731] By its wording, §7(1) Hungarian PIL Code 1979 would have been a counter-example, but it was interpreted not to target foreign law as such.[1732] Article 24 Latvian Civil Code seems equally vague.

All of the EU private international law regulations specify that the application of foreign law, not foreign law as such, must be incompatible with the public policy of the forum.[1733] There is, however, the special case of Article 10 Rome III; a provision that exists alongside the public policy clause of Article 12 Rome III. In a break from private international law tradition, it already leads to the *lex fori* if foreign law in the abstract runs afoul of certain tenets. It is not to be interpreted restrictively as a regular public policy provision.[1734]

Exceptional Character

Several domestic public policy rules contain some indication that they should not be employed easily. Typical operative words are "obvious(ly)" and "manifest(ly)" in relation to the contravention of public policy.[1735] In some cases, one can gather as much from the requirement that "fundamental" "principles" must be violated before the public policy exception can apply.[1736] In the case of Spain, Article 12(3) Spanish Civil Code does not contain

---

the content of foreign law enough to constitute a public policy violation: *ten Wolde*, Yearbook of Private International Law 13 (2011), 389, 396–397.

1729 See *Calvo Caravaca/Carrascosa González*, DIP I, 607.

1730 *Ballarino/Bonomi*, Yearbook of Private International Law 2 (2000), 99, 111; *Giardina*, Rev. crit. DIP 1996, 1, 15.

1731 *Dicey/Morris/Collins*, Conflict of Laws, at 5-005–5-006; *Bogdan*, PIL in Sweden, at 89; respectively.

1732 *Mádl/Vékás*, ZfRV 1982, 266, 280; §12(1) Hungarian PIL Act now seems clearer in this regard.

1733 Article 21 Rome I; Article 26 Rome II; Article 12 Rome III; Article 35 Succession Regulation; Article 31 M-/RP-Property Regulation.

1734 For the controversy surrounding Article 10 Rome III see *supra* section 2.9.5.3.

1735 Article 21 clause 1 Belgian PIL Code; Article 45(1) Bulgarian PIL Code; §4 clause 1 Czech PIL Act; §7 clause 1 Estonian PIL Act; Article 6 clause 1 EGBGB; Article 10:6 Dutch Civil Code.

1736 In this sense for §6 Austrian PIL Act *Beitzke*, RabelsZ 43 (1979), 245, 251; Article 22(1) Portuguese Civil Code *Neuhaus/Rau*, RabelsZ 32 (1968), 500, 506; for Article 2.564 Romanian Civil Code *Avasilencei*, Rev. crit. DIP 2012, 247, 260. As to Article 22 Portuguese Civil Code also see *Moura Ramos*, in: Symeonides (ed.), PIL at the End of the 20th Century, 349, 368: if, pursuant to Article 22(2) Portuguese Civil Code, Portuguese law even in the case

an express limitation, but Article 23 of Law 54/2007 on International Adoption does. In any case, a restrictive application of Article 12(3) Spanish Civil Code may be said to be necessary because the rule constitutes an exception to the principle of the application of foreign law.[1737] Even where there is no textual indication (or where one is not inclined to see one), national commentators often recommend making use of public policy rules only rarely and/or report a court practice to that effect.[1738] This even applies to the Italian example where the draft did contain a textual limitation that ultimately did not become law.[1739] It also applies to Polish private international law, even though a limitation has still not been inserted into the text.[1740] This is also a common position of member states without codified private international law.[1741]

All of the pertinent provisions in the EU private international law regulations require the incompatibility with the public policy of the forum to be "manifest".[1742]

Illustrations of Public Policy

Generally, the interpretation of "public policy" and its violation seems to be a matter left entirely to the courts.[1743] Only a few private international law codes give some indication of what they (do not) mean by "violation of public policy". As far as the definition of public policy is concerned, there are some

of a public policy violation only applies in a subsidiary way, this reinforces the exceptional nature of the entire provision.

1737 *Esplugues Mota/Azcárraga Monzonís*, Spanish Report, 21.

1738 §6 Austrian PIL Act: *Neumayr*, in: ABGB-Kurzkommentar, §6 IPRG at 2; *Wendehorst*, in: Verschraegen (ed.), Austrian Law, 79, 101. Article 33 Greek Civil Code: *Vassilakakis*, RHDI 63 (2010), 103, 107; see also *Vrellis*, in: Symeonides (ed.), PIL at the End of the 20th Century, 243, 254. §7 Hungarian PIL Code 1979: *Nagy*, PIL in Hungary, at 73; *Mádl*, RHDI 44 (1991), 227, 241; *id./Vékás*, ZfRV 1982, 266, 279. Article 22 Portuguese Civil Code: *Moura Ramos*, in: Symeonides (ed.), PIL at the End of the 20th Century, 349, 368–369.

1739 *Pocar*, IPRax 1997, 145, 152; the foreign observer can be somewhat sceptical, *Kindler*, RabelsZ 61 (1997), 227, 256.

1740 As to the identical predecessor (*Pazdan/Gralla*, WiRO 2011, 299, 300) of Article 7 Polish PIL Act: "rarely applied" (*Pazdan*, in: Lewaszkiewicz-Petrykowska (ed.), Rapports Polonais, 49, 59), "cautiously applied and narrowly interpreted" (*Pajor*, in: Symeonides (ed.), PIL at the End of the 20th Century, 329, 344); but also see *Mączyński*, Yearbook of Private International Law 6 (2004), 203, 209 ("extensive use").

1741 E.g. *Dicey/Morris/Collins*, Conflict of Laws, at 5-003 (England); *Wiwinius*, DIP, 61 (Luxembourg); *Bogdan*, PIL in Sweden, at 84; *Eek*, Swedish Conflict of Laws, 202.

1742 Article 21 Rome I; Article 26 Rome II; Article 12 Rome III; Article 35 Succession Regulation; Article 31 M-/RP-Property Regulation.

1743 E.g. the Lithuanian Supreme Court as to Lithuanian public policy (today: Article 1.11(1) Lithuanian Civil Code): Lietuvos Auksciausiojo Teismo Teiseju Senato Nutarimas No. 28 del Lietuvos Respublikos teismu praktikos taikant tarptautines privatines teises normas (21.12.2000), cited in: *Ravluševičius*, IPRax 2003, 272, 273 with note 5. As this statement precedes the new Lithuanian Civil Code, it is no contradiction when *Mikelėnas*, in: Yearbook of Private International Law 7 (2005), 161, 166, states that there is no case law yet concerning public policy.

domestic private international law provisions specifying that a country's constitution and/or human rights shape this concept.[1744] Occasionally, a rule sets forth what *cannot* constitute a violation of public policy. §7(2) Hungarian PIL Code 1979 provided that a judge is not to eschew the application of foreign law (i.e. assume a violation of public policy) simply because the socio-economic system of the foreign country was different from the Hungarian one. Historically, this referred to the application of bourgeois law; later it made sure that law from planned economies was not to be disregarded *per se*.[1745]

The European Commission had envisioned a similar negative illustration of public policy violations for the Succession Regulation. Article 27(2) of the Succession Regulation proposal[1746] clarified that

> [i]n particular, the application of a rule of the law determined by this Regulation may not be considered to be contrary to the public policy of the forum on the sole ground that its clauses regarding the reserved portion of an estate differ from those in force in the forum.

The statement was then relegated to being a recital;[1747] in the end, it disappeared altogether. One cannot argue, however, that the lack of this illustration means that a public policy violation *can* now be based "on the sole ground that its clauses regarding the reserved portion of an estate differ" from the *lex fori*, for this would amount to an *abstract* appraisal of foreign law not permitted by Article 35 Succession Regulation.[1748]

Conversely, Article 24 Rome II Proposal had established a positive *European Community* public policy standard, which would have been violated by the application of rules providing for non-compensatory damages.[1749] Recital 32 clause 2 Rome II now sets forth that *domestic* law may consider the application of such rules a violation of public policy.

Article 13 Rome III can be regarded as a similar positive illustration[1750] of the public policy clause that immediately precedes it. Pursuant to this provision,

---

1744 Article 4 Croatian PIL Act; Article 6 clause 2 EGBGB; Article 1.11(1) clause 1 Lithuanian Civil Code; Article 2.564(2) Romanian Civil Code.

1745 *Nagy*, PIL in Hungary, at 74. *Raffai/Szabó*, Acta Juridica Hungarica 51 (2010), 136, 145, provide a somewhat different interpretation (no application of public policy with "discriminatory intent").

1746 COM(2009) 154 final.

1747 See *Lechner's* draft report on the proposal for a regulation of the European Parliament and of the Council on jurisdiction, applicable law, recognition and enforcement of decisions and authentic instruments in matters of succession and the creation of a European Certificate of Succession (23.02.2011), 13 (PE441.200v02-00).

1748 *Wilke*, RIW 2012, 601, 607.

1749 Article 24 COM(2003) 427 final (40).

1750 See *Winkler von Mohrenfels*, in: MüKoBGB, Art. 13 Rom III-VO at 3; many others simply state that it is a "special public policy clause", see *Roth*, in: Calliess (ed.), Rome Regulations, Art. 13 Rome III at 1 (with further references).

no court of a participating member state is required to pronounce a divorce if its own law does not provide for divorce, or does not deem the marriage in question to be valid. The first alternative is already moot, for Malta, the last member state not providing for divorce, introduced it in 2011.[1751] The second alternative pertains in particular to same-sex marriages ("*such* a marriage"[1752]). If Article 13 Rome III did not exist, member states that do not provide for same-sex marriage might have had recourse to Article 12 Rome III in order to refuse the application of a foreign law under which a same-sex marriage is valid. Article 13 Rome III clarifies that they may indeed do so.

Link with the Forum

Pursuant to the Belgian and Bulgarian PIL Codes, it is necessary to examine the degree to which the given situation is connected to the forum state.[1753] The notion of a necessary link with the forum also appears in other member states.[1754] One might ultimately say that there can be no incompatibility with local public policy if the situation at hand is not (sufficiently) connected to the forum state.[1755]

Public Policy in Relation to Other Member States

In light of "[m]utual trust in the administration of justice" in the member states,[1756] one might consider limiting the application of public policy reservations to third states,[1757] or in some way loosening the standard when concerned with the application of the law of another member state.[1758]

1751 *Roth*, in: Calliess (ed.), Rome Regulations, Art. 13 Rome III at 2.

1752 Recital 26 subparagraph 2 clause 1 Rome III (emphasis added).

1753 Article 21 clause 2 Belgian PIL Code; Article 45(2) Bulgarian PIL Code.

1754 In Spanish private international law, there even is a statutory provision to this effect (Article 23 of the Law 54/2007 on International Adoption), albeit not in the general Article 12(3) Spanish Civil Code. See also, e.g., *Neumayr*, in: ABGB-Kurzkommentar, §6 IPRG at 1; OGH 4Ob199/00v; *Audit*, in: Bermann/Picard (eds.), Introduction to French Law, 453, 455; *Cachard*, DIP, at 643–645; *Loussouarn/Bourel/de Vareilles-Sommières*, DIP, at 403–410 (France); *Spickhoff*, Der ordre public im IPR, 97–99 (Germany); *Panopoulos*, RHDI 66 (2013), 319 (Greece); *ten Wolde*, Yearbook of Private International Law 13 (2011), 389, 397; *Rammeloo*, EuLF 2010, I-180, I-185 (the Netherlands). The idea and prevalence of a sufficient link with the forum was important enough for *Lagarde*, Public Policy, to include it in his "final observations" (at 64). See also *Wurmnest*, in: Leible (ed.), General Principles, §14.03[D].

1755 *Siehr*, Yearbook of Private International Law VII (2005), 17, 53.

1756 Recital 18 Enforcement Order Regulation; Recital 27 clause 2 Order for Payment Procedure Regulation.

1757 There seems to be general consensus that a public policy reservation is needed where the governing law is that of a third state, see only *Wurmnest*, in: Leible (ed.), General Principles, §14.02[B][1] with further references.

1758 See already *Zweigert*, RabelsZ 16 (1951), 387, 393.

No such idea, however, has found its way into the general public policy clauses in domestic private international law. If recent French Supreme Court practice in relation to the application of German law is any indication,[1759] things are not going to change soon either.

While the EU has refrained from inserting public policy clauses into several procedural instruments,[1760] the Brussels I regime still[1761] provides for such reservations despite also being based on the idea of mutual trust.[1762] While all EU private international law regulations contain public policy clauses, none of them offer any indication that a special standard should be applied when faced with the law of another member state.[1763] The Commission's idea to exempt the maintenance law of member states from the public policy clause did not become law.[1764] Nor have the erstwhile plans of the Legal Committee of the European Parliament[1765] to depart from the *ex officio* application of public policy reservations become reality in private international law (unlike in the Brussels regime[1766]).

The Consequences of a Violation of Public Policy

Once a violation of public policy has been determined, the respective court will refuse the application of the offensive foreign legal rule.[1767] But the case must be resolved, of course; some legal rule must be applied. Several domestic

1759 Cass 1e civ of 8.7.2015, No. 14-17.880. To be sure, the court did not say itself that there was a public policy violation, but it found fault with the appellate court's decision for not considering the question.

1760 See the Enforcement Order Regulation, the Order for Payment Procedure Regulation, and the Small Claims Procedure Regulation.

1761 The Commission had suggested to do away with the public policy reservation first when the Brussels Convention was turned into Brussels I (see COM(1997) 609 final, at 20), and again when Brussels I was recast (COM(2010) 748, 6).

1762 See Articles 45(1)(a), 58(1) subparagraph 1 and Recital 26 clause 1 Brussels Ibis; Articles 22(a), 23(a) and Recital 21 Brussels IIbis.

1763 *Wurmnest*, in: Leible (ed.), General Principles, §14.02[B][2].

1764 See Article 20 clause 2 of the Proposal for a Council Regulation on jurisdiction, applicable law, recognition and enforcement of decisions and cooperation in matters relating to maintenance obligations, COM(2005) 649 final.

1765 See the Report on the proposal for a regulation of the European Parliament and of the Council on the law applicable to non-contractual obligations ("Rome II") of 27.6.2005, A6-0211/2005, 33 (Amendment 50).

1766 See Article 45(1)(a) Brussels Ibis ("on the application of any interested party"). If important state interests are implicated, however, it has been suggested that a court is able to raise public policy of its own motion, *Leible*, in: Rauscher (ed.), EuZPR/EuIPR I, Art. 45 Brüssel Ia-VO at 3; but see *Fitchen*, in: Dickinson/Lein (eds.), Brussels I Recast, at 13.259 and at 13.275.

1767 Under EU private international law, the court "may" do so, but this wording is due to the EU perspective. It borders on the unthinkable that a court determines a violation of its public policy and does nothing about it.

private international law codes expressly provide the next step, usually in the final paragraph or clause of the respective public policy provision.[1768] In some countries, the judge must now apply the *lex fori* (Austria, Estonia, Hungary, Lithuania, and Romania). Others have the judge eventually apply the *lex fori*, too, but only if the foreign law does not have another relevant provision (Belgium, Bulgaria, and Portugal), or if an alternative connecting factor cannot be employed (Italy[1769]).[1770] Other countries have left the question entirely to the courts,[1771] even when the legislator was aware of foreign provisions setting forth the consequences of a public policy violation. This is the case in Germany: the German legislator, cognisant of §6 clause 2 Austrian PIL Act, wanted to facilitate "flexible and nuanced solutions", apparently not limited to application of German law.[1772]

5.7. SUBSTITUTION

Once the governing law has been determined, be it the *lex fori* or foreign law,[1773] a case with international elements can raise a further issue. What if a rule of the *lex causae* sets forth requirements that, in the case at hand, could only have been met abroad and/or[1774] pursuant to foreign[1775] law? Presumably, few legal systems will mind that, e.g. an offer or an acceptance is declared beyond the territorial reach of the legal system.[1776] Things are not as easy, however, if a requirement has strong legal implications. Common examples

---

1768 §6 clause 2 Austrian PIL Act; Article 21 clause 3 Belgian PIL Code; Article 45(3) Bulgarian PIL Code; §7 Estonian PIL Act clause 2; §7(3) Hungarian PIL Code 1979/§12(1) Hungarian PIL Act; Article 16(2) Italian PIL Act; Article 1.11(1) clause 2 Lithuanian Civil Code; Article 22(2) Portuguese Civil Code; Article 2.564(1) clause 2 Romanian Civil Code.

1769 The effect of Article 16(2) clause 1 Italian PIL Act is limited because there are only few of the presupposed conflicts rules with alternative connecting factors, *Pocar/Honorati*, in: Symeonides (ed.), PIL at the End of the 20th Century, 279, 294.

1770 See *de Lima Pinheiro*, Yearbook of Private International Law 14 (2012/2013), 153, 170, who expressly recommends Article 22(2) Portuguese Civil Code and Article 16(2) Italian PIL Act to the EU legislator.

1771 E.g. the Netherlands, *Boele-Woelki/van Iterson*, in: van Erp/van Vliet (eds.), Netherlands Report, 145, 155.

1772 BT-Drucks. 10/504, 44.

1773 It is generally acknowledged that the same issue arises irrespective of which law is the *lex causae: F. Sturm/G. Sturm*, in: Staudinger, Einl. zum IPR at 259; *Looschelders*, RabelsZ 64 (2000), 420, 423, against the position of the reviewed book, *Schulz*, Die Subsumtion ausländischer Rechtstatsachen, 63 and passim.

1774 See *Mansel*, in: FS Kropholler, 353, 365.

1775 "Foreign" and "abroad" in this context are to be evaluated from the perspective of the *lex causae*. It follows that "even" the *lex fori* can be "foreign" law.

1776 For another rather unproblematic example see Lawson v Fox, [1974] A. C. 803, 808 (references to "driving or being on duty" in the Transport Act 1968 not confined to "driving or being on duty in England only").

are procedural acts (does an action before the courts of another country temporarily halt the period of prescription?[1777]) or the involvement of certain legal personnel (public notaries, registrars). Typically, such requirements are set up with the respective institutions of the legal system at issue in mind. An example with particular European Union implications is the right to redress, as provided for by Article 4 Consumer Sales Directive. It requires that the final seller is liable to the consumer – a liability that could easily be governed by a law different to the one applicable to the contract between the final seller and her seller.

At least by and large, this is an issue of substantive law.[1778] Yet, as it only occurs in a case with "international elements",[1779] some connection to private international law is incontrovertible. As has perhaps already become obvious from the description in the previous paragraph, there is also a close connection to another (formally general) feature of private international law, the incidental question: if the incidental question is to be decided pursuant to a law different from the one applicable to the main question – which can happen regardless of one's stance on how to deal with incidental questions[1780] – the present issue arises.[1781] Accordingly, the topic appears, if at all, in private international law textbooks and other contributions by private international law cognoscenti. It is usually discussed in the context of "general" issues.[1782] After all, Lewald coined the term "substitution" in his discussion of *règles générales des conflits des lois.*[1783]

Similar to the issue of evasion of the law,[1784] the term "substitution", taken literally, proves rather elusive. Ultimately, if a requirement of domestic

---

1777 For a relatively recent Austrian example see *Budzikiewicz*, ZEuP 2010, 415, with comparative remarks.

1778 *Verschraegen*, IPR, at 1363; *Kropholler*, IPR, §33 I, II (231); already *Neuhaus*, Grundbegriffe, §46 IV (351); *Kegel/Schurig*, IPR, §1 VIII 2e (66); *von Bar/Mankowski*, IPR I, §7 at 240; *Schulz*, Die Subsumtion ausländischer Rechtstatsachen, 37–39; *Hug*, Die Substitution im IPR, 1; *Schmidt*, Sc. St. L. 12 (1968), 93, 94; but see *F. Sturm/G. Sturm*, in: Staudinger, Einl. zum IPR at 259; *Mansel*, in: FS Kropholler, 353, 364, considers substitution at the level of conflicts rules possible but unusual.

1779 Already *Lewald*, Règles générales, 134 (as part of the "application of foreign law"). Also see *Mansel*, in: FS Kropholler, 353, 371 (substitution being a problem area "relevant" for conflict of laws).

1780 Conflicts provisions of both the *lex fori* and the *lex causae* can lead to a different law than the *lex causae*; *Mansel*, in: FS Kropholler, 353, 364.

1781 *Mansel*, in: FS Kropholler, 353, 364–365; *von Bar/Mankowski*, IPR I, §7 at 242.

1782 *Kropholler*, IPR, §33 (231); *von Bar/Mankowski*, IPR I, §7 at 239–245; *Hug*, Die Substitution im IPR, 23. *Bogdan*, PIL in Sweden, at 78, likewise discusses problems of the interpretation of substantive rules of the governing law among the "basic terms", but under the heading "assimilation/adaptation". Differently *Kegel/Schurig*, IPR, §1 VIII 2e (66): part of the introductory chapters and of the discussion of the dichotomy of conflicts rules and substantive rules.

1783 *Lewald*, Règles générales, 132.

1784 *Supra* section 3.3.

substantive law can be met by something that occurred abroad, there is no need to substitute anything for anything *actually*; the domestic rule simply applies. If one of its requirements cannot be met by something that occurred abroad, "substitution" is impossible to begin with.[1785] Thus, the term should rather be read merely to designate the problem at hand: is it *possible* to fulfil a requirement set by the applicable law if the relevant facts occurred abroad? This is a question of interpretation of the *lex causae*, with the pivotal criterion generally assumed to be the "equivalence" of the foreign legal institution.[1786]

As the issue of substitution can occur regardless of the conflicts rule that led to the application of the *lex causae*, it is a formally general issue in the strict sense.[1787]

The general provisions of private international law of the member states do not deal with substitution; the topic mainly surfaces in German legal literature.[1788] EU private international law does not contain any rules on substitution either. As the issue concerns not only the content/interpretation of substantive law as such, but also the content/interpretation of substantive law of third states (i.e. non-members of the EU), the question of competence[1789] is presumably a factor influencing this lack of an EU rule, together with an apparent lack of interest in the topic across Europe. Yet there is a 2007 resolution by the Institute of International Law on "Substitution and Equivalence in Private International Law"; it is generally in line with the statements made here.[1790]

1785 See *Schulz*, Die Subsumtion ausländischer Rechtstatsachen, 54.

1786 *von Hein*, in: MüKoBGB, Einl. IPR at 235; *F. Sturm/G. Sturm*, in: Staudinger, Einl. zum IPR at 259; *Franzina*, in: LA Picchio Forlati, 185, 188; *Budzikiewicz*, ZEuP 2010, 415, 425–426; *Mansel*, in: FS Kropholler, 353, 368; *Kropholler*, IPR, §33 II 2 (232); *von Bar/Mankowski*, IPR I, §7 at 243; *Lewald*, Règles générales, 135. This is yet another point of contact between private international law and comparative law, see only *Basedow*, JZ 2016, 269, 278.

1787 Expressly for a (formally) general nature of the issue *Lüttringhaus*, in: Basedow/Rühl/Ferrari/de Miguel Asensio (eds.), Encyclopedia of PIL, s. v. "Substitution", I 2. See also *Kreuzer*, in: Jud/Rechberger/Reichelt (eds.), Kollisionsrecht in der Europäischen Union, 1, 4, who, however, considers a general *rule* on substitution impossible to make.

1788 *Jayme*, IPRax 2008, 298; see already the references in footnote 1781; but also see *Garcimartín Alférez*, DIP, at 21.18, *Schmidt*, Sc. St. L. 12 (1968), 93, 94 and 113–119, and the references in *Looschelders*, Die Anpassung im IPR, 66–67 (notes 33–35). Also see *Mayer/Heuzé*, DIP, at 273 (but conflated with "adaptation"); *Calvo Caravaca/Carrascosa González*, DIP I, 590 (as one of three techniques of "adaptation"). The English case referred to *supra* in footnote 1779 which could at least have functioned as a springboard into the topic of substitution does not seem to be cited in common law textbooks on private international law.

1789 But see *infra* Chapter 5, section 1.6.2. (Substantive Provisions).

1790 The resolution is published, e.g., in IPRax 2008, 297. See in particular its Article 2 (making equivalence the decisive factor) and Article 4 (leaving it to the *lex causae* to decide what is equivalent). *Kreuzer*, in: Jud/Rechberger/Reichelt (eds.), Kollisionsrecht in der Europäischen Union, 1, 4, had assumed that substitution would not lend itself to positivisation.

5.8. TRANSPOSITION

If legal positions/rights established under one (originally applicable) law are supposed to somehow continue existing under another (now applicable) law in which no exact counterpart for them exists, the issue called "transposition"[1791] arises. It follows from this description that it is essentially a product of a *conflit mobile*.[1792]

Substitution, transposition, and adaptation can be bracketed together as parts of the method of "consideration" in private international law.[1793] Yet for present purposes, they must be distinguished. Unlike the notion of adaptation, under which the applicable law can be adjusted to reach an adequate result,[1794] transposition concerns the adjustment of foreign legal positions to the applicable law.[1795] Similar to the idea of substitution, functional equivalence is generally regarded as the guiding principle.[1796] But transposition, as the term suggests, concerns the *transfer* of a foreign institution into the governing law, whereas substitution is only about a foreign phenomenon *fulfilling a requirement* set by an applicable legal rule. In the latter case, the foreign phenomenon "remains foreign", is still governed by foreign law.[1797]

As the issue of transposition is not confined to one area of private international law, it is at least[1798] formally general. As it only arises after the *lex causae* has been identified,[1799] it is most appropriately discussed as a question of the governing law.

Member States

No member state has enacted a formally general provision on transposition in its private international law code.[1800] Specific provisions occasionally touch

---

1791 *Lewald* also coined this term, Règles générales, 129–132.

1792 See *von Bar/Mankowski*, IPR I, §7 at 246; *Hug*, Die Substitution im IPR, 23; *Lewald*, Règles générales, 130. As to the *conflit mobile* itself see already *supra* section 4.2.

1793 *M.-P. Weller*, RabelsZ 81 (2017), 747, 775–779.

1794 *Infra* 5.10.

1795 *Looschelders*, Die Anpassung im IPR, 183; also see *von Hein*, in: MüKoBGB, Einl. IPR at 221.

1796 *von Hein*, in: MüKoBGB, Einl. IPR at 229; *Franzina*, in: LA Picchio Forlati, 185, 188; *Garcimartín Alférez*, DIP, at 21.19; *Kropholler*, IPR, §54 III 1 b (561); *von Bar/Mankowski*, IPR I, §7 at 246; *Lewald*, Règles générales, 131.

1797 See *von Hein*, in: MüKoBGB, Einl. IPR at 229.

1798 No cases of transposition easily come to mind e.g. in the field of (non-)contractual obligations.

1799 Also *Franzina*, in: LA Picchio Forlati, 185, 188 (about "adaptation", understood broadly, on the level of EU law).

1800 §3(2) Hungarian PIL Code 1979 dealt with legal institutions unknown to Hungarian law which makes it seem pertinent at first sight – see now §4(2) Hungarian PIL Act. It was generally regarded to be a provision solely for characterisation, however: *Nagy*, PIL in Hungary, at 50; *Raffai/Szabó*, Acta Juridica Hungarica 51 (2010), 136,143.

upon the issue, however.[1801] Some scholars (many do not make any mention of it at all) discuss the topic in a general manner, unconnected to specific choice of law provisions.[1802]

European Union

No Rome Regulation contains a provision on transposition either. There are, however, Article 31 Succession Regulation and Article 29 M-/RP-Property Regulation. By their wording and positioning (in the context of the provision on [certain] overriding mandatory provisions,[1803] and close to the provisions on *renvoi* and public policy), they are applicable regardless of which conflicts provision of the respective regulation determines the governing law. In this sense, therefore, they have a formally general character. While they do not concern all cases of transposition, they cover its paradigmatic[1804] instance: rights *in rem*.

Admittedly, Article 31 Succession Regulation and Article 29 M-/RP-Property Regulation go by their official title "adaptation" and require unknown rights *in rem* to be "adapted". As the corresponding term is consistently used in other languages too,[1805] a translation error can be excluded. The ECJ apparently saw no need not to stick with the terminology of Article 31 in its first decision on the Succession Regulation.[1806] The content of these provisions, however, clearly concerns what traditional private international law terminology designates "transposition".[1807] During the Brussels I recast proceedings – Article 54(1) subparagraph 2 Brussels Ibis likewise uses the term "adaptation"[1808] – several

1801 See e.g. §31(2) Austrian PIL Act: the existence of a foreign right is not called into question, but transposition can be necessary. Also Article 43(2) EGBGB, from which at least can be gathered *that* it is for German law to decide how to reconcile effects of a foreign right *in rem* with the now applicable German law, but not *how* to do that; see *Wendehorst*, in: MüKoBGB, Art. 43 EGBGB at 145 and 147–153.

1802 See already the references in footnote 1795; also *von Hein*, in: MüKoBGB, Einl. IPR at 220 (expressly stating that the issue is not only one relating to rights *in rem*); *Garcimartín Alférez*, DIP, at 21.18 (but in a section also separate from the "consecuencia jurídica"); *Calvo Caravaca/Carrascosa González*, DIP I, 590 (as one of three techniques of "adaptation"). *Franzina*, in: LA Picchio Forlati, 185, 186, considers Article 31 Succession Regulation and Article 54 Brussels Ibis as an indication of the emergence of an institute of the "general part".

1803 See *supra* section 2.9.5.4. for Article 30 Succession Regulation.

1804 *von Bar/Mankowski*, IPR I, §7 at 246; see also *Lewald*, Règles générales, 131.

1805 Dutch: "aanpassing"; French: "adaptation"; German: "Anpassung"; Italian: "adattamento"; Spanish: "adaptación".

1806 ECJ Case C-218/16, Aleksandra Kubicka, intervening party, v Przemysława Bac, acting in her capacity as notary, ECLI:EU:C:2017:755 at 61–64.

1807 See (for the Succession Regulation) *Dannemann*, in: Leible (ed.), General Principles, §15.02[C]; *Looschelders*, FS Coester-Waltjen, 531, 540; sticking with the terminology found in the regulations, however, *Martiny*, ZfPW 2017, 1, 27–28.

1808 The translations are consistent, too: Dutch: "aanpassing"; French: "adaptation"; German: "Anpassung"; Italian: "adattamento"; Spanish: "adaptación".

delegations also pointed out that "adaptation", as used by the EU legislator, "actually" means "transposition".[1809] One might read the sibylline reference of Recital 17 Succession Regulation and Recital 26 M-/RP-Property Regulation to "other forms of adaptation" as an indication that, for the purposes of EU private international law, "adaptation" is supposed to be the general term,[1810] encompassing both transposition as well as adaptation *stricto sensu*.

5.9. ERRONEOUS ASSUMPTIONS CONCERNING THE APPLICABLE LAW

Occasionally, parties adjust their behaviour – acts or omissions[1811] – to comply with one law, erroneously assuming it to be applicable to their case, when, from the beginning or later on, their case is actually governed by another law. Lewald classified such cases as an instance of (a need for) transposition.[1812] Under the supposition that as much content of the "wrong law" as possible must be preserved under the actual *lex causae*,[1813] the consequences of both notions are indeed rather similar. The requirement of an error, however, distinguishes both cases.

The conclusion that there has been an erroneous assumption concerning the applicable law can only be drawn once the actually applicable law has been determined. Therefore, it makes sense to regard the issue as one appropriately allocated to the "governing law" element of a conflicts rule.[1814] This should not detract attention from the fact that a solution does not necessarily have to be found at the level of the *lex causae*, although this is arguably the main

1809 See Council Document ST 9946 2012 INIT (15 May 2012), 2, in which the Italian, Portuguese and Spanish delegations distinguish "adaptation" in (now) Article 54 Brussels Ibis from "adaptation *stricto sensu*" and substitution, noting that the operation pursuant to Article 54 Brussels Ibis is "also" known as transposition. Also see *Fitchen*, in: Dickinson/Lein (eds.), Brussels I Recast, at 13.483, who seems hesitant at first to call the operation under Article 54 Brussels Ibis "adaptation" without inverted commas; quite similarly in this regard *Wendehorst*, in: MüKoBGB, Art. 43 EGBGB at 153, who also uses inverted commas to discuss "adaptation" under the Succession Regulation. *Franzina*, in: LA Picchio Forlati, 185, 187, expressly wants to avoid a strict distinction of all the terms associated with "adaptation" when analysing the provisions of EU law.

1810 Also see *Gössl*, RabelsZ 82 (2018), 618, 622, who considers transposition and substitution to be special cases of adaptation in general; similarly *Calvo Caravaca/Carrascosa González*, DIP I, 590.

1811 The German term for the issue, "Handeln unter falschem Recht", could be interpreted to mean only acts, *Münzer*, Handeln unter falschem Recht, 3–4.

1812 *Lewald*, Règles générales, 129.

1813 *von Bar/Mankowski*, IPR I, §7 at 247.

1814 *Symeonides*, Codifying Choice of Law, 198, analyses the pertinent Dutch provision (*infra*) as an escape device. As already pointed out *supra* (section 2.9.2.1.), this is a perspective on issues of private international law entirely different from the one employed here. Neither excludes the other.

way to deal with the issue (does the *lex causae* leave any room to take account of what the parties relied upon?[1815]). However, it is also a solution both theoretically possible[1816] and, as will be shown presently, found in the member states, to handle such erroneous assumptions at the level of conflicts rules. To the extent that conflicts rules provide the solution that the law assumed to apply actually applies, there has ultimately been no error.[1817] Once again[1818] a concept is at issue that does not deserve its name if viewed *ex post*.

As there is no telling in what context parties rely upon a law that is not applicable, the issue is formally general. If it is mentioned at all in scholarly writings, it often appears among statements that are separate from any specific conflicts provisions.[1819]

A search for a formally general provision concerning this issue, either in the domestic private international law of the member states or in EU private international law, comes to nothing – with two exceptions. First, §24 Czech PIL Act allows for the exceptional application of a law not determined by the pertinent rules if this conforms with, in particular, the parties' reasonable expectations regarding the application of another law. Second, Dutch private international law, among its general provisions, also contains a provision dealing with at least a subset of this issue. Pursuant to Article 10:9 Dutch Civil Code, if the law applicable under foreign private international law attributes certain consequences to a fact, these consequences may[1820] also be attributed to that fact where Dutch conflicts provisions deem a different law applicable – provided that not doing so "would constitute an unacceptable violation of the legitimate expectations of the parties or of legal certainty".

A provision like Article 10:9 Dutch Civil Code was not widely discussed prior to enacting it,[1821] in particular not as one applicable throughout all of Dutch private international law.[1822] Its content has been dubbed "*fait accompli* exception"[1823] or "doctrine of the accomplished fact".[1824] This description partly

1815 *Kegel/Schurig*, IPR, §1 VIII 2 d (66); *von Bar/Mankowski*, IPR I, §7 at 247; see already *Lewald*, Règles générales, 129 (implicitly). In particular, this concerns the interpretation of declarations made by the parties against the background of the law they assumed to be applicable, see *Dannemann*, in: FS Stoll, 417, 426–428.

1816 In detail *Münzer*, Handeln unter falschem Recht, 34–124.

1817 *Münzer*, Handeln unter falschem Recht, 4–5.

1818 See *supra* section 3.3. for evasion of the law and *supra* section 5.7. for substitution.

1819 See the references in footnote 1818.

1820 There is room for discretion: *Goldstein*, Rev. crit. DIP 2018, 3, 9; *Strikwerda*, Inleiding, 2 H 75; *Vonken*, Algemeen deel IPR, at 378; *ten Wolde*, Yearbook of Private International Law 13 (2011), 389, 401.

1821 *Vonken*, Algemeen deel IPR, at 445; *ten Wolde*, Yearbook of Private International Law 13 (2011), 389, 403; also see *Strikwerda*, Inleiding, 2 H 75.

1822 *ten Wolde*, NIPR 2010, 430, 432.

1823 *ten Wolde*, Yearbook of Private International Law 13 (2011), 389, 400; *id.*, NIPR 2010, 430; see also the Explanatory Memorandum, Kamerstukken II 2009/2010, 32317, No. 3, 19.

1824 *Symeonides*, Codifying Choice of Law, 198.

obfuscates that the rule concerns the parties' *assumptions* much more than established *facts*.[1825] Article 10:9 Dutch Civil Code seems to presuppose that the parties relied on the application of foreign private international law.[1826] This exceptional[1827] provision thus covers a case in which the parties assumed that the private international law of a foreign state would be applicable to their case and lead to one law, when, in reality/ultimately, Dutch private international law applies and leads to another law.[1828] In short: the provision is (at least[1829]) about an erroneous assumption concerning the law applicable to the case at hand. By making Dutch conflicts rules yield to foreign conflicts rules, the solution is clearly one of private international law.[1830]

In the Netherlands, one also comes across a special provision that seems to have been designed to prevent errors concerning the applicable law:[1831] Article 10:132 Dutch Civil Code. Where possession of an object has been lost involuntarily and the owner nevertheless makes dispositions in regard of the object, it is likely that the parties concerned assume that the law of the state applies in which the object used to be located. Yet if, in the meantime, the object has been moved to another state, regular conflicts rules would presumably deem that state's law to be applicable. Article 10:132(1) Dutch Civil Code resolves the problem by determining that the law of the state where the object was located prior to the loss of possession applies to the dispositions.

In EU private international law there is no general provision concerned with the problem of erroneous assumption of the applicable law. With Article 10(2) Rome I, however, a specific provision on consent exists that in part covers such mistaken assumptions.[1832] Article 26(3) subparagraph 1

1825 See *Goldstein*, Rev. crit. DIP 2018, 3, 7 and passim.

1826 *ten Wolde*, Yearbook of Private International Law 13 (2011), 389, 402; *id.*, NIPR 2010, 430, 431–432. One wonders whether the parties actually must have formed an idea about the applicable private *international* law. Arguably less strict *Vonken*, Algemeen deel IPR, at 381. Neither *Struycken*, RabelsZ 78 (2014), 593, 610, nor *Boele-Woelki/van Iterson*, in: van Erp/van Vliet (eds.), Netherlands Report, 145, 157, mention this narrow criterion; admittedly, however, neither contribution addresses the requirements in any detail, anyway.

1827 The Dutch legislator itself has stated as much: Kamerstukken II 2009/2010, 32317, No. 3, 19.

1828 It seems doubtful whether the parties must already have *acquired* a right for Article 10:9 Dutch Civil Code to apply (to this effect apparently *Symeonides*, Codifying Choice of Law, 198). While the doctrine enshrined here has also been called the "recognition of acquired rights" by *Boele-Woelki/van Iterson*, in: van Erp/van Vliet (eds.), Netherlands Report, 145, 157–158, the very same authors do not state that the prior acquisition of a right is a requirement. *ten Wolde*, Yearbook of Private International Law 13 (2011), 389, 401, makes no mention of such an element.

1829 See *Goldstein*, Rev. crit. DIP 2018, 3, 24–26, distinguishing Article 10:9 Dutch Civil Code from the concept of the *exception d'ignorance excusable du droit applicable*.

1830 See also *ten Wolde*, NIPR 2010, 430 and 433. *Strikwerda*, Inleiding, 2 H 75, considers it a limitation to Dutch conflicts rules.

1831 See already *Stoll*, IPRax 1997, 411, 413.

1832 See already *Münzer*, Handeln unter falschem Recht, 3 and 24–25 (for the now defunct Article 31(2) EGBGB). One can extend the idea to Articles 6(2) Rome III and Article 24(2) M-/RP-Property Regulation.

M-Property Regulation and Article 26(2) subparagraph 1 RP-Property Regulation can also be classified as pertinent specific provisions.[1833]

5.10. ADAPTATION

A further issue at the level of the governing law concerns – to this extent similar to the issue of public policy – the *result* of the application of foreign law. It is possible, albeit rare,[1834] that the application of different foreign laws to one set of facts leads to a result that none of the legal systems involved would have produced, or even intended, by itself. The *locus classicus* is the penniless widow (although she only seems to exist in the scholarly imagination):[1835] the inheritance law of state A does not provide the surviving wife with a share of her late husband's assets, but its matrimonial property law does. In state B, matrimonial property law does not give the surviving wife a share of the deceased's assets, but inheritance law does. Thus, both state A and state B have identified the same social problem, but dealt with it using different legal tools. (This, of course, brings us back to the need for functionalism in comparative law.) As long as a case is governed *in toto* by the law of state A or state B, no problem arises. Assume, however, that conflicts rules determine that for questions of inheritance law the substantive rules of state A apply, but for questions of matrimonial property law the substantive rules of state B do. It seems that the widow would be left out in the cold – even though, and this is crucial, neither state intends this outcome.

From the foregoing example it is apparent that the problem arises if there is "badly coordinated interplay between applicable rules from different jurisdictions",[1836] which manifests itself in particular[1837] in cases of "cumulation of applicable rules", as well as in cases of a "vacuum".[1838] Rules within one and the same legal system are (supposedly) attuned to each other – and, if not, typically some way of interpreting them to arrive at a satisfying outcome can be found, particularly by having one rule prevail over another. Yet when the applicable law consists of parts of one state's law and parts of another state's law, these parts have typically not been calibrated in a way

1833 For (somewhat strangely only) Article 26(2) RP-Property Regulation see *Goldstein*, Rev. crit. DIP 2018, 3, 28–29.

1834 *von Bar/Mankowski*, IPR I, §7 at 253.

1835 *Dannemann*, in: Leible (ed.), General Principles, §15.02[B].

1836 *Dannemann*, in: Leible (ed.), General Principles, §15.03[A].

1837 But not exclusively: in the wake of In Re Duke of Wellington [1947] Ch. 506, 523–524, a case used in common law textbooks (only) to discuss aspects of *renvoi*, a (possible) third class of cases has been identified, see *Looschelders*, Die Anpassung im IPR, 13–15 and 130–133; *Neuhaus*, Grundbegriffe, §47 II 3 (357); also see *Gössl*, RabelsZ 82 (2018), 618, 622–624, for another categorisation.

1838 *Wolff*, PIL, at 154; *Kahn-Freund*, General Problems, 232.

that takes account of each of the parts reciprocally – and, as they originate in different legal systems, no common solution exists as to which should prevail over the other.[1839]

In order to arrive at a tolerable outcome, some corrective measure is necessary. This is what Lewald calls "adaptation";[1840] in English, the issue also is known as "adjustment".[1841,1842] To use Wengler's famous simile:[1843] just as a mechanic must produce an operational car[1844] from parts from different manufacturers that themselves are fully functional but do not necessarily fit each other, a judge must come to a harmonious decision using different laws.

The problem to be resolved through adaptation stems from a fragmentation of the applicable law.[1845] As this fragmentation in turn results from the pertinent conflicts rules, i.e. the tessellated way in which they operate,[1846] the issue is one of private international law. Although it results from decisions made in the context of characterisation[1847] – it is a matter of course that all questions of the governing law depend in some way on prior characterisation[1848] – it is appropriate to allocate it to the "governing law".[1849] Only at this stage can one even decide whether there is any need for correction.[1850] Finally, the issue is formally general because it is not confined to one area of private international law.[1851]

1839 *Looschelders*, Die Anpassung im IPR, 7.

1840 *Lewald*, Règles générales, 139. The issue itself, as *Lewald* acknowledges, had been recognised much earlier: *Zitelmann*, IPR I, 144–149.

1841 *Wolff*, PIL, at 154; for a recent example see *Bogdan*, Rec. des cours 348 (2010), 9, 232.

1842 These terms seem preferable to those such as assimilation (but see *Bogdan*, PIL in Sweden, at 76–81) or "Angleichung" that might be understood to refer to the harmonisation of laws through legislative means, *Neuhaus*, Grundbegriffe, §47 (353–354).

1843 *Wengler*, Rev. crit. DIP 1954, 661, 682–683.

1844 Of course, the simile also works if the object to be produced is a bicycle: *Calvo Caravaca/Carrascosa González*, DIP I, 587.

1845 *Dannemann*, in: Leible (ed.), General Principles, §15.03[B]; *Garcimartín Alférez*, DIP, at 21.20.

1846 *Basedow*, in: Schlosser (ed.), Materielles Recht und Prozeßrecht, 131, 151.

1847 *Kahn-Freund*, General Problems, 231–234, discusses the issues of "cumulation"/"overlaps" and "gaps" as part of the section on characterisation; to the same effect *Wolff*, PIL, at 154, and *Wahl*, in: Schlegelberger (ed.), Rechtsvergleichendes Handwörterbuch, 343. *Wengler*, Rev. crit. DIP 1954, 661, 682, also emphasises the connection between characterisation and adaptation.

1848 Without the requirements of a rule having been met there can be no legal consequence.

1849 To this effect also *Strikwerda*, Inleiding, 2 E 52 (with a broader understanding of adaptation); implicitly *Calvo Caravaca/Carrascosa González*, DIP I, 587–591, and *Schwimann*, IPR, 47–48.

1850 Practically speaking, however, one might revisit the subject matter after one has recognised the problem, and re-characterise an issue in order not to end up with the problem; see *Kegel/Schurig*, IPR, §8 I (358); for the contention that it would be rather short-sighted not to consider the issue one of private international law (because it arises when applying substantive law), already *Schurig*, Kollisionsnorm und Sachrecht, 236.

1851 Also *Kreuzer*, in: Jud/Rechberger/Reichelt (eds.), Kollisionsrecht in der Europäischen Union, 1, 4.

No member state has ventured to make a general provision on adaptation. In some member states, the issue has not even come up in legal doctrine.[1852] For many years, the topic did not appear on the EU landscape either: Rome I, Rome II, and Rome III do not cover adaptation. Article 31 Succession Regulation, however, has possibly thrust the issue into the limelight now; an inchoate debate exists (and presumably will intensify because of Article 29 M-/RP-Property Regulation).[1853] This is ironic. As demonstrated already,[1854] neither Article 31 Succession Regulation nor Article 29 M-/RP-Property Regulation is actually about adaptation in its traditional sense, even though their official title and wording misleadingly suggest that, but about transposition.

A focus on Article 31 Succession Regulation for the issue of adaptation at the EU level is even stranger if one considers the following. First, the Succession Regulation does deal with a classic issue of a potentially absurd outcome: *commorientes*.[1855] If it is not possible to ascertain in what order the death of two or more persons occurred, different applicable laws can lead to irreconcilable results, in particular to the assumption that each person survived the other. In cases where the laws governing the successions[1856] at issue provide differently for this situation, or contain no provision at all, Article 32 Succession Regulation sets forth a substantive[1857] solution.[1858] Second, Article 29(2) subparagraph 2 Succession Regulation resolves an issue of a "vacuum" of rules. Third, Article 33 Succession Regulation gives precedence to a member state's right to appropriate the assets of a vacant estate over another state's right to claim the estate as an heir. These are all genuine instances of adaptation,[1859] even though the provisions themselves only betray that by their content and by the issues to which they pertain, not by their wording. Therefore, in the end there is the odd realisation that the one provision of EU private international law that actually uses the very term does not concern adaptation, while several others that do not use the term do concern it.

1852 *Vrellis*, in: Symeonides (ed.), PIL at the End of the 20th Century, 243, 260.

1853 See *Gössl*, RabelsZ 82 (2018), 618; *Dannemann*, in: Leible (ed.), General Principles, §15; *Franzina*, in: LA Picchio Forlati, 185.

1854 *Supra* section 5.8. (European Union).

1855 *Looschelders*, FS Coester-Waltjen, 531, 540; *Dutta*, in: MüKoBGB, Art. 32 EuErbVO at 1.

1856 The rule must be aligned with Article 1(2)(c) Succession Regulation pursuant to which the presumed death of a person is excluded from the scope of the Succession Regulation. See *Looschelders*, FS Coester-Waltjen, 531, 541, and *Dutta*, in: MüKoBGB, Art. 1 EuErbVO at 19, for two different ways of doing so.

1857 *Dutta*, in: MüKoBGB, Art. 32 EuErbVO at 7; *Wilke*, RIW 2012, 601, 607; *MPI*, RabelsZ 74 (2010), 522, 650.

1858 "[N]one of the deceased persons shall have any rights to the succession of the other or others."

1859 *Dutta*, in: MüKoBGB, vor Art. 20 EuErbVO at 56.

6. FORMALLY GENERAL ISSUES OF SUBSTANTIVE LAW

At the beginning of this chapter, the decisive criterion for the formal approach was identified to be relevance in more than one context. From the perspective of private international law, this means relevance for more than one area of conflicts rules. But what about conflicts rules that are relevant for more than one area of law[1860] because the substantive rules that they determine to be applicable have this kind of relevance? In other words, what about conflicts rules for formally general issues of substantive law?

In books that distinguish between general and special issues (maybe even between a general and a special "part") of private *international* law, "general" issues of *substantive* private law are found among the special issues.[1861] If one supposes a formal approach, it would thus seem that the respective authors apply it to private international law only. A legislator, however, is typically not bound by any such theoretical concept; it is at liberty to place conflicts provisions for formally general issues of substantive law among its "general" provisions of private international law. This part examines whether and to what extent European legislators have indeed done so.

Member States

Domestic private international law offers a couple of examples of respective provisions. For one thing, the general provisions on *certain* collateral questions[1862] can be analysed from this perspective. Neither the question of prescription nor the question of formal validity nor the question of capacity is relevant in only one field of substantive law. General provisions on these collateral questions are thus general provisions on formally general issues of substantive law. For another, there is the unparalleled general provision of §9 Estonian PIL Act that determines the law applicable to agency, as well as to the relationship between a *falsus procurator* and another party. As it does not respond to issues raised by other conflicts provisions, the only way of explaining it as formally general seems to be the overarching relevance of agency in substantive law.

Conversely, when the German legislator inserted a conflicts rule on agency into the EGBGB in the summer of 2017, it did not place it among the

1860 Relevance for more than one rule of substantive law would not be a useful criterion because a typical conflicts rule will determine the application of an entire group of rules within one field, see e.g. Article 12 Rome I for the scope of any the conflicts provisions of Rome I.

1861 For express examples see *Kegel/Schurig*, IPR, §17; *Spickhoff*, Der ordre public im IPR, 156–168; *Schwimann*, IPR, 62–65.

1862 As opposed to a formally general provision on the collateral question as such that does not exist, *supra* section 2.6. (The Collateral Question *de Lege Lata*).

"general provisions". Rather, making use of the vacancy in Article 8 EGBGB,[1863] the provision was put in the following section dealing with legal acts in general. This corresponds to the idea that agency is no issue of the "general part" of private international law, but of the private international law of the general part (of the BGB).[1864]

European Union

Only Rome II deals with certain collateral questions in a separate chapter.[1865] Nevertheless, this separation can be explained along the same lines as in domestic law: at issue are provisions for formally general issues of substantive law.

In both Rome I and Rome II, one also comes across provisions on legal subrogation[1866] and multiple liability.[1867] While they are found among the "Uniform [Conflicts] Rules" of Rome I – and not among its "Other Provisions" – they are supposed to be "Common Rules" in the context of Rome II. How can the latter phenomenon be explained? As the respective provisions determine the applicable law for the subject matters of legal subrogation and multiple liability, they do not relate to *conflicts* issues raised by other provisions of Rome II. If limited to private international law, the formal approach fails. Both subject matters, however, are not only relevant in the field of non-contractual obligations – as the inclusion of corresponding provisions in Rome I shows. Hence, one can analyse them as provisions for formally general issues of substantive law.

An EU conflicts rule on agency is missing as of yet. The topic was nevertheless included in the volume on "general principles" of EU private international law edited by Leible – yet wisely as a "further general issue",[1868] i.e. not allocated to the subject matter, the connecting factor, or the governing law. In his contribution, Gebauer ultimately expresses his preference not to include agency in a potential "Rome 0" Regulation.[1869]

1863 The former Article 8 EGBGB had concerned incapacitation and had become vacant in 1990.

1864 *Spickhoff*, RabelsZ 80 (2016), 481, 496; the legislator itself did not give an express explanation for the position of the new provision, see BT-Drucks. 18/10714, 24–27.

1865 *Supra* section 2.6. (The Collateral Question *de Lege Lata*).

1866 Article 15 Rome I, Article 19 Rome II (among the "Common Rules").

1867 Article 16 Rome I, Article 20 Rome II (among the "Common Rules").

1868 *Gebauer*, in: Leible (ed.), General Principles, §16. Admittedly, the "further general issues" also include the ascertainment and application of foreign law, and thus a topic that arguably can be regarded as an issue of the governing law (*supra* section 5.6.).

1869 *Gebauer*, in: Leible (ed.), General Principles, §16.04[B].

Conclusion

A handful of separate provisions on the domestic and EU levels can (only) be explained as formally general if one broadens the definition to include conflicts rules for issues of overarching relevance in *substantive* law. Private international law doctrine, however, has only very rarely acknowledged such provisions to belong among the "general provisions" of the field.[1870] Yet there are two recent exceptions to this rule. Kühn states that Article 16 Rome I and Article 20 Rome II rank among the rules of a developing "General Part" of EU private international law.[1871] Lehmann suggests "Rome 0" to be an appropriate place for EU conflicts provisions concerning the assumption of contract, as well as the liability for debts incurred by a business prior to takeover, based on the rationale that different kinds of obligations could be at issue.[1872] It appears that both writers' understanding of "general" provisions of private international law includes provisions on formally general issues of substantive law. On the other hand, Gebauer expressly recognises such an approach as potentially justifying the inclusion of agency in "Rome 0", but does not rely on it.[1873]

In conclusion, it would not be utterly unreasonable from a conceptual point of view if the EU legislator were to address (more) issues such as the ones discussed in this section separately from other conflicts provisions. To call the resulting provisions "general" or "common" would also be defensible conceptually, albeit largely not in line with domestic private international law tradition.

7. LEGISLATIVE DEFINITIONS

Finally, and perhaps most obviously, legislative definitions typically satisfy the requirements for being classified as formally general. Legislators usually only provide express definitions of their terms of art separate from the provisions employing those terms if the terms appear more than once. As the tripartite structure of conflicts rules is exhaustive, any term that in a

1870 Most authors simply say nothing at all on the subject. For a (potential) rejection, see *Kreuzer*, in: Jud/Rechberger/Reichelt (eds.), Kollisionsrecht in der Europäischen Union, 1, 4, who considers prescription to be out of place in a "general part". Translated into the categories used here, it appears that he is opposed to broadening the definition of "general" to include the recurring relevance of one subject matter for several areas of substantive private law.

1871 *Kühn*, Die gestörte Gesamtschuld im IPR, 199 – the location of Article 20 Rome II among the "Common Rules" is supposed to be an indication of this.

1872 *Lehmann*, IPRax 2015, 495, 499.

1873 *Gebauer*, in: Leible (ed.), General Principles, §16.02; see already *supra* footnote 1868.

legislator's opinion deserves a definition pertains to (at least) one of the elements. Hence, the majority of respective definition provisions have already appeared in this book. The remaining ones are those formally relevant only within one legal context, such as the clarifications surrounding the term "damage" in Rome II. Accordingly, the following observations by and large just provide a new (cross-section) perspective on issues already dealt with.

Member States

It is extremely rare for the general provisions of a domestic private international law code to contain provisions setting forth definitions. In fact, definitions of individual legal terms are rarely found in national private international law codes at all.[1874] The few existing examples all pertain to the connecting factor. Article 4 Belgian PIL Code, §3 Hungarian PIL Act, and Article 2.570(1) to (4) Romanian Civil Code are the only definitions found among general provisions; they concern the issues of (habitual) residence and domicile.

By its wording, Article 48(7) Bulgarian PIL Code defines habitual residence for the entire code. Yet it is located in a section of general conflicts provisions only for natural persons.[1875] Section 7 Latvian Civil Code (defining the "place of residence") is a special case because this code does not a have a formally separated section on private international law, let alone its general provisions. With Latvian conflicts rules found in Article 8 Latvian Civil Code onwards, and several of them relying on the "residence" of a party, one can at least point to the very close spatial and material proximity of Section 7 Latvian Civil Code to Latvian private international law.

European Union

In EU private international law, there are several provisions with definitions, always in sections separate from specific conflicts provisions. Both Rome I and II provide a meaning for "Member State"[1876] and a partial definition of

---

1874 There *is*, however, Section 9(7) and (8) Private International Law (Miscellaneous Provisions) Act 1995 [UK]. While this act does not meet the definition of code followed here (*supra* Chapter 2, section 1.2.), it does provide an example from national law that not only questions of residence may be subject to definitions in private international law legislation. Section 9(7) clarifies the meaning of "forum", Section 9(8) extends "delict" to quasi-delict.

1875 Similarly, §12 Hungarian PIL Code on domicile and habitual residence was located among rules regarding (natural) persons.

1876 Relevant e.g. for the subject matter of Article 7(1) Rome I, but also for the options for party autonomy in Article 7(3)(a) Rome I.

"habitual residence".[1877] There is also Article 2 Rome II which, judging from its title, seems to be a definition of "[n]on-contractual obligations" – which is only to the quite limited extent that it extends the term to non-contractual obligations likely to arise,[1878] Article 2(2) Rome II. It is actually more about defining "damage" (Article 2(1) and (3)(b) Rome II). Article 3 Rome III is captioned "Definitions" (defining "participating Member State" and "court"), as are Article 3 Succession Regulation and Article 3 M-/RP-Property Regulation. The latter define quite a few terms in their paragraph 1 – among them, in particular, definitions concerning the subject matter: Article 3(1)(a) through (d) Succession Regulation, Article 3(1)(a) and (b) M-Property Regulation, and Article 3(1)(a) through (c) RP-Property Regulation – and one ("court") in their paragraph 2.

Almost none of the terms defined by these provisions necessarily needs a definition in domestic private international law. This is because the respective term, such as "Member State", might not even appear in its conflicts provisions, or because the term, such as "court" or "succession", is well-known or defined elsewhere in national law. This may at least be part of an explanation for the lack of definitions in domestic private international law. For an instrument applying in several countries, however, the need for definitions is much bigger, lest a legal term is understood differently from country to country.

8. CONCLUSIONS

8.1. A COMPREHENSIVE MODEL

At this point, after a possibly overwhelming number of individual examples from domestic and EU law, the formal approach can be evaluated in broader terms. The approach has supposed that a reasonable understanding of "general" pertains to issues relevant in more than one context. For each issue identified by theoretical means, and on the basis of the elements of each conflicts rule, a comparative "empirical" (with statements about the law and legal rules as the objects) analysis was carried out: do domestic legislators and scholars concerned with domestic law recognise the issue? Do they consider it "general", or at least deal with it in a manner suggestive of its recurring relevance, i.e. separately from individual conflicts rules? Do the EU legislator and scholars concerned with EU law deal with the issue, and how?

1877 See Article 1(4) Rome I/Rome II (in the chapter on "Scope") and Article 19 Rome I/ Article 23 Rome II (in the chapter on "Other Provisions"), respectively. As to the latter provisions, already *supra* section 4.5.2.1.

1878 That this does not make any sense if taken literally – how would a non-existing obligation ever be the subject of court proceedings? (see *Halfmeier*, in: Calliess (ed.), Rome Regulations, Art. 2 Rome II at 9) – is of no relevance here.

The standard for an evaluation must be whether and how often issues identified here as theoretically formally general (in the strict sense) are indeed recognised in domestic, as well as EU, law as something "general", at least as something requiring or deserving treatment independent from individual conflicts rules. At the same time, existing law should not recognise too many issues as "general" that the theoretical model does not. The more instances of congruence between the model and the law in the (text-)books, the better the model.

8.1.1. Member States

The formal approach to private international law turns out to be a powerful way to conceptualise domestic "general" rules of the field. In several instances, an issue identified as formally general has a corresponding rule among the "general" provisions in *all* domestic private international law codes and mostly is considered separately from individual conflicts rules, even where there is no such code.[1879] Other issues identified here have corresponding "general" provisions in domestic codes and separate chapters in textbooks in a majority of domestic legal systems of the EU.[1880] Yet other issues have been enshrined in "general" provisions in about half of the member states, and appear as an overarching issue in many a member state's textbooks.[1881] On the other hand, only very few of these issues have *not* been the object of *any* domestic "general" provision;[1882] no issue at all has not at least been considered by scholars to be of overarching importance.

Yet this only is half the battle. The formal approach would still be a poor model if it left many "general" provisions in private international law unaccounted for, i.e. if the model did not comprehensively explain the scope of "general" sections of private international law legislation. But it holds up in this regard too. If one were to work one's way backwards from the issues, i.e. if one were to piece together legislative chapters with general provisions for each member state using the rules referred to in the course of the formal analysis,[1883] one would end up with almost exact replicas of the actual chapters for a vast majority of member states. In other words, while not every member state has a rule for every issue identified here as formally general, almost no member state has drafted a provision and called it "general" for an issue

---

1879 *Renvoi*, *supra* section 5.5.; public policy, *supra* section 5.6.

1880 Non-unified legal systems, *supra* section 5.2.; ascertainment and application of foreign law, *supra* section 5.3.; multi-nationals and stateless people, *supra* sections 4.4.1.2. and 4.4.1.3.

1881 Overriding mandatory provisions, *supra* section 2.9.; evasion of the law, *supra* section 3.

1882 In particular substitution, *supra* section 5.7.; adaptation, *supra* section 5.10.

1883 Admittedly, for many of those references one would need to have a look at the footnotes rather than the text.

not identified here as formally general. In fact, of *all* the domestic private international law provisions designated "general" by their respective legislator, *only four* have not yet appeared as examples of formally general provisions.[1884] Similarly, if one were to complete a table of contents for "preliminary matters", "parties générales" etc. of private international law textbooks, and the only material available was the references above, the result would look much like the originals.

8.1.2. *European Union*

The "Other Provisions" and "Common Rules" of Rome I and II, as well as the provisions without a subject matter clustered together after particular conflicts rules in Rome III, the Succession Regulation, the M-Property Regulation, and the RP-Property Regulation can also be and have already largely been explained from the formal perspective. Indeed, Articles 10 through 16 Rome III, Articles 29 through 38 Succession Regulation, and Articles 29 through 35 M-/RP-Property Regulation have *all* been covered as part of the formal approach.

Of the "Other Provisions" of Rome I, only Articles 26 and 27 are unaccounted for at this point. They set forth the duty of the member states to provide information regarding conventions and the Commission's duty to submit a report on the application of Rome I, respectively. As they have nothing to do whatsoever with the determination or application of the governing law, they can be regarded as foreign objects in a chapter of genuine private international law provisions. It is rather apparent that the EU legislator has (or had – prior to the M-Property Regulation and the RP-Property Regulation) not yet found a consistent location for provisions such as these: the counterparts of Articles 26 and 27 Rome I can be found among the "Final Provisions" of Rome II, and among the "General and Final Provisions" of the Succession Regulation, the M-Property Regulation, and the RP-Property Regulation.[1885] While the "Other Provisions" of Rome III do encompass rules on information to be provided by the (participating) member states and the review clause,[1886] they do *not* cover *renvoi*, public policy or non-unified legal systems, unlike the "Other Provisions" of Rome I.

1884 To wit: §1(1) Austrian PIL Act, Article 2(1) Bulgarian PIL Code, Article 10:3 Dutch Civil Code, and Article 24 Portuguese Civil Code. Article 10:3 Dutch Civil Code sets forth the application of Dutch law for Dutch court proceedings and thus constitutes a conflicts provision for *procedural* matters that is of no further interest here. Article 24 Portuguese Civil Code concerns legal acts aboard a ship or aircraft, and can thus be interpreted as a (formally general) concretisation of territorial connecting factors: *Neuhaus/Rau*, RabelsZ 32 (1968), 500, 505. As to the remaining two provisions, see *infra* Chapter 4, section 4.2.

1885 Articles 29 and 30 Rome II; Articles 78 and 82 Succession Regulation; Articles 64 and 68 M-/RP-Property Regulation.

1886 Articles 17 and 20 Rome III.

The formal approach has addressed all of the "Other Provisions" of Rome II; of its "Common Rules", only Articles 17 and 18 remain. Both provisions seem to concern questions relevant exclusively for non-contractual obligations. Because of this limitation to one context, they could not appear on the radar of the formal approach. Yet both *are* formally general provisions *within* this context: the "rules of safety and conduct" of Article 17 Rome II have (potential) relevance for *all* non-contractual obligations.[1887] The question of a "direct action against the insurer of the person liable" (Article 18 Rome II) is (potentially) relevant for all torts of Chapter II of Rome II.[1888] In other words, both provisions deserve the description "*common* provision"; unlike the formally general issues and provisions discussed before, however, they do not transcend the regulation in which they are found.

8.2. FORMALLY GENERAL ISSUES: A THEORETICAL NECESSITY

In light of this, it becomes questionable to call the issues identified here as formally general "venerable figures of thought",[1889] "essentially traditional points of dispute",[1890] "facteurs de complication" or "facteurs de perturbation",[1891] and the like. Such descriptions are not exactly wrong – many of the issues *have been* known for a long time and *have been* the subject of debate ever since; many of the issues *are* reasons why private international law is not the most accessible field of law; many of them do make the conflicts analysis more complex. There is no doubt, either, that many of these issues were among the "legal-theoretical niceties that American legal realism had come to abhor", and therefore served as a trigger for the "conflicts revolution".[1892]

Yet statements to this effect may also mislead to a great extent. They may suggest that the issues are essentially scholarly inventions, handed down from generation to generation for mostly traditional reasons. They may suggest that the issues in their abstractness are but philosophical concepts, perhaps without any real effect on the application of private international law in practice. To call solutions to general issues "general *principles*"[1893] may also have a

1887 See e.g. *Junker*, in: MüKoBGB, Art. 17 Rom II-VO at 4, noting that the main field of relevance of Article 17 Rome II nevertheless is torts, in particular (traffic) accidents.

1888 It also has a substantively general dimension, *infra* Chapter 4, section 5.

1889 *Siehr*, FS Drobnig, 443, 452, who himself, however, probably is not to be understood in the problematic way to be outlined here.

1890 *Aden*, RIW 2008, 700, 701.

1891 *Mayer/Heuzé*, DIP, at 221, and *Sinay-Cytermann*, in: Azzi/Boskovic (eds.), Quel avenir pour la théorie générale des conflits de lois?, 83, respectively.

1892 *Muir-Watt*, Transnational Legal Theory 2 (2011), 347, 415; *Michaels*, in: FS Kropholler, 151, 157; *Juenger*, in: LA Siehr (2000), 288, 298.

1893 See e.g. Leible (ed.), General Principles, and *Dolinger*, in: Essays in Honor of Juenger, 23.

problematic connotation of this kind, possibly making them seem to be more about abstract values than about concrete answers. If connecting each issue with a particular element of a conflicts rule and indicating why each issue is of relevance in more than one context have demonstrated anything, however, it is the inextricable relationship of these issues with private international law as such.[1894]

Because European private international law – in the member states, as well as on the EU level – consists of omnilateral rules determining the applicable law by way of a subject matter and a connecting factor, certain issues arise.[1895] The only way to avoid the issues is a complete system change; a system change that is highly unlikely for EU private international law at the very least. The entire field of private international law has a remarkable aptitude for absorbing change as it is.[1896] Where EU law creates (or is supposed to create) challenges for "traditional" private international law, they usually concern the content of particular rules, not their structure or way of functioning.[1897] Within the system, "formally general" is not a question of choice, nor is it the artificial product of the imagination of overzealous scholars;[1898] it is a theoretical necessity.

8.3. "FACTORING OUT" GENERAL ISSUES

An intuitively accessible way to summarise the formal approach is the idea of "factoring out" general issues. This figure of speech seems to be used almost exclusively in connection with German law or by German legal scholars. In that context, however, it is almost ubiquitous, with the puzzling exception (thus far) of private international law.

1894 There is, however, no entry on general issues/principles/parts as such in Basedow/Rühl/Ferrari/de Miguel Asensio (eds.), Encyclopedia of PIL, Volumes 1 and 2, and the contributors to the encyclopedia by and large seem to avoid express references to the "generality" of issues (based on a random sample of entries that, in light of the analysis above, could have given the respective author occasion to put an issue in the context of general issues). (*Basedow*, s. v. "Choice of Law", III, however, makes some observations similar to the ones made here.) By being entries in an encyclopedia with a comparative approach and with contributors from all over the world, the entries automatically have some "general" connotation, of course; yet it is not necessarily congruent with the one suggested here.

1895 Accordingly, the set of tools developed over the last century and a half is still suited to deal with EU private international law; *Schurig*, in: Mansel (ed.), IPR im 20. Jahrhundert, 5, 25.

1896 From a historical perspective *Ancel*, Éléments d'histoire du droit international privé, 19.

1897 *Kühne*, ZVglRWiss 114 (2015), 355, 361.

1898 To the same effect *Bogdan*, Rec. des cours 348 (2010), 9, 27; *Siehr*, in: Mélanges Overbeck, 205, 224 (more than mere "tricks").

Content of the Expression

The expression originates in high school arithmetic. According to the distributive law, (a + b)c = ac + bc. Hence, if all the addends in a sum contain the same factor, it can be "factored out". Instead of adding the addends immediately, one adds them only after they have been divided by the factor they share, and one then multiplies the result by that factor. For example, in the sum of ad + bd + cd, d is a factor common to all addends. Factoring it out yields d(a + b + c). To provide a more literal translation of the German "ausklammern" or "vor die Klammer ziehen": "d is drawn in front of the brackets".

History and Prevalence

The originator of the expression in relation to general legal rules is supposed to be Boehmer.[1899] He introduced it into German substantive private law in the 1930s,[1900] using it to describe the relationship between the general part of the BGB (Book 1) and its special parts (Books 2 to 5). Wolff also made use of it in the 1950s to explain the idea of classification in his textbook on private *international* law.[1901] The notion of "factoring out" thus appeared in English and in connection with private international law long ago. It was not supposed to have much impact in either context, however.

By contrast, the German version has enjoyed unprecedented success. There is hardly a German textbook or article on the general part of the BGB in which it does not appear.[1902] It has been picked up for English books on German (substantive) law too.[1903] The expression has also found its way (at least) into criminal law[1904] and environmental law.[1905] It is not limited to describing legislation, either, but has also been used, for example, to explain the line of thought of a doctoral thesis.[1906]

1899 See *Schmidt*, Zivilrechtskodifikation in Brasilien, 315 (with note 113). *Münch*, in: Behrends/Sellert (eds.), Kodifikationsgedanke, 147, 149 (with note 9); *Wieacker*, A History of Private Law in Europe, 376 (with note 8).

1900 Still in the 1954 edition available to me: *Boehmer*, Einführung, 66. For the prior edition see *Wieacker*, A History of Private Law in Europe, 376 (with note 8).

1901 *Wolff*, PIL, at 139.

1902 *Bitter/Röder*, AT, §2 at 12; *Boecken*, AT, at 45; *Boemke/Ulrici*, AT, §2 at 27; *Bork*, AT, §2 at 77; *Brox/Walker*, AT, at 37; *Köhler*, AT, §3 at 14; *Leipold*, BGB I, §3 at 2; *Medicus/Petersen*, AT, at 18; *Stadler*, AT, §1 at 9; *Wertenbruch*, AT, §2 at 1; *Wörlen/Metzler-Müller*, AT, at 64; *Wolf/Neuner*, AT, §7 at 12; *Säcker*, in: MüKoBGB, Einleitung at 27; *Petersen*, Jura 2011, 759; *Merz*, in: FS Larenz, 425, 431.

1903 *Foster/Sule*, German Legal System and Laws, 409.

1904 *Grünewald*, JZ 2011, 972, 975 (even for EU criminal law); *Tiedemann*, in: FS Baumann, 7 with further references.

1905 See *Gellermann*, in: Landmann/Rohmer, Umweltrecht, §22 BNatSchG at 1.

1906 *Müller*, Finanzinstrumente, 48.

Metaphorical Character (in Relation to the BGB)

The expression appears to be self-evident and has proved to be easily remembered. But it comes with a catch: taken literally in its connection with the BGB, it is a blatant lie. It would mean that every single provision in the special parts of the BGB, at some imaginary primordial stage, contained all the provisions found between §1 and §240 BGB, i.e. in Book 1. To give a deliberately obscure and bizarre example: it would mean that §236 BGB (in Book 1) on registered claims against the federal government is somehow a rule necessary for the provision on the merging of bee swarms (§963 BGB in Book 3). Not even the provisions on legal transactions (§§104–185 BGB) have been truly factored out;[1907] after all, they are already irrelevant for the most part in tort law (in Book 2).

The point is not that German legal scholars are poor mathematicians. Nor is it that the general part of the BGB is oversized.[1908] Rather, the point is that "factoring out" is only a metaphor. Those who explain the meaning of this expression in some more detail usually[1909] specify that the provisions of the general part of the BGB apply "to *several* of the subsequent books of the BGB",[1910] that they apply "*as a matter of principle* to the subsequent books of the BGB as well as to the supplementary private law acts",[1911] and that they are "common to all kinds of legal relationships, or at least to a number of important categories of these".[1912] Even with reservations such as these, quite a few rules in the BGB are in the wrong place if one assumes the formal perspective of relevance for more than one book.[1913] Indeed, the content of

1907 *Zitelmann*, GrünhZ 33 (1906), 1, 28, considered this the only issue suitable for general provisions.

1908 *Dannemann*, in: Adams/Bomhoff (eds.), Practice and Theory in Comparative Law, 96, 103 ("notoriously oversized").

1909 But see *Wörlen/Metzler-Müller*, AT, at 64, who even provide for a mathematical equation in relation to the provisions of the BGB.

1910 *Medicus/Petersen*, AT, at 18 (emphasis added) – but the reference to entire *books* is still rather broad.

1911 *Stadler*, AT, §1 at 9 (emphasis added); see also *Robbers*, Introduction, at 575 ("in principle [...] applicable to all of the following books") who does not speak of "factoring out".

1912 *Schmidt*, Scand. Stud. L. 9 (1965), 131, 139; very similarly *Zweigert/Dietrich*, in: Stoljar (ed.), Problems of Codification, 34, 36–37.

1913 §§21–89 BGB on associations and foundations constitute a self-contained set of rules (*Zweigert/Dietrich*, in: Stoljar (ed.), Problems of Codification, 34, 50; see already *Zitelmann*, GrünhZ 33 (1906), 1, 12). §§90–103 BGB on "things" can be said to belong in the third book of the BGB on the law of property (*Wieacker*, A History of Private Law in Europe, 386; *Zitelmann*, GrünhZ 33 (1906), 1, 25). Consumers and entrepreneurs (§§13, 14 BGB) virtually are irrelevant everywhere but in the law of obligations (*Schmoeckel*, in: HKK-BGB, vor §1 at 52). On the other hand, the definition of negligence (§276(2) BGB) and the principle of good faith (§242 BGB) are part of the law of obligations, although they are relevant all across the BGB and private law as a whole (*Zitelmann*, GrünhZ 33 (1906), 1, 27–28). Termination of an obligation because of fulfilment (§362 BGB) is relevant for all obligations, not just for the obligations of Book 2 where the provision is found.

the general part of the BGB does not follow any perspicuous (philosophical) principle.[1914]

An Expression Appropriate for Private International Law

Thus, in its supposed original context, the notion of "factoring out" shows some deficiencies. Perhaps it has already become apparent, however, that it largely corresponds with the formal approach to private international law adopted here. Rules on formally general issues in the strict sense, on issues that are relevant for each and every individual conflicts rule, can actually fulfil the *literal* definition of factoring out. A question like *renvoi* arises for every conflicts rule regardless of its subject matter: one can either make the same rule again and again, or one factors out the rule. To the extent that the same issue is supposed to be resolved differently depending on its respective context, one still can factor out the most common solution (if there is one) and provide for exceptions where needed. Rules for (only) formally general issues can be said to be factored out in relation to the conflicts rules in which the issue arises.

The expression of "factoring out" is therefore appropriate for the context of general rules of private international law, arguably even more so than for the context of (German) substantive private law. Against the backdrop that *all* domestic sets of general provisions of private international law meet the standard of "formally general", and thus are in line with the idea of factoring out, it is almost strange that the expression does not appear to have been used nearly as much for private international law as for substantive (private) law. If at all, it was usually a German-speaking scholar who used it.[1915] As the same issues necessarily arise in EU private international law, there is no reason not to use the expression in this context.[1916]

1914 *Schmoeckel*, in: HKK-BGB, vor §1 at 41.

1915 For the only non-German example that I have come across during my research for this book see *Mádl*, RHDI 44 (1991), 227 ("[l]ike a mathematical coefficient put in front of a pair of brackets") and 242, as well as *id./Vékás*, ZfRV 1982, 266, 268. The general provisions of the Italian PIL Act also have been described as factored out – by a German scholar: *Kindler*, RabelsZ 61 (1997), 227, 251. The same phenomenon can be observed for the Polish PIL Act: *Ernst*, RabelsZ 76 (2012), 598, 632. For the Austrian PIL Act, see *Wendehorst*, in: FS Heldrich, 1071, 1079.

1916 German examples in the context of EU private international law: *Stürner*, in: Langenbucher (ed.), Europäisches Privat- und Wirtschaftsrecht, §8 at 18; *Leible*, in: Reichelt (ed.), Europäisches Gemeinschaftsrecht und IPR, 31, 33; *Mansel/Thorn/Wagner*, IPRax 2013, 1, 2; I myself used the expression, too: *Wilke*, GPR 2012, 334. Also see *Jayme/Kohler*, IPRax 2006, 537, 541: "Es fehlt ferner ein Allgemeiner Teil, welcher die einzelnen Instrumente verklammert." As a matter of German language, "*ver*klammern" (to cotter) is not far from "*aus*klammern", but lacks the mathematical connotation.

CHAPTER 4
THE SUBSTANTIVE APPROACH

A second way to think about "general" issues and rules of private international law is to adopt a substantive perspective. The formal approach is all about quantitative relevance: issues occurring in more than one context. By contrast, the substantive approach is based on a qualitative criterion. It concerns issues considered so important, so fundamental,[1917] for private international law that they deserve special treatment. This would (also) be a reasonable explanation of why they are dealt with separately from individual conflicts issues and rules.

The use of the passive voice in the preceding two sentences poorly conceals one big problem with this approach: much of it depends on the *who*, on the person(s) considering something to be of special importance or not. One legislator or scholar might deem a certain topic to be particularly significant, while another might deem it entirely trite. Typically, there will be no *legal* reason proving one of them wrong, unless perhaps a legislator exceeds its constitutional boundaries. In other words, from a *legal* perspective, there is considerably less to say about substantively general issues as such than about formally general issues as such. It very much depends on policy. Substantively general provisions are not legally irrelevant, however. As they illustrate a legislator's policy decisions, they can play an important part in the interpretation of individual conflicts provisions.

If a domestic legislator does not make a provision setting forth its policy, the only way to discern any fundamental private international law policy is through interpretation, possibly taking into account extrinsic sources, i.e. legislative history and/or explanatory memoranda. By contrast, the EU legislator has a device at its disposal to set forth its policy considerations internally, both expressly and as part of the respective legal instrument, yet separately from

[1917] Indeed, the entire perspective has also been called the "fundamental" ("grundsätzlich") perspective, see *Schärdel*, Bücherkodifikation, 169; *Kindermann*, in: GS Rödig, 99, 106. *Schmidt*, Zivilrechtskodifikation in Brasilien, 317, refers to the "systematic" coherence of a legal system in this regard. This terminology is not ideal as the *formal* approach has also been described as being "systematic", see *supra* footnote 587. For *Groß*, Die Verwaltung, Beiheft 2 (1999), 57, 70, the fundamental character of provisions found in a "general part" even seems to be their most striking feature; along quite similar lines *Noll*, Gesetzgebungslehre, 213 (according to whom fundamental rights form part of a "general part" of a legal system in its entirety).

actual provisions: recitals.[1918] They deserve particular attention in the following. Indeed, several commentators concerned with the codification of EU private international law, or at least its general provisions, have already suggested relegating certain questions of principle to the recitals.[1919]

1. SUBSTANTIVE *APPROACH*, NOT SUBSTANTIVE *RESULT*

It would be a misunderstanding to think that the substantive approach necessarily pertains to substantive results being achieved. To be sure, the desire to bring about a certain result – instead of merely determining the applicable law with indifference as to the outcome – can and often will be a reason to attribute fundamental character to a rule of private international law. But it is a policy decision as well to have one's private international law rest on the idea that it does not generally depend on the outcome of a case. Whether or not to take such a decision is a question of fundamental policy, and thus a substantive issue for present purposes. Consequently, a general rule with that content would be a substantively general rule. In anticipation of the following section, one could also say that both the decision for an approach of conflicts justice and the one for an approach of substantive justice can be categorised as substantively general decisions.

2. PRIVATE INTERNATIONAL LAW AND (SUBSTANTIVE) POLICY IN GENERAL

Private international law lost its innocence long ago.[1920] Nobody would dispute today that private international law does not have to be an "aseptic" field of law marked by a "dearth of social values",[1921] that private international law is not necessarily a neutral instrument exclusively concerned with the most closely connected law, or that substantive policies can be pursued through conflicts rules. Thus, just a few remarks on (substantive) policy in private international law may suffice here.

1918 On the relevance of recitals in EU private international law *Requejo Isidro*, in: LA Kohler, 425, 434–438.

1919 See *Corneloup/Nourissat*, in: Fallon/Lagarde/Poillot-Peruzzetto (eds.), Quelle architecture pour un code européen de droit international privé?, 257, 264; *Lagarde*, ibid., 365, 367–368; *infra* footnote 1971.

1920 *Lüderitz*, in: FS Kegel, 31.

1921 For both expressions, see *Zweigert*, RabelsZ 37 (1973), 435 (English translation: 451) and 443. The foundational contribution on the different interests in private international law is generally regarded to be *Kegel*, in: FS Lewald, 259.

"Classical" private international law or private international law "à la von Savigny" – which is more a figure of speech than an entirely accurate description[1922] – is concerned not so much with the substantive outcome but with the application of the most closely connected law. It is about "seek[ing] out for each legal relationship the legal system to which, according to its own nature, that relationship belongs or to which it is subjected (where it has its seat)"[1923] – notably not the legal system whose rules provide for the "best", "(most?) just" substantive result from the perspective of the *lex fori*. Only where an outcome is entirely incompatible with the forum's ideas of substantive justice, does the public policy reservation provide for a ripcord. This is not only "justice pluralism",[1924] but "a specific justice of private international law which is independent from the justice that manifests itself in the substantive decision of social conflicts".[1925] It is, in short, conflicts justice.[1926]

Yet there are many ways other than the public policy exception in which considerations of a substantive nature influence (at least[1927]) modern European private international law, in which the values of a legal system affect its conflicts rules;[1928] always without leaving the functional[1929] boundaries of the traditional omnilateral system.[1930] This is especially obvious for rules favouring the validity of a juridical act[1931] or of a certain status, typically to be achieved by alternative references as in Article 11(1)–(3) Rome I. There are also rules favouring one of the parties involved, such as a consumer or employee. Respective rules bring about the desired favour by different means, e.g. by limiting the effects of party

1922 *Schurig*, in: Mansel (ed.), IPR im 20. Jahrhundert, 5–9; see *Kühne*, ZVglRWiss 114 (2015), 355, 360, for a critique of *Schurig*'s pointed view. Also see the contributions to Gössl (ed.), Politik und Internationales Privatrecht, in particular *Coester-Waltjen*, 1.

1923 *von Savigny*, System VIII, 108; translation by *Moura Vicente*, Yearbook of Private International Law 9 (2007), 257, 273; also see *van den Eeckhout*, in: Bergé/Francq/Gardeñes Santiago (eds.), Boundaries of European PIL, 399, 404.

1924 *Mills*, Confluence, 5–6. The main idea behind "justice pluralism" seems to be that the outcome of a case may be just even if the *lex fori* does not apply.

1925 *Basedow*, in: LA Borrás, 175, 180; also see *id.*, RabelsZ 73 (2009), 455, 458.

1926 For a short recent account see *Symeonides*, Codifying Choice of Law, 246–247; one of the earliest express statements to this effect seems to be *Zweigert*, in: FS Raape, 35, 49–52.

1927 See e.g. *Martinek*, Seven Pillars of Wisdom, 6.2. ("The substantive laws concerned were always taken into consideration to a certain extent, even by the clas[s]ical conflicts lawyer", with reference to different *favores*). For the "materialisation" of "traditional" private international law in general see e.g. *Audit*, Rec. des cours 305 (2003), 9, 327–357; *Siehr*, in: Mélanges Overbeck, 205, 232.

1928 *Bogdan*, Rec. des cours 348 (2010), 9, 78.

1929 It is correct, however, that the approach of looking for the closest connection is abandoned in these cases as *Kühne*, ZVglRWiss 114 (2015), 355, 362, points out.

1930 As opposed to replacing the entire system e.g. with a "better law approach" – see *Leflar*, N.Y.U. L. Rev. 41 (1966), 267, 295–304. Even though the "better law" only is one of *Leflar*'s five factors, it is appropriate to give this title to the entire approach, for it could be and often was regarded as dispositive, *Symeonides*, Codifying Choice of Law, 248.

1931 *Moura Ramos*, in: Symeonides (ed.), PIL at the End of the 20th Century, 349, 353.

autonomy (see Articles 6(2) clause 2 and 8(1) clause 2 Rome I), or by having the connecting factor focus on the protected party instead of on the one effecting the characteristic performance (see Article 6(1) Rome I).[1932] When Article 4(1)(e) and (f) Rome I use the franchisee's/distributor's habitual residence as their connecting factor, this is not only an identification of the place of characteristic performance, but also a measure of protection for these parties.[1933]

While private international law around the world seems to have had a certain resistance to being influenced by the respective political system,[1934] it has also been or can be employed for other policies,[1935] e.g. for migration policies.[1936] It can be used to safeguard, or even confer, fundamental rights, such as the right to marry for homosexual couples[1937] or the right to divorce.[1938] Already, the choice of a connecting factor, especially between nationality and (habitual) residence, reflects a policy decision.[1939] A state's stance on *renvoi* may seem to be a technical matter, but it is also governed by policy.[1940] In several member states at least, constitutional requirements or limitations have been observed to influence the content of conflicts rules.[1941] In particular, human rights concerns have an impact on conflicts rules.[1942]

1932 See *Symeonides*, Codifying Choice of Law, 251–282, for a detailed typology of all three favours.

1933 *Gebauer*, in: Calliess (ed.), Rome Regulations, Art. 4 Rome I at 27; *Leible/Lehmann*, RIW 2008, 528, 535; COM(2005) 650 final, 6.

1934 *Pauknerová/Pfeiffer*, Journal of Private International Law 10 (2014), 205, 207. To this effect probably also *Ancel*, Éléments d'histoire du droit international privé, 19 ("remarkable aptitude" of private international law for absorbing change). See also Article 4 Yugoslav PIL Act with its reference to the "basic principles of social organisation", and the relativisation by *Matić*, Neth. Int. L. Rev. 30 (1983), 220, 221 ("no substantial change" when compared to the term "public policy").

1935 *Muir-Watt*, Transnational Legal Theory 2 (2011), 347, 353–354 and passim.

1936 *van den Eeckhout*, in: Bergé/Francq/Gardeñes Santiago (eds.), Boundaries of European PIL, 407–408, with reference to Dutch law.

1937 *Erauw/Fallon*, in: Dirix/Lelen (eds.), The Belgian Reports, 227, 254, 256–257, for the Belgian PIL Code.

1938 See the first alternative of Article 10 Rome III, and *Lein*, in: Calliess (ed.), Rome Regulations, Art. 10 Rome III at 1.

1939 *Beaumont/McEleavy*, Anton's PIL, at 4.28; *Moura Vicente*, Yearbook of Private International Law 9 (2007), 257, 275; already *Zweigert*, RabelsZ 37 (1973), 435, 443.

1940 *Erauw/Fallon*, in: Dirix/Lelen (eds.), The Belgian Reports, 227, 254.

1941 See *Vrellis*, R.I.D.C 2017, 47, with examples from several member states and the EU. For Germany e.g. *von Hein*, in: MüKoBGB, Einl. IPR at 45; also the famous "Spaniard" decision by the German Federal Constitutional Court, BVerfGE 31, 58 [1971]; for Italy e.g. *Krätschmer*, Integration von Staatsverträgen, 44–48; *Giardina*, Rev. crit. DIP 1996, 1, 4; *Pocar*, IPRax 1996, 145, 146; for Portugal e.g. *Moura Ramos*, in: Symeonides (ed.), PIL at the End of the 20th Century, 349, 376–378; for Spain e.g. *Calvo Caravaca/Carrascosa González*, DIP I, 84–87. Generally *Cuniberti*, Conflict of Laws, 64–68.

1942 *Fawcett/Ní Shúilleabháin/Shah*, Human Rights and Private International Law, at 2.84–2.87 (with references to later parts of their book).

3. EUROPEAN UNION PRIVATE INTERNATIONAL LAW AND POLICY IN PARTICULAR

Considerations of both conflicts justice and substantive justice shape current EU private international law. Its legislative basis already serves as an indication of the former. As Article 81 TFEU – a provision in the "area of freedom, security and *justice*",[1943] after all – seems to presuppose harmonisation of conflicts rules *only*, i.e. without harmonisation of substantive law, it also presupposes that "there may be equal justice without equal (substantive) law".[1944] Article 4 Rome I in particular, and the many escape clauses in the regulations[1945] in general, show a commitment to the notion of the closest connection.[1946]

On the other hand, the examples from Rome I referred to in the preceding section demonstrate substantive policies at work. Indeed, the different policies of the TFEU, and potentially also the rights enshrined in the EU Charter of Fundamental Rights, are bound to have an effect on the content of EU private international law.[1947] While the concept of the EU as a "referee" in private international law has its merits,[1948] it meets its limitations in this context. A referee must be neutral – the EU has its own agenda. This agenda may not even be in line with the member states' interests and policies.[1949] It is namely one of economic integration.[1950] By way of primary EU law, private international law has become "politicised".[1951]

That Article 65(b) TEC tied EU private international law to the proper functioning of the internal market[1952] arguably did not influence the content of conflicts rules. A much clearer example is the "openly substantivist approach"[1953] of Article 7 Rome II. Recital 25 clause 1 Rome II justifies favouring the person sustaining the damage with the high level of environmental protection mandated

---

1943 Part Three, Title V TFEU (Article 67–89 TFEU) (emphasis added); also see *Meeusen/van Overbeeke/Verhaert*, RabelsZ 81(2017), 858, 878, on the (at first sight) "awkward" link between private international law and access to justice.

1944 *Basedow*, in: LA Borrás, 175, 180.

1945 *Supra* Chapter 3, section 4.1.2.

1946 See also *infra* section 4.2.

1947 See also *Meeusen/van Overbeeke/Verhaert*, RabelsZ 81(2017), 858, 880; the Charter has not yet featured much in ECJ judgments on private international law in the broad sense, however, *Düsterhaus*, ZEuP 2018, 10, 19.

1948 See *supra* Chapter 3, sections 2.9.5. and 5.2. (European Union).

1949 *Michaels*, in: FS Kropholler, 151, 160.

1950 In more detail on the influence of the economic goals of the EU on private international law *Düsterhaus*, ZEuP 2018, 10, 24–27.

1951 *M.-P. Weller*, RabelsZ 81 (2017), 747, 757–759.

1952 *van den Eeckhout* refers to this, in: Bergé/Francq/Gardeñes Santiago (eds.), Boundaries of European PIL, 399, 405; also see *Meeusen*, Liber Fausto Pocar, 685, 689–690.

1953 *von Hein*, in: Calliess (ed.), Rome Regulations, Art. 7 Rome II at 1; also see *Symeonides*, Codifying Choice of Law, 338; *Michaels*, in: FS Kropholler, 151, 160–161.

by Article 174[(2)] TEC (now Article 191(2) TFEU). Accordingly, Article 7 Rome II has been singled out as a rule revealing the "steering potential of choice of law rules".[1954] Similarly, conflicts rules favouring a consumer must be seen against the backdrop of the treaties,[1955] especially today with the prominent position of Article 12 TFEU. The existence of private international law policy interests of the EU (and/or of the member states) becomes particularly visible when it files amicus briefs with courts of third states in conflicts cases.[1956]

4. SUBSTANTIVELY GENERAL ISSUES

4.1. THE OVERLAP OF "SUBSTANTIVE" AND "FORMAL"

One can posit that issues identified above as formally general will quite often be regarded as substantively general. Formally general issues are an inherent part of every, or at least of more than one, conflicts rule. In a quite literal sense, these issues are fundamental: on them rests everything, or at least much, else. A legislator addressing such issues with formally general rules thus inevitably shapes the (substantive) character of its private international law.

In other instances, it may be the substantive character of an issue that prompts a legislator to make a certain general provision. The examples of public policy exceptions and overriding mandatory provisions of the forum are instructive. As outlined already, both issues have a strong connection to public interests.[1957] These public interests may very well have been the decisive aspect for a legislator to make a general provision, not so much the realisation that both issues are formally general,[1958] and could thus be dealt with efficiently in a single provision. In so doing, however, the legislator will very likely have created a rule that can be analysed as formally general. Perhaps the legislator was also aware of this character.

The relationship between formally and substantively general issues is thus one of two overlapping circles. If one assumes that a given legislator may have created at least one general rule only because of its formally general relevance, without any particular policy considerations, the circles would overlap in part.[1959]

1954 *Muir-Watt*, Transnational Legal Theory 2 (2011), 347, 388.
1955 See *Michaels*, in: FS Kropholler, 151, 161 (for the TEC).
1956 *Symeonides*, Codifying Choice of Law, 336, also for examples from recent US cases.
1957 *Supra* Chapter 3, section 2.9.2.2.
1958 *Supra* Chapter 3, sections 2.9.2. and 5.6.
1959 In an entirely different context, see *Förster*, JA 2014, 721, 724. When discussing the new §312a BGB on "general obligations and principles applying to consumer contracts", he states that the rules found in this provision are "general" *not* because of their fundamental content ("inhaltlich grundlegend") but because of their relevance for every consumer contract within the scope of §§312(1), 310(3) BGB.

If one – more reasonably (no legal rule without a policy decision[1960]) – assumes that their "fundamental" character makes all formally general issues substantively general to some degree at least, the bigger circle of substantively general issues encloses the smaller circle of formally general issues. For present purposes, a final verdict on whether the formally or substantively general character of an issue was decisive for a legislator is not necessary. It is only important that a given issue *can* be analysed/explained at least from one of these perspectives.

As formally general issues have been discussed extensively above, it remains to discuss substantively general issues outside of the overlap. A particular focus will be laid on those (few![1961]) existing rules of which the formal approach could not, or (arguably) not sufficiently, take account; perhaps the substantive perspective can do so now.

4.2. THE CLOSE(ST) CONNECTION

As already stated above, the search for the closest connection is generally regarded as the key feature of "traditional", "Savignian" private international law. The closest connection can appear in many roles,[1962] in particular as a subsidiary conflicts rule or as an escape clause. It can also be a leitmotif,[1963] the fundamental idea behind the choice of individual connecting factors. To put it another way, the closest connection can be one of the principles of a given system of private international law.[1964] One would not necessarily expect to find an express provision on the closest connection in this latter role; in accordance with classic legislative style, a principle "may linger elegantly in the background",[1965] should only be discernible from looking at (groups of) specific provisions.

Both §1(2) Austrian PIL Act and Article 2(1) clause 2 Bulgarian PIL Code, however, set forth that the principle of the strongest or closest connection manifests itself in the conflicts rules of the respective act. As formally general rules, these provisions would be simply redundant – unless (and then only to the extent that) one interprets them as subsidiary conflicts rules or escape clauses.[1966] But a substantive point of view does not have any difficulty dealing with such provisions. From this perspective, they enshrine guiding principles for the rest of each act.[1967]

1960 Policy considerations tend to appear even behind the most technical rule, see e.g. *Audit/Bermann*, in: Nuyts/Watté (eds.), International Civil Litigation in Europe and Relations with Third States, 55, 80, as to (territorial) scope of application rules.

1961 *Supra* Chapter 3, section 8.1.

1962 See *Symeonides*, Codifying Choice of Law, 176–188, in particular figures 4.2. and 4.3.

1963 *Geisler*, Die engste Verbindung, 62.

1964 See e.g. *Lagarde*, Rec. des cours 196 (1986), 9, 32–49.

1965 *Remien*, in: Leible (ed.), General Principles, §11.02[B], specifically for the closest connection.

1966 See *supra* Chapter 3, sections 2.10. and 4.1.

1967 Expressly to this effect *Schwimann*, IPR, 29. Arguably also *Palmer*, Am. J. Comp. L. 28 (1980), 197, 204, to the extent that she describes §1 Austrian PIL Act to be "set out like a preamble".

The lack of a similar general rule in other member states should not suggest that the concept of the closest connection is either unknown or not especially relevant there. The general provisions of Article 10:8 Dutch Civil Code and, to a lesser degree, Article 19(2) Belgian PIL Code openly *presuppose* that at least some conflicts provisions later in the respective codes are based on a presumed close connection. (If so, they provide for an escape if the presumption has been rebutted in a particular case, as already mentioned.[1968]) Elsewhere, the closest connection as a fundamental policy decision must be inferred from an overview of individual conflicts provisions.[1969]

The notion of the closest connection is also at least one of the background principles of EU private international law. While there is no pertinent provision, and while the recitals do not expressly call it a general principle or the like, Rome I and II, as well as the Succession Regulation, provide for quite a few escape clauses in favour of the law of a country with which the case is more closely connected.[1970] Moreover, Recitals 14 clause 1 and 21 clause 1 Rome III set forth that the group of laws that can be the object of party autonomy, as well as the connecting factors in absence of a choice, are based on the idea of a close connection. Similarly, Recital 37 clause 3 Succession Regulation, Recital 43 clause 3 M-Property Regulation, and Recital 42 clause 3 RP-Property Regulation provide that their main conflicts rule should make a succession be governed "by a predictable law with which it is closely connected". Accordingly, scholars of EU private international law have discussed the closest connection as an issue separate from individual conflicts rules, separate from a particular regulation.[1971]

4.3. PARTY AUTONOMY

The rise of party autonomy to a mainstay of private international law with increasingly substantive undertones has already been noted, but it has also been shown that only very few member states have drafted a general provision on party autonomy.[1972] Among them is Poland with Article 4 Polish PIL Act. Its first paragraph permits the parties to choose the applicable law whenever

---

1968 *Supra* Chapter 3, section 4.1.1.

1969 See e.g. *Pajor*, Rev. crit. DIP 2012, 5, 8; *id.*, Yearbook of Private International Law 13 (2011), 381, 384, for Poland.

1970 *Supra* Chapter 3, section 4.1.2.

1971 *Remien*, in: Leible (ed.), General Principles, §11.02[B] and §11.04 (conclusion No. 2); *Leible/Müller*, Yearbook of Private International Law 14 (2012/2013), 137, 147. These authors agree that the closest connection *as a principle* should not be enshrined in a provision, but, if at all, in a recital, even within a regulation on general issues of EU private international law. Also see *Sonnenberger*, in: FS Kropholler, 227, 236.

1972 *Supra* Chapter 3, section 4.3.3.

another provision of the Act allows them to do so. From a formal point of view, Article 4(1) Polish PIL Act is utterly useless. Instead of factoring out a rule, it repeats a rule that still exists multiple times elsewhere in the Act. The formal approach cannot properly take account of such a provision. From the substantive perspective, however, the existence of the provision as a general one can be explained quite easily: it serves to highlight the importance that the Polish legislator attributes to party autonomy.[1973]

Similar observations can be made for EU private international law. Recital 11 Rome I calls the parties' freedom to choose the applicable law "a cornerstone" of Rome I. This seems to say more than just pointing out that the connecting factor of party autonomy is of relevance not only for one of its conflicts rules. Rather, it seems to make the substantive statement that party autonomy is more than a mere "side-issue", more than a "maverick within the edifice of conflicts theory"[1974] for the purposes of Rome I. From this perspective, it is fitting that Article 3 Rome I and Article 14 Rome II are entitled "Freedom of choice". This is much less descriptive for the purpose of these rules (determining the applicable law, of course) than other titles of the same regulations that either mention a certain subject matter or the "applicable law".[1975] But it is testament to the importance of party autonomy, as are the respective positions of Article 3 Rome I – the very first conflicts rule of Rome I – and Article 14 Rome II – in a chapter of its own (and, at some point during the drafting process, also the very first conflicts rule of Rome II[1976]). The character of party autonomy as a mere connecting factor seems to take a back seat in all of these cases. Party autonomy as a guiding principle of private international law[1977] comes to the fore.

Other recitals further underline the importance of party autonomy in EU private international law, namely Recital 31 clause 1 Rome II ("*principle* of party autonomy"[1978]) and Recital 18 clause 1 Rome III ("The informed choice of both spouses is a *basic principle* of this Regulation").[1979] The wording of the recitals of the Succession Regulation, the M-Property Regulation, and the RP-Property Regulation is much more reserved with regard to the rationale

---

1973 Exactly to this effect *Pajor*, Yearbook of Private International Law 13 (2011), 381, 384.

1974 *Lehmann*, Vand. J. Trans. L. 41 (2008), 381, 383.

1975 See e.g. Article 4 Rome I: "Applicable law in the absence of choice", Article 5 Rome I: "Contracts of carriage", Article 6 Rome I: "Consumer contracts" etc.; Article 5 Rome II: "Product liability", Article 6 Rome II: "Unfair competition and acts restricting free competition" etc.

1976 See Article 4 of COM(2006) 83 final, and *supra* Chapter 3, section 4.3.4.

1977 See also e.g. *Calliess*, in: id. (ed.), Rome Regulations, Art. 3 Rome I at 1; *Mandery*, Party Autonomy in Contractual and Non-Contractual Obligations, 239; also see the references *supra* Chapter 3, section 4.3.1. Also *Kohler*, Rec. des cours 359 (2012), 285, 303 and passim, for "l'autonomie de la volonté" as a general principle of private international law.

1978 Emphasis added.

1979 Emphasis added.

behind party autonomy,[1980] although a reference to party autonomy as a general principle might have been warranted, at least in the succession context, for it is an innovation for many member states.[1981]

4.4. EQUAL TREATMENT

4.4.1. *Equal Treatment of Foreigners*

The formal approach struggles with general provisions found in private international law codes[1982] setting forth the equal treatment of foreigners. Among provisions concerned with the applicable law, they seem to be "an inconsistency".[1983] The best formal way to look at such rules seems to be from the perspective of the scope of application *ratione personae*, but this has proved to be somewhat of a stopgap.[1984] The substantive approach offers a more plausible explanation for provisions of this ilk in private international law. They concern the fundamental policy decision of equal treatment regardless of nationality. To set this forth as part of private international law specifically may be said to find its reason in (the French) tradition,[1985] and/or due to its intrinsic connection to a field of law (at least also[1986]) involving cases with *international* elements.

One also can point out that von Savigny's conceptualisation of private international law started with the desideratum of equal treatment of a state's nationals and foreigners everywhere, to the effect that the same law would apply regardless of the forum.[1987] While, soon after, the latter part of the statement took on a life of its own as the goal of decisional harmony,[1988] its historical connection to equal treatment of nationals and foreigners remains. This provides another aspect of intrinsic justification for such a rule in private international law specifically.

1980 "This Regulation should enable citizens to organise their succession in advance", Recital 38 clause 1 Succession Regulation; "[t]o facilitate to spouses the management of their property", Recital 45 clause 1 M-Property Regulation; "[t]o facilitate partners' management of their property", Recital 44 clause 1 RP-Property Regulation.

1981 See *Jud*, GPR 2005, 133, 136.

1982 To wit: §§26–27 Czech PIL Act; Article 14 Portuguese Civil Code. Also see Article 4 Greek Civil Code (which is the very first provision in the chapter on private international law) and Article 32 Slovak PIL Act (which is not positioned among the "common" provisions, but also not among the individual conflicts rules; it is found in a separate chapter on the status of foreigners that includes a rule on multiple nationalities and people without a nationality).

1983 For Article 8 of the 1965 Polish PIL Act expressly *Mączyński*, Yearbook of Private International Law 6 (2004), 203, 206.

1984 *Supra* Chapter 3, section 2.2.4.

1985 Ibid.

1986 *Supra* Chapter 3, section 2.2.1.

1987 *von Savigny*, System VIII, 27.

1988 *Lüderitz*, in: FS Kegel, 31.

Nevertheless, such provisions form the exception in domestic private international law, and EU private international law is devoid of them. At most, one might point to Recital 22 Rome III, Recital 41 Succession Regulation, Recital 50 M-Property Regulation, and Recital 49 RP-Property Regulation with their reference to the "general principles of the [European] Union", which mainly seems to mean non-discrimination on the grounds of nationality.[1989]

4.4.2. *Other Cases of (Potential) Discrimination*

The second alternative of Article 10 Rome III has already been analysed in detail.[1990] In the present context, however, its substantive dimension is worth emphasising. The provision constitutes a safeguard for a right to divorce/legal separation in which neither spouse is discriminated against on the basis of sex.[1991] No similar provision exists elsewhere in EU private international law, or among the general[1992] provisions of domestic private international law.

Finally, Recital 25 clause 2 Rome III, Recital 58 clause 2 Succession Regulation, Recital 54 clause 2 M-Property Regulation, and Recital 53 clause 2 RP-Property Regulation emphasise the principle of non-discrimination enshrined in Article 21 EU Charter of Fundamental Rights in the public policy context.

4.5. PROTECTION OF A WEAKER PARTY

The desire to protect a party that is perceived to be weaker than its counterpart manifests itself not only in substantive law, but also in private international law. Groups commonly thought to require protection (also) through conflicts rules are most notably consumers and employees;[1993] but also injured people in the tort context, passengers, (mass) insurance policy holders, tenants, and maintenance creditors.

It seems that the first code to contain conflicts rules for the protection of a weaker party was the Austrian PIL Act of 1979.[1994] In part catalysed by

---

1989 *Supra* Chapter 3, sections 4.4.2.2. and 4.4.2.3.

1990 *Supra* Chapter 3, section 2.9.5.3.

1991 *Lein*, in: Calliess (ed.), Rome Regulations, Art. 10 Rome III at 1.

1992 But see Article 107(2) subparagraph 2 Spanish Civil Code (outside of the provisions designated as rules of private international law, but referred to by Article 9(2) Spanish Civil Code), which, after all, was the model for Article 10 Rome III, *Calvo Caravaca/Carrascosa González*, CDT 2009, 36, 66.

1993 Also see *Düsterhaus*, ZEuP 2018, 10, 24–25, on the background of the protection of weaker parties (and the environment) in primary EU law.

1994 *Siehr*, in: Reichelt (ed.), 30 Jahre österreichisches IPR-Gesetz, 9, 17; also see *Palmer*, Am. J. Comp. L. 28 (1980), 197, 219–220.

the Rome Convention and/or instruments of EC/EU law, the idea appears everywhere across the EU nowadays.[1995] §67(3) Belgian PIL Code provides a striking example of taking the interests of a weaker party into account on the conflicts level.[1996] Pursuant to this provision, Belgian law applies to the conditions for adoption if the judge "considers the application of the foreign law clearly harmful to the higher interest of the adoptee". However, no domestic private international law code contains a provision marked as "general" that discernibly and specifically concerns the protection of weaker parties.

Similarly, EU private international law offers very little in the context of general *provisions* for the benefit of a weaker party. The "Other Provisions" of Rome I and II contain no such rule, nor do the groups of provisions of overarching importance in the other regulations. While Article 7 Rome II does discriminate in favour of the person who sustains the damage, the reason pursuant to Recital 25 clause 1 Rome II is not so much the protection of injured persons, but the protection of the environment.[1997] In other words, there is a favour for a party that one could consider to be in need of protection, but it is only an incidental consequence – not an indication of a policy to the same effect. Yet there is the "common provision" of Article 18 Rome II, permitting a direct action against the insurer of the person liable if *either* "the law applicable to the non-contractual obligation or the law applicable to the insurance contract so provides". This alternative reference is supposed to benefit the injured person by making fast and certain compensation more likely.[1998]

Even in light of only one overarching rule to this effect, the protection of certain groups[1999] of weaker parties is one of the fundamental policies of EU private international law, as evidenced by individual conflicts rules, and as set forth by numerous recitals. Recital 23 Rome I provides in general terms that "parties regarded as being weaker [...] should be protected by conflict-of-laws rules [...] more favourable to their interests than the general rules". Recitals 24 and 25 Rome I then specify this protection for consumers, Recital 32 Rome I for passengers and insurance policy holders, and Recital 35 Rome I for employees.

1995 See for Greece e.g. *Vrellis*, in: Symeonides (ed.), PIL at the End of the 20th Century, 243, 251; for Italy e.g. *Ballarino/Bonomi*, Yearbook of Private International Law 2 (2000), 99, 112; *Pocar/Honorati*, in: Symeonides (ed.), PIL at the End of the 20th Century, 279, 284; for Poland e.g. *Pajor*, Rev. crit. DIP 2012, 5, 11; *eund.*, Yearbook of Private International Law 13 (2011), 381, 386; for Portugal e.g. *Moura Vicente*, Yearbook of Private International Law 9 (2007), 257, 271.

1996 *Erauw/Fallon*, in: Dirix/Lelen (eds.), The Belgian Reports, 227, 244, with examples from Belgian court practice.

1997 Also see *von Hein*, in: Calliess (ed.), Rome Regulations, Art. 7 Rome II at 1–2.

1998 *Junker*, in: MüKoBGB, Art. 18 Rom II-VO at 1; *Gruber*, in: Calliess (ed.), Rome Regulations, Art. 18 Rome II at 5; *Heiss/Loacker*, JBl 2007, 613, 638.

1999 Somewhat strangely, EU private international law does not seem to regard tenants to be in need of special protection: *Rühl*, Journal of Private International Law 10 (2014), 335, 343.

All of these more specific recitals reiterate the term "protection", as if to remove any doubt as to the underlying policy. Recital 31 clause 4 Rome II expressly mentions the protection of weaker parties in the context of party autonomy in non-contractual obligations. Other recitals set forth that the protection of consumers has been one of the factors taken into account when drafting the individual conflicts provisions of Rome II.[2000]

5. SUMMARY

The substantive approach looks at the quality of a legal rule. From this perspective, a rule is "general" if it is sufficiently fundamental/important for the rest of the respective field of law. It is hard to narrow down the description further because importance is a policy decision to the extent that it does not already follow from the quantitative relevance of an issue/rule. Nevertheless, several substantively general provisions can be identified in domestic private international law. In EU private international law, there are mainly only several *recitals* of this nature. In particular, the substantive approach can explain the provisions with which the formal approach struggles. It thus complements the formal approach – or, going back to the image of two concentric circles,[2001] provides a further layer to it.

[2000] See Recitals 20 clause 1, 21 clause 3 Rome II.
[2001] *Supra* section 4.1.

PART III
STANDARDS

Thus far, it has first been shown that domestic, as well as EU, private international law distinguishes between at least two classes of private international law rules, with one often expressly called "general". This is not always done, however, in uniform fashion. It has then been demonstrated that, as a matter of theory, it is reasonable to approach the meaning of "general" from a formal and a substantive perspective, and that, as a matter of checking the theory against existing law and its academic presentations, both approaches together take account of virtually[2002] everything designated or treated as "general". As the future of European private international law clearly lies at the level of the EU, the final questions are whether the EU can and should make (formally and/or substantively) general provisions for *all*[2003] of its private international law.

"Can" implies the legal dimension (Chapter 5): does the EU have the competence to make general rules of this kind? Which legislative procedure is to be used? How would a respective instrument and the rest of EU private international law interact?

"Should" refers to the policy dimension (Chapter 6): does it make sense to create general provisions of EU private international law? What are the advantages and disadvantages of proceeding in this way? Is there any alternative scenario – and is it viable?

Accordingly, law and policy are the two standards by which the idea of general provisions of EU private international law will be examined in the following.

2002 See *supra* Chapter 3, section 8.1. for the few provisions not covered by the formal approach – of which the substantive approach has covered two (*supra* Chapter 4, section 4.).

2003 As demonstrated in Part II in connection with the different issues, the EU already has made quite a few (formally and/or substantively) general provisions and/or recitals in relation to *each* field of private international law, i.e. in relation to *each* private international law regulation.

CHAPTER 5

LAW

To ask whether the EU can *legally* implement any of the approaches discussed above mainly means to ask the questions of competence and procedure. This is not the place to give the nth overview of the development of EU private international law.[2004] The issue is simply: can the EU make general rules of private international law pursuant to the TEU and TFEU?

1. COMPETENCE IN THE AREA OF PRIVATE INTERNATIONAL LAW

There seems to be general agreement that Article 81(2)(c) TFEU, with its reference to "the rules applicable in the Member States concerning conflict of laws", pertains to rules that determine the applicable law.[2005] As a measure adopted on the basis of this article is not *required* to be necessary for the proper functioning of the internal market anymore,[2006] it can also encompass civil matters (arguably[2007]) without relevance for the internal market, such as family law.[2008] This statement finds further support in Article 81(3) TFEU – and found

---

2004 See for example *Beaumont/McEleavy*, Anton's PIL, at 1.43–1.45; *Leible*, in: Streinz (ed.), EUV/AEUV, Art. 81 AEUV at 1–3; *Basedow* in: LA Borrás, 175, 176–178; *eund.*, RabelsZ 73 (2009), 455–457; *eund.*, in: Essays in Honor of Juenger; *Fiorini*, ICLQ 57 (2008), 969–975; *Lequette*, in: LA Gaudemet-Tallon, 503, 504–508; *Weber*, Die Vergemeinschaftung des IPR; *Gaudemet-Tallon*, in: Essays in Honor of Juenger, 317, 323–329.

2005 Expressly *Stumpf*, in: Schwarze (ed.), EU-Kommentar, Art. 81 AEUV at 17; *Rosenau/Petrus*, in: Vedder/Heintschel von Heinegg (eds.), Europäisches Unionsrecht, Art. 81 AEUV at 7; *Weber*, Die Vergemeinschaftung des IPR, 124; implicitly (because of the connotation of "Internationales Privatrecht" in the German legal tradition) *Leible*, in: Streinz (ed.), EUV/AEUV, Art. 81 AEUV at 29; *Rossi*, in: Calliess/Ruffert (eds.), EUV/AEUV, Art. 81 AEUV at 22; *Kotzur*, in: Geiger/Khan/id., EUV/AEUV, Article 81 AEUV at 9; *Baratta*, in: Tizzano (ed.), Trattati dell'Unione Europea, Art. 81 TFUE, III 2 ("diritto internazionale private").

2006 In more detail *infra* section 1.2.2.

2007 But see e.g. *Dohrn*, Die Kompetenzen der EG im IPR, 109–113, already for Article 65 EC.

2008 *Stumpf*, in: Schwarze (ed.), EU-Kommentar, Art. 81 AEUV at 14; *Barrière Barousse*, JDI 2010, 3, 11; *Dethloff/Hauschild*, FPR 2010, 489, 490; *Fiorini*, ICLQ 57 (2008), 969, 977. This result also would seem to follow from a purposive interpretation of Article 81 TFEU in light of the freedom of movement and the Union citizenship, for "[s]timulating citizens to move across borders, and to reside in other Member States, necessarily requires that proper care is taken also of the private law effects which flow therefrom", *Meeusen*, in: Liber Pocar, 685, 692.

it in Article 67 TEC[2009] – that sets forth special rules for the establishment of measures concerning family law. That a lack of unanimity in the Council would entail that an area of private international law in family matters remains for the member states to deal with, does not mean that the EU does not have the competence in that area as a matter of principle;[2010] it just means that the EU was not able to make use of it in a certain matter yet. In sum, the EU can tackle all[2011] areas of private international law as a *subject matter*.

1.1. COMPETENCE FOR UNIFIED PRIVATE INTERNATIONAL LAW

Some scholars called into question whether Article 65 TEC gave the EU the competence to make unified provisions of private international law.[2012] They mainly relied on the wording of said provision as it only pertained to "promoting the compatibility of the rules applicable in the Member States concerning the conflict of laws". As it is well known, EU legislative practice did not seem much concerned. It was not necessary, either, to read Article 65 TEC this narrowly.[2013] Now that "promoting" has been dropped, that Article 81(1) clause 2 TFEU expressly mentions "measures for the approximation of the laws [...] of the Member states", and that Article 81(2)(c) TFEU requires a measure to be "aimed at ensuring [...] the compatibility", there is little room for similar doubts.[2014]

1.2. COMPETENCE FOR A *LOI UNIFORME*

There are two points of view from which one could doubt the existence of an EU competence to make conflicts provisions (also) determining the application of the law of a non-member state. First, there is the requirement of cross-border implications; second, there is the relevance for the internal market. Both aspects, however, turn out to be unpersuasive, at least nowadays.

2009 *Kroll-Ludwigs*, Die Rolle der Parteiautonomie, 21.

2010 But see *Barrière Barousse*, JDI 2010, 3, 25–26.

2011 *Struycken*, RabelsZ 78 (2014), 592, 601, considers Article 81 TFEU to be a "basis wide enough" for a "complete" EU codification of private international law.

2012 *Lequette*, in: LA Gaudemet-Tallon, 503, 515–516 (with further references); *Gaudemet-Tallon*, in: Essays in Honor of Juenger, 317, 326.

2013 In detail *Weber*, Die Vergemeinschaftung des IPR, 145–149.

2014 Also see *Wagner*, in: Leible (ed.), General Principles, §4.04 [B][2][a]; *Stumpf*, in: Schwarze (ed.), EU-Kommentar, Art. 81 AEUV at 17; *Roth*, in: Remien/Kieninger (eds.), Europäische Kollisionsrechtsvereinheitlichung, 11, 21; *Barrière Barousse*, JDI 2010, 3, 11; *Rossi*, in: Calliess/Ruffert (eds.), EUV/AEUV, Art. 81 AEUV at 22.

1.2.1. *Cross-Border Implications*

The subject matters of Article 81(2) TFEU are to be "ensured" "for the purposes of paragraph 1". This is a bit puzzling as Article 81(1) TFEU does not state any "purpose".[2015] Yet the reference to paragraph 1 at least makes sure that its limitation to "civil matters having cross-border implications" applies to paragraph 2 as well.[2016] Does that confine EU private international law to intra-Union cases?

It should be noted that the "cross-border implications" are not specified any further. Hence, it does not do violence to the wording to read the provision to also encompass cross-border implications involving a third state.[2017] Moreover, such an understanding is in line with the purpose of Article 81 TFEU, i.e. the notion that a citizen should not be put at a disadvantage by the mere fact that her civil matter is not confined to her home state.[2018] Therefore, the requirement of cross-border implications does not set any limitation in regard to whose law the EU can determine to govern a case.

1.2.2. *Relevance for the Internal Market*

Article 65 TEC required a Community measure to be necessary for the proper functioning of the internal market. This criterion suggested to some that Article 65 TEC conferred only a competence for intra-Community cases.[2019] Particularly due to the free circulation of judgments, however, the proper functioning of the internal market also required that the same conflicts rules apply across the European Community, even in cases involving a third state.[2020] In essence, "the *proper* functioning" constituted a quite ambitious goal;

2015 *Rossi*, in: Calliess/Ruffert (eds.), EUV/AEUV, Art. 81 AEUV at 10.

2016 *Rossi*, in: Calliess/Ruffert (eds.), EUV/AEUV, Art. 81 AEUV at 11.

2017 To this effect also *Leible*, in: Streinz (ed.), EUV/AEUV, Art. 81 AEUV at 9; *Baratta*, in: Liber Pocar, 3, 18; *id.*, in: Tizzano (ed.), Trattati dell'Unione Europea, Art. 81 TFUE, III 2; *Hess*, in: Grabitz/Hilf, Das Recht der Europäischen Union, Art. 81 AEUV at 30; but see *Hoppe*, in: Lenz/Borchardt (eds.), EU-Verträge, Art. 81 AEUV at 2; *Kindler*, IPRax 2010, 44, 48 (requiring a connection to another *member* state).

2018 *Rossi*, in: Calliess/Ruffert (eds.), EUV/AEUV, Art. 81 AEUV 12; *Dohrn*, Die Kompetenzen der EG im IPR, 90–92.

2019 *Lequette*, in: LA Gaudemet-Tallon, 503, 509–510; *Carruthers/Crawford*, Edin. L. R. 9 (2005), 65, 69; see also *Basedow*, in: Essays in Honor of Juenger, 175, 188–189.

2020 *Leible*, in: Streinz (ed.), EUV/AEUV, Art. 81 AEUV at 12; *id./Staudinger*, EuLF 2000/2001, 225, 230; *iid.*, AEDIPr 2001, 89, 102–103 (additionally relying on potential impediments to competition for suppliers in the EU); also see *Baratta*, in: Liber Pocar, 3, 18–19; *id.*, in: Tizzano (ed.), Trattati dell'Unione Europea, Art. 81 TFUE, III 4; *Rossi*, in: Calliess/Ruffert (eds.), EUV/AEUV, Art. 81 AEUV at 14; *Weber*, Die Vergemeinschaftung des IPR, 134–137; *Dohrn*, Die Kompetenzen der EG im IPR, 113–128, in particular 124–128; *Fletcher*, Conflict of Laws and EC Law, 52–56.

therefore, the threshold for measures by the Community was actually *lowered* in comparison to other bases of Community competence.[2021]

The TFEU has scuppered this debate anyway. In Article 81(2) TFEU, the relevance for the internal market is downgraded to an example ("particularly when" instead of "insofar as"). The criterion has ceased to be a limitation for the competence of the EU,[2022] if it ever was one. Accordingly, one cannot infer from it any statement on the inadmissibility of *lois uniformes*.

1.3. NO LIMITATION BY THE PRINCIPLE OF SUBSIDIARITY

The EU is limited in the exercise of its shared competence by the principle of subsidiarity. It requires, pursuant to Article 5(3) subparagraph 1 TEU, that "the objectives of the proposed action cannot be sufficiently achieved by the Member States", and that they can "be better achieved at Union level". It appears too sweeping a statement that the harmonisation of private international law "by its very nature" is in accordance with the principle of subsidiarity.[2023] To be sure, it generally does not necessitate changes of domestic substantive law, so that its "interference" with domestic law seems to be *relatively* moderate.[2024] It constitutes "shallow" integration as opposed to "deep" integration.[2025] Private international law is a significant tool to strike a "balance between centralised and more local systems of regulation",[2026] and is thus to be regarded favourably from the perspective of subsidiarity. But it does not follow that no interference at all, or perhaps interference limited to intra-Union cases,[2027] could not be even better (that is to say: mandated) from this point of view.

Yet the result seems to be correct. If one accepts that, in order not to have the citizen face any disadvantages from her civil matter having cross-border

2021 *Leible*, in: Streinz (ed.), EUV/AEUV, Art. 81 AEUV at 11; *id./Staudinger*, AEDIPr 2001, 89, 98; *Rossi*, in: Calliess/Ruffert (eds.), EUV/AEUV, Art. 81 AEUV at 13; *Dohrn*, Die Kompetenzen der EG im IPR, 107; but see *Bogdan*, in: Malatesta (ed.), The Unification of Choice of Law Rules on Torts, 33, 35.

2022 *Leible/Müller*, Yearbook of Private International Law 14 (2012/2013), 137, 141; *Barrière Barousse*, JDI 2010, 3, 11; *Dethloff/Hauschild*, FPR 2010, 489, 490; *Baratta*, in: Liber Pocar, 3, 13; *Hoppe*, in: Lenz/Borchardt (eds.), EU-Verträge, Art. 81 AEUV at 3; *Rossi*, in: Calliess/Ruffert (eds.), EUV/AEUV, Art. 81 AEUV at 13–14; more generally (change in the wording as an expansion of the EU's competence) *Fiorini*, ICLQ 57 (2008), 969, 976; *de Groot/Kuipers*, MJ 2008, 109, 111; but see *Kindler*, IPRax 2010, 44, 48.

2023 But see *de Groot/Kuipers*, MJ 2008, 109, 110; also the Commission's Rome II Proposal, COM(2003) 427 final, 7 ("The technique of harmonising conflict-of-laws [sic] rules fully respects the subsidiarity and proportionality principles since it enhances certainty in the law without demanding harmonisation of the substantive rules of domestic law.").

2024 To this effect also *Meeusen*, in: Liber Pocar, 685, 690.

2025 *Mills*, Confluence, 177.

2026 *Mills*, Confluence, 186.

2027 To this effect *Kindler*, IPRax 2010, 44, 48.

implications, the harmonisation of private international law is necessary, it is doubtful that the member states can sufficiently achieve this goal. Granted, they could negotiate and conclude pertinent international conventions, particularly also in the context of the Hague Conference with third states.[2028] Even if one agrees that Article 5(3) TEU envisions such international cooperation (it does not *exactly* fit any of the expressly mentioned "levels"),[2029] it is far from certain that all member states would agree to a given convention. While the Rome Convention was a successful instance of making a private international law convention in Europe, it cannot serve as a counterargument. Much fewer states were involved in its development than would be for a EU-wide convention nowadays. Furthermore, no other project of this kind came to fruition.[2030] It would seem that a legal act by the EU can achieve the objective of harmonisation better.[2031]

One might also wonder whether the principle of subsidiarity affects the competence to make *general provisions* of private international law. This question will be addressed momentarily.

1.4. COMPETENCE FOR GENERAL PROVISIONS

As a consequence, the EU has the competence to make provisions in all areas of private international law. The competence to make conflicts provisions (including for situations where a third state is involved) means the competence to make complete conflicts provisions, i.e. to set forth the subject matter, the connecting factor, and the governing law. When a solution pertaining to any of these elements is supposed to be the same for different conflicts rules, the EU could certainly make the same rule several times. It can just as well make a single rule that is relevant for more than one other rule, however, as this process

2028 *Lequette*, in: LA Gaudemet-Tallon, 503, 517; also to this effect, but seemingly undecided, *Pocar*, in: Malatesta (ed.), The Unification of Choice of Law Rules on Torts, 301, 304–305.

2029 The pertinent part of Article 5(3) subparagraph 1 reads, "[T]he Union shall act only if and in so far as the objectives of the proposed action cannot be sufficiently achieved by the Member States, *either at central level or at regional and local level* [...]" (emphasis added).

2030 As to both arguments, also see *Trüten*, Die Entwicklung des IPR in der EU, 204.

2031 To the same effect *von Hein*, in: Beaumont et al. (eds.), Cross-Border Litigation in Europe, 19, 27; *Weller*, in: id. (ed.), Europäisches Kollisionsrecht, at 36–37; *Trüten*, Die Entwicklung des IPR in der EU, §12 I 6 c (204–206); *Roth*, in: Remien/Kieninger (eds.), Europäische Kollisionsrechtsvereinheitlichung, 11, 25. With the EU having become a member of the Hague Conference, it itself now is able to use this setting to negotiate private international law conventions with third states. See also *Dohrn*, Die Kompetenzen der EG im IPR, 130–131, for disadvantages of (private international law) conventions in light of the goal of harmonisation.

of "factoring out"[2032] is merely a question of efficient legislative *technique*: the *content* of the legal act remains the same under either legislative approach. a(b + c) *equals* ab + ac, after all. If the Union has the competence to create a legal act with a certain content, it can choose either approach. It can also have fundamental policy decisions show through individual provisions, or set them forth expressly. Thus, the EU can make private international law rules or recitals of an overarching, formally and/or substantively general character.

It is important to recognise the limitation of the foregoing statement. It concerns general rules for *EU* private international law. It would be a much more doubtful endeavour if the EU were to draft general rules affecting specific domestic rules. It would be paradoxical, e.g. if the EU made a rule pursuant to which characterisation is to be carried out independently from domestic concepts, and wanted to have this rule apply to private international law at the domestic level that is not (yet) harmonised. This would certainly not make forum shopping less attractive: even if the subject matter "X" of country A and B had to be interpreted in a uniform (and autonomous) way, the private international law of A and B could still provide for different connecting factors for this subject matter; in the end, different laws could apply. One could already doubt if such a rule would be "aimed at ensuring [...] the compatibility of the rules", as Article 81(2) TFEU requires. In any case, such a measure would not achieve the objective better than domestic law could, and the principle of subsidiarity would be violated.[2033]

On a related note, this is also why the divergent geographical applicability of the existing private international law regulations is no theoretical problem. To be sure, the fact that not all regulations apply in all member states is considered to be one of the main roadblocks to an EU private international law code,[2034] or to general provisions of EU private international law in particular.[2035] This burdens political negotiations as to a respective instrument. However, as general provisions would only pertain to EU provisions to the extent that the latter are in force in, and binding upon, a given member state, a member state not participating in a given instrument would not be bound *in this regard* by general provisions. For example, a general provision would apply in a given member state in the context of Rome I and Rome II, but not for cases of divorce and legal separation.

2032 *Supra* Chapter 3, section 8.3.

2033 This is also why "the general part problem" of the idea of *lex specialis derogat legi generali* clashing with the idea of *lex superior derogat legi inferiori* (see *Schmidt-Kessel*, JZ 1998, 1135, 1137–1138) does not arise for general provisions of EU private international law as envisioned here. There can be no domestic *leges speciales* within the scope of application of EU private international law. Also see *Wilke*, GPR 2012, 334, 339.

2034 *Kieninger*, RW 2012, 406, 426–427.

2035 *Wagner*, in: Leible (ed.), General Principles, §4.04[B][3][c].

1.5. COMPETENCE TO MAKE A (GENERAL) PRIVATE INTERNATIONAL LAW *REGULATION*

As Article 81 TFEU does not contain any statement to the contrary, all types of legal acts are at the EU's disposal when it wants to make use of this competence.[2036] At the very least, one would have to interpret the references in Article 81(2) TFEU to the ordinary legislative procedure, and in Article 81(3) subparagraph 1 TFEU to the special legislative procedure, to mean that the EU can choose among the legal acts admitted by Article 289 (1) and (2) TFEU, respectively.[2037] Either way, the EU can make private international law regulations.[2038]

This means, first, that the EU was indeed able to adopt the six regulations at issue here *as regulations*.[2039] As a regulation does not require any implementation, this is the most suitable kind of legal act for private international law anyway.[2040] Second, if it decided to make general provisions of private international law, these could also be adopted as a regulation. To the extent that the EU has the competence to make the same rule *in* separate regulations, it has the competence to make the same rule *for* separate regulations in one (other) regulation.

1.6. COMPETENCE TO MAKE PROVISIONS ON CERTAIN GENERAL ISSUES

1.6.1. The Basic Answer

If the main steps taken in the field of competence are thus far correct, most issues identified above as general are accounted for already. The EU has the competence

---

2036 *Trüten*, Die Entwicklung des IPR in der EU, §12 I 4 (199); *Rossi*, in: Calliess/Ruffert (eds.), EUV/AEUV, Art. 81 AEUV at 16; *Basedow*, RabelsZ 73 (2009), 455, 460; *id.*, in: Essays in Honor of Juenger, 175, 191; *Dohrn*, Die Kompetenzen der EG im IPR, 139–141; *Baratta*, in: Tizzano (ed.), Trattati dell'Unione Europea, Art. 81 TFUE, II; *Leible/Staudinger*, EuLF 2000/2001, 225, 233; *iid.*, AEDIPr 2001, 89, 109–110; *Boele-Woelki*, in: LA Kurt Siehr, 61, 64; but see *Leible*, in: Streinz (ed.), EUV/AEUV, Art. 81 AEUV at 13–14 (all kinds of measures available for conflicts rules – in other areas possibly a different analysis, however).

2037 *Stumpf*, in: Schwarze (ed.), EU-Kommentar, Art. 81 AEUV at 6–8; similarly *Baratta*, in: Liber Pocar, 3, 16.

2038 According to *Basedow*, in: LA Borrás, 175, 183, "one great advantage" of Article 81 TFEU; as to doubts whether Article 65 TEC was a sufficient basis for private international law regulations *von Hein*, in: Beaumont et al. (eds.), Cross-Border Litigation in Europe, 19, 22–23.

2039 To the extent that regulations were adopted under Article 65 EC, the first point (i.e. the wording of said provision) applies as well.

2040 *von Hein*, in: Beaumont et al. (eds.), Cross-Border Litigation in Europe, 19, 23; *Basedow*, RabelsZ 73 (2009), 455, 460; *id.*, in: Essays in Honor of Juenger, 175, 191; *Leible/Staudinger*, EuLF 2000/2001, 225, 233. Even *Gaudemet-Tallon*, in: Essays in Honor of Juenger, 317, 325, who in general adopts a more sceptical perspective, admits that a directive would be inadequate.

under Article 81(2)(c) TFEU to make rules that determine the applicable law, which includes all issues raised by a conflicts rule itself. The EU legislator can thus specify what cases a given subject matter covers, as well as whether and to what extent domestic provisions are allowed to interfere with it etc.; it can lay down the connecting factor it deems appropriate for the respective subject matter, fixate it in time or not, and provide definitions and parameters for it etc.; and it can make its conflicts rules refer only to substantive law or to private international law, and determine whether and to what extent its conflicts rules can be disobeyed if the outcome under the governing law proves objectionable etc. The competence thus also includes rules on seemingly recondite issues like adaptation or the erroneous assumption concerning the applicable law, at least insofar as the rule concerned with any such issue is one determining the applicable law.[2041]

1.6.2. Special Cases

To the extent, however, that a conflicts provision implicates a question of court proceedings, or that the EU wants to make a substantive provision in the context of private international law, the basis of Article 81 TFEU may seem less firm.

Ascertainment and Application of Foreign Law

Among the less obvious issues, the questions with procedural overtones discussed in the course of this analysis still constitute a relatively easy case. To be sure, it is reasonable to consider Article 81(2)(c) TFEU too narrow a basis for rules on the ascertainment and application of foreign law. These issues may have a strong connection to conflict of laws (not really to "jurisdiction", the other matter covered by Article (81)(2)(c) TFEU), but most[2042] of their aspects do not concern the determination of the governing law. With Article 81(2)(f) TFEU, however, there is a basis for making pertinent provisions.[2043] Because of the connection to conflict of laws, the topic could suitably be dealt with alongside general rules of conflict of laws, i.e. in the very same regulation.[2044] A stand-alone legal act would also be possible, of course.[2045]

2041 It is possible to deal with these issues on the level of conflict of laws, see *supra* Chapter 3, sections 5.9.–5.10.

2042 A rule on the determination of the applicable law if the law deemed applicable in the first place cannot be ascertained, however, arguably could be based on Article (81)(2)(c) TFEU, for this is a genuine conflict of laws issue; see already *supra* Chapter 3, section 5.3.1.

2043 *Flessner*, in: LA Pintens, 593, 598–599; already *Hausmann*, EuLF 2008, I-1, I-13. Without any specific indication of which part of Article 81 TFEU is applicable *Basedow*, in: id./Pißler (eds.), PIL in Mainland China, Taiwan and Europe, 85, 87–88; *Trautmann*, Europäisches Kollisionsrecht und ausländisches Recht im nationalen Zivilverfahren, 410.

2044 Also *Trautmann*, Europäisches Kollisionsrecht und ausländisches Recht im nationalen Zivilverfahren, 413–414.

2045 *Kieninger*, in: Leible (ed.), General Principles, §17.04[B].

Substantive Provisions

More problematic are substantive provisions in or for the purposes of EU private international law. In principle, the subject matters of Article 81(2) TFEU indicate that harmonisation of substantive law cannot be based on Article 81 TFEU[2046] – even more so as the list, unlike its predecessor in Article 65 TEC, is exhaustive ("measures [...] aimed at ensuring" instead of "shall include").[2047]

From the outset, however, one can note that the wording of Article 81(2)(c) TFEU is not limited to making *conflicts* provisions. It allows for "measures" that ensure the "compatibility of the rules [...] concerning conflict of laws". This phrase covers substantive provisions that (merely) *pertain to* conflicts rules.[2048] *Within* the field of private international law, the EU can choose whether to make conflicts or substantive provisions.

A substantive provision that carries out an *adaptation* is an especially obvious candidate. As demonstrated above,[2049] the issue of adaptation only arises if at least one foreign law is applicable to a given case, i.e. exclusively when at least one conflicts provision has determined foreign law to be applicable. Adaptation and conflicts are joined at the hip. Moreover, cross-border implications, as required by Article 81(1) TFEU, exist *per definitionem* in such a case. The EU must simply be allowed to deal with a situation that its very own conflicts provisions created. Accordingly, e.g. it was perfectly within the EU's power to enact Article 32 Succession Regulation.[2050] By the same token, the EU has the competence to make a provision on *substitution*. Similarly, it has the competence to provide for *transposition*,[2051] to the extent that its conflicts provisions lead to a foreign law which in turn implicates a legal position unknown to the *lex fori*. Essentially, the EU competence for all these questions follows from them being genuine issues of private international law.[2052]

2046 *Kroll-Ludwigs*, Die Rolle der Parteiautonomie, 30; *Dethloff/Hauschild*, FPR 2010, 489, 490. But see *Barrière Barousse*, JDI 2010, 3, 29.

2047 *Haratsch/Koenig/Pechstein*, Europarecht, at 1123; *Kroll-Ludwigs*, Die Rolle der Parteiautonomie, 29; *Hoppe*, in: Lenz/Borchardt (eds.), EU-Verträge, Art. 81 AEUV at 3; *Stumpf*, in: Schwarze (ed.), EU-Kommentar, Art. 81 AEUV at 10; *Leible*, in: Streinz (ed.), EUV/AEUV, Art. 81 AEUV at 19; *Rosenau/Petrus*, in: Vedder/Heintschel von Heinegg (eds.), Europäisches Unionsrecht, Art. 81 AEUV at 10; *Rossi*, in: Calliess/Ruffert (eds.), EUV/AEUV, Art. 81 AEUV at 7; *Kotzur*, in: Geiger/Khan/id., EUV/AEUV, Article 81 AEUV at 6; but see *Hess*, in: Grabitz/Hilf, Das Recht der Europäischen Union, Art. 81 AEUV at 38 (without an explanation).

2048 Also see *Hess*, in: Grabitz/Hilf, Das Recht der Europäischen Union, Art. 81 AEUV at 29; *Baratta*, in: Tizzano (ed.), Trattati dell'Unione Europea, Art. 81 TFUE, III 2; similarly *Kuipers*, in: Basedow/Rühl/Ferrari/de Miguel Asensio (eds.), Encyclopedia of PIL, s. v. "European Union and Private International Law", III 2c.

2049 *Supra* Chapter 3, section 5.10.

2050 *Dutta*, in: MüKoBGB, vor Art. 1 EuErbVO at 20 and vor Art. 20 EuErbVO at 57; *Wilke*, RIW 2012, 601, 607.

2051 See *Dutta*, in: MüKoBGB, vor Art. 20 EuErbVO at 57 (for Article 31 Succession Regulation).

2052 Similarly *M.-P. Weller*, RabelsZ 81 (2017), 747, 779–780 (all questions of "consideration" in private international law covered by Article 81 TFEU).

2. LEGISLATIVE PROCEDURE

The legal "if" of a general part of EU private international law can thus be answered in the affirmative. The question of "how", however, threatens to pull the rug out from under the entire analysis.

2.1. TWO DIFFERENT LEGISLATIVE PROCEDURES FOR PRIVATE INTERNATIONAL LAW

Depending on the area of private international law, Article 81 TFEU provides for two different legislative procedures. In general, pursuant to Article 81(2) TFEU, measures are adopted "in accordance with the ordinary legislative procedure". But for measures concerning family law, Article 81(3) subparagraph 1 TFEU provides for a special legislative procedure. An instrument on general issues in the sense of the two approaches pursued in this analysis would pertain to family law, as well as to non-family law. Which procedure would have to be used?

If one could rely on an unequivocal focus of a regulation on general issues of private international law, one would end up with a clear answer. One would determine that such a regulation focuses either on family law or on non-family law, even if it touched side issues of the respective other area. As a consequence, one (and only one) of the two legislative procedures would apply in regard to the entire regulation. Alas, a classification along these lines seems impossible. Particularly as rules on general issues in the formal sense would affect the content of individual conflicts rules, they do not only concern isolated, secondary matters. A general regulation pertaining to the six current regulations would concern three family law regulations. Even when there was only one family law regulation in force, a potential regulation on general issues of the Rome Regulations and the Succession Regulation would not have clearly focused on non-family law,[2053] for its effect would have gone to the pith of the conflicts rules of Rome III, e.g. their legal consequence by allowing *renvoi*. On the other hand, even if family law measures at one point were to outnumber non-family law measures, a general regulation would still concern non-family law more than marginally for the reason just mentioned. One would not end up with a plain family law focus either.

If this were only a question of majorities, there would at least be no *theoretical* problem. A qualified majority (16(3) TEU) suffices for non-family law issues, whereas family law issues require unanimity pursuant to Article 81(3) TFEU. Yet unanimity is a special kind of qualified majority, so to speak. A general regulation pertaining to family law, as well as non-family law, would thus

[2053] *Wagner*, in: Leible (ed.), General Principles, §4.04 [B][2][b].

have to be passed unanimously. Political difficulties could and probably would ensue,[2054] but a legal obstacle would not exist.

The different legislative procedures, however, are not only a matter of different majorities.[2055] The ordinary legislative procedure means the *joint* adoption of a measure by the European Parliament and the Council, Articles 289(1) and 294 TFEU; in the special legislative procedure of Article 81(3) TFEU, the European Parliament is only *consulted*. Unanimity and consultation are no *maius* of qualified majority and joint decision. Rather, they form an *aliud*. To wit, fulfilling the requirements of the special legislative procedure of Article 81(3) TFEU cannot fulfil the requirements of the ordinary legislative procedure at the same time.

2.2. DOUBTS AS TO THE USEFULNESS OF THE PASSERELLE CLAUSE

The passerelle[2056]/rendezvous[2057]/bridging[2058] clause of Article 81(3) subparagraph 2 TFEU could be the way out. Pursuant to this provision, the Council, essentially in the course of the special legislative procedure of Article 81(3) subparagraph 1 TFEU, can determine "aspects of family law" to be subject to the ordinary legislative procedure. Afterwards, matters covered by Article 81(3) TFEU can be dealt with in the procedure of Articles 289(1) and 294 TFEU. As a result, there would solely be one kind of procedure for an entire regulation of general issues, even if it pertains to family law as well as non-family law.

This way out, however, only works if general issues can be considered "aspects" of family law. Those commentators who do not merely repeat the wording of Article 81(3) TFEU seem to assume that "aspects" essentially means "areas", i.e. that the passerelle clause makes it possible to subject certain areas of family law, such as custody or matters concerning birth or marriage certificates,

---

2054 As already happened concerning Rome III, see only *Basedow*, in: LA Borrás, 175, 182.

2055 Apparently overlooked by *Wagner*, in: Leible (ed.), General Principles, §4.04 [B][2][b]; certainly overlooked by myself, *Wilke*, GPR 2012, 334, 339.

2056 E.g. *von Hein*, in: Beaumont et al. (eds.), Cross-Border Litigation in Europe, 19, 24; *Kuipers*, in: Basedow/Rühl/Ferrari/de Miguel Asensio (eds.), Encyclopedia of PIL, s. v. "European Union and Private International Law", 2c; *Barrière Barousse*, JDI 2010, 3, 10; *Baratta*, in: Liber Pocar, 3, 21; *id.*, in: Tizzano (ed.), Trattati dell'Unione Europea, Art. 81 TFUE, IV; *Fiorini*, ICLQ 57 (2008), 969, 976; *de Groot/Kuipers*, MJ 2008, 109, 112.

2057 E.g. *Leible*, in: Streinz (ed.), EUV/AEUV, Art. 81 AEUV at 48; *Kotzur*, in: Geiger/Khan/id., EUV/AEUV, Article 81 AEUV at 16; *Hess*, in: Grabitz/Hilf, Das Recht der Europäischen Union, Art. 81 AEUV at 56.

2058 "Brückenklausel", e.g. *Kroll-Ludwigs*, Die Rolle der Parteiautonomie, 23 (note 122); *Dethloff/Hauschild*, FPR 2010, 489, 491; *Hoppe*, in: Lenz/Borchardt (eds.), EU-Verträge, Art. 81 AEUV at 13; *Rossi*, in: Calliess/Ruffert (eds.), EUV/AEUV, Art. 81 AEUV at 35.

to the ordinary legislative procedure.[2059] It is rather difficult to call a body of rules that, in principle, encompasses all conflict of laws in the field of family law (and more) an "area" of family law in this sense.[2060] To be sure, the wording itself does not exclude such an interpretation: an "aspect" is a part or a feature of something else. As amply demonstrated above, general rules of private international law, for the most part, deal with issues relating to different parts of a conflicts provision. Yet the idea behind Article 81(3) subparagraph 2 TFEU seems to be that there might be issues of family law that prove by and large uncontroversial,[2061] so that the member states feel comfortable relinquishing their *de facto* veto power in the Council (while at the same time giving a resulting measure more democratic legitimacy because of the bigger involvement of the European Parliament). From this perspective, "aspects" sounds much more like "subject areas", and much less like "issues potentially relevant for *all present and future* family law measures".

Even if one assumed, however, that Article 81(3) subparagraph 2 TFEU could be used to make general conflicts issues in family matters subject to the ordinary legislative procedure, subparagraph 3 causes a further, albeit only political, issue. Unlike its counterparts in Article 153(2) subparagraph 4 TFEU and Article 192(2) subparagraph 2 TFEU, the passerelle clause of Article 81(3) TFEU requires the national parliaments to be notified, and bestows veto power upon each and every single one of them. At the very least, to make use of the passerelle clause would thus be a move fraught with political risks.[2062]

2.3. A HYBRID PROCEDURE: COMBINING ARTICLE 81(2) AND (3) TFEU

Arguably, the EU legislator could proceed on the basis of a combination[2063] of Article 81(2) and (3) TFEU: one would join the criterion of joint adoption and the criterion of unanimity. This way, the "strongest" aspect of each

2059 *Rossi*, in: Calliess/Ruffert (eds.), EUV/AEUV, Art. 81 AEUV at 35; *Dethloff/Hauschild*, FPR 2010, 489; also see *Kotzur*, in: Geiger/Khan/id., EUV/AEUV, Article 81 AEUV at 16 ("Materien" instead of "Aspekte").

2060 *Wagner*, in: Leible (ed.), General Principles, §4.04 [B][2][b].

2061 Which means that Article 81(3) subparagraph 2 TFEU probably will only be made use of when consensus is likely already in regard to the individual provisions to be made later, *Dethloff/Hauschild*, FPR 2010, 489, 492.

2062 *Wagner*, in: Leible (ed.), General Principles, §4.04 [B][2][b]. See the generally pessimistic assessments of *Leible*, in: Streinz (ed.), EUV/AEUV, Art. 81 AEUV at 48–49; *Dethloff/Hauschild*, FPR 2010, 489, 491–493; and *Hess*, in: Grabitz/Hilf, Das Recht der Europäischen Union, Art. 81 AEUV at 56.

2063 For a combination apparently *Lagarde*, in: Fallon/id./Poillot-Peruzzetto (eds.), Quelle architecture pour un code européen de droit international privé?, 365, 367; touched upon by *Wiedemann*, in: Vaz de Sequeira/de Almeida Ribeiro (eds.), Católica Graduate Legal Research Conference 2014 - Conference Proceedings, 175, 196.

legislative procedure would be preserved, thus not curtailing the rights of any legislative body involved.[2064] Even so, the political uncertainties implicated by the requirement of unanimity[2065] would also arise, and be additionally paired up with a procedure arguably more prone to political uncertainties itself.

2.4. THE RESULTING DILEMMA – AND POSSIBLE REMEDIES

The analysis has produced an odd result: the EU has the competence to make a regulation on general issues of all (of its) private international law, but the TFEU does not expressly provide a legislative procedure for a regulation with such a scope. While the passerelle clause of Article 81 TFEU would produce the desired outcome (i.e. just one kind of procedure), its requirements appear ill-suited for general issues of private international law, to say nothing of political uncertainties. The latter would also exist if one were to rely on a hybrid procedure. Can the paradoxical predicament be solved other than by changing the TFEU?

2.4.1. Two Regulations

There is, of course, no legal obstacle keeping the EU from making *two* regulations on general issues of private international law: one for matters of non-family law pursuant to the ordinary legislative procedure, and one for matters of family law pursuant to the special legislative procedure. Such a course of action, however, would be at odds with one of the presumable objectives behind a regulation for general issues, i.e. the avoidance of repetitions.[2066] Moreover, even if both of these regulations were passed, they would also have to be changed at the same time in case that modifications are required or desired later. This would implicate the two different procedures again, with the risk that unanimity in the Council, or agreement in the European Parliament, cannot be reached anymore. As a result, two different versions of the general regulation could apply, which would also be clearly at odds with the unifying purpose behind a general regulation.

2.4.2. Reference to, *not* by *the General Regulation*

Thus far, the implicit assumption has been that a regulation on general issues would have a certain scope of application of its own: it would cover EU conflicts

2064 Unless one considered it a right under Article 81(3) TFEU that the European Parliament *only* is *consulted* and a right under the ordinary legislative procedure *not* to require unanimity in the Council.

2065 From an empirical perspective *Yüksel*, in: Beaumont et al. (eds.), Cross-Border Litigation in Europe, 35, 38.

2066 *Wagner*, in: Leible (ed.), General Principles, §4.04 [B][2][a]; *infra* Chapter 6, section 2.3.

rules in family as well as non-family law. But what if the regulation had an open scope, i.e. if it were only applicable if another instrument referred to it?

By definition, a regulation on general issues (at least in the formal sense as expounded above) not applicable on its own for matters of family law would not contain anything specific to family law. Therefore, it could be passed in the ordinary legislative procedure.[2067] In order for it to actually be applicable, however, other private international law regulations would need to refer to it. Such a reference would have to be made (or inserted into existing regulations) in the respective legislative procedure.

Static Reference

Problems arise if the general regulation is supposed to be changed at some point. If the reference to the general regulation by the special regulations is "static", i.e. limited to the content of the general regulation at the time the reference was made, there is a risk of different versions of the general regulation applying at the same time. This would happen if not all references by the special regulations were updated at the same time – a scenario that could be caused by one of the legislative procedures "working out" and the other not.

Dynamic Reference

The more practical solution would thus be a "dynamic" reference, a reference to the general regulation in whatever current form it has assumed. Unfortunately, it is again the different legislative procedures that come to haunt us at this point: a dynamic reference in the context of family law matters would be illegal.

In theory, a legislator can make dynamic references to other legal instruments of its own (internal reference) or to legal instruments of another legislator (external reference). The former alternative raises no problems. If the legislator later changes the object of reference, it could have changed the referring instrument at the same time. To avoid this kind of double work, the legislator can make a dynamic reference from the start. Much more problematic, however, is a dynamic reference to another legislator's instrument. In this scenario, another legislator can change the content of the referring legislator's rules without the latter necessarily even noticing. (As this cannot happen with a static reference, that type of reference causes no similar problem.) Functionally speaking, a dynamic reference to another legislator is thus a delegation of power; such delegations are usually subject to specific (constitutional) requirements.

Seen in this light, a dynamic reference in an EU regulation to another EU regulation seems to be innocuous at first; it seems to be an instance of

---

2067 *Wagner*, in: Leible (ed.), General Principles, §4.04 [B][2][c].

internal reference. Yet one must not forget that the family law legislator has to follow a special legislative procedure. Its requirements would be circumvented by a dynamic reference. Moreover, a dynamic reference to a regulation passed in the ordinary legislative procedure would be tantamount, in many respects, to making areas covered by Article 81(3) TFEU subject to the ordinary legislative procedure. Arguably the only way to do so in accordance with the TFEU, however, is through the passerelle clause. If its requirements are not met, or if the procedure prescribed by it is not complied with, there is no way of making aspects of family law subject to the ordinary legislative procedure. For these reasons, a dynamic reference by a family law regulation to a general regulation would be illegal from the perspective of the TFEU.

2.4.3. *Reference in Part to and in Part by the General Regulation*

A third option would be based on the notions just stated but would contain a twist. The starting point is the same: a regulation on general issues with an open scope could be passed in the ordinary legislative procedure, just like all private international law regulations with non-family law content. Hence, it is also possible to make a regulation on general issues that, on its own, pertains to all private international law regulations with non-family law content. Only the measures with family law content would need to refer to the general regulation in order for the latter to be applicable. To put it another way, the general regulation could have a split scope: in part *defined* to supplement all non-family law regulations of private international law, in part *designed* to be susceptible to application in family law regulations of private international law if they refer to it.

To be sure, the illegality of a potential dynamic reference by a family law regulation remains. But this approach is more efficient than the second model in that a later change of the general regulation at least does not require any separate change to any of the non-family law regulations.

2.4.4. *A Model Regulation*

If one arrived at the conclusion that the current setting of the EU Treaties makes it overly difficult to pass a single functional piece of legislation with general provisions of private international law, one could still think about passing it as a model – or even of only having a scholarly working group draft a model similar to the DCFR.[2068] Neither model regulation would be binding, obviously. But either option would at least provide the EU legislator with a check list, so to speak, of

[2068] For a scathing critique of scholarly codification efforts see *Riedl*, in: Jahrbuch Junger Zivilrechtswissenschaftler 2004, 31, who does point out pitfalls and weaknesses of such projects of which one at least better be aware.

which issues to consider and concrete examples of how to draft the respective solutions.[2069] Even if EU private international law remained fragmented, the separate instruments would be more coherent because they would be drafted, reviewed, and recast using a common yardstick.

3. SUMMARY

Pursuant to Article 81(2) TFEU, and for most issues Article 81(2)(c) TFEU in particular, the EU has the competence to create provisions for all private international law issues identified as formally or substantively general – to the extent that the resulting provisions relate to *EU* private international law. Paradoxically, however, the TFEU does not provide for a single procedure to make use of this competence. The passerelle clause of Article 81(3) subparagraph 2 TFEU, or a hybrid procedure not expressly provided for in the TFEU, does not seem to be a viable way out. By giving the general provisions a split scope, one would at least end up with a working solution, although it would be neither excessively elegant nor immune to political obstacles.

2069 Also see *infra* Chapter 6, section 2.4. for the "educational" value of general provisions.

CHAPTER 6
POLICY

Whether or not a legislator should make general provisions for a given area of law is obviously not a question confined to private international law. The pros and cons of a general part of a civil code have been a topic of discussion "[e]ver since the heyday of Pandectism".[2070] Pandectist textbooks following the structure introduced by Heise[2071] influenced the 1865 Saxon Civil Code, i.e. the "trial run" for the BGB,[2072] and then the BGB itself.[2073] But was it appropriate to transfer this structure of scholarly presentation and teaching, itself not free from critique, to legislation?[2074] Then again, criminal codes even before the 19th century had general parts, with the "technically exemplary"[2075] 1810 French *Code pénal* being a particularly influential model at the beginning of that century.[2076] Roughly two centuries later, the question of general provisions arises for EU private international law.

1. LEGISLATORS, SCHOLARS, TEACHERS: ANOTHER TRIPARTITE DISTINCTION

To begin with, it is worth emphasising that the following remarks only concern the legislator. The topic "general issues/rules" as such does not require this perspective. In particular, it can also be analysed in relation to scholars and teachers. These three dimensions must be set apart.[2077] At least as long as

---

2070 *Wieacker*, A History of Private Law in Europe, 385.

2071 *Heise*, Grundriß, 3; see *Brockmöller*, Die Entstehung der Rechtstheorie, 173.

2072 *Wieacker*, A History of Private Law in Europe, 367; *Zweigert/Dietrich*, in: Stoljar (ed.), Problems of Codification, 34, 38; *Schmidt*, Scand. Stud. L. 9 (1965), 131, 136.

2073 *Zitelmann*, GrünhZ 33 (1906), 1; *Medicus/Petersen*, AT, at 19.

2074 *Schmoeckel*, in: HKK-BGB, vor §1 at 30–42.

2075 *Vormbaum*, A Modern History of German Criminal Law, 66.

2076 See for example the 1851 Prussian Criminal Code whose first part concerns the punishment of felonies and misdemeanours *in general* and whose second part concerns *individual* felonies and misdemeanours; also *Schmoeckel*, in: HKK-BGB, vor §1 at 31; *Vormbaum*, A Modern History of German Criminal Law, 66. For the historical development in criminal law *Mertens*, Gesetzgebungskunst, 442; *Tiedemann*, in: FS Baumann, 7,.8–9.

2077 Expressly already *Zitelmann*, GrünhZ 33 (1906), 1, 4; nowadays e.g. *Schmidt*, Zivilrechtskodifikation in Brasilien, 312.

law is considered to be a systematic discipline[2078] – which is arguably (still) the European way of conceiving of law[2079] – the *scholarly* necessity of finding general patterns in the law and structuring it accordingly can hardly be questioned.[2080] This much is accepted even by those to whom a legislative general part in substantive private law is anathema.[2081] The often copious separate chapters on "general" or "preliminary" issues in books on private international law, even in member states without a respective code,[2082] demonstrate that this insight applies to private international law as well – and that it is anything but limited to the idea of law as "legal science". On the other hand, it has also rarely been disputed that general statements about (substantive private) law are not exactly the ideal place to start when *instructing* novices in the law.[2083] When faced with generalities, their interest in the law will probably wane quickly. As students of private international law seldom have no prior legal knowledge whatsoever, however, one can wonder whether this realisation applies to private international law with the same force.

In any case, the real bone of contention has been the *legislative* general part in substantive private law. Recently, Schmidt tautly summarised the arguments,[2084] so that there is even less reason to recount the debate here. Much more important for present purposes are the questions of whether the peculiarities of private international law in Europe warrant a different take on the issue, and whether the force of "traditional" arguments for and against a legislative general part of substantive private law increase or decrease when applied to this field of law.

2. THE LEGISLATIVE SOLUTION

2.1. "GENERAL PROVISIONS" vs. "GENERAL PART"

Thus far, the term "general part" has mostly been avoided when discussing private international law, unless conveying someone else's ideas has made it

2078 *Wieacker*, A History of Private Law in Europe, 386.

2079 *Reimann*, RabelsZ 78 (2014), 1, 6.

2080 See e.g. *Medicus/Petersen*, AT, at 39; *Zitelmann*, GrünhZ 33 (1906), 1, 19; *Azzi/Boskovic*, in: iidem (eds.), Quel avenir pour la théorie générale des conflits de lois?, 1; for a relatively rare express justification of this academic approach see *von Savigny*, System I, 391.

2081 *Schmidt*, Zivilrechtskodifikation in Brasilien, 312 (with note 98).

2082 *Supra* Chapter 2, section 1.2.

2083 See already *von Savigny*, System I, 392; *Zitelmann*, GrünhZ 33 (1906), 1, 30; also *Schmoeckel*, in: HKK-BGB, vor §1 at 45; *Wieacker*, A History of Private Law in Europe, 386.

2084 *Schmidt*, Zivilrechtskodifikation in Brasilien, 312–321 (general part in general), 321–326 (general part of the BGB in particular); also see *Münch*, in: Behrends/Sellert (eds.), Kodifikationsgedanke, 147, 149–150 (with note 11) for an overview of positions regarding the German BGB.

necessary to mention it. In the following, the "general part" will figure more prominently because the desirability of general provisions has been discussed most extensively in connection with the codification of substantive private law, and more specifically in connection with the BGB and its general part. This already highlights one of the topics to be touched upon momentarily, the relationship between the idea of general provisions and the idea of codification. Yet "general part" also concerns one of the ways of establishing general provisions within an area of law, i.e. a question of legislative technique. Both topics will be addressed in turn from the perspective of EU private international law.

2.1.1. *The Link to the Idea of Codification*

A part requires a whole. A "whole", i.e. comprehensive and relatively complete, legislative instrument is typically called a code. To mention the idea of a general part is thus likely to evoke positive or negative reactions associated with the idea of codification, particularly as the topic of a potential EU private international law code has been discussed over the last decade or so.[2085] As a general part by definition contains general provisions, even the latter term alone might produce this effect. Yet the concepts of "general part"/"general provisions" and "code" can and should be separated. Obviously, there can be codes without a general part – but a general part without a code is no oxymoron, either.

As demonstrated above, both formally and substantively general provisions of private international law require individual conflicts provisions to operate; without *them*, a general part indeed makes no sense at all. It does not matter, however, whether these conflicts provisions add up to a complete and comprehensive piece of legislation, nor whether they can be found in the same instrument as the general provisions. General provisions can fulfil their *function* of resolving recurring issues or enshrining policy considerations independently from these questions of content and structure. If a "proper" code were required to cover areas of law A through Z, but a given instrument only covered A through M, general provisions could still set forth solutions or standards for A through M. As long as there is no problem of competence, the general provisions could also pertain to conflicts rules of one or more entirely separate instrument(s). It would not even constitute a terminological atrocity

---

2085 See *Trüten*, Die Entwicklung des IPR in der EU, in particular §19 III–IV (660–679); *Kramer/de Rooij*, NIPR 2013, 1; *Ballester*, A European Code on PIL (including the estimated cost of not having such a code of €137,710,000); *Kieninger*, RW 2012, 406, 423–431; *Nourissat*, in: Douchy-Oudot/Guinchard (eds.), La justice civil européenne en marche, 174; Fallon/Lagarde/Poillot-Peruzzetto (eds.), Quelle architecture pour un code européen de droit international privé?; iid. (eds.), La matière civile et commerciale, socle d'un code européen de droit international privé?; *Czepelak*, ERPL 2010, 705; *Garcimartín Alférez*, EuLF 2007, I-77; *Siehr*, in: Jud/Rechberger/Reichelt (eds.), Kollisionsrecht in der Europäischen Union, 77.

to call a separate instrument of general provisions a "general part", as it would form a part, a portion, an aspect of private international law as an *area of law*, just not of a bigger *instrument*.

Transferred to EU private international law, this means that one's stance concerning a potential EU code of private international law should not necessarily influence one's opinion of general provisions of EU private international law, even if one were to compile them in a "general part". Even opponents or sceptics of codification efforts (on the EU level[2086] and/or in private international law) must face the existence of the six regulations[2087] discussed in this book and the common issues they raise. Conversely, even those who consider codification to be the best thing since sliced bread are not exempt from having to explain why the creation of general provisions of EU private international law is a good idea.

2.1.2. Legislative Techniques: Compilation, Insertion, Repetition

"General part" does convey, however, a certain idea of how general provisions are drafted, namely grouped together ("compilation technique"). But this is not the only way to resolve general issues uniformly; rather, it is only one of three.[2088] A legislator could insert a provision into one area of law and then refer to it from other areas ("insertion technique"), or it might as well repeat the same rule whenever the issue arises ("repetition technique"). While the law would be exactly the same in all of these scenarios,[2089] the three techniques imply different policy considerations.[2090] In this regard, the terms "general provisions" and "general part" cannot be used interchangeably.

2.2. COMPATIBILITY WITH DOMESTIC PRECONCEPTIONS ABOUT LAW

2.2.1. An Alien Structure?

"Imposing general parts on unwilling domestic legal systems can be just as problematic as the opposite, namely leaving the question hanging in the air

2086 For substantive private law see e.g. *Markesinis*, ERPL 5 (1997), 519, 524: "The idea of a European Code […] belongs to the 'Paradise of Legal Ideas' that would have appealed to some Pandectists but leave most of us on my side of the Channel sceptical to say the least."

2087 Also see *Czepelak*, ERPL 2010, 705, 726 (potential dissatisfaction of common lawyers with a private international law code as great as with the existence of individual regulations, anyway).

2088 *Heck*, AcP 146 (1941), 1, 15 (referring to his remarks on structuring the law for the purposes of lectures, 7); *Zweigert/Dietrich*, in: Stoljar (ed.), Problems of Codification, 34, 48.

2089 See *Zitelmann*, GrünhZ 33 (1906), 1, 24 ("self-delusion" to think that the insertion technique makes any difference as to content when compared to a general part).

2090 See in particular *infra* section 2.3.

as to how [...] issues blend in with the larger doctrine of private law."[2091] Transferred to our subject matter, the first part of this statement points out the potential problem of introducing compulsory general provisions to legal systems not used to this kind of structure in the respective field. The implication is at least twofold: for one thing, there is potential political controversy in the drafting process, caused by resistance of those legal systems to which the notion is alien. For another, if general provisions have (nevertheless) been created, their application might cause practical difficulties in these legal systems – at least in the beginning – simply because the legislative technique is unusual for those involved in legal proceedings.

These are grave concerns for substantive private law. It is rather questionable, however, whether they pertain to private international law as well. A knee-jerk defence reaction would be beside the point in any case. One of the findings of the country reports above was that about two-thirds of the member states have private international codes that provide for general provisions, more or less formally separate from other conflicts provisions. The idea of structuring private international law along the lines of "general vs. special" is known in all of the other member states too. To be sure, as pointed out in the preceding section, the existence of scholarly general parts does not allow for any inferences as to the desirability and usefulness of legislative general parts; political resistance cannot be ruled out. But, first, their widespread occurrence in contrast to other areas of (private) law of the respective legal systems can be seen as an indication that the idea of general rules of private international law has a certain reasonableness, perhaps even a certain appeal. It does not appear a foregone conclusion that common law member states will be opposed to the idea as such (unlike perhaps to the idea of codification[2092]). Second, where jurists are used to such a conceptualisation of private international law from their education, problems in application are not to be expected.

Moreover, EU private international law already contains sectoral general provisions. As such, they do not seem to have been the cause for any controversy. The legislative technique of separate sections for general provisions on an intermediate level is now known everywhere in the EU anyway.

2.2.2. Conceptual Parallels in Criminal Law

An intradisciplinary comparative perspective may help to shed further light on this issue. Legislative general parts in *criminal* law do not seem to have

2091 *Dannemann*, in: Adams/Bomhoff (eds.), Practice and Theory in Comparative Law, 96, 104 (as to EU rules of substantive contract law).

2092 *Kieninger*, RW 2012, 406, 425.

stirred up much controversy,[2093] although they have been around for more than two centuries and are a phenomenon known in most member states.[2094] If the distinction between general and specific provisions of criminal law is addressed, the applicability of the former in the context of the latter is usually stressed.[2095] General provisions are considered a necessary supplement of specific provisions.[2096] A qualitative criterion has even been expressly rejected.[2097] In the terminology used here, general provisions of criminal law are thus characterised by their *formally* general nature. This also explains why the metaphor of "factoring out" has caught on in German criminal law,[2098] although it is not "mathematically" correct here either.[2099]

One reason for the broad acceptance of general provisions in criminal law could be their formal nature. Two more reasons suggest themselves:[2100] first, compared with all of substantive private law, the field of criminal law appears to be manageable as regards the number of issues. This makes it easier to detect (and agree upon) commonalities, as well as to identify any need for exceptions. The creation of general provisions thus appears to be a great deal easier in criminal law than in substantive private law. Second, the principle of *nulla poena sine lege* particularly implicates the need for an exhaustive code, to be achieved in part by setting forth general rules.[2101] By contrast, in substantive private law, questions can simply be left to the courts and academia.

These three reasons can be transferred to (EU) private international law. Most general issues of private international law discussed (and enshrined in codes) today can be characterised as formally general.[2102] While private international law spans all substantive law, it typically raises much fewer issues because of its broad categorisations and its limited (albeit essential) function in determining the outcome of a case. To be sure, private international law is not subject to *nulla poena sine lege*, and domestic codification or reform efforts

2093 *Mertens*, Gesetzgebungskunst, 442–449.

2094 *Grünewald*, JZ 2011, 972, 975; *Tiedemann*, in: FS Lenckner, 411, 415 and passim; in particular, see *Mansdörfer*, in: id. (ed.), Die allgemeine Straftatlehre des common law, 1, 20–21, for the draft general part of criminal law under common law.

2095 See e.g. *Bohlander*, The German Criminal Code, 6.

2096 *Fincke*, Das Verhältnis des Allgemeinen zum Besonderen Teil des Strafrechts, 31.

2097 *Fincke*, Das Verhältnis des Allgemeinen zum Besonderen Teil des Strafrechts, 20–22.

2098 *Supra* Chapter 3, section 8.3. (History and Prevalence).

2099 See in particular *Tiedemann*, in: FS Baumann, 7, 11, who points out that specific rules of criminal law mandate certain conduct, while general provisions concern the application of criminal law and the attribution of (given) conduct.

2100 *Mertens*, Gesetzgebungskunst, 449.

2101 Also see *Tiedemann*, in: FS Lenckner, 411, 415–416; *Fincke*, Das Verhältnis des Allgemeinen zum Besonderen Teil des Strafrechts, 13–14.

2102 Just compare the size of the respective chapters in this book.

have often left questions, especially general ones, to the courts and academia. Yet the need for uniform application of *EU* law may at least encourage the EU legislator to leave as few (formally) general issues as possible without a legislative solution.

2.2.3. Summary

General provisions of private international law, even in a general part, are hardly an unusual concept for the member states. On the contrary, quite a lot of groundwork already exists, both on the domestic level and the EU level. Structural parallels to criminal law further underpin this view. General provisions of private international law are no Procrustean bed for the member states.

2.3. CLARITY, COHERENCE, AND ELIMINATION OF REDUNDANCIES

The three main arguments in favour of the legislative creation of general provisions are the goals of clarity, coherence, and elimination of redundancies.[2103] They overlap, of course, but will be considered separately (as much as possible) in the following.

2.3.1. Clarity

The goal of clarity is quite obvious, at least in its formal dimension. To expressly distinguish general and specific provisions in a legislative instrument by way of the compilation technique necessarily provides it with a rudimentary structure. Anyone turning to the instrument to ascertain how the law stands does not face a mere list of provisions,[2104] in which she would be left entirely on her own to orient herself. Rather, she immediately comes across a guidepost, channelling further research into the instrument. Moreover, where a question arises for which specific rules do not provide an answer, the law would still not be unclear as long as a general rule applies.

2103 For EU private international law recently *Wurmnest*, in: Leible (ed.), General Principles, §14.01; *Lurger/Melcher*, IPR, at 8/12–8/16; *Ballester*, A European Code on PIL, 11; in general e.g. *Schmidt*, Zivilrechtskodifikation in Brasilien, 313; for the general part of the BGB e.g. *Schmoeckel*, in: HKK-BGB, vor §1 at 41.

2104 For an extreme example, see English statutes up until the middle of the 19th century: no structure in the form of articles or even paragraphs, no numbering; *Mertens*, Gesetzgebungskunst, 429.

2.3.1.1. The Critique of Comprehensibility/Accessibility

From a more substantive perspective, however, the idea of clarity becomes a question of comprehensibility and accessibility of the law. This, in turn, has always been one of the main areas of critique lodged against general parts in substantive private law. The general part of the BGB in particular has been said to speak an "artificial language incomprehensible to the layman".[2105] The old joke goes that the difference between the BGB and the bible is that the bible has been translated into German. The abstractions of the BGB are supposed to remove it too far from social reality,[2106] making the law "anaemic".[2107] Medicus has furnished a telling example: in the BGB, it takes seven intellectual steps to arrive at the pertinent general provisions to analyse only the formation of a sales contract.[2108]

In this regard, the insertion technique may have an advantage over the compilation technique,[2109] as the general issue is resolved in concrete terms and potentially in a context where it is of particular relevance. The repetition technique could also produce more clarity because the reader is at no point in time required to jump back and forth between different parts. On the other hand, a legislative instrument could be said to become unclear simply because of the high number of provisions necessitated by the repetition technique.

2.3.1.2. Two Ripostes

For present purposes, the validity of the critique of the BGB and its general part/compilation technique[2110] can be assumed. Some have already expressed

2105 *Boehmer*, Einführung, 76; similarly *Medicus/Petersen*, AT, at 39. Then again, the fathers of the BGB did not really have the general population in mind, *Schmoeckel*, in: HKK-BGB, vor §1 at 7.

2106 *Wieacker*, A History of Private Law in Europe, 378 and 385; more recently *Koziol*, AcP 212 (2012), 1, 6–7. The abstractions of the BGB even were a target of national-socialism, see *Schmoeckel*, in: HKK-BGB, vor § 1 at 46, and *Schlegelberger*, Abschied vom BGB, in particular 12 and 21.

2107 *Hübner*, AT, at 79. The wording is somewhat problematic as it echoes the national-socialist attack on the general part of the BGB: *Schlegelberger*, Abschied vom BGB, 21.

2108 The example has been maintained in the new edition of the venerable textbook: *Medicus/Petersen*, AT, at 36–37; for similar examples in English, *Zweigert/Dietrich*, in: Stoljar (ed.), Problems of Codification, 34, 37 ("complicates the treatment" even of simple cases); *Rheinstein*, Ind. L. J. 34 (1959), 546, 550–551 (intended to demonstrate the *advantages* of the levels of abstraction).

2109 See *Bariatti/Pataut*, in: Fallon/Lagarde/Poillot-Peruzzetto (eds.), Quelle architecture pour un code européen de droit international privé?, 337, 339.

2110 The picture has been painted with a broad brush. As regards legislative definitions, for example, the BGB often adheres to the insertion technique.

similar worries in relation to EU private international law.[2111] There are two ways, however, to refute, or at least weaken, the argument in this regard. First, one has to call into question the comparability of the level of abstraction.[2112] It is indubitably high for the (general part of the) BGB that involves several layers of abstraction.[2113] But for private international law, the analysis above has demonstrated that (formally) general rules – theoretically and empirically – require just one operation of factoring out, just one step of abstraction: a certain issue arises for more than one conflicts rule and is consequently dealt with once for all of them.

Moreover, with the exception of purely *substantively* general provisions, of which there are none in EU private international law,[2114] general provisions of private international law reflect *concrete* recurring issues. They do not involve any potentially "artificial" or "philosophical" concepts that would need to be broken down before they can actually be applied. As Heck contended – quite courageously, considering the times – in defence of the general part of the BGB, the dichotomy of general and special is no feature of law specifically, but of every kind of collection of rules, from manuals for horticulture or for breeding chickens to cookbooks.[2115] The average citizen is quite used to such a level of abstraction. Conversely, no legislator can expect citizens to read a legal instrument from start to finish without taking account of its structure.[2116] Against the backdrop of every domestic private international law code having general provisions, it also appears that the fear of introducing an unmanageable level of abstraction has not deterred even one private international law legislator in the EU. On the contrary, several private international law codes, with their general provisions, have expressly been praised for facilitating access to the law.[2117]

Second, one can attack the premise of the critique. It clearly depends on the idea that the general population is the addressee of legislation, in the

2111 *Corneloup/Nourissat*, in: Fallon/Lagarde/Poillot-Peruzzetto (eds.), Quelle architecture pour un code européen de droit international privé?, 257, 261.

2112 Notably, *Schmidt*, Scand. Stud. L. 9 (1965), 131, 148, wonders in relation to the BGB whether "*all* these distinctions between different levels of abstraction are truly necessary" (emphasis added), perhaps implying that some level of abstraction would be fine.

2113 See e.g. *Zweigert/Dietrich*, in: Stoljar (ed.), Problems of Codification, 34, 37.

2114 Purely substantively general statements only can be found in the recitals, see *supra* Chapter 4, section 4.

2115 *Heck*, AcP 146 (1941), 1, 26–27; for the vivid illustrations, 8–9 (concerning the general part in legal education).

2116 See *Heck*, AcP 146 (1941), 1, 25 (refuting the alleged problem of the BGB's general part of dealing with heterogeneous issues).

2117 For Belgium: *Francq*, RabelsZ 70 (2006), 235, 278; similarly *Fiorini*, ICLQ 54 (2005), 499, 508. For Bulgaria: *Zidarova/Stančeva-Minčeva*, RabelsZ 71 (2007), 398, 407. For Italy: *Kindler*, RabelsZ 61 (1997), 227, 284. For the Netherlands: *Boele-Woelki/van Iterson*, in: van Erp/van Vliet (eds.), Netherlands Report, 145, 177.

sense that it should be able to grasp the law simply by reading the respective provisions.[2118] Yet, historically speaking, even when this was the fundamental legislative idea, the "general public could not be induced to use the [Prussian] General Land Law for bedside reading to any greater degree than had been the case with Justinian's *Digest*".[2119] The French *Code Civil* may have served as Stendhal's manual of style,[2120] but has also been recommended as a soporific.[2121] To expect the average citizen to comprehend the law through its perusal is simply a utopian vision,[2122] "romantic fancy".[2123]

If this observation is correct for substantive private law, i.e. legal rules that provide for an actual outcome (also) for cases of everyday life, legal rules determining the application of substantive rules will not fare any better. It may not be an accident that neither Rome I nor Rome II mentions the "citizen",[2124] not even in their recitals. It would be rather hard to pretend that private international law is not a field for jurists. Certain metaphors about private international law as a labyrinth,[2125] or a "swamp, [...] inhabited by learned but eccentric professors who theorize about mysterious matters in a strange and incomprehensible jargon",[2126] come to mind. A clear structure still would have the advantage of making access to private international law easier for general practitioners, who also increasingly face "demands for advice in the international setting",[2127] as has been emphasised in the context of several domestic private international law codes.[2128]

Admittedly, on the other hand, cross-border transactions and family relations are increasingly become part of everyday life in the EU. Rome III,

---

2118 For an historical overview see *Mertens*, Gesetzgebungskunst, 380–406. Of course, the general population *is* the addressee of legislation in the sense that the law concerns their (everyday) dealings.

2119 *Zimmermann*, ERPL 3 (1995), 95, 108 (italics in the original).

2120 Opinions are already divided as to whether this is to be praised or condemned, see *Newman*, Fr. Rev. 43 (1970), 434, 435.

2121 *Münch*, in: Behrends/Sellert (eds.), Kodifikationsgedanke, 147, 158.

2122 *Schmidt*, Zivilrechtskodifikation in Brasilien, 319; *Zimmermann*, ERPL 3 (1995), 95, 108. But there may be a constitutional limit for the complexity of legislation, see (for Germany) BVerfGE 5, 25, 31–34 [1956], and *Noll*, Gesetzgebungslehre, 182.

2123 *Zweigert/Dietrich*, in: Stoljar (ed.), Problems of Codification, 34, 53.

2124 Nor does the Council Resolution on the Quality of Drafting of Community Legislation for EU legislation in general (but guideline No. 4 at least mentions "those to whom the act is to apply").

2125 *Fränkel*, ZAIPR 4 (1930), 239.

2126 *Prosser*, Mich. L. Rev. 51 (1953), 959, 971.

2127 See *Leible/Müller*, Yearbook of Private International Law 14 (2012), 137, 152.

2128 For Belgium: *Pertegas*, IPRax 2006, 53, 61; *Francq*, RabelsZ 70 (2006), 235, 239–240. For the Czech Republic: *Pauknerová/Pfeiffer*, Journal of Private International Law 10 (2014), 205, 217. For Greece: *Vrellis*, in: Symeonides (ed.), PIL at the End of the 20th Century, 243, 257. For the Netherlands: *Rammeloo*, EuLF 2010, I-181, I-84. For Poland: *Pajor*, Rev. crit. DIP 2012, 5, 13; *id.*, Yearbook of Private International Law 13 (2011), 381, 388. As a reason in favour of a French private international law code: *Bourdelois*, in: Puigelier (ed.), La loi, 89, 103. For codes in general: *Zimmermann*, ERPL 3 (1995), 95, 110.

the Succession Regulation, the M-Property Regulation, and the RP-Property Regulation do repeatedly acknowledge the citizen as the person whose affairs are at issue, and whose mobility prompts the need for uniform private international law.[2129] One might even say that it is of particular importance for laypersons to at least know whether "their" law, of which they might have gained rudimentary understanding through socialisation, applies to their affairs or not.[2130] The intelligibility of private international law would then be of more relevance than that of substantive private law. Even from this perspective, however, the first argument would still apply: how problematic is *one* level of abstraction really?

2.3.2. *Coherence and Legal Certainty*

Coherence is one of the big issues in EU private international law.[2131] It is understood here to mean harmony among the different parts of a complex entity, i.e. either of private international law as a whole, or at least of one legal instrument. Formally general provisions further this goal because they ensure, in the absence of specific exceptions, that the same issues are resolved in the same way, regardless of the context in which they arise. Purely substantively general provisions also advance this goal by at least suggesting adherence to the same policies throughout one legal instrument. At the same time, both imply a higher degree of legal certainty,[2132] as issues or policy questions are not only resolved expressly (which itself promotes this goal), but also for all instances in which they occur.

2.3.2.1. *De Lege Lata*

Member States

The dual goal of increasing coherence and legal certainty figured prominently in domestic codification efforts, including the making of general provisions

[2129] See Recitals 9, 15 Rome III; 7 clause 1, 23 clause 1, 37 clause 1, 38 clause 1 Succession Regulation; 32 clause 1, 35 clause 3, and 43 clause 1 M-Property Regulation; 32 clause 1, 35 clause 3, and 42 clause 1 RP-Property Regulation.

[2130] Along similar lines *Garau Sobrino*, ZVglRWiss 117 (2018), 24, in particular 46–49, who after some astoundingly byzantine examples taken from current EU private international law in the broad sense expresses his wish for less complex rules with the "afflicted" ("leidgeplagt") citizen in mind.

[2131] Just see von Hein/Rühl (eds.), Kohärenz im Internationalen Privat- und Verfahrensrecht der Europäischen Union; *Wandt*, Rechtswahlregelungen (with the subtitle referring to *coherence*, comprehensiveness, and efficiency); *Crawford/Carruthers*, ICLQ 63 (2014), 1 (for the private international law of obligations); *Kramer et al.*, A European Framework for private international law, 11, 13, and passim; *supra* Chapter 2, section 2.1.2.

[2132] For a connection between coherence and legal certainty, also *Smits/Letto-Vanamo*, in: iid. (eds.), Coherence and Fragmentation in European Private Law, 1, 2.

of private international law specifically. The Dutch legislator, for example, justified the creation of an unprecedented[2133] general provision on the incidental question with the need for legal certainty.[2134] The goal of "systemic coherence" in Dutch private international law has been directly tied to the need for general provisions.[2135] Similarly, the Czech legislator has been said to have "felt the necessity to regulate some of the most important *general issues*, as there has been a certain degree of ambiguity connected with undesirable legal uncertainty".[2136] The new private international law provisions in the Romanian Civil Code have been described as progress towards legal predictability,[2137] as have been the older Yugoslav PIL Act and the Hungarian PIL Code 1979.[2138] The Belgian PIL Code is supposed to mark a big step forward in terms of the coherence of Belgian private international law.[2139]

European Union

Even *de lege lata* in its separate regulations, EU private international law reflects the ideas of legal certainty and coherence. The former appears several times in the recitals of all private international law regulations.[2140] The latter already manifests itself in the official names of Rome I and II:[2141] Rome II had no finalised convention as a predecessor after which it could have been named; its name can only be seen as an expression of its intimate relation to the Rome Convention/Rome I. Their recitals further underline this relation: Recital 7 Rome I calls for consistence with Rome II, Rome II essentially reciprocates in its Recital 7.[2142]

To be sure, later regulations did not receive official short names anymore. One can only speculate as to the reasons. As the Succession Regulation, the M-Property Regulation, and the RP-Property Regulation are about much more than conflict of laws, it makes sense not to align their name with the pure

2133 *Supra* Chapter 3, section 2.5.4.
2134 Kamerstukken II 2009/2010, 32317, No. 3, 12.
2135 *Struycken*, RabelsZ 78 (2014), 592, 603.
2136 *Pauknerová/Pfeiffer*, Journal of Private International Law 10 (2014), 205, 214 (emphasis added).
2137 *Avasilencei*, Rev. crit. DIP 2012, 247, 275.
2138 See *Matić*, Neth. Int. L. Rev. 30 (1983), 220, 222, and *Burián*, in: Symeonides (ed.), PIL at the End of the 20th Century, 263, 267 (with the caveat that fear of independent courts also might have been a factor in the socialist era), respectively.
2139 *Pertegas*, IPRax 2006, 53, 61.
2140 Recitals 6, 16, 39 Rome I; 6, 14, 15, 31 Rome II; 9, 15, 19, 21, 23, 29 Rome III; 37, 48 Succession Regulation; 15, 36, 43, 46–47, 49, 72 M-Property Regulation; 15, 37, 42, 45–46, 48, 70 RP-Property Regulation.
2141 *Kühn*, Die gestörte Gesamtschuld im IPR, 126.
2142 As Rome II is the older instrument, it could not expressly refer to "Rome I". Recital 7 does mention "the instruments dealing with the law applicable to contractual obligations", however.

private international law regulations Rome I and II.[2143] From this point of view, "Rome III" would have been a suitable *official* name for Regulation 1259/2010 – it has become, after all, its popular unofficial name. Perhaps, however, the EU legislator intended to reserve the "Rome" designation for a more or less commercial context, or for regulations applying in at least close to all member states.

Nevertheless, the regulations share a common bone structure, including clusters of provisions relevant for all individual conflicts rules.[2144] The structural similarities are also especially obvious between the Succession Regulation, the M-Property Regulation, and the RP-Property Regulation. Furthermore, the EU private international law legislator occasionally refers to other instruments of its law.[2145] Hence, it would be hard to argue that there has been no attempt by the EU to make its legislation coherent. The existence of false friends[2146] and cautionary statements from Luxembourg[2147] do not call this result into question. They only and rightfully provide warnings against *automatically* assuming coherence when interpreting existing EU private international law. On the other hand, the ECJ has also already spoken of, and thus arguably recognised, a "system" of EU private international law.[2148]

2.3.2.2. The Critique of "One Size Does Not Fit All"

Nobody seems to deny that general provisions promote coherence. A possible objection in this context, however, would be that they are essentially too much of a good thing. One might say that general provisions do not take sufficient account of the different policies underlying different areas.[2149] Yet such an

2143 Already *Wilke*, RIW 2012, 601 (with note 7).

2144 *Supra* Chapter 2, section 2, and Chapter 3, passim.

2145 See e.g. Articles 4(1)(h), 6(4)(b) and (c) Rome I. Also see Recital 7 Rome I and II as well as Recitals 17 and 24 Rome I for the connection between Brussels I and Rome I and II. There are also negative references in cases where the understanding of one term in one context is *not* supposed to be transferred to the present context, see Recital 39 Rome I.

2146 See *Briggs*, Private International Law in the English Courts, at 2.71.

2147 ECJ Case C-45/13, Kainz v Pantherwerke AG, ECLI:EU:C:2014:7, at 20: "It must be stated next that, although it is apparent from Recital 7 in the preamble to Regulation No 864/2007 that the EU legislature sought to ensure consistency between Regulation No 44/2001, on the one hand, and the substantive scope and the provisions of Regulation No 864/2007, on the other, that does not mean, however, that the provisions of Regulation No 44/2001 must for that reason be interpreted in the light of the provisions of Regulation No 864/2007. The objective of consistency cannot, in any event, lead to the provisions of Regulation No 44/2001 being interpreted in a manner which is unconnected to the scheme and objectives pursued by that regulation." Along similar lines also *Briggs*, Private International Law in the English Courts, at 2.61.

2148 See ECJ Case C-135/15, Hellenic Republic v Grigorios Nikiforidis, ECLI:EU:C:2016:774 at 45.

2149 *Bariatti/Pataut*, in: Fallon/Lagarde/Poillot-Peruzzetto (eds.), Quelle architecture pour un code européen de droit international privé?, 337, 338, touch upon this issue.

objection would be based on a misunderstanding. It presupposes that formally general *issues* in the strict sense require a formally general *solution* in the strict sense, that formally general *issues* require a common *solution*, and that a substantively general issue or solution is the *only one* relevant. None of these ideas, however, perforce follows from the idea of general provisions. To be sure, the smaller the number of exceptions, the greater the coherence. But as this is hardly the only policy to take into consideration, a legislator is not bound to make formally general provisions in the strict sense even for issues of this nature. It can always provide for exceptions where it sees fit. *Renvoi* is a good example on the EU level. The same question arises for all regulations, but the solution found in the Succession Regulation is different from the one adopted in the other five. Similarly, even though the issue of the incidental question must be resolved in respect of each individual conflicts provision,[2150] there is nothing barring a legislator from making a general decision in favour of the one solution that it considers to be the main rule. After all, two legislators in the EU recently opted to make such a decision.[2151]

General provisions are not tantamount to having one solution for all potential cases, not tantamount to the notion of "one size fits all". They do not gloss over existing differences *per definitionem*.[2152] A specific provision for a certain subject matter, or even an entire field of private international law, will prevail over a general provision. On the other hand, only if there are few or even no commonalities between the individual solutions should a legislator be discouraged from creating general provisions.[2153]

2.3.2.3. The "Correct" Point in Time

In a more refined version, the objection would consist in pointing out the risk that the legislator could generalise one solution too quickly, i.e. without realising that it is inappropriate for certain fields.[2154] Indeed, it would obviously be a mistake to begin rule-making in an area of law by making formally general rules (for purely substantively general rules, this is much more dubious[2155]).

2150 *Mansel*, in: FS Kropholler, 353, 358; *Siehr*, Yearbook of Private International Law VII (2005), 17, 51.

2151 *Supra* Chapter 3, section 2.5.4.

2152 Along these lines also *Heck*, AcP 146 (1941), 1, 6, attacking *Begriffsjurisprudenz*, i.e. "jurisprudence of constructs" (translation by *Weir*: *Wieacker*, A History of Private Law in Europe, 255).

2153 From the perspective of the theory of legislation see *Noll*, Gesetzgebungslehre, 227, referring to *Ball*, Vom neuen Weg der Gesetzgebung, 32–35.

2154 See already *Zitelmann*, GrünhZ 33 (1906), 1, 20; similarly *Wieacker*, A History of Private Law in Europe, 377; *von Savigny*, System I, 391–392, for the same risk in the academic context.

2155 On the contrary, it even might make sense to start by thinking about and drafting provisions that set forth the fundamental policies to be pursued through individual provisions. Along these lines exactly *Kindermann*, in: GS Rödig, 99, 106.

The EU legislator might even have shied away from certain provisions in the *individual* regulations for this reason, so as not to *de facto* pre-empt different solutions in other regulations.[2156] Again, the idea of factoring out proves illuminating: without knowing the addends, it is impossible to factor out anything.

It follows that any legislator must be cautioned against making general provisions before the bulk of individual provisions to which they would relate has at least been decided upon. It is necessary to proceed in an inductive manner when drafting general provisions.[2157] Moreover, when further areas of one general field of law are codified, and general provisions already exist for the areas codified prior, a legislator should not blindly have those general solutions apply to the new provisions, but consider whether they are appropriate for them too.

It should be noted, however, that all of this concerns the most appropriate *way* to draft general provisions; that is to say, these objections are not levied at general provisions as such. It is further submitted that, in light of the six existing regulations, it is not too early to think about general solutions of EU private international law. Similarly to the question of when to codify an area of law,[2158] consensus on the most propitious point in time to make general provisions is unlikely to be achieved anyway. As the parts of this book on EU law demonstrate, however, the EU private international law regulations do already provide quite a bit of material to work with. Should a solution now perceived as general turn out to be inadequate for future regulations, those regulations can (and are more likely to[2159]) provide for an exception themselves, or the general provision can be changed.

The goal of more coherent rules can already be achieved for the existing regulations. The risk of general provisions applying to specific issues for which they are neither suited nor intended is much lower for EU law than for domestic law. A domestic legislator might enact a general provision with areas of law A, B, and C in mind, overlooking that it will also apply to area D by virtue of the rule being general and the legislator having the competence to make rules for all areas of law. By contrast, general provisions of EU private international law cannot go further than those fields already harmonised

2156 If, e.g., one regulation contained a rule on the treatment of foreign law, it would likely be extended to other regulations; see *Fallon*, in: id./Lagarde/Poillot-Peruzzetto (eds.), La matière civile et commerciale, 1, 27.

2157 *Schmidt*, Zivilrechtskodifikation in Brasilien, 316 (with notes 127 and 128 as to the eventually different German practice at the end of the 19th century, as well as potential problems caused by it); already *Zitelmann*, GrünhZ 33 (1906), 1, 20.

2158 See *Bodénès-Constantin*, La codification du DIP français, at 172, and *Bureau*, in: Beignier (ed.), La codification, 119, 132–134, for the (domestic) codification of private international law; already *Neuhaus*, RabelsZ 37 (1973), 453, 460.

2159 See *infra* section 2.4.2. for the value of general provisions for the legislator.

by regulations.[2160] Even a provision expressly designated as "general" could not "accidentally" apply to a legal question for which there is no EU law yet.

2.3.2.4. Sufficient Coherence Through Interpretation?

One might further challenge the idea of coherence in part by pointing out that the (domestic) courts could make do with the existing rules, at least to the extent that provisions on general issues already exist (somewhere) in EU private international law. In a way, insights gained in the context of one regulation could cross-fertilise the interpretation of another regulation. Such an argument would not attack the need for, or usefulness of, uniform rules on issues not yet covered at all by provisions of EU law, but would suppose that where there is already material to draw upon in relation to certain issues, it is sufficient for the courts to arrive at coherent solutions.

To the extent that this argument is tantamount to saying that some areas of EU private international law do not need to change, at least not for reasons of coherence, the statements below on EU private international law without general provisions apply *mutatis mutandis*. Whether the courts, including the ECJ, are truly up to this task – or would not be better up to it with the existence of general provisions – is not obvious. Moreover, in light of the many, albeit sometimes small, divergences between the regulations, even within one and the same language, the task of finding a coherent interpretation is at least more difficult than it needs to be.

If this argument were to imply that the courts will be able to take account of parallel provisions in different regulations, however, it would miss the mark: if existing provisions of different regulations are (or were) really identical, general provisions (would) already exist – this would be an example of the repetition technique. The question would then only be to decide if the other techniques are not superior to this one. Yet this is not a question of coherence.

2.3.2.5. No Panacea

A final possible objection would consist in pointing out that even general provisions (on the issues analysed in this book) cannot remedy all incoherence in EU private international law. Indeed, incoherence, e.g. among the regulatory solutions regarding the protection of weaker parties,[2161] would not automatically cease to exist, not least because it already originates from the unclear premises as to which parties deserve protection and which do not.[2162]

2160 *Supra* Chapter 5, section 1.4.
2161 See *Rühl*, Journal of Private International Law 10 (2014), 335, 346–356.
2162 *Rühl*, Journal of Private International Law 10 (2014), 335, 340–342.

Yet, as long as no other option promises to eliminate all incoherence effectively,[2163] this observation is no argument against an approach that at least advances the cause of coherence in other aspects of EU private international law.

2.3.3. Elimination of Redundancies

The effect of general provisions of avoiding or eliminating redundancies borders on the self-evident for formally general issues. Instead of making use of the repetition technique, a legislator can either employ the compilation technique or the insertion technique. Both avoid – or, if they replace several existing rules of the same content, eliminate – redundancies, reducing the length of the legislative instrument as compared to the first option. This, in turn, can facilitate dealing with the instrument, as well as understanding the law.[2164] The effect is strongest for formally general issues in the strict sense, but it also exists for formally general issues, of course.

While the insertion technique avoids the verbatim repetition of entire rules, it still necessitates the creation of provisions that refer to the one emanation of the provision that is supposed to be formally general. To the extent that one is exclusively concerned with the size of a legal instrument, the compilation technique is therefore the best one,[2165] for every general solution only has to be stated once and does not require any further provisions. This is also the technique that domestic legislators have clearly favoured for private international law, as the comparative survey has demonstrated.[2166]

As has become apparent in the course of the analysis above, the EU legislator has thus far preferred to employ the compilation technique *within* each of the regulations, even reserving formally separate sections for general provisions in Rome I and II, and grouping them together in the other regulations. The Succession Regulation contains one exception to this approach in favour of the insertion technique, when its Articles 24(2) and 25(3) refer back to Article 22(1) subparagraph 2 concerning the issue of multiple nationalities. From the perspective of *all* of EU private international law, however, the legislator has followed the repetition technique when it inserted a relatively general provision on *renvoi*, non-unified legal systems, and public policy into *each* regulation. These redundancies would be eliminated by common general provisions.

2163 *Infra* section 3.

2164 *Rheinstein*, Ind. L. J. 34 (1959), 546, 552 ("economy of thought"); also see *Schmidt*, Scand. Stud. L. 9 (1965), 131, 147.

2165 Specifically for EU private international law, also *Wiedemann*, in: Vaz de Sequeira/de Almeida Ribeiro (eds.), Católica Graduate Legal Research Conference 2014 – Conference Proceedings, 175, 196.

2166 *Supra* Chapter 2, section 1.4.

Redundancies could also be avoided as regards the scope of application *ratione materiae* of EU private international law. A general provision – admittedly, most likely to be found in an EU code of private international law – would at least consist of all of the respective existing provisions, i.e. Article 1 of each regulation, rolled into one. As a consequence, some exclusions would become useless. As there *are* EU rules on obligations arising out of dealings prior to the conclusion of a contract (Article 12 Rome II), the exclusion of Article 1(2)(i) Rome I could not be maintained. As there *are* EU rules on wills and succession (see only Article 3 Succession Regulation), the respective exclusion of Article 1(2)(c) Rome I, Article 1(2)(b) Rome II, Article 1(2)(h) Rome III, and Article 1(2)(d) M-/RP-Property Regulation would be irrelevant.

Moreover, the elimination of redundancies would lower the risk of certain translation problems. In the course of this book, several instances of linguistic incoherence within one and the same language have come to light.[2167] Article 12 Rome I and Article 15 Rome II share the same title in most languages, but not in French.[2168] The French and Spanish public policy provisions are phrased differently from regulation to regulation.[2169] If one general provision replaces several others, the risk of a poor translation remains, of course – but at least it exists only once, not several times, and there can be no discrepancies within the same language.

2.4. THE "EDUCATIONAL" FUNCTION OF GENERAL PROVISIONS

Particularly in light of general practitioners,[2170] but also of non-specialist judges facing questions of private international law more and more, general provisions have a further potential advantage. Even where they set forth a solution to which later provisions make an exception, they flag the respective *issue* by their very existence. Domestic observers have often remarked that quite a few issues of private international law are simply missed in practice, or even deliberately ignored, due to their (supposed) complexity.[2171] The likelihood

2167 Also see *Fallon*, in: id./Lagarde/Poillot-Peruzzetto (eds.), La matière civile et commerciale, 1, 27–29.

2168 *Supra* footnote 793.

2169 *Supra* footnote 561.

2170 *Supra* section 2.3.1.2.

2171 *Ferreri*, in: Brown/Snyder (eds.), General Reports, 29, 36–37, and 39, from a comparative perspective. Also see for Belgium: *Francq*, RabelsZ 70 (2006), 235, 240; *Erauw/Fallon*, in: Dirix/Lelen (eds.), The Belgian Reports, 227, 269 (more pessimistically, even after the Belgian PIL Code entered into force). For Germany: *Mankowski*, in: Basedow/Kischel/Sieber (eds.), German National Reports, 133, 149. For Hungary: *Raffai/Szabó*, Acta Juridica Hungarica 51 (2010), 136, 142. For Latvia: *Strautins*, Yearbook of Private International Law 8 (2006), 289, 297.

of this happening by mistake is reduced where an issue is clearly visible in a general provision;[2172] where that provision is also drafted clearly, there should be less incentive to shy away from it.

Such an educational function can serve as a justification for all merely declaratory provisions.[2173] For example, the quite common references in general provisions of domestic private international law to EU law are legally unnecessary.[2174] EU private international law would apply regardless of them. Yet for a practitioner or judge used to relying only on domestic legislation, they might prove rather helpful by pointing her towards the pertinent legal instrument.[2175] Similarly, a formally useless general provision, such as Article 4(1) Polish PIL Act,[2176] can be said to alert the reader to the significance of party autonomy (besides its substantive value). General provisions on arguably easy-to-miss issues, like the incidental question or adaptation, might prompt a reader to actually consider these questions at all.

2.4.1. The "International Element" in Particular

As private international law as an area of law does *not* require an international or cross-border element, a respective rule is unnecessary from a legal perspective, even though it is quite common.[2177] Perhaps the policy idea of an educational, hortatory even, function of general provisions can "save" such provisions? One could say that they alert a judge or any other legal stakeholder to take private international law at least into consideration if the case at hand has any kind of international element.[2178]

While it is hard to see how such a provision could be harmful, it is submitted that its potential positive effect would be much greater if it were not found among general *private international law* provisions, but rather among general substantive private law provisions. Otherwise, only judges who already take private international law into consideration would find it. Yet nobody needs to alert those judges to the existence and relevance of private international law.

2.4.2. General Provisions as a Tool for the Legislator Itself

The legislator itself can benefit from general provisions in a similar way as their end-users. When *making* general provisions, the legislator is required

---

2172 To this effect also *Neuhaus*, RabelsZ 37 (1973), 453, 462.

2173 Also see *Noll*, Gesetzgebungslehre, 231 (propositions 1 and 3).

2174 See already *supra* Chapter 3, section 2.3. (Member States).

2175 Similarly for the Polish PIL Act (but with caveats as to the *concrete* provisions), *Ernst*, RabelsZ 76 (2012), 598, 632.

2176 *Supra* Chapter 4, section 4.3.

2177 *Supra* Chapter 3, section 2.2.1.

2178 Similarly *Kadner Graziano*, Journal of Private International Law 11 (2015), 585, 594.

to take account of existing rules, especially in order to identify an existing common solution. In doing so, it will notice gaps and inconsistencies. For example, if the EU were to create provisions common to at least Rome I and II, the potential gap between "contractual" and "non-contractual"[2179] might be more obvious than when creating instruments separately.

Once a legislator *has made* general provisions, they serve as the backdrop for making new specific rules, or for reforming existing ones – two tasks of significance for the EU legislator in the area of private international law because EU law does not (yet) encompass all of private international law, and because EU legislation generally progresses in an evolutionary manner[2180] (with the regulations themselves mandating to be reviewed[2181]). Not only would the general *issues* already be on the table, making sure that the legislator will not miss any, but there would also already be *solutions*, requiring the legislator to consider whether any exceptions are warranted in the given specific area of law.[2182]

2.5. UNIFORM LEGISLATION AND LEGAL UNIFORMITY[2183]

A possible further objection to EU general provisions of private international law would be that even they cannot guarantee that general issues (and consequently entire cases) will be decided uniformly. Generally speaking, uniform law is a relative concept from the beginning, as national courts interpret (typically only) a version of that law in the language of the court's country.[2184] Literal concord easily becomes substantive discord.[2185] Even in the most technical and minute areas of uniform law, interpretational divergences have arisen.[2186] Moreover, even if general provisions themselves are understood uniformly, there still might be divergences: courts might form different opinions as to whether a general provision "really" is supposed to apply in one particular field.[2187]

2179 As to the potential gap see *supra* Chapter 3, section 2.10.2 (Rome II).

2180 *Corneloup/Nourissat*, in: Fallon/Lagarde/Poillot-Peruzzetto (eds.), Quelle architecture pour un code européen de droit international privé?, 257, 262.

2181 See Articles 27 Rome I, 30 Rome II, 20 Rome III, 82 Succession Regulation, and 68 M-/RP-Property Regulation.

2182 See *Dannemann*, in: Adams/Bomhoff (eds.), Practice and Theory in Comparative Law, 96, 118, for the usefulness of the (D)CFR for national legislators as to "structure, concepts, drafting style and terminology".

2183 See *Kötz*, RabelsZ 50 (1986), 1, 7 ("durch Einheitsrecht [keine] Rechtseinheit").

2184 *Markesinis/Fedtke*, Engaging with Foreign Law, 334.

2185 *Zweigert*, RabelsZ 16 (1951), 387, 395.

2186 *Kötz*, RabelsZ 50 (1986), 1, 7; also *Zweigert/id.*, Introduction to Comparative Law, 27.

2187 See *Struycken*, RabelsZ 78 (2014), 592, 604–605, regarding the general "reasonableness and equity" principle of the Dutch Civil Code – does it apply in private international law, which formally is part of the Dutch Civil Code, too?

Nevertheless, the objection is not persuasive. First of all, one must ask whether uniform provisions do not at least further the aim of legal uniformity *more* than any alternative approach,[2188] even if problems of interpretation do arise. In part, such issues can also be eschewed by good drafting. Second, while interpretational divergences are a typical scourge of uniform legal texts, EU regulations have a distinct advantage. With the ECJ, there is "a central forum [...] capable of giving and enforcing authoritative interpretations of common rules as enacted by the European legislator".[2189] One should add that the Court is not only capable of doing so, but that the courts of the member states are obligated at some point to refer questions concerning the interpretation of EU law to the Court pursuant to Article 267(3) TFEU. The ECJ can thus prevent re-nationalisation of uniform law.[2190] To be sure, domestic courts sometimes tend to forgo referring a question to the ECJ, expressly or implicitly – and, in retrospect, quite often erroneously – assuming that there is "no scope for any reasonable doubt as to the manner in which the question raised is to be resolved".[2191] The workload of the Court must also be taken into account, possibly affecting the quality of the uniform response given.[2192] The institutional framework for legal uniformity through uniform legislation (of general provisions), however, is much better for EU law than for other sources of uniform law.

2.6. GENERAL ISSUES AS A SUITABLE OBJECT OF LEGISLATIVE ACTIVITY

2.6.1. The General Objection Refuted

One might object that general issues of private international law simply do not lend themselves to receiving legislative solutions. The underlying assumption would be not so much that it is not possible to find a general solution,[2193] but that it is impossible to draft respective provisions that prove useful. The usefulness would in turn be called into question on the assumption that a general provision is necessarily extremely broad and/or exceedingly complex.

2188 *Infra* section 3.

2189 *Markesinis/Fedtke*, Engaging with Foreign Law, 332; for the importance of a central court for uniform law, also *Simons*, EuLF 2007, I-1, I-4; *Juenger*, in: LA Siehr, 288, 303.

2190 *Mansel*, JZ 1991, 529, 532.

2191 ECJ Case C-283/81, Srl CILFIT and Lanificio di Gavardo SpA v Ministry of Health, Reports of Cases 1982, 3415 at 16. Under this condition, the Court does not object to domestic courts not referring a question.

2192 *Juenger*, in: LA Siehr, 288, 304; also see *infra* section 3.2.2.3.

2193 For this critique of "one size does not fit all" already *supra* section 2.3.2.2.

Indeed, many underscore the difficulty of drafting general provisions of private international law.[2194]

In this generality, the objection must be rejected flat-out, for both an empirical and a theoretical reason. First, such a broad objection clashes with the comparative realisation that all member states with a private international law code have enacted general provisions dealing with at least some of the general issues. Second, the foregoing analysis has shown that formally general issues of private international law are not about lofty principles, nor are predicated on academic vagaries; they implicate concrete questions, just repeated over and over again. This is also why one can be in favour of general provisions on party autonomy even if one is opposed to merely programmatic statements in legislation.[2195] Moreover, under the reasonable assumption that general parts require that only one legislator has the competence for the given area of law, and that they work best (or perhaps only) if the respective legal rules are all found on only one hierarchical level,[2196] EU private international law is a suitable area of law for general provisions (even in a general part): the general provisions as envisioned here would only pertain to EU private international law – thus to law enacted by one and the same legislator. They would only pertain to law found in regulations, not in delegated or implementing legal acts[2197] – thus to law on one hierarchical level.

2.6.2. The More Nuanced Objection

If at all, the question must be whether individual issues cannot "properly" be dealt with in a legislative way. That it is possible to make useful general provisions on *renvoi*, public policy, and non-unified legal systems requires no further explanation. Their ubiquity and the lack of voices questioning their *functionality* (save for critique regarding the particular *content* of a given rule) on both the domestic and the EU level speak volumes.

A prime suspect in this context would be characterisation, however. Legislators had even been diagnosed with "a state of despair" as to the potential creation of characterisation provisions.[2198] *General* guidance is supposed to be hardly possible.[2199] Still, legislators around the world,[2200] and in the EU

2194 E.g. *Loussouarn*, in: LA Droz, 191, 200; *Bureau*, in: Beignier (ed.), La codification, 119, 141; *Neuhaus*, RabelsZ 37 (1973), 453, 462.

2195 See *Kreuzer*, in: Jud/Rechberger/Reichelt (eds.), Kollisionsrecht in der Europäischen Union, 1, 4, who demonstrates opposition to the codification of (mere) principles "such as party autonomy", and *Wandt*, Rechtswahlregelungen, 215–216, who correctly points out that general provisions on party autonomy can consist in "factored out" concrete provisions.

2196 *Lepsius*, Die Verwaltung, Beiheft 10 (2010), 179, 196–197.

2197 See Articles 290, 291 TFEU.

2198 *Hernández-Breton*, in: FS Jayme I, 331, 332.

2199 *Sonnenberger*, in: FS Kropholler, 227, 240.

2200 *Hernández-Breton*, in: FS Jayme I, 331, 333–334.

in particular,[2201] *have* made general characterisation provisions. To speak of a "virtual absence of national model provisions"[2202] is highly misleading. To be sure, the fact alone that several member states have created a characterisation provision is no conclusive argument in favour of an EU provision, especially since characterisation in EU private international law follows somewhat different parameters than in domestic law.[2203] But it should caution against discarding the possibility of such a provision too quickly.[2204]

With two member states recently tackling the incidental question in a general way in their private international law codes,[2205] one should likewise be wary of any rash dismissal of the possibility of making such a provision. One can also understand this occurrence as a more fundamental reminder that even topics from which legislators traditionally shied away are not immune to positivisation. Maybe adaptation is next?[2206] In any case, the educational value of respective provisions[2207] should not be underestimated.

2.7. THE EUROPEAN UNION AS A SUITABLE LEGISLATOR FOR GENERAL PROVISIONS

Especially against the backdrop of the general part of the BGB that was created during the German empire, one might finally wonder if a more or less democratic legislator like the EU[2208] is even suited to tackling a complex and abstract endeavour such as the formulation of general rules. In particular, one might argue that ever-changing majorities and ever-changing political agendas – and all of that in a multi-level system – make the successful completion of such a project improbable. This would be in line with the somewhat romantic idea that "a code has to be the work of a single mind if it

2201 *Supra* Chapter 3, section 2.4. (Member States).
2202 *Heiss/Kaufmann-Mohi*, in: Leible (ed.), General Principles, §5.03[A].
2203 *Supra* Chapter 3, section 2.4. (European Union: The European Dimension of Characterisation).
2204 For such a provision: *de Lima Pinheiro*, Yearbook of Private International Law 14 (2012/2013), 153, 166. Doubtful: *Baratta*, in: id. (ed.), DIP, s. v. "Qualificazioni", 325; *Sonnenberger*, in: FS Kropholler, 227, 240. Against (the need for) such a provision: *Heiss/Kaufmann-Mohi*, in: Leible (ed.), General Principles, §5.04; *Kreuzer*, in: Jud/Rechberger/Reichelt (eds.), Kollisionsrecht in der Europäischen Union, 1, 53–54; *Siehr*, Yearbook of Private International Law VII (2005), 17, 40.
2205 *Supra* Chapter 3, section 2.5.4.
2206 See the proposal by *Dannemann*, in: Leible (ed.), General Principles, §15.03[G]; according to *Kreuzer*, in: Jud/Rechberger/Reichelt (eds.), Kollisionsrecht in der Europäischen Union, 1, 4, however, the topic eludes positivisation.
2207 *Supra* section 2.4. and *Mádl/Vékás*, ZfRV 1982, 266, 277, for the Hungarian characterisation provision in particular.
2208 This book stays clear of the minefield that is the debate concerning the democratic legitimacy of legal acts by the EU.

is to be all of a piece".[2209] But even without delving into the intricacies of democratic theory, there is at least some indication that the creation of general provisions of private international law at the EU level would not be systemically doomed from the start.

2.7.1. *Systematic Legislation at the Domestic and European Union Levels*

First, there is the observation that the majority of the domestic codes of private international law, with their sections on general issues, were drafted in liberal-democratic systems. Remember, moreover, that some of these codes (e.g. the Belgian PIL Code and the Bulgarian PIL Code) did not just replace existing codes that could have served as a framework, and that others have *introduced* the concept of general provisions of private international law (e.g. the Czech PIL Act).[2210] Apparently, then, it is far from impossible for democratic legislators to make general provisions, or even entire codes.[2211]

As far as the EU legislator is concerned, it first should be pointed out that it (and the Commission in particular) has a unique role in the field of uniform law. Unlike any other bodies creating uniform law, it "is given the chance to advance in a comprehensive approach towards solutions which are more than just patchwork", as though it was a "European Ministry of Justice".[2212] If one can expect uniform law to be coherent, the legislator most likely to be able to produce it is the EU. But is it really?

Thus far, the EU has not proved to be incapable of, or averse to, adopting measures of both a relatively broad scope and a relatively systematic character. A still recent example is the Consumer Rights Directive. Its Recital 2 speaks for itself:

> [The Doorstep Selling Directive and the Distance Contract Directive] have been reviewed in the light of experience with a view to simplifying and updating the applicable rules, *removing inconsistencies* and *closing unwanted gaps* in the rules. That review has shown that it is appropriate to replace those two Directives by a single Directive. This Directive should therefore lay down *standard rules for the common* aspects of distance and off-premises contracts [...][2213]

The Stockholm Programme referred specifically to the consolidation and consistency of the instruments adopted in the area of judicial cooperation

2209 *Wieacker*, A History of Private Law in Europe, 375; already *Ball*, Vom neuen Weg der Gesetzgebung, 15.
2210 In more detail *supra* Chapter 2, section 1.4.
2211 Also see *Schärdel*, Bücherkodifikation, 73–85, as to codification in pluralistic democratic systems.
2212 *Simons*, EuLF 2007, I-1, I-2.
2213 Emphases added.

in civil matters;[2214] in addition, the EU Justice Agenda for 2020 expressly mentions "the area of conflict of laws" when calling for an examination of whether EU law should be codified.[2215] Incidentally, the Commission's Better Regulation Guidelines identify "coherence" as one of the five main criteria for the evaluation of EU legal instruments.[2216] EU private international law as a whole could arguably also be subjected to a "Fitness check" by the Commission, i.e. the evaluation of an entire policy area, as opposed to the separate evaluation of individual instruments.[2217]

A technocratic institution like the Commission (with its Directorates-General) also seems less encumbered by the vicissitudes of democratic rule-making than, e.g. the European Parliament. Furthermore, private international law is not exactly an area of law that regularly sparks political outrage. One of the reasons why EU private international law has developed so quickly and continually may indeed be its relative distance from politics.[2218] The desideratum that private international law at the EU level should be free from policy concerns unrelated to private international law, and from politics in general,[2219] can be fulfilled at least in part.

2.7.2. *Support from Experts*

The involvement of (and the reliance of the legislator on) experts in the field is likely one reason why the features of democratic rule-making have not necessarily hampered the creation of systematic domestic private international law legislation. For example, a group of scholars was tasked by the Belgian Minister of Justice with drafting the Belgian PIL Code,[2220] and a group mainly consisting of scholars was tasked by the Polish Minister of Justice with drafting the Polish PIL Act.[2221] The Bulgarian Ministry of Justice relied on Bulgarian scholars and practitioners, supported by German scholars, for the draft Bulgarian PIL Code.[2222] The Deutsche Rat für IPR and the Max Planck Institute for Comparative and International Private Law laid important groundwork for the reform of German private international law.[2223] Several domestic codes

2214 Stockholm Programme, 3.1.2. (13).
2215 EU Justice Agenda for 2020, 4.2.
2216 Better Regulation Guidelines, 49 and passim.
2217 Better Regulation Guidelines, 8 and passim.
2218 *Kieninger*, RW 2012, 406, 429–430. One can doubt, however, that bodies of an international composition are better suited *per se* to arrive at the best solutions (see *Basedow*, The Law of Open Societies, at 443). National interests do surface regularly on the EU level.
2219 *Leible/Staudinger*, EuLF 2000/2001, 225, 235.
2220 *Erauw/Fallon*, in: Dirix/Lelen (eds.), The Belgian Reports, 227, 228–229; *Fiorini*, ICLQ 54 (2005), 499, 507.
2221 *Pajor*, Yearbook of Private International Law 13 (2011), 381, 382.
2222 *Zidarova/Stančeva-Minčeva*, RabelsZ 71 (2007), 398, 401.
2223 See *F. Sturm/G. Sturm*, in: Staudinger, Einl. zum IPR at 910–922.

of private international law are even said to bear the hallmarks of certain individual scholars: Kučera for the Czech PIL Act,[2224] Vitta and Monaco for the Italian PIL Act,[2225] and Pazdan for the Polish PIL Act.[2226]

The EU legislator has likewise demonstrated its willingness to rely on private international law experts. The 2005 Green Paper on succession and wills,[2227] which would ultimately lead to the Succession Regulation, was preceded by a comprehensive study by the German Notary Institute.[2228] In 2008, the Directorate-General for Justice tasked a team of different academic and legal institutions with researching the topic of "Application of Foreign Law by Judicial and Non-Judicial Authorities in Europe".[2229] The Committee on Legal Affairs of the European Parliament requested and received at least two studies on the status quo and the perspectives of EU private international law.[2230] On the other hand, scholarly efforts can form a counterweight where political contingencies affect EU legislative efforts after all.[2231]

3. EUROPEAN UNION PRIVATE INTERNATIONAL LAW WITHOUT GENERAL PROVISIONS

The preceding chapter and this one have demonstrated thus far that it would be possible (albeit in part tricky) to make general provisions for EU private international law, and that such an endeavour has many theoretical advantages. This does not mean, however, that such a project would succeed in practice. Even if everyone in, or at least a sufficient majority of, the EU were convinced that the *concept* does make a lot of sense, there could still be no agreement as to its *content*. Or a project could fall victim to other political factors. For this reason, this final section adumbrates the state of EU private international law without a set of general provisions. (Of course, one can also read the following remarks as an account of the alternatives to general provisions.)

At the outset, it is necessary to reiterate that (at least formally) general issues of private international law are questions that *actually* arise in connection with different conflicts rules. It follows that a legislator ignoring them does not

2224 *Pauknerová/Pfeiffer*, Journal of Private International Law 10 (2014), 205, 210.
2225 *Kindler*, RabelsZ 61 (1997), 227, 229–230; *Giardina*, Rev. crit. DIP 1996, 1, 3.
2226 *Ernst*, RabelsZ 76 (2012), 597, 602–604.
2227 COM(2005) 65 final.
2228 Deutsches Notarinstitut (ed.), Les Successions Internationales dans l'UE, 1–330.
2229 Esplugues/Iglesias/Palao, in: iid. (eds.), Application of Foreign Law, xxv.
2230 *Rühl/von Hein*, RabelsZ 79 (2015), 701; *Kramer et al.*, A European Framework for private international law: current gaps and future perspectives.
2231 In the context of the harmonisation of procedural rules *Stadler*, JZ 2017, 693, 701.

make them vanish. At least eventually, somebody has to come up with an authoritative solution.

3.1. NO RECOURSE TO GENERAL RULES OF DOMESTIC PRIVATE INTERNATIONAL LAW

As there are general provisions of private international law in the majority of member states, a judge of a respective legal system might be tempted to rely on her domestic solutions when faced with silence (or incoherence) in EU private international law. Evidently, however, this solution is not only not very sensible but, to a great extent, illegal. Formally general issues of EU private international law are issues *of* EU private international law. Unless it itself leaves them to domestic law as, e.g. for the time being the ascertainment of foreign law,[2232] an *EU* solution must be found.[2233]

3.2. JUDICIAL SOLUTIONS

If the legislator does not provide for an answer, one will have to be provided by the courts. First, this means domestic courts in their role as functional EU courts, applying EU private international law and developing solutions of EU law where the regulations do not contain a (clear) answer. Second, but strongly connected to domestic courts because of Article 267 TFEU, this implicates the Court of Justice of the European Union.

3.2.1. Common European Case Law?

The venerable history of the common law shows both that legal systems can do without sweeping codification and that the development of (a common) law does not have to be confined to the borders of one country.[2234] In light of this, the prospect of case law regarding general issues of private international law, to be developed by the courts of the member states, might not appear to be particularly horrific. Upon closer examination, however, serious doubts arise as to whether this approach would actually work – or would actually work well enough to satisfy the objectives of "predictability of the outcome of litigation [and] certainty as to the law applicable".[2235]

2232 *Supra* Chapter 3, section 5.3.3.1.

2233 See *Dutta*, in: MüKoBGB, vor Art. 21 EuErbVO at 48, for the general questions of the Succession Regulation.

2234 See also *supra* Chapter 1, section 1.2.1.2. for the *Ius Commune*.

2235 Recital 6 Rome I, Recital 6 Rome II; see also Recitals 9, 21, 23, and 29 Rome III, 37 Succession Regulation, 15, 36, 49, and 72 M-Property Regulation; 15, 37, 48, and 70 RP-Property Regulation.

In order for a case law approach to work, it seems that three conditions are essential: the courts must accept this approach, decisions from other courts must be accessible, and there must be a common high court able to resolve conflicting decisions. While the Court of Justice fulfils the third requirement, neither of the former two is met in the EU as of today. Moreover, it is questionable whether any of them could even be satisfied in the foreseeable future.

Acceptance by the courts is probably the smaller obstacle. Arguably, courts from common law countries are already well-suited to taking account of foreign decisions (if they were readily and reliably accessible), for dealing with other courts' decisions forms part of their judicial practice anyway. Civil law courts, while typically not used to a system of binding precedent, also regularly take account of other courts' decisions. Supreme courts typically have the role of ensuring uniform jurisprudence among the lower courts; the lower courts in turn take note of higher courts, as otherwise they would run the risk of having their decisions reversed. They will also often take a look at decisions by other courts from their legal system that have dealt with (seemingly) the same issue before, not least because lawyers regularly point them out to them. In both systems, the important step would be to regard *foreign* decisions as being in some way relevant, and to process them in one's own decisions. This thus appears less as a problem of having the right tools than as the psychological issue of being willing to use them – an issue perhaps not to be underestimated, even though resistance to taking account of foreign decisions will presumably be reduced under the purview of common provisions.

In order to make use of foreign decisions, however, one needs access to them.[2236] This requires some sort of collection/data base, and it requires that the judges be able to understand foreign judgments. Here, the problem becomes insurmountable for all intents and purposes. It might even be possible for the EU or the member states (with financial aid from the EU) to set up a comprehensive network for all domestic decisions regarding EU (private international) law.[2237] Yet, *pars pro toto*, how many Portuguese judges are there who are able to read an Estonian judgment – and the next day a Greek one?[2238] One should also not forget that average foreign language skills would not

[2236] See also *Rühl*, in: Zimmermann (ed.), Zukunftsperspektiven der Rechtsvergleichung, 103, 136; touched upon by *Markesinis*, ERPL 5 (1997), 519, 523.

[2237] There already is, of course, the European Judicial Network in civil and commercial matters (Council Decision 2001/470/EC of 28 May 2001, amended by Decision No 568/2009/EC of the European Parliament and of the Council of 18 June 2009) that could form the base of such a (more comprehensive) network.

[2238] Save for isolated cases where a judge possesses the necessary skills in the respective foreign language, of course.

suffice because legal documents are at issue. Hence, translations on a large scale would be necessary. But there are probably not enough qualified translators in the world for such a task, even assuming there is sufficient funding for it. Furthermore, language is not even the only problem. Divergent judicial styles, particularly regarding the way of legal reasoning, might render the best translations futile. This latter argument also applies if one were to limit a case law data base to decisions by a class of courts higher up in the judicial hierarchy, or even only to supreme court decisions, for which a sufficient number of translators might exist.

It is a matter of course that domestic courts will face general issues of EU private international law and will have to resolve them. They may or may not be up to that task.[2239] Maybe they can even discharge their duties in special European law,[2240] or even (EU) private international law chambers; the Court of Justice does not seem opposed *per se* to such ideas.[2241] At least appellate courts could have such specialised judicial bodies.[2242] To expect the resulting decisions *from* all over the EU to result in case law *for* all of the EU, however, is rather unrealistic. This is where the Court of Justice comes into play.

3.2.2. *General Solutions from the Court of Justice?*

3.2.2.1. Jurisdiction for the Authoritative Interpretation of EU Private International Law

Every domestic court can refer a question as to the interpretation of EU private international law to the Court of Justice: Article 267 TFEU. Courts of instance

2239 In France, it has been said that courts (even) are better suited than the legislator to deal with private international law (*Bureau*, in: Beignier (ed.), La codification, 119, 137). They supposedly can provide more flexible and "spontaneous" solutions, tailored to each given case (*Loussouarn*, in: LA Droz, 191, 203). This position, however, does not paint the most convincing picture of this field of law (also see *Bodénès-Constantin*, La codification du DIP français, at 187–188; see also ibid., at 64–82, for the refutation of the idea of a "codification jurisprudentielle").

2240 Touched upon by *Remien*, ZVglRWiss 115 (2016), 570, 581–582.

2241 When the compatibility of domestic legislation providing for the centralisation of jurisdiction in matters relating to maintenance obligations with the Maintenance Regulation was at issue (the case concerned the German Law on the Recovery of Maintenance in Relations with Foreign States – AUG), the Court was open to the idea of this "promot[ing] the development of specific expertise" in the field, which inter alia would serve the proper administration of justice: ECJ Joined Cases C-400/13 and C-408/13, Sophia Marie Nicole Sanders v David Verhaegen and Barbara Huber v Manfred Huber, ECLI:EU:C:2014:2461, at 45; also see *Rösler*, ZVglRWiss 115 (2016), 533, 547–548.

2242 *M. Stürner*, ZVglRWiss 117 (2018), 1, 23; *id./Krauß*, Ausländisches Recht in deutschen Zivilverfahren, at 527; also *Rösler*, ZVglRWiss 115 (2016), 533, 545–546, with the example of the Higher Regional Court Stuttgart. In Hamburg, there currently even exists a judicial chamber at first instance for cases in which foreign law is to be applied, see *M. Stürner/Krauß*, Ausländisches Recht in deutschen Zivilverfahren, at 526 with note 417.

in particular can accelerate the development of EU private international law in this way.[2243] But the important word is "can". The possibility of all domestic courts referring questions to the Court is the only necessary condition. Whether they will actually make use of it is an entirely different question, since even those courts that *must* refer questions have been known to show reluctance.

Still, one should point out that the conditions for uniform solutions in private international law are much better than before. Pursuant to Article 68 TEC, only courts against whose decisions there is no judicial remedy under national law were allowed (but also required) to request the Court to give a preliminary ruling concerning acts based on Title IV TEC. As this included Article 65 TEC, and thus private international law, lower courts were barred from referring respective questions to the Court. The European Community had created the goal of an "area of freedom, security and justice" (Article 61 TEC), but had effectively and paradoxically shut out the European judiciary.[2244]

3.2.2.2. The Scope of Decisions

By their very nature, judicial decisions concern the individual case before the judge(s). This characteristic makes lower courts rather ill-suited to providing solutions for entire sets of cases. High courts are also typically only concerned with one set of facts, even where their sole task lies in deciding points of law raised on appeal. Yet they find themselves in a better position because – *de iure* binding precedent or not – lower courts will typically bring their decisions in line with the decisions of the higher courts nevertheless. From this perspective, the Court of Justice must appear especially apt for offering solutions that are not just relevant for one set of circumstances: Article 267 TFEU only mentions the *interpretation* of EU acts, i.e. the level of the law; the facts do not seem to matter at all.

Even if one ignored that the Court does relate the facts in its preliminary rulings,[2245] however, its "general" pronouncements are inherently limited. To be sure, while *de iure* binding upon the referring court only, they are binding *de facto* upon all other courts as well.[2246] But binding only with respect to the question asked. This, in turn, will only concern a general issue *in its relevance for one particular conflicts rule*. A domestic court might request a decision on the treatment of an incidental question raised by a provision of Rome III. Can anybody be sure that the ruling applies to any other provision of Rome III?

2243 *Kramer/de Rooij*, NIPR 2013, 1, 2.
2244 *Basedow*, ZeuP 2001, 437.
2245 It would be fascinating to analyse how much of the Court's jurisprudence depends on the particularities of the case at issue.
2246 See only *Calliess*, in: id. (ed.), Rome Regulations, Introduction at 45.

To provisions of any other regulation? Even worse: to any other incidental question in the context of the *same* provision? The Court has not exactly demonstrated a willingness to make sweeping statements or conceptualisations. As concepts of law are only shaped by series of decisions, it is often difficult to deduce (correct) generalisations.[2247] The Court can and does serve as a lighthouse in EU law – but this also means that it leaves all those areas in the dark that its beam of light has not (yet) reached.[2248]

3.2.2.3. The Quality of Decisions

Regardless of the limited scope of the Court's rulings, the question is whether the field of general issues is in the best hands possible with the Court. Opinions are divided as to whether it has proved capable of adequately dealing with matters of private international law in particular.[2249] A question meriting further research is the legal background of the judges (as well as of the Advocates General) and its influence on decisions.[2250] If, for example, the assumption is correct that most of them are originally experts in public law,[2251] one could worry that the Court already lacks a sufficient understanding of the subject as a whole. Moreover, the importance of the judiciary approaching EU (private international) law from a comparative perspective was emphasised at the beginning of this book, but it was also mentioned that there is not much visible court practice to this effect.[2252]

To set up specialised chambers,[2253] or even a specialised court within the meaning of Article 257 TFEU,[2254] could be a sensible solution to these and other[2255] concerns regarding the quality of (private international law) judgments.

2247 See *Hess*, IPRax 2006, 348, 352 (as regards procedural law).

2248 *Simons*, EuLF 2007, I-1, I-4.

2249 See e.g. *Lequette*, in: LA Gaudemet-Tallon, 503, 529, on the one hand, and on the other *Pirrung*, in: FS Kaissis, 759, 762–763.

2250 The influence of the judge-rapporteur on the decisions of the ECJ was the object of *Kalbheim's* recent study, ZVglRWiss 115 (2016), 431, in which, however, he only touches upon the judges' background. Suggesting such an influence *Gebauer*, ZVglRWiss 115 (2016), 557, 568.

2251 See *Gebauer*, ZVglRWiss 115 (2016), 557, 569, arguing for a stronger orientation towards private law at the EU courts.

2252 *Supra* Chapter 1, section 1.2.2.; also see *Rühl*, in: Zimmermann (ed.), Zukunftsperspektiven der Rechtsvergleichung, 103, 134–135.

2253 Touched upon (in the context of private international law) e.g. by *Azzi*, in: Mélanges Audit, 43, 53; *Bergé*, in: Fallon/Lagard/Poillot-Peruzzetto (eds.), La matière civile et commerciale, 157, 159; also see *Streinz/Leible*, EWS 2001, 1, 5–7. For the specialisation of judges in general (and from a comparative perspective) see Opinion (2012) No. 15 of the Consultative Council of European Judges on the Specialisation of Judges, 13 November 2012, CCJE(2012)4, and RabelsZ 81 (2017), No. 3, with the introductory remarks by *Fleischer*, 497.

2254 *Rühl*, in: Zimmermann (ed.), Zukunftsperspektiven der Rechtsvergleichung, 103, 135.

2255 A further aspect is the potential relevance of having judges from both the common law world and the civil law world decide issues of private international law: see *Hartley*, in: Remien/Kieninger (eds.), Europäische Kollisionsrechtsvereinheitlichung, 101, 109 and 114,

As preliminary rulings concern relatively abstract legal questions and them only, it appears comparatively easy to identify cases warranting treatment by such a special judicial body. At the very least, one could and should consider the possibility of specialised (or, in any case, simply more[2256]) Advocates General. One main issue to be addressed would be that the Court has no control over the specialisation of the judges or Advocates General who are sent to serve on the court.[2257]

3.3. SUPPORT BY PRIVATE STAKEHOLDERS

The challenges in the absence of general provisions are daunting.[2258] However, at least some support could come from private stakeholders, namely legal scholars and practitioners with scholarly interests. While they lack the power of a legislator or judge to provide authoritative solutions as such, they could aid either of the former in fulfilling their task. This essentially brings us back to the beginning of this book and the idea of pan-European legal scholarship. Three particular ways in which private stakeholders could support the courts as regards general issues of EU private international law are through a respective model regulation, case law data bases, and an advisory council.

The idea of a model regulation has already been mentioned in the context of the difficulties of legislative procedure for general issues on the level of the EU.[2259] Data bases for case law have already appeared in the preceding section. At least two such projects exist: "Unalex"[2260] and the recently launched "EUFam's".[2261] Finally, the idea of an advisory council is inspired by the CISG Advisory Council. This private panel of experts has been created in light of the CISG facing many of the aforementioned problems germane to a normative text relevant for a plethora of countries.[2262] Its purpose is "[t]o issue and publish opinions and declarations on the interpretation, application, and in general the role of the [CISG]", and "[t]o promote a uniform interpretation of the [CISG]".[2263] This body has the possibility of structuring the discourse

who appears to state that the Court did not even understand certain ideas from the common law in famous cases under the Brussels regime.

2256 *Rühl*, in: Zimmermann (ed.), Zukunftsperspektiven der Rechtsvergleichung, 103, 135.

2257 See (from an empirical perspective) *Yüksel*, in: Beaumont et al. (eds.), Cross-Border Litigation in Europe, 35, 50–51, with further arguments against specialisation at the level of the ECJ.

2258 This is not to gainsay that to attain coherent EU private international law is quite the challenge even *with* general provisions.

2259 *Supra* Chapter 5, section 2.4.4.

2260 www.unalex.eu (last visited 12 October 2018).

2261 www.eufams.unimi.it (last visited 12 October 2018).

2262 See only *Herber*, IHR 2003, 201.

2263 Article II CISG-AC Bylaws; *Mistelis*, CISG-AC Publishes First Opinions.

and providing an overview of different solutions advanced all over the contracting states. A solution offered as a result not only receives its authority from this background, but also from its authors' renown.[2264] A similar panel for (not necessarily only) general issues of EU private international law would arguably likewise have positive effects. Its potential or desirable institutional framework, size, composition, procedure, etc., however, are beyond the scope of this book.

4. SUMMARY

When approaching the question of whether the EU should make (formally and/or substantively) general provisions of private international law, it is important not to confound the question with "general parts" in scholarly works and legal education. It is further important not to simply confound the (traditional) arguments for and against "general parts" in substantive private law with those for and against general provisions of private international law. When grouped together, general provisions of private international law further the triple objective of clarity, coherence, and elimination of redundancies. They would also be a useful tool for the EU legislator itself, and hardly too abstract to handle for domestic judges. In the absence of general provisions, precisely these judges face quite a few difficulties. As a common European case law is an unlikely prospect, the task of providing uniform solutions for general issues would largely (continue to) lie with the ECJ. While having a common court is better than not having a common court, it is not exactly obvious that the ECJ in its present form is suited and/or willing to resolve general issues in a general manner. Support for all courts, however, could at least come from private stakeholders.

2264 *Herber*, IHR 2003, 201, 202.

CONCLUSION

This book has explored the concept of general issues and rules of private international law in the EU. It adopted a (not necessarily traditional) comparative perspective (Chapter 1), taking into account the domestic law of all member states, as well as EU law as it stands in Rome I, Rome II, Rome III, the Succession Regulation, the M-Property Regulation, and the RP-Property Regulation. The main findings can be summarised as follows.

1. DOMESTIC PRIVATE INTERNATIONAL LAW AND GENERAL ISSUES *DE LEGA LATA*

General rules of private international law in the EU: *nihil sub sole novum.* A majority of member states have a private international law code, be it part of a civil code, an act combining rules on the applicable law with rules on jurisdiction and more, or a stand-alone legal instrument. Every single one of these codes contains a set of provisions on issues commonly considered "general". These provisions often even constitute a formally separate chapter whose title, in turn, often officially designates them as "general". In any case, these provisions always form an identifiable cluster. The size of these sets varies, however. Some consist of only a handful of provisions, whereas the number of provisions in others is in the double digits.

Moreover, particularly in the common law and French tradition without private international law codes, scholars have separated entire classes of issues from their discussion of individual conflicts rules. Empirically, the respective issues and the issues covered by general provisions in other member states' codes overlap to a great degree. In fact, the very designation "general" surfaces here and there in scholarly works on private international law, albeit in the vast majority of instances without any conceptual explanation (Chapter 2, section 2.1.).

2. EUROPEAN UNION PRIVATE INTERNATIONAL LAW AND GENERAL ISSUES *DE LEGE LATA*

Six regulations on separate areas of law make up the bulk of EU private international law. While they do isolate entire chapters from their sets of particular conflicts provisions, they do so neither uniformly nor according to any obvious pattern. Still, several of the provisions contained in these chapters correspond to issues with which domestic private international law deals by using provisions designated as "general". Even in the absence of overarching provisions for all of the regulations, the EU legislator has demonstrated an inclination to giving a rudimentary structure to its private international law (Chapter 2, section 2.2.) – one that, as the further analysis has demonstrated, can largely be explained with the same conceptual notions as the general rules in domestic private international law.

3. THE TWO MOST PROMISING WAYS TO CLASSIFY GENERAL ISSUES/RULES

Both the formal and the substantive approach have withstood scrutiny. They are the two most promising ways of thinking about the concept of "general" in European (Union) private international law because they have been shown to cover existing "general" provisions and "general" statements in scholarly contributions with only very few exceptions.

A formally general issue (and hence a formally general rule) is one relevant in more than one context of private international law, e.g. relevant not only in the determination of the law applicable to contractual and/or non-contractual obligations, but also in the determination of the law applicable to succession. There are even issues and rules with (potential) relevance for all contexts of conflicts rules. They have been designated "formally general in the strict sense" here.

A substantively general issue (and hence a substantively general rule) is one setting forth the underlying policies of a given system of private international law.

The formal and the substantive approach are not mutually exclusive but overlap (Part II).

4. THE FORMAL APPROACH AND THE TRIPARTITE STRUCTURE OF ALL CONFLICTS RULES

As the formal approach is based upon the idea that a reasonable understanding of "general" is one looking for issues or rules relevant in more than one context, it also seemed reasonable to use the structure of conflicts rules as a framework for coming across, identifying, and analysing formally general issues. For all conflicts rules share the same tripartite bone structure. The elements of subject matter, connecting factor, and governing law are common to all of them, regardless of the area of law. Hence, certain issues likewise arise regardless of the area of law. This at first more or less intuitive idea has been analysed element by element, and it has largely proved viable.

4.1. FORMALLY GENERAL ISSUES CONNECTED TO THE SUBJECT MATTER (CHAPTER 3, SECTION 2.)

It has been demonstrated that the question of the *mandatory nature* of conflicts rules is a formally general issue in the strict sense. It has been argued that EU private international law is of a mandatory nature, i.e. to be applied even when no party has raised the respective conflicts rule(s).

While the *scope of application* of conflicts rules is a formally general issue in the strict sense, it has been contended that the requirement of an international element is actually no (such) issue of private international law. It is relevant for *EU* private international law, however, but only because of the limited competence of the EU. The question of competence is also the reason why the scope of application *ratione materiae* is of much more relevance in EU instruments than in domestic law. The scopes of application *ratione temporis* and *ratione personae* are not customarily considered "general" issues, but at least in some way as separate issues.

The *hierarchy* of different instruments of private international law is another formally general issue in the strict sense. It is often addressed by an expressly "general" provision on the domestic level, and by a provision separate from individual conflicts (and jurisdictional etc.) provisions at the EU level.

The question of determining the applicable conflicts rule, i.e. *characterisation*, is universally recognised as a "general" issue of private international law; indeed, from the perspective adopted here, it is a formally general issue in the strict sense. Provisions on this issue are still relatively rare, although their number grew in recent years. At the EU level, an autonomous approach is warranted; the private international law regulations offer some (but only some) guidance in this regard.

If the applicable law to a given issue implies another legal concept, an *incidental question* is potentially raised. Should the conflicts rules of the *lex causae* or the *lex fori* be used in such a situation? The adjective "incidental" is to be preferred over "preliminary". Despite the obvious relation to the governing law, incidental questions should be considered an issue of the subject matter. For an internal conflicts decision, also implying a decision on the interplay of different subject matters of the *lex fori*, is needed in any case. The issue is (almost) universally known in the member states and is typically considered a "general" issue; pertinent provisions are rare, however. Yet, again, their number appears to be growing. At the EU level, there is no provision on the incidental question yet. The term "preliminary question", which occasionally appears in the EU private international law regulations, is both ambiguous and inconsistently translated. Arguably, and in spite of the lack of a written rule, a common default solution already exists: the conflicts rules of the *lex fori* should be used.

Collateral questions (in particular those regarding form, capacity, and prescription) can also be regarded as formally general issues in the strict sense connected to the subject matter. Some domestic "general" provisions on specific collateral questions exist; at the EU level, the picture is murkier.

Dépeçage has turned out (only) to be a description of a possible result of the application of conflicts rules. Formally general rules on it do not exist in domestic or EU private international law. Nor is there any apparent need for any such rule.

The question of the consequences of the existence of two or more in principle applicable conflicts rules, of which one is *more specific* than the others, is no genuine issue of private international law but of legal method in general. In accordance with this insight, no pertinent private international law provisions exist. Occasionally, EU private international law expressly draws attention to the issue, however.

A particular problem of private international law, however, is the phenomenon of *overriding mandatory provisions*: rules intended to apply regardless of the otherwise applicable law. It has been argued that this formally general issue in the strict sense must be understood to involve a conflicts decision; there is no such thing as an "immediate" application of a substantive rule. Against this background, it has also been argued that overriding mandatory provisions concern the subject matter. Essentially, they constitute a (potential or actual) restriction of an otherwise pertinent subject matter. While such a restriction raises no problems if it originates with the same legislator as the conflicts rule to be restricted, overriding mandatory provisions by another legislator pose the real challenge. As this scenario has become more prevalent – EU conflicts rules vs. domestic overriding mandatory provisions – the significance of the issue is clear. Of the domestic private international law codes passed since 1995, only two do not have a general provision on overriding mandatory provisions. With the exception of Rome III – in particular, Article 10 Rome III does not belong in this context – all EU regulations deal with them as well.

Finally, in cases where no particular subject matter applies, a *subsidiary conflicts rule* may be needed. In domestic private international law, such a general provision is rare. Due to the limited scope of application of each EU regulation, this issue could only be relevant for internal gaps, i.e. situations in which the conflicts rules of a regulation do not cover all situations within its scope of application. Only Rome II raises doubts in this regard.

4.2. FORMALLY GENERAL ISSUES IN CONNECTION TO THE CONNECTING FACTOR (CHAPTER 3, SECTION 4.)

The question of whether a *more appropriate connecting factor* exists in a given case constitutes a formally general issue in the strict sense, which obviously relates to the connecting factor. Several member states have, among their general provisions, an *escape clause* (as the solution to the issue is commonly known). EU private international law thus far only contains individual escape clauses. Arguably, a formally general escape clause with exceptions would be the more persuasive solution for at least some of the regulations.

When the factual basis for a variable connecting factor changes, the formally general issue known as *conflit mobile* arises. Only few member states provide for a general rule on this issue, whereas EU private international law by and large makes sure that the phenomenon cannot even occur.

The possibility to have the parties decide which law applies to their affairs – *party autonomy* – can give rise to formally general issues. They relate to the connecting factor because here the parties' determination provides the link between a subject matter and the governing law, i.e. functions in the same way as objective connecting factors do. Even where party autonomy seems to cause special problems in the context of *renvoi* and/or non-unified legal systems, they are best understood to be specific issues of party autonomy itself, namely of its limits. Only a few member states have made formally general provisions on party autonomy. EU private international law often does not provide for a formally separate rule on party autonomy. This makes sense against the background that it typically contains catch-all conflicts rules allowing for party autonomy, thus making any further abstraction within the respective legal instrument at the same time unnecessary and impossible.

Several formally general issues arise in relation to the connecting factor of *nationality*. While only few member states have a general provision on the determination of nationality, many more have tackled the questions of stateless persons and persons with multiple nationalities. It should be noted that Article 18 TFEU prohibits the member states from giving preference to the *lex fori* nationality in cases of the latter. Again, only few member states have a general private international law provision in the context of nationality dealing with the situation of refugees. Finally, these topics constitute one of the rare instances in which common law literature is largely silent on formally general issues identified here. This is likely due to the preponderance of domicile as a connecting factor under common law. EU private international law offers no provisions on stateless persons or refugees, and only a structurally inconsistent picture on multi-nationals. It has turned out that, each time contrary to appearances, Recital 22 Rome III is no formally general rule, while Article 22(1) subparagraph 2 Succession Regulation actually is. Only the Succession Regulation contains hints as to the determination of nationality.

Finally, the connecting factor of *(habitual) residence* (and other connecting factors relating to the location of a person, like domicile) has been dealt with only occasionally by the member states among their general provisions. Despite its prevalence, EU private international law does not say much about it either.

4.3. FORMALLY GENERAL ISSUES IN CONNECTION WITH THE GOVERNING LAW (CHAPTER 3, SECTION 5.)

Whether a conflicts rule, depending upon its connecting factor, can refer to all legal systems, or is restricted in this regard (e.g. by requiring reciprocity), is a formally general issue in the strict sense concerning the governing law. Two relatively modern private international law codes of the member states expressly state that reciprocity is not required. Conversely, the EU legislator has always clarified that *universal application* of EU private international law is intended.

As conflicts rules typically refer to the "law of the country [or state] where …", *non-unified legal systems* raise a problem to the extent that there is no pertinent law at the level of the state, but only at the level of its sub-units or for certain groups of people. This issue is (at least) formally general. A vast majority of member states have a general provision concerning this issue in their private international law codes, but do not seem to agree on the most appropriate sub-context for the topic (in particular: *renvoi* or ascertainment/application of foreign law?). All EU private international law regulations deal with the issue in a formally general way, and always in some way separately from individual conflicts provisions.

The *change of the lex causae* raises a formally general issue in the strict sense. Its overarching relevance generally seems to be recognised. Legislative solutions do not exist in Europe, however.

The notorious topic of *renvoi* constitutes a formally general issue in the strict sense: does a conflict rule refer to foreign substantive law or to (*not* "also to") foreign conflicts rules? All member states with a private international law code have a respective provision among their general ones. The topic is recognised virtually everywhere as being of overarching significance. Similarly, in EU private international law, *renvoi* provisions can be found in clusters of other provisions dealing with formally general issues.

Since and to the extent that a (omnilateral) conflicts rule can lead to the application of any law in the world, one makes the proverbial leap into the dark. A *public policy* reservation which ensures that a judge is not forced to render judgments in contravention of (at least) fundamental values of the *lex fori* is known in all member states; those member states with a private international code all have a respective general provision on this formally general issue in the strict sense. All EU private international regulations contain a public policy provision too. Structurally, it is always part of a group of provisions on formally general issues.

The *ascertainment and application* of foreign law have procedural undertones but can and should be discussed in the private international law context, and in particular as formally general issues in the context of the governing law. Only few member states with a private international law code do not deal with these issues among their general provisions. It has been argued that barring the review of the application of another member state's law contravenes Article 18 TFEU. While EU private international law itself leaves the issues of ascertaining and applying foreign law to the member states (for now), regard must be had to the principles of equivalence and effectiveness.

Lewald's triad of *substitution, transposition, and adaptation* has further been identified as constituting formally general issues. Substitution concerns requirements of the *lex causae* which can only have been fulfilled under a different law; transposition is about transferring a foreign concept (from the originally applicable law) into the (now) applicable law. For both concepts, the idea of equivalence serves as the guiding principle. General provisions on these questions do not exist in the member states or at the EU level, although, to the extent that the issues are discussed at all, their recurring relevance seems to be recognised. With Article 31 Succession Regulation and Article 29 M-/RP-Property Regulation there are at least formally general provisions on transposition of rights *in rem*; the official terminology "adaptation" is a poor choice. Adaptation in its traditional sense rather concerns situations in which the interplay of different applicable laws to a set of facts leads to a result not intended by any law on its own. No member state has made a respective general provision. The Succession Regulation provides some specific examples of adaptation which exclude, as just mentioned, the one provision actually called "adaptation".

Finally, it is a formally general issue whether private international law is responsive to *erroneous assumptions regarding the applicable law*. Some member states have enacted general provisions dealing with, or at least also covering, this issue, whereas no respective formally general provision exists at the EU level.

5. GENERAL ISSUES OUTSIDE THE TRIPARTITE STRUCTURE

The tripartite structure of conflicts rules provides no entirely exhaustive framework for formally general issues, however. There are a few issues that (at least occasionally) are treated as general in private international law across Europe, and that (at least partly) can be defined as formally general, but that cannot be assigned a (single) place in the structure of conflicts rules.

The topic of *evasion of the law* arises in the context of both the subject matter and the connecting factor, even though the latter context seems to be the much more relevant one – if one considers evasion of the law to be a relevant topic in the first place; not all member states do. Moreover, there are quite a few instances in which conflicts rules for *formally general issues of substantive private law*, often conflicts rules for certain collateral questions, are regarded as general rules of private international law too (Chapter 3, sections 3. and 6.).

6. "FACTORING OUT" FORMALLY GENERAL ISSUES/RULES

Typically, but not exclusively, formally general rules of private international law are no conflicts rules themselves, i.e. do not determine the law applicable to a given subject matter on their own. Rather, they complement conflicts rules with respect to one of their three elements. The image of "factoring out" serves as a very suitable description of these rules. In fact, it works much better in this context than in substantive private law, even though it originates there. The expression relates to the distributive law in mathematics and illustrates that formally general rules are relevant in more than one context (Chapter 3, section 8.3.).

7. COMPLEMENTING THE PICTURE: SUBSTANTIVELY GENERAL ISSUES (CHAPTER 4)

The concept of substantively general issues and rules complements the picture. Their "general" nature can be explained from a qualitative, policy-based perspective. In particular, the guiding principle of the *close(st) connection* and the idea of the *protection of weaker parties* come to mind. Furthermore, some expressly general provisions on *party autonomy* and *equal treatment* (of foreigners) can be explained better from this substantive perspective than from the formal perspective.

8. THE NECESSARY EXISTENCE OF GENERAL ISSUES

8.1. A THEORETICAL NECESSITY

Unlike snow and adolescence, general issues of private international law do not disappear if one simply ignores them long enough.[2265] Rather, especially in their formal manifestation, they are a theoretical necessity of systems based on omnilateral conflicts rules. There is no point in vilifying them. Accordingly, it comes as no surprise that not only private international law scholars but also legislators have addressed these general issues, albeit with varying levels of completeness.

[2265] The quote "Snow and adolescence are the only problems that disappear if you ignore them long enough" generally seems to be attributed to *Earl Wilson*.

8.2. A FINAL LITMUS TEST: THE PROPOSAL FOR A REGULATION REGARDING THE ASSIGNMENT OF CLAIMS

On 12 March 2018, the Commission put forth a proposal for a regulation "on the law applicable to the third-party effects of assignments of claims".[2266] Since it contains omnilateral conflicts rules, it must at least raise the formally general issues in the strict sense if they are indeed a theoretical necessity. Thus, this proposal can serve as a final litmus test for the ideas submitted throughout this book.

In the proposed regulation, one comes across provisions on the scope of application of the proposed instrument, on its terminology, and on its universal application (Articles 1–3), as well as on the scope of the applicable law, overriding mandatory provisions, public policy, *renvoi*, states with more than one legal system, and on the relationship with other instruments of private international law (Articles 5–11). There are also provisions on the application in time, and on the entry into force, of the proposed regulation (Articles 14–15). In short: one comes across rules for many formally general issues. In fact, if one neglects the provisions on certain technicalities of EU law-making,[2267] Article 4 is the *only* provision in the proposal *not* dealing with a formally general issue.

What is more, the explanatory remarks concerning Articles 8 to 11 expressly state that: "These articles deal with *general issues of application of conflict of laws rules* …".[2268] While this statement is not perfect from the perspective of this book – the other provisions mentioned above would have to be included in the list[2269] – it would appear that the Commission at least has a hunch about the formal approach to general issues.

9. A LEGISLATIVE COMPETENCE WITHOUT A CORRESPONDING PROCEDURE

If the EU wanted to make general provisions for its private international law, and to follow either or both concepts developed here, it would certainly have the

2266 COM(2018) 96 final.

2267 Article 12 concerns a list of pertinent international conventions to be drawn up, Article 13 contains the customary review clause.

2268 COM(2018) 96 final, 22 (emphasis added).

2269 It is also not perfect from the perspective of the views advanced in this book that the Commission seems to suppose that private international law as such (i.e. not only *EU* private international law) only applies in situations with a cross-border element, see COM(2018) 96 final, 4.

respective competence under the TFEU. All issues identified as general in the course of this analysis can be tackled under Article 81(2)(c) and (f) TFEU. The result of such legislative activity could be a regulation (Article 288(2) TFEU). The EU is not limited to dealing only with intra-EU situations; nor is it limited by the principle of subsidiarity in this regard (Chapter 5, section 1.).

The EU would face a procedural difficulty, however, if it were to make general provisions for its private international law. General provisions for family and non-family law matters would implicate *both* the ordinary legislative procedure and a special legislative procedure pursuant to Article 81(3) TFEU. To comply with both as such at the same time is impossible. A hybrid procedure not provided for in the TFEU might be legal, but the necessary combination of unanimity in the Council and joint adoption of the instrument by the European Parliament and the Council casts serious doubts on its chance of success. It is similarly doubtful whether the passerelle clause of Article 81(3) subparagraph 2 TFEU can be used to overcome this difficulty. For the time being, a moderately complex system of references seems to be the far from perfect, but only, way out (Chapter 5, section 2.).

10. THE CASE FOR THE CREATION OF GENERAL PROVISIONS OF EU PRIVATE INTERNATIONAL LAW

General provisions, particularly of the formal ilk, operate at a relatively low level of abstraction in private international law, much like in criminal law. It is therefore not sound to take policy arguments for and against "general parts" of substantive private law at face value when concerned with private international law. Whether one considers a "general part" of substantive law – in the wake of Pandectism – useful should not influence one's stance concerning general provisions of private international law (Chapter 6, section 2.).

The creation of general provisions of EU private international law is generally to be viewed favourably. They would not perplex domestic judges but rather lead to more clarity, more coherence, and fewer redundancies in this area of law. At the same time, they would positively affect future legislation in the field, be it entirely new instruments or revised ones. Without such provisions, harmonised private international law seems hard to achieve in practice. Divergent solutions in different member states cannot be prevented effectively. Even if a question finally reached the European Court of Justice, and if it was then resolved conclusively (and comprehensibly), the scope of the respective answer would likely still give rise to doubts. An "EU Private International Law Advisory Board" would probably be of some use; yet it could not resolve general issues as effectively as the EU legislator (Chapter 6, sections 2. and 3.).

11. A EUROPEAN CONCEPT FOR THE EUROPEAN UNION

Where does all of this leave us? Having worked oneself through the private international law of all the member states and of the EU itself, one can now state with confidence that – even though German scholars seem especially concerned with the topic at the EU level – general issues and rules of private international law are hardly a concept limited to one particular or only few member states. Rather, they are a European concept, recognised in all member states and at the EU level. Hence, the EU potentially making general provisions for its private international law cannot reasonably be challenged on conceptual grounds. As it has been passing individual private international law rules anyway, one should rather wonder how sensible it is to codify the flesh without the skeleton.[2270]

Criticism regarding the *content* of potential provisions could very well be valid, of course. But the EU should not be daunted in this regard either. First, as this book has demonstrated, there is almost no general issue without at least one domestic solution that could serve as a model. On the contrary, quite a few examples exist for several issues, and these examples are not always that different from one another. Second, the current political climate might not seem propitious for such an endeavour at first; yet it is even worse for the widespread harmonisation of substantive private law. This makes a uniform system of private international law all the more important. It would accompany, buttress, and complement the freedoms under the TFEU. In times of turmoil, it would thus serve as a shining example of the EU having a positive impact on the lives of its citizens, perhaps even simplifying them (see the optimistic Recital 32 Succession Regulation). The EU already has a voluminous body of private international law – but it will only end up with a well-oiled system if it adds an esemplastic part: general provisions.

[2270] See (in the context of French domestic law) *Bureau*, in: Beignier (ed.), La codification, 119, 141.

BIBLIOGRAPHY

ABGB-Kurzkommentar, see Koziol, Helmut/Bydlinski, Peter/Bollenberger, Raimund (eds.)

Aden, Menno, Das Internationale Privatrecht Rumäniens, in: Recht der internationalen Wirtschaft 2008, 700–707

Álvarez González, Santiago, ¿Qué norma de conflicto de leyes hay que adoptar para determinar la ley aplicable a las cuestiones previas a efectos de la sucesión?, in: Revista Española de Derecho Internacional 69 (2017), 19–48

Ancel, Bertrand, Éléments d'histoire du droit international privé (2017), Éditions Panthéon-Assas, Paris

Ancel, Bertrand/Lequette, Yves, Les grands arrêts de la jurisprudence française de droit international privé, 5th ed. (2006), Dalloz, Paris

Añoveros Terradas, Beatriz, La autonomía de la voluntad como principio rector de las normas de derecho internacional privado comunitario de la familia, in: Forner Delaygua, Joaquim/González Beilfuss, Cristina/Viñas Farré, Ramón (eds.), Entre Bruselas y la Haya, Estudios sobre la unificación internacional y regional del Derecho internacional privado, Liber Amicorum Alegría Borrás (2013), Marcial Pons, Madrid et al., 119–131

Antomo, Jennifer, Anerkennung ausländischer Privatscheidungen - Rom III-Verordnung analog?, in: Neue Juristische Wochenschrift 2018, 435–438

Association Henri Capitant des Amis de la Culture Juridique Française/Société de Législation Comparée (eds.), Principes Contractuels Communs (2008), Paris

Aubart, Andrea, Die Behandlung der *dépeçage* im europäischen Internationalen Privatrecht (2013), Mohr Siebeck, Tübingen

Auby, Jean-Bernard/Dutheil de la Rochère, Jacqueline (eds.), Traité de droit administratif européen, 2nd ed. (2014), Bruylant, Brussels

Audit, Bernard, Private International Law, in: Bermann, George A./Picard, Etienne (eds.), Introduction to French Law (2008), Kluwer Law International, Alphen aan den Rijn, 453–474

——, Le droit international privé en quête d'universalité, Cours général, in: Recueil des cours 305 (2003), 9–488

——, Le droit international privé français à la fin du vingtième siècle: progrès ou recul?, in: Symeonides, Symeon C. (ed.), Private International Law at the End of the 20th Century: Progress or Regress? (2000), Kluwer Law International, London, 191–220

——, La fraude à la loi (1974), Dalloz, Paris

Audit, Bernard/d'Avout, Louis, Droit International Privé, 7th ed. (2013), Economica, Paris

Audit, Bernard/Bermann, George A., The Application of Private International Norms to "Third Countries": The Jurisdiction and Judgments Example, in: Nuyts, Arnaud/Watté, Nadine (eds.), International Civil Litigation in Europe and Relations with Third States (2005), Bruylant, Bruxelles, 55–82

Audren, Frédéric/Halpérin, Jean-Louis, La culture juridique française, Entre mythes et réalités (2013), CNRS, Paris

Avasilencei, Catalina, La codification des conflits de lois dans le nouveau Code civil roumain: une nouevelle forme en attente d'un contentieux, in: Revue critique de droit international privé 2012, 247–275

Azzi, Tristan, La Cour de justice et le droit international privé ou l'art de dire parfois tout et son contraire, in: d'Avout, Louis/Bureau, Dominique/Muir-Watt, Horatia (eds.), Mélanges en l'honneur du Professeur Bernard Audit, Les relations privées internationales (2014), LGDJ, Issy-les-Moulineaux, 43–58

Azzi, Tristan/Boskovic, Olivera, Rapport introductif, in: idem (eds.), Quel avenir pour la théorie générale des conflits de lois? (2015), Larcier, Bruxelles, 1–17

Baetge, Dietmar, Auf dem Weg zu einem gemeinsamen europäischen Verständnis des gewöhnlichen Aufenthalts, in: idem/von Hein, Jan/von Hinden, Michael (eds.), Die richtige Ordnung, Festschrift für Jan Kropholler zum 70. Geburtstag (2008), Mohr Siebeck, Tübingen, 77–88

Baker, John Hamilton, An Introduction to English Legal History, 3rd ed. (1990), Butterworth, London

Ball, Kurt, Vom neuen Weg der Gesetzgebung (1921), Spaeth & Linde, Berlin

Ballarino, Tito/Ballarino, Elena/Pretelli, Ilaria, Diritto Internazionale Privato Italiano, 8th ed. (2016), Wolters Kluwer Italia, Milanofiori Assago

Ballarino, Tito/Bonomi, Andrea, The Italian Statute on Private International Law of 1995, in: Yearbook of Private International Law 2 (2000), 99–131

Ballester, Blanca, Cost of Non-Europe Report, CONE 3/2013, A European Code on Private International Law, Brussels (available online at http://www.europarl.europa.eu/meetdocs/2009_2014/documents/juri/dv/costonnoneuropreport_/costonnoneuropreport_en.pdf) (last visited 12 October 2018)

Bamberger, Heinz Georg/Roth, Herbert (eds.), Beck'scher Online-Kommentar BGB, C. H. Beck, Munich (cited as: *Commentator*, in: BeckOK BGB)

Baratta, Roberto (ed.), Diritto internazionale privato (2010), Giuffré, Milan (cited as: *Commentator*, in: Baratta, DIP)

Baratta, Roberto, Réflexions sur la coopération judiciaire civile suite au Traité de Lisbonne, in: Venturini, Gabriella/Bariatti, Stefania (eds.), Nuovi strumenti del diritto internazionale privato, Liber Fausto Pocar, Vol. 2 (2009), Giuffré, Milan, 3–22

——, The Process of Characterization in the EC Conflict of Laws: Suggesting a Flexible Approach, in: Yearbook of Private International Law VI (2006), 155–169

Bariatti, Stefania, *Forum shopping*, abus du droit et droit international privé européen: quelques réflexions, in: Forner Delaygua, Joaquim/González Beilfuss, Cristina/Viñas Farré, Ramón (eds.), Entre Bruselas y la Haya, Estudios sobre la unificación internacional y regional del Derecho internacional privado, Liber Amicorum Alegría Borrás (2013), Marcial Pons, Madrid et al., 161–173

——, Multiple Nationalities and EU Private International Law, Many Questions and Some Tentative Answers, in: Yearbook of Private International Law 13 (2011), 1–19

Bariatti, Stefania/Pataut, Étienne, Codification et théorie générale du droit international privé, in: Fallon, Marc/Lagarde, Paul/Poillot-Peruzzetto, Sylvaine (eds.), Quelle architecture pour un code européen de droit international privé? (2011), Peter Lang, Brussels, 337–361

Barrière Barousse, Isabelle, Le Traité de Lisbonne et le droit international privé, in: Journal du droit international 2010, 3–34
Bartin, Étienne, Principes de droit international privé selon la loi et la jurisprudence françaises (1930), Domat-Montchrestien, Paris
——, De l'impossibilité d'arriver à la suppression définitive des conflits des lois, in: Journal du droit international privé 1897, 225–255, 466–495, 720–738
Basedow, Jürgen, Hundert Jahre Rechtsvergleichung, in: Juristenzeitung 2016, 269–280
——, The Law of Open Societies, Private Ordering and Public Regulation in the Conflict of Laws (2015), Brill Nijhoff, Leiden
——, Gegenseitigkeit im Kollisionsrecht, in: Hilbig-Lugani, Katharina/Jakob, Dominique/Mäsch, Gerald/Reuß, Philipp M./Schmid, Christoph (eds.), Zwischenbilanz, Festschrift für Dagmar Coester-Waltjen (2015), Gieseking, Bielefeld, 335–348
——, The Application of Foreign Law – Comparative Remarks on the Practical Side of Private International Law, in: idem/Pißler (eds.), Private International Law in Mainland China, Taiwan and Europe, 85–97
——, 15 Years of European Private International Law - Achievements, Conceptualization and Outlook, in: Forner Delaygua, Joaquim/González Beilfuss, Cristina/Viñas Farré, Ramón (eds.), Entre Bruselas y la Haya, Estudios sobre la unificación internacional y regional del Derecho internacional privado, Liber Amicorum Alegría Borrás (2013), Marcial Pons, Madrid et al., 175–183
——, Theorie der Rechtswahl oder Parteiautonomie als Grundlage des Internationalen Privatrechts, in: Rabels Zeitschrift für ausländisches und internationales Privatrecht 75 (2011), 32–59
——, Das Staatsangehörigkeitsprinzip in der Europäischen Union, in: Praxis des Internationalen Privat- und Verfahrensrechts 2011, 109–116
——, The Communitarisation of Private International Law - Introduction, in: Rabels Zeitschrift für ausländisches und internationales Privatrecht 73 (2009), 455–460
——, Der Raum des Rechts - ohne Justiz, in: Zeitschrift für Europäisches Privatrecht 2001, 437–440
——, European Conflict of Laws under the Treaty of Amsterdam, in: Borchers, Patrick J./ Zekoll, Joachim (eds.), International Conflict of Laws for the Third Millennium, Essays in Honor of Friedrich K. Juenger (2001), Transnational, Ardsley, New York, 175–192
——, Qualifikation, Vorfrage und Anpassung im Internationalen Zivilverfahrensrecht, in: Schlosser, Peter (ed.), Materielles Recht und Prozeßrecht und die Auswirkungen der Unterscheidung im Recht der internationalen Zwangsvollstreckung - eine rechtsvergleichende Grundlagenuntersuchung (1992), Gieseking, Bielefeld, 131–156
Basedow, Jürgen/Rühl, Giesela/Ferrari, Franco/de Miguel Asensio, Pedro (eds.), Encyclopedia of Private International Law (2017), Edward Elgar, Cheltenham, Northhampton
Basedow, Jürgen/Hopt, Klaus J./Zimmermann, Reinhard/Stier, Andreas (eds.), The Max Planck Encyclopedia of European Private Law (2012), Oxford University Press
Basedow, Jürgen/Birds, John/Clarke, Malcolm/Cousy, Herman/Heiss, Helmut (eds.), Principles of European Insurance Contract Law (PEICL) (2009), Sellier, Munich
Beaumont, Paul R./McEleavy, Peter E., Anton's Private International Law, 3rd ed. (2011), W. Green, Edinburgh

Beck, Gunnar, The Legal Reasoning of the Court of Justice of the EU (2012), Hart, Oxford and Portland, Oregon

Beckmann, Martin/Durner, Wolfgang/Mann, Thomas/Röckinghausen, Marc (eds.), Landmann/Rohmer, Umweltrecht, Vol. 1, 84th instalment (July 15, 2017), C.H. Beck, Munich

BeckOK BGB, see Bamberger, Heinz Georg/Roth, Herbert (eds.)

Beitzke, Günther, Neues österreichisches Kollisionsrecht, in: Rabels Zeitschrift für ausländisches und internationales Privatrecht 43 (1979), 245–276

Benecke, Martina, Gesetzesumgehung im Zivilrecht (2004), Mohr Siebeck, Tübingen

Benicke, Christoph/Zimmermann, Andreas, Internationales Namensrecht im Spannungsfeld zwischen Internationalem Privatrecht, Europäischem Gemeinschaftsrecht und Europäischer Menschenrechtskonvention, in: Praxis des Internationalen Privat- und Verfahrensrechts 1995, 141–150

Bentwich, Norman, Westlake, A Treatise on Private International Law or The Conflict of Laws, with Principal Reference to its Practice in England, 7th ed. (1925), Sweet & Maxwell, London (cited as: *Westlake*, PIL (1925))

Bergé, Jean-Sylvestre, Dynamique interprétative de la Cour de justice et codification européenne du droit international privé, in: Fallon, Marc/Lagarde, Paul/Poillot-Peruzzetto, Sylvaine (eds.), La matière civile et commerciale, socle d'un code européen de droit international privé? (2009), Dalloz, Paris, 157–169

Bergmann, Hans Detlev, Hauptprobleme des finnischen internationalen Privatrechts (1987), Berlin

Bergquist, Ulf/Damascelli, Domenico/Frimston, Richard/Lagarde, Paul/Odersky, Felix/Reinhartz, Barbara, EU-Erbrechtsverordnung, Kommentar (2015), Otto Schmidt, Cologne (cited as: *Commentator*, in: Bergquist et al., EU-ErbVO)

Bernecker, Dietrich, Internationales Privat- und Prozessrecht im Großherzogtum Luxemburg, in: Rabels Zeitschrift für ausländisches und internationales Privatrecht 27 (1962), 263–346

Bernitt, Carmen Christina, Die Anknüpfung von Vorfragen im europäischen Kollisionsrecht (2010), Mohr Siebeck, Tübingen

Biagoni, Giacomo, Art. 9 [of Rome I], in: Le nuove leggi civili commentate 2009, 788–804

Binchy, William, Irish Conflicts of Law (1988), Butterworth (Ireland), Dublin

Bitter, Georg/Röder, Sebastian, BGB, Allgemeiner Teil, 3rd ed. (2016), Franz Vahlen, Munich

Bodénès-Constantin, Armelle, La codification du droit international privé français (2005), Defrénois, Paris

Boecken, Winfried, BGB, Allgemeiner Teil, 2nd ed. (2012), Kohlhammer, Stuttgart

Boehmer, Gustav, Einführung in das bürgerliche Recht (1954), J. C. B. Mohr (Paul Siebeck), Tübingen

Boele-Woelki, Katharina, For Better or for Worse: The Europ[e]anization of International Divorce Law, in: Yearbook of Private International Law 12 (2010), 1–26

——, Unification and Harmonization of Private International Law in Europe, in: Basedow, Jürgen/Meier, Isaak/Schnyder, Anton K./Einhorn, Talia/Girsberger, Daniel (eds.), Private Law in the International Arena, Liber Amicorum Kurt Siehr (2000), Schulthess, Zurich, 61–77

Boele-Woelki, Katharina/van Iterson, Dorothea, The Dutch Private International Law Codification: Principles, Objectives and Opportunities, in: van Erp, J.H.M. (Sjef)/van Vliet, Lars P.W. (eds.), Netherlands Report to the Eighteenth International Congress of Comparative Law (2010), Intersentia, Antwerp, Oxford, Portland, 145–183

Boele-Woelki, Katharina/Ferrand, Frédérique/González Beilfuss, Cristina/Jänterä-Jareborg, Maarit/Lowe, Nigel/Martiny, Dieter/Pintens, Walter (eds.), Principles of European Family Law Regarding Divorce and Maintenance Between Former Spouses (2004), Intersentia, Antwerpen, Oxford

——, Principles of European Family Law Regarding Parental Responsibilities (2007), Intersentia, Antwerpen, Oxford

Boemke, Burkhard/Ulrici, Bernhard, BGB Allgemeiner Teil, 2nd ed. (2014), Springer, Dordrecht et al.

Bogdan, Michael, Concise Introduction to EU Private International Law, 3rd ed. (2016), 1st ed. (2006), Europa Law Publishing, Groningen

——, Concise Introduction to Comparative Law (2013), Europa Law, Groningen

——, Private International Law in Sweden, 2nd ed. (2015), Kluwer Law International, Alphen aan den Rijn

——, Private International Law as Component of the Law of the Forum, General Course on Private International Law, in: Recueil des cours 348 (2010), 9–252

——, Refugees in Swedish Private International Law, in: Grimheden, Jonas/Ring, Rolf (eds.), Human Rights Law: From Dissemination to Application, Essays in Honour of Göran Melander (2006), Martinus Nijhoff, Leiden, Boston, 311–320

——, General Aspects of the Future Regulation, in: Malatesta, Alberto (ed.) The Unification of Choice of Law Rules on Torts and Other Non-Contractual Obligations in Europe (2006), CEDAM, Padua, 33–44

Bogdan, Michael/Maunsbach, Ulf, EU Private International Law: An ECJ Casebook, 2nd ed. (2012), Europa Law, Groningen

Bohata, Petr, Neugestaltung des tschechischen Zivilrechts – Teil 5: Internationales Privatrecht, in: WiRO 2012, 193–200

Bohlander, Michael, The German Criminal Code, A Modern English Translation (2008), Hart, Portland

Bonomi, Andrea, Protocol of 23 November 2007 on the Law Applicable to Maintenance Obligations, Explanatory Report (2013), edited by the Permanent Bureau of the Conference, The Hague

——, Mandatory Rules in Private International Law, The quest for uniformity of decisions in a global environment, in: Yearbook of Private International Law I (1999), 215–247

Bork, Reinhard, Allgemeiner Teil des Bürgerlichen Gesetzbuchs, 4th ed. (2016), Mohr Siebeck, Tübingen

Borrás, Alegría, Les ordres plurilégislatifs dans le droit international privé actuel, in: Recueil des cours 249 (1999), 145–368

Bourdelois, Béatrice, La loi comme source de droit international privé, in: Puigelier, Catherine (ed.), La Loi, Bilan et perspectives (2005), Economica, Paris, 89–104

Briggs, Adrian, Private International Law in the English Courts (2014), Oxford University Press

——, The Rejection of Abuse in International Civil Procedure, in: de la Feria, Rita/Vogenauer, Stefan (eds.), Prohibition of Abuse of Law, A New General Principle of EU Law? (2011), Hart, Oxford and Portland, Oregon, 261–277

——, The Conflict of Laws, 3rd ed. (2013), Oxford University Press

Brockmöller, Annette, Die Entstehung der Rechtstheorie im 19. Jahrhundert in Deutschland (1997), Nomos, Baden-Baden

Brox, Hans/Walker, Wolf-Dietrich, Allgemeiner Teil des BGB, 41st ed. (2017), Franz Vahlen, Munich

Budzikiewicz, Christine, Unterbrechung der Verjährung durch Auslandsklage, in: Zeitschrift für Europäisches Privatrecht 2010, 415–434

Bureau, Dominique, La codification du droit international privé, in: Beignier, Bernard (ed.), La codification (1996), Dalloz, Paris, 119–143

Burián, László, Hungarian Private International Law at the End of the 20th Century: Progress or Regress?, in: Symeonides, Symeon C. (ed.), Private International Law at the End of the 20th Century: Progress or Regress? (2000), Kluwer Law International, London, 263–277

Bussani, Mauro, Faut-il se passer du common law (européen)? Réflexions sur un code civil continental dans le droit mondialisé, in: Revue internationale de droit comparé 2010, 7–25

Cach, Christopher/Weber, Alexander, Privatautonomie im Internationalen Erbrecht, in: Zeitschrift für Europarecht, Internationales Privatrecht und Rechtsvergleichung (ZfRV) 2013, 263–269

Cachard, Olivier, Droit international privé, 6th ed. (2017), Larcier, Brussels

Calliess, Christian/Ruffert, Matthias (eds.), EUV/AEUV, Das Verfassungsrecht der Europäischen Union mit Europäischer Grundrechtecharta, 5th ed. (2016), C.H. Beck, Munich

Calliess, Gralf-Peter (ed.), Rome Regulations, Commentary on the European Rules of the Conflict of Laws (2015), Kluwer Law International BV, Alphen aan den Rijn (cited as: *Commentator*, in: Calliess (ed.), Rome Regulations)

Calvo Caravaca, Alfonso-Luis/Carrascosa González, Javier, Derecho Internacional Privado, Vol. I and II, 16th ed. (2016), Editorial Comares, Granada

Calvo Caravaca, Alfonso-Luis/Carrascosa González, Javier, La ley aplicable al divorcio en Europa: El futuro reglamento Roma III, in: Cuadernos de Derecho Transnacional 2009, 36–71

Caranta, Roberto, Judicial Protection against Member States: A New *Jus Commune* Takes Shape, in: Common Market Law Review 32 (1995), 703–726

Carpi, Federico, Specialisation of judges as an efficiency factor in civil justice, in: Adolphsen, Jens/Goebel, Joachim/Haas, Ulrich/Hess, Burkhard/Kolmann, Stephan/Würdinger, Markus (eds.), Festschrift für Peter Gottwald zum 70. Geburtstag (2014), Beck, Munich, 73–80

Carrascosa González, Javier, El reglamento Sucesorio Europeo 650/2012 de 4 de julio 2012, Análisis crítico (2014), Editorial Comares, Granada

Carruthers, Janeen M./Crawford, Elizabeth B., Variations on a Theme of Rome II, Reflections on Proposed Choice of Law Rules for Non-Contractual Obligations, Part I, in: Edinburgh Law Review 9 (2005), 65–97

Cavers, David F., A Critique of the Choice-of-Law Problem, in: Harvard Law Review 47 (1933), 173–208

Cheshire/North/Fawcett, see Torremans, Paul (ed.)
Chetail, Vincent, Les relations entre droit international privé et droit international des réfugiés: histoire d'une brève rencontre, in: Journal du droit international 2014, 447–475
Chong, Adeline, The Public Policy and Mandatory Rules of Third Countries in International Contracts, in: Journal of Private International Law 2 (2006), 27–70
Christandl, Gregor, Multi-Unit States in European Union Private International Law, in: Journal of Private International Law 9 (2013), 219–244
Cigoj, Stojan, Note [on the Yugoslav Private International Law Act], in: Revue critique de droit international privé 1983, 375–382
Coester-Waltjen, Dagmar, Die verpasste Chance – Der EuGH und die Privatscheidung, in: Praxis des Internationalen Privat- und Verfahrensrechts 2018, 238–242
——, „Totgesagte leben länger" – gilt dies auch für das klassische Internationale Privatrecht?, in: Gössl, Susanne L. (ed.), Politik und Internationales Privatrecht (2017), Mohr Siebeck, Tübingen, 1–17
Coester-Waltjen, Dagmar/Coester, Michael, Rechtswahlmöglichkeiten im Europäischen Kollisionsrecht, in: Michaels, Ralf/Solomon, Dennis (eds.), Liber Amicorum Klaus Schurig zum 70. Geburtstag (2012), Sellier, Munich, 33–47
Coing, Helmut, Europäisierung der Rechtswissenschaft, in: Neue Juristische Wochenschrift 1990, 937–941
——, Ius Commune, nationale Kodifikation und internationale Abkommen: drei historische Formen der Rechtsvereinheitlichung, in: Le nuove frontiere del diritto e il problema dell'unificazione, Atti del Congresso internazionale di Bari, Vol. 1 (1979), Giuffré, Milan, 171–199
——, European Common Law: Historical Foundations, in: Cappelletti, Mauro (ed.), New Perspectives for a Common Law of Europe (1978), Sijthoff et al., Leyden et al., 31–44
Lord Collins of Mapesbury with specialist editors (Briggs, Adrian/Dickinson, Andrew/Harris, Jonathan/McClean, J. D./McEleavy, Peter/McLachlan, Campbell/Morse, C. G. J.), Dicey/Morris/Collins, The Conflict of Laws, Vol. 1 and 2, 15th ed. (2012), Sweet & Maxwell, London
Conetti, Giorgio, La legge sul diritto internazionale privato della Repubblica di Slovenia, in: Rivista di diritto internazionale privato e processuale 2000, 569–578
——, Considerations sur la loi hongroise de droit international privé du 1979 en comparaison avec quelques lois recentes d'autres pay européens, in: Collisio legum, Studi di diritto internazionale privato per Gerardo Broggini (1997), Giuffré, Milan, 129–136
Conklin, William E., Statelessness, The Enigma of an International Community (2014), Hart, Oxford and Portland, Oregon
Cordero Álvarez, Clara Isabel, Incidencia de las normas imperativas en los contratos internacionales: especial referencia a las normas de terceros estados desde una aproximación europea, in: Cuadernos de Derecho Transnacional 2017, 174–193
Corneloup, Sabine, Zum Bedeutungsverlust des Renvoi, in: Praxis des Internationalen Privat- und Verfahrensrechts 2017, 147–152
Corneloup, Sabine/Nourissat, Cyril, Quelle structure pour un code européen de droit international privé?, in: Fallon, Marc/Lagarde, Paul/Poillot-Peruzzetto, Sylvaine (eds.), Quelle architecture pour un code européen de droit international privé? (2011), Peter Lang, Brussels, 257–280

Craig, Paul, EU Administrative Law, 2nd ed. (2012), Oxford University Press

Crawford, Elizabeth B./Carruthers, Janeen M., International Private Law: A Scots Perspective (2015), W. Green, Edinburgh

——, Connection and Coherence between and among European Instruments in the Private International Law of Obligations, in: International and Comparative Law Quarterly 63 (2014), 1–29

Csehi, Zoltán, Über das neue Gesetz Ungarns betreffend das internationale Privat- und Verfahrensrecht - Eine kurze Übersicht, in: Praxis des Internationalen Privat- und Verfahrensrechts 2018, 298–305

Cuniberti, Gilles, Conflict of Laws, A Comparative Approach (2017), Edward Elgar, Cheltenham

——, Brexit et contentieux international des affaires, in: Bahurel, Charles/Bernard, Elsa/Ho-Dac, Marion (eds.), Le Brexit, Enjeux régionaux, nationaux et internationaux (2017), Bruylant, Bruxelles, 197–211

——, The Discreet Influence of Abuse of Law in International Civil Procedure, in: de la Feria, Rita/Vogenauer, Stefan (eds.), Prohibition of Abuse of Law, A New General Principle of EU Law? (2011), Hart, Oxford and Portland, Oregon, 279–293

Cuniberti, Gilles (ed.), Code de droit international privé luxembourgeois, 2nd ed. (2014), Promoculture-Larcier, Windhof

Czepelak, Marcin, The Experience Concerning the Application of Community Instruments in the Recent EU Member States, in: Campuzano Díaz, Beatriz/idem/Rodríguez Benot, Andrés/Rodríguez Vázquez, Ángeles (eds.), Latest Developments in EU Private International Law (2011), Intersentia, Cambridge, Antwerp, Portland, 49–61

——, Would We Like to Have a European Code of Private International Law?, in: European Review of Private Law 2010, 705–728

Dannemann, Gerhard, Chapter 15, Adaptation, in: Leible, Stefan (ed.), General Principles of European Private International Law (2016), Kluwer Law International, Alphen aan den Rijn, 331–342

——, In search of system neutrality: methodological issues in drafting the European contract law rules, in: Adams, Maurice/Bomhoff, Jacco (eds.), Practice and Theory in Comparative Law (2012), Cambridge University Press, 96–119

——, Comparative Law: Study of Similarities or Differences?, in: Reimann, Mathias/Zimmermann, Reinhard (eds.), The Oxford Handbook of Comparative Law (2006), Oxford University Press, 383–419

——, Martin Wolff, in: Beatson, Jack/Zimmermann, Reinhard (eds.), Jurists Uprooted, German-speaking Émigré Lawyers in Twentieth-century Britain (2004), Oxford University Press, 441–461

——, Sachrechtliche Gründe für die Berücksichtigung nicht anwendbaren Rechts, in: Hohloch, Gerhard/Frank, Rainer/Schlechtriem, Peter (eds.), Festschrift für Hans Stoll (2001), Mohr Siebeck, Tübingen, 417–436

David, René, Le droit continental, la common law, et les perspectives d'un *jus commune* européen, in: Cappelletti, Mauro (ed.), New Perspectives for a Common Law of Europe (1978), Sijthoff et al., Leyden et al., 113–135

de Coninck, Julie, The Functional Method of Comparative Law: *Quo Vadis*?, in: Rabels Zeitschrift für ausländisches und internationales Privatrecht 74 (2010), 318–350 de Groot, Gerard-René, European Education in the 21st Century, in: de Witte, Bruno/Forder, Caroline (eds.), The common law of Europe and the future of legal education (1992), Kluwer, Deventer, 7–29

de Groot, Gerard-René/Kuipers, Jan-Jaap, The New Provisions on Private International Law in the Treaty of Lisbon, in: Maastricht Journal of European and Comparative Law 2008, 109–114

de la Feria, Rita/Vogenauer, Stefan (eds.), Prohibition of Abuse of Law, A New General Principle of EU Law? (2011), Hart, Oxford and Portland, Oregon

de Lima Pinheiro, Luís, Direito Internacional Privado, Volume I, 3rd ed. (2016), Almedina, Coimbra

——, The Methodology and the General Part of the Portuguese Private International Law Codification: A Possible Source of Inspiration for the European Legislator?, in: Yearbook of Private International Law 14 (2012/2013), 153–172

——, Choice of Law in Non-Contractual Obligations between Communitarization and Globalization, A First Assessment of EC Regulation Rome II, in: Rivista di diritto internazionale privato e processuale 2008, 5–42

de Witte, Bruno/Forder, Caroline (eds.), The common law of Europe and the future of legal education (1992), Kluwer, Deventer

Derleder, Peter, Ex promotione lux?, in: myops 11/2001, 12–22

Dethloff, Nina/Hauschild, Luise, Familienrecht im Rahmen der justiziellen Zusammenarbeit in Zivilsachen, Das besondere Gesetzgebungsverfahren gem. Art. 81 III AEUV, in: Familie Partnerschaft Recht 2010, 489–493

Deutsches Notarinstitut (ed.), Les Successions Internationales dans l'UE/Conflict of Law of Succession in the European Union/Internationales Erbrecht in der EU (2004), Deutsches Notarinstitut

Dicey/Morris/Collins, see: Lord Collins of Mapesbury with specialist editors

Dickinson, Andrew, Back to the future: the UK's EU exit and the conflict of laws, in: Journal of Private International Law 12 (2016), 195–210

——, The Rome II Regulation: The Law Applicable to Non-Contractual Obligations (2008), Oxford University Press

Dickinson, Andrew/Lein, Eva (eds.), The Brussels I Regulation Recast (2015), Oxford University Press (cited as: *Commentator*, in: Dickinson/Lein (eds.), Brussels I Recast)

Dobiáš, Petr, The New Czech Private International Law, in: Rivista di diritto internazionale privato e processuale 2015, 109–127

——, Die Neuregelung des Internationalen Privatrechts in der Tschechischen Republik, in: Recht der internationalen Wirtschaft 2012, 671–677

Dohrn, Heike, Die Kompetenzen der Europäischen Gemeinschaft im Internationalen Privatrecht (2004), Mohr Siebeck, Tübingen

Dolinger, Jacob, In Defense of the „General Part" Principles, in: Borchers, Patrick J./Zekoll, Joachim (eds.), International Conflict of Laws for the Third Millenium, Essays in Honor of Friedrich K. Juenger (2001), Transnational, Ardsley, New York, 23–51

d'Oliveira, Hans Ulrich Jessurun, Towards a 'European' Private International Law?, in: de Witte, Bruno/Forder, Caroline (eds.), The common law of Europe and the future of legal education (1992), Kluwer, Deventer, 265–283

Drago, Roland, General Introduction, in: Bermann, George A./Picard, Etienne (eds.), Introduction to French Law (2008), Kluwer Law International, Alphen aan den Rijn, xxxix–xl

Dreier, Horst (ed.), Grundgesetz, Kommentar, Vol. I, 3rd ed. (2013), Mohr Siebeck, Tübingen (cited as: *Commentator*, in: Dreier (ed.), Grundgesetz)

Drobnig, Ulrich, Das Profil des Wirtschaftskollisionsrechts, in: Rabels Zeitschrift für ausländisches und internationales Privatrecht 52 (1988), 1–7

——, Methodenfragen der Rechtsvergleichung im Lichte der „International Encyclopedia of Comparative Law", in: von Caemmerer, Ernst/Mentschikoff, Soia/Zweigert, Konrad (eds.), Ius Privatum Gentium, Festschrift für Max Rheinstein, Band I (1969), J. C. B. Mohr (Paul Siebeck), Tübingen, 221–233

Dübeck, Inger, Einführung in das dänische Recht (1996), Nomos, Baden-Baden

Düsterhaus, Dominik, Konstitutionalisiert der EuGH das Internationale Privat- und Verfahrensrecht der EU?, in: Zeitschrift für Europäisches Privatrecht 2018, 10–31

Dutta, Anatol, Der gewöhnliche Aufenthalt – Bewährung und Perspektiven eines Anknüpfungsmoments im Lichte der Europäisierung des Kollisionsrechts, in: Praxis des Internationalen Privat- und Verfahrensrechts 2017, 139–146

——, Gemeinsame oder getrennte Kodifikation von IPR und IZVR auf europäischer Ebene, Die bisherigen und geplanten Verordnungen im Familien- und Erbrecht als Vorbilder für andere Rechtsgebiete?, in: von Hein, Jan/Rühl, Giesela (eds.), Kohärenz im Internationalen Privat- und Verfahrensrecht der Europäischen Union (2016), Mohr Siebeck, Tübingen, 27–43

Eek, Hilding, The Swedish Conflict of Laws (1965), Martinus Nijhoff, The Hague

Eichel, Florian, Chapter 13, References to Non-unified Legal Systems, in: Leible, Stefan (ed.), General Principles of European Private International Law (2016), Kluwer Law International, Alphen aan den Rijn, 275–303

Einhorn, Talia, American vs. European Private International Law – The Case for a Model Conflict of Laws Act (MCLA), in: Boele-Woelki, Katharina/eadem/Girsberger, Daniel/Symeonides, Symeon (eds.), Convergence and Divergence in Private International Law, Liber Amicorum Kurt Siehr (2010), Schulthess, Zurich, 3–36

Erauw, Johan/Fallon, Marc, Flexibility and Conflict Justice in the Belgian Code of Private International Law, in: Dirix, Eric/Lelen, Yves-Henri (eds.), The Belgian Reports of the Congress of Washington of the International Academy of Comparative Law (2011), Bruylant, Brussels, 227–276

Erauw, Johan/Fallon, Marc/Guldix, Erna/Meeusen, Johan/Pertegás Sender, Marta/van Houtte, Hans/Watté, Nadine/Wautelet, Patrick (eds.), Het Wetboek Internationaal Privaatrecht becommentarieerd – Le Code de droit international privé commenté (2006), Intersentia/Bruylant, Anwerpen, Oxford/Brussels (cited as: *Commentator*, in: Het Wetboek Internationaal Privaatrecht becommentarieerd)

Erman BGB, see Westermann, Harm Peter/Grunewald, Barbara/Maier-Remer, Georg (eds.)

Ernst, Ulrich, Das polnische IPR-Gesetz von 2011, Mitgliedstaatliche Rekodifikation in Zeiten supranationaler Kompetenzwahrnehmung, in: Rabels Zeitschrift für ausländisches und internationales Privatrecht 76 (2012), 597–638

Esplugues, Carlos, with Iglesias, José Luis/Palao, Guillermo/Espinosa, Rosario/Azcárraga, Carmen (drafting team), General Report on the Application of Foreign Law by Judicial and Non-Judicial Authorities in Europe, in: idem/Iglesias, José Luis/Palao, Guillermo (eds.), Application of Foreign Law (2011), Sellier, Munich, 3–94

Esplugues, Carlos/Iglesias, José Luis/Palao, Guillermo (eds.), Application of Foreign Law (2011), Sellier, Munich (cited as: *National Reporter[s]*, in: Esplugues/Iglesias/Palao (eds.), Application of Foreign Law)

Esplugues Mota, Carlos Aurelio/Azcárraga Monzonís, Carmen, Spanish Report [to the XVIIIth International Congress of Comparative Law], (available online at http://ssrn.com/abstract=1953835) (last visited 12 October 2018)

Falconbridge, John D., Characterization in the Conflict of Laws, in: The Law Quarterly Review 53 (1937), 235–258, 537–567

Fallon, Marc, Les conditions d'un code européen de droit international privé, in: idem/Lagarde, Paul/Poillot-Peruzzetto, Sylvaine (eds.), La matière civile et commerciale, socle d'un code européen de droit international privé? (2009), Dalloz, Paris, 1–34

Fallon, Marc/Meeusen, Johan, Private International Law in the European Union and the Exception of Mutual Recognition, in: Yearbook of Private International Law 4 (2002), 37–66

Fallon, Marc/Lagarde, Paul/Poillot-Peruzzetto, Sylvaine (eds.), Quelle architecture pour un code européen de droit international privé? (2011), Peter Lang, Brussels

Faure, Michael/Smits, Jan/Schneider, Hildegard, Preface, in: idem (eds.), Towards a European Ius Commune in Legal Education and Research (2002), Intersentia, Antwerp and Groningen, I–IV

Fauvarque-Cosson, Bénédicte, Droit international privé et droit comparé: brève histoire d'un couple à l'heure de l'Europe, in: Azzi, Tristan/Bureau, Dominique/Fauvarque-Cosson, Bénédicte/Kessedjian, Catherine/Poillot-Peruzzetto, Sylvaine/de Vareilles-Sommières, Pascal (eds.), Vers de nouveaux équilibres entre ordres juridiques, Liber amicorum Hélène Gaudemet-Tallon (2008), Dalloz, Paris, 43–56

Fawcett, James J./Ní Shúilleabháin, Máire/Shah, Sangeeta, Human Rights and Private International Law (2016), Oxford University Press

Fentiman, Richard, Foreign Law in National Courts, in: Andenas, Mads/Fairgrieve, Duncan (eds.), Courts and Comparative Law (2015), Oxford University Press, 79–101

——, English Private International Law at the End of the 20th Century: Progress or Regress?, in: Symeonides, Symeon C. (ed.), Private International Law at the End of the 20th Century: Progress or Regress? (2000), 165–190

——, Foreign Law in English Courts (1998), Oxford University Press

Fernández Arroyo, Diego P., Private International Law and Comparative Law: A Relationship Challenged by International and Supranational Law, in: Yearbook of Private International Law 11 (2009), 31–71

Ferrari, Franco (ed.), Rome I Regulation, Pocket Commentary (2015), Sellier, Munich

Ferrer-Correia, A., Das Problem der Qualifikation nach dem portugiesischen internationalen Privatrecht, in: ZfRV 1970, 114–135

Ferreri, Silvia, Complexity of Transnational Sources, in: Brown, Karen B./Snyder, David V. (eds.), General Reports of the XVIIIth Congress of the International Academy of Comparative Law (2012), Springer, Dordrecht et al., 29–56

Fiala, Josef/Hurdík, Jan/Kirstová, Katarína, Contract Law in Slovak Republic (2010), Kluwer Law International, Alphen aan den Rijn

Fincke, Martin, Das Verhältnis des Allgemeinen zum Besonderen Teil des Strafrechts (1975), J. Schweitzer, Berlin

Finger, Peter, Verstärkte Zusammenarbeit im Scheidungskollisionsrecht, in: Familie und Recht 2011, 313–315

Fiorini, Aude, The Evolution of European Private International Law, in: International and Comparative Law Quarterly 57 (2008), 969–984

——, The Codification of Private International Law: The Belgian Experience, in: International and Comparative Law Quarterly 54 (2005), 499–519

Firsching, Karl, Einführung in das internationale Privatrecht (1987), C.H. Beck, Munich

——, Das neue jugoslawische IPR-Gesetz, in: Praxis des Internationalen Privat- und Verfahrensrechts 1983, 1–5

Fleischer, Holger, Spezialisierte Gerichte: Eine Einführung, in: Rabels Zeitschrift für ausländisches und internationales Privatrecht 81 (2017), 497–509

Flessner, Axel, Rechtsvergleichung und Kollisionsrecht – Neue Akzente in einer alten Beziehung, in: Mankowski, Peter/Wurmnest, Wolfgang (eds.), Festschrift für Ulrich Magnus zum 70. Geburtstag (2014), Sellier, Munich, 403–417

——, Das Parteiinteresse an der lex fori nach europäischem Kollisionsrecht, in: Verbeke, Alain-Laurent/Scherpe, Jens M./Declerck, Charlotte/Helms, Tobias/Senaeve, Patrick (eds.), Confronting the Frontiers of Family and Succession Law, Liber Amicorum Walter Pintens (2012), Intersentia, Cambridge et al., 593–606

——, Diskriminierung von grenzübergreifenden Rechtsverhältnissen im europäischen Zivilprozess, in: Zeitschrift für Europäisches Privatrecht 2006, 737–741

Fletcher, Ian F., Conflict of Laws and European Community Law (1982), North-Holland Publishing, Amsterdam/New York/Oxford

Foelix, Jean-Jacques Gaspard, Traité du droit international privé ou du conflit des lois de différentes nations en matière de droit privé (1843), Paris

Förster, Christian, Die Umsetzung der Verbraucherrechterichtlinie in §§ 312 ff. BGB – Eine systematische Darstellung für Studium und Examen – Teil I, in: Juristische Arbeitsblätter 2014, 721–730

Foster, Nigel/Sule, Satish, German Legal System and Laws, 4th ed. (2010), Oxford University Press

Foyer, Jacques, Requiem pour le renvoi?, in: Travaux du comité français de droit international privé, Années 1980–1981, Éditions du centre national de la recherche scientifique, Paris, 105–122

——, Le nouvel avant-projet de réforme du Droit international privé français, in: Journal du droit international 1971, 31–49

Franceskakis, Phoicon, Lois d'application immédiate et règles de conflit, in: Rivista di diritto internazionale privato e processuale 1967, 691–698

——, Quelques précisions sur les „lois d'application immédiate" et leurs rapports aves les règles de conflits de lois, in: Revue critique de droit international privé 1966, 1–18

——, La théorie du renvoi et les conflits de systèmes en droit international Privé (1958), Sirey, Paris

Francq, Stéphanie, Das belgische IPR-Gesetzbuch, in: Rabels Zeitschrift für ausländisches und internationales Privatrecht 70 (2006), 235–278

Fränkel, Rudolf, Der Irrgarten des internationalen Privatrechts, in: Zeitschrift für Ausländisches und Internationales Privatrecht 4 (1930), 239–243

Frankenberg, Günter, Critical Comparisons: Re-thinking Comparative Law, in: Harvard International Law Journal 26 (1985), 411–455

Franzina, Pietro, Note minime in tema di adattamento, sostituzione ed equivalenza nel diritto internazionale privato dell'Unione europea, in: Cortese, Bernardo (ed.), Studi in onore di Laura Picchio Forlati (2014), G. Giappichelli, Turin, 185–194

Freitag, Robert, Art. 9 Rom I-VO, Art. 16 Rom II-VO als Superkollisionsnormen des Internationalen Schuldrechts? – Gedanken zum Verhältnis zwischen internen und externen Lücken des EuIPR, in: Praxis des Internationalen Privat- und Verfahrensrechts 2016, 418–426

——, Rom I, Rom II – tertium est datur [sic] im Kollisionsrecht der Schuldverhältnisse!, in: Bernreuther, Jörn/id./Leible, Stefan/Sippel, Harald/Wanitzek, Ulrike (eds.), Festschrift für Ulrich Spellenberg (2010), Sellier, Munich, 169–176

Fuchs, Angelika, Mehrstaater im Internationalen Privatrecht, in: Witzleb, Normann/Ellger, Reinhard/Mankowski, Peter/Merkt, Hanno/Remien, Oliver (eds.), Festschrift für Dieter Martiny zum 70. Geburtstag (2014), Mohr Siebeck, Tübingen, 303–324

Garau Sobrino, Federico F., Welches Internationale Privatrecht wollen wir im 21. Jahrhundert?, in: Zeitschrift für Vergleichende Rechtswissenschaft 117 (2018), 24–49

Garcimartín Alférez, Francisco J., Derecho Internacional Privado, 3rd ed. (2016), Civitas, Cizur Menor

——, The Rome II Regulation: On the way towards a European Private International Law Code, in: The European Legal Forum 2007, I-77–I-91

Garnett, Richard, Substance and Procedure in Private International Law (2012), Oxford University Press

Gaudemet-Tallon, Hélène, De l'abus de droit en droit international privé, in: d'Avout, Louis/Bureau, Dominique/Muir-Watt, Horatia (eds.), Mélanges en l'honneur du Professeur Bernard Audit, Les relations privées internationales (2014), LGDJ, Issy-les-Moulineaux, 383–396

——, Quel droit international privé pour l'Union européenne?, in: Borchers, Patrick J./Zekoll, Joachim (eds.), International Conflict of Laws for the Third Millennium, Essays in Honor of Friedrich K. Juenger (2001), Transnational, Ardsley, New York, 317–338

Gebauer, Martin, Das Europäische Kollisionsrecht und seine Herausforderungen für den EuGH, in: Zeitschrift für vergleichende Rechtswissenschaft 115 (2016), 557–569

——, Chapter 16, The Law of Agency, in: Leible, Stefan (ed.), General Principles of European Private International Law (2016), Kluwer Law International, Alphen aan den Rijn, 345–356

——, Grundfragen der Europäisierung des Privatrechts (1998), C. Winter, Heidelberg

Gebauer, Martin/Teichmann, Christoph (eds.), Enzyklopädie Europarecht, Vol. 6, Europäisches Privat- und Unternehmensrecht (2016), Nomos, Baden-Baden

Geč-Korošec, Miroslava, Die Reform des slowenischen Internationalen Privat- und Verfahrensrechts und seine Anpassung an das Recht der Europäischen Union, in: Rabels Zeitschrift für ausländisches und internationales Privatrecht 66 (2002), 710–747

Geimer, Reinhold, Die europäische Erbrechtsverordnung im Überblick, in: Hager, Johannes (ed.), Die neue europäische Erbrechtsverordnung (2013), Nomos, Baden-Baden, 9–38

Geisler, Stephan, Die engste Verbindung im Internationalen Privatrecht (2001), Duncker und Humblot, Berlin

Giardina, Andrea, Introductory Note [to the Law Reforming the Italian System of Private International Law], in: International Legal Materials 35 (1996), 760–762

——, Les caractères généraux de la réforme, in: Revue critique de droit international privé 1996, 1–19

Gibbs, James Lowell, Law in Radically Different Cultures, An Experimental Course in Comparative Law, in: The American Behavioral Scientist 25 (1981), 37–42

Giuliano, Mario/Lagarde, Paul, Report on the Convention on the law applicable to contractual obligations (1980), OJ C 282/1

Geeroms, Sofie, Foreign Law in Civil Litigation, A Comparative and Functional Analysis (2004), Oxford University Press

Geiger, Rudolf/Khan, Daniel-Erasmus/Kotzur, Markus, EUV/AEUV, 5th ed. (2010), C.H. Beck, Munich

Geuenich, Berit, Die Bestimmung des anwendbaren Rechts im Falle der international-privatrechtlichen Verweisung auf einen territorialen Mehrrechtsstaat (2017), Mohr Siebeck, Tübingen

Gerber, David J., Sculpting the Agenda of Comparative Law: Ernst Rabel and the Facade of Language, in: Riles, Annelise (ed.), Rethinking the Masters of Comparative Law (2001), Hart, Oxford, Portland, Oregon, 190–208

Gogos, Demetrius/Aubin, Bernhard C.H., Das Internationale Privatrecht im griechischen Zivilgesetzbuch von 1940, in: Rabels Zeitschrift für ausländisches und internationales Privatrecht 15 (1949/1950), 240–285

Goldstein, Gérald, L'exception de prévisibilité, Vers une localisation subjective dans la résolution des conflits de lois?, in: Revue critique de droit international privé 2018, 3–29

González Beilfuss, Cristina, The Unification of Private International Law in Europe: a Success Story?, in: Boele-Woelki, Katharina/Miles, Jo/Scherpe, Jens M. (eds.), The Future of Family Law in Europe (2011), Intersentia, Cambridge/Antwerp/Portland, 329–340

Gordley, James, The Abuse of Rights in the Civil Law Tradition, in: de la Feria, Rita/Vogenauer, Stefan (eds.), Prohibition of Abuse of Law, A New General Principle of EU Law? (2011), Hart, Oxford and Portland, Oregon, 33–46

Gössl, Susanne L., Anpassung im EU-Kollisionsrecht, in: Rabels Zeitschrift für ausländisches und internationales Privatrecht 82 (2018), 618–653

——, Open Issues in European International Family Law: *Sahyouni*, "Private Divorces" and Islamic Law under the Rome III Regulation, in: The European Legal Forum 2017, 68–74

——, Preliminary Questions in EU Private International Law, in: Journal of Private International Law 8 (2012), 63–76

Gössl, Susanne L. (ed.), Politik und Internationales Privatrecht (2017), Mohr Siebeck, Tübingen

Gotlieb, A. E., The Incidental Question Revisited – Theory and Practice in the Conflict of Laws, in: International and Comparative Law Quarterly 26 (1977), 734–798

Gotsche, Heiko, Der BGH im Wettbewerb der Zivilrechtsordnungen (2008), Nomos, Baden-Baden

Gottschalk, Eckart, Allgemeine Lehren des IPR in kollisionsrechtlichen Staatsverträgen (2002), Duncker & Humblot, Berlin

Grabitz/Hilf, Das Recht der Europäischen Union, see Nettesheim, Martin (ed.)

Grafton, Anthony, The Footnote, A curious history (2003), Faber and Faber, London

Graveson, Ronald H., The Special Character of English Private International Law, in: idem, Comparative Conflict of Laws, Selected Essays, Volume I (1977), North Holland, Amsterdam et al., 1–13 (cited as: *Graveson*, Special Character)

——, Philosophical Aspects of the English Conflict of Laws, in: idem, Comparative Conflict of Laws, Selected Essays, Volume I (1977), North Holland, Amsterdam et al., 14–50 (cited as: *Graveson*, Philosophical Aspects)

——, The Doctrine of Evasion of the Law in England and America, in: Journal of Comparative Legislation and International Law 19 (1937), 21–31

Gray, Whitmore, E pluribus unum? A Bicentennial Report on Unification of Law in the United States, in: Rabels Zeitschrift für ausländisches und internationales Privatrecht 50 (1986), 111–159

Grellette, Matthew/Valcke, Catherine, Comparative Law and Legal Diversity – Theorising about the Edges of Law, in: Transnational Legal Theory 5 (2014), 557–576

Grimm, Alexander, Brüssel I-VO: Grenzüberschreitender Bezug und unbekannter Wohnsitz des Beklagten, in: Zeitschrift für Gemeinschaftsprivatrecht (GPR) 2012, 87–89

Grodecki, Jan K., Chapter 8, Intertemporal Conflict of Laws, in: Lipstein, Kurt (ed.), International Encyclopedia of Comparative Law, Vol. III, Private International Law (1976), Mouton, The Hague, and J. C. B. Mohr (Paul Siebeck), Tübingen

Groß, Thomas, Die Beziehung zwischen dem Allgemeinen und dem Besonderen Verwaltungsrecht, in: Die Wissenschaft vom Verwaltungsrecht = Die Verwaltung, Beiheft 2 (1999), 57–80

Grosswald Curran, Vivian, Cultural Immersion, Difference and Categories in U.S. Comparative Law, in: The American Journal of Comparative Law 46 (1998), 43–92

Group on European Tort Law (ed.), Principles of European Tort Law (2005), Springer, Vienna, New York

Gruber, Urs Peter, Scheidung auf Europäisch – die Rom III-Verordnung, in: Praxis des Internationalen Privat- und Verfahrensrechts 2012, 381–392

Grünberger, Michael, Alles obsolet?, Anerkennungsprinzip vs. klassisches IPR, in: Leible, Stefan/Unberath, Hannes (eds.), Brauchen wir eine Rom 0-Verordnung? (2013), Jenaer Wissenschaftliche Verlagsgesellschaft, 81–160

Grünewald, Anette, Zur Frage eines europäischen Allgemeinen Teils des Strafrechts, in: Juristenzeitung 2011, 972–977

Guillaumé, Johanna, [Case note on Cass. ass. plén., n° 14-21.323, and Cass. ass. Plén., n° 15-50.002], Journal du Droit International 2016, 104–117

Haratsch, Andreas/Koenig, Christian/Pechstein, Matthias, Europarecht, 11th ed. (2018), Mohr Siebeck, Tübingen

Harding, Maebh, Conflict of Laws, 5th ed. (2014), Routledge, London and New York

Hartley, Trevor, Choice of law, choice of court and mandatory provisions, in: Hess, Burkard/Jayme, Erik/Mansel, Heinz-Peter (eds.), Europa als Rechts- und Lebensraum, Liber Amicorum für Christian Kohler (2018), Gieseking, Bielefeld, 171–178

——, The Common Law and EU Private International Law, in: Remien, Oliver/Kieninger, Eva-Maria (eds.), Europäische Kollisionsrechtsvereinheitlichung (2012), Nomos, Baden-Baden, 101–116

——, Choice of Law for Non-Contractual Liability: Selected Problems under the Rome II Regulation, in: International and Comparative Law Quarterly 57 (2008), 899–908

Hartwieg, Oskar, Die Entstehung der Artt. 7–31 EGBGB, in: idem/Korkisch, Friedrich (eds.), Die geheimen Materialien zur Kodifikation des deutschen Internationalen Privatrechts 1881–1896 (1973), J.C.B. Mohr (Paul Siebeck), Tübingen, 23–56

Hathaway, James C., The Rights of Refugees under International Law (2005), Cambridge University Press

Hau, Wolfgang, Zivilsachen mit grenzüberschreitendem Bezug, in: Lorenz, Stephan/ Arnold, Stefan (eds.), Gedächtnisschrift für Hannes Unberath (2015), 139–158

——, Ein Rückzugsgefecht des BGH gegen die Revisibilität ausländischen Rechts, in: Praxis des Internationalen Privat- und Verfahrensrechts 2014, 397–400

——, Zur Durchführung der Rom III-Verordnung in Deutschland, in: Zeitschrift für das gesamte Familienrecht 2013, 249–255

Hauser, Paul, Eingriffsnormen in der Rom I-Verordnung (2012), Mohr Siebeck, Tübingen

Hausmann, Rainer, Le questioni generali nel diritto internazionale privato europeo, in: Rivista di diritto internazionale privato e processuale 2015, 499–522

——, Pleading and Proof of Foreign Law – a Comparative Analysis, in: The European Legal Forum 2008, I-1–I-13

Hayton, David J./Kortmann, Sebastian C. J. J./Verhagen, H. L. E. (eds.), Principles of European Trust Law (1999) Kluwer Law International, Deventer

Heck, Philipp, Der Allgemeine Teil des Privatrechts, Ein Wort der Verteidigung, in: Archiv für die civilistische Praxis 146 (1941), 1–27

Heeder, Oliver, Fraus legis, Eine rechtsvergleichende Untersuchung über den Vorbehalt der Gesetzesumgehung in Deutschland, Österreich, der Schweiz, Frankreich und Belgien unter besonderer Berücksichtigung des Internationalen Privatrechts (1997), Peter Lang, Frankfurt a. M.

Heinze, Christian, Bausteine eines Allgemeinen Teils des europäischen Internationalen Privatrechts, in: Baetge, Dietmar/von Hein, Jan/von Hinden, Michael (eds.), Die richtige Ordnung, Festschrift für Jan Kropholler zum 70. Geburtstag (2008), Mohr Siebeck, Tübingen, 105–127

Heise, Arnold, Grundriß eines Systems des gemeinen Civilrechts zum Behuf von Pandecten-Vorlesungen (1807), Mohr und Zimmer, Heidelberg

Heiss, Helmut/Kaufmann-Mohi, Emese, Chapter 5, Classification: A Subject Matter for a Rome 0 Regulation?, in: Leible, Stefan (ed.), General Principles of European Private International Law (2016), Kluwer Law International, Alphen aan den Rijn, 87–100

Heiss, Helmut/Loacker, Leander, Die Vergemeinschaftung des Kollisionsrechts der außervertraglichen Schuldverhältnisse durch Rom II, in: Juristische Blätter 2007, 613–646

Hellgardt, Alexander, Das Verbot der kollisionsrechtlichen Wahl nichtstaatlichen Rechts und das Unionsgrundrecht der Privatautonomie, in: Rabels Zeitschrift für ausländisches und internationales Privatrecht 82 (2018), 654–696

Helms, Tobias, Reform des internationalen Scheidungsrechts durch die Rom III-Verordnung, in: Zeitschrift für das gesamte Familienrecht 2011, 1765–1772

Henrich, Dieter, Zur Parteiautonomie im europäisierten internationalen Familienrecht, in: Verbeke, Alain-Laurent/Scherpe, Jens M./Declerck, Charlotte/Helms, Tobias/Senaeve, Patrick (eds.), Confronting the Frontiers of Family and Succession Law, Liber Amicorum Walter Pintens (2012), Intersentia, Cambridge et al., 701–713

——, Der Renvoi: Zeit für einen Abgesang?, in: Kronke, Herbert/Thorn, Karsten (eds.), Grenzen überwinden – Prinzipien bewahren, Festschrift für Bernd von Hoffmann (2011), Gieseking, Bielefeld, 159–167

Herb, Anja, Europäisches Gemeinschaftsrecht und nationaler Zivilprozess (2007), Mohr Siebeck, Tübingen

Herber, Rolf, Eine neue Institution: Der CISG Advisory Council, in: Internationales Handelsrecht 2003, 201–202

Hernández-Breton, Eugenio, An attempt to regulate the problem of "characterization" in private international law, in: Festschrift für Erik Jayme, Vol. I (2004), Sellier, Munich, 331–338

Hess, Burkhard, Back to the Past: BREXIT und das europäische internationale Privat- und Verfahrensrecht, in: Praxis des Internationalen Privat- und Verfahrensrechts 2016, 409–418

——, Methoden der Rechtsfindung im Europäischen Zivilprozessrecht, in: Praxis des Internationalen Privat- und Verfahrensrechts 2006, 348–363

Heß [sic], Burkhard, Intertemporales Privatrecht (1998), Mohr Siebeck, Tübingen

Hessel-Jolst, Christa, The Bulgarian Private International Law Code of 2005, in: Yearbook of Private International Law 9 (2007), 375–385

——, Current State and Future Perspectives of Bulgarian Private International Law, in: Yearbook of Private International Law 5 (2003), 143–153

Het Wetboek Internationaal Privaatrecht becommentarieerd (see Erauw, Johan/Fallon, Marc/Guldix, Erna/Meeusen, Johan/Pertegás Sender, Marta/van Houtte, Hans/Watté, Nadine/Wautelet, Patrick (eds.))

Hickey, Geraldine, Irish Private International Law, in: Rabels Zeitschrift für ausländisches und internationales Privatrecht 42 (1978), 268–303

Hill, Jonathan/Ní Shúilleabháin, Máire, Clarkson & Hill's Conflict of Laws, 5th ed. (2016), Oxford University Press

Hirse, Thomas, Die Ausweichklausel im Internationalen Privatrecht (2006), Mohr Siebeck, Tübingen

HK-BGB, see Schulze, Reiner (managing editor)

HKK-BGB, see Schmoeckel, Mathias/Rückert, Joachim/Zimmermann, Reinhard (eds.)

Hoffmann, Bernd von/Ortiz-Arce, Antonio, Das neue spanische Internationale Privatrecht, in: Rabels Zeitschrift für ausländisches und internationales Privatrecht 39 (1975), 647–691

Hoffmann, Bernd von/Thorn, Karsten, Internationales Privatrecht, 9th ed. (2007), C.H. Beck, Munich

Hohloch, Gerhard, Rechtswahl als Anknüpfungsprinzip (Zur Bedeutung des Parteiwillens im europäischen Internationalen Privatrecht), in: Frantzen, Torstein/Giertsen, Johan/Cordero Moss, Giuditta (eds.), Rett og tolerance, Festskrift til Helge Johan Thue (2007), Gyldendal, Oslo, 257–270

Holliday, Jayne, Reconciling the European Union Succession Regulation with the Private International Law of the UK, in: Bergé, Jean-Sylvestre/Francq, Stéphanie/Gardeñes Santiago, Miguel (eds.), Boundaries of European Private International Law (2015), Bruylant, Bruxelles, 297–309

Hollstein, Thorsten, Die Verfassung als "Allgemeiner Teil", Privatrechtsmethode und Privatrechtskonzeption bei Hans Carl Nipperdey (2007), Mohr Siebeck, Tübingen

Hood, Kirsty J., Drawing Inspiration?, Reconsidering the Procedural Treatment of Foreign Law, in: Journal of Private International Law 2 (2006), 181–193

Huber, Peter/Illmer, Martin, International Product Liability, A Commentary on Article 5 of the Rome II Regulation, in: Yearbook of Private International Law 9 (2007), 31–47

Hübner, Heinz, Allgemeiner Teil des Bürgerlichen Gesetzbuches, 2nd ed. (1996), Walter de Gruyter, Berlin/New York

Hübner, Rudolf, Ausländisches Recht vor deutschen Gerichten (2014), Mohr Siebeck, Tübingen

Hug, Sabine, Die Substitution im internationalen Privatrecht (1983), V. Florentz, Munich

Husa, Jaakko, Farewell to Functionalism or Methodological Tolerance?, in: Rabels Zeitschrift für ausländisches und internationales Privatrecht 67 (2003), 419–447

Illmer, Martin, Neutrality Matters – Some Thoughts About the Rome Regulations and the So-Called Dichotomy of Substance and Procedure in European Private International Law, in: Civil Justice Quarterly 28 (2009), 237–260

Jänterä-Jareborg, Maarit, Inter-Nordic Exceptions in EU Regulations on Matters of Family and Inheritance Law, in: Verbeke, Alain-Laurent/Scherpe, Jens M./Declerck, Charlotte/Helms, Tobias/Senaeve, Patrick (eds.), Confronting the Frontiers of Family and Succession Law, Liber Amicorum Walter Pintens (2012), Intersentia, Cambridge et al., 733–752

——, Foreign Law in National Courts, A Comparative Perspective, in: Recueil des cours 304 (2003), 181–386

Jayme, Erik, Kodifikation und Allgemeiner Teil im IPR, in: Leible, Stefan/Unberath, Hannes (eds.), Brauchen wir eine Rom 0-Verordnung? (2013), Jenaer Wissenschaftliche Verlagsgesellschaft, 33–49

——, Betrachtungen zu einer postmodernen Theorie der Rechtsvergleichung, in: idem, Rechtsvergleichung, Ideengeschichte und Grundlagen, Von Emerico Amari zur Postmoderne (2000) (= Gesammelte Schriften, Vol. 2), C. F. Müller, Heidelberg, 103–118 (cited as: *Jayme*, Postmoderne Theorie)

——, Rechtsvergleichung im internationalen Privatrecht – Eine Skizze, in: idem, Rechtsvergleichung, Ideengeschichte und Grundlagen, Von Emerico Amari zur Postmoderne (2000) (= Gesammelte Schriften, Vol. 2), C. F. Müller, Heidelberg, 45–56 (cited as: *Jayme*, Rechtsvergleichung im internationalen Privatrecht)

——, Zum internationalen Geltungswillen der europäischen Regeln über den Handelsvertreterausgleich, in: Praxis des Internationalen Privat- und Verfahrensrechts 2001, 190–191

Jayme, Erik/Kohler, Christian, Europäisches Kollisionsrecht 2006: Eurozentrismus ohne Kodifikationsidee?, in: Praxis des Internationalen Privat- und Verfahrensrechts 2006, 537–550

Jenard, P., Report on the Convention on jurisdiction and the enforcement of judgments in civil and commercial matters, [1979] OJ C 59/1–65

Jochem, Reiner, Die persönlichen Rechtsbeziehungen der Ehegatten in einer „hinkenden" Ehe – ein Sonderproblem?, in: Zeitschrift für das gesamte Familienrecht (FamRZ) 1964, 392–397

Johns, Fleur, Performing Party Autonomy, in: Law and Contemporary Problems 71 (2008), 243–271

Jud, Brigitta, Rechtswahl im Erbrecht: Das Grünbuch der Europäischen Kommission zum Erb- und Testamentsrecht, in: Zeitschrift für Gemeinschaftsprivatrecht (GPR) 2005, 133–139

Juenger, Friedrich K., The Problem with Private International Law, in: Basedow, Jürgen/Meier, Isaak/Schnyder, Anton K./Einhorn, Talia/Girsberger, Daniel (eds.), Private Law in the International Arena, Liber Amicorum Kurt Siehr (2000), Schulthess, Zurich, 288–309

Junker, Abbo, Internationales Privatrecht, 2nd ed. (2017), C.H. Beck, Munich

——, Der Reformbedarf im Internationalen Deliktsrecht der Rom II-Verordnung drei Jahre nach ihrer Verabschiedung, in: Recht der Internatationalen Wirtschaft 2010, 257–269

——, Empfiehlt es sich, Art. 7 EVÜ zu revidieren oder aufgrund der bisherigen Erfahrungen zu präzisieren?, in: Praxis des Internationalen Privat- und Verfahrensrechts 2000, 65–73

Kadner Graziano, Thomas, Gemeinsame oder getrennte Kodifikation von IPR und IZVR, Das schweizerische IPR-Gesetz als Modell für eine europäische Gesamtkodifikation – Lehren für die EU?, in: von Hein, Jan/Rühl, Giesela (eds.), Kohärenz im Internationalen Privat- und Verfahrensrecht der Europäischen Union (2016), Mohr Siebeck, Tübingen, 44–60

——, Codifying European Union private international law: The Swiss International Law Act – a model for a comprehensive EU Private international law regulation?, in: Journal of Private International Law 11 (2015), 585–606

——, Gemeineuropäisches Internationales Privatrecht, Harmonisierung des IPR durch Wisssenschaft und Lehre (am Beispiel der außervertraglichen Haftung für Schäden) (2002), Mohr Siebeck, Tübingen

Kahn, Franz, Gesetzeskollisionen, Ein Beitrag zur Lehre des internationalen Privatrechts, in: Lenel, Otto/Lewald, Hans (eds.), Franz Kahn, Abhandlungen zum internationalen Privatrecht, Vol. I (1928), 1–123 (= Jherings Jahrbücher für die Dogmatik des heutigen römischen und deutschen Privatrechts 30 (1891), 1–143)

——, Bedeutung der Rechtsvergleichung mit Bezug auf das internationale Privatrecht, in: Zeitschrift für Internationales Privat- und Strafrecht 10 (1900), 97–105

Kahn-Freund, Otto, General Problems of Private International Law (1976), Sijthoff, Leyden

Kakouris, Constantinos N., L'utilisation de la Methode [sic] Comparative par la Cour de Justice des Communautes Europeennes, in: Drobnig, Ulrich/van Erp, Sjef (eds.), The Use of Comparative Law by Courts (1999), Kluwer Law International, The Hague, London, Boston, 97–111

Kalbheim, Jan, Der Einfluss der Richter des Europäischen Gerichtshofs auf dessen Rechtsprechung – eine empirisch-statistische Analyse der Rolle des Berichterstatters, in: Zeitschrift für vergleichende Rechtswissenschaft 115 (2016), 431–482

Kegel, Gerhard, Begriffs- und Interessenjurisprudenz im internationalen Privatrecht, in: Festschrift Hans Lewald (1953), Helbing & Lichtenhain, Basel, 259–288

Kegel, Gerhard/Schurig, Klaus, Internationales Privatrecht, 9th ed. (2004), Beck, Munich

Kerameus, Konstantinos D., Procedural Implications of Civil Law Unification, in: Hartkamp, Arthur S./Hesselink, Martijn W./Hondius, Ewoud H./Mak, Chantal/du Perron, C. Edgar (eds.), Towards a European Civil Code, 4th ed. (2011), Kluwer Law International, Alphen aan den Rijn, 261–275

Kieninger, Eva-Maria, Chapter 17, Ascertaining and Applying Foreign Law, in: Leible, Stefan (ed.), General Principles of European Private International Law (2016), Kluwer Law International, Alphen aan den Rijn, 357–373

——, Kodifikationsidee und Europäisches Privatrecht, in: Rechtswissenschaft 2012, 406–431

Kindermann, Harald, Der Allgemeine Teil des Sozialgesetzbuchs, Eine Kritik aus der Sicht der Gesetzgebungstheorie, in: Klug, U./Ramm, Th./Rittner, F./Schmiedel, B. (eds.), Gesetzgebungstheorie, Juristische Logik, Zivil- und Prozeßrecht – Gedächtnisschrift für Jürgen Rödig (1978), Springer, Berlin/Heidelberg/New York

Kindler, Peter, Vom Staatsangehörigkeits- zum Domizilprinzip: das künftige internationale Erbrecht der Europäischen Union, in: Praxis des Internationalen Privat- und Verfahrensrechts 2010, 44–50

——, Internationale Zuständigkeit und anwendbares Recht im italienischen IPR-Gesetz von 1995, in: Rabels Zeitschrift für ausländisches und internationales Privatrecht 61 (1996), 227–284

Kinsch, Patrick, Un exemple d'ambivalence politique en droit international privé européen: la question de l'admissibilite de la protection unilateraliste, par des lois de police, des parties faibles aux contrats, in: Hess, Burkard/Jayme, Erik/Mansel, Heinz-Peter (eds.), Europa als Rechts- und Lebensraum, Liber Amicorum für Christian Kohler (2018), Gieseking, Bielefeld, 215–227

——, Préface à la première édition, in: Cuniberti, Gilles (ed.), Code de droit international privé luxembourgeois (2014), Promoculture-Larcier, Windhof, V–VI

Kirby, Michael, Precedent – Report on Australia, in: Hondius, Ewoud (ed.), Precedent and the Law (2007), Bruylant, Bruxelles, 75–83

Kischel, Uwe, La méthode en droit comparé, L'approche contextuelle, in: Revue internationale de droit comparé 2016, 907–926

——, Rechtsvergleichung (2015), C.H. Beck, Munich

Klami, Hannu Tapani/Kuisma, Eira, Finnish Law as an Option, Private International Law in Finland (2000), Kauppakaari, Helsinki

Klöpfer, Matthias, Missbrauch im Europäischen Zivilverfahrensrecht (2016), Mohr Siebeck, Tübingen

Kluth, David, Die Grenzen des kollisionsrechtlichen Verbraucherschutzes (2009), Jenaer Wissenschaftliche Verlagsgesellschaft

Koch, Harald, Kollisionsrecht und Auslandsbezug: Wie international ist das IPR?, in: Mankowski, Peter/Wurmnest, Wolfgang (eds.), Festschrift für Ulrich Magnus zum 70. Geburtstag (2014), Sellier, Munich, 475–482

Köhler, Andreas, Eingriffsnormen – Der „unfertige Teile" des europäischen IPR (2013), Mohr Siebeck, Tübingen

Köhler, Helmut, BGB, Allgemeiner Teil, 41st ed. (2017), C.H. Beck, Munich

Kohler, Christian, Abschied von der autonomen Auslegung des Begriffs "Zivil- und Handelssachen" in Art. 1 EuGVVO?, in: Praxis des Internationalen Privat- und Verfahrensrechts 2015, 52–56

——, L'autonomie de la volonté en droit international privé: un principe universel entre libéralisme et étatisme, in: Recueil des cours 359 (2012), 285–478

——, Entwicklungen im europäischen Personen und Familienrecht 2010–2011, in: Zeitschrift für das gesamte Familienrecht 2011, 1433–1440

Koopmans, Thijmen, Towards a New "Ius Commune", in: de Witte, Bruno/Forder, Caroline (eds.), The common law of Europe and the future of legal education (1992), Kluwer, Deventer, 43–51

Korkisch, Friedrich, Rechtsnatur und Funktion des Internationalen Privatrechts in den Gesetzen des 18. und 19. Jahrhunderts, in: Hartwieg, Oskar/idem (eds.), Die geheimen Materialien zur Kodifikation des deutschen Internationalen Privatrechts 1881–1896 (1973), J.C.B. Mohr (Paul Siebeck), Tübingen, 1–22

Kötz, Hein, Europäisches Vertragsrecht, 2nd ed. (2015), Mohr Siebeck, Tübingen

——, A Common Private Law for Europe: Perspectives for the Reform of European Legal Education, in: de Witte, Bruno/Forder, Caroline (eds.), The common law of Europe and the future of legal education (1992), Kluwer, Deventer, 31–41

——, Rechtsvereinheitlichung – Nutzen, Kosten, Methoden, Ziele, in: Rabels Zeitschrift für ausländisches und internationales Privatrecht 50 (1986), 1–18

——, Gemeineuropäisches Zivilrecht, in: Bernstein, Herbert/ Drobnig, Ulrich/ idem (eds.), Festschrift für Konrad Zweigert zum 70. Geburtstag (1981), J. C. B. Mohr (Paul Siebeck), Tübingen, 481–500

Kötz, Hein/Flessner, Axel, European Contract Law (1997), Clarendon Press, Oxford

Koziol, Helmut, Glanz und Elend der deutschen Zivilrechtsdogmatik, Das deutsche Zivilrecht als Vorbild für Europa?, in: Archiv für die civilistische Praxis 212 (2012), 1–62

Koziol, Helmut/Bydlinski, Peter/Bollenberger, Raimund (eds.), Kurzkommentar zum ABGB, 5th ed. (2017), Verlag Österreich, Wien (cited as: *Commentator*, in: ABGB-Kurzkommentar)

Kozyris, Phaedon John, Conflict of Laws, International Jurisdiction, and Recognition and Enforcement of Judgments and Awards, in: Kerameus, Konstantinos D./idem (eds.), Introduction to Greek Law, 3rd edition (2008), Kluwer Law Internationa, Alphen aan den Rijn, 379–408

Kramer, Xandra/de Rooij, Michiel/Lazić, Vesna/Blauwhoff, Richard/Frohn, Lisette, A European Framework for private international law: current gaps and future perspectives (2012), (PE 462.487, available online at http://www.europarl.europa.eu/document/activities/cont/201212/20121219ATT58300/20121219ATT58300EN.pdf) (last visited 12 October 2018)

Kramer, Xandra/de Rooij, Michiel, Naar een Europees wetboek van internationaal privaatrecht?, in: NIPR 2013, 1–2

Kramme, Malte, Die kollisionsrechtliche Behandlung der Erwerberhaftung bei Firmenfortführung vor und nach Inkrafttreten der Rom-Verordnungen, in: Praxis des Internationalen Privat- und Verfahrensrechts 2015, 225–228

Krätschmer, Stefan, Die Integration von Staatsverträgen in nationales IPR und IZPR am Beispiel der italienischen IPR-Kodifikation von 1995 (2004), Duncker & Humblot, Berlin

Kreuzer, Karl, Was gehört in den Allgemeinen Teil eines Europäischen Kollisionsrechts?, in: Jud, Brigitta/Rechberger, Walter/Reichelt, Gerte (eds.), Kollisionsrecht in der Europäischen Union (2008), Jan Sramek, Vienna, 1–62

Kroll-Ludwigs, Kathrin, Die Rolle der Parteiautonomie im europäischen Kollisionsrecht (2013), Mohr Siebeck, Tübingen

Kropholler, Jan, Internationales Privatrecht, 6th ed. (2006), Mohr Siebeck, Tübingen

——, Die Auslegung von EG-Verordnungen zum Internationalen Privat- und Verfahrensrecht – Eine Skizze, in: Basedow, Jürgen/Drobnig, Jürgen/Ellger,

Reinhard/Hopt, Klaus J./Kötz, Hein/Kulms, Rainer/Mestmäcker, Ernst-Joachim (eds.), Aufbruch nach Europa, 75 Jahre Max-Planck-Institut für Privatrecht (2001), Mohr Siebeck, Tübingen

——, Die vergleichende Methode und das Internationale Privatrecht, in: Zeitschrift für Vergleichende Rechtswissenschaft 77 (1978), 1–20

Kruger, Thalia/Verhellen, Jinske, Dual Nationality = Double Trouble?, in: Journal of Private International Law 7 (2011), 601–626

Kühn, Anna-Lisa, Die gestörte Gesamtschuld im Internationalen Privatrecht (2014), Mohr Siebeck, Tübingen

Kühne, Gunther, Internationales Privatrecht im 20. Jahrhundert, in: Zeitschrift für Vergleichende Rechtswissenschaft 114 (2015), 355–366

——, Rechtswahl und Eingriffsnormen in der Rechtsprechung des EuGH, in: Cascante, Christian/Spahlinger, Andreas/Wilske, Stephan (eds.), Global Wisdom on Business Transactions, International Law and Dispute Resolution, Festschrift für Gerhard Wegen zum 65. Geburtstag (2015), C.H. Beck, Munich, 451–462

——, Methodeneinheit und Methodenvielfalt im Internationalen Privatrecht – Eine Generation nach „Kollisionsnorm und Sachrecht", in: Michaels, Ralf/Solomon, Dennis (eds.), Liber Amicorum Klaus Schurig zum 70. Geburtstag (2012), Sellier, Munich, 129–146

——, Die Entsavignysierung des Internationalen Privatrechts insbesondere durch sog. Eingriffsnormen, in: Lorenz, Stephan/Trunk, Alexander/Eidenmüller, Horst/Wendehorst, Christiane/Adolff, Johannes (eds.), Festschrift für Andreas Heldrich zum 70. Geburtstag (2005), C.H. Beck, Munich, 815–830

Kunda, Ivana, Croatia, in: Kono, Toshiyuki (ed.), Intellectual Property and Private International Law (2012), Hart, Oxford and Portland, Oregon, 477–524

Lagarde, Paul, Embryon de Règlement portant Code europeén de droit international privé de droit international privé, in: Rabels Zeitschrift für ausländisches und internationales Privatrecht 75 (2011), 673–676 (= idem, En guise de synthèse, in: Fallon, Marc/idem/Poillot-Peruzzetto, Sylvaine (eds.), Quelle architecture pour un code européen de droit international privé? (2011), Peter Lang, Brussels, 365–376 [with further comments])

——, Présentation de la proposition de règlement sur les successions, in: Bonomi, Andrea/Schmid, Christina (eds.), Successions internationales, Réflexions autour du futur règlement européen et de son impact pour la Suisse (2010), Schulthess, Geneva, Zurich, Basel, 11–21

——, Le principe de proximité dans le droit international privé contemporain, Cours général de dróit international privé, Recueil des cours 196 (1986), 9–238

——, Chapter 11, Public Policy, in: Lipstein, Kurt (ed.), International Encyclopedia of Comparative Law, Vol. III, Private International Law (1994), J. C. B. Mohr (Paul Siebeck), Tübingen and Martinus Nijhoff, Dordrecht, Boston, Lancaster

Landmann/Rohmer, see Beckmann, Martin/Durner, Wolfgang/Mann, Thomas/Röckinghausen, Marc (eds.)

Lando, Ole/Nielsen, Peter Arnt, The Rome I Regulation, in: Common Market Law Review 45 (2008), 1687–1725

Lando, Ole/Clive, Eric/Prün, André/Zimmermann, Reinhard (eds.), Principles of European Contract Law, Part III (2003), Kluwer Law International, The Hague/London/Boston

Lando, Ole/Beale, Hugh (eds.), Principles of European Contract Law, Parts I and II (2000), Kluwer Law International, The Hague/London/Boston

Lalani, Shaheeza, Establishing the Content of Foreign Law: A Comparative Study, in: Maastricht Journal of European and Comparative Law 2013, 75–112

Lasok, Dominik, The Polish System of Private International Law, in: The American Journal of Comparative Law 15 (1967), 330–351

Lass, Christiane, Der Flüchtling im deutschen Internationalen Privatrecht (1995), C.H. Beck, Munich

Leandro, Antonio, Art. 10 [of Rome III], in: Le nuove leggi civili commentate 2011, 1503–1509

Leflar, Robert, Choice-Influencing Considerations in Conflicts Law, in: N.Y.U. Law Review 41 (1966), 267–327

Lehmann, Matthias, Chapter 2, Recognition as a Substitute for Conflict of Laws?, in: Leible, Stefan (ed.), General Principles of European Private International Law (2016), Kluwer Law International, Alphen aan den Rijn, 11–43

——, Eine Lücke im europäischen Kollisionsrecht der Schuldverhältnisse?, Die Haftung wegen Vermögensübernahme und wegen Fortführung eines Handelsgeschäfts, in: Praxis des Internationalen Privat- und Verfahrensrechts 2015, 495–500

——, Liberating the Individual from Battles between States: Justifying Party Autonomy in Conflict of Laws, in: Vanderbilt Journal of Transnational Law 41 (2008), 381–434

Lehmann, Matthias/Zetzsche, Dirk, Die Auswirkungen des Brexit auf das Zivil- und Wirtschaftsrecht, in: Juristenzeitung 2017, 62–71

Leible, Stefan, Der Beitrag der Rom II-Verordnung zu einer Kodifikation der allgemeinen Grundsätze des Europäischen Kollisionsrechts, in: Reichelt, Gerte (ed.), Europäisches Gemeinschaftsrecht und IPR (2007), Manz, Vienna, 31–54

——, Parteiautonomie im IPR – Allgemeines Anknüpfungsprinzip oder Verlegenheitslösung?, in: Mansel, Heinz-Peter/Pfeiffer, Thomas/Kronke, Herbert/Kohler, Christian/Hausmann, Rainer (eds.), Festschrift für Erik Jayme, Vol. I (2004), Sellier, Munich, 485–503

Leible, Stefan (ed.), General Principles of European Private International Law (2016), Kluwer Law International, Alphen aan den Rijn

Leible, Stefan/Lehmann, Matthias, Die neue EG-Verordnung über das auf außervertragliche Schuldverhältnisse anzuwendende Recht („Rom II"), in: Recht der Internationalen Wirtschaft 2007, 721–735

Leible, Stefan/Müller, Michael, The Idea of a „Rome 0 Regulation", in: Yearbook of Private International Law, Volume 14 (2012/2013), 137–152

Leible, Stefan/Staudinger, Ansgar, El artículo 65 TCE: ¿Carta blanca de la comunidad europea para la unificación del dereche internacional privado y procesal?, in: Anuario español de derecho internacional privado 2001, 89–115

——, Art. 65 EGV im System der EG-Kompetenzen, in: The European Legal Forum 2000/2001, 225–235

Leible, Stefan/Unberath, Hannes (eds.), Brauchen wir eine Rom 0-Verordnung? (2013), Jenaer Wissenschaftliche Verlagsgesellschaft

Leipold, Dieter, BGB I, Einführung und Allgemeiner Teil, 9th ed. (2017), Mohr Siebeck, Tübingen

Leitzen, Mario, Die Rechtswahl nach der EuErbVO, Zeitschrift für Erbrecht und Vermögensnachfolge 2013, 128–132

Lenaerts, Koen, Interlocking Legal Orders in the European Union and Comparative Law, in: International and Comparative Law Quarterly 52 (2003), 873–906

Lenaerts, Koen/Gutman, Kathleen, The Comparative Law Method and the Court of Justice of the European Union, Interlocking Legal Orders Revisited, in: Andenas, Mads/Fairgrieve, Duncan (eds.), Courts and Comparative Law (2015), Oxford University Press, 141–176

Lenz, Carl Otto/Borchardt, Klaus-Dieter (eds.), EU-Verträge Kommentar, 6th ed. (2012), Bundesanzeiger, Cologne/Linde, Vienna

Leonhardt, Peter, Das neue Internationale Privatrecht Rumäniens, in: Praxis des Internationalen Privat- und Verfahrensrechts 1994, 156–159

Lepsius, Oliver, Hat die Europäisierung des Verwaltungsrechts Methode?, Oder: Die zwei Phasen der Europäisierung des Verwaltungsrechts, in: Axer, Peter/Grzeszick, Bernd/Kahl, Wolfgang/Mager, Ute/Reimer, Ekkehart (eds.), Das Europäische Verwaltungsrecht in der Konsolidierungsphase = Die Verwaltung, Beiheft 10 (2010), 179–204

Lequette, Yves, De Bruxelles à la Haye (Acte II), Réflexions critiques sur la compétence communautaire en matière de droit international privé, in: Azzi, Tristan/Bureau, Dominique/Fauvarque-Cosson, Bénédicte/Kessedjian, Catherine/Poillot-Peruzzetto, Sylvaine/de Vareilles-Sommières, Pascal (eds.), Vers de nouveaux équilibres entre ordres juridiques, Liber amicorum Hélène Gaudemet-Tallon (2008), Dalloz, Paris, 503–544

——, [Case note concerning the *Caron* case], Revue critique de droit international privé 1986, 71–78

Letto-Vanama, Pia/Smits, Jan, Introduction, in: idem (eds.), Coherence and Fragmentation in European Private Law (2012), Sellier, Munich, 1–8

Lewald, Hans, Règles générales des conflits de lois, Contributions à la technique du droit international privé (1941), von Helbing & Lichtenhahn, Basel

Lippert, André, Der grenzüberschreitende Sachverhalt - Der Yeti des Europarechts, in: ZEuS 2014, 273–299

——, Der grenzüberschreitende Sachverhalt im Unionsrecht (2013), Mohr Siebeck, Tübingen

Lipstein, Kurt, Characterization, in: Feuerstein, Peter/Mansel, Heinz-Peter (eds.), Kurt Lipstein, Collection of Essays (2014), Mohr Siebeck, Tübingen, 623–676 (= Chapter 5, Characterization, in: id. (ed.), International Encyclopedia of Comparative Law, Vol. III, Private International Law (1999))

——, Unusual Bedfellows - Renvoi and Foreign Characterization Joined Together, in: Basedow, Jürgen/Meier, Isaak/Schnyder, Anton K./Einhorn, Talia/Girsberger, Daniel (eds.), Private Law in the International Arena, Liber Amicorum Kurt Siehr (2000), Schulthess, Zurich, 405–412

Lipstein, Kurt/Szászy, István, Chapter 10, Interpersonal Conflict of Laws, in: Lipstein, Kurt (ed.), International Encyclopedia of Comparative Law, Vol. III, Private International Law (1976), Mouton, The Hague, and J. C. B. Mohr (Paul Siebeck), Tübingen

Liukkunen, Ulla, Recent Private International Law Codifications, in: Hollo, Erkki J. (ed.), Studies on the Finnish Legal System, Finnish Reports to the 18th Congress of the International Academy of Comparative Law (2011), (available online to subscribers at www.edilex.fi/lakikirjasto/8070) (copy on file with the author)

Lookofsky, Joseph, Choice of Law in Denmark: Code-Light or Code-Tight?, in: Electronic Library on International Commercial Law and the CISG, (available online at http://www.cisg.law.pace.edu/cisg/biblio/lookofsky20.html) (last visited 12 October 2018)

——, Precedent and the Law in Denmark, in: Hondius, Ewoud (ed.), Precedent and the Law (2007), Bruylant, Bruxelles, 253–266

——, Danish Private International Law, in: Dahl, Børge/Melchior, Torben/Tamm, Ditlev (eds.), Danish Law in a European Perspective (2002), Forlaget Thompson, Copenhagen, 455–467

——, Danish Private International Law at the End of the 20th Century: Progress or Regress?, in: Symeonides, Symeon C. (ed.), Private International Law at the End of the 20th Century: Progress or Regress? (2000), Kluwer Law International, London, 147–164

Looschelders, Dirk, Die allgemeinen Lehren des Internationalen Privatrechts im Rahmen der Europäischen Erbrechtsverordnung, in: Hilbig-Lugani, Katharina/Jakob, Dominique/Mäsch, Gerald/Reuß, Philipp M./Schmid, Christoph (eds.), Zwischenbilanz, Festschrift für Dagmar Coester-Waltjen (2015), Gieseking, Bielefeld, 531–542

——, Internationales Privatrecht – Art. 3–46 EGBGB (2004), Springer, Berlin, Heidelberg, New York

——, [Besprechung von: Schulz, Carsten, Die Subsumtion ausländischer Rechtstatsachen] in: Rabels Zeitschrift für ausländisches und internationales Privatrecht 64 (2000), 420–429

——, Die Anpassung im Internationalen Privatrecht (1995), C. F. Müller, Heidelberg

Looschelders, Dirk/Smarowos, Kirstin, Das Internationalie Versicherungsvertragsrecht nach Inkrafttreten der Rom I-Verordnung, in: VersR 2010, 1–10

Loussouarn, Yvon, Les vicissitudes de la codification du droit international privé français, in: Borrás, Alegría/Bucher, Andreas/Struycken, Teun/Verwilghen, Michel (eds.), E pluribus unum, Liber Amicorum Georges A. L. Droz (1996), Martinus Nijhoff, The Hague, Boston, London, 191–204

Loussouarn, Yvon/Bourel, Pierre/de Vareilles-Sommières, Droit international privé, 10th ed. (2013), Dalloz, Paris

Lüderitz, Alexander, Anknüpfung im Parteiinteresse, in: idem/Schröder, Jochen (eds.), Internationales Privatrecht und Rechtsvergleichung im Ausgang des 20. Jahrhunderts, Bewahrung oder Wende?, Festschrift für Gerhard Kegel (1977), Alfred Metzner, Frankfurt am Main, 31–54

Lurger, Brigitta/Melcher, Martina, Handbuch Internationales Privatrecht (2017), Verlag Österreich, Vienna

Lurger, Brigitta/Faber, Wolfgang (eds.), Acquisition and Loss of Ownership of Goods (Pel. Acq. Own.) (2011), Sellier, Munich

Lüttringhaus, Jan D., Eingriffsnormen im internationalen Unionsprivat- und Prozessrecht: Von Ingmar zu Unamar, in: Praxis des Internationalen Privat- und Verfahrensrechts 2014, 146–152

——, Grenzüberschreitender Diskriminierungsschutz – Das internationale Privatrecht der Antidiskriminierung (2010), Mohr Siebeck, Tübingen

Mączyński, Andrzej, Polish Private International Law, in: Yearbook of Private International Law 6 (2004), 203–220

Mádl, Ferenc, System and Principles of the Hungarian Code of Private International Law, in: Revue hellénique de droit international 44 (1991), 227–250

Mádl, Ferenc/Vékás, Lajos, Über das ungarische IPR-Gesetz in rechtsvergleichender Betrachtung, in: ZfRV 1982, 266–286
Magnus, Robert, Der grenzüberschreitende Bezug als Anwendungsvoraussetzung im europäischen Zuständigkeits- und Kollisionsrecht, in: Zeitschrift für Europäisches Privatrecht 2018, 507–540
Magnus, Ulrich/Mankowski, Peter, Joint Response of the Green Paper on the Conversion of the Rome Convention of 1980 on the Law Applicable to Contractual Obligations into a Community Instrument and its Modernisation, COM (2002), 654 final (available online at http://ec.europa.eu/justice/news/consulting_public/rome_i/contributions/university_hamburg_en.pdf) (last visited 12 October 2018)
Makarov, Alexander N., Der allgemeine Teil des internationalen Privatrechts im Entwurfe des neuen französischen Kodifikationswerkes, in: von Caemmerer, Ernst/Hallstein, Walter/Mann, F.A./Raiser, Ludwig (eds.), Festschrift für Martin Wolff (1952), J. C. B. Mohr (Paul Siebeck), Tübingen, 247–269
Mandery, Maya, Party Autonomy in Contractual and Non-Contractual Obligations (2014), PL Academic Research (Peter Lang), Frankfurt a. M.
Mankowski, Peter, Über den Standort des Internationalen Zivilprozessrechts, Zwischen Internationalem Privatrecht und Zivilprozessrecht, in: Rabels Zeitschrift für ausländisches und internationales Privatrecht 82 (2018), 576–617
——, Das Staatsangehörigkeitsprinzip – gestern und heute, in: Praxis des Internationalen Privat- und Verfahrensrechts 2017, 130–139
——, Chapter 10, Dual and Multiple Nationals, Stateless Persons, and Refugees, in: Leible, Stefan (ed.), General Principles of European Private International Law (2016), Kluwer Law International, Alphen aan den Rijn, 189–210
——, Zur Nichtanwendung des von den Parteien eines Handelsvertretervertrags gewählten Rechts zu Gunsten zwingender Vorschriften der lex fori („Unamar"), in: EWiR 2014, 11–12
——, Das Bündelungsmodell im Internationalen Privatrecht, in: Michaels, Ralf/Solomon, Dennis (eds.), Liber Amicorum Klaus Schurig zum 70. Geburtstag (2012), Sellier, Munich, 159–179
——, Interessenpolitik und europäisches Kollisionsrecht, Rechtspolitische Überlegungen zur Rom I- und zur Rom II-Verordnung (2011), Nomos, Baden-Baden
——, The Codification of Private International Law since the 1960s, in: Basedow, Jürgen/Kischel, Uwe/Sieber, Ulrich, German National Reports to the 18th International Congress of Comparative Law (2010), Mohr Siebeck, Tübingen, 133–160
Mann, Frederick Alexander, The Formal Validity of Wills in Case of Dual Nationality, in: ICLQ 35 (1986), 423–425
——, Der „gewöhnliche Aufenthalt" im Internationalen Privatrecht, in: Juristenzeitung 1956, 466–470
Mansdörfer, Marco, §1, Die Grundlagen des Straftatsystems im common law, in: idem (ed.), Die allgemeine Straftatlehre des common law, Eine Darstellung unter besonderer Berücksichtigung des englischen Strafrechts (2005), C. F. Müller, Heidelberg, 1–21
Mansel, Heinz-Peter, Chapter 8, Party Autonomy, Legal Doctrine on Choice of Law, and the General Section of the European Conflict of Laws, in: Leible, Stefan (ed.), General Principles of European Private International Law (2016), Kluwer Law International, Alphen aan den Rijn, 131–169

——, Eingriffsnormen im internationalen Sachenrecht, in: Ackermann, Thomas/Köndgen, Johannes (eds.), Privat- und Wirtschaftsrecht in Europa, Festschrift für Wulf-Henning Roth zum 70. Geburtstag (2015), C.H. Beck, Munich, 375–382

——, Zum Verhältnis von Vorfrage und Substitution, Am Beispiel einer unterhaltsrechtlichen Vorfrage des iranischen Scheidungsrechts, in: Baetge, Dietmar/von Hein, Jan/von Hinden, Michael (eds.), Die richtige Ordnung, Festschrift für Jan Kropholler zum 70. Geburtstag (2008), Mohr Siebeck, Tübingen, 353–371

——, Das Staatsangehörigkeitsprinzip im deutschen und gemeinschaftsrechtlichen Internationalen Privatrecht: Schutz der kulturellen Identität oder Diskriminierung der Person?, in: Jayme, Erik (ed.), Kulturelle Identität und Internationales Privatrecht (2003), C. F. Müller, Heidelberg, 119–154

——, Rechtsvergleichung und europäische Rechtseinheit, in: Juristenzeitung 1991, 529–534

——, Personalstatut, Staatsangehörigkeit und Effektivität (1988), C. H. Beck'sche Verlagsbuchhandlung, Munich

Mansel, Heinz-Peter/Thorn, Karsten/Wagner, Rolf, Europäisches Kollisionsrecht 2012: Voranschreiten des Kodifikationsprozesses – Flickenteppich des Einheitsrechts, in: Praxis des Internationalen Privat- und Verfahrensrechts 2013, 1–36

Markesinis, Basil S., Why a code is not the best way to advance the cause of European legal unity, in: European Review of Private Law 5 (1997), 519–524

Markesinis, Basil/Fedtke, Jörg, Engaging with Foreign Law (2009), Hart, Oxford and Portland, Oregon

Martinek, Michael, The Seven Pillars of Wisdom in Private International Law – The German and the Swiss Experience with the Codification of Conflicts Law Rules, in: Chinese Yearbook of Private International Law and Comparative Law 2001, 15–54 (also available online at http://archiv.jura.uni-saarland.de/projekte/Bibliothek/text.php?id=221) (last visited 12 October 2018) (cited as: *Martinek*, Seven Pillars of Wisdom)

——, Wissenschaftsgeschichte der Rechtsvergleichung und des Internationalen Privatrechts in der Bundesrepublik Deutschland, in: Simon, Dieter (ed.), Rechtswissenschaft in der Bonner Republik (1994), Suhrkamp, Frankfurt a. M., 529–619

Martiny, Dieter, Die Anknüpfung güterrechtlicher Angelegenheiten nach den Europäischen Güterrechtsverordnungen, in: Zeitschrift für Privatrechtswissenschaft 2017, 1–32

——, Lex rei sitae as a connecting factor in EU Private International Law, in: Praxis des Internationalen Privat- und Verfahrensrechts 2012, 119–133

——, Neues deutsches internationales Vertragsrecht, in: Recht der Internationalen Wirtschaft 2009, 737–752

Mäsch, Gerald, Chapter 6, Preliminary Question, in: Leible, Stefan (ed.), General Principles of European Private International Law (2016), Kluwer Law International, Alphen aan den Rijn, 101–116

——, Der Renvoi – Plädoyer für die Begrenzung einer überflüssigen Rechtsfigur, in: Rabels Zeitschrift für ausländisches und internationales Privatrecht 61 (1997), 285–312

Matić, Zeljko, The Yugoslav Act Concerning Private International Law, in: Netherlands International Law Review 30 (1983), 220–222

Mattei, Ugo, Comparative Law and Critical Legal Studies, in: Reimann, Mathias/Zimmermann, Reinhard (eds.), The Oxford Handbook of Comparative Law (2006), Oxford University Press, 815–836

Maultzsch, Felix, Party autonomy in European private international law: uniform principle or context-dependent instrument?, in: Journal of Private International Law 12 (2016), 466–491

Max Planck Encyclopedia of European Private Law, see Basedow, Jürgen/Hopt, Klaus J./ Zimmermann, Reinhard/Stier, Andreas (eds.)

Max Planck Institute for Comparative and International Private Law, Comments on the European Commission's Proposal for a Regulation of the European Parliament and of the Council on jurisdiction, applicable law, recognition and enforcement of decisions and authentic instruments in matters of succession and the creation of a European Certificate of Succession, Rabels Zeitschrift für ausländisches und internationales Privatrecht 74 (2010), 522–720

Mayer, Otto, Deutsches Verwaltungsrecht, Vol. 1 (1895) (= Binding, Karl (ed.), Systematisches Handbuch der Deutschen Rechtswissenschaft, Sixth Section), Duncker & Humblot, Leipzig

Mayer, Pierre/Heuzé, Vincent, Droit international privé, 11th ed. (2014), Montchrestien, Paris

McBryde, William W./Flessner, Axel/ Kortmann, Sebastian C. J. J. (eds.), Principles of European Insolvency Law (2003), Kluwer, Deventer

McCrum, Robert, Globish, How the English Language Became the World's Language (2010), Viking, London

McParland, Michael, The Rome I Regulation on the Law Applicable to Contractual Obligations (2015), Oxford University Press

Medicus, Dieter/Petersen, Jens, Allgemeiner Teil des BGB, 11th ed. (2016), C. F. Müller, Heidelberg

Meeusen, Johan, Who Is Afraid of European Private International Law?, in: Venturini, Gabriella/Bariatti, Stefania (eds.), Nuovi strumenti del diritto internazionale privato, Liber Fausto Pocar, Vol. 2 (2009), Giuffré, Milan, 685–700

——, Instrumentalisation of Private International Law in the European Union: Towards a European Conflicts Revolution?, in: European Journal of Migration and Law 9 (2007), 287–305

Meeusen, Johan/van Overbeeke, Fieke/Verhaert, Lore, The Link Between Access to Justice and European Conflict of Laws After Lisbon, in: Rabels Zeitschrift für ausländisches und internationales Privatrecht 81 (2017), 858–883

Meidanis, Haris P., Part I, Choice of Law/General Questions, in: Vrellis, Spyridon (ed.), Private International Law in Greece, 2011, Kluwer Law International, Alphen aan den Rijn, 43–54

Melchior, George, Die Grundlagen des deutschen internationalen Privatrechts (1932), Reprint 1971, Walter de Gruyter, Berlin, New York

Merten, Detlef/Papier, Hans-Jürgen (eds.), Handbuch der Grundrechte in Deutschland und Europa, Vol. 1 (2004), C. F. Müller, Heidelberg

Mertens, Bernd, Gesetzgebungskunst im Zeitalter der Kodifikationen (2004), Mohr Siebeck, Tübingen

Merz, Hans, Stellung und Funktion des Obligationenrechts im System des schweizerischen Privatrechts, in: Canaris, Claus-Wilhelm/Diederichsen, Uwe (eds.) Festschrift für Karl Larenz (1983), C.H. Beck, Munich 1983, 425–441

Metzger, Axel, Abuse of Law in EU Private Law: A (Re-)Construction from Fragments, in: de la Feria, Rita/Vogenauer, Stefan (eds.), Prohibition of Abuse of Law, A New General Principle of EU Law? (2011), Hart, Oxford and Portland, Oregon, 235–251

Michaels, Ralf, Die Struktur der kollisionsrechtlichen Durchsetzung einfach zwingender Normen, in: id./Solomon, Dennis (eds.), Liber Amicorum Klaus Schurig zum 70. Geburtstag (2012), Sellier, Munich, 191–210

——, Die europäische IPR-Revolution, in: Baetge, Dietmar/von Hein, Jan/von Hinden, Michael (eds.), Die richtige Ordnung, Festschrift für Jan Kropholler zum 70. Geburtstag (2008), Mohr Siebeck, Tübingen, 151–173

——, The Functional Method of Comparative Law, in: Reimann, Mathias/Zimmermann, Reinhard (eds.), The Oxford Handbook of Comparative Law (2006), Oxford University Press, 339–382

Mikelėnas, Valentinas, Reform of Private International Law in Lithuania, in: Yearbook of Private International Law 7 (2005), 161–181

Mills, Alex, Party Autonomy in Private International Law (2018), Cambridge University Press

——, The Confluence of Public and Private International Law (2009), Cambridge University Press

Mirkovic, Aude, Précisions de la Cour de cassation quant aux conséquences du recours à la GPA à l'étranger, in: La Semaine Juridique, Èdition Générale, 2013, 1731–1734

Mistelis, Loukas, CISG-AC Publishes First Opinions, (available online at http://www.cisg.law.pace.edu/cisg/CISG-AC.html) (last visited 12 October 2018)

Mosconi, Franco/Campiglio, Cristina, Diritto internazionale privato e processuale, 4th ed., Volume I (2007), UTET Giuridica, Roma

Moura Ramos, Rui Manuel, Le droit international privé portugais à la fin du vingtième siècle: progrès ou recul?, in: Symeonides, Symeon C. (ed.), Private International Law at the End of the 20th Century: Progress or Regress? (2000), Kluwer Law International, London, 349–382

Moura Vicente, Dário, Sources and General Principles of Portuguese Private International Law: An Outline, in: Yearbook of Private International Law 9 (2007), 257–275

Mugdan, Benno (ed.), Die gesammten Materialien zum Bürgerlichen Gesetzbuch für das Deutsche Reich, Vol. I, Einführungsgesetz und Allgemeiner Theil (1899), R. v. Decker, Berlin

Muir-Watt, Horatia, Private International Law Beyond the Schism, in: Transnational Legal Theory 2 (2011), 347–428

——, The role of the conflict of laws in European private law, in: Twigg-Flesner, Christian (ed.), The Cambridge Companion to European Union Private Law (2010), Cambridge, 44–57

Müller, Michael, Objektive Anknüpfungsmomente für Schuldverhältnisse im europäischen IPR und IZVR, Die Behandlung vertraglicher Sachverhalt, in: von Hein, Jan/Rühl, Giesela (eds.), Kohärenz im Internationalen Privat- und Verfahrensrecht der Europäischen Union (2016), Mohr Siebeck, Tübingen, 243–278

——, Mehrdeutige Begriffe im Internationalen Privatrecht, in: Juristische Ausbildung 2015, 1319–1325

——, Finanzinstrumente in der Rom I-VO (2011), Jenaer Wissenschaftliche Verlaggesellschaft

MüKoBGB, see Säcker, Franz Jürgen/Rixecker, Roland/Oetker, Hartmut/Limperg, Bettina (eds.), Münchener Kommentar zum Bürgerlichen Gesetzbuch

Münch, Joachim, Strukturprobleme der Kodifikation, in: Behrends, Okko/Sellert, Wolfgang (eds.), Der Kodifikationsgedanke und das Modell des Bürgerlichen Gesetzbuches (BGB) (2000), Vandenhoeck & Rupprecht, Göttingen, 147–173

Münzer, Cornelia, Handeln unter falschem Recht (1992), Peter Lang, Frankfurt a. M.

Nagy, Csongor István, Private International Law in Hungary (2012), Kluwer Law International, Alphen aan den Rijn

Nehne, Timo, Methodik und allgemeine Lehren des europäischen Internationalen Privatrechts (2012), Mohr Siebeck, Tübingen

Neocleous, Andreas/Koundourou, Maria/Monou, Efrosini, Private International Law, in: Neocleous, Andreas (ed.), Neocleous's Introduction to Cyprus Law, 3rd edition (2010), Neocleous & Co., Limassol

Nettesheim, Martin (ed.), Grabitz/Hilf, Das Recht der Europäischen Union, 63rd instalment (December 2017), C.H. Beck, Munich

——, Die Begründung der Entscheidungen des EuGH, in: Tichý, Luboš/Holländer, Pavel/Bruns, Alexander (eds.), Odůvodnění Soudního Rozhodnutí – The Judicial Opinion – Begründung von Gerichtsentscheidung [sic] (2011), Centrum právní komparatistky, Prague 343–356 [Czech translation: 331–342]

Newman, M. L., Stendhal and the *Code civil*, in: The French Review 43 (1970), 434–442

Neuenbäumer, Anke, Ernst Zitelmann – Die Begründung der Rechtsvergleichung als Wissenschaft (2014), Dr. Kovač, Hamburg

Neuhaus, Paul Heinrich, Die Grundbegriffe des Internationalen Privatrechts, 2nd ed. (1976), J. C. B. Mohr (Paul Siebeck), Tübingen

——, Empfiehlt sich eine Kodifizierung des Internationalen Privatrechts?, in: Rabels Zeitschrift für ausländisches und internationales Privatrecht 37 (1973), 453–465

N[euhaus], [Paul] H[einrich], [Statement concerning *Franceskakis*, Conflits de lois (Principes généraux)], in: Rabels Zeitschrift für ausländisches und internationales Privatrecht 33 (1969), 194–196

Neuhaus, Paul Heinrich/Rau, Hans, Das Internationale Privatrecht im neuen portugiesischen Zivilgesetzbuch, in: Rabels Zeitschrift für ausländisches und internationales Privatrecht 32 (1968), 500–512

Niboyet-Hoegy, Marie-Laure, [Case note concerning the *Caron* case], Journal du droit international 1987, 87–94

Noll, Peter, Gesetzgebungslehre (1973), Rowohlt, Reinbek

Nordmeier, Carl Friedrich, Grundfragen der Rechtswahl in der neuen EU-Erbrechtsverordnung – eine Untersuchung des Art. 22 ErbRVO, in: Zeitschrift für das Privatrecht der Europäischen Union (GPR) 2013, 148–155

Nourissat, Cyril, La codification de l'espace judiciaire civil européen, in: Douchy-Oudot, Mélina/Guinchard, Emmanuel (eds.), La justice civil européenne en marche (2012), Dalloz, Paris, 175–185

Nowicka, Aurelia, Private International Law, in: Dajczak, Wojciech/Szwarc, Andrzej J./ Wiliński, Paweł (eds.), Handbook of Polish Law (2011), Wydawnictwo Szkolne, Warsaw, 573–607

Ömür, Susan, Rechtswahl als Rechtsgeschäft, Wirksamkeitsvoraussetzungen und das auf sie anwendbare Recht nach europäischem internationalen Privatrecht (2016), Jenaer Wissenschaftliche Verlagsgesellschaft

Oppermann, Thomas/Classen, Dieter/Nettesheim, Tübingen, Europarecht, 7th ed. (2016), Beck, Munich

Örücü, Esin, Developing Comparative Law, in: idem/Nelken, David (eds.), Comparative Law, A Handbook (2007), Hart, Oxford and Portland, Oregon, 43–65

Pajor, Tomasz, La nouvelle loi polonaise de droit international privé, in: Revue critique de droit international privé 2012, 5–13

——, Introduction to the New Polish Act on Private International Law of 4 February 2011, in: Yearbook of Private International Law 13 (2011), 381–388

——, Polish Private International Law at the End of the 20th Century: Progress or Regress?, in: Symeonides, Symeon C. (ed.), Private International Law at the End of the 20th Century: Progress or Regress? (2000), Kluwer Law International, London, 329–347

Palmer, Edith, The Austrian Codification of Conflicts Law, in: The American Journal of Comparative Law 28 (1980), 197–234

Panopoulos, Georgios, La jurisprudence grecque de droit international privé en 2012, in: Revue hellénique de droit international 66 (2013), 319–333

Parra-Aranguren, Gonzalo, *Fraude à la loi* in Recent Codifications of Private International Law in the American Hemisphere, in: Einhorn, Talia/Siehr, Kurt (eds.), Intercontinental Cooperation through Private International Law, Essays in Memory of Peter E. Nygh (2004), T.M.C. Asser Press, The Hague, 263–298

Pauknerová, Monika, Escape Clauses and Legal Certainty in Private International Law, in: Yearbook of Private International Law 18 (2016/2017), 61–82

——, Treatment of Foreign Law in a Comparative Perspective, in: Revue hellénique de droit international 64 (2011), 5–25

Pauknerová, Monika/Pfeiffer, Magdalena, The New Act on Private International Law in the Czech Republic: Starting Points and Perspectives within the European Union, in: Journal of Private International Law 10 (2014), 205–226

Pazdan, Maksymilian, Das neue polnische Gesetz über das internationale Privatrecht, in: Praxis des Internationalen Privat- und Verfahrensrechts 2012, 77–81

——, Recent Codifications of Private International Law: The Polish Experience, in: Lewaszkiewicz-Petrykowska, Biruta (ed.), Rapports Polonais (2010), Wydawnictwo Universytetu Łódzkiego, Łodz, 49–68

Pazdan, Maksymilian/Gralla, Erhardt, Polen: Gesetz über das Internationale Privatrecht, Einführung, in: WiRO 2011, 299–301

Peari, Sagi, The Foundation of Choice of Law (2018), Oxford University Press

Pertegas, Marta, The Belgian Code on Private International Law: a tour d'horizon, in: Praxis des Internationalen Privat- und Verfahrensrechts 2006, 53–61

Pesce, Angelo, Die Reform des italienischen Internationalen Privat- und Verfahrensrechts, in: Recht der internationalen Wirtschaft 1995, 977–983

Peters, Anne/Schwenke, Heiner, Comparative Law beyond Post-Modernism, in: International and Comparative Law Quarterly 49 (2000), 800–834

Petersen, Jens, Die systematische Stellung des Allgemeinen Teils vor der Klammer der anderen Bücher, in: Jura 2011, 759–761

Philip, Allan, The Scandinavian Conventions on Private International Law, in: Recueil des cours 96 (1959-I), 241–348

Piek, Sarah, Die Kritik an der funktionalen Rechtsvergleichung, in: Zeitschrift für Europäisches Privatrecht 2013, 60–87

Pirrung, Jörg, Bemerkungen zur Zusammenarbeit zwischen EuGH und Gerichten der EU-Staaten zum IPR, insbesondere in der Rechtssache C-29/10 Koelzsch gegen Luxemburg, in: Geimer, Reinhold/Schütze, Rolf A. (eds.), Recht ohne Grenzen, Festschrift für Athanassios Kaissis zum 65. Geburtstag (2012), Sellier, Munich, 759–776

Pisani, Christian, Nachlassspaltung im maltesischen Erbrecht und deren Folgen für die Nachlassplanung in deutsch-maltesischen Erbfällen, in: Praxis des Internationalen Privat- und Verfahrensrechts 2007, 359–363

Plender/Wilderspin, European PIL of Obligations, see Wilderspin, Michael, The European Private International Law of Obligations Pocar, Fausto, Concluding Remarks, in: Malatesta, Alberto (ed.) The Unification of Choice of Law Rules on Torts and Other Non-Contractual Obligations in Europe (2006), CEDAM, Padua, 301–305

——, Das neue italienische Internationale Privatrecht, in: Praxis des Internationalen Privat- und Verfahrensrechts 1997, 145–161

Pocar, Fausto/Honorati, Costanza, Italian Private International Law at the End of the 20th Century: Progress or Regress?, in: Symeonides, Symeon C. (ed.), Private International Law at the End of the 20th Century: Progress or Regress? (2000), Kluwer Law International, London, 279–294

Pozzo, Barbara, Comparative law and language, in: Bussani, Mauro/Mattei, Ugo (eds.), The Cambridge Companion to Comparative Law (2012), Cambridge University Press, 88–113

Prosser, William L., Interstate Publication, in: Michigan Law Review 51 (1953), 959–1000

Puharič, Krešo, Private International Law in Slovenia, in: Yearbook of Private International Law 5 (2003), 155–167

Raape, Leo, Internationales Privatrecht, 5th ed. (1961), Franz Vahlen, Berlin, Frankfurt a. M.

Rabel, Ernst, Aufgabe und Notwendigkeit der Rechtsvergleichung, in: Leser, Hans G. (ed.), Ernst Rabel, Gesammelte Aufsätze, Vol. 3, Arbeiten zur Rechtsvergleichung und zur Rechtsvereinheitlichung (1967), J. C. B. Mohr (Paul Siebeck), Tübingen, 1–21 (cited as: *Rabel*, Aufgabe und Notwendigkeit)

——, Die Fachgebiete des Kaiser-Wilhelm-Instituts für ausländisches und internationales Privatrecht, in: Leser, Hans G. (ed.), Ernst Rabel, Gesammelte Aufsätze, Vol. 3, Arbeiten zur Rechtsvergleichung und zur Rechtsvereinheitlichung (1967), J. C. B. Mohr (Paul Siebeck), Tübingen, 180–234 (cited as: *Rabel*, Die Fachgebiete des Kaiser-Wilhelm-Instituts)

——, The Conflict of Laws: A Comparative Study, Volume I, 2nd ed., prepared by Drobnig, Ulrich (1958), Michigan Legal Studies, Ann Arbor

——, Deutsches und amerikanisches Recht, in: Zeitschrift für Ausländisches und Internationales Privatrecht 16 (1951), 340–359

——, Das Problem der Qualifikation, in: Zeitschrift für Ausländisches und Internationales Privatrecht 5 (1931), 241–288

Radbruch, Gustav, Einführung in die Rechtswissenschaft, 13th ed., prepared by Zweigert, Konrad (1980), K. F. Koehler, Stuttgart

Raffai, Katalin/Szabó, Sarolta, Selected Issues on Recent Hungarian Private International Law Codification, in: Acta Juridica Hungarica 51 (2010), 136–155

Rammeloo, Stephan, The Long Road towards Codification of Netherlands Private International Law: Book 10 Civil Code (Draft Bill), in: EuLF 2010, I-181–I-190

Ranieri, Filippo, Europäisches Obligationenrecht, 3rd ed. (2009), SpringerWienNewYork, Vienna

Rauscher, Thomas, Internationales Privatrecht, 5th ed. (2017), C. F. Müller, Heidelberg

Rauscher, Thomas (ed.), EuZPR/EuIPR, Europäisches Zivilprozess- und Kollisionsrecht, Vol. I, Vol. III, 4th ed. (2016), Otto Schmidt, Cologne

Ravluševičius, Pavel, Die Reform des Internationalen Privatrechts in Litauen, in: Praxis des Internationalen Privat- und Verfahrensrechts 2003, 272–275

Reichelt, Gerte, Der neue französische IPR-Entwurf, Einige Anmerkungen zum Allgemeinen Teil, in: ZfRV 1971, 249–260

Reimann, Mathias, The American Advantage in Global Lawyering, in: Rabels Zeitschrift fur ausländisches und internationales Privatrecht 78 (2014), 1–36

——, Comparative law and neighbouring disciplines, in: Bussani, Mauro/Mattei, Ugo (eds.), The Cambridge Companion to Comparative Law (2012), Cambridge University Press, 13–34

——, Was ist wählbares Recht?, in: Verschraegen, Bea (ed.), Rechtswahl, Grenzen und Chancen (2010), Jan Sramek, Vienna, 1–31

——, Comparative Law and Private International Law, in: idem/Zimmermann, Reinhard (eds.), The Oxford Handbook of Comparative Law (2006), Oxford University Press, 1363–1396

——, The Progress and Failure of Comparative Law in the Second Half of the Twentieth Century, in: The American Journal of Comparative Law 50 (2002), 671–700

——, The End of Comparative Law as an Autonomous Subject, in: Tulane European & Civil Law Forum 11 (1996), 49–72

Reithmann, Christoph/Martiny, Dieter (eds.), Internationales Vertragsrecht, 8th ed. (2015), Otto Schmidt, Cologne

Reitz, John C., How to Do Comparative Law, in: The American Journal of Comparative Law 46 (1998), 617–636

Remien, Oliver, Die Anwendung und Ermittlung ausländischen Rechts im System des Europäischen Internationalen Privatrechts, in: Zeitschrift für vergleichende Rechtswissenschaft 115 (2016), 570–585

——, Chapter 11, Closest Connection and Escape Clauses, in: Leible, Stefan (ed.), General Principles of European Private International Law (2016), Kluwer Law International, Alphen aan den Rijn, 211–224

——, Über die Anwendung fremden mitgliedstaatlichen Zivilrechts in anderen Mitgliedstaaten des Europäischen Rechtsraums – Anwendbarkeit, Ermittlung und Revisibilität, in: Ackermann, Thomas/Köndgen, Johannes (eds.), Privat- und Wirtschaftsrecht in Europa, Festschrift für Wulf-Henning Roth zum 70. Geburtstag (2015), Beck, Munich, 431–442

——, Proof of and Information about Foreign Law, in: Schmidt-Kessel, Martin (ed.), German National Reports on the 19th International Congress of Comparative Law (2014), Mohr Siebeck, Tübingen, 223–260

——, Variationen zum Thema Eingriffsnormen nach Art. 9 Rom I-VO und Art. 16 Rom II-VO unter Berücksichtigung neuerer Rechtsprechung zu Art. 7 Römer Übereinkommen, in: Kronke, Herbert/Thorn, Karsten (eds.), Grenzen überwinden – Prinzipien bewahren, Festschrift für Bernd von Hoffmann (2011), Gieseking, Bielefeld, 334–347

——, Illusion und Realität eines europäischen Privatrechts, in: Juristenzeitung 1992, 277–284

Remy, Benjamin, Les codifications récentes du droit international privé, in: Revue internationale de droit comparé 2010, 291–323

Rentsch, Bettina, Der gewöhnliche Aufenthalt im System des Europäischen Kollisionsrechts (2017), Mohr Siebeck, Tübingen

——, Die Zukunft des Personalstatuts im gewöhnlichen Aufenthalt, in: Zeitschrift für Europäisches Privatrecht 2015, 288–312

Requejo Isidro, Marta, Reflections on the Preambles to the EU Private International Law Regulations, in: Hess, Burkard/Jayme, Erik/Mansel, Heinz-Peter (eds.), Europa als Rechts- und Lebensraum, Liber Amicorum für Christian Kohler (2018), Gieseking, Bielefeld, 425–439

Requejo, Marta/Cuniberti, Gilles [case note on ECJ Case C-327/10, Hypoteční banka a.s. v Udo Mike Lindner], Rev. crit. DIP 2012, 421–430

Reuter, Stefan, Die „Nachfrage“ im Internationalen Privatrecht: Rechtsgrund-, Rechtsfolgen- und andere Verweisungen im grenzüberschreitenden Kontext, in: Zeitschrift für Privatrechtswissenschaft 2017, 475–496

Rheinstein, Max, Einführung in die Rechtsvergleichung, 2nd ed. (1987), C. H. Beck, München

——, The Approach to German Law, in: Indiana Law Journal 34 (1959), 546–558

Riedl, Kristina, Vom Unsinn wissenschaftlicher Kodifikationsprojekte, in: Tietze, Andrea/McGuire, Mary-Rose/Bendel, Christian/Kähler, Lorenz/Nickel, Nicole/Reich, Barbara/Sachse, Kathrin/Wehling, Eileen (eds.), Jahrbuch Junger Zivilrechtswissenschaftler 2004, Europäisches Privatrecht, Über die Verknüpfung von nationalem und Gemeinschaftsrecht (2005), Richard Boorberg, Stuttgart et al., 31–59

Riehm, Thomas, Vom Gesetz, das klüger ist als seine Verfasser – Zur Revisibilität ausländischen Rechts, in: Juristenzeitung 2014, 73–78

Ring, Gerhard/Olsen-Ring, Line, Einführung in das skandinavische Recht, 2nd ed. (2014), 1st ed. (1999), Beck, Munich

Rigaux, François/Fallon, Marc, Droit International Privé, 3rd ed. (2005), Larcier, Brussels

Robbers, Gerhard, An Introduction to German Law, 6th ed. (2017), Nomos, Baden-Baden

Rödig, Jürgen/Baden, Eberhard/Kindermann, Harald, Vorstudien zu einer Theorie der Gesetzgebung (1975), Gesellschaft für Mathematik und Datenverarbeitung, St. Augustin

Rogerson, Pippa, Collier's Conflict of Laws, 4th ed. (2013), Cambridge University Press, Cambridge

——, Quantification of Damages: Substance or Procedure?, The Cambridge Law Journal 2006, 515–518

——, Habitual Residence: The New Domicile?, in: International and Comparative Law Quarterly 49 (2000), 86–107

Roth, Wulf-Henning, Drittstaatliche Eingriffsnormen und Rom I-Verordnung, in: Praxis des Internationalen Privat- und Verfahrensrechts 2018, 177–186

——, Der Grundsatz der loyalen Zusammenarbeit in der Europäischen Union und das Internationale Privatrecht, in: Heid, Daniela/Stotz, Rüdiger/Verny, Arsène (eds.), Festschrift für Manfred A. Dauses zum 70. Geburtstag (2014), C.H. Beck, Munich, 315–335

——, Europäische Kollisionsrechtsvereinheitlichung, Überblick – Kompetenzen – Grenzen, in: Remien, Oliver/Kieninger, Eva-Maria (eds.), Europäische Kollisionsrechtsvereinheitlichung (2012), Nomos, Baden-Baden, 11–49

——, Handelsvertretervertrag und Rom I-Verordnung – Eine Skizze, in: Bernreuther, Jörn/Freitag, Robert/Leible, Stefan/Sippel, Harald/Wanitzek, Ulrike (eds.), Festschrift für Ulrich Spellenberg (2010), Sellier, Munich, 309–328

——, [Case Note on *Ingmar*], in: Common Market Law Review 39 (2002), 369–383

Rösler, Hannes, Die Europäisierung von IZVR und IPR als Herausforderung für die deutsche Gerichtsorganisation, in: Zeitschrift für vergleichende Rechtswissenschaft 115 (2016), 533–556

——, Rechtswahlfreiheit im Internationalen Scheidungsrecht der Rom III-Verordnung, in: Rabels Zeitschrift für ausländisches und internationales Privatrecht 78 (2014), 155–192

Rudolf, Claudia, Slowenien: Neues Internationales Privat- und Prozessrecht, in: Praxis des Internationalen Privat- und Verfahrensrechts 2003, 158–162

Rugullis, Sven, Die Rechtswahl nach Art. 27 Abs. 1 EGBGB – Sachnorm- oder Gesamtverweisung?, in: Zeitschrift für Vergleichende Rechtswissenschaft 106 (2007), 217–227

Rühl, Giesela, Judicial Cooperation in Civil and Commercial Matters after Brexit: Which Way Forward?, in: International and Comparative Law Quarterly 67 (2018), 99–128

——, Die Wahl englischen Rechts und englischer Gerichte nach dem Brexit, in: Juristenzeitung 2017, 72–82

——, Rechtsvergleichung und europäisches Kollisionsrecht: Die vergessene Dimension, in: Zimmermann, Reinhard (ed.), Zukunftsperspektiven der Rechtsvergleichung (2016), Mohr Siebeck, Tübingen, 103–138

——, Commercial agents, minimum harmonization and overriding mandatory provisions in the European Union: *Unamar*, in: Common Market Law Review 53 (2016), 209–224

——, The Protection of Weaker Parties in the Private International Law of the European Union: A Portrait of Inconsistency and Conceptual Truancy, Journal of Private International Law 10 (2014), 335–358

——, Rechtswahlfreiheit im europäischen Kollisionsrecht, in: Baetge, Dietmar/von Hein, Jan/von Hinden, Michael (eds.), Die richtige Ordnung, Festschrift für Jan Kropholler zum 70. Geburtstag (2008), Mohr Siebeck, Tübingen, 187–209

Rühl, Giesela/von Hein, Jan, Towards a European Code on Private International Law?, in: Rabels Zeitschrift für ausländisches und internationales Privatrecht 79 (2015), 701–751 (with the original presentation being available online at http://www.europarl.europa.eu/RegData/etudes/STUD/2015/510003/IPOL_STU(2015)510003_EN.pdf) (last visited 12 October 2018)

Sacco, Rodolfo, Legal Formants: A Dynamic Approach To Comparative Law (Installment I of II), in: The American Journal of Comparative Law 39 (1991), 1–34

——, Droit commun de l'Europe, et composantes du droit, in: Cappelletti, Mauro (ed.), New Perspectives for a Common Law of Europe (1978), Sijthoff et al., Leyden et al., 95–109

Säcker, Franz Jürgen/Rixecker, Roland/Oetker, Hartmut/Limperg, Bettina (eds.), Münchener Kommentar zum Bürgerlichen Gesetzbuch, Vol. 1, 7th ed. (2015), Vol. 2, Vol. 3, 7th ed. (2016), Vol. 11, Vol. 12, 7th ed. (2018), C.H. Beck, Munich (cited as: *Commentator*, in: MüKoBGB)

Salomon, Max, Grundlegung zur Rechtsphilosophie, 2nd ed. (1925), Rothschild, Berlin

Sana-Chaillé de Néré, Sandrine, Les questions préalables, in: Azzi/Boskovic (eds.), Quel avenir pour la théorie générale des conflits de lois? (2015), Larcier, Bruxelles, 123–138

Sánchez Lorenzo, Sixto A., El principio de coherencia en el derecho internacional privado europeo, in: Revista Española de Derecho Internacional 70 (2018), 17–47

Sandrock, Otto, Über Sinn und Methode zivilistischer Rechtsvergleichung (1966), Alfred Metzner, Frankfurt a. M., Berlin

Šarčević, Petar, The New Yugoslav Private International Law Act, in: The American Journal of Comparative Law 33 (1985), 283–296

Schacherreiter, Judith, Der missglückte Legal Transplant des Art. 9 Abs. 3 Rom I-VO – Eine Kritik an der Regelung fremder Eingriffsnormen im europäischen internationalen Vertragsrecht, in: Zeitschrift für Europäisches Privatrecht 2015, 497–516

Schaeffner, Wilhelm, Entwicklung des internationalen Privatrechts (1841), Sauerländer, Frankfurt am Main

Schärdel, Florian, Die Bücherkodifikation (2012), Nomos, Baden-Baden

Schilling, Johannes, Eingriffsnormen im europäischen Richtlinienrecht, in: Zeitschrift für Europäisches Privatrecht 2014, 843–860

Schlechtriem, Peter, Restitution und Bereicherungsausgleich in Europea, Vol. 1 (2000), Vol. 2 (2001), Mohr Siebeck, Tübingen

Schlegelberger, Franz, Abschied vom BGB (1939), Franz Vahlen, Berlin

Schlegelberger, Franz (ed.), Rechtsvergleichendes Handwörterbuch für das Zivil- und Handelsrecht des In- und Auslandes, Vol. 4 (1933), Franz Vahlen, Berlin

Schmidt, Folke, The German Abstract Approach to Law, in: Scandinavian Studies in Law 9 (1965), 131–158

Schmidt, Jan Peter, Zivilrechtskodifikation in Brasilien (2010), Mohr Siebeck, Tübingen

Schmidt, Torben Svenné, The Preliminary Question and the Question of Substitution in Conflict of Laws, in: Scandinavian Studies in Law 12 (1968), 93–119

Schmidt-Kessel, Martin, Zahlungsverzug im Handelsverkehr – ein neuer Richtlinienentwurf, in: Juristenzeitung 1998, 1135–1145

Schmitz, Melanie, Die Rechtswahlfreiheit im europäischen Kollisionsrecht (2017), Duncker & Humblot, Berlin

Schmoeckel, Mathias/Rückert, Joachim/Zimmermann, Reinhard (eds.), Historisch-kritischer Kommentar zum BGB, Vol. I, Allgemeiner Teil (2003), Mohr Siebeck, Tübingen (cited as: *Commentator*, in: HKK-BGB)

Schneider, Jens-Peter/Hofmann, Herwig C. H./Ziller, Jacques, Die ReNEUAL Model Rules 2014: Ein Verwaltungsverfahrensrecht für Europa, in: Juristenzeitung 2015, 265–271

Schröder, Vincent, Die Verweisung of Mehrrechtsstaaten im deutschen Internationalen Privatrecht (2007), Mohr Siebeck

Schulz, Carsten, Die Subsumtion ausländischer Rechtstatsachen (1997), Duncker & Humblot, Berlin

Schulze, Reiner (managing editor), Bürgerliches Gesetzbuch, Handkommentar, 9th ed. (2017), Nomos, Baden-Baden (cited as: *Commentator*, in: HK-BGB)

Schulze, Reiner/Zoll, Fryderyk, European Contract Law (2016), Nomos/C. H. Beck/Hart, Baden-Baden/Munich/Oxford

Schulze, Ulrich W., Zur Rechtsentwicklung in den baltischen Staaten, in: Roggemann, Herwig/Kuss, Klaus-Jürgen (Hrsg.), Wirtschaften und Investieren in Osteuropa (1994), Berlin Verlag Arno Spitz, Berlin, 187–213

Schurig, Klaus, Das Fundament trägt noch, in: Mansel, Heinz-Peter (ed.), Internationales Privatrecht im 20. Jahrhundert, Der Einfluss von Gerhard Kegel und Alexander Lüderitz auf das Kollistionsrecht (2014), Mohr Siebeck, Tübingen, 5–25

——, Eine hinkende Vereinheitlichung des internationalen Ehescheidungsrechts in Europa, in: Kronke, Herbert/Thorn, Karsten (eds.), Grenzen überwinden – Prinzipien bewahren, Festschrift für Bernd von Hoffmann (2011), Gieseking, Bielefeld, 405–414

——, [Besprechung von: Oliver Heeder, Fraus legis], in: Rabels Zeitschrift für ausländisches und internationales Privatrecht 65 (2001), 746–758

——, Zwingendes Recht, „Eingriffsnormen" und neues IPR, in: Rabels Zeitschrift für ausländisches und internationales Privatrecht 54 (1990), 217–250

——, Die Gesetzesumgehung im Privatrecht, Eine Studie mit kollisionsrechtlichen und rechtsvergleichenden Aspekten, in: Heldrich, Andreas/Sonnenberger, Hans Jürgen (eds.), Festschrift für Murad Ferid zum 80. Geburtstag am 11. April 1988 (1988), Verlag für Standesamtswesen, Frankfurt a. M., 375–422

——, Die Struktur des kollisionsrechtlichen Vorfragenproblems, in: Musielak, Hans-Joachim/idem (eds.), Festschrift für Gerhard Kegel (1987), Kohlhammer, Stuttgart et al., 549–598

——, Kollisionsnorm und Sachrecht, Zu Struktur, Standort und Methode des internationalen Privatrechts (1981), Duncker & Humblot, Berlin

Schuz, Rhona, A Modern Approach to the Incidental Question (1997), Kluwer Law International, London, The Hague, Boston

Schwander, Ivo, Wie kann nationales IPR zu vermehrt internationaler Optik gelangen?, in: Basedow, Jürgen/Meier, Isaak/Schnyder, Anton K./Einhorn, Talia/Girsberger, Daniel (eds.), Private Law in the International Arena, Liber Amicorum Kurt Siehr (2000), Schulthess, Zurich, 673–684

Schwartze, Andreas, Die Ermittlung und Anwendung des Vertragsrechts anderer EU-Staaten im deutschen Zivilprozeß nach § 293 ZPO – ein besonderer Fall, in: Yessiou-Faltsi, Pelayia/Jost, Fritz/Kaissis, Athanassios/Apalagaki, Charoula (eds.), Recht in Europa, Festschrift für Prof. Dr. Dr. h.c. Hilmar Fenge zum 65. Geburtstag am 28.10.1996 (1996), Dr. Kovač, Hamburg, 127–146

Schwarze, Jürgen, European Administrative Law (2006), Sweet and Maxwell, London

Schwarze, Jürgen (ed.), EU-Kommentar, 3rd ed. (2012), Nomos, Baden-Baden

Schwimann, Michael, Internationales Privatrecht einschließlich Europarecht, 3rd ed. (2001), Manz, Vienna

Seifert, Achim, Das europäische Arbeitsrecht im Gesamtgefüge des europäischen Privatrechts, in: Zeitschrift für Europäisches Privatrecht 2015, 241–272

Sein, Karin, The Development of Private International Law in Estonia, in: Yearbook of Private International Law 10 (2008), 459–472

Siehr, Kurt, Österreichisches IPR-Gesetz und europäische Ideengeschichte, in: Reichelt, Gerte (ed.), 30 Jahre österreichisches IPR-Gesetz, Europäische Perspektiven (2009), Manz, Vienna, 9–22

——, Die Kodifikation des Europäischen IPR – Hindernisse, Aufgaben und Lösungen, in: Jud, Brigitta/Rechberger, Walter/Reichelt, Gerte (eds.), Kollisionsrecht in der Europäischen Union (2008), Jan Sramek, Vienna, 77–95

——, General Problems of Private International Law in Modern Codifications – *de lege lata* and *de lege Europea ferenda*, in: Yearbook of Private International Law VII (2005), 17–61

——, „False Conflicts", „lois d'application immédiate" und andere „Neuentdeckungen" im IPR, Zu gewissen Eigengesetzlichkeiten kollisionsrechtlicher Systeme, in: Basedow, Jürgen/Hopt, Klaus J./Kötz, Hein (eds.), Festschrift für Ulrich Drobnig zum siebzigsten Geburtstag (1998), Mohr Siebeck, Tübingen, 443–454

——, Rechtsangleichung im IPR durch nationale Kodifikationen, in: Stoffel, Walter A./ Volken, Paul (eds.), Conflits et harmonisation, Mélanges en l'honneur d'Alfred E. von Overbeck (1990), Éditions Universitaires Fribourg, 205–243

——, Normen mit eigener Bestimmung ihres räumlich-persönlichen Anwendungsbereichs im Kollisionsrecht der Bundesrepublik Deutschland, in: Rabels Zeitschrift für ausländisches und internationales Privatrecht 46 (1982), 357–383

Siems, Mathias, Comparative Law (2014), Cambridge University Press

Simons, Thomas, European and International Uniform Law, in: The European Legal Forum 2007, I-1–I-8

Sinay-Cytermann, Anne, Présentation générale des facteurs de perturbation affectant la règle de conflit (lois de police, questions préalables, renvoi), in: Azzi/Boskovic (eds.), Quel avenir pour la théorie générale des conflits de lois?, 83–89

Singer, Philippe/Engel, Jean-Charles, L'importance de la recherche comparative pour la justice communautaire, in: Journal du droit international 2007, 497–513

Smits, Jan M., Rethinking methods in European private law, in: Adams, Maurice/Bomhoff, Jacco (eds.), Practice and Theory in Comparative Law (2012), Cambridge University Press, 170–185

——, European private law and the comparative method, in: Twigg-Flesner, Christian (ed.), The Cambridge Companion to European Union Private Law (2010), Cambridge, 33–43

Société de legislation comparée (ed.), L'application du droit étranger (2018), Paris

Solomon, Dennis, Die Renaissance des Renvoi im Europäischen Internationalen Privatrecht, in: Michaels, Ralf/idem (eds.), Liber Amicorum Klaus Schurig zum 70. Geburtstag (2012), Sellier, Munich, 237–263

——, Die Anknüpfung von Vorfragen im Europäischen Internationalen Privatrecht, in: Bernreuther, Jörn/Freitag, Robert/Leible, Stefan/Sippel, Harald/Wanitzek, Ulrike (eds.), Festschrift für Ulrich Spellenberg (2010), Sellier, Munich, 355–370

Sonnenberger, Hans Jürgen, Chapter 7, Overriding Mandatory Provisions, in: Leible, Stefan (ed.), General Principles of European Private International Law (2016), Kluwer Law International, Alphen aan den Rijn, 117–128

——, Anerkennung statt Verweisung?, Eine neue internationalprivatrechtliche Methode?, in: Bernreuther, Jörn/Freitag, Robert/Leible, Stefan/Sippel, Harald/Wanitzek, Ulrike (eds.), Festschrift für Ulrich Spellenberg (2010), Sellier, Munich, 371–391

——, Randbemerkungen zum Allgemeinen Teil eines europäisierten IPR, in: Baetge, Dietmar/von Hein, Jan/von Hinden, Michael (eds.), Die richtige Ordnung, Festschrift für Jan Kropholler zum 70. Geburtstag (2008), Mohr Siebeck, Tübingen, 227–246

Sonnentag, Michael, Die Konsequenzen des Brexits für das Internationale Privat- und Zivilverfahrensrecht (2017), Mohr Siebeck, Tübingen

Spickhoff, Andreas, Kodifikation des Internationalen Privatrechts der Stellvertretung, in: Rabels Zeitschrift für ausländisches und internationales Privatrecht 80 (2016), 481–542
——, Der ordre public im internationalen Privatrecht, Entwicklung – Struktur – Konkretisierung (1989), Alfred Metzner, Neuwied/Frankfurt
Stadler, Astrid, Allgemeiner Teil des BGB, 19th ed. (2017), C.H. Beck, Munich
J. von Staudingers Kommentar zum Bürgerlichen Gesetzbuch mit Einführungsgesetz und Nebengesetzen, Einleitung zum Internationalen Privatrecht (revised ed. 2012), Art 3–6 EGBGB (IPR – Allgemeiner Teil) (revised ed. 2013), Art 7, 9–12, 47, 48 EGBGB (Internationales Recht der natürlichen Personen und der Rechtsgeschäfte) (revised ed. 2013), Rom I-VO (revised ed. 2011), Sellier/de Gruyter, Berlin
Stoll, Hans, Parteiautonomie und Handeln unter falschem Recht bei Übereignung beweglicher Sachen, in: Praxis des Internationalen Privat- und Verfahrensrechts 1997, 411–413
——, Bemerkungen zu den Vorschriften über den „Allgemeinen Teil" im Gesetzesentwurf der Bundesregierung zur Neuregelung des IPR (Art. 3–9, 11–12), in: Praxis des Internationalen Privat- und Verfahrensrechts 1984, 1–5
Stone, Peter, EU Private International Law, 3rd ed. (2016), Edward Elgar, Cheltenham
Story, Joseph, Commentaries on the conflict of laws, 3rd ed. (1846), Little and Brown, Boston
Strautins, Edgars, Two 2005 Latvian Supreme Court Decisions on International Jurisdiction and Procedure, in: Yearbook of Private International Law 8 (2006), 289–297
Streinz, Rudolf (ed.), EUV/AEUV, 3rd ed. (2018), C.H. Beck, München
Streinz, Rudolf/Leible, Stefan, Die Zukunft des Gerichtssystems der Europäischen Gemeinschaft – Reflexionen über Reflexionspapiere, in: Europäisches Wirtschafts- & Steuerrecht 2001, 1–12
Strikwerda, Luc, Inleiding tot het Nederlandse international privaatrecht, 11th ed. (2015), Kluwer, Deventer
Struycken, A. (Teun) V.M., The Codification of Dutch Private International Law, A Brief Introduction to Book 10 BW, in: Rabels Zeitschrift für ausländisches und internationales Privatrecht 78 (2014), 592–614
Stuij, Steven, De wetsontduiking in het ipr: de opleving van een leerstuk?, in: Nederlands Internationaal Privaatrecht 2015, 217–225
Sturm, Fritz, Wegen Verletzung fremden Rechts sind weder Revision noch Rechtsbeschwerde zulässig, in: Juristenzeitung 2011, 74–78
Stürner, Johannes, Die Rom III-VO – ein neues Scheidungskollisionsrecht, in: Jura 2012, 708–713
Stürner, Michael, Wie kann der Zugang zu ausländischem Recht in Zivilverfahren verbessert werden?, in: Zeitschrift für vergleichende Rechtswissenschaft 117 (2018), 1–23
Stürner, Michael, Internationales Privatrecht, in: Langenbucher, Katja (ed.), Europäisches Privat- und Wirtschaftsrecht, 4th ed. (2017), Nomos, Baden-Baden, 465–525
Stürner, Michael/Krauß, Franziska, Ausländisches Recht in deutschen Zivilverfahren, Eine rechtstatsächliche Untersuchung (2018), Nomos, Baden-Baden
Sundström, G. O. Zacharias, Foreign Ships and Foreign Waters – British, American, German and Scandinavian Court Practice in Collision Cases (1971), Almqvist & Wiksell, Stockholm

Symeonides, Symeon C., Codifying Choice of Law Around the World, An International Comparative Analysis (2014), Oxford University Press

——, General Report, in: idem (ed.), Private International Law at the End of the 20th Century: Progress or Regress? (2000), Kluwer Law International, London, 3–79

ten Wolde, Mathijs H., Codification and Consolidation of Dutch Private International Law: The Book 10 Civil Code of the Netherlands, in: Yearbook of Private International Law 13 (2011), 389–411

——, De mysteries van het *fait accompli* en Boek 10 BW, in: Nederlands Internationaal Privaatrecht 2010, 430–436

Thomale, Chris, Verstärkte Zusammenarbeit als Einigungsersatz? – Eine Gegenrede am Beispiel des Europäischen Privat- und Gesellschaftsrechts, in: Zeitschrift für Europäisches Privatrecht 2015, 517–545

Tichý, Luboš, Die Verhinderung von Rechtsmissbrauch im Prozess am Beispiel der Brüssel I-Verordnung, in: Witzleb, Normann/Ellger, Reinhard/Mankowski, Peter/Merkt, Hanno/Remien, Oliver (eds.), Festschrift für Dieter Martiny zum 70. Geburtstag (2014), Mohr Siebeck, Tübingen, 351–863

Tiedemann, Klaus, Der Allgemeine Teil des Strafrechts im Lichte der europäischen Rechtsvergleichung, in: Eser, Albin/Schittenhelm, Ulrike/Schumann, Heribert (eds.), Festschrift für Theodor Lenckner zum 70. Geburtstag (1998), C.H. Beck, Munich, 411–434

——, Zum Verhältnis von Allgemeinem und Besonderem Teil des Strafrechts, in: Arzt, Gunther/Fezer, Gerhard/Weber, Ulrich/Schlüchter, Ellen/Rössner, Dieter (eds.), Festschrift für Jürgen Baumann (1992), Gieseking, Bielefeld, 7–20

Tizzano, Antonio (ed.), Trattati dell'Unione Europea, 2nd ed. (2014), Giuffrè, Milan

Torremans, Paul (ed.), Cheshire, North & Fawcett, Private International Law, 15th ed. (2017), Oxford University Press

Trautmann, Clemens, Europäisches Kollisionsrecht und ausländisches Recht im nationalen Zivilverfahren (2011), Mohr Siebeck, Tübingen

Troge, Thorsten, Europarecht und das Staatsangehörigkeitsprinzip im Internationalen Privatrecht (2009), Nomos, Baden-Baden

Truchot, Claude, Languages and supranationality in Europe: The linguistic influence of the European Union, in: Maurais, Jacques/Morris, Michael A. (eds.), Languages in a globalising world (2003), Cambridge University Press, 99–110

Trüten, Dirk, Die Entwicklung des Internationalen Privatrechts in der Europäischen Union, Auf dem Weg zu einem europäischen IPR-Gesetz (2015), Stämpfli/Nomos, Bern/Baden-Baden

Twigg-Flesner, Christian, Introduction: key features of European Union private law, in: idem (ed.), The Cambridge Companion to European Union Private Law (2010), Cambridge, 1–19

Ulmer, Peter, Vom deutschen zum europäischen Privatrecht?, in: Juristenzeitung 1992, 1–8

Valcke, Catherine, Reflections on comparative law methodology – getting inside contract law, in: Adams, Maurice/Bomhoff, Jacco (eds.), Practice and Theory in Comparative Law (2012), Cambridge University Press, 22–48

van Caenegem, Raoul C., Judges, Legislators, and Professors, Chapters in European Legal History (1987), Cambridge University Press, Cambridge

van Calster, Geert, European Private International Law, 2nd ed. (2016), Hart, Oxford and Portland, Oregon

van Dam, Cees, European Tort Law, 2nd ed. (2013), Oxford University Press
van den Eeckhout, Veerle, The Instrumentalisation of Private International Law: Quo Vadis?, Rethinking the "Neutrality" of Private International Law in an Era of Globalisation and Europeanisation of Private International Law, in: Bergé, Jean-Sylvestre/Francq, Stéphanie/Gardeñes Santiago, Miguel (eds.), Boundaries of European Private International Law (2015), Bruylant, Bruxelles, 399–418
van Gerven, Walter, A Common Law for Europe: The Future Meeting the Past?, in: European Review of Private Law 4 (2001), 485–503
——, Non-contractual Liability of Member States, Community Institutions and Individuals for Breaches of Community Law with a View to a Common Law for Europe, in: Maastricht Journal of European and Comparative Law 1994, 6–40
van Hoogstraten, M. H., Le droit international privé néerlandais et la question préalable, in: Netherlands International Law Review 9 (1962), 209–225
Vassilakakis, Evangelos, Recent Private International Law Codifications, in: Revue hellénique de droit international 63 (2010), 103–112
Vedder, Christoph/Heintschel von Heinegg, Wolff (eds.), Europäisches Unionsrecht, 2nd ed. (2018), Nomos, Baden-Baden
Verschraegen, Bea, Internationales Privatrecht (2012), Manz, Vienna
Verwilghen, Michel, Conflits de nationalités, Plurinationalité et apatridie, in: Recueil des cours 277 (1999), 9–484
Vitta, Edoardo, Chapter 9, Interlocal Conflict of Laws, in: Lipstein, Kurt (ed.), International Encyclopedia of Comparative Law, Vol. III, Private International Law (1976), Mouton, The Hague, and J. C. B. Mohr (Paul Siebeck), Tübingen
von Bar, Christian, Gemeineuropäisches Sachenrecht, Band I (2015), C. H. Beck, Munich
——, Privarecht europäisch denken!, in: Juristenzeitung 2014, 473–479
——, The Common European Law of Torts, Vol. 1 (1998), Vol. 2 (2000), C. H. Beck, Munich
von Bar, Christian/Clive, Eric/Schulte-Nölke, Hans/Beale, Hugh/Herre, Johnny/Huet, Jérôme/Storme, Matthias/Swann, Stephen/Varul, Paul/Veneziano, Anna/Zoll, Fryderyk (eds.), Principles, Definitions and Model Rules of European Private Law, Draft Common Frame of Reference (DCFR) (2009), Sellier, Munich
von Bar, Christian/Mankowski, Peter, Internationales Privatrecht, Volume I, Allgemeine Lehren (2003), C. H. Beck, München
von Hein, Jan, EU Competence to Legislate in the Area of Private International Law, in: Beaumont, Paul/Danov, Mihail/Trimmings, Katarina/Yüksel, Burcu (eds.), Cross-Border Litigation in Europe (2017), Hart, Oxford and Portland, Oregon, 19–34
von Hein, Jan/Rühl, Giesela (eds.), Kohärenz im Internationalen Privat- und Verfahrensrecht der Europäischen Union (2016), Mohr Siebeck, Tübingen
Vonk, Olivier W., Dual Nationality in the European Union (2012), Martinus Nijhoff, Leiden, Boston
Vonken, A. P. M. J., Mr. C. Assers Handboek tot de beoefening van het Nederlands burgerlijk recht, Vol. 10, Internationaal privaatrecht, Deel I: Algemeen deel IPR (2013), Kluwer, Deventer (cited as: *Vonken*, Algemeen deel IPR)
von Mehren, Arthur Taylor, The Contribution of Comparative Law to the Theory and Practice of Private International Law, in: Butler, William E. (ed.), International Law in Comparative Perspective (1980), Sijthoff & Noordhoff, Alphen aan den Rijn, Germantown, Maryland, 153–165

von Savigny, Friedrich Karl, System des heutigen römischen Rechts, Vol. 1 (1840), Vol. 8 (1849), 2nd reprint 1981, Scientia, Aalen

Vormbaum, Thomas, A Modern History of German Criminal Law (2014) (edited by Michael Bohlander, translated by Margaret Hiley), Springer, Berlin Heidelberg

Vrellis, Spyridon, Quelques réflexions sur l'influence des droits fondamentaux en droit international privé, in: Revue internationale de droit comparé 2017, 47–64

——, Le droit international privé grec à la fin du vingtième siècle: progrès ou recul?, in: Symeonides, Symeon C. (ed.), Private International Law at the End of the 20th Century: Progress or Regress? (2000), Kluwer Law International, London, 243–261

Wagner, Gerhard, Die neue Rom II-Verordnung, in: Praxis des Internationalen Privat- und Verfahrensrechts 2008, 1–17

Wagner, Rolf, Chapter 4, A 'Rome 0' Regulation from a Political Point of View, in: Leible, Stefan (ed.), General Principles of European Private International Law (2016), Kluwer Law International, Alphen aan den Rijn, 61–83

——, Änderungsbedarf im autonomen deutschen internationalen Privatrecht aufgrund der Rom II-Verordnung?, in: Praxis des Internationalen Privat- und Verfahrensrechts 2008, 314–318

——, Das Vermittlungsverfahren zur Rom II-Verordnung, in: Baetge, Dietmar/von Hein, Jan/von Hinden, Michael (eds.), Die richtige Ordnung, Festschrift für Jan Kropholler zum 70. Geburtstag (2008), Mohr Siebeck, Tübingen, 715–731

Wandt, Sandra, Rechtswahlregelungen im Europäischen Kollisionsrecht, Eine Untersuchung der Hauptkodifikationen auf Kohärenz, Vollständigkeit und rechtstechnische Effizienz (2014), PL Academic Research (Peter Lang), Frankfurt a. M.

Watson, Alan, The Making of the Civil Law (1981), Harvard University Press, Cambridge, Massachusetts, and London

Weber, Anja, Die Vergemeinschaftung des internationalen Privatrechts (2004), Tenea, Berlin

Weber, Helmut, Die Theorie der Qualifikation (1986), J. C. B. Mohr (Paul Siebeck), Tübingen

Weckesser-Georgi, Beate, Die letztinstanzliche Überprüfung der Behandlung ausländischen Rechts in zivilgerichtlichen Verfahren, Eine Untersuchung aus europäischer Perspektive (2006), dissertation.de - Verlag im Internet, Berlin

Weis, Paul, Nationality and Statelessness in International Law, 2nd ed. (1979), Sijthoff & Noordhoff, Alphen aan den Rijn/Germantown, Maryland

Weller, Marc-Philippe, Vom Staat zum Menschen: Die Methodentrias des Internationalen Privatrechts unserer Zeit, in: Rabels Zeitschrift für ausländisches und internationales Privatrecht 81 (2017), 747–780

Weller, Marc-Philippe/Benz, Nina/Thomale, Chris, Rechtsgeschäftsähnliche Parteiautonomie, in: Zeitschrift für Europäisches Privatrecht 2017, 250–282

Weller, Marc-Philippe/Hauber, Irene/Schulz, Alix, Gleichstellung im Internationalen Scheidungsrecht - talaq und get im Licht des Art. 10 Rom III-VO, in: Praxis des Internationalen Privat- und Verfahrensrechts 2016, 123–132

Weller, Matthias, Allgemeine Lehren, in: idem (ed.), Europäisches Kollisionsrecht (2016), Nomos, Baden-Baden, 19–125

Wendehorst, Christiane, Kollisionsnormen im primären Europarecht?, in: Lorenz, Stephan/Trunk, Alexander/Eidenmüller, Horst/ead./Adolff, Johannes (eds.), Festschrift für Andreas Heldrich zum 70. Geburtstag (2005), C.H. Beck, Munich, 1071–1088

Wendehorst, Christiane C., The Austrian IPRG as a Recent Codification of Private International Law, in: Verschraegen, Bea (ed.), Austrian Law – An International Perspective (2010), Jan Sramek, Vienna, 79–115

Wengler, Wilhelm, Die Vorfrage im Kollisionsrecht, in: Zeitschrift für Ausländisches und Internationales Privatrecht 8 (1934), 148–251

——, Réflexions sur la technique des qualifications en droit international privé, in: Revue critique de droit international privé 1954, 661–691

Wertenbruch, Johannes, BGB Allgemeiner Teil, 4th ed. (2017), C.H. Beck, Munich

Westermann, Harm Peter/Grunewald, Barbara/Maier-Remer, Georg (eds.), Erman, Bürgerliches Gesetzbuch, 15th ed. (2017), Otto Schmidt, Cologne

Westlake, John, A Treatise on Private International Law or The Conflict of Laws, with Principal Reference to its Practice in England, 7th ed. (1925), see Bentwich

——, A Treatise on Private International Law or The Conflict of Laws, with Principal Reference to its Practice in the English and other Cognate Systems of Jurisprudence, and Numerous References to American Authorities (1859), T. & J. W. Johnson & Co., Philadelphia (reprint (1986), Fred B. Rothman & Co., Littleton, Colorado) (cited as: *Westlake*, PIL (1859))

Wieacker, Franz, A History of Private Law in Europe with particular reference to Germany (1995), Clarendon Press, Oxford

Wiedemann, Denise, Convergence and Divergence in the EU's Judicial Cooperation in Civil Matters: Pleading for a Consolidation through a Uniform European Conflict's Codification, in: Vaz de Sequeira, Elsa/de Almeida Ribeiro, Gonçalo (eds.), Católica Graduate Legal Research Conference 2014 – Conference Proceedings, Lissabon 2015, 175–198

Wilderspin, Michael, Plender/Wilderspin, The European Private International Law of Obligations, 4th ed. (2015), Thomson Reuters, London

Wilke, Felix M., Offensive Doppelsechs: Das IPR der Verbandsklage gegen AGB, in: Zeitschrift für das Privatrecht der Europäischen Union (GPR) 2017, 21–24

——, Chapter 1, Introduction, in: Leible, Stefan (ed.), General Principles of European Private International Law (2016), Kluwer Law International, Alphen aan den Rijn, 1–8

——, Verbraucherschutz im internationalen Zuständigkeitsrecht der EU – Status quo und Zukunftsprobleme, in: EuZW 2015, 13–19

——, Einführung, in: Leible, Stefan/Unberath, Hannes (eds.), Brauchen wir eine Rom 0-Verordnung? (2013), Jenaer Wissenschaftliche Verlagsgesellschaft, 23–31

——, Brauchen wir eine Rom 0-Verordnung? Eine Skizze anlässlich einer Bayreuther Tagung, in: Zeitschrift für Gemeinschaftsprivatrecht (GPR) 2012, 334–341

——, Das internationale Erbrecht nach der neuen EU-Erbrechtsverordnung, in: Recht der internationalen Wirtschaft 2012, 601–609

Wilson, Richard J., The Role of Practice in Legal Education, in: Brown, Karen B./Snyder, David V. (eds.), General Reports of the XVIIIth Congress of the International Academy of Comparative Law/ Rapports Généraux du XVIIIème Congrès de l'Académie Internationale de Droit Comparé (2012), Springer, Dordrecht et al., 57–83

Winkler von Mohrenfels, Peter, Art. 10 Rom III-VO: Kollisionsrechtliche Eingriffsnorm oder Spezialfall des ordre public?, in: Witzleb, Normann/Ellger, Reinhard/Mankowski, Peter/Merkt, Hanno/Remien, Oliver (eds.), Festschrift für Dieter Martiny zum 70. Geburtstag (2014), Mohr Siebeck, Tübingen, 595–615

Wiwinius, Jean-Claude, Le droit international privé au Grand-Duché de Luxembourg, 3rd ed. (2011), Paul Bauler, Luxembourg

Wolf, Manfred/Neuner, Jörg, Allgemeiner Teil des Bürgerlichen Rechts, 11th ed. (2016), C.H. Beck, Munich

Wolff, Martin, Private International Law, 2nd ed. (1950), Clarendon Press, Oxford

Wörlen, Rainer/Metzler-Müller, Karin, BGB AT, 14th ed. (2016), Franz Vahlen, Munich

Wortley, B. A., The General Principles of Private International Law from the English Standpoint, in: Recueil des cours 71 (1947), 3–109

Wurmnest, Wolfgang, Chapter 14, *Ordre Public* (Public Policy), in: Leible, Stefan (ed.), General Principles of European Private International Law (2016), Kluwer Law International, Alphen aan den Rijn, 305–329

——, Grundzüge eines europäischen Haftungsrechts (2003), Mohr Siebeck, Tübingen

Yntema, Hessel E., The Historic Bases of Private International Law, in: The American Journal of Comparative Law 2 (1953), 297–317

Yüksel, Burcu, An Analysis of the Effectiveness of the EU Institutions in Making and Interpreting EU Private International Law Regulations, in: Beaumont, Paul/Danov, Mihail/Trimmings, Katarina/eadem (eds.), Cross-Border Litigation in Europe (2017), Hart, Oxford and Portland, Oregon, 35–53

Zajtay, Imre, Chapter 14, The Application of Foreign Law, in: Lipstein, Kurt (ed.), International Encyclopedia of Comparative Law, Vol. III, Private International Law (1972), Mouton, The Hague, and J. C. B. Mohr (Paul Siebeck), Tübingen

Zidarova, Jordanka/Stančeva-Minčeva, Vessela, Gesetzbuch über das Internationale Privatrecht der Republik Bulgarien, in: Rabels Zeitschrift für ausländisches und internationales Privatrecht 71 (2007), 398–456

Zimmermann, Andreas (ed.), The 1951 Convention Relating to the Status of Refugees and its 1967 Protocol, A Commentary (2011), Oxford University Press (cited as: *Commentator*, in: Zimmermann (ed.), The 1951 Convention)

Zimmermann, Reinhard, The Present State of European Private Law, in: The American Journal of Comparative Law 57 (2009), 479–512

——, *Ius Commune* and the Principles of European Contract Law: Contemporary Renewal of an Old Idea, in: MacQueen, Hector L./idem (eds.), European Contract Law: Scots and South African Perspectives (2006), Edinburgh University Press, 1–42

——, Comparative Law and the Europeanization of Private Law, in: Reimann, Mathias/idem (eds.), The Oxford Handbook of Comparative Law (2006), Oxford University Press, 539–578

——, Codification: history and present significance of an idea, in: European Review of Private Law 3 (1995), 95–120

——, Der europäische Charakter des englischen Rechts, in: Zeitschrift für Europäisches Privatrecht 1993, 4–51

——, Das römisch-kanonische ius commune als Grundlage europäischer Rechtseinheit, in: Juristenzeitung 1992, 8–20

Zimmermann, Reinhard/Whittaker, Simon (eds.), Good Faith in European Contract Law (2000), Cambridge University Press

Zitelmann, Ernst, Der Name „internationales Privatrecht", in: Niemeyer's Zeitung für internationales Recht (NiemZ) 27 (1918), 177–196

——, Der Wert eines „allgemeinen Teils" des bürgerliche Rechts, in: Zeitschrift für das Privat- und öffentliche Recht der Gegenwart (GrünhZ) 33 (1906), 1–32

——, Internationales Privatrecht, Vol. I (1897), Duncker & Humblot, Leipzig

Zweigert, Konrad, Zur Armut des internationalen Privatrechts an sozialen Werten, in: Rabels Zeitschrift für ausländisches und internationales Privatrecht 37 (1937), 435–452

——, Méthodolgie du droit comparé, in: Université de Toulouse, Faculté de droit et des sciences économiques (ed.), Mélanges offerts à Jacques Maury, Vol. 1 (1960), Dalloz, Paris, 579–596

——, Die Rechtsvergleichung im Dienste der europäischen Rechtsvereinheitlichung, in: Rabels Zeitschrift für ausländisches und internationales Privatrecht 16 (1951), 387–397

——, Rechtsvergleichung als universale Interpretationsmethode, in: Zeitschrift für Ausländisches und Internationales Privatrecht 15 (1949/1950), 5–21

——, Die dritte Schule im internationalen Privatrecht, in: Festschrift für Leo Raape zu seinem siebzigsten Geburtstag, 14. Juni 1948 (1948), Rechts- und Staatswissenschaftlicher Verlag, Hamburg, 35–51

Zweigert, Konrad/Dietrich, Hartmut, System and Language of the German Civil Code 1900, in: Stoljar, Samuel J. (ed.), Problems of Codification (1977), Australian National University, Canberra, 34–62

Zweigert, Konrad/Kötz, Hein, Introduction to Comparative Law, 3rd ed. (1998), Clarendon Press, Oxford

INDEX

ABOUT THE AUTHOR

Felix M. Wilke is a senior assistant and university lecturer at the Law and Business School of the University of Bayreuth, Germany. He holds an LL.M. from the University of Michigan Law School, which he attended as a Grotius Fellow. Before returning to the University of Bayreuth for his current position, he was a law clerk at the Hanseatic Higher Regional Court of Hamburg.

www.ingramcontent.com/pod-product-compliance
Ingram Content Group UK Ltd.
Pitfield, Milton Keynes, MK11 3LW, UK
UKHW051846100926
8556IPUK00005B/478

9 781780 6869